NAPOLEON and the DARDANELLES

VERNON J. PURYEAR

UNIVERSITY OF CALIFORNIA PRESS
Berkeley and Los Angeles : 1951

NAPOLEON

and the

DARDANELLES

UNIVERSITY OF CALIFORNIA PRESS

Berkeley and Los Angeles

California

CAMBRIDGE UNIVERSITY PRESS

London, England

The title page shows Napoleon receiving
Persian Ambassador Mirza
at Finkenstein, April 27, 1807.
From the painting by Mulard,
now at the Musée de Versailles.

Printed in the United States of America
By the University of California Press

Preface

STATESMEN still may learn from the opportunities and mistakes of Napoleon's era. The collapse of the once mighty Napoleonic empire may be attributed significantly to the ultimate failure of its policies for the Near East. These policies involved the deception of Turkey and Persia and the withholding of the Dardanelles from Russia.

This account of Napoleon's policies for the Near East is based on original manuscript sources, drawn primarily from among the documents in the archives of the Ministry of Foreign Affairs in Paris. The documents reveal not only French policy but also the significant Turkish, Persian, Russian, and English reactions to it.

Special thanks are due M. Amédée Outrey, director of the French foreign ministry's Service des Archives, for the permission accorded the author to utilize the original documents. The reports of the secret discussions with Russia in 1808 were studied in the Archives Nationales. A grant-in-aid by the Social Science Research Council enabled the author to carry on his research while on sabbatical leave.

V. J. P.

Davis, California

Contents

I   *Observer on the Bosporus* (1802–1803)   1

II   *"Emperor and Padishah"* (1804)   23

III   *Scheming for Persian Coöperation* (1805)   41

IV   *Ottoman Policy Veers Toward France*
     (OCTOBER, 1805–FEBRUARY, 1806)   61

V   *New French Courses Are Charted*
     (MARCH–JULY, 1806)   75

VI   *Breaking the Russo-Turkish Alliance*
     (AUGUST–DECEMBER, 1806)   99

VII   *"That Infernal Strait"*
     (JANUARY–FEBRUARY, 1807)   127

VIII   *Persia Enters the French Orbit*
     (MARCH–MAY, 1807)   149

IX   *Napoleon Abandons the Ottoman Empire*
     (JUNE–JULY, 1807)   171

X   *An Unratified Armistice*
     (JULY–SEPTEMBER, 1807)   201

XI   *Testing the Franco-Russian Alliance*
     (OCTOBER–DECEMBER, 1807)   225

XII   *Shall Turkey Be Partitioned?*
     (JANUARY–FEBRUARY, 1808)   251

[*CONTINUED*]

XIII *The Dardanelles—"La Langue de chat"*
   (MARCH, 1808)   281

XIV *"The Bases Cannot Be Accepted"*
   (MARCH—JUNE, 1808)   307

XV *Post-mortem at Erfurt*
   (JULY—NOVEMBER, 1808)   329

XVI *Near Eastern Policy at Loose Ends*
   (1808—1809)   355

XVII *Rim of the Blockade* (1809—1814)   379

XVIII *Epilogue: The Last Phase* (1814—1815) 403

   NOTES   411

   BIBLIOGRAPHICAL NOTE   421

   INDEX   431

I

Observer on the Bosporus

1802–1803

NAPOLEON's policies for the Near East accounted in great part for the ultimate collapse of his imposing empire. Observable unity and continuity for several years, only to be followed by vacillation, marked the French dictator's diplomatic activities that centered at Constantinople. One forgotten result of General Napoleon Bonaparte's invasion of Egypt in 1798 was Russia's reversal of its usual policy of aggression against Turkey to one of support. It was Bonaparte who forced these two traditional enemies into alliance, partly in consequence of his implied threat to march from occupied Egypt through Syria and perhaps take possession of the Dardanelles. His pro-Turkish policy extended from his treaty of peace with Sultan Selim III of the Ottoman Empire in 1802 to his alliance with Tsar Alexander I of Russia in 1807. In 1806 Emperor Napoleon wished Turkey to form an alliance with France against Russia and Great Britain, whereas in 1808 he discussed with Alexander a partition of Turkey. Whether as friend of Turkey or ally of Russia, however, the French emperor never permitted the tsarist realm to possess the Dardanelles. With Persia he signed a military alliance in 1807, only to leave that state to itself in its conflict with Russia. It is thus understandable that Napoleon's continental blockade was not enforced in the Levant, and that Turks and Persians determined not to become his pawns in 1812, the year memorable for his defeat in Russia and Spain.

That is a broad outline of the significant French policies discussed in this book. The heretofore neglected story of their evolution and results, as recorded in the archives, begins when the French Revolutionary wars ended in 1802 with the general pacification of Europe. A halting step toward the ultimate return of France to an impressive position in the Near East befitted the power that had suffered complete military defeat in Egypt at the hands of Turkey and Great Britain. First Consul Napoleon Bonaparte announced that he wished to be friends with the theo-

I

cratic Ottoman Empire, the state he had attacked by invading Egypt in 1798.

Yet the occupation of the land of the Nile until 1801 by French forces had so seriously wounded the prestige of Turkey that only a cautious peacetime nurturing of the new policy could make real the official pledge of the Franco-Turkish peace treaty negotiated in mid-1802. Bonaparte in 1802 apparently had no political policy for Turkey; he sought only to save face and restore France's economic profits.

This chapter recounts the hesitant diplomatic efforts of the First Consul, acting through Foreign Minister Talleyrand in Paris and through Chargé d'Affaires Pierre Ruffin and Ambassador General Brune in Constantinople, the latter being Bonaparte's first observer of Russia stationed on the Bosporus.

The pain of the Turkish wounds from invasion had been somewhat assuaged by victory. The handicaps to Brune's implementation of the policy of friendship, or even to winning Turkey's faithful fulfillment of stipulated treaty terms, dated also from the latter's arguments over terms for an armistice in 1801 and for the treaty in 1802. Turkey had not wished to concede to France the commercial navigation of the jealously guarded Black Sea. Even in peacetime it did not relish restoring full equality of treaty status to Bonapartean France. French ships nevertheless won admission to that sea for the first time when, by treaty, the French invasion of Egypt and the consequent war were terminated. Paradoxically, the Egyptian adventure conceded England the same right, both victor and vanquished winning the same legal authority to sail the Black Sea with their commercial vessels.

The search for added profits made Bonaparte insist on penetrating the Black Sea for the first time. In the course of the negotiations for the Franco-Turkish treaty, he had secretly guaranteed the sultan's territories against possible retaliatory action by the Russians and the British. The foreign ministers, Talleyrand of France and Galib Effendi of Turkey, included this long-debated requirement in the treaty, which they signed in Paris on June 25, 1802. The commercial opening to France of the Turkish Straits and the Black Sea was thus positively stipulated:

The Ottoman Empire agrees that French vessels of commerce henceforth shall enjoy without contestation the right of entrance and of free navigation in the Black Sea under the French flag. The Ottoman Empire agrees, moreover, that the said French merchant vessels, in their entrance into and in their departure from that sea, and in everything which can facilitate their free navigation, will have privileges entirely comparable to the merchant vessels of the nations which have obtained the right to navigate the Black Sea. The Ottoman Empire and the government of the French Republic will concert in efficacious measures to purge from piracy the seas which serve their commercial vessels. The Ottoman Empire promises to protect against all piracy the French commercial navigation of the Black Sea.

Another stipulation—which Turkey neither understood nor applied —provided that the sultan, no less than France, had to pay indemnities for the French civilian losses suffered during Bonaparte's invasion of his territory. The treaty called for a special convention to indemnify equitably and reciprocally the losses of property by confiscation or sequestration during the war.[1]

Encouraging Turkey's prompt approval of the treaty, Bonaparte issued his formal ratification on July 2, and dispatched a friendly letter to his "perfect friend," the sultan. Galib accepted the French executive instrument but could himself transmit no ratification because it was not authorized by Sultan Selim III. The First Consul also decided to dispatch a special envoy to Constantinople for diplomatic effect and to undertake certain investigations in the Levant. He at first appointed Horace Sebastiani, who had made a very good impression on the Turks the year before. Under the drafted instructions, the envoy would have made suitable clarifications and could have begun the negotiation for indemnities. He might have instituted the commission, whose purpose was to collect, verify, and liquidate all the French claims. Indemnities were to be paid to merchants and other claimants from a general fund supplied by Turkey. That Turkey would ratify the treaty this time, in contrast with its failure to do so in 1801, was almost assured by the circumstance that Turkey's allies now also had signed with France. The contrasting lack of urgency this time led Bonaparte to commission Ruffin to see the ratification through, while Sebastiani was to investigate conditions in the Levant.

The treaty's reciprocal guarantee of territory required prompt explanation, for otherwise it might frighten Turkey into repudiating the treaty. Ruffin was directed to convey the First Consul's interpretation of this guarantee. Bonaparte himself dictated the vague language to be used, language which Talleyrand phrased for Ruffin as follows: "The First Consul wishes that nothing respecting this be discussed in detail. The guarantee, in view of the circumstances in which Turkey is found in respect to some of its possessions, must remain vague, indeterminate, and general." The chargé d'affaires was instructed to say that Bonaparte had added the secret stipulation only to avoid alarm on Turkey's part at the possible consequences of the guarantee; such a "liberal concession" attested the disinterested and benevolent spirit of France.[2]

The Ottomans interposed no objections to the treaty, and ratifications were exchanged in Paris on September 8. Talleyrand agreed with Ruffin and the others that sailing the Black Sea should strengthen political relations with Russia as well as with Turkey and should contribute to the maintenance of peace and stability. The chargé d'affaires was directed to notify the merchants and to support them in order that French commerce "might properly enjoy the advantages and extensions which the treaty assured it." The foreign minister affirmed that French merchants would be welcomed again throughout the Ottoman Empire. Turkey should protect the French merchants and ships, and it should concert with France to destroy piracy in all "the seas which serve their commercial vessels."[3]

A treaty which covered commercial privileges throughout the Ottoman Empire, in place of the old unilateral capitulations, of itself represented a notable advance in the French position. All the powers at once reëxamined their restored tariff rates effective in Turkey. They discovered approximate equality in the over-all rates, although Frenchmen believed they possessed advantages in their prewar tariff, while Englishmen believed that Russia held some slight advantages.[4] The impatient Council of Commerce of Marseille wrote Talleyrand on July 17 that its merchants were eager to trade in the Black Sea and throughout the Near East. The council recalled Bonaparte's assurance in January, 1802, that freedom for commerce in the Black Sea would be stipulated by treaty. It reviewed the limited French trade in the Black Sea during the 1780's —carried on of necessity under the protection of foreign flags. Because France had not shared with Russia and Austria the duty-free commercial passage through the Bosporus into the Black Sea, the council believed similar privileges would be "of the greatest advantage to French commerce." Marseille did not doubt that French commerce there would soon reach a high degree of usefulness and profit.[5]

The profits and other potentialities from France's commercial navigation of the Black Sea became a subject of Talleyrand's inquiries. Typical is the reply by E. Gandin, secretary of the embassy at Constantinople and former consular agent in Wallachia. He predicted an expanded trade with Russia, Danubian Europe, and western Asia. The tsarist realm would purchase French wines, liquors, fine oils, perfumes, sugar, coffee, and textiles, while France would take Russian grains, salted meats, tar, hemp, flax, potash, and tobacco. Trade could be carried on with Ottoman Bulgaria and Rumelia through the port of Varna, and more considerably with Moldavia and Wallachia. Connections could be established with such centers as Tiflis and trade opened in Circassia, Georgia, and the adjacent regions. Means could be found from the Black Sea concession to open up interesting political relations with Persia, in order to combat English influence there. In Gandin's opinion, the peacetime development of commercial routes to Russia, the Ottoman Empire, and the east generally would prove of "incalculable" value during any naval war. The knowledge of the Black Sea gained by merchant sailings could perhaps later prevent the collapse of the Ottoman Empire.[6]

Ruffin relayed information received from, among others, A. Raubaud, a former French agent at Smyrna personally known to Talleyrand. Raubaud duplicated many of Gandin's predictions, advancing the thesis that France would have little to fear from competition by the English Levant Company. V. T. Fourçade, former vice-counsul at Crete, suggested, as a means of extending French trade, the use of Varna and Galatz as the most important depots for Danubian produce, and Odessa, Kherson, Nikolaev, Kaffa, and Taganrog as centers for trade with southern Russia. For Asia Minor, Ottoman Sinop and Trebizond could serve. Other less well-founded or reasonable predictions reflected a considerable variety of new economic hopes. Some Frenchmen believed that gold and copper mines and vast forests only awaited exploitation. Others wished for a Black Sea route to the Indies.[7]

Bonaparte complemented his policy of peace with one of collaboration with the Ottoman Empire. To the ambassadorship he appointed General Brune, a distinguished former commander in chief of the French army in the Netherlands. The selection of such a figure of itself suggested Bonaparte's purpose. By his instructions Brune, a known proponent of closer commercial relations with the Ottoman Empire, must regain the position and respect in the Near East which France had held for two centuries. The new ambassador's ostensible instructions were of the generalized type customary for French ambassadors to Turkey during Bourbon days. Most of their details we may omit from consideration, as did Brune himself. It is important that the government wished Brune to build up Turkish confidence in the good will of the French Republic and to restore and extend commerce. Bonaparte wished to stress the

reciprocal guarantee of territories. Although Turkey assumed no responsibility to participate in French wars, the French Republic guaranteed
all the Ottoman territory. Obviously Brune must have observed the
omission of any explanation of what constituted the Ottoman territory
thus guaranteed.[8]

In the secret instructions to Brune, we can see Bonaparte beginning
to occupy himself with the opportunities of the Ottoman Empire.
Egypt itself no longer lured him. The French Republic intended by all
the means in its power to recover the supremacy it enjoyed under the
Ottoman capitulations. The ambassador was directed to take back under
his protection the Roman Catholic hospitals within that empire, the
Roman Catholics of Syria and Armenia, and the pilgrims who visited
the Holy Places of Palestine. He had to protect French commerce in
all ways, protesting every infraction of capitulatory privilege. He had
to make a personal friend of the Ottoman foreign minister, or of someone close to the minister. Because Russia and Austria possessed local
interests within certain of the Ottoman states, it would be to French
advantage to hold the balance between these two. Brune might concert
with the ambassador of Russia but be more friendly with the ambassador of Prussia, "the state more sincerely within French interests." He
should offer Turkey his mediation whenever occasion arose. The ambassador of France should always be in the limelight and should see that
Turkey focused attention on him. As an example borrowed from his
experience in Egypt, the First Consul directed that the French palace be
fully lighted on Mohammedan holidays. Two French frigates should be
stationed regularly "in the seas of Syria and at Constantinople" in order
to protect French commerce in coöperation with the French consuls.
Brune must forward exact information respecting the Ottoman provinces, extending his research in the direction of Persia.[9]

General Brune's characteristic, leisurely departure—to facilitate preparations for a more pompous arrival—permitted his stop for entertainment by the merchants of Marseille. He came at last to Constantinople
with a considerable staff, transported for show by a small naval squadron;
the disembarkation at the Ottoman capital in December, 1802, awed
even Ruffin. It offered a marked contrast to that day in 1798 when,
upon Bonaparte's invasion of Egypt, the chargé d'affaires had been led
away to an Ottoman prison. Brune believed the honors accorded him by
the sultan and the grand vizir to be superior to those given others. Following the example of Madame Brune, several wives of the new officials

accompanied their husbands. Brune appeared at a moment when it was not difficult for Frenchmen to capitalize on whatever anti-British feeling had resulted from the latter's overlong military sojourn in Alexandria. Would France take diplomatic possession of the Levant?

Brune brought new commissions for the existing staff. Interpreter Kieffer became secretary-interpreter; Citizen Parandier, the agent for foreign affairs, became first secretary; and Citizen Lamarre became second secretary. The observer on the Bosporus was given adequate assistance throughout the Ottoman Empire; French consular services were promptly reëstablished. Among the consuls ("commissioners of commerce"), a consulate general for the Morea had a shifting official residence. A vice-consul came to Athens, and agents appeared again in Crete and Cyprus. For Syria there were French consuls in Acre, Aleppo, and Tripoli. New positions were opened for the Black Sea, including vice-consulates for Heraclia and Trebizond. V. T. Fourçade became consul general at Sinop. Odessa for the first time received French consular representation, and an agent was sent to Kherson. Brune placed consular agents in Moldavia and Wallachia. A geographer mapped the newly opened regions.[10]

Brune and Ruffin did not at first get on well together. The ambassador needed the latter as the principal translator of documents and as an adviser, but he did not wish him to be in the limelight. It was owing to Brune that Kieffer, Ruffin's ablest associate during the previous eight years, went back to Paris in company with the new Ottoman ambassador, Halet Effendi. So low were Ruffin's spirits that (unsuccessfully) he requested his own recall to France. Kieffer was appointed to teach Oriental languages in Paris. In publishing a French-Turkish dictionary he collaborated by mail with Ruffin, his lifelong friend. Bianchi, coauthor of the dictionary, was another who had studied with Ruffin and with the most famous French Oriental language teacher of the day, Antoine Silvestre de Sacy.[11]

It had been intended that Pierre Ruffin's title be "commissioner-general of commerce"—really consul general, except that during the First Consulate this title was not in use. Such a status did not satisfy Brune, probably because it did not satisfy Ruffin. On Brune's recommendation Talleyrand appointed Ruffin to be counselor of embassy, but thereafter he always signed himself "ex-chargé d'affaires" as well as counselor. In another change of consequence—because the embassy's interpreters were in a sense the real ambassadors—Eugene Franchini gradually replaced Dantan as the principal interpreter and liaison officer. This Franchini and his brother Antoine had been inherited by the French from the defunct Republic of Venice in 1797.

Brune's first dispatch from Constantinople bore the date of January 7, 1803. The Russian minister, A. Italinski, had arrived on an English frigate some ten days earlier. The French ambassador overcame the difficulties raised by the Ottomans upon the passage through the Bosporus into the Black Sea of the first French ship from Marseille, the *Epaminondas*. He debated Italinski's claim of Russia's right to issue bills of health at Constantinople for all foreign ships entering the Black Sea. Captain David awaited authorization to proceed to Odessa while Brune debated the question of the quarantine. Italinski intimated that David's ship would not be permitted to anchor in a Russian port unless he submitted to the usual quarantine and inspection. Brune wished treatment in Russia similar to that accorded in Turkey—or at least that David be charged no more than a nominal payment for clearance papers and suffer no delays for quarantine. Russia, he contended, needed this extra opportunity to develop its commerce in the Black Sea. Evidently he won out for specific ships, if not for the principle, because on March 10, 1803 he reported that other ships from Marseille would proceed to Odessa.[12]

After conferences with French merchants, Brune forwarded their recommendations to Talleyrand. These merchants desired the reëstablishment of the eighteenth-century privileges of the Chamber of Commerce of Marseille, in the hope of again directing and unifying French commerce in the Levant and in Barbary. They wished the construction and repair of certain public ships and the status of a free port for Marseille and its environs, like that of Genoa, Leghorn, and Trieste. Although Bonaparte had granted a nominal 2 per cent, they wished restored the former duty of 20 per cent, or an equivalent protective measure against foreigners who imported French manufactures into the Levant or who imported raw materials from the Levant into France.[13] Brune thought it might be a good plan for France to establish for the Black Sea a privileged company of merchants, directed and encouraged by the government. He observed the jealousies of Turkey and Russia; each seemed to desire to monopolize trade on the Black Sea. He reported that Odessa was ahead in winning Russia's southern trade.[14]

The new ambassador actively protected and extended French interests in collaboration with the French merchants. He restored the former commercial deputies in the Levant and sent investigators to various

points in Turkey and southern Russia. Turkey reaffirmed France's traditional privilege of protecting the Roman Catholics. Brune urged French
subjects to utilize their privileges. Paris newspapers credited this initial
success to him by anticipation, using the fictitious date lines which
Bonaparte so often employed: on February 2, 1803, the foreign ministry
prepared a note—published in the *Moniteur* and datelined Constantinople—which announced that several Roman Catholic churches of the
Levant, deprived of French protection during the war, now possessed
it again. Bonaparte's government, the official gazette concluded, should
be congratulated for its resumption of the protector's role.[15]

Enthusiasts for French trade did not foresee the brevity of the general
peace. While it endured, considerable commercial activity began in the
Black Sea. Approximately 815 foreign ships called at Russia's southern
ports in 1803. Twenty-five per cent of the grain from southern Russia
went to Marseille. A grain scarcity, with consequently augmented profits,
increased France's share. Only fifteen ships under France's own flag
loaded at Odessa, however, before the renewal of the Anglo-French war
forced this commerce to go into new channels or to cease altogether.[16]

The Ottoman Empire, on the whole, accepted France's commercial
navigation of the Straits and Black Sea with good grace. The least disposed of all Ottoman subjects to accept the peace settlement with
France, as anyone could guess, proved to be Bonaparte's implacable foe
during the invasion of 1799, namely Djezzar Pasha (Ahmed Pasha) of
Syria. Under pretext that peace had not been concluded, Djezzar took
action against the first French ship to appear off his coast. He confiscated it, sequestered its merchandise, and arrested its captain and
crew. Once more Bonaparte angrily revealed his bellicose disposition of
1799; he personally issued the order for Brune to make strong representations against Djezzar. If the Turkish government appeared too weak
to require that justice be done to that pasha, said Bonaparte, he himself
would do it. The matter was readily adjusted.

Attention was called to another anti-French governor by Alexandre
Romieu, who represented Bonaparte in Corfu as consul general and
chargé d'affaires. He said that Ali Pasha of Albania seemed to be sunder-
ing the last slender bonds which connected him with the sultan's central
administration. Romieu feared that the pasha might declare his independence. If, believed Romieu, Ali Pasha were once master of Albania
and his strong ambition held, no obstacle could bar his conquering
Greece. Afterward he could even develop a naval power manned by

Greek sailors. Romieu added, "He supremely detests the French."[17]
Meanwhile the resourceful Brune did not neglect to use, for rebuilding
French prestige, the tendencies toward insubordination in the provinces.
He protested against Ali Pasha's arbitrary arrest of a servant of the
French consul in Albania. He submitted to the grand vizir early in
March a list of other grievances against provincial officers. These in-
cluded slights or insults to French consuls in Coron, Patras, Athens,
Crete, and Alexandria, and at the Dardanelles. He enumerated the hand-
icaps to the complete restoration of trade. As a result the sultan decreed
better protection to Frenchmen and their commerce throughout the
empire.[18]

More important, neither Britain nor Russia took recriminatory action
against Turkey for opening the Black Sea to France. Instead the former
promptly obtained for itself the same privilege of navigation as France
by transforming its wartime concession into a permanent treaty concession. Britain, as Turkey's fighting ally, had earned nothing less than
peacetime equality of treaty rights with a France defeated in Egypt.
British statesmen suspected in advance what France would accomplish
and officially informed Turkey that they expected the free navigation
of the Black Sea to be conceded to them permanently by treaty, "should
the subjects of any other powers than those of Turkey and Russia participate in that navigation." Turkey replied that any privileges to France
or other powers would be conceded immediately to England, indeed
"two days sooner to Britain than to any other nation."[19] The phraseology of Britain's request caught Turkey off guard, for it had seemed
that only France was meant. But Austrian ships already were sailing the
Black Sea, as were also the vessels of the new Ionian Republic. Turkey
therefore did not wait until the treaty with France was ratified to redeem
its promise to Britain. On July 24, 1802, it delivered an official note
authorizing to British vessels free access to the Bosporus and the Black
Sea. Turkey also confirmed and clarified the equality of Great Britain's
tariff rates in Turkey with those of Russia—another matter of interest
to the privileged English Levant Company.[20] Logic, rivalry, and the
commercial potentialities of the area dictated the treaty status, although
Great Britain did not depend extensively upon the commerce of the
Black Sea. Moreover, since 1581 whatever extensions of the Levantine
trading rights came to other powers usually accrued to England also.

With respect to Russia, obviously a more difficult problem, France
did what it could to render the settlement palatable and thereby avoid

any occasion for upholding the territorial guarantee given Turkey. As an illustration of Bonaparte's approach, one speaker argued before the French Senate on September 7, that France, far from wishing to diminish the power and prosperity of Turkey, had in view "the introduction of new elements of civilization, and the opening up of the great world commercial route in the center of its provinces." Turkey had negotiated without constraint only upon the pacification of Europe. "The access to the Black Sea opens a new commercial route for us," the speaker continued, "and the sphere of our commerce is now expanding through its direct communications with southern Russia." He encouraged Tsar Alexander to put aside possible "vulgar jealousy" and agree that "the expansion of industrial relations between France and Russia would be advantageous to the industry of both." Turkey had sought only the friendship of France.[21]

Russia acquiesced because foreign economic access to the Black Sea would indeed aid its commerce. The tsar nevertheless remained watchful of his Turkish ally and was a jealous protector of Russian interests. In 1802 two new hospodars took office in Moldavia and Wallachia. These chief executives of the Principalities were given additional privileges; their terms of office were lengthened to seven years. In accordance with friendly action under the Russo-Turkish alliance, the sultan agreed that the hospodars should not be deposed except in cases of misconduct established by joint Russian and Turkish inquiry. As we shall see (chap. vi), Turkey's violation of this agreement at French behest in 1806 proved exceedingly important. Russia's military sailing of the Straits conformed with the alliance signed with Turkey against General Bonaparte in September, 1798. A continuing basis for such passage was the Russian communications with the Ionian Islands, which dated from the agreement of March, 1800. This agreement provided for their joint Russo-Turkish occupation.

French resistance to this passage engendered Franco-Russian political rivalry everywhere for several years. France met the competition in part by becoming more and more a Balkan power in its successive treaties with Austria. Brune reported his first observation of impressive Russian military forces passing the Straits for Corfu on May 30, 1803. That day he saw at anchor before Constantinople a Russian vessel of the line of 74 guns and another of 60 guns, their crews totaling 1,190 men. Periodically he sent reports of similar observations to Paris.

Soon after his arrival, the French ambassador recounted to "Citizen

First Consul" Bonaparte an important debate with Italinski. The Russian minister affirmed the Black Sea to be "a great lake appertaining to Russia," for the sailing of which Russia might enforce whatever quarantine or other rules it liked. Brune held that because this "great lake" possessed at least two masters, namely, Turkey and Russia, its key could not pertain exclusively to the latter. Italinski cited the case of a British frigate long stationed at Constantinople; in order to enter the Black Sea at all this ship had to sail furtively for Odessa and Sevastopol.[22]

Talleyrand reacted violently against the procedure followed at Constantinople for the *Epaminondas*. He labeled as a "pretension" the Russian intention to clear all French ships entering the Black Sea. Italinski's additional claims infuriated him. He advised Bonaparte of his decision to direct all French captains thereafter not to ask for Russian authorization but to seek Turkish authorization alone. He boldly notified the captains that only Turkey controlled the Straits. After studying Italinski's claims further, Talleyrand, on May 14, directed the French minister at St. Petersburg to seek to have countermanded at its beginning a Russian practice of inspection and quarantine not supported by treaty. Only the Turks might authorize the sailing into the Black Sea. In addition, French commercial relations with Russia were required to follow the Franco-Russian treaty of 1787, which authorized no Russian inspection at Constantinople.[23]

Brune in 1803 displayed some of the nervous irritation shown in 1853 by Ambassador Stratford Canning of Great Britain in contributing to the coming of the Crimean War. He requested Paris to authorize a French frigate and two brigs to come to Constantinople to be at his disposal; ostensibly these ships were to map the coasts of the Black Sea but actually they were to protect and facilitate French commerce. Talleyrand forwarded this proposal to the navy on May 18, 1803. From there it was sent to the war department. The evasion had not ended by the time everyone in Paris agreed that the approaching rupture with Great Britain must terminate the discussion of this interesting possibility. Had the new war not intervened, the navy would have favored Brune's plans—and so it was finally decided upon, when too late to have any effect.[24]

The debate between Talleyrand and Italinski suggests a parallel present-day problem. The Soviet Union in 1946 might have won passage for its warships, had not the Turkish, American, and British governments resisted its diplomatic efforts. Launching the move on August 7,

1946, the Soviet Union sought to place the defense of the Straits under the joint control of itself and Turkey. Consulted by Turkey, the Anglo-American policy-makers insisted upon the continued control of the Straits by Turkey, or alternatively by the United Nations.[25] Brune's skirmish with Italinski in 1803 over quarantines seemed trivial as compared with the dispute over Russia's treaty privilege of that time to pass the Straits with its warships and military transports. Russia temporarily possessed then, by virtue of its Ottoman alliance, what the western Allies of the Second World War actually conceded to the Soviet Union, contingent upon treaty arrangements, in the Potsdam Conference of 1945.

In due course Ruffin opened negotiations in Constantinople intended to adjust reciprocally the pecuniary claims that accumulated during the invasion of Egypt. The Turks seemed to believe they might require France to pay reciprocal indemnities for Bonaparte's invasion of Egypt. In the treaty stipulation, however, the French held the advantage because only civilian losses were mentioned. Damages by Turkey arose from its arrest of some 1,842 French civilians and the seizure of their property. No such numbers of Turks lived in France, and Bonaparte would not even discuss the counting of Ottoman civilians in Egypt who had suffered in consequence of almost three years of French rule. Like a faithful servant Ruffin remained—if unsuccessfully—at the task for several years; the conferences were stenographically recorded and officially attested. Talleyrand considered the negotiations to be Ruffin's special assignment, and his alone. The 18 official sessions dragged from August, 1802, to February, 1804, without achieving any significant results. The negotiators authorized a few restitutions of houses and property but failed in all attempts to devise a formula for general settlement.

Indirectly these conferences were of enormous benefit to later Napoleonic policy. During the sterile negotiations Ruffin met and grew to like Ibrahim Effendi, whom Turkey kept returning as negotiator to most of the conferences. The friendship was mutual, and Ibrahim proved a genuine friend of France. He held the position of kiaya bey, strategically important with respect to Ottoman policy-making. The position was variously described by contemporary writers as that of private secretary to the sultan, or Greek agent of the minister of the interior, or first lieutenant of the grand vizir. Owing to his position, Ibrahim Effendi knew the leading court secrets and had direct access to Sultan Selim III. We shall read of Ruffin's secret political discussions with him in 1805 and 1806 (chap. iv).

At the same time as he appointed Brune, Bonaparte ordered Sebastiani to Alexandria to learn whether the British had evacuated the country as required by the Treaty of Amiens. Ostensibly he would "obtain information respecting the status of the former French commercial establishments and concerning means for their prompt reorganization." Sebastiani traveled impressively on the *Cornélie*, a French frigate authorized to visit several ports in the Levant. He embarked at Toulon on September 17; he was expected to visit Tripoli, Alexandria, Jaffa, Acre, Smyrna, Zante, Corfu, and Cephalonia—some of these places known personally to Bonaparte. Remembering his naval defeat at Aboukir in 1798 and the subsequent Anglo-Turkish blockade, Bonaparte doubtless welcomed this opportunity for the undeterred sailing of a French frigate in the eastern Mediterranean. As secretary-interpreter went young Amédée Jaubert, an interesting linguist, whose activities in behalf of Napoleon's policies for Persia will loom large in our story. He had been with Bonaparte in Egypt, becoming the chief interpreter following the death of his superior. Bonaparte liked him. He pleased Sebastiani during this particular voyage.

The secret instructions on which Sebastiani acted reveal many of the major objectives of the First Consul at the time. Sebastiani induced the pasha of Tripoli to recognize the flag of Italy, not a difficult assignment. Although ordered to fight Bonaparte as the invader of Egypt in 1798, all the pashas in North Africa had either feared or admired him enough to be lukewarm antagonists. Sebastiani transmitted a communication from Talleyrand to the pasha, who stated his liking for Bonaparte.

Fortified by a letter in hand from the Ottoman ambassador in Paris to the pasha of Cairo, Sebastiani anchored his frigate before Alexandria on October 15. He investigated the English status and sought to learn whether French consuls could be stationed in Egypt. For a moment the British mistook the French vessel for one of their own so commonly seen in that port. The scene represented a stark contrast to the French humility during the enforced evacuation of 1801. An arrogant French officer reported the English as in strong positions at Alexandria. Sebastiani called on General Stuart, the British commandant. He stated bluntly that the French government had believed Alexandria to be evacuated in conformity with the treaty and announced that he possessed authority to claim the execution of that stipulation. Stuart replied, as Sebastiani had surmised he would, that he as yet had received no orders to evacuate. The commandant nonchalantly added that he believed he would spend the winter in Alexandria. The French could make the best or worst of these challenging words, spoken in the city so intimately associated with Bonaparte's rise to power. Such talk, by a prominent officer of the nation in large part responsible for the First Consul's failure in Egypt and Syria, probably would hasten the reopening of the Anglo-French war.

"The people of Alexandria evince great joy at seeing us," Sebastiani reported, doubtless pleasing Bonaparte. Some gossip placed Sebastiani in the city in order to take possession of it in the name of the "Great Consul." Sebastiani found Egypt disunited, a condition attributed to the rival Mamelukes. With three or four thousand men the Mamelukes held Faiyum and the district up to a short distance from Cairo. Rumor had it that Djezzar Pasha would align himself with them to force a change of Ottoman governors at Cairo. The English with 4,430 men occupied Alexandria, while the Turks with some 20,000 governed most of the remainder of Egypt. Sebastiani discovered bad feeling between the Turks and the English, another encouragement to Bonaparte's still bellicose attitude. Sebastiani believed the Turks probably could not hold their major military positions for long.

The investigator's report excited Bonaparte further. It stated that the English were generally detested in Cairo and that Egypt as a whole seemed anxious for their departure. The country admittedly would fall into disorder afterward, the situation accordingly inviting Bonaparte to return. Sebastiani reported Osman Bey, one of the three principal Mameluke chiefs, as devoted to the French. The envoy, basing his belief on his own friendly reception, wrote: "Today 6,000 French soldiers would be sufficient to reconquer Egypt." Egyptians held in great respect the well-remembered French army of Egypt.[26]

According to Sebastiani's survey, disorders of all kinds marked Syria. Djezzar still mastered the coast, held Palestine, and controlled Damascus, whose pasha appeared to be in full revolt against the sultan. Sebastiani inquired whether the Christians suffered vexations and whether Turkey duly observed all the privileges assured to them under the French protectorate. In November he visited Acre, Djezzar's capital, which had withstood a Bonapartean siege in 1799. He covered up reality with reports that Bonaparte doubtless would like to read. He stated the unlikely, that the Syrians received him with the same enthusiasm as had the Egyptians. He visited Smyrna and returned to France by way of the Ionian Islands. He reported an impressive welcome at Zante.[27]

An order by Talleyrand and the reactions to it supply us from time to time with useful bits of hitherto unpublished information respecting the Straits. He requested precise information of the actual passage of Russian ships through the Straits from the Black Sea and around to the Adriatic.[28] Reports from Constantinople and St. Petersburg meanwhile detailed the latest gossip concerning Russia's Black Sea fleet. Brune advised, in a ciphered dispatch of February 19, of the arrival at the Turkish capital of a large armed Russian vessel. It anchored near the "stationary" frigate, so called by Brune because the Russians always had one there "under one pretext or another." Cargoes of wine had arrived for the crews of the ships transporting Russian troops to Corfu.

The French legation in St. Petersburg seldom communicated directly with the embassy in Constantinople, news from Russia being forwarded to Brune from Paris or Vienna. Minister Hedouville reported that Russia was "arming a force in the Black Sea, and particularly at Sevastopol." Thus already began to appear what would be the principal strategic objectives of the Crimean War of the 1850's. A regiment of artillery was moved southward to the Sea of Azov. Hedouville believed Russia advanced the charge of French ambitions for southern Greece in order to cover up this armament.[29]

General Brune reported the coming in mid-April of two Russian frigates and three transports en route from Sevastopol to Corfu. They took on provisions at Constantinople, in conformity with the Russo-Turkish alliance. At the same time a dozen small English commercial boats under escort of a brig of war entered the port of Constantinople; they were destined for Odessa and were to return to Malta with grain. Italinski later assigned Ambassador Elgin's calling that British brig into the Dardanelles as one reason for Russia's insistence upon maintaining the military passage of the Straits. For over two months Russia's diplomats avoided the French ambassador's palace in Pera. Brune reported that Italinski actually belonged to the pro-British crowd in St. Petersburg.[30]

Events soon pointed to another Anglo-French war. The numerous French plans—including many ephemeral ones—for peaceful penetration of the regions bordering the Black Sea would have represented a substantial economic challenge in the Levant. They were halted almost at their inception because, as every student of history knows, the general pacification proved only temporary. Recriminations in the press between England and France had become an important factor when (in August, 1802) Bonaparte threatened to intervene in Switzerland. Belatedly

France evacuated Otranto. Commercial relations had not been restored with England; certain Frenchmen attached to the *ancien régime* were welcomed across the English Channel; British troops remained in Malta.

The discussions soon broadened, and Bonaparte became increasingly hostile. Sebastiani's report of the pro-French and anti-English feeling he found in Egypt created a sensation when published in the *Moniteur* of January 30, 1803. The report incensed the British, whose object in Egypt had been to render compatible the particularistic Mamelukes and the restored Ottoman military authority. The British government heeded the implied warning. It withdrew from Egypt in March, thus complying belatedly with the Treaty of Amiens. Not to be too greatly intimidated, however, it declared that British troops would not be withdrawn from Malta until France fulfilled the conditions of the treaty.

Bonaparte's annoyance changed to anger. Taking a lesson from Sebastiani's success in discovering or promoting a pro-French spirit in the east, Bonaparte, in mid-January, 1803, ordered General Charles Decaen to prepare an expedition for Mauritius Island (then known as Île de France) in the Indian Ocean. France still held tiny outposts in India. France under cover of the Treaty of Amiens thereupon fitted out a colonial expedition. To many this project seemed to raise more than the question of routes to India. Bonaparte intended Decaen to enter into discussions with native Indian princes who manifested hostility to British rule and to learn how large an army from Europe would be needed to help them eject the British.

Decaen and his contingent of soldiers sailed early in March, 1803. Tariff discussions between France and Turkey opened without enthusiasm late that month, when General Brune could relay the official Turkish news of the departure of the English troops from Alexandria. General Stuart withdrew after arranging with the beys for a government there. He had been prodded by a hostile letter from the grand vizir—to which he rejoined that he "saw with chagrin this letter, based on poorly represented facts." A Turk friendly to the French, probably Ruffin's new friend Ibrahim, turned over the original of Stuart's reply, which still reposes in the French archives in Paris.[31] The British general sought to contradict Sebastiani's story of Egypt's anti-English sentiment by stating to his government that Turkish officers evinced cordiality at the time of the evacuation and gave "the strongest testimonies of affectionate attachment on the part of the inhabitants at large." Stuart hoped for the "permanent preponderance of British influence in that country."[32]

Not yet knowing of the evacuation, Talleyrand near the end of March directed Ambassador Brune to neglect no opportunity to express the view that Turkey should not be deceived. "The English pretension to conserve Malta," he said, "of itself should suffice to reveal British policy the same as the long sojourn in Egypt." If, in spite of the wishes of the First Consul, England should again disturb the peace, it would be important for the Ottoman Empire to reassert its sovereignty over Egypt by insisting upon a prompt evacuation.

Threats followed from both sides of the Channel. Warlike preparations in England and France stimulated the martial spirit. Great Britain forced the issue by declaring war against France on May 18. This freed England of the treaty stipulation to evacuate Malta. Decaen's efforts were circumscribed, although Mauritius would not be taken until 1810. The new war suspended action on all French plans for economic expansion in the Levant. Tensions had prepared the people for the news in Constantinople, where spreading word of the event required several weeks to arrive. When the British ambassador withdrew from Paris on May 12, Marseille spread the report. French commerce became uncertain when Constantinople learned of this on June 23. Precautionary measures thus had intervened before news of the official announcement of the war was received a week later. A British squadron—consisting of a ship of the line, two frigates, and two brigs—anchored immediately at Tenedos, just outside the Dardanelles.[33]

There was a momentary danger that Turkey would join the English and thus return the assistance accorded from 1798 to 1801. But the sultan soon indicated his desire to remain neutral by presenting to Bonaparte a diamond-encrusted jewel box (July 20, 1803). France reopened its consular establishments in Egypt. Mathieu de Lesseps served there until his departure for reasons of health in November, 1804.[34] The sultan's government waited several weeks before announcing on September 20 its policy of neutrality.

Brune's initial successes in advancing French interests terminated abruptly, however, except for the Turkish neutrality, as we shall see. Moreover, he had to complain on August 22 of the "culpable conduct" of several French merchants who, not trusting Bonaparte's ability to protect them, sought Prussia's protection. The merchants remembered well their plight during the French adventure in Egypt. By mid-October, Bonaparte found time to express annoyance and astonishment at their attitude, especially since France and Turkey were still at peace.[35]

For several months Brune conducted the routine business of a wartime embassy in relations with a neutral state. Among other things, he offered France's good offices in the interminable quarrels between the local beys and the Ottoman military administrators in Egypt—an offer Turkey deferred for future acceptance, although De Lesseps relayed it to the beys. Reports had it that Turkey once more feared a French landing in southern Greece by the forces stationed in Italy, as had been expected in the summer of 1798. Brune explained away the story as "an English trick," and Talleyrand later instructed him to deny it officially.

France's General Council of Commerce, a subdivision of the Ministry of the Interior, drafted a new proposed tariff for Turkey which stipulated the most-favored-nation privileges. Talleyrand sent Brune full authority to negotiate it (December 23, 1803), meanwhile authorizing language at Constantinople that would keep alive the French expectation of being able to sail the Black Sea some day. "I deign to remark," the foreign minister wrote, "that the epoch of our admission to the Black Sea has been that of a sort of revolution in the commercial relations of that part of the world with all the powers. Before our admission, almost all the other flags were excluded from the Black Sea. Today most of the great powers are admitted. It is natural that France wishes to extend its trade there." The more powers admitted, he reasoned, the more difficult would it be for England "to realize its projects for an exclusive commerce." He said the embassy should still do its best to have French merchants indemnified for their losses from 1798 to 1801.[36]

Bonaparte's Levantine policy was conditioned by his general European policies. Meanwhile he began for Turkey and Egypt the contradictory policy that in the long run would mark almost all his Near Eastern actions. On September 19 he directed by ciphered instructions that De Lesseps assure the Mamelukes at Cairo of his friendship for them. Any communication they wished to make could be sent safely, without the Turks' knowledge. He played the other side also. He did not wait to learn of the favorable reception accorded Mathieu de Lesseps in Alexandria; without pledging France to anything, he ordered the Mameluke beys and the pashas to be played against the sultan. Among the First Consul's "Letters and Orders" in the archives is an instruction of August 6, 1803, to Talleyrand: "Inform General Brune that the English are disembarking arms at different points in southern Greece, using ships bearing the French flag and commanded by captains speaking French. This is a ruse to indispose Turkey against us."[37]

British policy, in contrast, supported the interests of the sultan in Egypt. When in October, 1803, a Mameluke chief came to London to lobby, the British government announced that he did so without official approval. Its "fixed determination" forbade listening to proposals that might "affect the interests or the rights of the Ottoman Empire in Egypt."[38] Britain belatedly followed France in restoring official representation to Egypt. The reactivation began with the appointment of a consul general on January 30, 1804. By instructions this official could not take sides in local quarrels but must devote his efforts to seeing that the pashas upheld all the privileges and immunities of the English Levant Company.[39]

British moves for its consuls in Egypt annoyed Brune. He complained to Bonaparte against the new titles for Consul General Missett (who was given the additional title of chargé d'affaires), and for Vice-consul Briggs of Alexandria, an influential trader who was also appointed commercial agent of the English Levant Company. Brune thought France should at least match the titles by promoting several French agents. He suggested promotions for Consuls Rousseau of Bagdad, Corancez of Aleppo, Choderlos of Smyrna, Fourçade of Sinop, Vice-consul Dupré of Trebizond, Consul General de Lesseps of Cairo, and Vice-consul Drovetti of Alexandria.[40] Drovetti became especially renowned, for it was he who, in 1829, after distinguished service in Egypt, encouraged France to venture the conquest of Algeria by using Mehemet Ali of Egypt as its strong lieutenant.[41]

Franco-Russian relations turned cool, a factor of subsequent importance. Count Markov complained bitterly to Talleyrand respecting the treatment of himself by Bonaparte during a conference on September 25, 1803. The Russian minister had come out second best when he called on the First Consul to discuss the personal affairs of two French citizens. Talleyrand handed Markov a blistering reply. Through General Hedouville, Bonaparte's minister in St. Petersburg, the foreign minister won Markov's recall by Tsar Alexander. Easygoing Baron Pierre d'Oubril, left in charge of Russia's affairs in Paris, elicited Bonaparte's and Talleyrand's approval. Meanwhile, although Italinski followed courteous and correct forms with Brune, he manifested none of the intimacy so obvious in his official relations with Lord Elgin.

Talleyrand directed observations to be undertaken by an attaché of the French legation in St. Petersburg of the coast of the Black Sea, including its population, customs, and commerce. Hedouville could report only scant headway in assuring Russia's neutrality in the Anglo-French war. Bonaparte complained that Hedouville's reports were neither frequent enough nor adequately instructive. The latter's dispatches justify the rebuke, for only occasionally did he transmit inside information. Somewhat earlier he had explained he could not come into possession of any Russian secrets, owing to the interdiction of communications between the staff of the foreign ministry with the foreign diplomatic corps, and owing to the relative isolation of members of the diplomatic group from one another. At the end of December, he divulged the names of the four men having Alexander's full confidence—namely, Noviltsov, Kochubei, Czartoryski, and Tolstoi. An expedited courier required at least 17 days for the journey from Paris to St. Petersburg. Hedouville claimed that he was doing his best and was sending in a report not less than once each week.[42]

As another illustration of the friction, early in 1804 France and Russia disputed the treaty status of the Ionian Islands, while Russia objected to Chargé d'Affaires Romieu and his functions in Corfu. A specific complaint was the nature of the financial functions assigned to him, said to impinge upon the stipulated full independence of the Ionian Republic. Bonaparte insisted that the pertinent article of the Franco-Turkish treaty of 1802 authorized France to guarantee the Ionian Republic jointly with Russia; he meant that France must share the protecting. Russia argued that the guarantee of the Ionian constitution, the technical phrasing of the treaty, stood quite apart from any right or obligation to protect the islands. It contended that Russia alone possessed the latter right, under its treaty with Turkey. The sultan did not dislike the stipulation, Russia said, for it protected islands which were still under his suzerainty; only France objected.[43]

In this chapter we have become oriented to Bonapartean policy for the Levant during both peace and war. French preoccupations in 1802 called for restored and expanded peacetime trade, the rebuilding of prestige, and the creation and maintenance of political interests at the Dardanelles and the Bosporus. The chief French policy of the moment achieved success by holding Turkey to neutrality. Thus was rendered ineffective the Ottoman military alliance with Great Britain. In addition, French Near Eastern policy awaited the general developments elsewhere. Perhaps anticipating Russia's joining the Third Coalition, jealous France focused its attention on the military navigation of the Straits authorized by Turkey to the tsar.

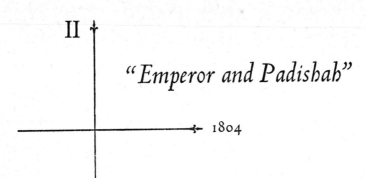

II

"Emperor and Padishah"

1804

The Levant still held in official French thinking that unique and detached place it had always occupied. France's greatest difficulty lay in forming a policy which would hold the respect and confidence of the sultan's closest advisers. Although Turkey maintained its neutrality during 1804, it gravitated toward a more friendly treatment of Russia and Great Britain, with whom it had formal alliances. The First Consul had not yet convinced such neutrals that France could win the war against the new coalition. When Brune appraised Ottoman attitudes at the beginning of 1804, he tabulated more diplomatic reverses than successes for France. He had unsuccessfully solicited approval to place consular agents at Rosetta and Varna, and he had been left unsatisfied in a new request for the satisfaction of Ottoman property sequestrations during the French invasion of Egypt. On February 8, Ruffin finally confessed the failure of his prolonged negotiation, although Marseille, supported by the Ministry of the Interior in Paris, nevertheless kept alive the claims.[1]

This chapter will discuss French news, rumors, and views of the Near East during the first half of 1804 and will stress what became the strained Franco-Turkish relations during the rest of the year. The failure of Turkey to recognize Napoleon's new imperial title annoyed ambitious Ambassador Brune perhaps more than did the covert opposition of Russia and Great Britain back of Turkey's refusal. Napoleon for his part unsuccessfully encouraged a strong anti-Russian policy for Constantinople, the key to it being to persuade Turkey to close the Dardanelles to Russia. Brune at first attributed his reversals to the anti-French foreign minister. He soon confessed that opposition to France seemed to be gaining throughout the Turkish ministry. In a report to Paris he eventually seemed to consider the governing party to be "all-English and all-Russian."[2] As watchdog on the Bosporus, he probed in another direction. He questioned Italinski on January 24 about the rumor that the tsar's fleet at Sevastopol intended to pass the Straits. The Russian minister reportedly "answered with embarrassment that he knew nothing." Brune heard that Russia would break off relations shortly with the French Republic. Another and more persistent rumor held that Russia would send its Black Sea fleet—reputedly a squadron of eight vessels of the line and six frigates—into the Aegean to be combined with the Ottoman squadron.[3]

Such adverse reports spurred Paris to action. On February 29, 1804, Talleyrand enjoined Brune to make his best effort to wean the Ottoman ministry away from England and Russia. The ambassador might argue that everything these powers did injured the dignity of the Ottoman Empire. Bonaparte personally called in Ambassador Halet to renew the assurances of his interest and to express his affection for the sultan and his empire. The First Consul followed this move on March 14 with a secret autographed letter to Sultan Selim III. He denied any attempt on the part of France to invade Egypt or Greece—rumors to that effect notwithstanding. He hoped that Ambassador Brune was satisfactory and that Selim would communicate with the latter unreservedly. He wished Turkey to be strong. He desired to be Turkey's friend. He advised the sultan to clean up the Serbian rebellion. As for Egypt, the sultan should constitute a strong council to reëstablish order there. Syria, always a center of interest for France, should be governed well. Doubtless in reply to reports of growing British influence in Arabia, he advised that Mecca and Medina be controlled effectively.

According to positive instructions, Brune must obtain a special audience at which Citizen Amédée Jaubert would present Bonaparte's letter. The First Consul explained to General Brune the secret letter to Selim. Jaubert carried a French version and a Turkish translation, the latter in order that the Sultan could read it personally and privately. Jaubert would permit Brune to read the French version. Bonaparte revealed to Brune that he had also explained to Ambassador Halet the issues discussed in his letter to the sultan.[4] Brune was to utilize the letter and the occasion for all possible personal contacts with the sultan. The ambassador's statements could supplement Bonaparte's letter. The latter wrote to him: "I desire to support the Ottoman Empire. I desire that it recover a little energy."[5]

As pertinent news, Paris had heard of Decaen's arrival in the Indian Ocean and of his joining forces with the Dutch squadron. The principal diplomatic affair of 1804—quite outside the scope of the present work —was France's military execution of the Duke of Enghien. Russia reacted so violently against it that by April 25 Hedouville awaited with impatience his recall to Paris. His opportunity for a leave of absence permitted him to depart on June 7, when Rayneval took over as chargé d'affaires. France, like Russia, thereupon contented itself with second-rate representation in the other's capital.[6]

At the same time Napoleon sought to impress the Turks by spreading rumors of an alliance with the United States. Thus, in the French archive series for Turkey and Russia, one occasionally reads of French relations with the United States. Isolationist Americans of 1804 hardly suspected the French use of such propaganda as the existence of a *de facto* concert between France, Spain, and the United States. Bonaparte let it be known that French relations with the Western Hemisphere were greatly improved in consequence of his sale of Louisiana to the United States. President Thomas Jefferson's earlier annoyance with him—so strong as to lead to the threat of alliance with Britain—gave way to resumption of the characteristic attitude of friendliness for France. On April 9 Talleyrand penned this farfetched note to Brune for Turkish consumption: "No disquiet on the part of foreign powers can distract France from its preparations for war. The arrangements contemplated with the United States are consummated. They have entered into possession of Louisiana, and the assent of the Spanish government to this measure consolidates the union that subsists between the three powers."[7]

The diplomats were busy with rumors in the spring of 1804. Ruffin did what little he could to revive the discussions of the pecuniary claims.[8] When, on April 28, Citizen Jaubert arrived bearing Bonaparte's letter and the dispatches to General Brune, the French embassy stirred. The special envoy announced he must deliver the letter to Selim in person, a method that did not conform with Ottoman court practices. The sultan's foreign minister loyally revealed this news to the allied Russian minister, who, according to French reports, suggested several pretexts to forestall the audience. Supposedly, the Russian minister delivered to the Ottoman government two communications injurious to the French government and disagreeable for Jaubert. In order to counter Russia's advice, as much as to fulfill his pointed instructions from Bonaparte, Brune insisted that the sultan grant the audience for the purpose. Jaubert added the menacing statement that he was counting, for personal report to Bonaparte, the number of days Turkey kept him waiting. If the delays continued very long, he would return to Paris without leaving the letter.[9]

This adamant attitude won new respect for France. The sultan eventually agreed to receive Jaubert, provided Brune would be present. Accordingly, Brune, Jaubert, and Eugene Franchini, the French embassy's interpreter, were conducted to the sultan's palace by Prince Callimachi, rival of anti-French Prince Moruzzi. In the company of several high officials of his government Sultan Selim received the letter. In the brief ceremony, Brune introduced Jaubert and stated in French the latter's object. After the translation of this into Turkish, the grand vizir replied for the sultan. Turkey wished "to consolidate the bonds of friendship and good intelligence" with France. Jaubert announced in Turkish he must deliver the letter only to the sultan. Having received permission he did so. Selim thereupon pleasantly requested news of Bonaparte, giving Brune an opportunity to say that the sultan could not find a better friend anywhere than the First Consul.

"Bonaparte is my friend," the sultan replied.[10]

The sultan's answer to Bonaparte's letter was dated May 18, some twenty days from the time of Jaubert's coming. Selim addressed it "to the very magnificent Bonaparte, First Consul of the French Republic," and agreed that there must be "perfect harmony" between the two governments. He said the rumors of a French invasion of his domains had had no effect upon him, but if they had, he would have requested a friendly explanation from General Brune. Indeed, if anything came up requiring negotiations with France, he would speak with confidence to Bonaparte's ambassador. Meanwhile, Brune should deal with his ministers. Selim detailed the steps leading to the formation of a Turkish army on the western European model.[11]

Brune advised Paris that the letter was in large part phrased by Selim's ministers. The grand vizir delivered it to Jaubert for transmission. From Brune's reports of the details it appears that Ibrahim Effendi, the friend of France, twice conferred with the sultan to counter adverse counsels given by the Moruzzi family and others who disliked the friendly exchanges with France. Upon departure with the reply, Jaubert was directed by Brune to visit en route the princes of Moldavia and Wallachia. He carried Brune's recommendation to Talleyrand that all French consuls in the Near East be directed not to leave their posts without specific authorization from the ambassador. He requested two additional promotions: Ruffin to be secretary-counselor and Eugene Franchini to be the embassy's first interpreter (dragoman).[12]

Six days before Jaubert departed with the personal letter from the sultan, Foreign Minister Talleyrand at Paris was notifying him (May 19,

1804) of a significant change in the nature of Bonaparte's dictatorial regime. To Ambassador Brune he recounted the First Consul's assumption of the imperial title, Napoleon I. At the same time he revealed it impressively to Halet Effendi, the ambassador of the Ottoman Empire, who, like everyone else in the French capital, already knew. Napoleon's famous first-name signature replaced the family-name signature of "Bonaparte" formerly used. Gone was the characteristic flourish of the B and p, familiar to all researchers in the official documentary records covering the preceding eight years. There was now the flourish of the N, penned so often during the ensuing years.

One month later, this breath-taking news having been rushed to him, Brune gave due notice at Constantinople. Still a month later he could proudly display to the Ottoman government his own recommission as ambassador. Bearing the date of June 27, this was signed by Emperor Napoleon at the "Imperial Chateau of St. Cloud." For a time Talleyrand and Hugues Bernard Maret, Napoleon's secretary of state, had forgotten in their excitement to issue the new commission. The St. Cloud advisers would neglect little else thereafter, during at least eight of the eleven years of the Napoleonic empire.

Brune had just reported Russia's latest ship movements in the Straits: the appearance from Corfu early in June of several ships—a frigate of 40 guns, five other armed vessels, and three transports. Now for a time he too almost forgot his duties in contemplating the imperial title and its exciting possibilities for the fulfillment of his ambitions. He wished to be "Marshal of the Empire." In his own words, written somewhat later, he longed to return to Paris to sit at the foot of the new throne.[13]

More important was the question of whether or not the Ottoman government would accord Napoleon recognition. The Ottomans had long appreciated titles. High-ranking Turks held many, often accompanied by numerous adjectives of glorification mostly unknown in the western world. Of titles, the sultan possessed most, such encumbrances taking considerable time to read in his official communications. If the Turks had ever been reduced to finding a single-word title for the sultan, a circumstance never officially necessary, they had the word—padishah, or great king. Borrowed from the Persians, it combined the ideas of various elements of earthly and heavenly authority that adhered to the sultan's magnificence. The word sultan—originally only a title of birth appropriated by the Ottoman princes destined to rule—meant less than padishah. Furthermore the word padishah possessed a local significance for the Turks neither generally known nor understood in the west. When infrequently mentioned there, the intelligentsia might set the translation down as emperor, the title which now weighed down Napoleon I. To the Turks, on the other hand, emperor meant less.

As a close student of Ottoman institutions Ruffin knew all this. The Turks at first paid scant attention to Napoleon's title, that is, the official few who learned of him as "Emperor of the French" during that summer. In no sense did they share Brune's seemingly genuine enthusiasm for it. The annoyed ambassador changed his tactics, probably upon Ruffin's explanation of the important Ottoman word padishah, which, if translated at all, certainly included emperor among its renderings.

"Napoleon is padishah," Brune told the Turks.

Yet that would hardly do either, for to the French public this word would appear as less significant than emperor and certainly too little for "His Imperial Majesty" who ruled from St. Cloud. Brune therefore amended his statement to: "Napoleon is emperor *and* padishah."

Brune's eventual break with Turkey grew out of the debate over the use of these titles. They had conceded padishah to the allied Tsar of Russia, who likewise jealously guarded it against a commoner who claimed a throne. Alexander I liked the title, appreciating its business value, and encouraged the allied Ottomans in their anxious custody of it. Applying their coveted words emperor and padishah to another foreign ruler seemed too much to the Turks.

The Ottoman foreign ministry at first did not reveal the hesitation expressed later. It appeared cordial, acknowledging with "real satisfaction" Brune's notice of Napoleon's imperial titles. The ambassador erroneously first reported that the ministry recognized the titles; nevertheless he admitted that some questions of form remained for the new letters of credence he had requested to be sent to Ambassador Halet in Paris. Nothing coming of this, he demanded that Turkey "recognize absolutely" the title (June 29, 1804). An evasive Ottoman reply to the demand interpreted Turkish policy as not certain whether Napoleon had observed all the usages common to Christian rulers. Turkey would have to follow other Christian powers on the issue. Brune bluntly stated he could not transmit such a response to Paris because French kings had long been recognized by all the powers. The Ottomans replied that they had recognized Bourbon kings as padishahs but never as emperors. If Napoleon wished recognition of that title only and should request it in writing, no difficulties should be encountered.[14]

Meanwhile on July 27, Emperor Napoleon acknowledged to Brune the sultan's reply delivered to him by Jaubert. At the same time he authorized an anti-Russian attitude, an opposition to specific Turkish policies in behalf of the tsar's realm. The French complained that Turkey had authorized a Russian establishment at Corfu, favored their passage of the Straits, and permitted Greek ships to navigate under the Russian flag. The French ruler announced he had recalled Romieu from Corfu and Hedouville from St. Petersburg and might not permit the latter to return.[15] In mid-August, 1804, Napoleon sent Jaubert to warn Ambassador Halet of the danger of an attack by Russia against Turkey.

Because the uncertain relations of France with Russia had called for comment at Constantinople, Talleyrand gave Brune certain interpretations to be used in his conversations: among these, that Russia lacked capable ambassadors, and that the recalled Minister Markov had been much too clever. Brune could say:

Russia understands that it cannot trouble itself about the affairs of southern Europe any more than France can about those of Persia. But it does not yet realize adequately that to France alone may be attributed, that is to say to the concert recently established between the two cabinets, the influence in Germany which has produced several great and honorable results.

As the key policy, Brune must request Turkey to close the Straits (August 26). Talleyrand authorized alarmist prophecies for the continued Russian use of the Dardanelles and Bosporus. "If Russia goes ahead and openly joins England," he stated, "it can expect a colossal enlargement of French forces and powers." Russia's forces in the Ionian Islands concerned Napoleon. "He is pained," stated Talleyrand, "that the Ottoman Empire closes its eyes to the inherent dangers if Russia builds its power there and at the same time covets the Principalities. The Ionian situation does not really require Russian troops. Thus these presumably are for use elsewhere, conceivably to attack Naples but more likely for use against Turkey. They could be intended to aid Ali Pasha of Albania to revolt." Turkey should realize that Russia could win the Ionian Islands and Albania only by means of troops transported there by way of the Dardanelles. Of the Straits, Turkey was mistress; it should open them to foreign passage only when its own safety so required. The transport of 5,000 troops to Corfu did not by any means end the matter. The Ottoman government should appreciate all the inherent dangers: in urgent self-interest Turkey must close the Straits against foreign soldiers who conceivably might be prepared to act against the Ottomans.

It should be Turkey's duty likewise to close the Dardanelles and the Bosporus to any forces which, if not directed against Turkey, could be intended only against France. Britain would profit from the situation, not Turkey. The fewer facilities Russia possessed for moving its troops into the Mediterranean, the better the Ottoman chances for keeping the peace with its northern neighbor. With Russia excluded from the Mediterranean, the respective geographic positions of France and Russia did not place their interests in conflict. Such language anticipated the Anglo-American argument with the Soviet Union in 1945 and 1946.

Talleyrand once put into a characteristically long sentence Napoleon's dislike of Russia's navigation of the Straits. He said, "As a French grievance against Russia, the latter, while having an express obligation by convention to protect the Ionian Republic in concert with France and the Ottoman Empire and to conserve the integrity of the Ottoman Empire, in fact by maritime expeditions overtly menaced that empire."[16]

Russia steadily reinforced Corfu. Its fourth convoy of troops since Brune's arrival sailed through the Straits in July. The issue of Napoleon's title soon became involved with many other things, including the break between Emperor Napoleon I and Tsar Alexander I.[17] The question in St. Petersburg concerned only one word: emperor. There, on June 19, Rayneval first learned of the title from the columns of the *Moniteur*. He, like Brune, must have felt exhilarated. He knew he must before long present new letters of credence signed by His Majesty, the Emperor of the French. The Russians read the news and made the title an issue. They permitted that new issue to combine with the existing general state of friction to intensify the anti-French feeling.

Russian newspapers would not permit publication by the French chargé d'affaires of a notice to Frenchmen in Russia to cast their ballots of preference respecting a hereditary title (July 2). Rayneval evaded this ban, however, by notifying Frenchmen personally. He carefully observed the mixed reactions, as did Consul General Barthélemy de Lesseps. An early rumor had it that Russia would recognize the title, the majority of the tsar's council being favorable. But Russia's adverse reaction was soon manifest in Paris. On July 21 Chargé d'Affaires d'Oubril submitted a series of four demands on France, the granting of which would arrange the affairs of Italy in concert with Russia and restore German neutrality. He stated that he would depart if these were not conceded.

Napoleon's personal handwriting may be seen in a marginal comment on D'Oubril's note. "Send it to the ministry," he ordered, meaning to

Talleyrand; but he issued the rejoinder personally. He made two demands on Russia: the French and Russian governments should forego any communications directly or indirectly with the enemies of the two states, and Russia should permit France to participate, in fact, in the guarantee of the independence and the constitution of the Ionian Republic.

The exchanges with St. Petersburg proceeded rapidly. D'Oubril replied for the tsar on August 28, in effect rejoining that the troops originally in the Ionians had been withdrawn. Those at that time in the islands had come from Naples and had entered Corfu with the consent of the sultan and upon the request of the local inhabitants.

The upshot may be guessed. The "minister of external affairs" for His Majesty, Emperor Napoleon I, announced that D'Oubril must wait in France until the arrangements were completed for Rayneval's simultaneous exit from Russia. St. Petersburg had permitted the French chargé d'affaires to wait in Riga, hence D'Oubril must wait at the French frontier. Talleyrand and Czartoryski validated the respective passports for September 30.[18] This severance of diplomatic representation seemed too friendly, and Baron d'Oubril did not hurry his return to St. Petersburg. It was not a complete break, for Talleyrand directed De Lesseps to remain in the Russian capital and all other French consuls in Russia to stay at their posts.

Napoleon directed a war department which was preparing the Grand Army of the empire for significant action—a matter pertaining to the general history of Europe rather than pertaining to Napoleon's policies at the Straits. Jaubert received the eagle of the Legion of Honor. Brune's military status advanced from general to marshal in the manner of which he had dreamed. It made him more anxious than ever to reënter the military service. He wished to come back to Paris; perhaps he thought of glorying at close range in the breath-taking capital *N* which painters were so busily placing everywhere.

With greater concern than ever, Brune reported new Russian forces arriving at Constantinople. On September 10 there appeared an old Russian ship of the line converted into a troop transport, two packet boats, a frigate, and a vessel of the line armed as a cargo carrier. Close surveillance by the crews prevented Brune and his agents from obtaining more definite information; but he supposed the ships transported 3,000 or more troops. He estimated the total number of Russians dispatched to the Ionians up to that time as approximating 16,000.[19]

Although the Turkish foreign minister at first seemed to agree to accept "padishah" immediately, and "emperor" whenever most of the states of Europe recognized it, the Ottoman government did not use either title officially. In contrast to their friendly language otherwise, they did not even accidentally employ the term emperor for Napoleon. Nor did they say padishah. There the matter rested for three or four months. Brune repeated his demand for reaccrediting to the emperor the resident Ottoman ambassador in Paris. Brune submitted his own revised credentials to Turkey and always spoke of Emperor Napoleon as his "august sovereign," or "His Majesty."

Near the end of September, Brune determined to force the issue: Napoleon must be recognized in writing as emperor and padishah. He demanded that the new letters for Halet signify both titles, emperor for its international meaning and padishah for its local significance. The Ottoman foreign minister informed the ambassador in confidence that Turkey considered itself bound, owing to the alliance, to consult Russia in matters of interest to Russia. Tsar Alexander personally interested himself in opposing such recognition by Turkey, for it would concede Napoleon a dignity equal to his own. The foreign minister hinted, however, that Turkey would finally accede to the French request. Meanwhile, he promised that Turkey as the friend of both might mediate between France and Russia.

Brune would not be thus sidetracked. He contended that the Russo-Turkish alliance had been abrogated by the general settlement of 1802 and declined to discuss the offer to mediate.[20] With some misgivings he attended a meeting and debated the issues with several of the Ottoman ministers on September 20, having been vaguely told in advance that they did not intend to refuse him. Soon afterward he was shown an imperial order, signed by Selim personally, which directed all Ottomans "to give every insistence to the arrangement." This evasiveness did not fool Brune, for nobody knew what constituted "the arrangement." Brune's position would suffer loss of dignity and luster, so he wrote Talleyrand, if he compromised much longer. Ruffin alternated with Brune in the surveillance of the Russian military transports seen in the Bosporus. From confidential advices given the Prussian legation, Brune understood that the Turks adopted their dilatory tactics in order to gain time to refer the new issue to Russia.[21]

Brune requested his passports on October 4 as a trial coercive measure. Italinski advised the Turks not to permit French pressure to lead them to recognize "Bonaparte," whose military action in Italy and underhand tactics in Greece demonstrated his "perfidious designs" against the Ottoman Empire. He further stated that Tsar Alexander expected Turkey, in concert with him, to accord no recognition either of the title emperor or of padishah. Britain's chargé d'affaires supported Italinski by stating that Ambassador Arbuthnot, then en route to Constantinople, would suspend his journey until assured that Turkey would not give way.[22]

Brune maintained his diplomatic offensive. On October 14 he again enumerated the French grievances against the Turks, reproaching them especially for their dependence on Russia. Neutral Turkey, allied with Russia and recently so friendly with France, was caught in a pincer by Brune's decision to force acceptance of the titles. The Ottoman foreign minister now handed him a note that could be interpreted in both pro-French and pro-Russian senses. It assured Brune that Turkey would consent to add the title of emperor to that of padishah, which had been recognized for French kings, as soon as it could harmonize this with its own interests. Selim refused his consent to Brune's departure, asserting that the ambassador lacked sufficient motive.[23] Brune waited a week, then declared again that he must depart. He renewed the request for his passports.

French over-all relations with Russia had reached a critical stage by this time. Diplomatic conversations everywhere reflected this. In Constantinople everyone observed how Brune and Italinski avoided each other, the latter especially avoiding the former. Italinski countered the Napoleonic pressure courageously. It appeared as though the Turks might yield. He demanded in a strong letter that they live up to their alliance, or he himself would go home, and Russia would thereafter consult its own interests. He said that Turkey must promise not to recognize Napoleon either as padishah or as emperor until Russia did so.

Brune wished to consider this as a Russian threat of war, although the Turkish hesitation to open hostilities angered him. He pressed his speculative advantage of the moment by claiming that he had been insulted and France humiliated. He would depart for Paris immediately, he said, unless Turkey without further delay recognized both titles. After scoring what he considered at least a partial victory, he privately explained to Talleyrand that he really did intend to come to France, although for other reasons. While awaiting the Turkish reply, he shaped his course of action. He would leave, but claim the move was taken solely upon his own initiative. This would leave Talleyrand free to disavow the action. Ruffin, together with two secretaries, would remain at the embassy to conduct the routine business. Thus Brune would not really break off diplomatic relations with Turkey but simply depart in a huff as a warning. He once more expressed his desire to visit Emperor Napoleon's capital, to sit at the foot of the throne. And, he said, a marshal of France must not let his emperor be insulted by the Turks.[24]

For several days early in October, it remained uncertain whether Brune or Italinski would win out. The sultan further delayed matters by personally issuing an imperial order to be shown Brune, requiring his agents "to do what they had agreed to do." Because no one knew what had been agreed to respecting the titles and because the order mentioned no details, Brune became very angry. He announced on November 7 that his decision to depart had become irrevocable. He complained to the Ottoman foreign office once again of Turkey's bad treatment of France, "its oldest and most respectable ally," at a time when Turkey needed French friendship more than ever.

The Turks now reversed their previous use of the words: they admitted it would not be inconvenient for them to say emperor but wondered what advantage there would be in adding padishah. This new approach Brune hopefully interpreted as pure and simple acceptance— their promise to accept both terms. At least so he wrote the Turks, perhaps in order to have the advantage of making them wonder whether they had not at last committed themselves. Brune wondered what the Russians would do next.[25]

Brune's ruse did not succeed, for the Turks made no direct reply. They simply continued to outwait the French. For a moment he considered that he had won the recognition, for which he was complimented by his colleagues. But eventually, with resignation, he left the capital, assuming an air of abused innocence.

He turned the embassy over to Parandier as chargé d'affaires, not to Ruffin. Before departure, he held long and earnest discussions with the Ottoman foreign minister about Russia's navigation of the Straits. He argued as Talleyrand had directed but got nowhere. Russia meanwhile sailed its transports through the Dardanelles and the Bosporus. Brune's unsuccessful negotiation ended his important, if heretofore almost forgotten, tenure at Constantinople.[26] Had the Russo-Turkish alliance really lapsed? The germ of an idea is detected in Brune's argument that it had been cancelled in 1803, owing to the failure of Britain, Russia, or Turkey to employ it. At least Italinski and his fellow Russians did not long delay their negotiations for the formal renewal of that alliance.

Although he would have been strongly seconded on the issue, Brune had not waited for new instructions from Paris. When the ambassador's dispatches reported in mid-November his first request for passports, Talleyrand pointed out to Halet that France's reaction was one of surprise and chagrin. He said that Turkey apparently intended to withhold recognition of Napoleon's title until Russia granted it. Such action would be tantamount, he said, to turning away from friendship with France, Turkey's ancient ally, in preference for Russia, the power which for a century had aggrandized itself at Ottoman expense. He charged that the replies to Brune had been "of an incoherent nature, betraying confusion" and revealing "humiliating dependence on Russia." Talleyrand wrote Brune that Emperor Napoleon could not conceal his surprise at the continued Ottoman hesitation to recognize his new dignity. If the ambassador did not obtain the formal recognition of the imperial title within three days, he must leave Constantinople. This represented, he said, Napoleon's "irrevocable determination" to recall Brune if the Ottoman government did not recognize the titles exactly as Brune had demanded.[27]

Halet rather than Brune transmitted this threat to the sultan. A copy of it came into Brune's hands on December 12, several days before he actually departed from the French palace in Pera. Even yet he could not be certain, so noncommittal were the Turks, whether he actually had them pledged to recognition, or even whether they had sent their ambassador in Paris some message conceding it. In fear of undoing remotely possible success, he could not bluntly tell the Turks why he was leaving. For all he knew, the new credentials he had demanded might even then be on their way to Halet. He did know that the Turks revealed nothing more to him one way or the other.

Talleyrand's three-day limit seemed impressive, notwithstanding that there appeared no way to determine officially when to start the counting. Brune decided upon an ingenious procedure. Instead of announcing anything directly to the Ottomans, he made the solemn announcement of Talleyrand's stipulated three-day limit to the Frenchmen called together in the ambassador's palace. He did this exactly three days before his announced day of departure for Vienna. During that brief remaining interval, he phrased instructions for Parandier. "The reason I am leaving," he stated, "is the nonrecognition of Emperor Napoleon under the titles of emperor and padishah."

On December 20 Brune detailed to Napoleon his reasons for quitting his post. The status of the negotiation did not permit his remaining longer. The preponderant pro-Russian segment of the Ottoman council had taken the adverse decision, although one faction clearly liked France. The issue of the titles played right into the hands of the group in the council who wanted to keep France and Russia at odds out of the fear that they might reach an understanding and perhaps partition Turkey in the Balkans.[28]

The three days being up on December 22, 1804, Brune left the French palace, but not Constantinople as yet. The chief interpreter of the Ottoman foreign ministry talked him into waiting four days longer for a final reply, and accordingly he waited in a suburban village. Meanwhile, ex-Foreign Minister Atif wrote him that he had been named by Selim to arrange the affair by means of confidential conferences. Brune replied that he did not reject such conferences but that he could not agree with the further request to return to the French palace for them. He gathered from various verbal communications that it was intended, as he wrote to Paris, "to seduce him with friendly demonstrations."[29] During the four days, Atif made but did not keep an appointment with him. Brune hoped to the last he would not really have to depart.

Loudly protesting against the recognition of either title, Britain and Russia meanwhile made sure the Sultan did not give in. Slight recriminations resulted from the first news in Paris of Brune's threat to leave. The minister of police, upon Napoleon's orders, arrested the chief interpreter of the Ottoman legation in Paris, in order to examine his papers (January 10, 1805). Jaubert of the foreign ministry translated the papers, which the police had discovered to be mostly in Turkish and Greek.[30]

Ambassador Halet patiently waited for the delayed comment by his government, after which he addressed Napoleon on February 21. He said Brune's departure had "given rise to a thousand sinister conjectures concerning the relations of France and Turkey." As for himself, he was worrying more over his personal finances. Although desolated by the appearance of coldness thus manifested, he counted just as before upon Napoleon's good will.[31] General Brune eventually returned to service in the French army.

The internal as well as international position of the Ottoman Empire concerned official Russia as its ally. Internal problems included numerous provincial issues, among them the insubordination in Egypt, the questionable loyalty of formerly rebellious Passvan Oglu of Vidin, the Albanian objective of greater autonomy, and, above all, the pretentious

Serbian revolt under way in 1804. The ardent young Pole, Prince Adam Czartoryski who became foreign minister for Tsar Alexander I, deliberated upon the best means of connecting Turkey's confused affairs with the rebirth of Poland under Russian sponsorship. In a well-known memorandum of 1804 he discussed the reorganization of Europe, contingent upon the success of a coalition war against "Emperor" Napoleon. According to him, Russia might win Constantinople and the Dardanelles. Russia's attitude toward tyrannical Turkey should depend on the latter's policy respecting France. Turkey should not be molested if it did not side with France. If during the war, however, it appeared that the Ottoman Empire would fall, Great Britain and Russia must take a hand. Meanwhile Russia might renew its alliance with Turkey and introduce changes looking toward the stipulated autonomy for Serbia, Montenegro, and the Ionian Islands.

Czartoryski considered alternate plans to be needed, if the question ever arose of definitively settling the fate of the Ottoman Empire. The mass of Turkish territories in Europe could be divided into locally governed states, federated under Russian leadership. If a general partition were arranged, Austria might acquire Croatia, part of Bosnia, Wallachia, Belgrade, and Ragusa, and Russia could take Moldavia, Cattaro, Corfu, "and, above all, Constantinople and the Dardanelles, together with the neighboring ports, which would make Russia master of the Straits." France and Britain could be offered several Aegean islands or portions of Turkey in Asia or Africa.[32]

Czartoryski omitted all these contingent details in writing the instructions for De Noviltsov, ordered to London in November, 1804, to arrange an alliance against Napoleon. His general proposal would leave Turkey intact, provided it did not align itself with France. He solicited Britain's agreement to the principle of common action with Russia, should Turkey join France.[33] Students of history will note that this was precisely the approach adopted in 1844 by Tsar Nicholas I. He arranged a secret agreement with British statesmen, the collapse of which contributed so greatly to the coming of the Crimean War.[34] In 1804 and 1805 Britain insisted on the preservation of Turkey, and Russia actually followed that principle.

As a corollary to this general policy and in response to the reports of Brune's urging the acceptance of the titles, Russia in mid-December 1804 authorized Italinski to renew the alliance with Turkey. It was expected that the new treaty would bind Turkey more and more to

Russia and retard its attachment for France. It should engage Turkey to join the coalition of powers which Russia wished formed against imperial France. Czartoryski forwarded his draft treaty to Italinski. Its projected secret annexes foretold the coöperation of Turkey with Russia and Great Britain to circumscribe Napoleon's conquests and to expel him from Italy. Respecting the Ionian Islands, Turkey would continue to permit Russian vessels of war to sail into and from the Black Sea, and it would facilitate their passage of the Straits.[35]

Brune's departure left Ottoman policy uncertain and Napoleon's titles of emperor and padishah unrecognized. The debate thus deprived France of top-rank representation at Constantinople at the moment that a renewed alliance with Russia confronted the sultan. As soon as Napoleon learned of it, he ordered the remaining official Frenchmen to do what they could to prevent the negotiation of the renewal or to prevent its ratification.

Talleyrand could not yet know, in November, 1804, of Brune's personal break with the Ottoman government. He could guess it, however, from the urgency manifested late in September. The deceptive policy for Egypt must be modified, if France hoped to encourage Turkey's friendship. A beginning might be made by a change in the policy which had sought to play off Egypt against Turkey. He modified the directive for French agents in Egypt by cautioning Drovetti not to interfere with Egypt's government, thereby dodging any possibility of embarrassing discussions of internal politics. The latter must protect commercial affairs and must not leave his post if revolutions came.[36]

On December 10 Barthélemy de Lesseps wrote from St. Petersburg to say that Lord Gower, the British ambassador, appeared to play a much less brilliant role in the Russian capital than was commonly believed.[37] By the time of Brune's return to Paris, the urgency of steps to meet the menace of a third coalition impelled a softer tone respecting the titles than Brune would like. The changing of personalities often reorients international problems. Some said another ambassador might be sent to Constantinople. Talk of returning Verninac could be heard as far away as Constantinople. This was the Verninac who had been sent by the Directory in 1795, and who in 1804 occasionally gleaned bits of inside information from secret talks with Ambassador Halet's interpreter. He was always more showman than ambassador, although he had succeeded in reopening diplomatic relations after appearing in 1795 with a military flourish in the wake of grenadiers. Ruffin had not liked

Verninac then. Now, in reply to the rumor of the latter's return, Ruffin frankly wrote Hauterive, chief of the political division of the foreign ministry, that he did not wish to serve under him. Ruffin had demonstrated his own worth too well for such advice to be ignored; Verninac would not do. It was decided to leave Parandier and Ruffin to perform their creditable work without a regular ambassador.

The momentary tension in Paris eased when Jaubert, upon Talleyrand's orders, officially visited the Ottoman ambassador on January 29, 1805. Jaubert desired to learn what communication the Turks wished to make, and Halet replied in quite conciliatory language. A letter from the grand vizir told of Brune's departure and explained that Turkey simply could not accede to Brune's demand, owing to threats of war by Russia and Great Britain. The grand vizir had assured France that the sultan did not wish to break off relations. More important, Halet also dropped the hint that Turkey agreed with Russia only for the moment, in order to gain time before declaring war against its erstwhile ally. No evidence of such an interpretation, however, is found in any conversations of the Ottoman foreign minister with Parandier or Ruffin in Constantinople. There the discussions of Brune's departure indicate that the Turks took it quite casually or ignored it altogether. Parandier sought to minimize the basic quarrel and the Turks sought to forget all comment respecting the reasons for Brune's withdrawal.[38]

Parandier never won Ruffin's complete confidence and, more detrimental to French policy, he had little opportunity for contacts with the Turks. He sat in the French embassy lamenting that, from everything he heard, the Russians and British were pushing Turkey hard for a break with France. They had persuaded the Turks to believe, he wrote Paris, that a French expedition had sailed from Toulon for a landing in Greece and Egypt. Parandier never judged next-door developments very well. Although he did not know it, this language by France's enemies had probably been intended to expedite Italinski's authorized quest for a new Russo-Turkish alliance in advance of the termination of the old one.

Meanwhile the Ottomans recognized their existing alliance with the tsar, permitting his warships to sail the Straits in order to discharge his legal or imagined responsibility in the Ionian Islands. We might here suggest a parallel and contrast for this situation in our own times. The Soviet Union offered at the Conference of Potsdam in 1945 to accept responsibility for a share of the control of Libya. If this had been granted by its Allies of the Second World War, the inevitable parallel would be found in the Straits opened for the Soviet Union's naval vessels to sail from the Black Sea to North Africa. The western Allies agreed among themselves, however, not to assign a part of Libya to the Soviet Union, and thus they avoided for themselves and Turkey the difficulty in which Turkey found itself in 1804.

In this chapter we have discussed a significant if transitory setback for French policy at the Straits. Napoleon and his advisers considered that they must take positive steps to detach Turkey from its concert with the tsar, Russia rather than Great Britain looming as the larger French foe. Complementary to this, they must court the friendship of Shah Feth Ali of Persia, already the military opponent of Tsar Alexander I.

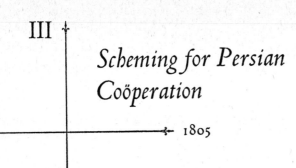

III

Scheming for Persian Coöperation

1805

PROBLEMS repeat themselves and historical parallels recur often. French policy for the Ottoman Empire, like the Russian, possessed a contingent character. Napoleon foresaw his break with Russia and by early 1805 associated Turkey and Persia in his mind as aides in meeting it. The documents of the period reveal that Napoleon was convinced Sultan Selim would follow only a pro-British and pro-Russian policy in 1805; hence the French advantage lay in continued Ottoman neutrality. On the other hand, the French emperor—like Britain and Russia—courted assistance wherever he could find it. Turkey and Persia could be quite useful to him because of their strategic locations—Turkey's with respect to Russia and Persia's with respect to British India. If pursued with caution and persistence, a policy of alliance with both might be evolved ultimately.

French relations with Persia, as well as with Turkey, reveal how Napoleon's policy gradually created a close friendship with those eastern nations. Persia itself sought to open relations with the French emperor late in 1804, after an attack by a Russia seeking to annex Georgia, the province claimed by Persia and sometimes also by Turkey. In this chapter we discuss the attempts of France to smooth over its partial break with Turkey early in 1805, and we tell the story of the difficulties and delays experienced in shaping a Persian policy. This is the year (1805) when the expected Third Coalition formed against France.

Talleyrand, after waiting a month to test the effect of Brune's departure, directed Parandier (on February 28, 1805) to keep a distinct reserve in all his dealings with the Ottomans. He intended to build up an air of expectancy. Instead of naming a new ambassador he announced that Amédée Jaubert, secretary-interpreter of the foreign ministry, who had studied under Sylvestre de Sacy, would come to Constantinople to deliver personally another autographed letter written by Napoleon to the sultan. Although the letter had been drafted a month earlier, Napoleon held it back to await Parandier's reports. When these revealed that Turkey was doing nothing to meet Brune's demand, the French government authorized Parandier to leave Constantinople after making another special effort to deliver the letter. Specifically, he must leave if an audience for Jaubert should be refused by the sultan, or if, after the presentation of the letter, the Ottoman government did not immediately recognize Napoleon's titles by issuing new letters of credence to Ambassador Halet. Thereafter, only Ruffin would remain at the embassy, and he would confine himself to commercial matters. Thus, if Jaubert failed, all regular diplomatic communication by the French embassy would be totally disrupted.[1]

Napoleon's letter to Selim by no means left unchallenged the Turkish concert with Russia. Brune's reports of Russian sailings through the Dardanelles thus bore considerable fruit, as did also the dispute over Turkey's refusal to recognize Napoleon as emperor and padishah. Napoleon taunted the sultan by asking, "Have you ceased to reign? Why suffer the Russians to give you the law?" If they sent as many as 15,000 troops to Corfu, could anyone imagine they would use so few against powerful France? Their armed vessels in the Straits would have made them feel at home in Constantinople. Could the sultan be blind to the possibility of a sudden attack on Constantinople? That would mean the end of the Ottoman dynasty. He branded Selim's foreign minister as a betrayer and said half of the sultan's ministers had sold out to Russia. Selim ought to dismiss his council and the foreign minister or he might lose everything. Napoleon wished to be friendly, but should the sultan persist in refusing recognition, he must align himself with the other side. That he had never been a weak enemy Selim should know. In response to information from French Consul General Rousseau, Napoleon advised the Ottoman council to take prompt steps to prevent the loss of Mecca and Medina. Moreover, Turkey should support Persia, now at war against Russia. "Your enemies are the Russians," he concluded, "because they wish to rule over the Black Sea. They cannot do this without possessing Constantinople." He reminded the sultan that the Russians were Greek Orthodox Christians, of the same faith as half the sultan's subjects.[2]

In a note to the Ottoman ambassador dated March 19, Talleyrand conveyed Napoleon's "extreme and just dissatisfaction" at the result of the negotiations by General Brune. Turkey's refusal to recognize the French emperor by both titles represented "an offense and a scandal in

the eyes of all Europe." Napoleon did not charge Sultan Selim personally with this result, but rather the pro-Russian segment of the Ottoman council. Because the emperor did not wish to abandon the Ottoman
Empire, whose preservation he considered essential, he had written the
sultan. Talleyrand also issued an overture to Prussia for a concert "to
reëstablish a just equilibrium of influence at Constantinople."[3]

The foreign minister doubtless appreciated the fact that Parandier
could not meet the needs of the high diplomacy Napoleon intended for
the Near and Middle East—perhaps General Brune had erred in leaving
affairs in his hands. In an instruction carried by Jaubert, Talleyrand
directed Ruffin to observe carefully all the Turkish schemes, measures,
embarrassments, and fears. What had led the sultan into dependence on
Russia? Talleyrand stated that Parandier had been named chargé d'affaires only for the purpose of leaving Ruffin free to work in a personal
way with his Ottoman friends.

Before Jaubert departed, two important communications from western
Asia reached Paris, the letter from Rousseau and an offer of Persian
alliance carried by the returning Ambassador Brune. An Armenian messenger, Osep Vassilovitz, delivered Persia's overture for alliance, allegedly from Shah Feth Ali himself. It came to the French embassy at
Constantinople at the moment Brune was leaving. The ambassador directed the messenger to wait at Constantinople for Napoleon's answer.
The shah invited the renewal of commercial relations between France
and Persia. Because of Russia's invasion of Georgia, he proposed the
common action of France and Persia against Tsar Alexander I. Ruffin
translated the Persian message and Brune took it to Napoleon.

In devising the reply to Persia, the foreign ministry discussed the
proper salutation. Everyone preferred a short and simple phraseology.
Someone recalled that King Louis XIV had sent several letters to the
"King of Persia," but emperor was decided upon to match Napoleon's
own title. In a friendly tone the letter opposed the British and the
Russians. Napoleon advised Persia to fear and watch them. He pictured
Russia as a poor and greedy trespasser against Turkey, and England as
building more redoubtable power in India every day. He warned that
Persia could be conquered with 25,000 foreign troops, although not if
the Persians learned to make their own arms and to handle their de-
fenses with well-drilled troops, frontier forts, and a squadron in the
Caspian Sea.[4]

The threads of a Napoleonic policy for Persia go back to mid-1804, when Bonaparte rediscovered an interest in western Asia, a region he had all but ignored after his humiliating round trip from Egypt to Syria at the head of an army in 1799. Talleyrand had taken the initiative on September 30, 1803, by instructing Consuls General Corancez of Aleppo and Rousseau of Bagdad to communicate with the chief of the Wahabis, the Mohammedan puritans of the day, and to solicit their friendship. He desired prompt news of any conflict between them and Syria or Egpyt. He said Bonaparte considered it important for the French Republic to be the first to know of any significant political changes in western Asia. He especially wished to learn of conditions in Persia.[5]

When Corancez advised in February, 1804, against soliciting Wahabi support, Rousseau proposed as a substitute that Talleyrand dispatch a letter to Persia, carried by special courier in order to avoid the publicity attending a person of diplomatic rank.[6] These suggestions quickened Napoleon's interest and aroused his imagination. From them developed what became in 1805 the missions of Napoleon's two special messengers to Teheran. These were Alexandre Romieu, just recalled from Corfu, and Amédée Jaubert, a Bonapartean favorite from the days in Egypt.

On June 26, 1804, about a month after the excitement caused by Napoleon's new title had died down, Talleyrand concurred in the advice of Corancez. A reason can be seen in Rousseau's report, received in February, 1805, that the English were negotiating with the Wahabis. Moreover, the Ottomans had beaten the Wahabis before Jedda, probably weakening French confidence in their military potentialties. Talleyrand agreed that the situation had changed.[7]

Jaubert was now given the Persian negotiation as a second responsibility, with Ruffin to aid him in delivering Napoleon's letter to the sultan and to handle and second the correspondence for Jaubert's secret mission to Persia. In advance Napoleon rewarded with the eagle of the Legion of Honor both Jaubert and the embassy's interpreter at Constantinople, Eugene Franchini.

St. Cloud palace prepared Jaubert's trip to Constantinople and beyond so secretly that the archives of the foreign ministry are still without complete records of it. Napoleon outlined the trip personally and ordered secrecy. According to the instructions, the principal object of Jaubert's mission was to inform himself of the situation in Persia, province by province, and of the attitude of the governors there. He must learn how Persians equipped their forces. If possible he was to travel northward as far as the valley of the Araks (Araxes) River and to push on to Russia's frontier. "He will inform himself of past events," said Napoleon, "and of everything else for a good understanding of the country. Ordinarily he will be quite reserved in all his comments, but in speaking with ministers of the shah, he will say I wish to enter an alliance and tender Persia some support."[8] Jaubert thus won another opportunity to become celebrated as translator, interpreter, traveler, orientalist, and diplomat of consequence during the Napoleonic empire.

On March 18, 1805, as Napoleon was busy creating a Kingdom of Italy for himself and his marshals, Russian Minister Italinski was holding a three-hour conference with the principal Ottoman officials. Parandier transmitted to Paris what was doubtless Ruffin's version of the presumably secret discussion. Turkey wished to know the significance of Russian troop landings in Turkish ports on the southeastern shores of the Black Sea, where a Turkish governor had considered them enemy troops rather than allies. Several of the ships sailed on to Constantinople. Italinski explained that the transports had been en route to Corfu and had been blown ashore.[9] The Turks suggested that Italinski had mentioned the number of Russian troops destined for Corfu as 30,000 or 40,000, obviously much exaggerated. Some 2,000 actually passed through the Straits early in March, transported on two Russian ships of the line, the dreadnoughts of that day.[10]

A new letter by Corancez, dated December 19, 1804, was responsible for a second French mission to Persia, that of Adjutant Commander Romieu. It came to Paris in April, 1805, after Jaubert's departure and seemed to confirm the genuineness of the offer by Persia. As soon as he read it, Napoleon penned directions to Talleyrand. Corancez must be told of the secret instruction for Jaubert to open up diplomatic relations with Persia. Romieu would be sent to Persia also, and he would deliver en route ciphered letters for Jaubert and Corancez. Jaubert's object might be revealed by Corancez to Abbas Mirza, the reportedly pro-French young crown prince in command at Tabriz against the Russians. "As in the nature of things it is possible that Jaubert cannot reach Persia," the emperor directed. "Romieu, you will apprize Corancez of my intention to pursue in the most efficacious manner a liaison with Persia. I should like the shah to send an agent to Paris. Also, write Rousseau at Bagdad to continue his correspondence with the vizir with whom he is in touch."[11]

Napoleon directed Romieu to depart immediately, with the same instructions as those given Jaubert. The second envoy would be consul-

general to Persia. Acting upon the advice of Ruffin, he and Jaubert
should follow different paths, one going by way of Bagdad and the other
by Trebizond and Erzurum. Acquiring information would be their
principal object, learning among other things "the character and power
of the sovereign of Persia, the character and talents of his ministers,
the power and degree of subordination of the generals and of the governors of the provinces." Napoleon desired "exact knowledge of the
resources of the country and of its over-all status." Romieu must coöperate with Jaubert, directly if he overtook him, indirectly if the latter
already had left Constantinople. Corancez at Aleppo would be notified,
as well as Rousseau, supposedly at Bagdad. As Talleyrand explained it
to Ruffin on April 27, "The mission of Romieu has absolutely the same
object as that of Jaubert, and their instructions are common."[12]

Talleyrand sent further instructions on March 19, carried by Romieu.
The emperor's interest in Persia had been stimulated, Talleyrand wrote,
by the letters from Corancez and Rousseau. He repeated the emperor's
decision "to pursue in the most efficacious manner a liaison with Persia."
Napoleon informed Talleyrand of his plan. He wished information of
Persia and he wished that a diplomatic agent of the shah be stationed
in Paris. Talleyrand's staff might make researches respecting Persia,
study the reports from Rousseau and others, and study the newspapers
published in St. Petersburg that revealed English activities in Persia, all
"to give the emperor an idea of the situation." Romieu would carry to
Persia a duplicate of Napoleon's letter to the "Emperor of the Persians."

The French foreign ministry's fabricated news report in the *Moniteur*
of Jaubert's journey had it appear (under date line of Constantinople on
April 23) that he had been presented to the sultan and had delivered
Napoleon's letter. The Turks had judged the letter to possess high importance, and several meetings of the Ottoman council had been held.[13]
The actual events happened in a different way. Jaubert departed from
Paris on March 2. He came to Constantinople on April 8, according to
the foreign ministry's later calculation, or on April 12, according to
official dispatches sent from Constantinople. Jaubert's announcement of
his intention to deliver Napoleon's letter into the sultan's own hands
led the Russian minister to hold an earnest conference with the Ottoman foreign minister throughout the afternoon of April 15.

Through the embassy's interpreter, Eugene Franchini, Parandier verbally solicited an audience in which Jaubert might deliver the letter. The
Turks replied that the sultan's personal acceptance could not be per-

mitted without the presence of a French ambassador. Jaubert countered that Brune's absence rendered the new Napoleonic letter all the more important, addressed as it was "from the first Emperor in Europe to the first Emperor in the Orient." He hinted that the sultan's refusal to receive him and the letter "would have the most serious consequences." The Turks suggested that the request be placed in writing.

Parandier's written request on April 20 significantly added that Jaubert's orders required him to depart if the letter were not received by the sultan himself. Turkey replied verbally on April 24 that the sultan could not accept the letter personally. Parandier insisted that it could be delivered only in that way and invited the sultan's advisers to reconsider. Still they procrastinated, although the grand vizir and the foreign minister talked with Jaubert a second time that day. Jaubert gave an urgent character to the matter by stating that if the reply still remained negative, he would ask for his passports a few hours later and for Parandier's the next day. Again the French were put off. A day or so later, when the grand vizir discussed the issue with Jaubert, Franchini threw in a further threat. Always clever at invention, the interpreter made the unauthorized comment that Turkey's refusal would be considered "as a commencement of hostilities against France."

Secret discussions followed, in an attempt to break the impasse. The Turks revealed that they held back from fear that Russia would march into Turkey, and England would sail to the Dardanelles. They finally arranged, however, for Jaubert to deliver the letter secretly to Sultan Selim. The French envoy accordingly appeared incognito on May 2 at the place indicated, the *Kiosk des Eaux douces*. As prearranged, he discovered Selim taking a walk and engaged him in conversation much as if a surprise encounter. In the ceremonial transfer, Jaubert did not actually hand over Napoleon's letter to Selim. Instead, an officer accepted it from Jaubert and gave it to the sultan. Ruffin reported, "The sultan received the letter by the simple intermediary of an officer, according to custom." Immediately upon acceptance of the letter, the sultan handed it unopened to another aide. Making no pretense at reading it, Selim told Jaubert it would be answered. In substance, the French had won their point after two weeks of delay. The letter had been delivered into the sultan's own hands, in Jaubert's presence.

Jaubert conferred secretly with the grand vizir five days later. The discussion is not recorded in the French archives. One report hints the unlikely, that Jaubert revealed that his second destination was Persia.

In any event, he stated he would leave Constantinople within a few days, presumably for France, as soon as he received the sultan's reply to Napoleon's letter. Parandier encouraged Paris by relaying the rumor that the Turks had broken off their presumed negotiations for a renewal of their alliance with Russia. The Russians were furious. On May 17, Parandier reminded the grand vizir that he and Jaubert would turn their backs upon Constantinople if any Ottoman official except the sultan himself signed the reply. Ruffin's personal and secret negotiations with his friend, Ibrahim Effendi, more than anything else produced a friendly reply. The grand vizir had been apprized of the secret, but the hostile foreign minister was circumvented. Ibrahim and Ruffin worked together most of one night to write and translate into Turkish a strong note stressing the advantages of friendship with Napoleon. This Ibrahim put under the eyes of Selim.

The sultan's letter, handed Jaubert on May 21, was dated back to April 8, so anxious were the Turks to have no new black marks against them. They antedated it to the time Jaubert reached the Dardanelles, remembering that in the similar situation of 1804, he had counted the intervening days. The Turkish original of the letter bears the French foreign ministry's appended heading without other comment, "Letter of Sultan Selim to Emperor Napoleon, dated back to April 8, 1805." The reply committed the sultan to no policy. He addressed his answer to "His Majesty, our very august friend Napoleon." Napoleon's agent in Bucharest reported that Turks there said the sultan's letter had been addressed "To Napoleon Bonaparte, our friend," without recognizing the imperial dignity. The ministry's French translation of the reply gives the salutation as follows: "To His Majesty, our very august, very sublime, very magnificent, and very affectionate friend." There is no mention of royalty, no title of emperor, or padishah, or king, but only "His Majesty." Nor is there any mention of Napoleon's name. The overleaf of the original bears the name Napoleon alone.

Selim thanked the French emperor for the confidential letter, which Jaubert, "our friend," had put into his own hands. Although the sultan did not salute Napoleon as emperor or padishah in the letter, he termed him eminent and a genius. Selim wished the happy concord between Turkey and France to be "consolidated more and more." He reciprocated all of Napoleon's friendly personal expressions. Napoleon's letter contained many counsels, the sultan stated noncommittally, at a time when everyone hoped the friendship of long standing between France and Turkey would grow anew. The attachment that Napoleon's "glorious majesty" had expressed for Selim's "august person" had been particularly demonstrated. Napoleon's entire letter unmistakably marked his friendship for Turkey. The letter had been read with all the attention it merited, and it had given the sultan much satisfaction. The latter had known for a long time that Napoleon possessed great energy and elevation of soul, and had been convinced of Napoleon's personal regard for himself. The opinions and advice in the letter offered such proof of Napoleon's friendship as did not have to be demonstrated by long arguments. The sultan liked especially Napoleon's sentence, "To everything is assigned its opportune moment," for in that statement one found "the source of all kinds of success." So the reply ran, for what would require two additional paragraphs to condense. It was signed, "Old friend, Sultan Selim."[14] It included not one word of Russia, or of naval ships, or of the Black Sea, or of politics. "That is all we have been able to obtain," Ruffin explained. He considered the reply sentimental yet significant because of the peculiarities of the moment.[15]

All these developments occurred while Ruffin and Jaubert conferred together about plans for the latter's secret journey to Teheran. Throughout 1805, France sent no ambassador to the Ottoman capital. Counselor of Embassy Ruffin, of all the staff, especially overworked himself during these days. He negotiated with the Turks; he served as embassy paymaster; he assembled material for the official dispatches, which he himself wrote, revised, and copied; he ciphered and deciphered. For the first time he began to complain, at sixty-three, that he could no longer do the active things he did as a young man of twenty-five, when he had followed the famous Gueray Khan's campaigns in the Crimea in 1769. He appeared pleased to receive official confirmation of what the Turks already had told him from Brune's explanation: that Parandier had been named chargé d'affaires because he himself had been reserved for a higher place in Ottoman counsels.

It is interesting that by the instructions Ruffin, rather than Chargé d'Affaires Parandier, handled all the secret details at the Turkish capital, the intermediary point for Persia. Parandier was completely ignored while the clever negotiations were going on to arrange the two journeys to the Persian capital. Jaubert planned with Ruffin and Eugene Franchini to depart for Persia instead of for his announced destination in the west. Ruffin's friend, Ibrahim Effendi, the kiaya bey, became another actor in the drama, giving Ruffin the inside track on secret information.

Parandier did not learn of these plans, so secret were they. With the reply in hand, Jaubert now publicly announced he would soon leave to meet the emperor at Milan and deliver it. Jaubert reported that no one at Constantinople except those sharing the secret knew he had any object other than to deliver Napoleon's letter and receive the reply. The Turks liked him. One minister proposed that he become the regular intermediary between Ambassador Halet Effendi and the foreign ministry in Paris. Ruffin on April 24 acknowledged the ciphered instructions for Jaubert's mission to Persia, a journey he considered as difficult as it was important. He thought Jaubert could return to Constantinople from Teheran within four months, but he foretold difficulties. The "barbarous jealousy" of the English most certainly would be a factor in his success. Remembering the assassination of a French engineer in the desert in 1782, Ruffin advised Jaubert to travel to the north, by way of Erzurum, Erivan, and the towns south of the Caspian. Vassilovitz confirmed this as the better and more rapid route.

In withholding their Persian schemes from Parandier, Ruffin explained that the secrecy over the delivery of Napoleon's letter to the sultan was necessary in order to prevent Italinski's learning the details. Parandier's dispatches confirm his ignorance of the arrangements. When applying to Parandier for a passport to France for Antoine Franchini, Jaubert simply told the chargé d'affaires he had been directed to bring one of the Franchinis back to Paris. Ibrahim Effendi and Eugene and Antoine Franchini were the local men who helped in the secret arrangements for Jaubert's departure.

The unexpected fortnight's delay before Jaubert had in hand the reply to Napoleon's letter found the first special envoy still at Constantinople when Romieu appeared on May 19. The latter apparently was little noticed at first, being taken simply as a diplomatic courier. Yet his incognito had not been preserved. He was surprised to learn from Jaubert, Ruffin, and Eugene Franchini that his coming had been announced by the Prince of Wallachia, whose courier preceded him to Constantinople by two days. Romieu reasoned this must have been revealed by his letter of introduction addressed by Undersecretary Hauterive to Consul Saint Luce at Bucharest. That letter mentioned him as being on a secret mission. In conferences the three outlined Romieu's trip, Jaubert's already having been prepared. One slip by Paris respecting Parandier had to be covered up. In their preoccupation when sending Romieu, Talleyrand and Napoleon neglected to write the chargé d'affaires. Embarrassed, Ruffin saw Romieu appear with a large packet of documents but no letter for Parandier. Before long everyone speculated —Turks, Russians, and English—about Romieu. Eugene Franchini, who could be counted upon for inventing reasons whenever required, schemed to throw the curious off guard by whispering an approximation of the truth. Revealing an eastern destination, he confidentially stated to the Turks that Romieu was en route to Muscat, feeling this most certainly would suggest Romieu's going in the opposite direction. He even told this to Parandier. To put the Russians off Romieu's scent, Eugene Franchini proposed that Romieu be announced as the new French consul at Basra, with the explanation that the hopes for general peace would render that point important for trade. The British and the Russians, Ruffin also believed, "would fix their eyes on that area but finish by concluding he must be going somewhere in the opposite direction, to Greece, Albania, or Rumelia." If one revealed a part of the correct information, it might throw them off the trail completely.[16] Romieu joined Jaubert and Ruffin in lauding Ibrahim as the "intimate and unqualified friend of the French government."

By June, their funds were available to both envoys, and their assistants were hired. Jaubert departed first, on June 8, together with Antoine Franchini and the original Armenian messenger and a French domestic servant. They knew it would be difficult if not impossible to obtain Turkish authorization for Jaubert to go to Persia. Hence he traveled on an unused passport issued to Antoine for a trip to Trebizond. Before departing by ship, Jaubert solemnly accepted the sultan's letter to Napoleon. Antoine and he set out together, and each took the other's place after leaving the Bosporus. Jaubert was presumably sailing for Varna, the route he had followed in 1804 after having received another such letter. Ruffin had arranged for a second boat to be waiting at the northern outlet of the Bosporus. To carry out the deception, instead of going to Paris as publicly announced, Jaubert transferred to this boat for Trebizond, and Antoine's boat continued to Bulgaria. Antoine remained in Bucharest for 15 days, and late in July delivered the sultan's letter and other dispatches to Talleyrand in Geneva. This was intended to allow Jaubert time to arrive in Trebizond and perhaps to travel beyond.

Romieu set out for Aleppo on June 15, accompanied as far as Scutari by Eugene Franchini. This envoy carried the letters from Talleyrand to Corancez and Rousseau, together with the signed duplicate of Napoleon's letter to the shah and its translation into Persian. Napoleon's letter he

kept separately and secretly on his person. He took with him to Aleppo
an interpreter and a considerable quantity of books and papers. Thus
the two left unnoticed, Jaubert to travel by the northern route and
Romieu by the southern route through Alexandretta and Aleppo.

Jaubert had reached and passed Erzurum and Romieu had left Aleppo
when, near the end of July, Eugene Franchini, back in Constantinople,
again displayed his ingenuity. Parandier listened to his story about Jaubert's movements. Eugene first set the stage by appearing ignorant of
any unusual plan for Jaubert. He then revealed, as a "discovery" from
a friend in Vienna who had written a member of his brother's wife's
family in Constantinople, that Napoleon had departed from Italy on
June 12, taking Jaubert with him. This "inside" information was nullified by the French consul at Trebizond, who reported to Parandier of
seeing Jaubert in that place. Ruffin was questioned, and frankly stated
he could not reveal the details until so instructed by Paris. Early in
August, when the boat that transported Jaubert to Trebizond returned,
everyone knew the truth—because Jaubert had requested the same boat
to call for him a month later. All this proved too much even for gullible
Parandier.[17]

By mid-July opinion in Constantinople held that Turkey would give
in to Russia's insistent demand to renew the alliance. France's official
staff reasoned that Turkey would either make an alliance or agree with
Russia's demand that one be signed soon. Turkey did not wish to include
stipulations foreign to the alliance proper, among them Russia's request
that Turkey confirm the autonomy of the Principalities of Moldavia and
Wallachia.[18] A Russian argument put before the Turks held that France
and Austria were scheming together to prepare a partition of the Balkans.
Talleyrand again directed Ruffin to try his best to forestall new Ottoman alliances with Russia and Britain. He could state that a renewal
would discontent France and weaken Turkey. The foreign minister
thought that fictitious news reports in the *Moniteur* might possibly help
to discourage Turkey's pro-Russian policy. Late in June, 1805, a foreign
ministry article datelined Constantinople told of Russian troops coming
to the Adriatic and of pressure in the region between the Caspian and
Black Seas. The article significantly hinted that Turkey had not failed
to notice these moves. Another news item stated that Turkey would take
steps to defend the interests and dignity of its empire, perhaps by closing
the Dardanelles.

Britain's Ambassador Arbuthnot appeared on June 21. Reports had it that the new envoy threatened to depart if Turkey did not express in writing an attitude antipathetic to France and did not meet all of Russia's requests. If the sultan did not renew the Russo-Turkish alliance, the Russians reportedly threatened to invade Turkey. The Turks, on the other hand, could excuse their procrastination since the existing eight-year alliance of 1798 by its terms still had fourteen months to run.[19]

Russia joined Britain against France. Nothing suggesting a partition of the sultan's domains appeared in their alliance, ratified July 28, 1805. Russia could appraise Napoleon's ambitions from the general European situation. As for the Levant, it could judge from Brune's activities, Napoleon Bonaparte's imperial and colonial objectives in Egypt in 1798, and from his underhand negotiations with Tsar Paul I in 1800. The tsar's advisers interpreted these episodes as predicated upon certain fixed ideas, among them the desire to open up commercial contacts between Marseille and Russia in the Black Sea and thus fully utilize the ports of Italy and southern France. These advisers believed the imposing position of Russia disquieted the French emperor more than the state of war with Britain. Feeling persisted in Russian quarters that General Menou, the last commander of the French expedition to Egypt, had been stationed in Turin for the express purpose of opening and maintaining Napoleon's contacts with Egypt. They also reasoned that Brune had been sent as ambassador in order to keep before the Turks interpretations of a military kind. Napoleon planned to break up the Russo-Turkish alliance and expel the Russians, whom Frenchmen represented as the true oppressors of the Turks. Napoleon would militarize the Italians and let their country be his route to the Ottoman Empire.[20]

In point of fact, imperial France concerned itself less with the pro-British orientation of Russian policy than with Russia's over-all objectives as reflected in its sailing of the Straits. In his correct analysis for Napoleon, submitted in August, Talleyrand argued that Turkey held far greater importance than did Great Britain in Russia's calculations. He believed that if no serious quarrel with Austria intervened, "every serious subject of a quarrel with Russia could be postponed to the time when the Ottoman Empire would be destroyed."[21]

Ruffin twice complained to Turkey early in September of Russia's sailing of the Straits. But he tempered Talleyrand's arguments, justifying himself to Paris by observing that at the time they were phrased Talleyrand did not know of the Ottoman cabinet changes. Esseid Ismail

Jafez, the new grand vizir, in replying to Talleyrand's letter on September 11 discussed the traditional friendship of France and the Ottoman Empire, remarking on its "freedom from all interruption." He said Talleyrand's comments tended "constantly to consolidate the edifice of mutual affection." Jafez accepted Ruffin's appointment as a good one, one which "no doubt would contribute to doubling the forces of the ancient friendship." The Ottoman said nothing of politics, of Ruffin's opposition to Turkey's alliance with Russia, or of Russia's sailing the Straits.[22]

Among Selim's troubles were provincial revolts and insubordination. Serbia's revolt seemed to point the way to revolts elsewhere in the Ottoman Empire. Over in Egypt incessant troubles had marked the gradual restoration of Ottoman authority. The Mamelukes, nearly always masters of Upper Egypt, warred intermittently with Lower Egypt, governed by pashas in the service of the sultan. Caravans were stopped; commerce was ruined. The insubordinate Mameluke leaders lacked unity among themselves. Drovetti forwarded summaries of the news fortnightly. To his friends among official Turks in Egypt he strongly argued against any further alliance with Russia and especially against aid to England. Sultan Selim decided in mid-1805 to end his lack of direct authority in Egypt. He appointed Mehemet Ali as governor. This thirty-six-year-old Albanian had helped command the regiment of Albanian irregulars who took part in the Turkish fighting against Bonaparte's forces in Egypt.[23]

French influence in Egypt had been and continued to be largely personal. Drovetti won Mehemet Ali's good will, forecasting the considerable influence by Frenchmen in the pasha's colorful career until his death in 1849. Mehemet Ali built on the foundations laid by the French army in Egypt from 1798 to 1801. He initiated and identified himself with various internal improvements that contributed greatly to the building of modern Egypt. He expanded the army and navy and launched agricultural and scientific advances. The French convinced the Egyptians so thoroughly of their military superiority that Mehemet Ali long favored French military instructors and technicians. He restored commerce, particularly that of interest to Europeans. However, he established a state monopoly of foreign trade, which foreigners disliked. He duplicated French financial methods in Egypt, paying and provisioning his army through forced loans.[24] In short, during the Napoleonic period Mehemet Ali laid the foundations for a personal rule which permitted him in the 1830's to challenge the sultan in two wars over Syria and in 1840 to establish his family as the hereditary rulers of Egypt.

Assuming a fighting war with Russia to be inevitable, Napoleon's preference for the suggested alliance with Persia lent special significance to the mission of the two envoys en route to Teheran, in mid-1805. Jaubert almost cleared the last Ottoman frontier town without causing suspicion. After leaving Trebizond, he traveled to Erzurum in the company of Osep Vassilovitz. There he outfitted himself in Oriental dress, an act sufficient to arouse the suspicions of a true Oriental. The French capital—unaware of Jaubert's approaching difficulties—about that time discovered an omission in the envoy's original instructions. What must he do upon his return from Persia? Talleyrand directed that he must not wait for new instructions at Constantinople, but must report to Napoleon immediately.[25]

The lateness of the season spurred the travelers on. They finally came to Bayazid, an Armenian Kurd village in Turkey named after the early Ottoman sultan. It was the focal frontier point for Turkey, Armenia, and Persia. There Mehmed Pasha, the local ruler, detained Jaubert by force, for either ransom or inquiry or for both. Like most Ottoman pashas in Anatolia and on the frontiers of the sultan's empire, Mehmed governed his territory in virtual independence of the central authority. He separated Vassilovitz from Jaubert, forced the guide to reveal Jaubert's nationality, and arrested the French envoy (July 7). Jaubert had accepted Mehmed's proffered escort of Kurds to conduct him to Erivan. This proved a ruse, for they conducted him only to the outskirts of the city. At an isolated house he faced Mehmed, who pretended to place him in protective custody upon orders from Constantinople.

Jaubert was imprisoned in an underground part of the citadel of Bayazid, where he lived a miserable life during the ensuing months. The many reports of approaching relief proved false. Thus until February 19, 1806, and even later, Jaubert's furtherance of Napoleonic policy remained at a complete standstill. He tells of his imprisonment in a nonpolitical travelogue published in 1821. He relates that in 1806 an epidemic worse than any for 80 years decimated the district. It killed Mehmed and his son. Ibrahim Pasha, an uncle of the deceased governor, then succeeded to power. Meanwhile Jaubert acquired friends, who got word of his captivity through to Persia. When the shah interceded, the newly installed Ibrahim solicited the orders of the sultan. Thereupon Yousef Pasha, the sultan's governor of Ottoman Asia, negotiated Jaubert's release. Upon receipt of the Turkish orders, February 19, 1806, Jaubert and his small group left Bayazid for Teheran.[26]

Romieu came to Aleppo by the southern route on July 14, 1805. There he met not only Consul Corancez but also the two Rousseaus, father and son. Jean François Rousseau was a son of Jacques Rousseau, who had accompanied Louis XIV's Ambassador Michel to Persia to negotiate the treaty of commerce of 1708. Jean François Rousseau had first appeared in Basra in 1756, as a student of Oriental languages; later he became an agent of the Compagnie Française des Indes Orientales. Then Louis XVI appointed him consul and transferred him to Bagdad. There he served during the Revolution, the Consulate, and the Empire, until his death in 1808. Both father and son traveled widely. The son, Joseph Rousseau, whom Napoleon appointed consul at Basra, ceded nothing to his father in *savoir-faire* or scientific value. He learned Persian while a student at Bagdad, an exceptional accomplishment for a young Frenchman. He made himself known to Talleyrand in 1805 by submitting a long report concerning the general situation of the shah's realm and by writing poetry in Persian which eulogized France and Emperor Napoleon. Some of this poetry, translated by Ruffin, is in the French archives today.[27]

According to the Napoleonic instructions which Romieu transmitted, Jean François Rousseau must return to Bagdad to collect data dealing with political, geographical, civil, and military matters in Persia. Romieu invited Joseph Rousseau to accompany him to Teheran. Thereupon the Rousseaus found excuses to object. The father alleged the son's illness. Joseph promised to come later, however, perhaps the next year. As a substitute he recommended his brother-in-law, Georges Outrey, vice-consul at Bagdad. Joseph had married Elizabeth Outrey, the daughter of Christophe Outrey, a French physician long in the service of the pasha of Bagdad. Romieu thereupon employed Outrey as his guide-interpreter, aide-de-camp, and secretary. It may be noted that a great-grandson of Georges Outrey is Amédée Outrey, the present-day director of the archives of the French Ministry of Foreign Affairs and long in the French consular service; his daughter is the namesake of the earlier Elizabeth Outrey.

Georges Outrey spoke Arabic, and could wear the Oriental costume like a true Ottoman. Ruffin had cautioned Jaubert and Romieu to clear the Turkish frontier as rapidly as possible, this being one reason for Romieu's pushing on from Aleppo immediately, on July 25. En route to Teheran he and Outrey and their small party encountered brigands and other dangers. A special courier dispatched after them by the elder Rousseau warned them of possible attacks from English sympathizers. If details later supplied by Outrey are of interest: he and Romieu traveled from Aleppo by way of Birijik, crossing the Euphrates, then by Urfa, Mardin, Mosul, Kerkuk, Kermanshah, and Hamadan. Between Urfa and Mardin they were in constant danger of assassins. J. F. Rousseau and Corancez later accused England's Consul General John Barker of inspiring their attempted arrest, perhaps murder, a charge that engendered a fierce debate in Bagdad and Aleppo. Romieu and party arrived in Teheran on September 24, 1805, too ill to render impressive services for Napoleon.

The shah received Romieu in a ceremonious secret audience at which Napoleon's letter was duly presented. In Romieu's only extant communication from Teheran after his arrival, he sent meager details to Joseph Rousseau on October 3. He said he had arrived a week earlier, thoroughly tired, after braving suffering, dangers, and sickness. He charged that English partisans attempted to assassinate him. He had been received by the shah. He expected to be presented again, when he would deliver the gifts he had brought. The Persians accused the English of perfidy for having intimate official relations with Russia, their enemy. Romieu said that if young Rousseau returned to Persia he would hardly recognize the country, so much had it changed. He found the Persian court in deplorable relations with Russia, with no end of the impasse in sight. Although Jaubert should have arrived a month earlier, he had not yet appeared. The Persians readily agreed to send an envoy to Paris, but only after Joseph Rousseau arrived—a qualification proposed, Romieu believed, merely to gain time to learn the British reactions. He urged young Rousseau to hasten his coming to Persia.[28]

The envoy died shortly afterwards. Young Outrey and another companion of the trip recovered, being more habituated to the climate and possessing robust constitutions. When Outrey carried the news back to Bagdad, many believed Romieu and his companions had been poisoned by English partisans. From Aleppo, Corancez later confirmed Outrey's report of Romieu's death and burial with honor by the Persians. Outrey, after the demise of his chief and his own recovery from several days of similar illness, received from Shah Feth Ali a "diploma" for Napoleon, and from the grand vizir a dispatch for Talleyrand. The shah announced to him the approaching appointment of one of the big men of Persia,

Mirza Mohammed Riza, as ambassador to France.[29] Thus Outrey
brought real news to Bagdad and Aleppo. Napoleon seemed on the
way to winning his first objective, the shah's promise of an ambassador
(chap. viii).

Talleyrand reminded the French navy that the French government
always had possessed the title of protector of Roman Catholic establishments in the Levant.[30] He thus appraised for Napoleon the general situation of the Ottoman Empire in respect to Russian policy: unless Austria
raised issues, any serious French quarrel with Russia should await the
time when the Ottoman Empire must be partitioned. For circulation
to the French foreign missions he stated on July 23 that Russia menaced
Turkey and fomented provincial revolts.[31]

The foreign minister late in July phrased special instructions which
Parandier must have expected. Ruffin was ordered to replace the latter
as chargé d'affaires. Talleyrand came to appreciate Ruffin at this time,
after having read of the latter's secret conferences with Ibrahim which
had aided so greatly in attaining both of Jaubert's objectives. Ruffin's
promotion, he stated, came "in consequence of happy changes in the
counsels of the sultan, to which his zeal had contributed." Parandier
was directed to have his colleague accredited immediately, with little
formality and without calling for a personal audience with Sultan Selim.

As soon as Turkey accepted Ruffin in the new capacity the latter had
to deliver an official note calling attention to the "constant passage of
Russian troops by the Bosporus," this being clearly interpreted as a
menace to the safety of the Ottoman Empire. "Under pretext of simple
passage," Talleyrand warned, "they might stop before the capital and
burn its walls." Napoleon considered all these Russian transports to be
passing the Straits with a simulated destination. "Russia is at war with
no one," Talleyrand continued. "But its vessels and the troops it sends
pertain to a system of war that sooner or later might develop. The strong
Russian forces at Corfu have no other object than to foment agitation
in Turkey's European provinces." These small forces could not be for
use against Napoleon. "What are 20,000 troops, in starting war against
France?" So small an army would be the first victim. Turkey possessed
enough troubles without thus making it easy for Russia to attack it.
Talleyrand advised Turkey to adopt strong language. Napoleon said he
did not wish to incite war, but he recommended that Turkey's duty,
following "active and assiduous surveillance," should lead it to declare
war against Russia. Talleyrand stated, "Emperor Napoleon regards the

passage of Russian troops into the Bosporus and the navigation by armed Russian vessels within the Ottoman Straits as an infraction of treaties. Otherwise this is a formal and positive authorization for navigation there by the armed vessels of France." France trusted that the new Ottoman grand vizir would change Turkey's policy.

The foreign minister did not refer bluntly to the refusal to recognize Napoleon's title. He said simply, "Turkey hesitates to recognize Emperor Napoleon's new dignity." He continued, "I may suppose that, our position having progressively ameliorated since your last dispatches, the question will be resolved in the sense of the instructions to Marshal Brune." A Russian negotiator might come to Paris, with instructions reportedly amicable. The coldness between France and Russia might therefore end; hence it did not appear in Ottoman interest to base its policy too much on their friction. Talleyrand wrote in a friendly tone to the grand vizir, ostensibly to notify him of Ruffin's new title.[32] Thereafter questions concerning Napoleon's title simmered. Talleyrand said little or nothing more of it. He seemed far more concerned with Russia's possible interference in the Balkans, including possible aid to Serbia. Turkey would be concerting against itself, he concluded, by continuing to permit Russian ships of war to navigate the Straits.[33]

Ruffin relayed to Talleyrand something of Parandier's disquiet respecting the secrecy surrounding Jaubert's departure from Constantinople. Upon the announcement of Ruffin's new title, Parandier could only prepare to return to Paris. General affairs occupied the displaced chargé d'affaires during his last weeks in office. Gossip held that Arbuthnot had dispatched a British agent to Persia, on Romieu's heels. Parandier noted a "change in the tone and manner" of the Austrian internuncio, the latter complaining that France seemed to want everything in sight. The Austrian predicted, so Parandier heard, that "All Europe would be obliged to send troops to stop the torrent."

Parandier often could duplicate Brune's several reports of 1804 relating to Russian troop transports and naval vessels arriving in the Straits, with more such ships always expected. Ruffin got nowhere with the Ottoman foreign office when raising the issue of the Straits in September, 1805, as directed. Eugene Franchini thereupon created an opportunity to confer directly with the grand vizir. He asked him to read a Turkish translation of that part of Ruffin's note which he stated to be "very serious, respecting the passage of Russian ships by the Bosporus." Jafez merely read it, without comment.[34] Thus Napoleon failed to halt sailing the Straits at that time. The emperor must have known what Ruffin and the others on the spot understood as the reason for the failure, namely that France must establish a far more imposing position in Europe before speaking with vital effect on that subject.

Ruffin, the indispensable and indefatigable professor of Oriental languages, we should note here, enjoyed an exceptionally long academic leave of absence. It extended from 1795 to 1822. An imperial decree divided the functions of his dual chair at the Collège de France in November, 1805. Kieffer, his colleague for years at Constantinople and fellow-prisoner during the time French forces held Egypt, became acting professor of Turkish. Silvestre de Sacy, the noted French teacher of Oriental languages, replaced Ruffin as professor of Persian. Only in 1822—when Ruffin had reached the age of eighty—did the officials finally cancel his claim to Kieffer's position.[35]

This chapter has discussed a segment of the transitional year in the evolution of an effective Napoleonic policy for the Near and Middle East. Until there should be a significant new orientation of general European policy, Paris knew the government at Constantinople would not concede the recognition of Napoleon's titles. Napoleon thought he must find military support from within that region. Persia's overture for an alliance found him responsive and eager. Owing to difficulties of communication with Persia and the lack of definite information on the shah's military potential, his best initial opportunity seemed to be in neutral Turkey. There he could plan to halt Russia's sailing of the Dardanelles. He reasoned that if it should be possible later to bring Turkey and Persia into the French orbit, a gigantic pincer could be created against the tsar. Napoleon had begun to secure the aid of both countries in implementing his general policies.

IV

Ottoman Policy Veers Toward France

UNTIL 1812 Emperor Napoleon challenged his enemies front by front, and usually nation by nation. His opportunity soon came to build up French prestige in the eyes of the hesitant Ottoman ministers. When, late in August, 1805, Austria joined Russia and England to form the Third Coalition, it became the principal immediate objective of his Grand Army. Tsar Alexander hoped to remain neutral in 1805 and yet to aid Russia's allies with measures short of war. French aggrandizement, however, so menacing to those allies, forced him to take up arms in September. Even so, he never considered that he participated in a fighting war that year. Consul General de Lesseps did not even quit his post at St. Petersburg. At that time the tsar declared Russia's war objectives to be: preserving the sacred inviolability of treaties and reëstablishing the general tranquillity. Many people in the Europe of that day must have believed that nothing could withstand his third blitzkrieg against the Habsburgs, just as many in 1939 and 1940 doubtless believed that Hitler would win. Napoleon's one-by-one conquests anticipated Hitler's successive if transitory victories. The purpose was the same. Napoleon's war at sea figured on the deficit side of the French ledger, for Admiral Nelson won the great victory of Trafalgar over the allied French and Spanish fleets off Cadiz on October 21. After that, Napoleon could produce no navy worthy of challenging the British.

In this chapter we discuss the influence on Russia's Near Eastern policy of the significant Napoleonic military campaigns against Austria. Although Sultan Selim III, over French protest, renewed the Ottoman alliance with Russia in September, 1805, he became so convinced by February, 1806, of Napoleon's impregnable military position in Europe that he climbed aboard Napoleon's band wagon. He heralded this policy in one way by recognizing fully and publicly the French ruler's imperial titles, over the continued strong Anglo-Russian opposition and despite having previously acceded to Tsar Alexander's demand. More significant, a few of Selim's closest advisers eventually talked him into putting into writing a secret statement later handed Napoleon's agents to the effect that cordiality no longer existed in Russo-Turkish relations.

In September, Talleyrand sent to Ruffin the first news of the new war against Austria. He hoped Turkey "would not be involved." Ruffin at the moment was discussing a new tariff with Turkey and analyzing the news of Mehemet Ali's changes in Egypt. Napoleon ordered a general survey of the tsar's military potential, with his blitzkrieg against Austria about to be undertaken at a time when Russia's military policy remained uncertain. He used the French diplomatic clearing centers of Berlin, Dresden, Copenhagen, and Constantinople. Ruffin's special assignment from Talleyrand stated, "You will add precise information of the Russian regiments that have passed the Dardanelles to sail to Corfu and send exact information respecting any new troops for that destination."[1]

Turkey might have veered either toward Russia or toward France in policy, and against a possibly recalcitrant Turkey either of these powers could favor the extreme solution of bringing about its collapse. Having a military alliance with Turkey, Russia possessed the initial advantage. Among the recurrent projects to partition the sultan's empire that concerned Napoleon, one, in September, 1805, favored the freeing of Greece under Napoleonic sponsorship. The project is an unsigned memorandum among the papers of the diplomatic series for Turkey in the archives of the French Ministry of Foreign Affairs. It is a note that doubtless influenced Talleyrand's new scheme, which we shall consider below. The memorandum—mailed from Marseille—was not written by Parandier,[2] that ex-official still being in Constantinople. Its unnamed author would partition the Ottoman Empire as a means of containing Russia. The author took into consideration all the major powers except Prussia. "The way to deal a terrible blow to Russia and to Austria," he stated, "is to reëstablish the Eastern Greek Empire." Turkey's weakness invited action. If Austria and Russia did the partitioning, there would be difficulty for France. A better plan would be to send a French army into European Turkey, at the same time calling upon all the Greeks to throw off the Ottoman "yoke." If Turkey did not align itself with the enemies of France it would be impolitic to attack it, the memorandum continued. "Today, however, the Turk is entering a coalition against France and we are justified in attacking it by every means."

The author's proposed invasion in order to establish an "insurmountable barrier" against Russia and Austria, did not require the reëstablishment of independent Poland along with Greece, although both these were the natural allies of France. If Prussia did not join France's enemies, Napoleon might establish only the Greek monarchy and compensate Prussia in the north. France for its part would take compensation for liberating Balkan Europe, especially Crete, from Turkey. Crete's location would favor commerce with the Black Sea and with Turkey in Europe, Asia, and Africa. The territorial spoils from Turkey, however, represented merely a detail. The memorandum desired to justify a French attack on Turkey for the purpose of partitioning it. This partition might come by means of an agreement with Russia and Austria, in which event France would acquire the territory stretching from Salonica to the Morea, together with Crete and most of the islands of the Archipelago. If France invaded without aid it should take only Crete, and its enemies would acquire nothing.[3]

This memorandum illustrated a trait of Napoleon's planning. If ever Sultan Selim III ignored Napoleon's imperial titles, the latter would have a way of dealing with that. Napoleon preferred the opposite course, however: to establish his position impregnably in order to encourage the Ottoman support of French policy. The germ had been planted, nevertheless, and when, within six weeks, Napoleon's military victories prepared the Austrian question for a new treaty solution, Talleyrand himself recommended a plan of partition.

Talleyrand had long expected a new Russo-Turkish alliance to be signed. His usually pro-Turkish feelings gave way for a moment to a determination to meet menace with menace. In mid-October he "meditated on the future peace" and drafted for Napoleon a scheme for detaching parts of the Ottoman Empire. This he would have put through in concert with Austria. He recommended that Austria be made strong in the Balkans, to be a balance for Russia and what remained of the Ottoman Empire. He reasoned on the basis of only four great powers, Russia being excluded from that rank and France being the greatest. By virtue of location Austria and Russia stood as France's "natural enemies." Russia, while not the enemy of France, indirectly became one because it was the natural foe of France's allies, including the Ottoman Empire. Located on either side of France, Austria and Britain should be its rivals; yet in view of the Russian menace they should be considered natural and necessary allies. A French alliance with Prussia seemed out of the question. If Austria could be separated from England and its interests thrown into opposition to Russia's, the Ottoman Empire would be guaranteed. Talleyrand would push Austria away from all direct territorial contact with France in Italy. Independent Venice and Trieste might be interposed, preferably as a republic under French influence. This would exclude Austria from one of the principal keys to Switzerland and in general push Austria toward the east. He admitted that the result would be, as always, a revenge-seeking enemy, if such sacrifices were imposed without compensation. One might support one's rival in the face of greater dangers elsewhere. France should therefore fortify Austria against Russia. Austrians should not be unwilling to exchange Venice, Tyrol, and the neighboring regions for Moldavia, Wallachia, Bessarabia, and northern Bulgaria.

Such an exchange would bar Russia from the Balkan land route to Constantinople and the Straits and direct the tsar's territorial aspirations toward Asia. Thus, it should strengthen the remaining portion of the Ottoman Empire, even though weakening the whole. In any event the Turks, by not having made progress, had lost their relative power-position in Europe. They became weaker because they were too far extended in the Balkans. They held Moldavia and Wallachia only nominally. They were, according to Talleyrand, definitely encumbered with too many lands for their weak central government. In Austrian hands the Danubian Principalities would constitute a real barrier to Russia. Placed on a common frontier there, Russia and Austria would moreover become "rivals and natural enemies." With Turkey between them, as then, they were natural allies. Austria's task of governing them would be difficult because, he believed, these provinces would prefer Russia. With the Russian menace and the native population keeping Austria desirably occupied, the latter perforce would gravitate toward France. Turning Russia toward Asia would pit the tsar against Great Britain in India. Talleyrand drafted a French treaty with Austria embodying these principal ideas. This pledged France to intervene "in an efficacious manner" to win these concessions from Turkey in favor of Austria and guaranteed Austria's hold over the new provinces as against Russia.[4]

Foreign Minister Czartoryski's preliminary draft for the tsar of the renewed alliance with Turkey mentioned only the privilege of sailing Russian war vessels through the Straits. Minister Italinski at Constantinople deemed it necessary to specify this amply, however, as had been true in 1798. Thereby the entrance of the Black Sea could be kept closed to the ships of war of other foreign nations. Italinski explained that his insistence was due to the sailing of an English frigate to Constantinople. If the action became a precedent, Napoleon would follow it.

Turkey's new defensive military and naval alliance was signed with Russia on September 23. It was intended to be effective for nine years. The terms were similar to those of 1798, including authority for Russia to navigate the Straits. Russia and Turkey agreed to consider the Black Sea closed to all naval forces except the Russian and the Turkish. (This suggests the virtually parallel demand of the Soviet Union in 1946, which the United States and Great Britain positively opposed.) Russia and Turkey reciprocally guaranteed the integrity of their territories as then held.

The alliance admitted Russian warships and transports into the Straits in order to defend their closure, but it specifically excluded from the Black Sea all other foreign vessels of war, including carriers of munitions. It also stipulated the right to enter each other's ports for repairs or as winter havens. The attempt of another power to violate the stipulated closure would be considered hostile to both. If Russia and France went to war, the sultan must either furnish a contingent of troops or coöperate with the tsar in other ways. Presumably this meant the closure of the Straits except to Russia's warships, although this was not so stated. Russia's vessels of war might pass the Straits on all occasions, and specifically they could communicate with the Ionian Islands. Russia promised to treat Turkey kindly in any alliances formed against Napoleonic France.[5]

This alliance was presumably secret but Ibrahim, or another Turkish friend, revealed it to Ruffin, whom we find demanding on October 5 a categorical statement as to whether or not the alliance with Russia had been renewed. The Ottoman foreign office replied that as yet nothing could be said. Ruffin took this reply literally and transmitted a long argument against renewal. Although he suspected the actual signing, he hoped by his action to delay or prevent the ratification. He protested vigorously, always contending that the general peace in 1802 had annulled the sultan's alliances with England and Russia.

In St. Petersburg, Czartoryski impatiently awaited the result. He reflected during the first half of October on the outcome of Italinski's negotiations. He presumed the delay of news was caused by the poor roads. Since the situation when Bonaparte held Egypt in 1798 was different, he believed the alliance would be renewed—a renewal that would not be due to Turkey's loyalty or good will or need. He reasoned that Italinski may have caused the downfall of Mahmed, the grand vizir heading a group of Turkish ministers unfavorable to Russia. If so, it would indicate a Turkey ready to fulfill new engagements to Russia. If Italinski should succeed, it would be in order to present the customary gifts at the exchange of ratifications. Although Ottoman ministers did not deserve any gifts at all, the tsar should send inexpensive presents.[6] The foreign minister of Russia meanwhile schemed in the direction of a Pan-Slavist federation.

Not only did Napoleon ignore Talleyrand's recommendation to arrange with Austria to amputate the Ottoman Empire, but he also flirted with Russia. He sent General Savary to the Russian military field headquarters to speak for the restoration of general peace (November 27, 1805). That officer received a cool reception, although Tsar Alexander did write a short letter in his own hand, addressed simply to the "Chief of the French Government." Two days later Savary appeared again, this time inviting a personal meeting of the two sovereigns. Whereas Russia's impatient military advisers declined this offer, the tsar compromised. He sent Dolgoruki, an aide-de-camp, to meet the French emperor at the French outposts on November 30. Napoleon suggested that Russia annex Moldavia instead of quarreling with France, a suggestion the Russians rebuffed.[7]

Successive war bulletins sent to Constantinople by special couriers both anticipated and confirmed the French victories that would aid French policy there. A rumor placed Napoleon's armies in Vienna as early as October 10, whereas they actually entered it on November 13. Having lost his fight against the ratification of the Russo-Turkish alliance, Ruffin was encouraged to new efforts by the rapid advances of the Grand Army.

From the vantage point of occupied Vienna Talleyrand enthusiastically detailed the military successes on December 9, by which time speculation within Napoleon's court circles placed Jaubert and Romieu as almost certainly at their destination of Teheran. Wishful thinkers looked ahead to a triple alliance of France, Turkey, and Persia against Russia and Great Britain. On Christmas Day of 1805, Ruffin wrote with equal enthusiasm: "The miraculous victories of our august emperor have weakened the attachment of the Greeks for the Russians. May they diminish also the fear of them held by the Turks!"[8]

Napoleon surveyed affairs, likewise in Vienna, when the ratifications of the Russo-Turkish treaty of alliance were being exchanged on December 30. It might have been expected that Russia would ask Turkey to join immediately in the war against France, an obvious object of the alliance. Turkey's neutral position and the news that day, however, contrasted with the situation of 1798; it was almost impossible for Turkey to enter the war. The news recounted the Battle of Austerlitz on December 2, in which Napoleon annihilated the principal army opposing him. Russia at such an embarrassing moment could hardly ask Turkey to join the war. One is reminded of the parallel of June, 1940, when, upon the defeat of France by Nazi Germany, Britain could not ask Turkey to act on its alliance and go to war against Fascist Italy, which had entered as Hitler's ally.

Napoleon's agents believed that the power of the emperor's sword would give an edge to his words. In order to forestall an English duplication of Russia's treaty success, Ruffin issued a veiled threat against any alliance with "the enemies of His Majesty, the Emperor of the French." Indeed, English politics at Constantinople alerted Ruffin hardly less than Russian policy, and his warnings against Turkey's Russian alliance had been predicated on the assumption that Turkey also would renew with Britain. Logically, the next item on its anti-French agenda would be for the Ottoman council to renew the alliance made with Great Britain when that nation had gone to Egypt in 1798 to defeat the French. Ruffin utilized the favorable impressions of Napoleon's military march against Austria to address a strong note to the Turks against such action (January 15, 1806). He maintained that the peace between France and Turkey signed in 1802 had nullified the English as well as the Russian alliance. Moreover, he said that Turkey itself had nullified the treaties through its neutrality in 1803 after the new Anglo-French war. He contended that no practical reasons existed in 1806 for Turkey to think of remaining Britain's ally.[9]

Ottoman appeasement of Napoleon began immediately. A vizirial letter officially recognized Napoleon's asserted titles of emperor and padishah (January 10, 1806); this recognition reveals a victory over former Turkish policy by the selfsame blitzkrieg that defeated Austria. Ruffin stated that such recognition would constitute ample reason for Napoleon to forget his previous displeasure with the Turks. Yet he sought more than a mere announcement by the grand vizir. Hence the acknowledgment was published in an imperial decree. This appeasement thus occurred very soon after the exchange of ratifications of the Ottoman alliance with Russia which had been protested by the French. Ruffin observed that the Turks seemed to flounder much like men who, unable to swim, have been thrown into the sea.

Following Austerlitz, the French emperor dictated the Peace of Pressburg on December 26, 1805. Napoleon's Italy acquired Venice and Dalmatia, together with Istria, except for Trieste. With bad grace Austrian officers turned over the ex-Venetian coastal strip.[10] Talleyrand jubilantly wrote Ruffin that through these territorial gains France "happily approached the states of the Ottoman Empire, and would thereby multiply the relations between the two neighbors." On January 22 a special courier to Constantinople, coming in twenty days by way of Vienna, brought the news of the Peace of Pressburg and Talleyrand's glowing comments upon the rapidity and continuity of Napoleon's military victories. French agents freely surmised that the new general situation of itself might forestall a renewal of the Turkish alliance with England.[11]

Dalmatia had been held by the later defunct Republic of Venice until 1797; then by Austria until this moment in 1805. This, and the neighboring Illyrian Provinces (acquired by France in 1809), were the only territories France had ever held in the Balkans. Of the nine years of French rule in Dalmatia, the first four stressed a constructive administration under General Marmont and the last five the procurement of manpower and supplies for war. Among numerous constructive improvements were equipping the harbors of Gravoza and Cattaro (see chap. ix); founding the first newspaper; starting a high school; instituting the code Napoléon; and building numerous roads, which represented the most permanent of the physical improvements. The French pacified the Greek Orthodox clergy, even though at the same time they aroused the enmity of the Roman Catholics. The important commercial and postal affairs in the Balkans about which Napoleon was concerned related to a great highway the emperor desired to establish between the Adriatic and the Bosporus. Although all the French agents worked to organize a fairly satisfactory postal service, this project became primarily a responsibility of the military. But they never developed the commercial route.[12]

News of Napoleon's occupation of Vienna touched off studies in St. Petersburg of the policy Russia must now adopt. Tsar Alexander created a special council of the key men of his court, as the upshot of their debates early in January 1806. The Peace of Pressburg speeded up Russia's adoption of alternate policies for the Near East. Princes Lupchin,

Kurakrin, and Czartoryski, together with Counts Stroganov, Zavadov-ski, Vassiliev, Rumiantsov, and Kochubei, concluded that France had acquired in Dalmatia "the means of changing the nature of existing relations between Russia and the Ottoman Empire, and of enforcing its views upon the latter." All but two of these same advisers favored a policy of unity with England and efforts to preserve the confidence of the Ottoman council. Stroganov and Rumiantsov demurred, the lat-ter thereby notably stamping himself as pro-French. Nine advisers favored attempting to discover Napoleon's real sentiments toward Rus-sia: namely, Soltykov, Stroganov, Zavadovski, Kurakrin, Vassiliev, Lup-chin, Troschinski, Chichagov, Czartoryski. Five favored a more spirited policy, a policy intended to prevent a Franco-Austrian concert in the Balkans. General Viasmitinov, together with Kochubei, Troschinski, Chichagov, and Czartoryski advised Tsar Alexander: "In any case, and in all events, to hold Russia's land and sea forces on a most respectable footing, and dispose them in such manner as to be able to employ them where necessity dictated, and particularly in Moldavia and Wallachia, if the Austrians wish to occupy these Principalities or if the French attack the Ottoman Empire."[13]

No hint of these significant secret discussions reached French ears at the time, although Consul General Barthélemy de Lesseps in St. Peters-burg could hardly fail to see the frigidity in Russian attitudes as well as in the Russian weather. He stated he could depend little on the announcements of the Russian cabinet. He felt, more than knew, that for two months his correspondence with Paris had been opened and read. On the other hand, Franco-Russian relations perceptibly improved in recent weeks. Foreign Minister Czartoryski suggested confidentially to De Lesseps on January 29 that Russia neared a *rapprochement* with France, provided France felt the same way. This put a question which Napoleon's envoy could not answer.

The terms of the Austro-French treaty also led Russia to reveal to Great Britain some of the considerations listed by the tsar's advisers, because the favorable side of Russian policy was the new friendship with Britain. Of the unsatisfactory factors, the French successes in the field suggested a reason for Turkey's possible vacillation in policy. Russians reasoned, according to their statements to London, that the territorial cessions by Austria reflected Napoleon's firm attachment to projects against the Ottoman Empire. The ex-Venetian territories gave France "all imaginable facilities for realizing such projects." How could the situation be met? Turkey itself could do little, and might even "abandon itself without reserve to France." Russia and Great Britain, as the two powers most interested in preserving the Ottoman Empire, should there- fore concert in their policies. Russia proposed to support Turkey if it should, on the off-chance, make war against France. Russia meanwhile should keep 100,000 troops on the frontier of the Principalities. It must retain in the Mediterranean and send to Corfu its army units in Italy theretofore earmarked for return to Russia, and concentrate a naval squadron off Corfu. A Balkan landing, which did not seem improbable, would require support by Britain's forces at Malta—and Britain could make an easy chore of occupying Egypt.

Principal among the Russian steps, if Turkey evinced any serious disposition to sunder Russia's communications through the Dardanelles and Bosporus, would be to occupy Moldavia and Wallachia. Contacts with the sultan's Slavic and other Christian provincials might be de- veloped, in anticipation of an official pro-French policy by Turkey.[14] Unrevealed to England, Russia listed for its own guidance the points any one of which should lead it to employ the 100,000 troops against Turkey. These would move if a French army entered Ottoman territory or if there were any military demonstration by Austria with the apparent object of detaching Ottoman provinces. Likewise, they should act upon the assembling of Turkish forces on the Danube or upon a marked re- inforcement of the garrisons in Bessarabia.

The same result should follow any convincing proof obtained by the Russian minister at Constantinople that Turkey had adopted a pro- French policy and was reversing its alliance with Russia. The hypothet- ical cases which would constitute proof were listed: a categorical demand by Turkey for Russia to evacuate Corfu, or the least difficulty Turkey made in the passage of the Straits by Russian ships, especially those Russian vessels of war returning from the Aegean. If called into action by one of the foregoing situations, the military departments would set the pattern for Russia's army and navy. The army should occupy Molda- via, Wallachia, and Bessarabia, and it should return to Corfu all the Russian troops debarked at Naples. Corfu would have naval reinforce- ments from the Baltic, and immediately get back the naval contingents previously ordered home to the Black Sea. The naval commander in that sea would hold himself in readiness for a demonstration against Constantinople, when notified that Russian soldiers had entered Molda- via and Wallachia. If Turkey declared war against Russia, the tsar's forces must occupy the Principalities immediately and coöperate with Britain in dispatching fleets to the Dardanelles.[15]

It was reasoned that if the Russian army on the Dniester moved promptly, and if the Anglo-Russian squadron appeared at the Dardanelles, Turkey's Christian subjects would be encouraged to revolt. Thus Russia's military and naval forces could support the Ottoman Empire or alternatively speed its dissolution. If Turkey dissolved, the best solution for its European provinces probably would be to create a series of independent states. Serbia, Montenegro, and Herzegovina could be organized quite readily. Macedonia and Albania probably would ask for monarchial regimes. Moldavia, Wallachia, and Bessarabia would be booked for the tsar's annexation.[16]

The admitted basis for Russia's nervous planning was the fact that more than ever France had become the immediate neighbor of the Ottoman Empire. No longer did a weak Austria alone confront it in the Balkans. What could prevent Napoleon from organizing the Balkan provinces, with or without the blessing of the sultan? At first Russia feared that France and Austria had made such an agreement. Russia thus credited Napoleon with a Balkan and Ottoman policy far removed from the actual one he planned. In one of its immediate aspects, as we shall see, Russia appraised the situation with absolute correctness: Turkey could be talked into closing the Straits against Russian vessels of war and troop transports. This was the most insistent demand of the French palace in Pera during the ensuing months. Russia also guessed the sultan's long-range policy, for Napoleon's apparently invulnerable military position in Europe eventually would encourage him to war against the tsar.

By February the Turks revealed to the French the halting attitude of Russia, and indicated that they did not expect to be called upon to fight against Napoleon. They spoke of this to Ruffin and Roux (Talleyrand's secretary who was on special mission to Constantinople). Except for permission for Russia to sail the Straits, the Turkish alliance with Russia seemed dead.[17]

To the friendly Ibrahim, Talleyrand wrote a letter which Roux delivered. The missive conveyed assurances of Napoleon's best intentions toward Turkey (chap. iii). This led to the important negotiations at Constantinople in February; these were conducted by Roux, who really had been sent there to persuade Ibrahim Effendi to influence Turkish policy. Roux, Ruffin, and Ibrahim held several secret conferences. Ostensibly they clarified the types of notification to be issued for Turkey's recognition of Napoleon's titles. More significantly, the French attempted to persuade the Ottomans to end Russia's military navigation of the Straits. In a conference especially authorized by Sultan Selim, Ibrahim spoke in a friendly manner with Roux for three hours one afternoon. Ibrahim made inquiries about ex-Ambassador Brune whom, since his secret departure (chap. ii), the Turks had hitherto disdained to mention. The official recognition of Napoleon became Ottoman public law. It was of utmost significance that the kiaya bey promised to see that the sultan recorded in writing his verbally expressed sentiments, which had now been secretly announced as favorable to Napoleon. Roux could report triumphantly to Talleyrand, "The Ottoman Empire has been delivered by the victories of the Emperor of France."

Ibrahim kept his word. On February 28—after Roux's departure— he delivered to Ruffin a letter written to him by the sultan in which Selim revealed quite friendly feelings for the French people, nation, and emperor. He stated that his alliance with Russia lacked cordiality, as could be surmised from the language of his ministers. His relations with Russia thereafter would be "commanded by policy and by circumstances." He stated that his inclination and esteem from childhood had been completely for the French. "I am myself the ancient friend and partisan of France," he said. He ordered special instructions issued to Halet Effendi to announce his recognition of Napoleon's titles.[18] The Ottoman foreign minister further explained that because France required that the titles emperor and padishah be used in a letter by the sultan himself, such a letter would be sent. The researcher in the archive records of the period can find the Turks using this form of address at least once: ". . . the very magnificent and very celebrated Emperor and Padishah of France, Napoleon I."[19]

Discussions such as these proved the new prestige of French diplomacy in Constantinople, as compared with the lean months after Brune's departure in December, 1804. This was also a notably successful period in putting into effect the pro-French views of Ibrahim Effendi. The latter wrote Talleyrand a long letter on March 2. He reciprocated the French assurance of excellent intentions. He stated, "The bonds that so happily unite the Ottoman Empire and the court of France are indissoluble." They would "assume a new degree of solidarity, in consequence of this mutual assurance."

Writing more at length and less formally to Ruffin, Ibrahim revealed the changed and changing attitude of the sultan's advisers. He explained that in response to Roux's request he had written out a summary of what he had stated verbally in the secret conferences. He had shown the sultan this précis, which resulted in the sultan's letter to him. It is of highest significance that he stated the sultan had given assurance that France could count on his "perfect reciprocity" if Napoleon took an interest in the affairs of the Ottoman Empire. Ruffin observed that such papers as these never before had been communicated by the Ottomans to a European legation. When questioned by the English about some of his pro-French utterances, the kiaya bey stated openly that Turkey held nothing against France. Although allied with Russia and England, Turkey desired peace.

The Ottomans sought other ways to convey their change of feeling toward France. Ambassador Halet presented to the French foreign ministry a "confidential" verbal note which replied to a charge that Ottoman suspicions of French intentions lay behind the publicized defensive preparations they were making in Greece and elsewhere. The new measures were only natural precautions, Halet stated, and were not directed against France. The preparations included some 30,000 or more soldiers who would be moved into Rumelia to establish order. Turkey believed itself able to place under arms some 80,000 to 100,000 well-equipped troops.[20]

Sending Mouhib Effendi as the new Ottoman ambassador to Paris left no doubt of the shift of Turkish policy. According to Ruffin, Mouhib seemed a tranquil partisan of the French. Ruffin had come to know him earlier as the official reporter of the conferences he held with Ibrahim from 1802 to 1804—conferences respecting the unpaid indemnities which were no longer mentioned. Ruffin made friends with Ibrahim in those conferences, we recall, despite his failure to collect any money for the Frenchmen.[21]

Thus in this chapter we have seen that, paradoxically, the greatest impulse to a new French policy of friendship with Turkey came soon after the renewal of the Russo-Turkish alliance. Napoleon's victory over Austria materially affected that alliance by reducing Turkey's will to apply it. Napoleon soon planned his complementary military campaigns against Prussia and Russia. He launched a vigorous new diplomatic offensive against Russia and Britain and, as we shall see, soon supplemented it with a policy of alliance with Turkey and Persia.

V

New French Courses
Are Charted

BY LATE MARCH, 1806, Napoleon had received full re-
ports of the friendly Turkish policy. For the first time since taking over
the helm of the French state he could proceed with a Russian policy
based on Franco-Turkish collaboration. His decision to collaborate became the turning point in French policy for the Straits. He sought first,
however, to test the sultan's changed attitude. He could do so by attacking the authorization for Russia's naval vessels and transports to pass
the Straits in order to carry troops and supplies to the Ionian Islands.
Russians no less than Frenchmen admitted that if Napoleon could win
Turkey's termination of Russia's passage of the Straits, the Russo-
Turkish alliance would be killed. Everyone recognized that Ottoman
general policy could and should be gauged from that specific action.

In this chapter we discuss Napoleon's general Eastern policy, which
by May, 1806, contemplated defeating Russia through military action
in the north with simultaneous diversions by Turkey and Persia in the
south. Transitory negotiations with Russia only delayed this policy without altering it. The specific object for Turkey should be, as Napoleon
himself interpreted it, to end the Russo-Turkish alliance and to exclude
Russia from the Dardanelles and the Bosporus.

Official news from Constantinople reaching St. Petersburg on March
7 confirmed Turkey's recognition of Napoleon as emperor and padishah.
Unofficial reports from the Principalities revealed the need for prompt
measures to meet contingencies there. Several pashas of Rumelia reportedly formed a military garrison of 10,000 at Ismail. More important, the pasha of Scutari (opposite Constantinople) reportedly entered Rumelia with an army of 40,000, both moves reflecting possible
anti-Russian policies at Constantinople. The Ottoman central administration seemed to believe it must clean its house there by deposing
the pro-Russian hospodars of Moldavia and Wallachia.

These moves also were evidence that the Turks felt safe on Napoleon's

Dalmatian frontier of their Balkan empire. In contrast was Russia's Balkan policy, where Cattaro became an issue with France in 1806. The tsar's forces crossed the narrow neck of water between Corfu and the mainland and occupied Cattaro, antagonizing Napoleon. Although he smiled at the four or five thousand Russian troops in the region, he did not admit Russia's right to a counterpoise to his hold on Dalmatia. A lively debate at St. Petersburg marked the initial period of Russia's occupation of Cattaro. Should it not be turned over to Austria? Strategic factors dictated a negative answer, some of the tsar's officials maintaining that the troops stationed there were worth twenty times as many troops stationed elsewhere. Cattaro gave Russia one more reason for its passage of the Straits. Like Corfu, it kept alive the necessity for such passage. The fleet unit first stationed off Cattaro, however, sailed there from the Baltic—with Britain's blessing. Already the principle seemed established whereby Russia restricted its use of the Straits to vessels of the Black Sea fleet. In St. Petersburg no one took for granted that Turkey, wavering as it was, would readily admit the Baltic units into the Black Sea.[1]

The general attitude of the Ottoman government, rather than specific grievances, at first accounted for Russia's holding its Turkish ally suspect. A warning threat to occupy the Principalities of Moldavia and Wallachia, it was reasoned, might deter the Ottomans from their apparent tendency toward concert with Napoleonic France. General Michelson, commander on the Dniester, was authorized in the spring of 1806 to make good on the threat if it were necessary. Russians freely predicted a complete change of Turkish policy: the alliances with Russia and Great Britain would give way to coöperation with France. Contingent orders were issued to Michelson to be prepared for an immediate occupation of the Principalities. Well in advance of need, St. Petersburg prepared a proclamation for Moldavia and Wallachia which said the Russians came only with the intention of saving the Ottoman Empire from France.[2] By direction of March 8, Minister Italinski communicated to Turkey the reasons for Russia's military reconnoiter beyond the Dniester. More important, he requested that orders be issued for Ottoman troops to desist from any hostile preparations against Russia. He stated that otherwise the tsar would be forced to occupy the Principalities in order to assist Turkey to regain its independence.[3]

Russian reasoning was sound because, the long debate respecting Napoleon's titles having ended, Turkey—although unsuccessfully—now appeased Napoleon in a practical anti-Russian way. It moved to withdraw Russia's right to military navigation of the Straits. Turkey overstressed the defensive character of the alliance, however, stating that Russia's operations against France should be considered as obviously offensive. The passage of the Straits thus could not apply, said this diplomatic appraisal, because Turkey might be drawn into the war against France for permitting Russia's vessels of war to sail the Straits. Turkey took this bold initiative on April 26, asking Russia to cease sending such vessels through the Dardanelles and Bosporus.

As one would expect, Minister Italinski promptly refused. He charged Turkey with attempting to evade "the only interesting article" of the covenant of alliance and warned that, the case arising, Russia "reserved the faculty of having recourse to force." He held his ground with success. In a test on June 24, when Russia's war brig *Jason* passed the Straits, he stated that Turkey itself would have to employ force if it wished to prevent the passage. The same terse statement put the frigate *Kildan* through, on July 23. The Ottomans frankly admitted they did not intend exclusion by force, but merely had issued a "friendly request" in fear of French reprisals.[4]

With Austria out of the way and Prussia for the moment frightened away from England and Russia, Napoleon was able to continue to divide and conquer his enemies. He attempted to separate Britain and Russia by seeking a treaty of peace with one or the other. His negotiations with England soon failed. On the other hand, Russia for a time in 1806 expected an agreement to be arranged with France. In addition to the overture by Czartoryski on January 29 (chap. iv), Count von der Goltz, Prussia's minister at the tsar's court, after informing himself of Russia's dispositions toward France, conferred with Consul General de Lesseps about a possible *rapprochement*. He stated that the tsar and his ministers held no hatred for France and that Russia's ruler followed no project of territorial aggrandizement. He minimized the importance of Russia's conquest of Georgia in the war then under way against Persia, and gave assurance that Alexander would not adopt plans for an invasion and partition of Turkey. The Prussian envoy admitted hearsay evidence for his conjecture. De Lesseps agreed with it, however, as a result of his own discussions with Foreign Minister Czartoryski.

After a special French courier reported this indirect information to Paris, Napoleon's anti-Russian but obedient foreign minister forwarded a cautious overture inviting whatever proposals Russia might have for restoring normal relations. Talleyrand reminded De Lesseps that the tsar possessed the abstract right to expel the French consul general and that hence the latter must consider himself as recalled if such a tendency should be revealed. However, not wishing "to aggravate anew the unjust quarrel, without object or utility, which he would be pleased to see terminated," Napoleon did not recall the French consul general. As if to cover quickly this diplomatic opening, the emperor added that he did not contemplate entering into any sort of political relationships with St. Petersburg. De Lesseps must be certain to reveal these sentiments to Russia.[5]

The way now being cleared on both sides for possible negotiations, De Lesseps went into immediate conference with Czartoryski. He stated that now he could answer with pronounced assurance Czartoryski's question of January 29 as to whether France felt disposed to reach a *rapprochement*. As of that day, April 12, Napoleon "would see with pleasure an unjust quarrel finished—a quarrel having neither object nor utility." Czartoryski listened attentively during the two-hour meeting. Several times he asked for a repetition of the startling if veiled phraseology. The question soon narrowed to whether Russia should proceed alone to peace with France in the face of its new alliance with Great Britain. Czartoryski admitted, however, that he could see no objection to preliminary discussions directly with France—and in all probability Britain also desired to terminate the war. Czartoryski rushed a courier to London, and discussed the matter with Ambassador Lord Gower in St. Petersburg.

A week later, immediately before De Lesseps again dispatched his courier to Paris, Czartoryski summoned him and the courier to a conference. He stated to them that Tsar Alexander had been very well satisfied with the response. The three then discussed various methods for the proposed negotiation and fell to mentioning possible actual terms of settlement. De Lesseps threw out the idea that French commerce in the Mediterranean must be restored and trade between France and Russia extended into the Black Sea.[6]

The alert Czartoryski could not miss this reference to the unrestricted commercial navigation of the Dardanelles and Bosporus by France. Ten days later he summoned De Lesseps to correct any admission of agreement respecting that commerce until political affairs should be adjusted. He said he had questioned the aged Count Rumiantsov, Alexander's minister of commerce, the latter in turn having consulted several merchants. The entire matter remained quite inconclusive, with Russia consequently embarrassed.

A majority of the tsar's advisers recommended direct negotiations with Napoleon. In consequence, Alexander authorized Baron Pierre d'Oubril to go to Paris to negotiate. Everything now hinged on the result. When D'Oubril departed from St. Petersburg on May 27, De Lesseps observed, "political events were in the most perfect stagnation." Although secrecy was supposed to mark the D'Oubril mission, it was not well preserved. When advising Talleyrand two weeks earlier that D'Oubril would treat with the French government, Czartoryski explained that while technically D'Oubril would be the agent for Russian prisoners of war held by France, he might also discuss anything that could further the peace of Europe. Russia sought a frank survey of possibilities preliminary to a general peace. The envoy might participate also in similar discussions between France and Britain.[7] As another means of communicating with Talleyrand, Czartoryski mentioned to De Lesseps that he expected Cattaro to be an issue between France and Austria. This De Lesseps interpreted as an overture for a separate treaty. In private discussions arranged in Vienna between the French and Russian ambassadors, Russia repeated its general desire for an understanding with France. The reason publicly assigned for the mission—but disbelieved in foreign circles—was a discussion of purely commercial affairs. Nor did anyone take seriously D'Oubril's title, "agent for Russian prisoners."[8]

Meanwhile Napoleon had by no means been awaiting Russia's attitude. He had carefully considered Turkish policy in the light of its possible pro-French orientation. He decided on a two-fold program for Constantinople: to negotiate for an alliance with Turkey, and to do so by means of a distinguished military officer in whom he had the utmost confidence. General Horace Sebastiani was such an officer. It was he who had undertaken missions to the Levant in 1802 and 1803, when he won respect for Napoleon and himself. Napoleon had promoted him to general of division in 1805, and appointed him ambassador to Turkey on May 2, 1806. Talleyrand also believed Sebastiani's earlier services in the Levant should render him "more useful to Napoleon, and more agreeable to the Turkish government." Thus it happened that Ambassador Sebastiani was the clever negotiator given the chance to achieve success for the new French policy in Turkey. Then thirty-four years old, he later became an important figure of the Bourbon Restoration; he once served as foreign minister under King Louis Philippe.

More important was the French policy for the Near East, now authorized in the instructions to Sebastiani. Issued in May, 1806, these comprise some twenty-eight manuscript pages containing Talleyrand's considerable revisions. The essentials of these instructions may be given here.

Talleyrand affirmed that the internal situation of the Ottoman Empire had changed little. There were the customary ravages of the plague, the rebellion in Serbia, the frequent insubordination. The sultan directly controlled only the center of his empire, while the pashas beyond ruled over detached provincial governments. Not even regular communications could be maintained with the extremities of the sprawling empire. As an observer Sebastiani must send Napoleon positive information about Egypt, Arabia, and Persia. Egypt, reportedly standing in virtual revolt against the Ottoman government, was a special problem. Various stages of civil war had been in progress since the enforced evacuation of French troops in 1801. Turkey possessed no real authority there. Napoleon believed, or pretended to believe, that England encouraged the class, religious, and sectional rivalries within Egypt.

The need for accurate information applied generally to Turkey's Balkan provinces. Ali Pasha of Albania, anti-French before Napoleon's last war with Austria, might be induced to send several thousand troops against Russia, the "common enemy." Passvan Oglu of Vidin had lost a segment of his followers, his reconciliation with the sultan in 1802 proving unpopular. Napoleon reacted adversely to the Russian occupation of the Cattaro. Talleyrand stated that the Emperor concerned himself with the Adriatic only "in the spirit of true benevolence and protection." Cattaro, Ragusa, and the Ionian Islands must be taken from Russia. While the uncertainties of war made it impossible to designate in advance all the results to accrue, Sebastiani should impress upon Turkey the advantages of that new phase of French policy. In fact, the entire Ottoman Empire must be wrested from Russia. The latter's location on the Black Sea and its treaty position in Moldavia and Wallachia facilitated attacks on Turkey. There were the Russian bonds of religion with the Greeks and the new Russian outposts on the Adriatic. Although Sultan Selim had renewed the Russo-Turkish alliance, Talleyrand considered that Turkish opinion had changed. Ottoman ministers were now less fearful of displeasing Britain and Russia. They had recognized Napoleon as emperor and padishah, and France had become an immediate neighbor of Turkey in Europe.

No result had come from Ruffin's repeated claim for indemnities for Turkish confiscations at the time Bonaparte attacked Egypt in 1798. Rather than further prolong the debates over individual claims, the ambassador might simply agree upon a flat sum. Talleyrand held to the principle of compensation by Turkey but admitted that the losses by French merchants of Smyrna and elsewhere had been exaggerated. Sebastiani must deny Turkey's counterclaim for indemnities to Ottoman subjects in Egypt. Although the Franco-Turkish treaty of 1802 stipulated that both parties should pay, Sebastiani must assert the inequality of the conditions: the beys and not France had been primarily responsible for the losses in question during the French occupation. He must contend that such losses were nothing as compared with Turkey's arrest of 1,842 French officials and merchants in 1798 and their consequent suffering.

Talleyrand believed Sebastiani should find it equally simple to adjust the disputed tariff. France might agree to an upward adjustment to cover variations of exchange values, or stipulate a flat increase for all tariffed items. England and Russia had negotiated new tariffs with Turkey. Much had to be done to restore confidence in France, in French merchants, and in French exports. The commercial monopoly effective for Marseille under the Bourbons might be reëxamined and everything recommended for reëstablishment that accorded with then existing conditions. Marseille recognized, however, that maritime peace would be requisite for substantial commercial betterment.

France could strike a blow at Russia and England by surrendering a privilege enjoyed in common with them and equally distasteful to Turkey —the granting of foreign warrants of protection within Turkey. Foreign commerce had been extended in part by special warrants issued to the hundreds of persons who handled it, Turkish subjects as well as foreigners. Talleyrand stated that Russians had abused the common privilege. Sebastiani might propose to restrict such warrants to fifty, provided Turkey held other nations to that number.

The foreign minister reminded Sebastiani of the longest of the lists of capitulatory prerogatives, which was obtained in 1740. Everyone at the Ministry of Foreign Affairs knew of that prized document in the treaty room, of the richly ornamented Turkish original which summed up and extended the several commercial and jurisdictional grants to Bourbon France. This large, illuminated, rolled manuscript tabulated the series of eighty-five concessions, some dating back to 1535. From a dubious interpretation of one phrase, but more from long custom, France conceded to itself the protector's role for Roman Catholics of the Levant. "The first power of Europe must conserve that rank, in all its relations with the Ottoman Empire," Talleyrand directed.

In fear of another persecution such as they suffered at Turkey's hands from 1798 to 1801, many Frenchmen had gone over to foreign protection. Sebastiani must make these persons realize that no other power in Europe could offer the protection extended by Napoleonic France. The ambassador must fulfill the functions of the consul general and also care for the interests of Napoleon's Italian subjects, for whose shipping the emperor held high hopes. French establishments meriting the ambassador's particular care included the naval hospitals at Constantinople and Smyrna.

Napoleon desired to protect especially the foreign religious missions, those of the interior possessing also the political function of aiding French communications with India and Persia. Through communications from western Europe to the Persian Gulf (a Paris-to-Bagdad route) would benefit France and Turkey both politically and commercially. Geography placed Turkey astride all the Near Eastern routes and made it a barrier to the invasion of Europe from Asia. In like manner, it should become a bar to Russia. It should also possess all the coasts of the Black Sea in addition to the Straits. Constantinople was the nexus of the land routes to the Middle East. The death of Alexandre Romieu and the "cruel uncertainty" over Amédée Jaubert revealed the desirability of regular communications with that part of Asia. In the interest of French policy Turkey should set up its own regular communications with Persia and reopen diplomatic relations with that country. Constantinople might supervise regular routes eastward to Persia, and Paris might do likewise for the Balkans. The segment between Constantinople and coastal Albania required protection against bandits, Talleyrand said. He charged the Russians at the Cattaro with employing the Montenegrins to support the rebellious Serbs.

France, the instructions continued, had decided to occupy Ragusa and its district, in order to beat the Russians, who had reportedly proposed to go there. Napoleon had already sent General Lauriston with a force to this spot. Sebastiani should deliver suitable explanations to Turkey, and Turks and French together could proceed against the Montenegrins, thus cutting Russia's communications with Serbia.

Talleyrand stated that the Greeks probably never would be able to recover their independence and that Russians worked through them to develop an internal influence within Turkey. He authorized a neat straddling position: Napoleon thought that the Greeks as a group required protection, whereas numerous individual Greeks did not. Sebastiani could stress another contrast: Napoleon would never protect rebels, whereas Russia maintained communications with the Serbians, whose revolt they incited. The war between France and Russia backed up on each side to the neutral Ottoman frontier; Napoleon only desired to utilize his geographical position to safeguard Turkey from Russia. Russia's "usurped" influence within the Principalities must be ended.

Sebastiani might use the issue of the Straits to cover Napoleon's move into Ragusa. What if Russia should be discontented? This French step, admittedly taken against Russia, could become a pretext for requesting the passage of the Dardanelles for additional tsarist troops destined for the Adriatic coasts or for Montenegro or Serbia. Sebastiani must oppose formally any such concession. If the Russians, when refused, forced the passage of the Straits, Turkey could interpret this as a direct act of hostility. Sebastiani must immediately convey information of such a development to General Marmont, commander of Napoleon's 25,000 troops in Dalmatia.

Thus, according to French policy, if France could not sail the Dardanelles neither could Russia. If more Russian troop transports bound for the Adriatic sailed to Constantinople, Sebastiani should request Turkey to refuse passage. Turkey also might be advised to pay careful attention to its own naval establishments. Although Napoleon possessed adequate land forces on the continent to enforce respect for his friends, he would welcome Ottoman naval support.

Talleyrand recorded that Turkey had made some progress toward westernizing its army (the instructions continued). Napoleon sincerely desired to aid the Ottoman central government in restoring its internal authority, and he favored any other measures intended to cast off the "yoke of Russia." If necessary, Sebastiani might hint the prospect of Turkey's recovery of the Crimea by saying Napoleon would promise in a peace treaty with Russia to seek annulment of all the treaty stipulations considered hostile to France or onerous to Turkey. Napoleon did not need any additional territory in the Balkans. What he held there he intended to use as an aid to Turkey. Dalmatia thus represented the means for prompt support of his friends and, in addition, the means to set and hold the peace of Europe.

Sebastiani must invariably oppose England, which sought territorial acquisitions in the Levant to equal Gibraltar and Malta and to assure its dominance of the Mediterranean. By its geographical location, England could be either a natural friend or a natural enemy of remote Turkey. Its Mediterranean ships and expanding power in Asia, however, placed it directly adjacent; hence, it appeared to be the natural enemy of the Ottoman Empire.

The instructions concluded with references to Jaubert's route to Persia. If he had not yet returned when Sebastiani arrived in Constantinople, the ambassador must ask the Ottomans to assure his safe return. If he was still in Persia, Sebastiani could send him the news of Europe and ask him to procure information respecting the English in Asia, perhaps from the French consul at Bagdad. In all these matters the new French ambassador to Turkey would be well seconded by Pierre Ruffin.[9]

Among the many internal problems of the Ottoman Empire was the Serbian revolt. Not only was the revolt enmeshed in factionalism, but also it might at any time become an issue for Russia or Austria—or for France, owing to Napoleon's position in Dalmatia. In order to acquire information about Bosnia, Albania, and Greece, Napoleon appointed Pierre David as consul in Bosnia, intending thereby to "multiply" the neighborly relations with Turkey in Europe. David must increase commerce across Turkey's common frontier with Dalmatia, obtain information, watch Albania, and seek to encourage Bosnian attitudes favorable to France.[10] The new French policy focused on Albania. Hugues Poqueville went to Arta to report on affairs there, in the Ionian Islands, and in Dalmatia. Mathieu de Lesseps, at first directed to return to Egypt, found himself transferred to Leghorn where he served until 1810. (This De Lesseps is not to be confused with Barthélemy de Lesseps, Ruffin's son-in-law, who served in Russia.) Although Consul David's voluminous reports were mostly trivia, he did win some recognition for the information on Balkan Europe he supplied down to 1814. His reports covered also the gossip of neighboring Serbia. Zealous and efficient as a report-writer and defender of Napoleon, he engendered some personal rivalry.

Napoleon's letter accrediting Sebastiani to the sultan stated that the ambassador would employ his best efforts to maintain the Franco-Turkish treaties and the Ottoman capitulations. Talleyrand directed Ruffin (now reduced to counselor of embassy, the position he held under Ambassador Brune) to request the Ottoman government to order the disquieted pashas in Bosnia to correct their false interpretations of the coming of French troops into Dalmatia. A French consul general was stationed at Scutari (Albania), and the general French attitude foretold an armed clash on the Balkan rim with General Lauriston's forces. Ruffin should ask the Turks to direct the pasha at Scutari to assist the French in every way. Talleyrand reverted to Napoleon's idea of an alliance, the wedge for it being the Balkans adjacent to Dalmatia. The French troops there also could aid the Turks in Bosnia and might assist against the Montenegrins. Russian military and naval forces in the Ionian Islands had been responsible for Napoleon's order to arm merchant vessels against the Russian-Ottoman-controlled Ionian flag. The Russian forces, he stated, exposed the Ionians to attack, simply by being permitted to sail through the Dardanelles to the Adriatic.[11]

Even as Talleyrand was revising instructions for Sebastiani, Napoleon expanded his political policy for Turkey, probably due to two arrivals in Paris from Constantinople. One of them was Antoine Franchini, brother of the Constantinople embassy's clever first interpreter. Napoleon directed Talleyrand to relay everything Antoine said and to ask for advice respecting the means of sustaining French influence at the Ottoman capital (May 19). One means should be the sending of prompt and frequent couriers between Paris and Constantinople. A special courier was sent to announce Sebastiani's appointment. Napoleon required frequent correspondence with Turkey because, if the Turks let themselves be drawn into new mischief against him, his affairs in Dalmatia would suffer. Ruffin was authorized to compensate Osep Vassilovitz and others for their good treatment of Jaubert.[12]

Turkey's Ambassador Mouhib arrived on May 21, duly accredited to the emperor and padishah. Talleyrand utilized the Ottoman courier, who was returning to Constantinople with the report of Mouhib's arrival, to announce Sebastiani's appointment and to express appreciation for the several evidences of friendship for France during the visit of Roux to Constantinople (chap. iv). Napoleon received Mouhib in formal audience on June 5. The latter said that Sultan Selim, the "master of two continents and two seas," had sent him to salute "his Imperial and Royal Majesty, Napoleon I, greatest among sovereigns of Christian believers" and the "oldest, truest, and most necessary friend" of the Ottoman Empire. The sultan had deemed ordinary diplomatic channels inadequate to convey his felicitations on Napoleon's accession, the magnitude of which accounted for Mouhib's appointment.

Everyone understood how belated were the felicitations. Ex-Ambas-

sador Brune, who failed to win recognition for Napoleon in 1804, would
have gloried in Mouhib's pronouncement. Mouhib's point that Napoleon had become "most necessary" is credible, whereas not even
Napoleon himself could take seriously the phrase, "truest friend." After
all, Selim had waged war against him when he occupied Egypt. Emperor
Napoleon I was never one to quibble over extravagant recognition of
himself, however, and his response met the occasion. He stated to
Mouhib that these expressions touched his heart. One of the greatest
results of his military successes had been to give him the opportunity
to aid "the most useful and oldest of his allies." Thereafter, everything
that made the Ottomans happy or unhappy would make Frenchmen
happy or unhappy. The sultan need never fear him nor when united
with him need he ever fear anyone.[13]

Talleyrand wrote Ruffin that Napoleon had showered Mouhib with
attention and had declared the cause of Turkey's empire inseparable
from that of his own. He wished to use his neighbor's frontier in the
Balkans to help defend it, since such defense would, for one thing,
break the Russian grip on Cattaro.[14] France sought reward for the reception accorded Mouhib. As an initial test of the new Ottoman policy,
"the good harmony between France and Turkey being perfectly reëstablished," Talleyrand requested (on June 19) the complete restoration of
the claim of France to a religious protectorate over the Christians' holy
places. He also requested pro-French Ibrahim Effendi to treat Napoleon's new ambassador with the same consideration he would give Talleyrand himself. He thanked Ibrahim for helping to restore the best of
relations between France and Turkey.[15]

Because June, 1806, is the date of a significant development in Teheran, let us now catch up the threads of French policy in Persia (chap.
iii). Ruffin's dispatches in February and March had dealt with the growing speculation over the circumstances of Romieu's death and Jaubert's
fate, together with the discussions he and Roux, Talleyrand's secretary,
held with leading Turks. Ruffin then relayed Corancez's version of
Romieu's death, the French consul holding to his charge of poisoning
by English partisans. In the argument between Corancez and Britain's
Consul General John Barker, the former said a plot to assassinate Romieu
while en route to Teheran had been discovered immediately after Romieu
departed from Aleppo late in June. Corancez said Barker had sent an
English Tatar named Sarcos Hali to follow Romieu and Outrey and
do them harm—basing this story on a ciphered dispatch from Romieu

allegedly sent en route on August 21. The plot being discovered, Corancez had speeded a messenger to warn them of it. Ruffin doubted this evidence.[16] The only extant letter from Romieu, that written to Joseph Rousseau, told of the dangers of the voyage but did not mention Sarcos Hali.

But what of Jaubert? The foreign ministry had not yet learned of his imprisonment in Bayazid. Speculation for a long time had it that Jaubert had died—perhaps in consequence of the efforts of English partisans. This story thus shifted over to Jaubert the discredited story of the foul murder of Romieu. Talleyrand issued directions in February, 1806, for Joseph Rousseau to go from Aleppo immediately and collect Romieu's papers and to try to learn the fate of Jaubert and his party.

The documents eventually reveal the latter's movements. Early in March Ibrahim related the encouraging news that Jaubert was still alive. Partially incorrect details had come through from Bayazid to the effect that he and his group had been arrested before they left Ottoman territory, taken to the mountains by a hundred Kurdish brigands, and robbed of their papers and effects.[17] Jaubert himself reported to Constantinople his decision to proceed upon release directly to Persia instead of returning to the Turkish capital. At the end of March, 1806, he was actually en route to Persia. His former native costume having fooled no one, he now employed the name of Daniel and purported to be a Danish merchant. He traveled under the escort of 12 picked horsemen and an officer. He avoided Sinop upon advice that the Russian consul there had orders to arrest him.[18]

We recall that Jaubert carried the original copy of Napoleon's letter to Shah Feth Ali, the duplicate having been delivered in the autumn of 1805 by Alexandre Romieu. As late as mid-May, 1806, Talleyrand could do no more than admit to Sebastiani he did not know Jaubert's fate. From fragmentary reports the story was finally patched together. French consul Dupré at Trebizond confirmed on April 24 Jaubert's release at Bayazid in mid-February. Georges Outrey, secretary-interpreter of the deceased Romieu, outlined from Bagdad on June 6 his own negotiations while in Teheran. He had won the shah's decision to send as ambassador to France a distinguished Persian, who would carry gifts for Napoleon. He had solicited the shah's aid to obtain the release of Amédée Jaubert. Although as late as June 4 Consul Corancez of Aleppo could relay no news of Jaubert's arrival in Teheran, his letter confirmed Outrey's statement that the shah had named a principal officer to be envoy to Paris. Everyone considered this decision to be quite exceptional, because Persia had sent few ambassadors anywhere. It had received only one from France, Ambassador Michel, sent out by Louis XIV in 1798.[19] Corancez wrote again later in June, to relate that Outrey, who returned to Bagdad on May 27, brought further word that the shah's envoy would deliver a reply to Napoleon's letter. The Persians at first desired Outrey to deliver it, but Corancez proposed that a courier take it as far as the French embassy at Constantinople, whence regular diplomatic messengers would relay it.[20]

Jaubert came to Teheran early in June. Illness, the winter weather, and a visit to Crown Prince Abbas Mirza and others in Persian provinces along the way, had delayed his arrival. He meanwhile obtained information of the potentialities of Persia's none-too-promising military power. His letter of June 5 detailed his good treatment at the hands of the shah. A line of troops flanked by several cannons and white horses marked his path to the initial ceremonial audience in the spacious inner court of the palace. He presented Napoleon's letter, the principal object of his coming, and the official gifts of arms, textiles, and jewelry. He wrote that he arrived at Teheran without funds and found none available to him. But, he said, so jealously did he guard Napoleon's prestige that he would walk back to Constantinople rather than appeal to the Persian government for aid. Illness again overtook him, weakening him so much that he could not mount a horse. Owing to the dangers at Bayazid, sadness shadowed his spirit.

Jaubert's second letter, penned on June 20 from a point near the shah's military headquarters in the field, related that the solicitous Feth Ali had sent one of his ministers on daily visits during his illness. The envoy here explained that he could not dispatch his courier with the first letter, because that individual also fell ill. Jaubert found himself too weak to use his authorized cipher. Thus he could not yet reveal what he would report in person to Napoleon early in 1807—that Feth Ali offered to support France against Britain in India if Napoleon would support Persia against Russia.[21] The shah wrote a reply to Napoleon's letter, giving it to Jaubert. He congratulated the emperor on defeating Austria. He recounted Persia's military successes against Russia's forces in Georgia, and suggested that a regular French ambassador be stationed in Teheran.[22] As we shall see in Chapter VIII, this idea appealed strongly to Napoleon. When Jaubert eventually returned to Paris, he was assigned an important post, auditor of the Napoleonic Council of State.

He was honored by the French government and by learned societies for many years.

Jaubert addressed to Ruffin the two letters of June. Their delivery was delayed until December, however, by which time Jaubert himself had returned to Constantinople. As a sidelight on the subsequent developments respecting Persia, it is noteworthy that once Ruffin had learned of Jaubert's release at Bayazid, he concerned himself with personnel to assist that intrepid traveler. This suggests that in their secret planning he and Jaubert probably intended to keep open the relations with Persia, should the latter succeed in his mission. Joseph Rousseau still appeared disinclined to go to Teheran and at sixty-six the elder Rousseau was too old. Ruffin next preferred Georges Outrey, whom the elder Rousseau already had recalled to Bagdad. Hence the chargé d'affaires sent Joannin out from Constantinople late in July, to act as the French chargé d'affaires in Persia's capital. Joannin, like the two Franchinis, was a former Venetian aide inherited by the French when General Bonaparte ended the Venetian Republic in 1797. He came to the embassy with General Brune in 1803 and had since learned Persian. Andrea de Nerciat, born in Hesse-Cassel, also followed Joannin's program of training after 1803. Somewhat later (March, 1807) he also went from Constantinople to Persia to become a secretary and interpreter. Joannin and Nerciat figured in the transitory French ascendancy in Teheran in 1808, as we shall see. Late in August, 1806, Jaubert was on his way back to Constantinople when Joannin met and discussed affairs with him at Erzurum. Joannin arrived in Teheran on November 5. Illustrative of the ways in which news came out of western Asia at that time is Consul Corancez's writing (in the form of a bulletin) at Aleppo that a Tatar from Teheran had revealed to him on November 19 that Joannin had been well received at the Persian frontier and that a large house had been hospitably assigned for his residence.[23]

In Paris, Napoleon's pro-Turkish policy expanded. From St. Cloud palace on June 11, he directed Talleyrand to pen for Mouhib a note violently critical of Russia's policy in the Balkans. This contended that Russia, in reinforcing its territories facing Turkey, acted as neither friend nor ally of the sultan. If Russia really wished to be friendly, the note said, it would not encourage the Serbian rebels with advice and money. By what right did the tsar interfere in Moldavia and Wallachia? Did these provinces appertain to Russia or to Turkey? France warned that such a process would soon free the Morea also and, after that, the other areas in which Greeks lived; eventually, the entire Ottoman Empire would collapse. Ruffin was directed to say much the same, with suitable variations: Turkey could judge between France and Russia by the contrast in policy: if Napoleon should be requested by the Serbs for support, he would not even talk with them until they had laid down their arms.[24] Meanwhile, Ruffin used as a talking point against Russia the false report that Russia had excited the Serbian revolt.[25]

A letter by Napoleon might help to render his own move into Ragusa acceptable. On June 20 he replied to Selim's communication which had been transmitted by Mouhib. He stated that he had discussed fully and secretly with the new ambassador the true interests of the Ottoman Empire. He assured the sultan of his personal intention to follow the course of interposing obstacles before Turkey's enemies. He hoped Frenchmen in Turkey would be treated as subjects of the only western nation that had been allied with the Ottoman Empire for three centuries and also as subjects of the most favored nation. By way of advice —in words suggesting American advice to Greece in 1947, in a somewhat parallel situation—Selim must not permit any foreign power (Russia) to participate in his negotiations with the Serbs, and should employ rigorous methods to force into submission the Serbian rebels who had been excited and encouraged by Russia. The latter had requested Serbian independence in order to create a splinter state. The Phanariot Greeks who governed Moldavia and Wallachia were nothing more than Russian agents—a hint for the sultan to get rid of them. Napoleon said the sultan should prevent Russian ships from entering the Bosporus and should not permit Greek ships to sail under Russia's flag. Turkey need not fear Russia. The tsar's forces were weaker than they would like others to believe, and in any event Turkey could count on the assistance of France. He suggested that in order to be in better position to help Turkey, France should probably occupy Albania.[26]

Talleyrand's several letters recounted Napoleon's expectations. He wrote cordially to the sultan's first interpreter and penned Mouhib a friendly, anti-Russian, anti-Serbian letter. He directed Ruffin to emphasize the French thesis that Russia would have employed Ragusa only to supply the Serbs, this being the French reason for appropriating it.[27] Napoleon simultaneously ordered the 2,400 Italian and other troops in Albania reinforced by 800 men from Prince Eugene's command. When he learned that Lauriston skirmished with Montenegrins and Russians near Ragusa on July 8,[28] he claimed to Mouhib that the latter had violated Ottoman territory (July 28). He offered to pay the expenses if Turkey wished to send 1,000 or 1,200 troops there, and he gave the ambassador the services of the French courier to convey this urgent message to his government.[29]

General Marmont, who was to become another familiar figure, took over the command in Dalmatia from General Beauharnais and distinguished himself there for a number of years. Later he served in Spain and Portugal. Napoleon gave preciseness to Marmont's authority on July 26, 1806, to prevent misunderstandings with Lauriston. Young General Marmont (who had attained that rank with Bonaparte in Egypt) was named commander in chief of all French forces in Dalmatia and Albania, specifically of the troops in Dalmatia, at Ragusa, and at Cattaro.[30] He is best remembered in Dalmatia for building the coastal road from Zara to Spalato.

Apparently, the Turks first learned officially on June 22, 1806, of General Lauriston's entrance. Resourceful Ruffin rendered the move palatable to Turkey without awaiting instructions. Characteristically adroit, he wrote on June 19 an unofficial and unsigned note of explanation about Ragusa and took it during the night to the kiaya bey. Thereby the information was given the sultan secretly, without its going through the foreign minister. During the French embassy interpreter's regular conference with the Turkish ministers the following day Ruffin observed no visible reactions; apparently the note had "calmed the spirits."

Napoleon attempted to explain away the absence of a respectable French squadron off Corfu. Through Talleyrand, he informed Ali Pasha of Albania that he had sent a part of his fleet to the Indian Ocean and needed the remainder for a descent on England. Attempts at amphibious landings by Russia would be met from his land base. Through Hugues Pocqueville it was intended to hint secretly that if ever Albania came into Napoleon's hands, the latter could not hope to find a more able lieutenant than Ali Pasha himself. For that communication, Talleyrand protected France against adverse reactions in Constantinople. The statement was so confused that anyone finding it would be unable to figure out whether the comment to Ali Pasha emanated from Napoleon or merely from an agent.[31]

Sebastiani could not actually be on the scene for several weeks, for new ambassadors never proceeded promptly to their stations. New instructions to him matched the successive manifestations of Turkey's friendliness. Talleyrand's supplemental directions to Sebastiani on June

21 conformed with Napoleon's policies as announced in the letter to
Selim. Turkey's very friendly attitude had altered affairs. Napoleon desired no Turkish territory and personally authorized the statement that
he would not favor a partition of the Ottoman Empire "even if he
should be offered three-fourths of it." He would support no Turkish,
Greek, or Egyptian rebel, even if among the fifth columnists of his own
expeditions to Egypt and Syria. Napoleon promised to center his entire
Levantine policy in the Ottoman Empire and earnestly wished Turkey
to treat France as the most-favored power. Talleyrand cautioned the
French ambassador against intimacy with the Russians, although after
peace he might be friendly with the Austrian and the Prussian agents
and even with the English.

Sebastiani should oppose all advices to the Turks from the Russians
and the British, and especially create disfavor against the one foreign
power possessing the privilege of navigating the Dardanelles.[32] A great
object, Talleyrand directed, "must be the closure of the Bosporus to the
Russians, and the prohibition of the passage from the Mediterranean
to the Black Sea of all their ships, whether armed or unarmed." Turkey
should be encouraged to retain Moldavia and Wallachia, these to serve
as a more effective barrier against the tsarist realm in the future.[33] The
supplemental instructions outlined the essential French object in the
Levant, namely, to establish implicitly or indirectly against Russia a
triple alliance of France, Turkey, and Persia.

Sebastiani's entourage included as second secretary his favorite, young
Latour-Maubourg, whose name we shall later encounter repeatedly. The
merchants of Marseille sought many things through the new ambassador.
Once again they called for the illogical, but probably promised, indemnities for Turkish confiscations during Bonaparte's invasions of Egypt
and Syria. Antoine de Saint-Joseph requested new efforts to reopen the
Black Sea to French commerce. He thought that France ought somehow
to find ways to utilize the authorization for such navigation stipulated
in the Franco-Turkish treaty of 1802.[34] Two French consuls, sent to
Jassy and Bucharest, worked to free Moldavia and Wallachia from Russian influence. Often subjected to arrest, they became the unhappiest
Frenchmen in the Levant.[35]

The stream of French dispatches hinted nothing more for Turkey
than a persistent expectation of friendship and alliance with France.
Even before Baron d'Oubril came to Paris the French foreign ministry's
archives for Turkey suggest that Talleyrand and others almost forgot

the Baron's scheduled mission. His coming in no sense changed the instructions for Sebastiani. The sole brief official mention of D'Oubril to the Near East at the moment was for Ruffin's private information.

Russia meanwhile noted the altered tone of all the official exchanges with presumably allied Turkey. The tsar's subjects in Constantinople could not be unaware of the change. Fright gripped some of them, leading the commissioner of the Galata sector to call all the resident Russians together on May 23. He told them of the false rumor that measures would be taken by the Ottoman government against every Russian found there. They need not fear, he stated, a duplication of such sad Russian experiences as the Ottoman arrests during the Russo-Turkish war of 1768–1774, and the French treatment in 1798–1801. The Russo-Turkish alliance had been renewed only four months before, he said; the good relations between the two countries were continuing and anyone molesting a Russian would be severely punished.[36]

Czartoryski's summary of the political situation at the end of June, when he prepared to surrender the foreign ministry to Baron Budberg, listed Turkey alone among Russia's neighbors as making the most equivocal dispositions with respect to Russia. The Ottoman council, long amenable exclusively to Russia, seemed to be falling under Napoleon's influence. "Bonaparte acts, and will act, at Constantinople by fear," he warned. He said Russia still possessed intact "all its means of action against Turkey," including the attachment of the Slavic peoples and of the Greeks within the Ottoman Empire.[37]

D'Oubril arrived in Paris at the moment of Napoleon's new dreams of territorial expansion, dreams in which the Near and Middle East figured. He needed Near Eastern allies promptly, if they were to be of service in the coalition war against him. Talleyrand did not clear the path for D'Oubril very well, an illustration of the scant attention paid his coming. At Strasbourg on June 29 the envoy met some delay over passport formalities. Czartoryski's conferences with Ambassador Gower had clarified the limitations of D'Oubril's negotiations in Paris and had arranged for Britain's participation from the sidelines. France declined to negotiate with Russia and England together, whereas Britain would not enter a general negotiation in advance of an understanding with Russia. It was agreed that Russia might discuss individual issues, among them the possible return of Cattaro to Austria. Charles James Fox, foreign secretary of the day at London, on June 14 commissioned Ambassador Lord Yarmouth to concert with D'Oubril.[38]

Gossip in Constantinople at first had it that the Russians told the Turks that France was sending an envoy to St. Petersburg to offer peace. Early in June Talleyrand revealed for Ruffin's private information that Baron d'Oubril would come to the French capital, and he suggested that the arrangements to be made could conceivably lead to peace. France prepared in advance to claim credit for any pro-Turkish stipulations negotiated with D'Oubril. He announced that Napoleon felt disposed to free Turkey from all its engagements to Russia which hindered a more intimate connection with France.[39]

In contrast to the divergence of views between Russia and France immediately after the battle of Austerlitz, D'Oubril's conversations sought peace between them. During the same month (July, 1806), Napoleon was busy setting up the Confederation of the Rhine with himself as protector, while Talleyrand basked in the glitter of his new title, Prince of Benevento.

Everyone agreed that Britain would temporize. Yarmouth arrived on July 6. Believing Napoleon would accord more favorable terms for peace than were originally expected, he encouraged D'Oubril to hope for a settlement. D'Oubril boldly announced that Russia intended to retain Corfu. He suggested that France might be asked to give up Ragusa, Albania, and Dalmatia to Sicily and thus destroy French influence in Turkey.

Talleyrand worked to split apart D'Oubril and Yarmouth.[40] He appeared impatient, as if wishing to hand D'Oubril a treaty which must be signed to avoid disrupting the negotiations. D'Oubril seemed willing to sign without Yarmouth's concurrence a preliminary treaty with France. He once went so far as to indicate to Talleyrand that Napoleon's occupation of the coasts of the Adriatic held the first place in Russian calculations. We can see the reason for this. Russia's pretext for navigating the Straits might disappear if clashes with Napoleon's superior forces under Marmont should eliminate the Russian toe holds in the Adriatic. France's foreign minister retorted that the occupation would not be ended.

Talleyrand tried to discuss the alleged complaints by Turkey against Russia for its frequent sailing of war vessels through the Dardanelles without, he said, any right. D'Oubril replied with the positive statement that treaties established the Russian right. Talleyrand changed the subject; Napoleon could bide his time. The issue did not yet involve a possible change of ownership of the Dardanelles, as it would in the big debate of 1808 which will be discussed in Chapter XIII.

Talleyrand argued with D'Oubril over the disposition of Venice, Istria, Dalmatia, and Albania. When Russia proposed that France evacuate Ragusa, and France suggested that Russia evacuate Corfu, neither gave the other any encouragement.[41] With a view to stimulating D'Oubril to a more prompt acquiescence in the terms really desired, Napoleon directed Talleyrand on July 12 to publish in the *Moniteur* news allegedly from Constantinople and Serbia to the effect that Russia wished to attack Constantinople.[42] Talleyrand produced a draft of an armistice for discussion. From its terms D'Oubril believed that France sought to win Russia's recognition of Napoleon's title and to split Russia from England. The Russian envoy wrote the tsar that Napoleon obviously desired peace but "without any sacrifices—or at least without any important restitutions."

As one means of breaking the stalemate, Talleyrand cleverly stepped out of the negotiations, and Napoleon commissioned General H. J. G. Clarke of the Ministry of War to continue them. This change brought affairs to a head quickly, timorous D'Oubril being no match for a key military man. Within a week Clarke put over the French point of view through overstating all the French demands. Clarke's extreme version of the counterrequests of France listed the Russian abandonment of their protectorates over Moldavia and Wallachia and of the privilege of sending troops and armed vessels through the Dardanelles. He asked them to evacuate Corfu and promise to recall the troops concentrated along the Turkish frontier. They should agree, he said, not to accord their flag to ships of any non-Russian subjects, meaning the Greek or other provincials of the Ottoman Empire. D'Oubril termed this "a strange project,"[43] and even before Clarke finished reading it, he interrupted to say that he would never sign it and that any discussion of several of the terms was out of the question. But D'Oubril did state what he would sign, so far as Turkey was concerned—and even here conceded more than he had intended.

The methods of Talleyrand and Clarke were thus bringing results. The latter unsuccessfully sought to stipulate an end to Russia's passage of the Dardanelles, a subject in particular on which D'Oubril refused to treat. Finally Napoleon, through Talleyrand and Clarke, impatiently demanded on July 20 the signing of what had been agreed upon, under penalty of according less favorable terms should there be further delay. Thereupon Clarke and D'Oubril that day signed the Franco-Russian treaty of peace. Russia's negotiator sent word to his court that he signed it only when France made him understand the impossibility of obtaining better terms. He thus admitted being browbeaten into the agreement.

For convenience we shall term this the Clarke-Oubril treaty. It is of special interest, that among its formal stipulations was the reciprocal promise of the independence and territorial integrity of the Ottoman Empire. This signified in part that the French diplomatic position in the Near East had advanced from one of inferiority to one of equality with Russia, notwithstanding the Russo-Turkish alliance. Other stipulations for the Near East required the evacuation of Montenegro, the independence of Ragusa under Turkey's guarantee, and the recognition of the independence of the Ionian Islands. France retained her communications with Cattaro. By an annex of secret stipulations concerning minor Turkish matters, France and Russia each played for the support of the sultan.

Napoleon desired to have the Near Eastern terms applied immediately, without awaiting the tsar's ratification. D'Oubril coöperated to the extent of certifying a copy of the treaty and of the French request to Russia's Admiral Seniavin, the commander off Corfu. The envoy possessed no authority to do even that, and the negotiators must have thought better of the plan, because the originals of the papers still remain in the Paris archives.[44] It was reasoned that the tsar should be the person to approve or disapprove a treaty which his agent had been browbeaten into signing. Baron Budberg, Russia's new foreign minister, might disapprove or disavow the negotiations. England, disapproving nearly all the terms, might talk Russia into repudiating the signed treaty. Moreover, whether the negotiators at Paris appreciated the factor or not, Russia's military and naval commanders possessed a remarkable capacity for refusing to listen to orders from subordinate diplomatic officials, especially when these orders appeared indirectly through Napoleonic channels.

Budberg's immediate and persistent view of the Clarke-Oubril treaty was that D'Oubril had departed from his instructions in signing it, a viewpoint which Consul General Barthélemy de Lesseps labeled as absurd. The latter fruitlessly called attention to the fatal consequences of disapproval. In a dramatic gesture one day, he delayed the dispatch of his courier to Paris a few hours in an appeal for a last-minute change of Russian plans. But the Russian representatives were adamant.

Had Russia ratified the treaty, it most certainly would have given a different orientation to French planning for the Near East. On August 16 Budberg notified Talleyrand of Tsar Alexander's decision. He astutely avoided stating his objections to the treaty's several terms favorable to Turkey. He reminded France that D'Oubril had been directed to conclude "a peace that could be durable and equally honorable for the tsar and his allies." This had not been realized. The treaty only mentioned the eventual withdrawal of the French troops from the Germanies and left France in Albania and Dalmatia. Tsar Alexander did not like the terms for the Kings of Naples and Sardinia and did not wish such a treaty before the ending of war between France and Britain.[45]

On August 30 Tsar Alexander clarified for the Russian public his reasons for resuming war against Napoleon. He had sought a general peace by means of negotiation. Events had prevented his assisting the allies as much as he had desired, he said, although he had held to the principles originally announced for a just settlement. He stated that when the French government evinced attitudes favorable to peace early in 1806, he had once more proposed certain general bases for it. The discussion aimed at the restoration of peace on terms in accord with the honor and security of the Russian Empire, together with the interests of Russia's allies and the tranquillity of Europe. To the tsar's great regret, the Clarke-Oubril treaty did not conform with these principles, and he therefore had not ratified it. He would renew his negotiations with Napoleon at any time, however, on the conditions stated.[46]

When Paris circulated Russia's explanation to its diplomatic agents, it directed them to remark that the spirit of the French troops in the Germanies was still the same as during the blitzkrieg of 1805. Clearly Napoleon was looking eastward and to another blitzkrieg. Talleyrand authorized the expression to Turkey of French official belief that the treaty's favorable stipulations for Turkey represented Russia's secret motive for refusing ratification.[47]

Napoleon as yet knew nothing of several important simultaneous anti-Russian developments at Constantinople—which we shall discuss in the next chapter. In this chapter we have traced the course of Franco-Turkish friendship, reflected notably in Ambassador Mouhib's statements at Paris and in Napoleon's instructions to his new ambassador to Turkey. We have witnessed a slight extension of French territorial control in the Balkans and the beginnings of success of the policy with respect to Persia. Conditions, diplomacy, and policy had combined to set the stage for France to demolish the Russo-Turkish alliance.

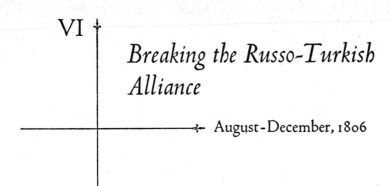

VI

Breaking the Russo-Turkish Alliance

⟶ August-December, 1806

FRENCH DIPLOMATS recognized that the general policy of the Ottoman Empire would stand or fall by its efficacy in the Dardanelles and the Bosporus. The impressive French successes of early 1806 in Turkey seemed little in comparison with the French diplomatic gains late in the year when Turkey declared war against Russia, its former ally. Meanwhile through lightning land campaigns Napoleon brought his empire to its zenith. He had beaten Austria in 1805 before Prussia could intervene and would humble Prussia in 1806 before Russia could intervene. The defeat of Tsar Alexander I in 1807 came with the precautionary advantage of a Turkish attack on Russia. French policies in the Near East preliminary to Napoleon's success against Russia are discussed in this chapter.

Overtures for peace with Great Britain and Russia had failed. That France should replace Russia and Britain as Turkey's ally was the purpose of the instructions given Ambassador Horace Sebastiani, as we have seen (chap. v); one means to this end would be the closing of the Straits to Russian naval vessels. The instructions also proposed the joint military action of France and Turkey against Montenegro and directed Sebastiani to notify the commander in Dalmatia of any Russian action which might be interpreted as hostile to Turkey. Such instructions approximated a proposal of a general Franco-Turkish military alliance.

One means of winning Turkey and Persia to the French side might be found through the prestige accruing from a defeat of Prussia. Napoleon's military campaigns—including the Russian operation in 1812, which covered some seven hundred miles in less than three months—were accomplished in short, hard blows. He spent much more time in and near Paris than is commonly realized. Perhaps the most striking Napoleonic blitzkrieg was the Grand Army's prompt victory over Prussia in 1806, when Frederick the Great's bedroom clock was captured at Potsdam.

Plans for the blitzkrieg of 1806 were directly related to Napoleon's new policy of military alliance with the Ottoman Empire and Persia. Of the two, Turkey was the more important by virtue of its geographical location, the tradition of Russo-Turkish hostility, and the long Franco-Turkish friendship of Bourbon days. An opening wedge against Russia could be found in the relatively insignificant warrants of foreign protection which on Sebastiani's authorization Talleyrand might curtail almost to the vanishing point. The warrants extended a given foreign nation's privileges of trade to their individual holders regardless of nationality. All the foreign ambassadors, ministers, and consuls enjoyed the privilege of issuing these warrants, and the common practice of selling them to numerous subjects of the Sultan represented a source of considerable profit. Sharp curtailment of these sales would sharply affect Russia as well as the English Levant Company. Russia's officials issued Russian protection to Greeks and others, including Frenchmen; hence when Britain's Lord Elgin personally relinquished the privilege for himself in 1804, his salary thereafter was paid by the government rather than by "The Company of Merchants of England Trading to the Levant Seas." The company still controlled the British consuls, however, and sales of the warrants continued until an Anglo-Turkish war in 1807.[1]

For Russia the reauthorized military and naval navigation of the Straits represented the most interesting stipulation of the alliance with Turkey, according to Minister Italinski. The breaking of that alliance was deemed by Napoleon to be his first duty. With the launching of militant diplomacy to terminate the alliance in May, 1806, he made a correct appraisal of Turkey's attitude. Victory in this policy for the Straits would be tantamount to success for his general policy of alliance with Turkey, a success perhaps to be won if French military prowess could again assert its supremacy in central Europe. Turkey from this point of view thus represented a sort of jury as Napoleon proceeded with his principal task of 1806, the defeat of enterprising Prussia.

Sebastiani had set out for his important post before the arrival in Paris of Russia's Baron d'Oubril to sign an ill-advised treaty of peace (chap. v). The new ambassador to Turkey was unaware of the existence of the Clarke-Oubril treaty, which if ratified would nullify a great part of the political instructions he had been given. After taking several weeks for preparations he traveled overland in a special coach drawn by four specially harnessed horses—the gift of General Caulaincourt upon Napoleon's orders.[2] The slow journey placed him in Vienna on July 12 and in Bucharest late in July. In Bucharest he learned of the Clarke-Oubril treaty—still two weeks before its rejection by Russia and a week before news of it reached St. Petersburg.

Five days earlier, Napoleon's foreign minister had stated that an armistice prevailed and that ratifications would be exchanged in St. Petersburg. According to Talleyrand's clarification of the pertinent terms, French acquisition of the Cattaro would force the retirement of all Russians on the mainland of the Adriatic to Corfu, where only 4,000 would be retained. Ragusa would become an independent republic under Turkey's guarantee. Napoleon went to Ragusa only in order to cut the Russian lines, Talleyrand said, whereas Russia now had agreed to evacuate the mainland. He remarked that Russia's strong efforts had failed to make Napoleon yield the Adriatic territories that established him as an immediate neighbor of the Ottoman Empire. The French emperor would never surrender this common frontier which could be so useful to Turkey. Talleyrand credited Napoleon with the treaty's formal requirement of the independence and integrity of the Ottoman Empire, together with the more obvious if less important agreement to recall French troops from Montenegro. The Russo-Turkish alliance was not mentioned in the treaty, which pledged that France and Russia would employ their best efforts to end the Franco-Prussian war; French negotiations with England would ensue.[3]

It appears from this evidence that the French government had taken for granted approval of the treaty. Within ten days of the signing, nonetheless, Napoleon ordered strong measures planned in Paris against the Montenegrins and recommended similar action by the Ottomans. Ruffin's announcement of the stipulation for Turkish independence and territorial integrity created a good impression for France at Constantinople.

Soon Napoleon's military prestige combined with Sebastiani's personality to make the French ambassador the principal foreign figure in the Turkish capital, where the latter's unhurried journey ended on August 22. By the end of Sebastiani's first month at his post, his influence was felt in a number of ways. Because of the Clarke-Oubril treaty he delayed the overtures originally intended for the triple alliance, but he advised Paris that his first observations seemed favorable for the alliance, if this were still desired by Napoleon. He came to an understanding with Turkey not to permit navigation by Greek, Armenian, or Turkish ships under foreign flags, with particular reference to the Russian.

The hospodars of Moldavia and Wallachia were removed at about the time of Sebastiani's appearance, and pro-French hospodars were named. Prince Callimachi replaced Prince Moruzzi, and Alexander Suzzo replaced Prince Ypsilanti. Moruzzi and his influential family represented the chief anti-French faction. Observers—including to a certain extent Sebastiani himself in his own reports to Paris—incorrectly credited this significant anti-Russian move exclusively to him. Since Turkey had announced the step earlier, it is not clear that Sebastiani was justified in claiming that the shift resulted from his advice on behalf of the French emperor. Everyone observed that the removals might result in a Turkish break with Russia because of the obvious violation of the Russo-Turkish agreement of 1802, whereby such action required joint inquiries. England joined Russia in protesting the move.[4]

Russia's complaint and Sebastiani's obviousness caught other foreign agents unawares. Neither Italinski nor Ambassador Arbuthnot could check the immediately apparent development of French political influence. Italinski, despite the Clarke-Oubril proposal, still cautiously observed with Sebastiani that understandably strict aloofness in neutral capitals which always marks the personal conduct of the envoys of belligerent powers. He made no move to speak with Sebastiani and the French ambassador likewise kept silent. Italinski frankly advised the Turks of the uncertainty of peace, owing to the factor of ratification. He "threw fire and flame" at Turkey, Sebastiani reported, and rushed off a special courier for instructions.

The Clarke-Oubril treaty had favored Turkey so appreciably that its nonratification by Russia, news of which reached Constantinople on September 6, played right into Sebastiani's hands. Because Napoleon had approved the treaty, it followed almost automatically that Turkey could find a better friend in France than in its military ally. On that same September 6 the *Moniteur* announced to the French public Russia's refusal to ratify the Clarke-Oubril treaty, and Napoleon had already departed for his campaigns in the Germanies.

Sebastiani interpreted the news as signifying that the Franco-Russian war had been resumed and acted accordingly. As the upshot, on September 8 the excited Italinski issued a veiled ultimatum to Sultan Selim. By his formal note of complaints he definitely intended to prevent the anti-Russian hospodars from assuming their duties. He regretted having to complain so soon after renewal of the Russo-Turkish alliance, but he explained that Russia's grievances had mounted. He particularized, in addition to the removal of the hospodars, Turkey's nonfulfillment of the arrangements of 1800 respecting the Ionian Republic and Albania (ex-Venetian), and the frequent failure to yield to Russia's recommendations in behalf of Moldavia and Wallachia. He stressed the ambiguity of Turkey's general intentions, apparent from its refusal to renew the parallel alliance with Great Britain. In the brief interval since the coming of Sebastiani, Italinski continued, not only had Turkey failed to renew relations with England but had, under guise of a "formal request," halted Russia's passage of the Straits by its land and sea forces and thus had nullified the "most interesting provision" of the Russian alliance. Tsar Alexander, he declared, had reason to suspect a change of Turkish policy. Therefore Turkey must fulfill its treaty obligations, and punctually. Russia "would regard as an evidence of rupture with it every species of act or of pretension" contrary to stipulations; whether of the Russo-Turkish treaties of commerce and alliance; or the convention of 1800 for the passage of the Straits; or the autographed commands of successive sultans, known as the capitulations, in benefit of Russia. The note added another ominous threat. Tsar Alexander expected Turkey in its own interest to end this state of affairs; the Russian army on the Dniester would be ready at all times to support Turkey, if it should be attacked. Upon the least hostile move by Turkey, however, the tsar regretfully would employ that same army against the sultan. Russia demanded a categorical written response as to whether or not Turkey intended to discharge fully all its commitments to Russia.

Italinski requested that Turkey hold up the departure for their posts of the two new hospodars and insisted that no subterfuge be practiced such as the dispatch of lieutenants to discharge their functions. He proposed that the boyars of each Principality might assemble in extraordinary session and choose a first boyar from among themselves to act as their provisional executive.[5] The specific complaint against changing hospodars without consultation seems well founded. It obviously was far less important, however, than the other matters—notably the Ottoman request for Russia's ships of war to keep out of the Straits. Sebastiani correctly reported to Paris the core of the complaints to be Turkey's refusal to renew the British alliance and the announced intention to terminate Russia's passage of the Dardanelles and Bosporus. Turkey's version of Italinski's note—translated by Sebastiani on September 8—revealed Turkey's thorough understanding of the several Russian complaints.[6]

Arbuthnot, in Russia's general interest, warned Turkey against favors to France. He set forth several British complaints, including the exceptional honors accorded the French ambassador and the removal of the hospodars. Turkey had refused to renew the military alliance, had violated the capitulations in tariff matters, and had restricted the privilege of foreign protection of Ottoman subjects.[7]

Turkey minimized all the argument, stating it wished to be on friendly terms with Russia and Britain. It suggested that Italinski followed rumor more than facts. A rebellion in Rumelia constituted the chief immediate internal problem for Turkey in mid-September, with the mutinous forces standing at the gates of the capital city. In order to calm the rebels, the Sultan shifted almost all his ministers. The grand vizir was replaced by the chief of the janissaries, the kiaya bey by the chief clerk in the offices of the grand vizir. The affair (a curtain raiser for the three palace rebellions we shall see staged in 1807 and 1808) produced a temporary stagnation in official business. For several days there was little chance for a reply to Russia. Sebastiani could not conclude any of the business under discussion before the cabinet shake-up. He wrote that he hoped the Straits would be closed against Russia by the Turks—who had merely requested an end to such navigation—although Italinski's note left no doubt whatever that Russia would deny the request. Sebastiani now advised the new council to close the Straits by Turkey's sovereign action alone. "The Russians are agitating with violence here," he reported, and the British ambassador "was playing the role of agent for Italinski." Sebastiani claimed that both envoys threatened "a prompt and terrible war" in order to win their objectives. All the clamor had not led the new Ottoman ministry to change the former policy, he said, since the appointed hospodars were being ordered to their posts as scheduled. Greek merchant vessels sailing under the Russian flag no longer might pass the Straits. The new Ottoman ministers seemed to hold friendly sentiments for France. The deposed Moruzzi and Ypsilanti, however, revealed "quite an aversion to France." They reviled Napoleon and circulated false reports belittling France's position in Europe.[8]

Sebastiani faced the new ministers with the same sort of threat with which Italinski had tried to intimidate the old. He wrote to the sultan's foreign minister on September 16 that he had been advised "in an indirect but positive manner" that Russia had refused to ratify the Franco-Russian treaty of peace concluded on July 20. Europe thus had returned to the position of six weeks earlier. Sebastiani reminded the Turks of the treaty's favorable stipulations to Turkey and, anticipating Talleyrand's unsubstantiated contention, charged that Russian disapproval of the terms in question had primarily accounted for the nonratification. Sebastiani explained that he had been authorized to declare in the name of Napoleon that principles of friendship as well as the laws of strict neutrality forbade navigation of the Straits by Russian vessels of war, transport, or military supply. If Russia were permitted to sail the Straits, France should reciprocally be granted the privilege of troop passage by land across Balkan Turkey in order to reach the banks of the Dniester. He said the renewal or continuance of alliance with the enemies of "Napoleon the Great" manifestly infringed on Ottoman neutrality. In response to such hostility the emperor would be forced to adopt measures to conform with his interests and his dignity. The strong French army in Dalmatia could be employed to defend the Ottoman Empire, if Turkey did not yield to Russia and England. He thereby implied that the same army could be sent against Turkey. Similarly demanding a written reply, he declared that Napoleon had no interest in Turkey, except to see it prosper.[9]

During most of that critical month of September, Italinski waited and watched. Turkey did not respond with any complete or formal reply and certainly sent no note of compliance. The tsar's envoy could properly interpret the response that was made as "negative for some objects, contradictory toward facts and treaties for others, evasive and illusory for all the remainder." The sharply pro-French orientation of Turkish policy dated from September 24, when Turkey notified Sebastiani of its acquiescence in his principal demand. Being a friend of Napoleon, it desired to please its French neighbor in Balkan Europe. Although France seemed disquieted because Russia sailed the Straits, Turkey remained also a good friend and good neighbor of Russia. Both its friends had renewed their war. Accordingly, in order to be "scrupulously neutral," it was notifying Italinski he must tell his court not to sail the Straits with Russian vessels of war or troop transports. Thus, true to his prediction, Sebastiani soon could report triumphantly that Turkey's new ministers had closed the Bosporus against Russia, even in the face of the threat of a naval coalition of Russia, Prussia, and England against France. When Turkey announced its decision to Italinski, on the same day, it again assigned its strict neutrality as the reason for the closing.[10]

Hence by successive steps the Russo-Turkish alliance had been virtually nullified—although no one dared announce the fact. Turkey had dismissed the hospodars on August 24—at least in part at French instigation—and thereby had violated a special agreement with Russia. It had reasserted its sovereignty over the Ionian Islands. Despite the stipulation of the Russo-Turkish alliance, the announcement of the closure of the Straits against all foreign warships had been made. Reference must be to Russia, the only nation whose vessels were claiming such passage. Turkey at the same time refused to renew its expiring military alliance with Great Britain.[11]

With the receipt of new orders from St. Petersburg on September 27, Italinski found himself fully confirmed in his opposition to Turkey's dismissal of the hospodars. In a formal protest against the dismissals, he demanded restoration of the former hospodars and stated that neither an evasive reply nor further dilatory tactics would be tolerated. He repeated the other grievances and added that Russia desired to continue to protect Greek shipping. If Turkey did not comply, he would ask for his passports and leave Constantinople immediately.[12]

The British ambassador now had reasons for summoning the British fleet to the Dardanelles. Without awaiting the decision of his government he prepared the Mediterranean commanders for such a summons. The largest sailing vessels of that day, known as ships of the line, carried from 74 to 96 or more cannons. The presence of two British ships of the line at the Dardanelles had been suggested earlier by Ambassador Arbuthnot to Sidney Smith, the naval officer who had assisted in the successful Ottoman and Syrian defense of Acre against Bonaparte's siege in 1799. Now a rear admiral, Smith was Britain's expert on the affairs of the Near East.

Arbuthnot suggested that the fleet's commander send him at least a frigate on which to remove his family. His nervousness was based on seemingly reliable reports which indicated that France was seeking an alliance with Turkey, because the proposals at least had not been rejected. He said France had demanded the end of Ottoman alliances with England and Russia and the halting of the passage of Russian naval vessels. As an equivalent France would demand authority to send troops from Dalmatia across Balkan Turkey to the Dniester. The request for Russia to cease the sailing of the Straits represented concrete evidence of Turkey's new policy. Although he had not as yet been instructed on the point, Arbuthnot on his own initiative supported Italinski's point of view—including the demand for the continued military passage of the Dardanelles and the Bosporus. He almost took the decision at the end of September to suspend his official functions in further warning to Turkey.[13]

When Arbuthnot summoned the war vessels to stand ready outside the Dardanelles in September, 1806, we digress to remark, he set what became Britain's standard procedure for handling such crises at Constantinople. Entire British fleets—not merely isolated ships—were actually to enter the Dardanelles in 1807, 1849, 1853, and 1878, while Britain remained at peace with Turkey. A British ambassador in each instance gave the signal. Only in 1807—and this problem will concern us in the next chapter—did the squadron force its way past the resistance of Turkey's ships of war and coastal guns. The British ambassadors liked to seek the coöperation of their nearest admirals well in advance of need. They wished ships of war anchored at Tenedos, just outside the Dardanelles. Sometimes—although not in 1807—such a display of naval power influenced Turkish policy. Always the ships were deemed near enough to be called up to Constantinople quickly, in order to remove British personnel in consequence of any anti-British development. In each case the presence of British official personnel represented the plausible pretext for anchoring warships just outside the forbidden Dardanelles.

The most interested observer and opponent of Turkish policy at the Straits has always been Russia, except for the short period from 1798 to 1806, when Russia itself navigated that body of water. Napoleonic France had become the interested observer desirous of breaking up the authorized sailings through the Straits by Russian vessels of war or troop transports. Since September, 1806, there have been no such sailings.

Turkey's official reply was delivered to Russia on October 1 by Galib Effendi, the new Ottoman foreign minister, in a long statement which Sebastiani had approved in advance. According to this document, Turkey had never refused to comply with the commercial provisions of existing treaties, nor would it do so in the future. The issue of protecting Greeks within Turkey, applying as it did only to Turkey's own subjects, did not really concern Russia. By demanding passage of the Straits, Russia had indirectly transgressed one of the principal conditions of the Russo-Turkish alliance. The tsar should not insist on a measure that would destroy Turkish neutrality. The sultan did not consider the removal of the hospodars to be a treaty violation. Italinski immediately restated the grievances and demanded his passports if the Ottoman answer should prove unsatisfactory (October 10).[14]

Sebastiani gleefully wrote Talleyrand that matters were now so poised that Russia's note could be tantamount to a declaration of war, if Turkey should not comply. Yet, owing to Arbuthnot's mediation, the tension eased for several weeks. The Russian minister agreed to delay his departure, and these uncertain circumstances accounted for the British hopes, as of October 13, for an amicable adjustment. Britain's home government understood the situation in that light in November, when it nevertheless ordered a large squadron to sail through the Dardanelles and up to Constantinople, with or without the blessing of the Ottoman government.

Sultan Selim reduced the strain by restoring the former hospodars. Sebastiani could never be sure how this came about. Certainly the increasingly friendly tone apparent in letters to France seemed dictated by the conditions. The crisis of the first ten days of October appeared a very good time for the sultan to reply to Napoleon's confidential and friendly letter, delivered by Sebastiani. Selim wrote Napoleon, and Galib Effendi addressed Talleyrand, on October 6. The sultan detailed the negotiations with Russia. Here, we may note, he more than complied with his own order to respect Napoleon's titles; his salutation read, "Very magnificent, very powerful, very excellent Emperor and Padishah, our great friend Napoleon." Galib spoke of mutual friendship.

Selim stated he felt his "spirit embarrassed" because he did not understand why Russia had refused the Clarke-Oubril treaty. He liked its terms favoring Turkey, terms he credited to Napoleon. He recounted his dilemma. Because he had dismissed the hospodars, Italinski had threatened formally to depart, together with all his staff, while the British had stated that if Russia and Turkey went to war, their fleets would assist Russia. The sultan admitted that the understanding of 1802 during a seven-year term required notice to Russia before the dismissal of a hospodar and that he had not given such notice. He had proceeded, in August, on the seemingly valid assumption that the Clarke-Oubril treaty had restored full Ottoman independence, thereby presumably annulling all the restrictive treaty arrangements for the Principalities. Because the treaty had not been ratified, however, the antecedent situation had been restored. Everyone knew with what good faith Turkey strictly fulfilled her treaty commitments, he continued. The court of Russia had seized upon this deviation as the pretext for its demand. The Ottoman government had waited in vain some fifteen or twenty days for advice from Napoleon and then proceeded to make strong replies to Italinski. It was clear from the manner of Italinski's threatened departure that war might break out. Selim played down the fact that Arbuthnot had accorded Russia his strong support, although he did believe that the English envoy had received "vast and absolute" instructions to coöperate with Italinski—instructions which conceivably could form the basis for an official notification of the declaration of war by Great Britain against Turkey.

Several of the sultan's ideas were clearly Sebastiani's and thus revealed the close relations between the two. The Ottoman ruler stated that he desired to spare lives and did not wish to make war against these two powers. Such conflict would be contrary to his religion and in any event would be premature. The fact that the Russian fleet stood ready in the Black Sea was an important factor in his decision to restore the hospodars. Italinski had shown the Ottoman foreign minister the dispatches he had prepared for delivery to the military and naval commanders upon his departure. Thereupon Selim had agreed to restore the hospodars, meanwhile attempting to bring Italinski into a conference in which his ministers might argue him down. He desired friendship with France.[15] Napoleon liked a letter of such tenor even if he greatly disliked the decision it announced. Thereafter he must always consider as his personal friend any fellow ruler so friendly, so frank, and so unstinting in the use of coveted titles. Neither Napoleon nor Selim seemed to remember that this was the same sultan who had gone to war against Bonaparte for invading Egypt in 1798.

Sebastiani's revelation of the over-all situation enables us to understand why the sultan gave way in the matter of the hospodars. The "sad truth," as Sebastiani stated it, was Turkey's utter unpreparedness for war. Consternation had seized the people, the rebels in Rumelia had to be appeased, Ottoman forts were poorly armed, and the sultan could count on only a small and poorly organized army. All these discouraging facts and more the Ottoman ministers revealed to him in a conference of October 9. The French ambassador's promises provided them with some consolation and enabled them to display a little courage; so they took the "firm resolution"—which proved quite transitory—not to restore the hospodars. An additional pledge not to renew Turkey's alliance with England was actually fulfilled. They ordered additional military preparations on the Danube and in the Balkans and Asia. The menacing Russian army of some 90,000 on the Dniester, where they had been stationed for just such a contingency as this, appeared ready to march.

Sebastiani advised Paris that only France could save the weak and demoralized Turks, who required support proportional to the great danger
confronting them. The sultan's wish to gain time accounted for his request that Arbuthnot forestall Italinski's departure. The Ottoman ministers threw out the proposal to wait, at least until the governments of
Russia and England decided whether Turkey had not been justified in
upholding its dignity in the matter of the hospodars. Italinski had
simply accorded with Arbuthnot's suggestions and the crisis had been
postponed.

Sebastiani admitted that he had not expected such an early concession.
In the event of war, he wrote Talleyrand, he would give military advice
to the sultan's ministers. He might even enter the Turkish army, turning the embassy over to Ruffin. Galib Effendi, who had not proved to
be too great a friend of France, would, Sebastiani believed, become
amenable. At least the ambassador did not want to compliment the new
foreign minister too much. This dispatch, which Talleyrand deciphered
in French-occupied Berlin, on November 7, 1806, did not mention the
sultan's consent to reintegrate the deposed hospodars but did recount
the ministerial decision of October 9 against that course. Selim's letter
to Napoleon, received at the same time, gave that account.[16]

The Turkish reply having been presented to Russia, secret discussion
now turned to a possible Ottoman agreement with France. From Sebastiani's initial reports of the controversy with Russia over the hospodars, Talleyrand considered the Russo-Turkish alliance as terminated.
The partial Turkish rebuff of Russia especially encouraged Napoleon's
advisers, who sensed the evident opening of a new anti-Russian policy.
From Mainz, which was three or four weeks by mail from Constantinople, Talleyrand on October 9 eagerly encouraged Turkey in its course.
He authorized assurances that the sultan might count upon French support. He cautioned Turkey to look to its own defenses by maintaining
good garrisons and putting down the Rumelian rebels, and advised that
all Russian vessels of war or troop transports should be prohibited from
passing the Bosporus and Dardanelles. France did not require all its
available forces for its war against Prussia; hence it could increase the
garrison in Dalmatia. He reiterated that Napoleon was refusing to evacuate that province because of its splendid geographical location for according aid to the Ottoman Empire.

The disparity between the dates of events and the reception of information concerning them at Napoleon's headquarters is well illus-

trated in the documents which record Persian affairs. When Talleyrand wrote from Mainz on October 18, to Consul Rousseau at Bagdad, of the paucity of news from Persia, he as yet had received no word of Amédée Jaubert's safe arrival in Teheran in June. He directed Rousseau to attempt to have France's friends press Persia's war against Russia vigorously. Actually, Jaubert, still weak from his prolonged illness, already had returned to Constantinople on October 10. He brought direct word of the imminent arrival from Persia of Ambassador Mirza Riza, who had been instructed to negotiate a military alliance with Napoleon. General Sebastiani welcomed the latter at Constantinople on October 21. It was arranged to send him, together with Jaubert, to Napoleon's winter headquarters as soon as their whereabouts had been learned. Mirza Riza visited for several weeks in the Turkish capital.[17] Talleyrand, thinking along the same line, confidently directed Sebastiani to ask the Persian ambassador to obtain authority to sign an alliance between France, Turkey, and Persia.

Military events soon furthered the French policy. Prussia, which had not been at war for over a decade, joined the allies against Napoleon late in September and made a poor showing. The record of Napoleon's blitzkreig against Prussia can be sketched by a statement of his brief stopping places along the route. He was at Metz on September 26, at Mainz three days later, at Wurzburg on October 3, and at Bamberg four days later. He badly defeated the Prussians in the famous battle of Jena, on October 14. He entered Naumburg October 18, Merseburg on the 19th, and Potsdam on the 25th. He established himself in Berlin on October 27, the fighting in that blitzkrieg finished.

The treaty of peace had to wait until Russia could be beaten also. Three days before Jena, already looking ahead to Russia, he had ordered a strong effort to obtain a military alliance between France, Turkey, and Persia. He also rediscovered Poland, another potential bulwark against Russia, and announced his intention to protect it. Talleyrand—who moved the French foreign ministry's headquarters to Berlin on November 2—repeated his encouragement to Turkey. Napoleon prepared to move farther to the east.

Sebastiani needed news, not of the significant war with Prussia, but of another blitzkrieg won by France. The British at Constantinople communicated on October 12 the first news of the Franco-Prussian war and of Russia's advancing a large army to aid Prussia. Thus the Prussian campaign was in fact nearly over by the time Turkey learned of its beginning. The difference between the dates of events and news of them elsewhere must be kept in mind constantly, for these events took place more than three decades before the telegraph. Jena had been won when, in mid-October, the people at Constantinople were informed of the sultan's decision to restore the deposed hospodars. Sebastiani related that certain ministers—notably Foreign Minister Galib—had acquiesced upon hints of a new coalition to be formed against France. Perhaps the sultan doubted that Napoleon would have available the suggested 100,-000 men to support Turkey—the figure whispered in June. Sebastiani expressed extreme disapproval of several of the Ottoman ministers, although he thought their vacillation could be attributed in part to the uncertain times. In his opinion, Russia's fleets might still navigate the Bosporus without difficulty and the Ottoman alliance with England probably would be renewed; he had accomplished all that he could.[18]

Sebastiani soon had different news. Everyone at Constantinople for a moment lost sight of Russo-Turkish arguments. Speculation was rife that Napoleon's defeat of Prussia at Jena would prove to be virtually a one-battle knockout of a nation at war. The victory gave Sebastiani the concrete evidence he required to advance French policy, news of it more than balancing Russia's threat to Turkey by land and England's by sea. It seemed that Napoleon could now contain the warlike Russians through pressure at the north. The Turks did not yet know of the British threat to come at the Dardanelles (chap. vii), although a British policy favorable to Russia was easily conceivable. Under Sebastiani's direction the Turks proceeded by anticipation; they began to fortify both Straits. At first they thought more of the Bosporus, in Russia's direction. At Sebastiani's request—relaying Talleyrand's advice—they began to re-fortify both banks of both Straits.

Talleyrand on November 9 received Sebastiani's gloomy dispatch of October 16. His reply—as a statement by the representative of the most powerful military state in Europe—was intended to restore full confidence. He could scarcely focus his attention on Turkish affairs, however, so eager was he to report Napoleon's startling achievements.[19] Motivated by Austria's halting attitude, Napoleon sent General Andreossy, a stronger representative, as minister to Vienna. Andreossy—like so many of the emperor's key men—had fought in Egypt.[20]

The official British reaction is seen in the cabinet order of October 22, which directed the approach to the entrance of the Dardanelles of the imposing squadron commanded by Admiral John T. Duckworth.

That squadron anchored at Tenedos a month later, with the authorization either to attack or defend Turkey, depending upon the latter's conduct. Thus Russia, France, and Great Britain now menaced Turkey with precisely the same alternative policy of friendship or hostility.

The British fleet was intended to bolster English and Russian prestige at Constantinople. The actual effect was the opposite, however, because the presence of the fleet further stimulated the Franco-Turkish friendship. News of French military successes in Prussia outweighed the British success at Trafalgar, although the latter obviously sharpened the British squadron's view of its objectives. In new instructions of November 21, the cabinet directed the squadron to sail to the Straits immediately and "to take up such a hostile position as would enable the ships to act effectively against Constantinople." Not neglecting Egypt, the cabinet authorized the squadron to capture Alexandria, "in the event strong measures became necessary" to prevent the French from establishing themselves there.[21]

Napoleon's letter of November 11 to the sultan was the principal influence on Turkey's decision to change to a policy of war against Russia. The victor over Prussia wrote with heightened confidence; amply reciprocating titles, he saluted the "very high, very excellent, very powerful, very magnanimous, and invincible Prince, great Emperor of the Moslems, Sultan Selim, his very dear and perfect friend." He recounted his significant victory, his hold of Berlin and Warsaw, and his command of 300,000 troops. Thus could he counter the enemy's claims of disaster to his arms, especially in a communication to the ruler whose Principalities had been threatened unless he restored the deposed Princes Callimachi and Suzzo. He advised the sultan to regain confidence and Turkey to renew its energy. Destiny willed the maintenance of the Ottoman Empire: "I have the will to save it, and I put my victories at our common disposal," he promised. If Turkey sent its army to the north of the Danube all the way to the Dniester, the Russians would be obliged to retreat. He himself would deflect them from the Principalities by compelling them to use their forces against himself at the north.[22] To the sultan such a course appeared simple. Talleyrand advised Sebastiani that this letter should give the Turks the courage they had lacked in mid-October.

The economic warfare during the Anglo-French conflict of Napoleon's time is often termed the Continental Blockade, an operation which met many difficulties in Egypt and in the region of the Straits. This economic

war began in earnest in 1806. Napoleon's confidence in his star knew
no bounds as he sat in the palaces of Prussia's revered Frederick the
Great. What if he had lost his best fleet a year earlier, off Trafalgar?
There remained two alternatives against England, the blockade of Europe
on the land side, and subsequent attacks against India—the latter in coöperation with Turkey and Persia and possibly also with a defeated
Russia.

To Sebastiani went a copy of the famous decree, issued in Berlin on
November 21, establishing the Continental Blockade against English
commerce. As a reaction to what he termed Britain's "highhanded
conduct on the high seas," Napoleon prohibited all commerce and
correspondence with the British Isles and forbade the sale of English
merchandise. No ship coming directly from England or the English
colonies could be received in any port under his control. Any neutral
ship contravening the rule would have its cargo confiscated exactly as
though it were English merchandise.[23] Britain struck back hard in January, May, and November, 1807, with "orders in council" which
required neutrals to sail to British home ports or its ports in the Mediterranean.

Sebastiani in mid-November, 1806, could transmit officially to the
Turks the details of Jena and its aftermath. He gave them a brief period
to grasp the full significance of the humiliation of Prussia. Then, in a
conference with Galib on November 22, the ambassador virtually issued
orders to the Turks. He replied evasively when the Ottoman minister
inquired about the reason for Napoleon's entrance into Poland, stating
merely that Napoleon could be trusted.

Galib at length admitted that the sultan had awaited just such general
circumstances as these to unite with France. Turkey's only means of
accomplishing its end, Sebastiani explained, would be to send a distinguished envoy to "Napoleon the Great" with full authority to sign
an alliance. Must the alliance be offensive and defensive, or of only the
defensive nature which Turkey would prefer? Sebastiani advised that
the ambassador be given considerable discretion and sign whatever Napoleon wished. He should take with him complete information about
Turkey's army, finances, and military potential in general, and from all
of these facts Napoleon would form his decision.

It will be recalled that Russia had not complied with the "request"
that it desist from sailing the Straits. In answer to Sebastiani's questioning, Galib announced he would issue an order temporarily closing the

Straits against Russian ships and that he would so notify the Russian minister. This significant statement was made on the day the decree for Napoleon's Continental Blockade against British commerce was circulated by Talleyrand's staff. The fact that the Turks were climbing aboard Napoleon's band wagon was illustrated further by their promise of action against the English at the Dardanelles—precisely at the time when rumors told of the approach of an English squadron. Turkey promised to fulfill Sebastiani's request to prohibit the British entrance into the Dardanelles. Two English vessels—one a war frigate—nevertheless entered the Dardanelles and sailed to the port of Constantinople. Upon Sebastiani's inquiries the Turks told him no others would pass. The Ottoman ministry accordingly restricted all the foreign powers, not expressly singling out England. European warships thereafter must not pass the Dardanelles without *ad hoc* permission. The English rear admiral—on November 22, Sebastiani presumed—asked for the admission of the entire squadron.

St. Petersburg's reaction to Italinski's diplomatic rebuffs was, as can be surmised, the determination to permit Turkey no concessions. Foreign Minister Budberg's significant instruction to that effect, dated November 27, led within a month to the breaking of relations and to war. In the absence of news of the complete satisfaction of Russia's demands, Budberg stated, Tsar Alexander considered that Turkey was merely playing for time to prepare its means of resistance. This action was being taken flagrantly, in coöperation with the "common enemy." France occupied a position of menace to Turkey in Dalmatia, from which French forces could cross Balkan Turkey and attack Russia on the Dniester. He had heard that Sebastiani had suggested this to Turkey.[24]

Budberg considered France's position, apart from the issue of the deposed hospodars, as adequate reason for the tsar's order of mid-October whereby General Michelson was directed to enforce Turkey's alliance obligations. On October 23, Budberg received Italinski's dispatch announcing the restoration of the hospodars. The tsar expected immediate clarification of the other issues also, but all the dispatches received at St. Petersburg from Italinski that week were confined to the single subject of the hospodars. Russia now sought not merely an isolated demonstration in its favor, so Budberg stated, but a more favorable Ottoman general policy. He charged that even the one concession had been executed in bad grace.

Russia noticed especially that Turkey had given only partial satisfaction, as a result of Sebastiani's frequent conferences with pro-French Ibrahim Pasha and with several other key Ottomans. Confusion marked the Principalities and Passvan Oglu was invading their frontiers. Tsar Alexander could not assume the sultan's sincerity from the concession. Russia, like France, would consider Turkey's policy for the Straits as the test of general policy. The treaty grant-of-passage represented a guarantee proportionate to its importance; Russia must request "a solemn and authentic declaration by which Turkey will never in any case infringe this right, under any pretext whatsover." Budberg also demanded the renewal of the alliance between Turkey and Great Britain, and the setting up of a national army in the Principalities. This was Russia's unyielding official position. Budberg also advised Italinski to indicate to Turkey that St. Petersburg was well aware of the Turkish violations of treaty and of alliance. Turkey thus conducted itself with the intention of winning French approval and aid—which explained Sebastiani's success from the moment of his arrival and the illegal removal of Princes Moruzzi and Ypsilanti.[25]

The documents reveal similar sharp objectives for France. That same day, from Berlin, Talleyrand wrote Sebastiani that after further mopping-up operations in Prussia the push against Russia would begin. "It is necessary," he stated, "that the Ottoman Empire not hesitate any longer to make a diversion, all along its frontiers."[26] This warning foretold the reasoning Napoleon employed in his personal letter to Selim on December 1. The emperor wrote the letter in terse telegraphic language and dispatched it from Posen—from which point he commanded the region from the Rhine to the Vistula. He exulted that the Prussia which had aligned itself with Russia had disappeared. His own armies stood on the Vistula, and Warsaw was within his power. Prussia and Poland would form armies to recover Polish independence from Russia. The time had come, he urged, for the sultan to recover his independence, "to chase out and declare traitors the rebel hospodars whom unjust foreign violence had forced him to restore," and reëstablish hospodars of his own choice. Selim should march against Russia and not accord the Serbians concessions demanded with arms in hand. From Russia he had nothing to fear. "I have charged my ambassador to contract all the engagements necessary," Napoleon stated. "If you have merely been prudent until now, any further condescension toward Russia will be weakness and lose you your empire." He related to Sebastiani that the Russians, wishing to defend Warsaw, had been beaten and dispersed.

He desired that Turkey take the necessary steps, beginning by restoring its own hospodars. He further stated to his ambassador, "You are authorized to sign a secret offensive and defensive treaty by which I guarantee Turkey the possession of Moldavia, Wallachia, and Serbia." He would agree to make peace only in common with Turkey.[27]

Russia's losing policy could be seen at Constantinople at the end of November. Sebastiani reported triumphantly the rapid development of pro-French moves. Napoleon's lightning victory over Prussia changed the outlook of a majority of the sultan's ministers. Sebastiani had invited them to form an alliance with France to deliver Turkey from the yoke imposed by Britain and Russia. Because he possessed no authority to sign an agreement, the Ottoman ministry appointed a special envoy to negotiate with Napoleon. Much divided opinion existed in the sultan's council, the English and the Russians still having many partisans. Conforming to French advice, the Turks had repaired and armed the castles of the Bosporus and the Dardanelles. Sebastiani reported: "The sultan possesses two considerable army corps. One is at Sofia, to require the Serbians to submit, the other at Ismail, to oppose the Russians if they cross the Dniester—and even to act offensively if Napoleon desires." [28]

Not the least of Sebastiani's successes lay in his encouragement of the friendly exchanges of messages with the French government. As the dispute with Russia approached a showdown, the sultan and Napoleon quickly wrote two letters to each other. Upon the French ambassador's suggestion, Selim congratulated Napoleon for his successes in a friendly and confidential letter of November 30. He addressed it to the "very majestic, very powerful, very august Emperor and Padishah of France," and mentioned the "pure and simple affection subsisting physically and naturally since time immemorial" between the two empires.

As much as anything, the nonratification of the Clarke-Oubril treaty pointed the way to things to come. Selim considered that Napoleon's victories had thrown terror into the hearts of certain enemies—especially so because he counted France "the sincere and natural ally" of Turkey. He had previously made silent and secret military preparations against Russia; now he would proceed quite openly. His armies would assemble at essential centers, and depots would be established for military supplies and provisions. Turkey's forts and castles would be fortified and its naval forces armed. His ministers were revealing these preparations regularly to Sebastiani, who in turn had been giving them advice. In brief, Selim announced that France and Turkey held common interests.[29]

Down to the opening week of December, 1806, the documents pointed not to the imminence of Russo-Turkish war but only to its inevitability. Because General Michelson was entering the Principalities, whatever Italinski might say presumably would have less effect than the commander's words. Michelson wrote, on December 2, that whereas Turkey previously had observed the Russian alliance, one now noted infractions of every kind. He warned, "Bonaparte's real intention is to make himself master of the Ottoman Empire." Russia desired peace and friendship with Turkey and demanded the explicit fulfillment of the renewed alliance, including the passage of the Straits.[30]

Before Selim learned of this letter he addressed another friendly communication to Napoleon, on December 6. One week of his open military preparations to meet Russia's threat of invasion had produced a new crisis in Russo-Turkish relations. Hence the sultan almost anticipated Napoleon in first proposing an outright military alliance. He apprized Napoleon of the "doubling and tripling of Ottoman preparations," and asked for such an alliance. Sebastiani's arguments, he said, had convinced him of the ancient and natural conformity of interests between the French and Turkish empires; he wished to enhance the power and dignity of the Ottoman Empire and at all times to maintain its independence and glory. In view of the reciprocal expressions of interest and confidence he had decided to send a special negotiator to treat with Napoleon for an alliance.[31]

The sultan not only accepted the principle of military alliance with France but began immediately to act as Napoleon's ally; Sebastiani hoped his emperor would be content. Selim also offered to dismiss his anti-French secretary and adviser, if Napoleon should request it by confidential letter. Sebastiani—correctly or incorrectly—reported that the Russians were already marching across Moldavia, and the Turks asked Italinski to explain the advance of that army. Meanwhile two other English vessels, in addition to the two already at Constantinople, anchored within the Dardanelles. Physical pressure to influence policy thus came from two directions—England's by sea, Russia's by land.[32]

An essential development was Russia's actual occupation of parts of Moldavia and Wallachia. Letters addressed late in November to Berlin and Constantinople from the Principalities carried the first reports of Russia's crossing over into Moldavia—although Russia later claimed to have crossed only on December 10. Perhaps the first units were small. French dispatches of December 13 record a debate over responsibility

for a frontier clash; by mid-December Constantinople took for granted
that Russians had entered the Principalities in force. Sebastiani dated
the initial crossing of the Dniester as early as November 22—the date
eagerly accepted by Napoleon's officials in Paris. Whatever the precise
date, between November 22 and December 10 a considerable Russian
army crossed into Moldavia with Jassy as its immediate goal. The Ottoman reaction was of importance because in mid-December Turkey decided to resist the Russians. A report stated that the Russian army—
exaggerated to 140,000—had crossed or would cross the Dniester in
order to restore the already-restored hospodars. The serious developments thus were due in part at least to the slowness of the communications of that day.

Thus by December 11 Napoleon had new pretexts to call for an urgent communication with Turkey; he had heard that the Russians entered Jassy on November 25. From Posen, he directed that this news be
expedited to any Ottoman ambassador who in turn should send it
promptly to Constantinople. The sultan must be informed also that
Napoleon was now master of Warsaw, and that this was the time for
Turkey to act. Selim must not neglect this opportunity to regain his
independence; Napoleon "liked the sultan, and took much interest in
him." He rebuked certain wishful thinkers, including French agents at
Warsaw, who prematurely announced the opening of a Russo-Turkish
war.[33] The beginning of the fighting war between France and Russia
may be set as December 10, the day when St. Petersburg published a
decree against all French subjects resident in Russia. The Holy Synod
issued a religious appeal, to protect the Greek Catholic Church against
Napoleon Bonaparte.[34]

Persia, like Turkey, by this time was ready for a Napoleonic alliance.
Napoleon did not as yet know the details of the complete success of
his initial overture to Persia; of Jaubert's views and results no details
had been received. That envoy's first letters from Teheran went astray,
and because he had been too ill to use his cipher he had written only in
cautious generalities. His most important letters in any event failed to
arrive at Constantinople until December, 1806—a circumstance which
again reminds us of the constant problem of slow communications. Jaubert himself returned to Constantinople several weeks before these letters. He wrote Talleyrand on November 14, but the letter never reached
its destination; the foreign minister asked for a duplicate of it on January 6, 1807.[35] Mirza Riza arrived, and likewise waited at Constanti-

nople to learn where Napoleon would be. Georges Outrey, who accompanied Mirza Riza, handed to Sebastiani in mid-December the shah's reply to Napoleon's letter of early 1805. Everyone lauded the work of Jaubert, so Ruffin wrote Talleyrand at the end of December; his success spoke for itself.[36]

Sebastiani gave Napoleon's first urgent letter to Selim on December 15, together with its translation by Ruffin. The Ottoman ruler read the letter in Sebastiani's presence, after which he revealed the significant decision soon to be taken by his government. He stated that his honor, safety, and religion commanded a declaration of war against Russia for invading his provinces; all the Ottoman resources would be employed in the struggle. The foreign minister—whom Sebastiani still called anti-French—opposed with vigor the declaration of war and advised further temporizing. This hedging presented Sebastiani an opportunity to state his reasons for Turkey's going ahead. At the sultan's personal invitation, he conferred with the Ottoman ministers as a group on December 16, preliminary to the final decision. The decision for war also proved difficult because of Ottoman inertia and the respective pro-Russian and pro-English division of official opinion. English partisans were especially active; the British squadron as well as a Russian army stood menacingly near. As a gesture toward an easier decision for war, Sebastiani suggested that there be no detention of Russians or confiscation of their property.

The formalities for declaring war against Turkey's erstwhile ally soon would be completed, everyone knew, and these formalities would conform with customary Mohammedan procedures. Before the learned ulema, on December 18, the mufti of Constantinople (the respected spiritual judge) supplied the requisite ecclesiastical justification. Italinski had no discretion left; he understood he would be ordered to leave Constantinople. The grand vizir announced in martial spirit that he would personally command the army of the Danube—although no one expected actual fighting during the winter months. Fresh orders to the commanders of the castles of the Dardanelles and the Bosporus prohibited Russian ships from passing the Straits. Turkey at that time issued no similar specific prohibition against British ships.

Through Sebastiani Selim requested Napoleon to send him as soon as possible "some French artillery officers, engineers, infantry officers, naval officers, and even some generals," all of whom would be treated with distinction. In the lend-lease of military personnel the ambassador himself could be useful; he wished either to fight alongside the Turks or to join the French army in Dalmatia. Sebastiani strongly recommended the sending of artillery officers and engineers of the type he had sought from Generals Lauriston and Marmont some three months earlier, when they had replied evasively that none were available.[37]

The sultan made good his promise to inform Sebastiani of developments. The ambassador did not lack for full details even of secret affairs during this period when Turkey rushed through the formalities for the declaration against Russia. He knew immediately of the Ottoman council's debates, of Russia's threats, and of the menacing character of Britain's "advice." Whereas Italinski no longer commanded attention, the spotlight turned to Britain's Ambassador Charles Arbuthnot. The latter's presumably secret communications with the Ottoman government passed through the hands of the most-favored ambassador, Napoleon's —and the copies remain in the French archives today. In consequence of the debate over a reported frontier clash between Russian and Ottoman forces in the Principalities, the Ottomans solicited Arbuthnot's intervention. He called the clash nothing more than pure accident. In a communication of December 13, he justified Russia's reasoning for sending in the troops. Basing his remarks on what Italinski had told him, he stated that the Russians would not act in a hostile manner against their Turkish ally. He would deplore any reaction by Turkey against this necessary and precautionary move intended to guarantee the safety of Turkey. Budberg, in the frigid St. Petersburg of December, realistically justified the tsar's order to move into Moldavia. Some 30,000 of General Michelson's forces occupied Jassy on December 16 and advanced in the direction of the Danube. The commander announced these moves as "friendly."[38]

Late in November, details finally reached St. Petersburg of Turkey's yielding on the issue of the hospodars. The decision must now be taken whether or not to stand on the order to occupy the two Turkish Principalities. Budberg in the following eight points thus appraised the many elements of the situation: (1) The Ottoman concession might be a ruse to gain time for further military preparations; (2) France might strike at Balkan Turkey from its position in Dalmatia; (3) a Russian withdrawal from the Principalities would have an adverse moral effect upon all peoples opposing Napoleon; (4) to remain there would encourage the Serbians; (5) there was always fear that Turkey's internal dissolution might begin at any time; (6) Sebastiani's successes at Constantinople indicated the reversal of Ottoman foreign policy by giving France the preponderant influence; (7) because Russia did not really know Turkey's intentions, it must await more positive evidence before withdrawing; (8) Russia could interpret its occupation as merely a strategic equivalent to the French hold on Dalmatia.[39]

Turkey declared war with great solemnity, Sebastiani's dispatch of December 24 recording the details. An assembly of the ulema, the janissaries, and the great of the empire formally advised that course. They ceremoniously announced to Sultan Selim their unanimous opinion that he must "repress the unjust aggression of Russia in Moldavia and Wallachia, and thus avenge the outraged national honor." Sebastiani observed great enthusiasm among the people, the ulema, and the janissaries. Only the ministry held back, being "timid, cold, and still almost uncertain." The ambassador recounted that he had had to speak for war with vigor—even after the Sultan's announcement of December 16—owing to the foreign minister's last-minute negotiations through Ambassador Arbuthnot, in an attempt to win Russia's promise to evacuate the Principalities. Sebastiani in contrast emphasized Turkey's honor, security, religion, and national sovereignty. The breaking note—which Sebastiani considered weak—demanded Russia's evacuation of Turkish territory.

The English ambassador, Sebastiani reported, labeled the Turkish action as violent and absurd. He gave himself over to "outrageous menaces" against the Ottoman government which Sebastiani, in his turn, considered as "absurd ravings." The two British vessels at Constantinople and the five at the Dardanelles bolstered Arbuthnot in his policy and for a short time forced the Turkish ministers to caution. They did not, however, change what Sebastiani described as the "truly national" decision. Arbuthnot spoke to the Turks of French weaknesses and circulated several rumors—said to emanate from Ambassador Robert Adair of Vienna—which in effect said that half of the French army had been lost since the opening of Napoleon's latest campaigns. It was added that Prussia would refuse to uphold the armistice with France in order to join forces with Russia, that France's weak position in Spain and Portugal indicated those two powers would carry the war to the heart of France, and that Paris itself faced revolt.

Italinski embarked on December 25, on board an English vessel. Pro-French Prince Suzzo once again became the hospodar of Wallachia—an almost meaningless appointment unless Russia's army could be importuned to retreat. Sebastiani advised Turkey to take "severe measures" simultaneously against Great Britain. "If the ministry were as Moslem as the inhabitants of Rumelia," he chided, "the brave English would not be suffered long at Constantinople." However, he wrote Talleyrand, "Except for the ulema and the military, all are corrupt to the point where it is difficult to put over the idea." He considered everything prepared for effective war against Russia in the Balkans and in Asia when moderate weather came in the spring. "Some Turks," he remarked, "consider this war only as a useful diversion for France. Today, more than ever, the appearance here of French officers in all categories is needed." An Ottoman squadron of twenty vessels would soon be ready. Turkey lacked adequate officers, especially artillery officers, to repair the forts of the Dardanelles and the batteries defending Constantinople.

Alexander's forces moved forward quickly, since no effective Turkish military opposition had as yet materialized. Bucharest was occupied on December 27, 1806. Perhaps Napoleon's scheming through Sebastiani might prove a fiasco, if these advances could be sustained despite the weather and if effective British naval pressure came from the south. On that December 27 the sultan answered Napoleon's letter of November 11. He told of his declaration of war, and of the appointment of Vahid Effendi as the special envoy named to negotiate for a military alliance with Napoleon.[40]

Sebastiani claimed to be on quite intimate terms with several high Turkish officials, the group always attached to France; it was they who had taken the vigorous measures. The principal minister opposing the policy apparently was Galib, who, Sebastiani said, revealed his real attitude by terming the French ambassador a minister of the sultan. Galib delivered over to the Russians and English five pro-French Ionian sailors —an action against which Sebastiani protested. "You have no idea how many intrigues go on here," he wrote Talleyrand, "and how little one may count on promises, whether of ministers or of the Turks in general or of the Greeks." The situation so tended toward demoralization that he himself wished to leave; having accomplished what his "august master" desired, he announced himself as ready to retire.[41]

Napoleon ordinarily was approximately one month behind with official news from Constantinople. Late in December Talleyrand acknowledged from Berlin Sebastiani's dispatches up to November 30 and the sultan's letter of December 1. He forwarded these curtain raisers of the developments in December to Napoleon in Poland, at the same time assuring Sebastiani that the emperor would be "infinitely pleased" with his work.[42] In Algeria, Frenchmen were in such disfavor that Talleyrand instructed Sebastiani to solicit Turkey's correction of abuse of them there.[43]

Turkey published a manifesto of its declaration against Russia and also announced the war by a circular to the foreign diplomatic missions. The sultan's government charged several infractions of treaties, including the annexation of the Crimea and the push into Ottoman-claimed Georgia. Russia had been accorded certain privileges in Georgia, only to finish by annexing the province. Russia had encouraged the non-Moslem inhabitants of Turkey and assisted the rebel Serbs. Russia itself had nullified the Russo-Turkish alliance. Strictly speaking, Russia possessed no rights in the Ionian Republic other than those of coguarantor. Yet it had regulated and removed the Ionian police, made of those islands its warehouse for the Balkans, and built up a fighting force there to be used in Italy. Russia had abused its authorization to sail the Dardanelles and Bosporus, and thereby forced Turkey to violate the strict neutrality proclaimed in the Franco-Russian war. Russia sent money and supplies through the Straits, destined for Albania. Its warrants of protection which should have been intended only to facilitate foreign trade had been issued to "incalculable numbers" of Ottoman subjects, especially in Moldavia and Wallachia. In the latter provinces Russia's consul interfered with the domestic administration. Russia not only had contested Turkey's appointment of new hospodars, but also had invaded those provinces. The last circumstance was the breaking point meaning war, Turkey concluded, although any of the others would have constituted adequate reason.[44]

As a further illustration of the appeal of Napoleon's new military prestige in southeastern Europe, Prince Moruzzi of Moldavia, one of the deposed and subsequently reinstated anti-French hospodars, offered to bury the hatchet and thus end the long-standing feud of his family with the French. He sent John Ghika, his secretary, to Napoleon with this overture. He protested his loyalty to the sultan, wrote of aiding that ruler against Russia, and expressed confidence in Napoleon. Talleyrand's reply on January 11 combined recriminations with the olive branch. Ironically, he listed Moruzzi's permitting Moldavia to fall into dependence upon Russia and his facilitating the passage of Russian troops into Moldavia. Without recalling "the just grievances of the past," however, it was announced that from then on Napoleon's appraisal would depend on Moruzzi's wartime activity toward the common victory. The foreign minister confidentially explained to Sebastiani that this apparent acceptance of Moruzzi's overture was intended to win Moldavian support in the war effort. Moreover, Moruzzi seemed tied up with Passvan Oglu of Vidin and Mustapha Bairakdar of Ruschuk, both of whom commanded large provincial armies and could be powerful aids to Turkey.[45] The exchange of letters brought no result; in contrast, the anti-French attitudes of the Moruzzis seemed to grow. As late as November, 1808, we find M. Champagny, Talleyrand's eventual successor at the foreign ministry, inquiring about the Moruzzi letter. The matter ended when Moruzzi did not answer Talleyrand's reply. Champagny stated that Napoleon's embassy at Constantinople still considered the Moruzzi faction a strong one and still the enemy of France.[46]

In summary, we have seen that negotiations with Turkey late in 1806 indicated the essential anti-Russian role of the Near and Middle East in Napoleon's general policies. He sought military alliances with Turkey and Persia and wished to see a reconstructed Polish state. He calculated that political alliance with Turkey and Persia might be complemented with commercial treaties, to bring permanent economic profits to France. The *de facto* alliance with Turkey was already being applied: the sultan, on January 7, 1807, proclaimed the Dardanelles and the Bosporus closed to foreign navigation for the duration of his war with Russia.

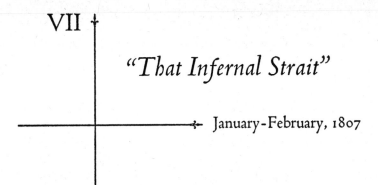

VII

"That Infernal Strait"

January-February, 1807

DESPITE Napoleon's impressive land victories, the naval primacy of Great Britain caused new losses of French prestige throughout Mediterranean lands. On the other hand, Turkey's declaration of war against Russia—its own as well as Britain's ally—indicated how sharply British influence had declined at the important center of Constantinople. By its shift of alliance from Russia to France, Turkey earned for itself, moreover, the unsavory reputation of vacillation in policy— a reputation to last ever afterward. As the tsar's Foreign Minister Budberg revealed, no longer might Russia and Great Britain have confidence in their alliances with a sultan of Turkey. The Ottoman Empire would learn a lesson from the six-year aftermath of climbing aboard Napoleon's band wagon late in 1806—that it must never again go to war to support an apparent winner in Europe. Imperial Turkey did not follow the lesson in 1914, but the Republic of Turkey during Hitler's transitory days of victory could have used the earlier episode to justify its neutrality.

Even if the potential invader of Britain should possess the requisite sea power, he also must adequately protect his land flanks all the way from Spain to the Dardanelles and north to the Baltic. Neither Napoleon nor Hitler could win that protection because of Russia. Napoleon well knew that he could not invade Britain successfully unless— an unlikely prospect—he could build up supremacy in sea power. No more squadrons existed to take over from countries with which he had or might make alliances, save possibly the Danish and the Turkish. His naval construction proceeded at snail's pace.

Anxious Britons reacted promptly to Napoleon's plan of sealing off the coasts of Europe by alliance and blockade all the way round from Constantinople to the Baltic. Their reply, apart from extensive measures to enforce shipping restrictions against neutrals, was to attack in 1807 that giant arc of Napoleon's power at both its presumably weak ends: they penetrated the Dardanelles and bombarded Copenhagen. In this chapter we deal with the background and immediate aftermath of the British fleet's sailing into the Sea of Marmora in February, 1807, Turkish guns and Ambassador Sebastiani notwithstanding.

Britain decided upon a course of naval activity in the Mediterranean much more forceful than one of mere counterblockading. It took the unprecedented action of ordering Sir John Duckworth, on January 13, 1807, to sail through the Dardanelles with his fleet. "Some late proceedings on the part of the Turkish government," Admiral Collingwood said upon cabinet authority, "indicate the increasing influence of the French and a disposition by Turkey to abandon the alliance which happily has subsisted with the British government." Everyone recognized the factor of slow communications; matters might meanwhile be adjusted at Constantinople. Britain's threatened "prompt and decisive measures" therefore were given a contingent character—except that Admirals Duckworth, Sidney Smith, and Thomas Louis must sail their respective squadrons through the Dardanelles and up to Constantinople. They must be prepared "to act with vigor and promptitude, as circumstances and the state of affairs upon arrival might make necessary." If the differences should be found settled they must act amicably. If not, the orders were to open fire against the Ottoman capital after demanding the transfer to British ships of Ambassador Arbuthnot and all the British subjects. Even if these demands should be met, the fleet nevertheless should begin hostilities whenever Arbuthnot so directed.

Significantly, Duckworth under his orders also must "demand the surrender of the Turkish fleet, together with a supply of naval stores from the arsenal sufficient for its complete equipment," and this demand was to be accompanied with "a threat of immediate destruction of the town." Britain anticipated the customary Turkish dilatoriness. If the Turks offered to negotiate, Duckworth must not permit them to delay longer than half an hour. If they refused absolutely, he must cannonade the city "or attack the Ottoman fleet, wherever it may be, holding it in mind that the getting the possession of the Turkish fleet, and next to that its destruction, is the object of first consideration." Upon the opening of hostilities against Turkey, General Fox in Sicily must detach 5,000 men for the occupation of Alexandria, in order to forestall a possible French collaboration with friendly Turks. According to the original plan, Russians would coöperate from Corfu. Prompt action was so essential, however, that Duckworth was directed to proceed without awaiting the requested support of four Russian vessels.[1]

Owing to the time lag between events at Constantinople and Napoleon's receipt of news of them, he could not as yet know how quickly the Russo-Turkish quarrel had come to a head. His reports received on December 27 authenticated the events of a month earlier; the tendency of Turkish policy gave him much ground for conjecture. He directed that Turkey be informed he had beaten Russia's General Kameski in three engagements.

Napoleon did not really need to know of the Ottoman declaration of war. His imagination inferred, if for the most part incorrectly, the developments of the ensuing weeks from the encouragement the Turks had given Sebastiani down to November 30. He directed Talleyrand to publish fictitious news at Paris, datelined from Bucharest, detailing "the hypocritical conduct of Russia and the status of its relations with Turkey." He personally worded a fictitious news summary for the *Moniteur*, indicating that Britain's passions guided Russian policy. He ridiculed the Russian claim that it had entered Moldavia by agreement with the sultan and cast aspersions on its "pretended" alliance with Turkey. Passvan Oglu and Mustapha Bairakdar had crossed the Danube and occupied Bucharest, the article said, stopping the advance of Russia's armies. The statement was further made that nonplussed Italinski had been unable even to reply to Turkey's request for information. The Russians had arrested the French consul; in rejoinder to this action, the two pashas had arrested the Russian consul. Frenchmen would also read: "Four English vessels have appeared before Constantinople to impose their will on Turkey. They will not succeed, and England will act against its best interests if it seconds the Russian pretensions." Moreover, Napoleon chided, what could they do? They had ships, but Turkey would close all its ports to them. "All the pretended treaties of alliance have proved false, and war is declared between the two powers. . . . The shah of Persia is preparing to repress the unjust agression of Russia, and reënter Georgia."[2] Another faked story presents this gem of December 31, addressed to Napoleon's minister of police:

The last bulletins will show you the great successes we have had over the Russian armies. The supposed treaty of alliance between Russia and Turkey is an invention. The Turks entered Wallachia the very moment the Russians entered Moldavia. Have articles written in this sense, and dated from Bucharest. The thing is true, but still public opinion must be enlightened. Have the same thing done with respect to Persia, dated from Tiflis. The fact is that the Russian Empire is attacked on every side.[3]

Napoleon planned to coördinate France's war effort against Russia with that of all Turkey and part of Poland, perhaps also involving Persia and, if need be, the Barbary Regencies of northern Africa. New Year's greetings dispatched from Warsaw to Sultan Selim offered the occasion for a letter to his "very great and true friend," to encourage actual happenings such as he had announced in the newspapers. War had been declared on Turkey, not provoked by Turkey, Napoleon stated; enemies had invaded its territories. He understood that the sultan's forces stood ready to resist invasion from across the Dniester. The Ottoman envoy could now be expected to negotiate an alliance and thereby to guarantee the sultan's power. "The moment has arrived to restore the Ottoman Empire to its former grandeur," he encouraged. "There is not a moment to lose; your frontiers are invaded." Ottomans should be called to the colors to defend their towns, mosques, and everything Mohammedan —which the Russians wished to destroy. He prayed God to bless Selim's arms.[4]

In mid-January he advertised Russia's army as being in "precipitous retreat" toward the Niemen, at the time he issued his decree for a provisional government for Poland.[5] Napoleon's march eastward had stimulated Polish national feeling. Statesmanlike and respected Adam Czartoryski reëntered the scene with the proposal that Russia sponsor a plan for a Slavic federation.[6] The emperor turned over to General Jean Baptiste Gouvion the governing of the city and province of Warsaw. For three weeks he and his entourage amused themselves there with fêtes, balls, and concerts. Napoleon appeared in public with a new favorite, the beautiful twenty-two-year-old Polish Countess Maria Walewska, who followed him to Osterode and Finkenstein. Their son, Count Walewski, became a French foreign minister of the 1850's.

Talleyrand remained at Warsaw to conduct diplomatic operations and to watch Gouvion. The farther such an empire as Napoleon's extends, the weaker it becomes and the more it costs the homeland and its foreign friends to defend it and extend it still farther. The Duchy of Warsaw —into which the provisional regime graduated—would pay as heavily as Turkey for its breathing spell. Warsaw, like the Ottoman state, hoped to extend its boundaries as compensation for work done for Napoleon and from his generosity. Such an empire must be sure never fully to satisfy its friends but instead merely to dangle before them the prospect of achieving all their desires. In such a manner Napoleon dealt with Turkey, Poland, and Persia in 1807.

Gradually all the details of Russo-Turkish relations filtered through to Napoleon. On January 20, in reply to the sultan's second friendly letter of December, Napoleon stated that he also had read the proclamations issued by Russia's generals and that they had made him as indignant as they had his "very dear and perfect friend." Selim could be certain of Napoleon's complete support. The time had come, he repeated, "to consolidate the empire of the Ottomans."[7] Talleyrand sent news, opinions, and directions to Sebastiani. He asked for diversionary attacks. Russian troops in the Principalities, he affirmed, numbered only 35,000, an insufficient number to cross the Danube. There they would be further weakened if Turkey forced them to place a second southern army in action by invading the Crimea; he asked for action by Turkey's squadron in the Black Sea. Persia should make further efforts in Georgia; Turkey could assist by ordering the pasha of Erzurum to move into Georgia. Thus there would be simultaneous Turkish attacks in Georgia, the Crimea, and Bessarabia.[8]

Napoleon's presence in eastern Europe, together with the centralization of diplomacy at Warsaw, enabled him to learn of the events at Constantinople somewhat sooner than was usually the case—ordinarily within a month. Nearly always unrealistic in naval matters, he was unaware of the fact that the British at the moment were effectively barring his path at the entrance of the Dardanelles. Belatedly he issued an offer to sail several French and Italian ships of the line secretly through the Straits, in order to maneuver in the Black Sea with the Turkish fleet. By what means these ships could have pushed up to the Dardanelles is open to surmise, since the large British squadron stood at Tenedos and several Russian vessels were in the Adriatic. Probably he considered the offer another means of luring Turkey into war against England without a formal alliance. He may have expected the English themselves to attack Turkey. Success in such a maneuver would have had the effect of enabling Napoleon to stand astride the Dardanelles. He lent Turkey the requested French military officers and tendered several companies of French artillery troops to aid in defending the Bosporus—"if that would be expedient and not alarm the Ottoman government." He cautioned Sebastiani to discuss this proposal secretly and to deal only with the sultan himself. He replied to the Turkish request for a military diversion simply by himself asking for a diversion. His wish that Turkey attract Russian forces obviously reflected his desire that the tsar maintain some forces elsewhere while the French assaulted him at the north.[9]

Official confirmation of the Russo-Turkish war was received at Warsaw on January 29. Upon Napoleon's order, Marshal Berthier explained
to General Marmont that, war having been solemnly declared, Italinski
with some 500 or 600 "Greeks and others" had departed from Constantinople. General Michelson commanded 30,000 men, including 10,-
000 at Bucharest. The Turks had 15,000 and Passvan Oglu 20,000,
while some 60,000 were being mobilized to come from Asia. Berthier
and Marmont did not like the Asiatic troops, some of whom they had
easily defeated in pitched battles in Syria in 1799; Berthier considered
the European Turks the better fighters, although they too lacked the
European type of training. He considered it unlikely that the Russians
would be able to cross the Danube. Napoleon desired that Marmont
send five officers to Constantinople and write the pashas of Bosnia and
Scutari to solicit their protection en route. Twenty or thirty officers
might also be lent these pashas, on their request, and aid be accorded
them in other ways.

The possibility existed that the sultan would request an army corps
to defend the Danube. The emperor was willing, the clarification continued, to send Marmont with his 25,000 troops by way of Vidin.
These troops, with the Ottoman forces to be available soon, would force
the Russians to augment their inadequate 30,000—obviously rendering
the campaign easier for Napoleon at the north. This matter remained
purely hypothetical, Berthier cautioned. Napoleon directed Marmont to
take for granted that he could count on the Turks as sincere allies and
hence furnish them whatever arms and munitions they wished. The
Persian and Ottoman ambassadors were, at the moment, en route to
Warsaw to sign alliances to counter Russia's ambitions. Marmont might
publicize the fact that he only awaited Ottoman authorization to pass
the Danube and oppose the Russians. The sight of French officers in
various areas of European Turkey would have a good effect.[10]

Talleyrand confirmed these statements to Sebastiani, adding that
French troops would not cross the Dalmatian frontier unless Napoleon
came to an understanding on the matter with Turkey. He would be
willing to send 25,000 to the Danube if Turkey requested. Might not
his forces occupy the forts adjacent to Ragusa? The Bosporus had been
closed against Russia. Napoleon considered taking over the management of the principal defenses of the Straits and the Black Sea. He was
proposing, upon Turkey's request, to send six vessels of the line to master
the Black Sea in company with the Turkish fleet. He frankly admitted

he could send these six vessels only if they escaped the English. Once in the Black Sea, these large vessels, supported by twelve or fifteen Turkish ships, should assure superiority over the Russians there. Napoleon also could disembark in the Straits several artillery companies to aid in defending the Bosporus.[11]

Upon the receipt of Sebastiani's dispatch of December 17, 1806—officially revealing the sultan's personal decision for war against Russia—Napoleon planned to coördinate all the common efforts against the tsar. These plans seemed to hint at effective alliance action with Turkey, although Talleyrand, carefully dodging a statement of stipulations for an actual alliance, spoke generally, to the effect that Napoleon would second the Ottoman efforts. Talleyrand said that if Turkey desired a corps of French troops to come to the Danube and even to proceed to Constantinople, the request would meet with no other question than that of their provisioning; a convention could be arranged by the Turkish negotiator expected at Warsaw. Talleyrand took cognizance of the pro-English faction at Constantinople and of the baneful effects on Turkish commerce to be expected from war in the Near East. It should be Sebastiani's responsibility to keep the Turks war-active, in one way by suggesting the expedition to the Crimea which would force Russia to divide its armies in the south.

The ambassador should emphasize that the closing of the Straits against Russia would not only render useless the eight Russian vessels of war stationed in the Adriatic, but also would isolate the Russian forces on Corfu and at Cattaro. An attack from all sides could be launched against the common enemy already defeated in Poland. Sebastiani should request the sultan to urge Feth Ali's coöperation, as Napoleon had done. The officer-messenger carrying Napoleon's letter to Persia must emphasize that France's advanced position before Russia in eastern Europe was similar to Persia's position in western Asia. Sebastiani must engage the Turks to assure the prompt arrival of that messenger in Persia. Both France and Turkey should encourage Persia to turn action in Georgia into a powerful diversion, a storm center where Russia would be obliged to maintain strong forces.

Couriers must be sent to Tripoli, Algeria, and Morocco, to tell of the four wars: the Franco-Russian, the Franco-Prussian (ended with French victory), the Russo-Persian, and the Russo-Turkish. In consequence of Russia's invasion of Turkey, these Regencies should be encouraged to declare war. Under the direction of Ambassador Andreossy at Vienna, a French military informer, Meriaze, was stationed at Vidin to act as the clearing agent for much of the correspondence between Warsaw, Constantinople, and Dalmatia.[12] Napoleon directed that nothing be said as yet respecting the results which might be expected from the treaty ending the Russo-Turkish war. He once spoke of territorial profit to Turkey, in the form of the reacquisition of the Crimea—although the suggestion preceded news of the sultan's declaration of war.

Jealous Ambassador Arbuthnot well understood Sultan Selim's willingness to conclude an alliance with France. He correctly reported that Napoleon had expressed personal confidence in Selim and that Sebastiani by his advice to the latter's ministers not only had stimulated Ottoman suspicions of England but had rendered them warlike. This British appraisal unquestionably helped to set the stage for Admiral Sir John Duckworth's forced passage of and withdrawal from the Dardanelles. Staging an exploit still remembered in the annals of naval history, Duckworth intended his squadron to support new British negotiations at Constantinople but, as we shall see, when his fleet had forced itself into the Sea of Marmara he became afraid that his naval force would be bottled up there.

With increasing vigor Arbuthnot had sought throughout January to renew the expiring and unenforced Anglo-Turkish alliance. He wished to add clauses requiring the unrestricted admission of British warships into the Straits and to induce Turkey to abandon Moldavia and Wallachia to Russia, at least while a state of war persisted. Thus it was necessary for Duckworth to enter the Straits by force, if at all. Alert Britons could foresee the certain breakdown of negotiations which had such one-sided objectives. The inevitability of Turkey's declaration of war against Britain's ally was obvious; equally clear was the need for taking other measures than negotiation to stem the wave of French successes at Constantinople. Wishful thinkers might indulge in the hope that although Turkey had declared war against Russia, actual war might never be waged. The British had friends among the Ottoman ministers and knew, as did the French, that Turkey's fighting ability and equipment were none too good.

Arbuthnot's task was to deal not with a prospectively inactive war, however, but with the existing Russo-Turkish conflict. His negotiations reached a high pitch on January 26, 1807, when he resignedly affirmed to Galib that Turkey had evinced partiality for France ever since the coming of Sebastiani; an illustration of this fact was the closure of the

Straits against Russian vessels of war. The hospodars—deposed, reinstated, and deposed again—proved the preponderance of French influence. Accordingly, he threatened joint action by Britain and Russia, the latter to operate by land and the British primarily by sea. He declared their joint squadrons would sail through the Dardanelles to Constantinople, if Turkey did not change its policy and make this change clear to all by the expulsion of Sebastiani. The war with Russia would cease, he promised, if Turkey followed this course. Otherwise the rupture of friendship with England also became inevitable. He added that the relatively small British squadron at Tenedos would soon be reinforced by a larger and more complete combined squadron which would include four large Russian vessels that would sail from the Adriatic and pass the Dardanelles. Upon Turkey's negative response, he would order all British subjects to depart from Turkey, and he himself would depart together with his family. A British vessel of war waited to take them on board.[13]

For weeks officials harked back to this declaration by Arbuthnot on January 26. Friendly Ottomans turned over to the French ambassador several of Arbuthnot's letters menacing Turkey—letters transmitted by the English embassy's interpreter, Pisani (who rivaled Eugene Franchini). These communications announced that the British squadron intended to restore affairs to their condition before the Turkish declaration of war and to expel all of Napoleon's representatives. No act of hostility would be committed by the Anglo-Russian squadron, provided it encountered no obstacles in sailing into and through the Dardanelles.

In reporting the British threat, General Sebastiani also submitted his private reactions. From his military background he predicted, "The Dardanelles will not offer resistance very long, owing to the poor state of its fortifications." The delay in the coming of Marmont's five engineers and artillery officers annoyed him. Had they arrived during the preceding month, there would have been ample time to prepare the Dardanelles for effective resistance. Even in the capital city itself he observed little active preparation to meet the threat of British invasion. "Nevertheless, the council has taken the courageous resolution to resist," he could report; it had rejected Arbuthnot's "humiliating propositions."

The sultan promised Sebastiani he would issue precise orders to the officers at the Dardanelles to resist passage of the British fleet. Galib told Sebastiani that Selim's reply to Arbuthnot had been "suitable to the dignity of the sultan." The Ottoman foreign minister requested that the Emperor of France, the "natural ally of the Ottoman Empire since time immemorial," be notified immediately of the new imminence of war with Great Britain, at a time when Turkey had gone to war with Russia. Sebastiani in contrast took the entire matter quite calmly, boldly proposing that the sultan himself take the initiative by declaring war against the English and arresting them or confiscating their property. Less distasteful to the Turks was his further recommendation of immediate improvements of the defenses of the Dardanelles, a project in which he promised his personal assistance.[14]

On the credit side of the Turkish ledger, Sebastiani mentioned privately to Talleyrand the geographical position of Constantinople, which rendered the city naturally quite strong against naval attack. The British had on the scene no land forces with which to attempt the conquest of Constantinople with its population of some 800,000. The invading fleet would encounter the Turkish squadron and the coastal defenses. The frightened Turkish ministry would not really go over to the English and Russians, according to Sebastiani, because the presence of strong French armies stationed in Poland and Dalmatia seemed to bolster the Turkish position. There seems little doubt that Sebastiani promised them as much, at this time of crisis. The ambassador in any event ignored the fact that the possible pillaging of Constantinople would mean the ruin of the empire. He applauded the energy of the Turks and emphasized the "alliance" with France which would culminate in victory. Sebastiani communicated all this argument in a long letter sent directly to Napoleon and in condensed version to Talleyrand. He mentioned his distrust of Austria, whom he did not believe a stranger to the Serbian capture of Belgrade. As pro-French or at least anti-Russian news, he mentioned that the elder Prince Ypsilanti, father of the deposed Prince of Wallachia, had been ordered decapitated; Prince Suzzo soon would depart for the Danube, to attempt to resume his "off-again, on-again" position of hospodar.[15]

Galib's comments to Arbuthnot and to Sebastiani left no doubt that Turkey almost certainly would accelerate its pro-French policy. It was Arbuthnot who took fright. He broke off his personal relations with Turkey on January 27 and secretly quit his post. From his refuge on a nearby British man-of-war he negotiated for several days. The Ottoman foreign ministry caught the spirit of Sebastiani's calm during those days while the British fleet and possibly a Russian squadron also were approaching. Everyone understood that adverse weather conditions would force the land war with Russia in the Balkans to remain a *sitzkrieg* for some time.

Ottoman foreign affairs became oriented more and more toward the French. Napoleon now possessed another title, that of "King of Italy." When Sebastiani called attention to this fact, Galib accredited Mouhib Effendi in Paris as ambassador to Napoleon as the King of Italy.[16] Public opinion at first expected the British squadron to appear before Constantinople within a matter of days. As the fright disappeared, however, almost everyone minimized Britain's striking power; Sebastiani's military logic had seen to that. Although Arbuthnot's flight served to give the Turks added confidence, it nevertheless indicated an inevitable rupture with Britain which would render Sebastiani's position more difficult than it would otherwise have been. Ottoman confidence in the working alliance between France and Turkey was reflected when the sultan, on January 27, decorated Sebastiani and Ruffin. The ambassador attested the coöperation by personally undertaking the direction of new defenses. He conferred with the entire Ottoman council respecting the defenses. He gave assistance at Constantinople and, through Vice-Consul Jerome Mechain, also at the Dardanelles. He officially summoned the Turks to greater activity in mid-February, recommending that they keep 4,000 or 5,000 defense workers engaged every day.[17]

Upon his departure the British ambassador had stated that he believed it his duty to take with him the resident British subjects and to leave the embassy property entirely under Turkey's protection. As his specific reason for leaving—an interpretation revealed by Baron Hubsch of Denmark—he charged that Turkey refused a passport for his courier and thus "had cut off all communications between himself and England." The practical reason for his flight was his hearing a rumor that the Turks would soon take hostages, as they had done against the French in 1798 and against the Russians in 1768.

When Turkey refused all his requests, he revealed his instructions and threatened to order the British squadron to force the passage of the Dardanelles. From his safe position on board the *Endymion* he wrote on January 29 in a tone of abused innocence. He complained of Turkey's iterated refusal to grant a passport to the British courier. He stated he would "wait a reasonable time before having recourse to more efficacious measures to obtain reparation for the injuries committed against the King of England and against the king's ally, the Tsar of Russia. But

Turkey must realize that the response, a simple affirmative or negative, must be given without delay."[18]

Let us digress for a moment to speak of Persia. Full news of and by that state eventually came through to Napoleon's headquarters. The French emperor could always apply to letter-writing his mastery of the techniques for encouraging troops. From the piecemeal reports of Jaubert's trip to Teheran he penned from Warsaw a letter to Shah Feth Ali, in mid-January, 1807. He offered Persia friendship, in order to be able to utilize that country which, by its location, had a bearing on both Russia and British India. Of his two faithful servants sent to visit the shah's court, he stated, Romieu had died. Jaubert had told of Feth Ali's friendly disposition and of Persia's military successes against the Russians. He announced his conquest of Prussia, his significant advance against Russia, and his establishment of a provisional government at Warsaw. Reminiscent of his lectures to troops, his letter continued, "On your side, attack with vigor the enemies who are being weakened and discouraged by my victories. Take Georgia from them, together with all the provinces bordering Persia's empire. Close the gates of the Caspian against them. France, Turkey, and Persia are at war against Russia. Let all three concert, and form an eternal alliance." He awaited the shah's ambassador. In the midst of his victories, he renewed his assurances of personal affection for Feth Ali.

Jaubert and Georges Outrey became unofficial hosts for Mirza Riza, by arrangement at Constantinople. Outrey served as his guide-companion to Warsaw, with Jaubert traveling ahead. The Persian envoy always proceeded leisurely. His fondness for hesitant movement, combined with the general uncertainty of Napoleon's whereabouts, delayed the voyage from the Turkish capital for several weeks. It was finally learned that Napoleon would winter in eastern Europe.

Jaubert thus heralded the Persian who finally came, in March, to French headquarters (chap. viii). On January 3 Jaubert left Constantinople, to make investigations en route and to report to Napoleon. In the Balkans he observed the greatest confidence in the French emperor. He visited Passvan Oglu, being received unhesitatingly at Vidin not so much out of friendship for France as because he delivered a packet of official dispatches from the Ottoman government. Passvan Oglu reviled the Ottoman ministers as "donkeys and treacherous," who took advantage of Sultan Selim's weakness. He stated that although he would not enter Wallachia to fight the Russians, he would close the pashalic of Vidin against them. He prepared for the coming of a French army to his city —with many reservations. Jaubert considered it doubtful whether this pasha would willingly even see at Vidin a regularly resident French officer who would easily be able to report the pasha's movements. Eventually the French would learn that Ottoman pashas did not welcome French troops within the Ottoman Empire. The intrepid traveler observed a considerable movement of Ottoman troops all along his route and noted their great zeal for defending their country. Their army on the Danube reportedly numbered some 30,000 men. They told him they had lost 700 or 800 men in a small battle before the Russians entered Bucharest, while only 200 or 300 Russians had been killed, in an engagement that served to awaken the Turks to the real danger confronting them.[19]

When phrasing the secret instructions for the Ottoman plenipotentiary to negotiate with Napoleon, Selim again wrote to Napoleon as emperor and padishah (February 9). He suggested that the two sovereigns exchange their "most secret thoughts." He had read of Napoleon's "glorious victory over the common enemy." Ottoman troops for their part were at Ismail waiting out the winter weather and intending ultimately to expel the Russian enemy who had launched the surprise invasion of the Principalities. The "very judicious Sebastiani" would send the full details of every move. Upon the ambassador's request, the sultan gladly accorded recognition to King Joseph of Naples and King Louis of Holland. Sebastiani sent the big news by cipher: the special Ottoman envoy would possess authority to conclude an offensive and defensive alliance, including authority to stipulate the passage of French troops across Ottoman territory.[20] As we shall discover, Napoleon's ace ambassador in this case let his enthusiasm outrun his judgment.

Sebastiani's promises on behalf of the mighty Napoleon—together with his calm and his direction of the defenses at the Straits—encouraged the Turks. Believing that the British squadron had come to Tenedos determined to force the renewal of Turkey's alliances with Russia and England, he did not as yet suspect its actual object: to take over the Ottoman fleet. Sebastiani advised his Ottoman friends, on February 10, that "a noble resistance could assure the political existence of the Ottoman Empire." The Ottoman squadron and the prompt armaments would oblige "the enemy" to return to England.[21]

Admiral Duckworth at length prepared to move, by force if necessary, into the Dardanelles and up to Constantinople. He did not feel justified in waiting any longer for Admiral Seniavin's smaller Russian squadron to sail to Tenedos. It eventually arrived, too late to participate in Duck-worth's unwise exploit. Might not a display of naval power influence Turkey to change its attitude toward England and Russia? Could the admiral indeed capture the Ottoman fleet by threatening force, as London seemed to expect? The British admiral's warnings, at intervals down to February 17, summoned the sultan to halt his war against Russia.

Napoleon at this time publicly announced a policy for peace. When it was read by the envoys of Turkey and Persia, it seemed to promise them the restoration of all territories conquered by Russia—even if no such assurance were actually stated. The special message by the emperor on the subject was sent to a special session of the French Senate convoked on February 18 to hear it. Dangers confronted the Ottoman Empire, the statement read. "How long it would take to repair the damages resulting from the loss of the empire of Constantinople! Let not Russia ensconce itself from the Baltic to the Mediterranean. Persia, like Turkey, is motivated by the same spirit as France. Hence if France would win the peace, it must guarantee the complete independence of these two great empires."[22]

Talleyrand communicated to the Senate the reasons for Napoleon's decision respecting the Ottoman Empire. He saw its "independence menaced by an ambitious neighbor, and considered its preservation essentially bound up with the security of Europe." In consequence of Napoleon's measures to preserve the Ottoman Empire, the foreign minister explained that it might be necessary to postpone the date for peace. He promised that peace, when at last it came, would be durable. For the time being, Napoleon must guarantee other powers against the ambitions of Russia. An indication of the danger to Turkey was the fact that the Russians had captured two key fortresses on the Danube.

That session of the Senate was intended to notify Russia, Turkey, and Prussia of the official French viewpoint and especially to warn England. Talleyrand reviewed the developments that had preceded the Russo-Turkish war. He fixed the disputed date of Russia's occupation of Moldavia and Wallachia at the earliest anyone had reported, namely on November 22. In referring to the hospodars he labeled Ypsilanti of Wallachia as a traitor to Turkey, and Moruzzi of Moldavia—who had secretly proffered aid to Turkey and France against Russia—as an individual who did not inspire full confidence. He recounted that during the course of the debate over Turkey's replacement of the hospodars, "an inconceivable war" had emerged at the north between France and

Prussia, disuniting the two powers most eager to preserve Turkey. An English fleet had sailed to the Dardanelles, with an announcement by its admiral that he would make common cause with Russia. Hence Turkey had "ceded to necessity" and restored the hospodars. Since Russia and England had not been thereby satisfied, the Russo-Turkish war had opened. The French consul at Jassy had been taken prisoner by Russia.[23]

The British took action in the Near East on February 19, the day after this Senate session in Paris. They had allowed Turkey several days to consider and reply to their several "final" notes. From Tenedos they forced their way through the Dardanelles, opening operations with a squadron of five ships of the line, four frigates, and two bombers. Turkey's shore batteries fired without great effect. The attackers also brushed aside the intercepting squadron near Point Nagara, deep within the Dardanelles, with losses to the Ottomans. Hostilities thus opened without a declaration of war.[24]

The news of Britain's forced passage electrified Constantinople. Sebastiani put into cipher a special dispatch reporting his first intelligence of the move. He learned, late on February 20, that some nine English vessels already had entered in spite of Turkey's resistance and that the remainder of the fleet was following, awaiting favorable winds; he expected to see the entire squadron before Constantinople quite soon. Anything could happen, he concluded; he himself might be arrested, upon English demand. The grand vizir apparently desired to prepare Constantinople for defense, but most of the ministers revealed fright or lethargy. "My position is difficult," he admitted. They could not locate a horse that evening to carry the courier intended to depart with the letter; so M. Latour-Maubourg appended a note the next morning in which he revealed Sebastiani as one of the busiest men in Constantinople, and one who was beginning to get real action for the defense.[25]

On that February 21, Arbuthnot informed the Turks of what they knew already. He stated from the *Royal George*—to which he had moved—that his demands of January 26 had not been met. Because the Turks had treated the entire matter with indifference, the British had fulfilled their threat. Duckworth sent a statement expressing his great surprise at discovering the Turks firing upon his ships from the castles guarding the Dardanelles. He affirmed that the ships had entered in consequence of their prerogative based on the alliance dating back to the French expedition to Egypt. That alliance, however—as everyone knew—had never permitted British navigation of the Straits.

Duckworth anchored his invading fleet before Constantinople on February 24. Turkey not only declined to yield to such a menace but thereupon displayed unexpected nonchalance. Frenzied efforts by the admiral for six days failed even to approach a settlement. All the documents passed through the hands of Sebastiani, who tabulated the now-enlarged British demands: Turkey must (1) expel the French embassy or at least Sebastiani; (2) surrender for six months nineteen ships of the line and as many frigates, together with provisions; (3) relinquish the Dardanelles to English garrison troops; and (4) renew the alliances with Britain and Russia.[26] The British attempted to negotiate on these extreme demands for the fleet and the Dardanelles, with the probable intention of yielding on some points. They found the Turks so adamant as to refuse even to enter a conference.

These events are recorded for us in the French archives by a British letter of February 26—surreptitiously delivered to Sebastiani—and by Sebastiani's complete report dated March 3. Duckworth replied with ridicule to Galib Effendi's note alleging that the Turks possessed no power to designate a definite place at which to hold the conferences which Britain proposed. After a delay of five days, the Turks finally informed Arbuthnot and Duckworth of the people's irritation against the English, an irritation so great that no safe meeting place could be designated either on the European or the Asiatic side of the Dardanelles. More important, the Ottoman council curtly decided not to negotiate with the English until after their fleet had departed from Constantinople and the Straits. "All this," reported Sebastiani, with apparent good reason, "the Turks did in concert with me and according to my suggestions."

On his own initiative Duckworth began to bargain by reducing his demands to the original request for the expulsion of Sebastiani and the renewal of Turkey's military alliances. He promised British mediation to end the Russo-Turkish war. The Turks really lacked authority over their own subjects, he chided. He regretted the evidence of Sebastiani's influence, an influence at work behind what he somehow interpreted to be a Turkish overture for peace, an overture he said the British could not for a moment entertain. (The French archives do not indicate the issuance of such an offer by Turkey.) Duckworth for his part transmitted a copy of Vice-Admiral Thomas Louis' antecedent instructions to sail into the Dardanelles which, he said, "left no room for doubt that, upon the official termination of Arbuthnot's mission, no possible means could have prevented the passage of that strait by the British squadron." He cited the ambassador's authority to declare his mission terminated.[27]

No one replied to the British offers, explanations, cajolery. As a strategic precaution, Duckworth notified the Turks on February 27 that he would change the position of anchorage of his squadron off Constantinople, in the Sea of Marmara. He changed it "without the least intention of committing hostilities until the last means of conciliation had been tried without result."

During these days the Turks prepared feverishly. Except for declining to participate in conferences, they disregarded the English messages. They tried to ignore officially the impressive British squadron. With the aid of a few French officers lately arrived from Dalmatia, Sebastiani directed several thousand Ottomans in the preparations of their new defenses. Everyone at the French embassy assisted, together with the Spanish minister and his staff. Sebastiani's encouragement and example spurred on the Turks, whom he reported as laboring with energy, rather than with their original "fright and fear." Within the ten days following February 17 there were placed some 306 additional cannons and 16 mortars along the banks of the Dardanelles. The Turks meanwhile summoned 100,000 troops to the colors.

While they thus prepared, they employed dilatory tactics in the so-called "negotiations." Constantinople at length possessed what Sebastiani termed "a respectable state of defense." Vice-Consul Mechain was directing the new defenses at the Dardanelles, where all the defenses were prematurely pronounced ready by February 28. Thereupon the sultan turned a defiant face to the British admiral. The contest remained what it had been on both sides, a battle of nerves. The Turks refused further discussion with the British so long as British vessels of war remained inside the Straits. This adamant stand rendered the British fleet's position impotent, and the new defenses were rapidly making its position precarious. One incident, the accidental burning of a British ship, resulted in heavy loss of life.

The British yielded first, the Turks winning the battle of nerves. From British admirals down the feeling grew that the venture would fail. Duckworth became alarmed at the possibility of having his squadron bottled up in the Sea of Marmara. He began a hasty retreat, on March 1. Mechain viewed the flight from Point Nagara, where it anchored briefly. From a mountain top and with strong lenses the French vice-consul watched the sailing resume the next day. He dispatched runners to Nagara's fort and horsemen to the Dardanelles castles, to warn the Turks to be wary. He reported that the British fired on Nagara, only to be met by Turkey's answering fire. They lost no ships at that point, although they were forced to abandon a small Turkish prize vessel.[28] On March 3 the British repassed the entrance of the Dardanelles under fire.

When he was once more back at Tenedos, Duckworth expressed himself as thankful to be outside "that infernal Strait." He had entered without any complementing land forces, against his better judgment, and had departed before bad matters became worse. The episode recalls a lesson which should have been heeded in 1915, during the First World War, when the British and French launched their initial naval advance into the Dardanelles without complementary land forces—to fail almost as soon as they began. Meanwhile, for over a century the easy success in 1807 had given the Turks unwarranted confidence. They still had great faith in guns and torpedoes strategically placed along the banks—it was their unsuccessful panacea of 1915 for defending the Straits.

Ottoman police sealed the British embassy in February, 1807, and impounded the stores and warehouses of British merchants. Sebastiani reported an order by the sultan to arrest all Englishmen and confiscate their property. This order was apparently lip service to France, however, because we hear nothing more of it. A more significant reaction was the request by the sultan and grand vizir on March 2 that the French ambassador send for 500 Napoleonic troops, for the most part cannoneers, to aid in defending Constantinople against any recurrent British attempt of that character. Sebastiani solicited General Marmont to send these troops from Dalmatia if his instructions permitted. The sultan dispatched orders to forestall a possible resistance by the local governors to the troops' passage through the Balkans; these small forces were authorized to travel in groups of 50 mounted men. Sebastiani requested that some of the 500 men be assigned to the Dardanelles rather than that all of them be employed at the capital.[29] Everyone feared that the passage of even a small number of French military personnel through turbulent Bosnia would present difficulties. Most of the force eventually arrived at the Turkish capital in May, as we shall see (chap. ix), only to be precipitately sent home by Ottoman revoluntionaries. Was Sultan Selim III a military reformer at heart—as it is customary to say—or was he merely a yielder to strategic necessity?

Few of the regular diplomatic corps of western Europe stationed in Turkey in those days spoke the Turkish language. It is sometimes af-

firmed with justice that the real ambassadors were the principal interpreters, who served as the liaison officers of the respective ambassadors
and ministers and of the Ottoman foreign office itself. Thus one might
argue that Franchini had merely outwitted Pisani in the negotiations
with the sultan's interpreter. Diplomatic communications halted between Turkey and England. An agent of the British interpreter, however, managed to ensconce himself at the castles of the Dardanelles, to
provide Pisani with precise information respecting the military operations there. Hassiz Effendi, governor at the Dardanelles, seemed to be
a friend of Pisani, according to Mechain's report. Constantinople had
issued no instructions for dealing with Pisani or his agents. By contrast,
the French embassy's interpreters felt that their own presence was justified and that all others were mere interlopers.[30]

On March 10 Sebastiani received Napoleon's offer to send six French
ships of the line into the Black Sea, where they might be combined
with the Ottoman squadron. In order to fulfill directions with the
required secrecy, only the Ottoman foreign minister was present at the
private audience with the sultan. Selim appeared "charmed" with Napoleon's willingness to lend the ships. Morover, he not only would not
be alarmed at the arrival of a few French troops in Constantinople, but
he suggested that two companies of light artillery, rather than one, be
sent to help defend the Bosporus and the Dardanelles. In his opinion,
the British fleet had escaped not because of the Turkish lack of cannon
but rather because of the dearth of trained personnel to man the artillery.

The British might return. The sultan said that arrangements must be
made in advance for signaling, in order to permit the French ships to
enter the Dardanelles despite the British squadron at Tenedos. He
offered to dispatch a naval convoy to Gallipoli, at the mouth of the
Dardanelles, and stated that he would accept several French officers for
his naval vessels. Incensed at Duckworth's adventure, he was seriously
considering the French recommendation to arrest all Englishmen found
in Turkey, confiscate their property, and prohibit English commerce
within his empire.

Selim by personal letter to Napoleon expressed his satisfaction with
the French offers. He also directed the dey of Algeria to attack English
commerce and to treat the French as friends and allies. In addition to
his other titles Napoleon was now termed the "very generous" emperor
and padishah of France. The sultan detailed the circumstances of the
British attack on the Dardanelles—at just the moment when Ottoman

imperial forces were preparing themselves to march against the "common enemy" in the Balkans. Because Arbuthnot's insulting propositions could not be accepted, that ambassador summoned the naval squadron to embarrass the Ottoman government. Still winning no diplomatic advantage, the ambassador himself had made a "furtive departure" but had called the squadron into the Dardanelles. He mentioned that Sebastiani had aided the preparations that forced the British fleet into "ignominious retreat."[31]

Admiral Seniavin with eight vessels of the line and two smaller vessels joined the British at Tenedos. He is said to have urged a return to Constantinople, this time with the combined fleets. Instead, Duckworth turned late in March to support General Mackenzie Fraser's abortive military occupation of Alexandria. Seniavin meanwhile blockaded the Dardanelles—and held it for months without reinforcement.

Why did the British occupy Alexandria in 1807? A French author suggests that the action was taken because of an unsupported suspicion that Napoleon intended to appear there again, a natural British reaction. Britons recalled the difficulties attendant on their arrival at the port of Alexandria on August 1, 1798, a month after the establishment of General Bonaparte's expedition. Although Admiral Nelson had immediately defeated the anchored French squadron, the subduing of the entire Bonapartean force required almost three years. We might also recall the fact that Britain had recovered "face," three weeks after the precipitate flight from the Dardanelles. Another suggestion is that, having failed at the center, the British could proceed to enter another Turkish province for vengeance. The strategic justification of the action in Egypt was explained by England's "war" with Turkey, whether the conflict was a *sitzkrieg* or not. Certainly Britain might properly attack any Ottoman province, if indeed Arbuthnot possessed the authority to engage England in warfare. In the longer and larger perspective, moreover, England desired good government in Egypt. The resulting orderly affairs would eliminate all pretexts for foreign intervention and make the country capable of repressing any new aggression, from France or any other nation. Thus Britain, even if it did not covet Egypt, at least took precautions against any reëstablishment of the French rival there. Order and stability were prerequisites for Egyptian preparations for defense.

Hence the British landing at Alexandria on March 20 should be considered a preventive measure against French aggression, a further warning to Turkey, and a means of face-saving after the British failure in the

Dardanelles. Belated official objectives were revealed by new orders from London. The Duke of Portland's ministry, with George Canning as the foreign secretary, was not formed until April. Orders stated that forces sent to Alexandria, a convenient war station, might possibly be employed later anywhere in the Ottoman Empire. For purposes of publication and propaganda the British cabinet clarified the move as anti-French and anti-Turkish but not anti-Egyptian. This policy recalls Talleyrand's and Bonaparte's myth of 1798—which no one even at that time took seriously—that the French had moved into Egypt in order to attack the English (who were not there). The publicized French claim had stuck in the popular imagination, but the British actually went to Egypt in order to extrude the French. The British cabinet in 1807 admitted that the new venture might prove too costly if British agents "should be led to engage too deeply in the local politics of the country." It authorized no reinforcements and contemplated no permanent occupation of Alexandria; it authorized no advances into the interior of Egypt. Many soon considered that it might be expedient to withdraw.[32] Before receiving these orders, the British on the scene attempted to include Rosetta in their zone of occupation, a move which stirred Mehemet Ali to resistance. He broke up their siege and chased them back into Alexandria— a setback which gave the French a new advantage for propaganda in Constantinople.

The Duckworth affair added new laurels to Napoleonic policy. Thus began an Anglo-Turkish "war" which remained unfought, except for the fleet episode and the sterile British intervention of some six months' duration in Alexandria. In this chapter we have discussed the most significant of the British episodes that occurred in reaction to Napoleon's position of influence at and near the Dardanelles. After failing to intimidate Turkey into renewed coöperation with Russia and Great Britain, British squadrons implemented their ill-advised general policy by attacking both ends of Napoleon's arc of land power which extended from the Near East to the Baltic. The British neither bombarded Constantinople nor captured the Turkish fleet nor mastered the Dardanelles; they simply forced their way through the Dardanelles and fought their way out again. They invaded Egypt and in September would render Denmark helpless. At the north, they would burn Copenhagen, take away the Danish fleet, and master the Sound. The French emperor's imposing military position meanwhile influenced Persia—as we shall see in the next chapter—to execute its policy of forming a military alliance with France.

VIII

Persia Enters the French Orbit

⟶ March-May, 1807

WITH THE COMING of Ambassador Mirza Riza of Persia momentarily expected, Napoleon penned another letter to Shah Feth Ali on February 2, 1807. Persia for centuries had been "the most brilliant empire in the east," he stated, while Russia remained "uncultured and its people ignorant and barbarous." With the same type of enthusiasm reflected by his exaggerated or fictitious accounts of news events, he intended to render Persia receptive to an alliance with France and Turkey. Unmindful of the facts reported by Sebastiani, he estimated that 200,000 Turks were marching against the tsar. He withheld sending the letter, however, and revised it after Amédée Jaubert's report in person at his headquarters had discouraged his expectation of much military aid from Persia.[1]

Napoleon himself interpreted as a most notable event his first meeting with Mirza Riza. Witness the command painting of the event, the meeting in 1807 at his headquarters in Finkenstein, Poland, the temporary unofficial capital of Europe. The scene realistically depicts the indomitable, peregrinating Jaubert presenting to the emperor the ambassador extraordinary of Shah Feth Ali, on April 27. This painting, together with the many others in a series of Napoleonic highlights, may be seen in the Bourbon palace museum at Versailles. The emperor did not intend that this painting be used for propaganda purposes in Persia. The famous painter, Mulard, who did not paint it until 1810, months after the brief alliance of 1807 between France and Persia had become merely a memory, depicts with brilliant effect the moment of the introduction. In the large reception room the beturbaned Mirza Riza steps toward a doorway, his hand about to be extended to greet the emperor. As Jaubert does the honors, groups of Persians and French watch respectfully. A painting within a painting faithfully reproduces the high background mural. It shows Napoleon standing just inside the open door of his own adjacent room. Mirza Riza is posed for a traditional greeting, while the artist portrays the emperor as almost everyone now mentally pictures him, standing serenely with the overdone characteristic of his right hand in the opening of his coat. That day was indeed a memorable one for the "Emperor of the French and King of Italy."

This chapter recounts from the material in the archives the story of the French alliance with Persia.

The Duckworth adventure of late February (chap. vii) was obviously as yet unknown to Napoleon at the opening of March. French envoys had just arrived in Poland from Constantinople and Persia. Jaubert had arrived somewhat earlier, bringing a recent letter from the sultan to Napoleon, together with that written by the shah in mid-1806. Vahid Effendi, the special Ottoman negotiator appointed to arrange an alliance with the dazzling French Empire, appeared in Warsaw on March 1, at precisely the moment when Duckworth fled the Sea of Marmara. Mirza Riza appeared with a like purpose, guided by Georges Outrey.

Talleyrand at this time occupied the emperor's Near and Middle Eastern calculations with letters describing the discussions that anticipated alliances with Turkey and Persia. Since Napoleon's Russian campaign was the big order of business, a friendly relationship with Turkey and Persia was more desirable than ever. From the very beginning of the Prussian campaign Napoleon had seemed to be merely en route to Russia. He pushed on in that direction, impatiently allowing a stop of only a month in Berlin, a delay which ended on November 24. He set up imperial headquarters to the east for the winter—for a time at Posen and during the heart of the winter at Warsaw, from December 21 to February, 1807. Talleyrand remained in Warsaw to handle diplomatic operations and to oversee the Napoleonic invention, the Duchy of Warsaw. Napoleon stopped at Osterode for a few weeks and established his headquarters at Finkenstein from April 3 to June 15.

Jaubert gave news and views personally to Talleyrand and further recounted his own experiences. At the time of his departure from Persia in September, the war against Russia seemed to be proceeding with vigor. He told of Persia's army, the greatest disadvantage of which was a lack of artillery. Commanded by the inspiring if youthful Crown Prince Abbas Mirza, however, the Persians fought with courage and hatred. Mirza frankly stated that he and his father liked Napoleon. As an item of particular interest, Jaubert revealed the fact that the two English frigates were no longer anchored at Constantinople, for Italinski and his staff had been transported on these ships to Malta. Jaubert described the events of late December, including his departure from Constantinople, and the way in which Arbuthnot's threat to leave had been followed by the Ottoman declaration of war against Russia. In the hope of preventing a frankly dreaded war against England, the Ottoman ministers had dispatched a special Turkish courier with a letter from Sultan Selim to King George III in London, justifying the declaration against Russia. Vahid had accompanied Jaubert as far as Adrianople, and then had traveled directly to French headquarters while Jaubert stopped to visit Vidin (chap. vii). In common with Persia's envoy, Vahid possessed authority to negotiate an alliance but he had been given little discretionary power; and his instructions stipulated manifold details of procedure and the logic to be employed.[2]

Before negotiating with Mirza Riza, Talleyrand wisely questioned both Outrey and Jaubert concerning the nature and extent of the relations Napoleon might hope to establish between France, Turkey, and Persia. Most of their conclusions, based on their own observations and inquiries on the scene, must have jarred him. For one thing, the shah's army had been greatly overrated in general speculation before this time.

Outrey considered that there would be no commercial problem for France in Persia. The obsolete Franco-Persian treaties could be renewed without difficulty and several new concessions could be obtained. More significantly, both Turkey and Persia would enter willingly into a temporary or permanent military alliance with France against Russia. Outrey cautioned, however, against pushing either prospective ally into a two-front war against both Russia and England; neither Turkey nor Persia wished to fight England. Nor could Outrey or Jaubert assure the same friendly disposition toward an anti-Russian alliance, if this were also directed against England. Lacking a naval force, Persia could not attack by sea. By land, it need not confine itself exclusively to its own territories; its forces could proceed to India by way of Afghanistan and Kurdistan, although this could be done only after arrangements had been made with the countries concerned.

Jaubert believed that Persia, embarrassed by the losses suffered in the conflict with Russia, would be ready to extend its influence in these countries. On the other hand, during a Persian war against England, Russia would be England's ally. If it were on the defensive against Russia's army at the north and the British navy at the south, could Persia at the same time send a considerable force to India? In Jaubert's opinion, the nature of Persian soldiering seemed to preclude the possi-

bility. He had heard of 50,000 Persians being held in check by no more
than 10,000 Russians.

Persia nonetheless could damage the English considerably by prohibiting the passage through its territory of English troops or merchants;
certainly it could interrupt all land communications between England
and India. Instead of war between Persia and England Jaubert preferred
a state of coldness and misintelligence in relations that might result
in the severance of communications and contacts. Similarly, Turkey did
not possess adequate forces to resist Russia on the Black Sea and simultaneously to fight a maritime war against Great Britain. A two-front
war inevitably would place Turkey, like Persia, at serious disadvantage.

Talleyrand listened carefully on that March 1 and determined to proceed cautiously and slowly. He procrastinated by referring unnecessary
questions to Napoleon at Osterode. Should the alliance be a triple affair
or should it bring on two bilateral treaties? The foreign minister favored
one document, while Jaubert—because Turkey's and Persia's interests
differed greatly—would have liked two. Which did Napoleon wish, a
temporary alliance only for the existing war, or a permanent coalition?
Must the policy be directed against Russia alone or against both Russia
and England? Did Napoleon desire an immediate treaty or a later one
to be negotiated in Paris? Talleyrand himself preferred to come to terms
in Paris, where the appearance of the two special ambassadors would
also influence public opinion across the English channel.

Napoleon replied realistically that the Persian treaty could be signed
at Paris since he hoped to have ended his Russian blitzkrieg before the
time that would necessarily elapse if communications were made with
Teheran. Jaubert, who had been gone almost two years, wished the
Turkish alliance consummated as soon as possible. To begin with, Napoleon must know precisely what the Ottoman ambassador expected in
the way of territorial compensation from Russia and what he had been
authorized to sign.[3] Napoleon replied (March 3) with some impatience
to Talleyrand's questions. How could he answer, when he had not as
yet received Jaubert's report? The Persian treaty, less pressing than the
Turkish, could be negotiated at Paris. Talleyrand must be watchful that
Austria and Russia did not secretly agree to grant each other equivalents
if Russia expanded its territories at Ottoman expense in consequence of
the new war.[4] Outrey's and Jaubert's advice obviously had had its effect
on Napoleon's advisers in Warsaw. Talleyrand sent Napoleon another
convenient excuse for delay with the advice that the Turkish and Persian

ambassadors awaited the French signal to depart for Paris. Sebastiani supported the alliance, writing his belief that Abbas Mirza intended to execute the requested Persian diversion against Russia by sending 50,000 troops into contested Georgia.

French military alliances with the Ottoman Empire and Persia might indeed have become a reality. Many dispatches by Talleyrand for several weeks related to the proposed alliances. Turkey at first seemed to intend to sign and to give the alliance any scope Napoleon desired. The projected triple alliance which the foreign minister submitted for approval might be changed to a compact applying to Turkey and France alone, he wrote, should Napoleon wish to proceed with Turkish negotiations immediately.[5]

Perhaps Napoleon could alter the Ottoman attitude of reserve which Talleyrand had detected at the outset. The emperor had proposed to send some 25,000 soldiers to Vidin and to the Dniester, together with several French garrisons intended to man Ottoman forts. Napoleon now estimated that he could dispatch 20,000 soldiers to Persia, provided both Turkey and Persia assigned suitable numbers of their own troops for the joint purposes of the alliances.

In his conversations with Mirza Riza and Vahid, the foreign minister was easily able to conceal his real attitude. When these diplomats came to Warsaw, they found Talleyrand quite excited respecting Napoleon's brilliant military successes. Impressed, Mirza Riza believed the time propitious for negotiating confidently with the mighty Frenchman. Soon the Persian negotiations assumed the primary position in importance. Talleyrand's brief preparatory discussions with the two envoys occurred on March 3, at the time when Duckworth's squadron was withdrawing from the Dardanelles. The early talks were reported to Napoleon, and Talleyrand proceeded to submit his projected separate treaties with Turkey and Persia, each of which would reinforce friendship and commerce by political alliance. The latter would be positive against Russia and eventual against England. During the existing war the three powers would not for the time being make common cause against England but only against Russia. In this manner Turkey would fight England only if England attacked, and Persia agreed to do nothing more than break off commercial relations. Talleyrand did not know that England and Turkey were already technically at war, as a result of Duckworth's operations in the Dardanelles.

Talleyrand based his draft for Persia on the old commercial treaties which were reminiscent of the far-flung power of King Louis XIV and which because of their vagueness required new clarifications. As for results, Persia, regaining territory conquered by Russia, must be the sovereign over Georgia. Napoleon would agree to send a number of French officers to Persia, thus duplicating his offer to Turkey. In exchange, he would ask for the cession of an island or two in the Persian Gulf. His proposed treaty with Turkey would primarily confirm and interpret the capitulations. France would agree to a new tariff based on existing prices, provided that no other nation enjoyed lower rates.[6]

Jaubert's harrowing experiences of 1806, now fully revealed to Napoleon, led the emperor to seek improved means of communication with Persia. As a side issue neither to be fulfilled nor taken seriously, he authorized substitute measures by sea. He wished the French navy to transport the French ambassador to the Persian Gulf by frigates. In two or three months, so Talleyrand anticipated—and he so notified the minister of the navy, in apparent seriousness—the French frigates would sail to that gulf again, in order to return with the ambassador or his dispatches.[7]

Vahid Effendi got off to a bad start with Talleyrand. Impatiently, he solicited an audience with Napoleon at the very first interview with the foreign minister. This Talleyrand would not arrange in advance of an exchange of opinions. In the preliminary discussions the French and Turkish friendliness so much in evidence at Constantinople was markedly absent. Vahid possessed authority to negotiate an offensive and defensive alliance and appeared willing to agree that French troops should pass through whatever Ottoman territory the treaty stipulated. As its minimum expectation, however, Turkey required absolute independence and the integrity of its territory; Russia must withdraw from the Principalities. If the joint efforts could produce other territorial gains, Turkey would like to recover the Crimea. The sultan would permit French troops to enter Moldavia and Wallachia, under French command and Ottoman provisioning. These forces must come, however, by way of Poland and not through Constantinople, where they would cause "more fright than satisfaction."

Talleyrand proposed sending some 30,000 French troops immediately to the Danubian provinces. Vahid countered by insisting that Turkey had many troops—although these were poorly equipped—and did not need Napoleon's forces; further, Vahid lacked instructions to invite them in the absence of an over-all treaty arrangement. The failure to achieve unquestioning acceptance of all the French proposals annoyed Talleyrand. Napoleon compromised by having the foreign minister suggest that both Turkey and Persia employ a number of French officers immediately. The Persian ambassador, to whom Napoleon wrote personally, at once agreed in principle by saying Persia could accept twelve or fifteen. So small a number could not impress Napoleon, even if he valued the opening wedge which the presence of any number of his officers would represent.

The Ottoman ambassador considered that no request for French officers should precede the formal alliance, whereupon Talleyrand praised the Persian ambassador as a man "of ardor, spirit, and amiability," and criticized Vahid as "reserved, constrained, and quite disagreeable." He added that the Ottoman ambassador "says and repeats that he needs officers but that he can request them only after the conclusion of a treaty of alliance. He would prefer that the treaty stipulate they be sent."[8]

Napoleon's factual information of Jaubert's mission to Persia in 1806 was considerably more detached and fragmentary than this account, drawn from the chronological files accumulated later in the Ministry of Foreign Affairs, has been. Up to March, 1807, Napoleon had received few of the letters describing the situation, but his impatient demand for Jaubert's written report brought quick results. In Warsaw on March 6 Jaubert wrote a detailed account of his mission. The secret character of his report, which is still in manuscript even today, may be deduced from the great differences between the original account and the longer travelogue published in 1821. The secret report, certified by Jaubert as "rigorously exact," is preserved in France's National Archives. It here serves us for a recapitulation of his journey, setting the stage as Napoleon himself saw it at the time when the French alliance with Persia was being negotiated. The report will also supply the background for Minister Gardane's impressive French military mission to Teheran later in 1807, as we shall see.

According to the secret report of Jaubert, he was commissioned by Napoleon to carry the emperor's reply to a letter of 1804 from Shah Feth Ali. Jaubert left Constantinople on May 15, 1805, disguising his identity and object. Upon reaching Bayazid he was detained in "long and cruel captivity" for several months in a subterranean prison near the Turkish frontier (chap. iii). When he was finally released, inclement weather temporarily interfered with the continuance of his journey. Discovering that he needed Turkish passports to assure his prompt passage to Persia, he abandoned secrecy and openly applied to Constantinople. By that time, news of Napoleon's victory over Austria at Austerlitz had fortunately softened Ottoman policy toward France and furnished the principal reason for the granting of his request.

After further delay he arrived at Khoi, a frontier town in Persia. Even then he did not proceed directly to Teheran but turned off the road to visit the army camp of Abbas Mirza, the twenty-year-old crown prince and commander. His observations during that phase of his visit to Persia account for the succinct analysis of the Russo-Persian military situation which he presented Napoleon in the report. News of Austerlitz preceded him to Persia, causing a strong sensation and lightening his task. Following a stay of several days with the crown prince, he visited Mohammed Ali Mirza, another son of the shah and a provincial governor ambitious to command a projected expedition against the pasha of Bagdad. Persia's army was greatly in need of reform in both organization and discipline. Would Napoleon, Jaubert inquired, fulfill Abbas Mirza's request for a certain number of French officers to serve as instructors and cannoneers? With such assistance Persia could oppose Russia with a real army instead of with its existing "undisciplined horde."

When Jaubert at last approached Teheran, he was already being heralded as the Frenchman who carried the orders of the "Great Emperor." Received in solemn audience, he duly submitted Napoleon's letter to Feth Ali. Jaubert said that the Persian court accorded him exceptional honors, perhaps the more impressive because of Romieu's sad misfortune in 1805. As he observed the internal situation in Persia, the dynasty seemed solidly established and the people loyal. The country feared an invasion from Russia, the Russo-Persian war being fought in Georgia not yet having interrupted all regular communications. The Persians, pacific by nature, nevertheless represented a military potential of consequence, if they could be suitably trained. All Persians would welcome reforms that might enable them to humiliate tsarist Russia.

Feth Ali consistently revealed himself as friendly to Napoleon and as discontented with the English. It was not yet surmised, in the summer of 1806, that France itself would now be on the point of invading Russia. The shah requested a military alliance with Napoleon, "founded on the reciprocal character of their interests." He believed that the French emperor's diplomatic support alone would be a powerful weapon against his enemy. In Jaubert's opinion, the shah possessed the power and the will to assist Napoleon to accomplish his ends against the English in India; Feth Ali had pointedly stated that he would support his promises. If, after Napoleon dealt out to the Russians their just punishment, he wished to send one of his powerful armies to India, Feth Ali not only would accord the passage but would himself march there beside Napoleon. The shah repeated this promise to Jaubert several times and affirmed further that he would welcome French merchants and missionaries to Persia.[9]

During that first week of March, Warsaw and Osterode were still unaware of the fact that the English fleet had entered and fled the Dardanelles. On March 7, Talleyrand received Sebastiani's dispatch of February 9, with its news of approximately a month earlier, when the preliminaries of Admiral Duckworth's exploit were under way. We recall that the message revealed the vigor of the Turkish council's resistance to the English, by contrast with the apathy of the public. Sebastiani believed that Turkey would be pushed into war by the English, who had one squadron already stationed at Tenedos and another on the way. He believed that the English intended to attack Constantinople in order to create a powerful diversion in Russia's favor. After decapitating the elder Prince Ypsilanti and confiscating his property, Turkey offered that individual's country home to France as a summer palace for the French ambassador. Napoleon promptly accepted the offer.[10]

Such was Napoleon's current information from the Persian and Turkish capitals. From the Principalities—closer sources of information—came word that Russian forces under Michelson late in November, 1806, had occupied large portions of Moldavia and Wallachia. Turkey in rejoinder had declared war late in December and planned to organize a fighting force to extrude the Russians. Russia had no wish for a two-front war and certainly none for a three-front war including the conflict with Persia. Napoleon did not know that the tsar's minister of foreign affairs was laboring behind the scenes, even at that late date, to bring Turkey back into line with "justice and equity"—to restore the alliance and friendship which Napoleon had disrupted.

Foreign Minister Budberg's communication of March 10 to the grand vizir, who presumably commanded the Turkish army on the Danube, ignored the fact that direct diplomatic relations had been wanting since Italinski's withdrawal from Constantinople. Budberg argued that Bonaparte could never be Turkey's friend. "His sole permanent object is to reverse all legitimate governments," Budberg stated, "in order to establish his pretended universal monarchy over their ruins." Russia, by contrast, interested itself directly in the independence and integrity of the Ottoman Empire. To avoid the seemingly inevitable diversion, Budberg authorized General Michelson to treat for peace, if Turkey should reveal such a disposition. With respect to terms, Turkey must confirm the alliance with Russia and renew that with England, hold the Straits open to Russian vessels of war and troop transports, fully observe the stipulated autonomy of the Principalities, and authorize the hospodars to maintain and control their own armed forces.[11]

Napoleon wrote Talleyrand on March 11 from Osterode that he would not make an issue of French troops traversing the Balkans. If Vahid Effendi should say that the troops were unwelcome in Turkey, he must be assured by the foreign minister that this project would be dropped. As for the requested officers it would be necessary only to specify their number, rank, and equipment—and the same policy would apply to Persia. Probably as a propaganda measure intended to soften the Turkish envoy's attitude, Napoleon directed that Talleyrand should insert in the journal of Warsaw a fabricated report of Turkish successes against the Russians, together with "their reported capture of two Russian ships in the Dardanelles, etc." He frankly wrote Marmont that the plan for a large force to cross the Balkans had fallen through.[12]

Napoleon could tolerate no "cold war." Sebastiani must write the Persians, if their enthusiasm appeared to be weakening, to make strong attacks against Russia. He foresaw the danger to his general policy in a Persian or Turkish war against Russia devoid of real fighting. "I have written a letter to the shah," he advised Talleyrand on March 13. "It is to be given the ambassador. Hand him also a statement in French—which he might translate into Persian—of the events of the last six months in Europe. Request the Turkish envoy to send the same statement to his court to counter some of Russia's propaganda there. Also direct Sebastiani to send to Persia an officer bearing a letter from him to the grand vizir to advise of what has passed, and to take steps to establish regular communications with Teheran." It appeared desirable, indeed necessary, to plan for a courier to start to Persia every week. This arrangement would require concert with Turkey and with the shah's agents. The emperor now preferred that neither Mirza Riza nor Vahid go to Paris, but that they conclude their business and depart without delay for their respective capitals.[13]

Napoleon's letter to the "Emperor of the Persians" stated that Jaubert had reported to him a good reception by the Persian court. Feth Ali

would have learned already that French armies now stood on the frontiers of Russia. Napoleon's victories in two battles had frightened the
Russians into massing to defend their capital. Mirza Riza had come
to Warsaw—although Napoleon had not as yet met him; being the commander, Napoleon must be with the advance guard of the French army.
Napoleon desired that the Persian ambassador, before returning home,
plan to visit Paris, where he might make a full report concerning Napoleon's power and the temper of the French people. Upon Talleyrand's reminder, Napoleon also addressed the crown prince, whose letter
he acknowledged with congratulations on Persia's victories over the Russians, and an expression of hope for further victories. "Fortune is for
the brave," he encouraged. Talleyrand prepared the directed special propaganda covering Napoleon's successes during the preceding six months;
Outrey checked the translations into Turkish and Persian.[14] Thus a
second packet of official letters for Teheran had at last been prepared,
some two years after the first venture when Jaubert and Romieu were
dispatched over different routes with Napoleon's initial letter to Feth
Ali. No one rushed the departure of a courier to be sent on such a long
voyage, whereas the French ruler invariably failed to allow adequate
time for exchanges of messages anywhere in the Near or Middle East.
He was looking beyond Russia to British India.

Talleyrand and Vahid by now could take for granted the Ottoman
recovery of the Principalities, an attitude which reduced the talking
value of Talleyrand's draft treaty with Turkey. As a further inducement
Napoleon's minister reacted favorably if haltingly to the Ottoman request for recovery of the Crimea, if Turkey definitely considered this
territory essential to its complete independence from Russia. Whether
in a real or fancied manner, France already had accorded considerable
support to the Ottoman interpretation. When Austria seemed to reveal
that Russia would accede to the former Russo-Turkish treaties as a basis
for a settlement with Turkey, Talleyrand rejoined that Turkey would
not thereby recover its full independence. Everyone appreciated that
such recovery hinged on the nature of the treaty furnishing the basis for
a settlement. A return to the treaty of 1774 and its aftermath would
lead to retrocession of the Crimea; a return only to the Russo-Turkish
alliance of 1805 would result in Russian evacuation of the Principalities
but retention of the military passage of the Straits. Someone suggested
that these terms might merely represent Russia's first offer.

Because Warsaw was approximately a month behind on general news from the Near East, Talleyrand ordinarily summarized the dispatches received in bunches for Napoleon's examination. The belated news of Duckworth's threat to sail his fleet up to Constantinople at first impressed neither Napoleon nor Talleyrand. In mid-March appeared Sebastiani's report of February 19, telling of the Turkish decision to resist a British passage of the Dardanelles and of the weakness of Turkey's defenses. The still unimpressed officials at Talleyrand's headquarters went right ahead with routine business, as if they had not the remotest expectation of a foreign occupation of Constantinople.[15] Ambassador Andreossy first officially reported from Vienna the British naval movement into the Dardanelles, together with the demands on Turkey issued from February 19 to 26. Talleyrand read this news on March 26 and speeded it to Napoleon. The latter stormed, "If the Turks have any courage, the English will be the dupes."

Talleyrand was soon able to relay to him Sebastiani's reports up to March 3, expedited by way of Vidin rather than Vienna. The English had sailed out of the Sea of Marmara, the Turks having fully prepared their defenses under Sebastiani's direction. It will be recalled that only at this time did the sultan notify Admiral Duckworth that he would not negotiate as long as the British fleet remained within the Straits. Talleyrand presented to Vahid Effendi a summary of the British exploit, since the Turkish envoy at Warsaw received only occasional news directly from his government. The negotiators at Warsaw did not wholly neglect commercial affairs. Napoleon had no way of knowing the ineffectiveness of his Continental Blockade throughout the Levant. Apparently his Italian subjects grumbled at the superior privileges for trade enjoyed by Marseille, for we note an imperial decree of May 3 extending to Genoa the same legal privileges for the Levant which Marseille held.[16]

At Constantinople, Ruffin and Sebastiani were saddened early in 1807 by the deaths of Madame Ruffin in January and Madame Sebastiani in April. It seemed only a question of time until Sebastiani would leave —and Ruffin secretly desired to be his successor. Ruffin's flourishing signature attested his continuing activity, even though Sebastiani held the responsibility and signed most of the dispatches. Ruffin translated all the important Turkish documents and advised behind the scenes. He was to be ambassador in fact on four occasions, although Napoleon never accorded him that coveted title.[17]

Napoleon on April 3 issued instructions to Talleyrand that a statement be made at Constantinople. The foreign minister complied only on April 29; the reason for delayed action is not recorded. According to this document Sebastiani was to inform the Ottomans that Russia had offered peace, with Austria acting as mediator. The emperor had declared, however, that "he would never negotiate without his allies, among whom Turkey stood in the front rank." He would like Vahid Effendi to be instructed to attend a peace congress, should one be called. He would "never separate his cause from that of Turkey." All additional comment must minimize the talk of peace. Any mention of peace by a belligerent, Sebastiani would say, should cause his opponent to redouble preparations. Napoleon's pleasure in the (incorrect) news that the grand vizir had crossed the Danube led to Talleyrand's urging the vizir's departure from Constantinople for the front, if this move had not already been made. Napoleon planned strong action against Russia as soon as he could occupy Danzig, the capture of which had been delayed by the weather.[18] The grand vizir actually departed from Constantinople on March 30, to command the small Turkish army on the Danube. Russia opened the spring battles; the advance of its armies toward the Danube was reported by the French agent at Ruschuk on March 26.

Napoleon personally addressed Selim from Finkenstein on April 3. He stated that at his own expense he had authorized the loan to Turkey of the officers and the requested small number of 500 troops. He had issued blanket authorization, moreover, for Dalmatia and Naples to forward to Turkey arms, munitions, or other requisites. Already, several cannons and gunners had been lent the pasha of Albania. Napoleon needed only to know Turkey's further requirements. He tendered French generals, officers, arms of every kind, even money. As a result of both friendly and political motives his interest in Selim's success was so great that he could refuse no request. Napoleon did ask that the sultan come to an understanding with the Shah of Persia, also Russia's enemy, in order to make possible a complete attack on the common foe. Although Russia was talking of peace, Napoleon would refuse to sanction the Russo-Turkish territorial treaty of 1774 as expanded by the treaty of 1792. On the contrary, absolute independence for Turkey must be stipulated.[19] We shall see Sebastiani apply the latter statement with telling but completely misplaced effect on June 14, the day on which Napoleon defeated Russia in the battle of Friedland (chap. ix). Napoleon also wrote Feth Ali on April 3, asserting that he desired Persia to be a friend of Turkey and to abandon quarrels over minor grievances in order that the two nations might jointly face the real enemy. Moreover, the shah could coöperate by halting all British communications with India and intercepting their couriers. "They are the friends of the Russians and our enemies," he wrote.[20]

Talleyrand more than utilized all the favorable news from Sebastiani, as his summaries present affairs in a better light than was actually justi- fied. A private letter from Prince Suzzo, the pro-French hospodar of Wallachia, expressed the belief that a French army corps might cross the Balkans for the Dniester. After the arrival of detailed reports con- cerning Duckworth's failure, Talleyrand's summary on April 4 stated:

That Your Majesty proposed to join six French vessels to the Turkish squadron to act in the Black Sea and there embark some companies of artillery, charmed the sultan. He desires that your Majesty add two companies of light artillery for a landing in the Crimea. His intention, if you approve, is to send 10,000 men there. He would like also several naval officers and first mates. General Sebastiani reports that the sultan will re- ceive with pleasure 25,000 French troops at Vidin, from there proceeding directly to the Dniester. French garrisons will be accepted for the forts you wish to occupy near Ragusa. The English at Constantinople have been arrested, their property confiscated, and the sale of their merchandise prohibited. The sultan dispatched a letter to the dey of Algiers, upon French request, directing that ruler to attack the English and treat the French as friends. The present capitan pasha being the dey's father, one does not doubt the order will be obeyed—at least insofar as regards the French. Hostilities have been launched in Georgia. The Greeks are conducting themselves well. Public spirit is ex- cellent.[21]

It is little wonder that Napoleon by decree of April 7 authorized as Se- bastiani's encouragement and reward *la grande décoration* of the Legion of Honor; the sultan later presented the award, upon Napoleon's request.

Napoleon recommended that the Dardanelles be defended with a large number of cannon, and especially with mortars. Upon the receipt of further satisfactory reports from Sebastiani, he thanked Selim (April 8) for the measures undertaken to enforce the Continental Blockade against English commerce. He countered the sultan's suggestion that French ships be conveyed into the Dardanelles by stating that he needed the Turkish fleet in the Black Sea rather than in the Mediterranean. Turkey had indeed intimated that it might send some vessels of war into the Black Sea to ravage the southern coasts of Russia and create the diversion Napoleon requested.[22]

Sebastiani's encouraging words, and the obvious need of support for the poorly equipped Ottoman army opposing Russia, explain the re- ported request that Napoleon send five or six large vessels of war to

Constantinople. The ships could help to break up Seniavin's blockade of the Dardanelles, provided Britain did not interfere. Napoleon on April 22 directed Decrès, minister of the relatively weak French navy, to rush the completion at Toulon of the ships *Robuste* and *Commerce de Paris*. These, with three other available vessels, would bring the total to five. Meanwhile, Sebastiani forwarded reports narrating some adverse developments, notably the opposition by the pashas and the janissaries to the tentative assignment of the 25,000 French troops to Vidin.[23]

The official offer of the good offices of the Emperor of Austria for the reëstablishment of peace in Europe arrived in Warsaw on April 7. Talleyrand's view that Turkey must be included in any discussion of a general pacification prevailed. Napoleon at first refrained from comment. Several days later, Talleyrand threw out the idea that an armistice based on the status at the time of signing would probably suit everyone, but Napoleon reproached him for being too forward in discussing the possibility of an armistice with Russia. The latest news received from Constantinople, on April 24—news dated March 22—continued to favor France in southeastern Europe. The Dardanelles were well defended and the British fleet was back at Malta.[24]

Our scene now shifts to the drafting of the Franco-Persian alliance, the outstanding development of April, 1807. In the general picture, Napoleon insisted that the French navy must expedite all its construction then in progress, so that in four or five months the twenty-nine vessels he counted upon for long-range service would be available. This total included the Spanish and Dutch vessels and the French ships stationed or under construction at Brest, Lorient, Cadiz, and Toulon. He directed an investigation of a possible naval expedition to the Persian Gulf. The shah had requested 4,000 infantry troops, 10,000 rifles, and 50 cannons. "When can they leave," he asked minister Decrès, "and where can they debark?" Their object would be to support the shah's 14,000 cavalry and to force upon Russia "a considerable diversion." Decrès was advised that General Gardane and some army officers would be dispatched, and Napoleon suggested that a naval engineer not really needed in France would be quite useful to the legation in Teheran.[25]

In Persia, Joseph Rousseau, the French consul in Basra, prepared the way for a resident French ambassador in Teheran. In April, 1807, Joseph departed from Aleppo and with five French and Italian companions traveled by way of Mosul and Bagdad. He avoided the route by way of Erzurum, from fear of bandits and a knowledge of Jaubert's experiences.

He distributed generous gifts along the route to Bagdad, as is shown by his submitted expense account of some 31,000 francs, at a time when 1,500 francs would pay the salary for a year of a French consul appointed to the Persian Gulf. The expenses also included the wages of his escort; yet the French government questioned the figures and never fully refunded his unauthorized expenditures. (As late as 1817, he still sought a settlement.) He came to Teheran late in May, 1807, in the capacity of embassy secretary, a misnomer since France as yet had neither embassy nor legation in that city. Consul Rousseau arranged that a minister be received.

Because the preparatory discussions between Talleyrand and Mirza Riza had assured a Franco-Persian alliance, Napoleon promptly commissioned a resident minister and legation staff for Teheran. The necessary imperial decrees were dated April 12, at the very time when Joseph Rousseau was trudging his weary way from Bagdad. Appointed minister plenipotentiary to Persia was Brigadier General Antoine Gardane, an officer of Napoleon's imperial household. The minister's brother, Ange Gardane, became first secretary of the legation. Joseph Rousseau was appointed second secretary, perhaps as a concession to his known popularity with Persian officials. Joannin, who was already in Teheran and who was one of the two interpreters reassigned from the staff of the embassy at Constantinople, would be the first interpreter. Four students of Oriental languages were commissioned to receive instruction in Persian. Several officers from various French military units must accompany the minister, in accordance with the request of Persia's special ambassador and with Jaubert's personal word from Crown Prince Abbas Mirza.

Persia's ambassador at Warsaw meanwhile found himself the center of considerable attention. Governor Gouvion arranged to escort him on April 23 to Thorn, from which city the ambassador was to proceed to Finkenstein. Mirza Riza appeared "enchanted," Talleyrand reported, to be permitted at last to meet Napoleon personally. He and his staff required four carriages and were accompanied by two Polish officers speaking French and German. Jaubert assisted in the negotiations with Mirza Riza at Warsaw and Finkenstein; Outrey was also on hand as an interpreter. Talleyrand commended the latter as "a man of merit and of courage, strongly devoted to the service of Napoleon."[26]

Napoleon doubtless considered Persia an additional aid in the defeat of Russia and in the possible eventual extrusion of Britain from India. The acme of his interest in Persia was reached with the alliance signed at Finkenstein. Whether Napoleon's evaluation of Persia related primarily

to India or to Russia is open to question. Years later, when General
A. J. M. R. Savary, the Duke of Rovigo, once Napoleon's envoy to
Russia, argued that the French emperor wished to push Persia against
Russia, he quoted from Napoleon's instructions to the navy respecting
the Black Sea. Napoleon's scheming for a combined naval assault against
Russia in that sea may be contrasted with his direction to Minister
Gardane to survey Persia's over-all military potential, and to include details concerning routes and possible supplies for an expedition to India.
That Napoleon desired Persia to strike at Russia with full force cannot
be denied; certainly he so instructed Gardane. He likewise had asked
Turkey to attack the Russians in Georgia, and the probability is that
the latter course offered the more immediate potential aid. Communications were quicker and Turkey could strike at three points simultaneously: on the Dniester, at the Crimea, and in Georgia. Persia, on the
other hand, would be the stronger bulwark in a later campaign against
British India. In addition its ability to hurl itself against Napoleon's
land enemy, Persia represented in 1807 a pivot of French policy supplementary or alternative to Turkey, which might not only prevent the exclusion of France from the Near and Middle East but also be a possible
aid in increasing French power in those regions. Both Turkey and Persia
were already at war against Russia. After Napoleon had finished with
Russia, Persia as well as Turkey might be pushed into a fighting war
against England.

Audiences granted him by Napoleon doubtless seemed quite impressive to Mirza Riza, occurring as they did in the midst of big campaigns.
Danzig and Königsberg had been occupied; the Russians were preparing
to retreat to the Niemen; a welcome reportedly awaited the emperor in
Lithuania, if the war should take that turn. Mirza Riza many times
held the spotlight; everything must be done to create and maintain a
favorable impression for him to carry back to the shah's court. Napoleon
always appeared as the busy, conquering hero. The Persian ambassador
was guided to Danzig to witness a European army in action when
Marshal Lefebvre entered the city in mid-May. General Savary recounted
in his memoirs that Mirza Riza once expressed himself as not understanding why Napoleon did not decapitate the inhabitants of Danzig.
French troops marching in unison to martial music entertained him, and
he wondered aloud whether the emperor could not give him some of the
musicians.[27] He reviewed other French forces in action, in the wake of
the distinguished reception given him late in April at Finkenstein. Later,

on May 29, we find the emperor having a long visit with him in the park adjacent to the imperial castle. Jaubert interpreted the conversation, which turned on the literature and monuments of Persia, as one intended to confirm Napoleon's general interest in everything Persian. Jaubert was pensioned that year and soon was named auditor of the Council of State. In that post he won conspicuous recognition and thereafter was always available to translate Napoleon's most important Persian documents.

Everyone expected Mirza Riza to complete his negotiations and return to Persia. Napoleon himself took the initiative and asked that resident representatives be exchanged. Word came through of the arrival at Constantinople of a second Persian officer en route to visit Napoleon. The emperor in unwarranted enthusiasm spoke of the officer as an ambassador, although the latter merely brought a new letter from the shah. The basis for Napoleon's misinterpretation was a notice at hand early in April, heralding without explanation the shah's second envoy. Letters from Aleppo indicated the courier's or "officer's" objects to be to felicitate Napoleon on his victories, to reveal Persia's intention to suppress English privileges, to request an alliance, and to suggest Joseph Rousseau as the resident French agent in Persia. The officer visited in the Turkish capital for several weeks instead of proceeding to Napoleon's headquarters.

At the outset, Talleyrand warned Napoleon that this envoy in no sense could be classed as an ambassador; rather he was a simple aide-de-camp of the shah who had turned the letter over to Sebastiani for transmission. The foreign minister yielded to the emperor later in the year, however, when both showered unmerited attention on the individual in Paris. They soon learned his name, Yousef Bey; much later they learned from Gardane how much less important he was in Persia than Mirza Riza. Napoleon continued to misinterpret the courier's standing. Doubtless to Yousef's surprise, the French capital that autumn accorded him all the courtesies and entertainment due a distinguished ambassador. Yousef Bey, in short, made a good thing out of his messenger service.[28]

How much the French accomplished with Mirza Riza is revealed by the successive draft treaties of alliance left in the manuscript archives. Without considering the complete details, we may observe that the French steadily gained advantages, from the time of Talleyrand's first draft presented at Warsaw to the signing of the final treaty at Finkenstein.

The amicable French and Persian relations culminated auspiciously with the signing of their alliance on May 4. Napoleon's headquarters announced that the alliance bore no terminal date. Directed against Russia and Great Britain, it stipulated Napoleon's guarantee of Persia's existing territory and specifically recognized the shah's sovereignty over Georgia. Persia promised to declare war—and make war—against British India. As initial steps Persia agreed to recall its envoy to Bombay and to expel from Persia all consuls and all agents of the English East India Company. It would attempt to influence the Afghans to attack India and, if access to India could be won, it would itself send an army against India. French ships would be accorded facilities in the Persian Gulf. Gardane later successfully interpreted the latter secret stipulation as requiring the cession of two islands. He won them on paper, but Britain prevented Napoleon's taking them over.

Because Napoleon had stated his intention of sending an army against India, the treaty insisted that French troops must possess the exclusive foreign privilege of passage across Persia. Equivocally he promised his "best efforts" to obtain Russia's evacuation of Georgia. Military supplies must be furnished to the French in Persia, at prices comparable to those charged its own nationals. The reciprocal establishment of legations was agreed upon. Persia promised to Europeanize its army, for which Napoleon would supply on request the necessary weapons and officers for military instruction. A new treaty of commerce would be negotiated in Teheran.[29]

French headquarters gave Mirza Riza no encouragement to tarry in Poland after the signing. His object fulfilled, his entertainment virtually ceased. He remained in Warsaw only four days during the return journey (May 8-12). An item of minor interest is that upon departure he left his hotel bill unpaid. The bill amounted to some 227 Polish ducats, which the innkeeper, one Karl Friedrich Dückert, took the precaution of having approved and signed by Outrey, whom he incorrectly assumed to be Mirza Riza's secretary. Mirza Riza having ignored the accumulated charges for food, lodging, fuel, and other items, the irate Dückert appealed in June for his money by letter addressed with a penman's flourish to "Senator Gouvion, General of Division and Governor of the City and Province of Warsaw." Gouvion transferred the plea to Talleyrand, in order to learn Napoleon's wishes in the matter. Evidently the emperor authorized payment, for otherwise we should discover additional documents concerning the matter. He was to humor Yousef Bey in the same manner in Paris that year. Being official guests, the Persians seemed to expect free entertainment. Such expectations, alien to both

French and European protocol, irked Talleyrand. He utilized the first opportunity to check up on Persian reciprocity to Gardane, and free entertainment by Persia was confirmed, as we note in Chapter XIV.[30]

By no means through accident did Napoleon appoint as minister to Teheran a strong man with a military background. The emperor wished to capitalize promptly upon his treaty with Persia. In the European manner he set Gardane's annual salary liberally, at 120,000 francs a year. He appointed several French engineers and artillery officers, young men who could serve the policy of the alliance by working on the inside, as instructors of the Persian troops. The instructions to Gardane issued on May 10 reveal Napoleon's analysis of Persia's place in his scheme of things. He said, "Persia is considered by France from two points of view, as the natural enemy of Russia and as a means of passage for an expedition to India." Gardane must employ his best efforts to keep Persia and Turkey friendly and importune Persia to give effect to the alliance by going to war with England. He must always emphasize that Russia, because of its geographical location, stood as Persia's natural enemy. France also considered Persia important as a means of land access to India. The several French military officers could help to prepare the Persian army for better service against Russia and for possible service in India. A French army of 20,000 could be provided against India, the instructions stated; how many could Persia furnish? Were suitable numbers of horses available for the cavalry? Gardane should report promptly on the geography and topography of the country and on its coasts, population, finances, military potential, and commercial resources.

He must advance all possible personal contacts. Regular couriers to and from Teheran must be started promptly. He could arrange at Constantinople for the rapid transit of correspondence between himself and Paris, with courier service at weekly intervals. The immediate French object of a triple alliance between France, Turkey, and Persia involved Persia's aid against both Russia and British India. A long-range object was the goal of a favorable Franco-Persian commercial treaty which Gardane must negotiate.[31]

Napoleon's quest for information of strategic value should by no means be considered an end in itself. He had looked ahead to Russia immediately before smashing Prussia. Here he looked ahead to British India immediately before defeating Russia. Indirectly he admitted as much, when in November, 1807, he explained to Russia, his ally at the time, that Gardane's mission was really directed against India. On

May 10 Gardane departed for Warsaw, his first key stop en route to Constantinople and Teheran. No French defeat of Russia had as yet taken place, nor did one seem imminent. Talleyrand notified Sebastiani of the approach of the new minister and ordered regular correspondence and coöperation with the latter after his arrival at his destination.[32]

Summarizing information concerning events throughout the Near East in the spring of 1807, we may say that Mehemet Ali's repulse of the British attack against Rosetta (chap. vii), of itself important to French policy, becomes doubly so. On May 20, the Ottoman foreign ministry's chief interpreter and liaison officer, Alexander Suzzo, announced to the French embassy that the governor of Egypt would "reinforce Alexandria against the common enemy." This pronouncement meant that the British sojourn even there would be rendered as unpleasant as possible. It seemed evident that the Serbian rebellion would soon be subdued by Turkey. The pasha of Vidin had improved his conduct toward France; Finkenstein recognized the latter's "good dispositions," on the basis of reports from Meriaze spurring him to action. Early in May the Turks exiled the anti-French Moruzzi family from Constantinople. In answer to Sebastiani's letter Mustapha Bairakdar, the governor of Silistria and war commandant of the Danube Valley, reported that the Ottoman forces were assembled and that they had repulsed the Russians more than once. The Turks tended to exaggerate their minor successes against the Russians, and Napoleon's headquarters also overstated the importance of the engagements. Gossipy Consul David of Bosnia erroneously reported on May 18 that the Russians were in precipitous retreat from the Principalities. Advices declared that the Persians would soon launch a mighty effort against Russia's forces in Georgia.[33]

In this chapter we have seen Napoleon proceed with an alliance and a plan for utilizing Persia in his Asiatic program which involved Russia and Britain. Turkey's failure to form an alliance with Persia represented one weakness in Napoleon's pattern of diplomacy. More important, the best available information indicated that Persia's strategic aid would remain a highly problematical factor, at least until training and supplies of the European type could be given the shah's army. The tendency of the impatient emperor was to set in motion many projects for both Turkey and Persia, and then to lay his plans aside while he concentrated on the big campaigns. We shall see in the next chapter how Napoleon's blitzkrieg and victory against Russia eliminated most of the need for the aid originally called for from Turkey and Persia.

IX

Napoleon Abandons the Ottoman Empire

— June-July, 1807

FRIENDLY TURKEY had by no means issued carte blanche authority to Napoleon for the strategic use of the Balkan area and the strait of the Dardanelles. Because Vahid Effendi, the Ottoman negotiator at Warsaw, had been less amenable to advice than Mirza Riza, he had been forced to await events and, "patiently enough," his turn for Napoleon's attention. It seemed possible that if he, like the Persian ambassador, could discuss matters with Napoleon personally, the vacillating negotiations with Turkey might enter a new course. There were no urgent reasons for a formal Franco-Turkish alliance, since both France and Turkey were already at war against Russia. In this chapter the various approaches in 1807 to such an alliance will be discussed, and the more important course of the reversal of Napoleon's position through his alliance with Russia will be traced.

Fighting weather prevailed in the north, permitting the French emperor to begin in May, 1807, his urgent attempt to defeat the main Russian army. Concerning the proposed alliance with Sultan Selim, we do not possess adequate records of Talleyrand's discussions with Vahid. It may be readily inferred from subsequent reactions, however, that the French demands grew so large as to force the Ottoman negotiator to accept Talleyrand's principal proposals *ad referendum*. We may surmise from the dissatisfaction with the Turkish envoy expressed by Napoleon's minister that the envoy also favored submitting the issue to higher authority, respectively to the emperor and the sultan. Whatever the position Vahid may have assumed, two of Talleyrand's proposals engendered special objection later. We learn of these difficulties from Vahid's debate with General Armand Caulaincourt and from the subsequent debates in the Turkish capital.

Talleyrand thus drafted one of the debated stipulations:

If the concert to be established in the military operations of France and Turkey requires the passage of troops across their respective territories, such troops shall enjoy during

their stay in the territories of their ally every support and means of transport and subsistence.

Vahid possessed no authority to accept such a requirement, nor this one:

France and Persia being united by a similar treaty of alliance [chap. viii], it is agreed
that in case France should find it necessary to send support to Persia or to the French
possessions in India, they will enjoy for the passage of such troops through the Ottoman
Empire the same freedom of movement.

Talleyrand wished these stipulations to apply to France alone, upon
Turkey's promise that the privileges would be granted to no other
powers. He required that within its borders the Ottoman government
protect Frenchmen traveling to Persia in political, military, or commercial capacities. Persians en route to France would enjoy the same safeguard in Turkey. As an end to a long dispute, Turkey would agree to
pay from the Ottoman government's customs receipts the indemnities
for French losses suffered during Bonaparte's expedition to Egypt. There
must also be complete restitution or compensation for French property
taken by Turkey in Smyrna. France would accept a new tariff conforming with the existing higher prices of merchandise, provided that no
other power were given greater advantages. The French must enjoy
greater commercial benefits than those accorded the English. Talleyrand
excluded a separate peace; he intended the alliance to apply in all French
and Turkish wars against Russia and England. The two powers would
agree later upon the character and amount of support to be reciprocally
accorded during time of war and for outbreaks in the Balkans or Dalmatia.

According to Talleyrand's treaty draft, the sultan further must close
the Bosporus to Russian vessels of war and the Dardanelles against the
ships of both Great Britain and Russia. There must be no renewal of the
Russo-Turkish alliance, with its permission for Russia to navigate the
Straits. He must reëstablish French privileges in all the ports of the
Levant and in the Barbary Regencies and require the latter to declare
war against Russia. These and other projected terms favored France,
which in return would guarantee Turkey's repossession of the Crimea,
if that province should be occupied by Turkey during its war with Russia. France would also guarantee to Turkey all of its former rights in the
Principalities and its empire's "full and entire integrity."[1]

Because Vahid made no move to accept such terms, Napoleon, employing the device which had worked so effectively in 1806 against re-

luctant Baron d'Oubril of Russia (chap. v) again substituted a principal negotiator. He transferred the discussions to Finkenstein and the French negotiation to trusted General Caulaincourt. There Napoleon might also personally advance the French case—perhaps as impressively and successfully as he had done with Mirza Riza a few weeks earlier. The documents record the Ottoman envoy's departure from Warsaw for Thorn and Finkenstein on May 25. As Mirza Riza had been, he was guided by two Polish officers who spoke French and German.

Meanwhile Turkey failed to issue a request for the proffered French troops. Napoleon's generous offer of all-out assistance, of anything that Sultan Selim requisitioned, seemed to be virtually ignored. The first call for aid was the modest solicitation that Sebastiani request of General Marmont the loan of 15 cannons and ammunition for the pasha of Bosnia.

General Caulaincourt was commissioned to negotiate when Vahid appeared at the emperor's headquarters. Talleyrand remained in Warsaw, and the aide-de-camp and Vahid were now supposed to negotiate while they followed Napoleon around. Inevitable confusion marked this stage of the negotiations, which opened on May 28, only a fortnight before Napoleon's significant military victory over Russia at Friedland. Roux of the foreign minister's staff assisted. Jaubert was on hand with the Turkish ambassador, serving as guide, companion, interpreter, and general aid to French policy.

Following a first conference at Finkenstein, the French archives record a conference in Danzig on June 1, when Caulaincourt and Vahid fully debated the projected alliance. Their discussions already had advanced far enough for Vahid to present his counterproject for a treaty. He proposed a purely defensive alliance, directed exclusively against Russia. According to the terms of this concert, France and Turkey would obligate themselves not to enter a separate truce or treaty with Russia. France must guarantee to the Ottoman Empire the restitution and conservation of its lost provinces, namely the Crimea and the other lands on the Black Sea. Turkey would attack the Crimea by land and sea, utilizing the support of a French army. After a three-year term circumstances would dictate the policy, under the stipulation that any independent action by either ally must always assume a mutual policy of peace.

The first disagreement related to limiting the term of alliance. Vahid would offer friendship forever but military alliance for only three years.

Nor would Turkey accept the obligation to attack other powers than Russia. Caulaincourt in rejoinder held that England was also at war with Turkey, but the Turkish ambassador stated that he had not received official news of an Anglo-Turkish war. We know from Sebastiani's reports that official Turks in Constantinople really did not expect another attack by England.

Caulaincourt pointed to the warlike character of the newspaper accounts which told of the coming of an English squadron to Constantinople and its enforced withdrawal through the Dardanelles. He argued that Turkey's duty to itself rendered inevitable its own defensive action against England. In response, the Ottoman envoy inquired what support France could offer Turkey against England, particularly against the loss of certain islands in the Aegean. Indeed, by what means could France acquire naval superiority over Britain in the seas of the Levant?

Caulaincourt evaded these embarrassing issues by observing that France could be useful in other regions than the Levant. France could attack England in its home islands, in its colonies, and wherever in Europe the British attempted commerce; France could also assist Turkey to regain the provinces lost to Russia. He proposed that they discuss Talleyrand's suggested treaty.

Vahid wished instead to discuss his own proposal, a draft of a shorter treaty which conformed with his instructions. Caulaincourt admitted the advantage of brevity but considered this document to be entirely too brief. The Turkish draft entirely omitted any references to England, to French privileges, to commerce, and to other significant matters. Talleyrand's longer treaty should provide, Caulaincourt insisted, the basis for the discussion. France desired constant alliance, not merely constant friendship; the one should endure as long as the other. France did not seek merely an alliance of circumstances but rather one based on the long-range and geographically dictated policy toward Russia as located where it could at any time attack Turkey.

Vahid abandoned part of his objections but, because his instructions authorized only an alliance strictly defensive in character, continued to oppose an offensive alliance. Caulaincourt thoughtfully but unsuccessfully observed that nations always assert their wars to be exclusively defensive. The Ottoman insisted upon a stated distinction; he maintained that Ottoman institutions, laws, and religion would render impossible an alliance that favored an aggressor. Why, he asked, did France offer only 100,000 troops while pledging Turkey to all-out war against Russia?

Caulaincourt retorted that such a number was large; 100,000 effective bayonets represented more than the total of all potential Turkish aid to France. The real difference, he argued, arose from geographical position, because Russia's location bore directly on Turkey. Turkey held a similar advantage in naval policy because France asked that it furnish only ten ships of the line or frigates, which would serve exclusively in the Mediterranean. When the envoy interrupted the general to request that France recognize the independence of Ragusa and the Ionian Islands under Turkish suzerainty, Caulaincourt refused to discuss such subjects.[2]

Thus, more than ever, deadlock marked the negotiations. France and Turkey by now had only delimited their areas of disagreement. Each sought terms to suit its own requirements. Napoleon in a long personal conference with Vahid likewise failed to bring the ambassador around to the French viewpoint. The emperor's best argument held that an alliance with the Ottoman Empire was a necessary safeguard not for his own empire, but for the Ottoman Empire. He stated that he would continue to regard as his own the interests of the sultan's empire. The negotiators went to Marienburg on June 4 and then returned to Warsaw. Talleyrand's summary to Sebastiani on June 6 frankly admitted that "the negotiations had made little progress." Inviting the assistance of Napoleon's ambassador at Constantinople, he authorized the tender of the Crimea to Turkey.[3]

Vahid remained adamant, and the Franco-Turkish military alliance was not signed, either at that phychological moment or later. It is unlikely that even Sultan Selim, had he continued in power, would have accepted the hard terms of protectorate proposed by France.

Special circumstances both in the north and in Turkey interposed themselves. Napoleon won the battle of Friedland on June 14, after which event he no longer really needed the Turkish alliance. Unknown to Napoleon and Vahid, some two weeks earlier a palace revolution had overthrown Selim, Napoleon's friend. The successor was soon able to discover a plausible excuse for refraining from an attack against southern Russia; he averred that he could not spare many ships for the Black Sea because a Russian fleet of nine vessels stood just outside the Dardanelles, at Tenedos.

General Marmont had eventually sent into and through Balkan Turkey the 500 well-armed French cannoneers to man the newly placed shore batteries guarding the Dardanelles, in accordance with the request

made early in March by Sultan Selim and the grand vizir. The troops
were intended to serve as protection against any further venture such as
Admiral Duckworth's forced passage of the Dardanelles in February.
They appeared in the Ottoman capital late in May, just in time to
witness the many anti-French reactions that followed the revolution,
and were ordered by the overthrowers of Selim III to depart without delay.

Only after Napoleon came to Tilsit to negotiate with Tsar Alexander
—with a humbled Russia behind him and a different French policy for
Turkey ahead—did he discover from the official dispatches all the anti-
French details incidental to the palace revolution. His new information
furnished him with a convenient pretext for reversing his former policy
for Turkey. He read piecemeal Sebastiani's finally complete story of the
ending of Selim's reign. As one immediate effect, the newly arrived
French soldiers were banished, and Ottoman foreign policy was left uncertain.

Sebastiani's general news of May 23, all encouraging to France, had
foretold nothing of the imminence of revolt against the collaborator
Selim. That dispatch, deciphered at Napoleon's headquarters at Tilsit
on July 2, indicated that France as yet had no cause for complaint in
Turkey. One of Marmont's officers had inspected the shores of the Dardanelles and found them adequately prepared for defense against any
new British attack. The ambassador commended to the emperor the
fidelity and devotion of Eugene Franchini, the embassy's first interpreter
and liaison officer.[4]

From Sebastiani's next reports came the shock. The dispatch of four
days later, dated May 27 and deciphered at Tilsit on July 4, told of the
beginnings of revolution against Selim in the castles commanding the
Bosporus. Revolt was centered in the janissaries, the traditional core of
the Ottoman infantry. By now these soldiers lived mostly on their reputation, being much less efficient in war and far more corrupt than their
fighting predecessors of other centuries had been. With salaries unpaid
for two months before, they had already shown a tendency to revolt.
Their taking over the castles of the Bosporus precipitated the major
revolution. The revolt spread. The janissaries opposed the new levies
of troops, foreign influence, and Sultan Selim's little understood and
always overstated zeal for reform.

Sebastiani reported on May 28 that "the insurrection has assumed a
very alarming character." Extremist janissaries demanded the head of
every minister and the deposition of the reforming sultan. Foreign en-

voys for several days found it impossible to conduct any business at all with the rebel leaders. Napoleon had no way of knowing at Finkenstein or Danzig of these developments and their results. On this May 28 he had authorized Caulaincourt to negotiate the Turkish military alliance based on the terms proposed by Talleyrand. Consul David could write that day in a gloomy vein, that "anarchy seemed rampant in Bosnia, as in the remainder of the Ottoman Empire."

Sebastiani recounted the important subsequent events at Constantinople. His detailed report of June 1 (deciphered at Tilsit on July 4) revealed the effect of the announcement of the prospective arrival of the 500 French officers and men. He perforce wrote as an observer, admitting that he had had no official contacts during the disturbances. The coming of the French forces seemed to presage the enforced introduction of a French type of military discipline and drill, the prospect of which angered the janissaries. Already a few French officers had arrived at the Turkish capital. Dissatisfied with belated salary payments on May 25, they led the palace revolt against the sultan.

The deep-seated quarrel really transcended any personalities or groups of soldiers, or Selim's slight tendency toward reform. It in fact presented the native-born Mohammedans with a long-sought opportunity to take over the government. Under a different sultan, they might at least dominate the regime. This long-range contest stemmed from a conflict behind the scenes waged ever since the all-out struggle in the fifteenth century. Native-born Mohammedans were pitted against the recruited Mohammedans who actually controlled the theocratic government. (Pretender Jem in 1481 had disputed with and fought Sultan Bayazid over the problem.) The bone of contention was the control of the political institutions of the Ottoman theocratic state.

The Moslems born of Mohammedan parents had always controlled the ecclesiastical institutions. The political theory of the Ottoman state, however, held that there must be no division of sovereignty. One religious law, the Mohammedan, bound sultans as well as commoners in all temporal as well as spiritual affairs. The learned men, the ulema as a class, the interpreters of the law, and the muftis of the empire as individuals and as a group, held the essential religious direction and interpreted the theology. The greatest power resided in the judge of the sacred law, the mufti of Constantinople, who was often termed by foreigners the grand mufti, to distinguish him from the ordinary mufti who could be seen in any important Ottoman city.

The political government, on the other hand, had long been controlled by the Mohammedans recruited from Christian families, the so-called "slave family" maintained by the successive sultans. The rulers preferred as their ministers, military commanders, and top-grade administrators in general these men who had as boys been conscripted from Christian homes and afterwards trained in the Mohammedan faith. The sultan legally owned them as his slaves. Few persons reached places of real power in the civil and military administration who did not belong to this recruited group. During several centuries they paradoxically proved themselves the most fanatical Mohammedans of all and until the late eighteenth century were the most loyal partisans of all sultans.

The native-born Moslems wished to control the state. In concert with some anti-janissary troops and with the support of certain disaffected, reform-hating, and jealous janissaries, they seized power. Both the ulema-theocrats and the janissaries, at opposite poles on the Moslem issue, joined in conservative opposition to Selim's real or fancied reforms. Neither was willing to see Turkey's army transformed according to the Napoleonic pattern.

On the last Friday of the month, May 29, 1807, began the thirty-six-hour palace revolution. It effected the deposition of Selim III, the first deposal of a sultan since 1730. Many contemporary observers considered the revolt and its result a catastrophe for Turkey. The ulema leveled two charges against Selim III. (1) He had formed various Turkish army corps on the European model. This action had furthered hatred and lack of discipline among the janissaries, already unsettled by their desire for supremacy, extreme disdain for Europeans, and fear of loss of the sovereign's favor. They especially feared seeing their corps entirely reformed or eliminated. All of this, said the charge, helped to exasperate the violently troubled spirits and excited revolt. (2) According to Mohammedan religion and law, Selim, like any other sultan, should descend from the throne, since in seven years of rule he had fathered no children. For this reason intrigues respecting the succession had marked court affairs for several years.

Commanded by a new chief, some 3,000 janissaries comprising the militia of Constantinople seized the reforming Selim that night. They tried him before a special tribunal constituted by themselves. On the following morning the decision and deposition were more formally established by the mufti of Constantinople, and Selim was led away to jail. Leadership of the Ottoman state went to one of the two available princes of the Ottoman line, namely to Mustapha IV, who was Selim's cousin and who was a son of Sultan Abdul Hamid I.

Twenty-eight-year-old Mustapha IV proclaimed that "the people" had summoned him to occupy the throne. He subscribed to the janissaries' conditions but after a fortnight decided to continue Selim's foreign policy by carrying on the wars against Russia and England.[5]

The new regime held power for fourteen months, often against the active efforts of the intermittently turbulent janissaries. These slave-family members, important figures par excellence through several centuries, now fought to preserve at least the vestiges of their once-dominant position in the army and state. For a time the new government held Selim prisoner in his palace. A little more than a year later, as we shall see in a subsequent chapter, the revolutionaries murdered him in order to prevent his rescue by the regular troops whom he had usually favored over the caste-system janissaries.

A great many Turks celebrated the announcement of the accession of Sultan Mustapha IV on May 29, 1807, by insulting the French generally. The janissaries demanded and won the dismissal of the French troops. These anti-French factions became quite angry when the new ruler, instead of changing the former political system, within two weeks indicated his wish to cultivate French friendship and even to march in person to do battle with the Russians as Napoleon's ally.

At the outset, however, Sebastiani could do no more than observe developments, his influential position counting for little or nothing. Indeed the French embassy itself was momentarily threatened at the end of May by the English and Russian partisans.[6] Fictitious reports reached St. Petersburg as late as November 4 to the effect that Sebastiani's family had been removed to Odessa on board an Italian vessel, in consequence of the anti-French phase of the palace revolution.[7]

Because Selim had been a friend of France, the friends of the revolutionaries at first conveniently supposed that his successor would favor the factions hostile to France. That Napoleon probably shared this view may be seen by an examination of the communications first received at Tilsit. One circumstance in particular confirms such an interpretation. A member of the pro-French party was beheaded, and all the French officers except Juchereau de Saint-Denys were dismissed. Apart from the immediate facts, anyone might logically assume that no French policy in Turkey could be permanent. This view Napoleon could and did adopt at Tilsit.

So much and no more did Napoleon know respecting the palace revolt, during his several days' conference with Alexander at Tilsit. Manifestations of anti-French feeling were many. "We therefore preferred coming to an adjustment with Russia, independently of the Turks," General Savary, another aide-de-camp to the emperor, frankly explained later. "We availed ourselves of the circumstance of the sultan's removal to abandon the country."[8]

Sultan Mustapha willingly joined the pro-Napoleonic forces, nonetheless, in the hope of profit for Turkey. A certain Cheleby Mustapha Pasha was named grand vizir. Halet Effendi, the foreign minister, had once been ambassador in Paris. Mustapha issued orders to enforce the Continental Blockade, although France was to learn later that the policy was one of lip service only. More important was the fact that Mustapha's advisers believed that the suggested French alliance would provide Turkey with the long-sought opportunity to overthrow the hated treaties whereby Russia acquired the Crimea—a possibility at which French officials had many times hinted. The treaty that in 1774 had detached the Crimea also had stipulated that considerable autonomy be enjoyed by the Principalities and had, moreover, forced open the Bosporus and Dardanelles to Russia's commercial navigation. The Turks hoped that the powerful Napoleon would force Russia to terminate all these onerous stipulations. Mustapha's government demonstrated hostility toward England as well as Russia, and ordered further discussions of a military alliance with Napoleon.

Once again we may see the inevitable results of the belated arrival of news events. Dispatches concerning incidents in the Franco-Russian war reached Constantinople about a month after they had occurred. Thus Turkey could not know immediately of the French victory at Friedland on June 14, a day on which Foreign Minister Halet Effendi affirmed in quite a positive manner that the revolution had effected no changes in Ottoman foreign policy. Indeed his formal note had cleared the revolution of its anti-French aspects. At least the note satisfied Sebastiani and gave France relief from the ambassador's original fear that Ottoman foreign policy would reverse itself. News of all these occurrences reached Napoleon a month later—or whenever reports could catch up with him in his ceaseless peregrinations. By then he would already have negotiated peace and formed an alliance with Russia.

On June 14 Halet offered to sign a reciprocal pledge to continue the common fight against Great Britain and Russia, and to agree reciprocally to conclude a joint peace with France. In its anticipated treaty of peace with Russia, Turkey desired to have full restoration of its independence and specifically demanded the elimination of the obnoxious stipulations that favored Russia. Primarily such an agreement would amount to the retrocession of the Crimea and its guarantee by France.

"The intention of the present government of the Ottoman Empire," stated Halet, "is not only to continue the alliance recently established between the Ottoman Empire and the august emperor of France, but to corroborate and fortify it even more. In consequence, Turkey takes the formal engagement to continue with all vigor the existing war against Russia and England. It will not enter a separate peace with these two powers, but will make war and peace together with the court of France. It is understood that France for its part will not enter a separate peace. Turkey will be called to the treaty conference between the belligerent powers, and admitted as a contracting party."

The actual signing of the Franco-Russian treaty at Tilsit on July 7 was to be accomplished with neither time nor thought of inviting Turkey.

"The treaty will reassert the independence and integrity of the possessions of the Ottoman Empire," Halet continued, "that is to say, abolish the prejudicial conditions challenging the independence and liberty of the Ottoman Empire that are found in the treaty whereby Russia annexed the Crimea. France will guarantee formally that in the future such conditions will not be executed. All this will be stipulated explicitly in the general treaty of peace, upon Turkish request of France."

Sebastiani at the moment could not know the will of his Imperial Majesty, Napoleon I. He knew nothing of Friedland, nor of the emperor's intention to form an alliance with Russia. Nonetheless, on that June 14 he in turn formally affirmed these conclusions. He blandly stated in writing that he, "knowing the intentions and the will of his august master, Emperor Napoleon, did not hesitate to declare them officially. France would never separate its interests from those of Turkey, he promised unequivocally. War and peace would be made by the two nations only on terms of mutual agreement. When general peace was reëstablished, he pledged that its first and principal stipulation would be a guarantee of the integrity and independence of the Ottoman Empire. The treaty must eliminate the "miserable and outrageous" conditions that restricted Turkey's complete sovereignty. That is to say, any treaty which France signed with Russia would abolish the severance of the

Crimea and formally guarantee Turkish possession of that territory in the future.

Because Napoleon had not canceled the instructions made early in the year, Sebastiani was justified in adding that France would furnish men and munitions, upon Turkish request. No French troops would enter Turkey without Turkish authorization, provided that the Russians did not cross the Danube nor advance toward Dalmatia. In the latter contingencies it would become necessary for French armies to advance against the common enemy.[9]

As a result of Napoleon's victory that day, these were to prove hollow words. Soon Russia would be Napoleon's ally, under terms held secret from Turkey and by no means favorable to Turkey. In the north it could be perceived after Friedland that the French quest for Near Eastern allies would be necessary only to support its anti-English policy, and even that power might agree to peace. The attitude is reflected in Caulaincourt's stalemated negotiations with Vahid as well as in the halting policy now adopted with regard to Persia, despite the auspicious inauguration of that policy only a month earlier.

Gardane and certain members of his party had set out for Persia, traveling overland rather than by the impractical sea route at first proposed for them. Letters written by the new minister to Persia place him in Vienna on June 16. Arriving in Temesvar on June 27, he rested for several days. Despite Friedland, Talleyrand from his position in Finkenstein prodded Gardane to greater speed on June 26, with instructions, however, that the talk of a third bilateral treaty be toned town. The "alliance" between Turkey and Persia must give way to "friendship" between them. Also, Gardane must seek to obviate Turkey's jealousy or opposition to the concession made by the Persian ally for passage of French troops to British India.

Gardane obviously was now on very unsure ground. We know from his letters that he proceeded quite slowly, obeying orders but apparently looking back while traveling in the hope of learning the outcome of any negotiation with Russia, and making sure he did not outrun any countermanding orders. He had not moved beyond Vidin by July 10, the day after Napoleon and Alexander had ratified their alliance at Tilsit.[10]

Paradoxes were present in Britain's position in the Near East from February to June, 1807. British agents there twice made war in commando fashion and then retreated to a "cold war" position. Everyone recognized the fact that the British naval expedition to Constantinople

in February had been unfortunate. Alexandria now ironically represented
a stronghold from which the cabinet at London thought it desirable that
the British retreat. Directives confined the occupying forces to Alexandria alone. Turkey generally ignored the state of "war" existing between
itself and England. Astute French observers, including Jaubert and Outrey particularly, advised against a two-front war for the sultan, whose
hands were full with the Russian venture into which Napoleon's ag-
gressive policy and ambassador had pushed him.

Imprisoned Selim no longer could make the decision. Although he
was still in power when Britain's Arbuthnot fled Constantinople, he
did not recall his ambassador from London. On the other hand, Selim
had not communicated with his envoy in England for four months, nor
could the Ottoman ambassador find any convenient means of getting reports through to Constantinople. On June 17 dispatches arrived from
the Turkish ambassador belatedly revealing the British cabinet's complete disavowal of the actions of Arbuthnot and Duckworth in forcing
the Dardanelles. It was announced that Arthur Paget, the new British
ambassador, charged with the restoration of the former friendly relations, would arrive before long at the Dardanelles.

The situation presented an adequate opportunity, had Sultan Mustapha's advisers wished one, to reverse the pro-French policy of his predecessor. The Ottomans, however, held to their exchange of commitments
with Sebastiani on June 14. A strong pro-French policy was indicated.
The mufti and the Ottoman council promised Napoleon's ambassador
not to negotiate with England until after the evacuation of Egypt and
the recall of the fleet from Levantine waters. Paget would not be received,
they stated, nor would the English frigate bearing him be allowed to
enter the Dardanelles. Soon afterwards, news came of Napoleon's victory
at Friedland. Because the Turks did not at first foresee the really adverse
effect of this event on their own position, the cheering news of the defeat
of their enemy momentarily increased their regard for France.[11]

Hence Paget, who proved arrogant, really appeared at the Dardanelles
at an inopportune time. He and others slowly appreciated the fact that
a Turkey supported by the Napoleonic regime could not be brought to
terms by threats. Duckworth's diplomacy had stalled, as a result of the
forced passage of the Dardanelles; the occupation of Alexandria could
not bring Turkey back to the Anglo-Russian camp nor indeed could it
achieve any worthwhile purpose. Officialdom in London anticipated the
British agents in the Near East in their acceptance of these demonstrated

conclusions. Hence George Canning ordered an attempt to return Turkey to a position of alliance with Russia and Britain.

Russia likewise sent its own special negotiator, Pozzo di Borgo, who was to play an intermittent and colorful part in Russia's relations with Turkey for many years thereafter. He stationed himself at Tenedos, with Russia's blockading squadron, and awaited an opportunity to negotiate. Paget, following instructions, must coöperate with Pozzo di Borgo and the Russian fleet, and withhold any pacific overtures until the Turks evinced receptivity. His and Pozzo's efforts might prove doubly important; if Russia and Turkey could be persuaded of the advantages of peace, Napoleon's employment of Turkish forces for a diversion at Russia's southern areas would terminate.

Paget at first believed he could employ the British hold at Alexandria as a lever for terms. He discovered that the Dardanelles were under rigid blockade, primarily of Russian nature. He offered the evacuation. When rebuffed, he temporarily suspended the contemplated withdrawal from Alexandria, a step approved later by the government. He changed his mind by July, convinced at last the Turks could not be intimidated, and the voluntary evacuation got under way in September.[12]

Unknown to Mr. Paget, on June 16 London had ordered a somewhat different course. The troops in Alexandria must be withdrawn, but the fleet must remain in the Levant to intercept all supplies intended for Constantinople. The purpose of the naval operations might be achieved either at Alexandria, or at Smyrna by an extension of the blockade in effect for the Dardanelles. The admiralty suggested the blocking off of Alexandria after the departure of the British, by sinking Turkish vessels at the entrance of the channel of the Nile River.[13] Russia in 1854 would sink a half dozen ships of the line at the entrance of Sevastopol harbor, in action taken against Great Britain and France during the Crimean War.

Napoleon's victory of June 14 subdued Russia's fighting fervor. The armistice came a week later. Because he was no longer in need of a Turkish alliance, we hear little more of it. Once more the conqueror looked ahead. If Turkish territory should be required for marches to India, Russia and France, allied but ignoring the niceties of other alliances, would simply push their way through it. In a practical sense the Turks, although they did not know it, from this point on were to be spectators observing French policy from the sidelines. Like the Poles and the Lithuanians, they could only hope for favorable consideration. All these groups followed with interest the evolution of the new relations between France and Russia. Even the Prussian king, as a result of his military disaster at the hands of Napoleon, must anxiously await the fate of his country, of which the territorial diminution was doubted by nobody. Napoleon after Friedland had prepared to march ahead into Lithuania, directing a segment of Franco-Polish troops toward Grodno. Russia's army, surprised at the rapidity of the French advance, decided not to defend Vilna. Instead, on June 27 the Russians began to evacuate that city, and Napoleon's prompt entry served as a curtain raiser for the campaign of 1812. He had expected an enthusiastic reception, but faced instead a silent, virtually deserted city.

Russian officials appraised affairs philosophically, in advance of the peace conference at Tilsit between Napoleon and Alexander and their advisers. The upholding of the integrity of Russian territory was emphasized as one of the most important of the proposals made to Tsar Alexander by his counselors; all these proposals evolved into instructions for the negotiations. The restitution of the French conquests in Prussia possibly could be stipulated, to balance Russia's evacuation of Moldavia and Wallachia and departure from the Ionian Islands and Cattaro. So far as the Ottoman Empire was concerned, the tsar must hold himself ready to arrange affairs under the mediation of France and on the basis of previous treaties. Two peacetime advantages might be sacrificed: the passage of ships of war through the Straits, and the issuance of the traditional foreign warrants of protection to certain Turkish subjects.[14]

Meanwhile, although Vahid Effendi would not agree to complete compliance in the proposed alliance with France, he expressed enthusiasm over Friedland and the capture of Königsberg. Napoleon's successes gave him as much joy as if they had been Ottoman victories, he wrote Talleyrand on June 23. He did not suggest any prospect of immediate settlement by treaty; doubtless he wished to encourage Napoleon to proceed with his campaigning until Turkey was also a victor. On that day, however, he learned of the French armistice with Russia, signed the previous afternoon. Was Turkey now to be abandoned? All serious Franco-Turkish negotiations came to an abrupt end obviously as a direct result of the Franco-Russian armistice rather than as a result of the evident divergence between Caulaincourt's and Vahid's views.

Entering into direct communication with Tsar Alexander on June 24, Napoleon directed that Turkey be informed of the armistice and that Sebastiani state that the interests of Turkey would be "treated gently." His seasoned foreign minister, almost distracted by the rapidity of vic-

tories and other events, on June 26 wrote a long dispatch in terms that
were almost gibberish concerning current affairs. Talleyrand's letter to
the grand vizir three days later likewise appeared almost meaningless,
unless compliments paid to Napoleon for a continuous string of successes could mean anything to a Turkey that clearly must now fear
desertion by its ally.[15]

Much unfinished business remained in the Near and Middle East at
the time when the Franco-Russian truce suddenly and dramatically interposed itself. The British held Alexandria and the Russians blockaded
the Dardanelles. Mehemet Ali had restored a semblance of order in
Egypt, in place of the previous internal confusion. No Franco-Turkish
military alliance had been negotiated. Could the Ottoman Empire survive with evidence of its internal decay everywhere apparent, and with
Russia in the Principalities? Gardane was traveling slowly toward Persia,
where rival Britain's Hartford Jones was also traveling in the hope of
negotiations.

The city of Marseille never liked Napoleon's thundering campaigns,
because it rarely profited from their attendant complications. Bonaparte's
career in 1798 almost ruined the city's shipping, for Marseille had furnished most of the 280 vessels that transported the French expedition
to Egypt. The greater portion of these ships never returned; Admiral
Nelson saw to that. Only once during the ensuing years did trade prospects improve, as we have seen during the interlude of peace in 1802.
Always Marseille planned ahead for stable peace, biding its time and
hoping for future profits from renewed trade in the Levant. Deposed
Selim's favoritism for France was now being appreciated by French merchants. Shortly before the arrival of news of Selim's deposition, Marseille interested itself anew in the prospects of Levantine trade during
peacetime. Selim wanted French textiles to replace those which had
theretofore been furnished by England. The Council of Commerce so
wrote the Ministry of the Interior (June 12). The council wished to cooperate, if British control of the Mediterranean could be circumvented.
The realistic suggestion was made that France could fully meet the
Turkish needs only after the restoration of peace.[16]

France and Russia at the time of the armistice did not yet know of
the palace revolution in Constantinople. Nevertheless both nations were
on the point of reversing their policies for the Near East, as a result of
the alliance of Tilsit. The period of impressive French diplomatic successes at Constantinople was to end, on paper immediately in the treaty

of secret alliance, in practice slowly in the actions of the French official personnel in Turkey. The earlier French policy would be replaced by an experiment, only partially announced, with an impractical if geographically plausible Franco-Russian combination of power. Turkey and Persia could have seen themselves, had they known the secret details, as mere pawns in a hemispheric game played by emperor and tsar.

It is common knowledge that at the Tilsit conference Emperor Napoleon I concluded with Tsar Alexander I the most significant of his many diplomatic undertakings. The principals and their advisers spent several days in discussion, from June 23 to July 12, 1807. They interspersed their secret negotiations with troop maneuvers, reviewing, and elaborate dining. With an abruptness unusual in peace settlements in those days, France and Russia entered states of both peace and alliance. Their failure to admit Vahid Effendi to the talks was explained by Talleyrand as arising from Turkey's failure to sign a military alliance with France, but the true explanation might have been found in the new situation in the north, and in Turkey's declining to give France carte blanche to stipulate the terms. The official news from Constantinople received on July 2 and 4, as we have seen, revealed the deposal of Sultan Selim III late in May. These dispatches could not reveal Turkey's foreign policy, however, for at first the new sultan had none. The anti-French phases of the revolution thus supplied Napoleon with a convenient excuse for casting Turkey aside in favor of the larger profits to be derived from coöperation with Russia.

Victorious Napoleon and defeated Alexander held their most famous secret conference during the afternoon of June 27, on a raft moored in the Niemen. Their associates left them to themselves after dinner that evening. On following days the two rulers eluded their advisers for lesser periods. The King of Prussia, who had not been invited to participate in the meeting, waited in the rain on the shore during the three-hour conference of the 27th. Then and there emperor and tsar settled the broad outlines of the policy of peace and alliance, leaving the details to their subordinates. They would accept peace and an alliance between themselves. In addition, France and Prussia would come to terms, on the basis of an appreciable diminution of Frederick William III's territory.

During the discussions Alexander unsuccessfully sought to achieve a solution of various territorial and strategic problems in the Balkans and at the Straits. Napoleon did not wish to go to this extreme. Having accepted the tsar as his principal ally, however, he encouraged the Russian ruler's hope of a later partition of the Ottoman Empire. When the subject of partition was once again broached during the following February, Alexander recognized in the discussion "the language of Tilsit." Napoleon revealed the same significant afterthought, in cautious instructions to Ambassador Caulaincourt, dated November, 1807. The two emperors, Napoleon at that time admitted, had agreed at Tilsit to take no action respecting a partition of the Ottoman Empire until an understanding should be reached at a later meeting for that specific purpose, in Paris or elsewhere.[17] No one knows the exact nature of their confidences in the personal conferences of June 27 and later. Enough can be deduced from their secret negotiations early in 1808, however (chap. xiii), and from the events that transpired as a result of the conference, to indicate that they frankly debated an eventual and at least partial partition of the Ottoman Empire. They discussed the strategic importance of the Straits and in passing considered France's emerging territorial ambitions in Balkan Europe.

Napoleon immediately perceived that Russia had designs on the Straits, and he retired into impassive silence. Hence the new allies stipulated in the Franco-Russian treaty that if Turkey refused to make peace (no specific terms being prescribed in advance) it must lose most of its Balkan provinces. It would be permitted to retain only Constantinople and Rumelia, the hinterland of the Straits. It was Napoleon who contended that the discussion of a partition should await developments. He desired a state of general peace as a prerequisite to further parleying, since he planned to put an end to his own war with England as well as Alexander's war with Turkey. The two nations might reciprocally assist each other to the achievement of conditions of peace.

The suggestion of a partition of the Ottoman Empire was no new concept either to the Russians or the French. Napoleon simply added the idea of a possible partition to his general policy, and to his own territorial plans. Significantly, several times he had often emphasized to the tsar the idea that whereas bordering states are permanently hostile, permanent natural friendship exists between geographically noncontiguous states. He said that if friendship were to persist, the French and Russian frontiers must never touch. Other powers must always stand between them, especially in the Balkans. Alexander admitted the logic of this argument, adopted it, and later reminded Napoleon of it. He did not wish to stand too near Napoleon's military might again.

A prime point of encouragement to the tsar was Napoleon's unhesitating agreement to the principle that the Ottoman Empire had not long to live, a probability to which the provincial revolts alone pointed. News of the palace revolt at Constantinople more than amply confirmed the speculation. Months later, Alexander confided to General Caulaincourt that news of the revolt had caused Napoleon at Tilsit to be as convinced of that inevitable conclusion as was Alexander himself; and Russia long had held that point of view. The news could not have come more opportunely than in early July to bring Napoleon and Alexander to the common opinion.

The change of sultans at Constantinople and the overthrow of Selim gave Napoleon a twofold advantage for his altered policy. He now possessed a pretext to abandon Turkey, as well as an excuse for requiring Russia to await further news before carrying on a detailed discussion of the precise terms of succession to the Ottoman territories. Dispatches from Sebastiani at the time reported noticeably anti-French overtones; yet Napoleon considered general peace rather than partition to be the chief issue. If a partition of Turkey were arranged, Britain by virtue of its naval power would inevitably seize the lion's share. As a preliminary to an agreement calling for general peace, therefore, the two emperors agreed in writing upon a double mediation. Russia must encourage and mediate an Anglo-French peace; France must work for peace between Russia and Turkey. Each ally pledged to take the other's part in continuing the struggle, moreover, if either Britain or Turkey, or both, rejected the proffered peace.

Evidently the Russo-Persian war was little discussed. Napoleon doubtless had been convinced by the arguments of Jaubert and Outrey that this conflict was of minor importance. No Persian was on hand to demand and be denied a hearing. Napoleon later excused his lack of consideration for Shah Feth Ali, his most recent ally, by stating the obvious fact that it had not as yet been physically possible to ratify the alliance. Russia could and did contend that the agreed mediation related only to Turkey and England, and not to Persia.

One might argue that the failure of the Tilsit bargainers to make any stipulation respecting Persia of itself conceded to Russia the annexation of Georgia, provided that Russia could enforce such an action by military measures. So Persia would also be abandoned. France and Russia must obviously join their forces everywhere, or their new alliance would be meaningless. In the vital regions of the Near and Middle East, neither nation must act so as to arouse the other's suspicions—a policy to which

Napoleon rigorously adhered, to the acute exasperation of his agents in the field.

Regarding the later territorial spoils anticipated in Europe, however, the allies had to find equivalents for each other. At Tilsit and afterwards Napoleon gave Alexander considerable reason to hope that a partition of the Ottoman Empire in the Balkans might be arranged. The tsar in turn conceded to the French emperor authority to decide when the partition would be made. Both mentioned specific Balkan territory on which they had designs.

As a talking point Napoleon trumped up a palliative measure which the tsar accepted, a measure intended to influence Turkey to accept with confidence French mediation without the advantage of advance stipulations. The tsar would agree to withdraw his army from Moldavia and Wallachia during the negotiation of a Russo-Turkish treaty. As an equivalent, they stipulated Napoleon's evacuation of Prussian Silesia. When phrasing the seemingly reciprocal policy, however, Napoleon cleverly inserted a precise date for the Tsar's withdrawal and none for his own. Several months later, he was to direct his ambassador, General Caulaincourt, to read and explain that overlooked stipulation to the tsar's foreign minister.

Immediately after a crushing military defeat would be no time for a vanquished tsar to win the best possible share in an allocation of the spoils from the Ottoman Empire. Promptly after the conference, on July 24 he reminded the French emperor of the latter's statement that the Ottoman Empire could not long survive; the message was conveyed through General Savary, whom Napoleon had named to Russia as temporary *chargé de mission*, in advance of Caulaincourt. The tsar stated that when Turkey crumbled, and at a time to be specified by Napoleon, Russia would hope to win a share of the spoils.[18]

There is evidence that Napoleon at Tilsit vigorously objected to the tsar's hopes for acquisition of Constantinople. This came at a time, however, when no specific equivalent for France had been discussed. Possession of the Dardanelles and Bosporus had not been debated in detail, although in the secret sessions the French emperor repudiated any idea of conceding ownership of Constantinople to Russia. He encouraged the hope that Russia and France might some day share several of the European provinces of the Ottoman Empire, excluding Constantinople and Rumelia. One of Napoleon's private secretaries, De Meneval, described the proposed division of territory to the historian, A. Thiers, who accepted the conclusion because it was substantiated by other evidence. According to De Meneval's account, upon their return from a walk during one of the very secret conferences, the tsar and emperor kept right on talking. Napoleon asked De Meneval for a map of Turkey, and then put his finger on Constantinople. As if in reply to a demand, he shouted to Alexander, with much excitement and heedless of the fact that De Meneval was listening, "Constantinople, Constantinople, never! That is the empire of the world."[19]

Neither side proceeded so far at Tilsit as to discuss a possible division between themselves of the zone of the Straits. This principle we shall see Napoleon suggest in March, 1808, with General Caulaincourt as his spokesman. Alexander will emphatically demur (chap. xiii).

Mention was made of Russia's possible acquisition of Moldavia and Wallachia in exchange for French equivalents, and of the strategic desirability of France's possession of Albania and southern Greece. These incidental hints Napoleon quickly brushed aside with his argument that other equivalents must be found. With more urgent logic, he stressed that all the details bearing on Turkey must await a state of peace, especially the French peace with Britain, in order that the English share of the spoils might be held within reasonable bounds. If England were at peace, it would need to be given only Egypt and the Ionian Islands, smaller spoils than the British might appropriate in time of war. In this connection Austria was barely mentioned, although it was agreed that the Habsburg state might be needed to stand as a geographical and political barrier between the continent's two superpowers. So far as the Germans in general were concerned, the problems of Prussia demanded immediate solution.

From the position taken by Napoleon at Tilsit, it may be seen that Russia could never be conceded the mastery of Balkan Europe. At best it might share that region with France, if another power stood between the two as a buffer. If Austria were included in a three-way partition, the respective shares would diminish; and they would further diminish if and when England should be included. Napoleon doubtless considered it unwise to decide any details at all. Even Russia's willing concessions to France might be contested. Although from a military standpoint it was obvious that Turkey could be pushed aside, France's ability actually to occupy its assigned shares of the Ottoman Empire admitted serious question. The French share of southern Greece, for example, would inevitably be exposed to the naval arm of England which dominated the

Mediterranean. Such suppositions would become actualities if the war between France and England continued, a possibility which Napoleon seems to have taken for granted in spite of Russia's authorized role as mediator.

Of far more importance was Russia's pledge to join France, if and when Britain did not accept the proffered mediation. It was necessary only to reach the point of agreement on a general policy of alliance, which should immediately become operative through the two mediations for peace. Detailed terms affecting England and Turkey could be discussed later. Even so, Napoleon's major achievement of firmly attaching defeated Russia to his general policy must be accompanied by prospects of suitable territorial reward to the tsar. Turkey by no means represented the only available alternative. Georgia represented a bird in Russia's hand; Finland could be detached by force from Sweden. Napoleon would control Silesia, Albania, and southern Greece in exchange for equivalents. Other territories except for the Straits could be conceded also under the same principle, in order that Russian and French policy might be made so harmonious that an Anglo-Russian war would result. The principle of finding equivalents would give Napoleon a chance to invalidate Russia's gains—just as Hitler invalidated Stalin's advantages in 1939 and 1940.

Napoleon could be, and was, purposely vague respecting details for the eventual partition of the entire Ottoman Empire. From England he desired not India, but peace, and he raised no issue of equivalents that would affect India. His territorial share must come from Prussia and from Turkey. Obviously the agreement to agree later respecting a partition of Turkey represented a complete reversal of Napoleon's policy of 1806 to maintain Turkey and see it enlarged by a repossession of the Crimea. He had announced that policy to the French Senate, and he had affirmed his support of Turkey's integrity as essential to general peace. Unknown to Napoleon, Sebastiani had conceded the same point, and more, in his exchange of official notes on June 14 with Turkey's new government.

Napoleon's position as a result of the treaty was thus by no means the middle-ground position it appears with respect to his mediation between Russia and Turkey. He merely hoped that his stand could be made to appear moderate to Turkey, an interpretation which he authorized in order to avoid the charge of absolute repudiation of his publicly announced policy. If in the end the new sultan should be unwilling to arrange matters satisfactorily with Russia, what territories could be conceded the tsar? At Tilsit one concession and one only Napoleon dangled as a possibility, namely the acquisition of the Principalities, in exchange for a suitable equivalent for France. Even this solution must await the prescribed French mediation, which would follow their careful appraisal of Mustapha IV's regime. Later the new allies could consider splitting up Balkan Turkey. Napoleon's afterthought, when he learned within the same month of July that the new Ottoman council would be friendly to France, extended the claims he had made at Tilsit to demands of territories for himself in eastern Europe outside of Balkan Europe as well as within it. Specifically, he demanded Silesia from Prussia, a nation of which the tsar by the Treaty of Tilsit had required French evacuation.

Napoleon had not realized that Mustapha would be friendly. At Tilsit he was aware only of the primary fact of the palace revolution, that his recent collaborator, Sultan Selim, had been removed from power in a revolution manifesting a number of anti-French tendencies. General Savary in his memoirs apologizes for, and partially explains, Napoleon's change to Russia as an ally, probably gleaning some of his ideas in Russia immediately after Tilsit. It is not difficult to conjecture as to Napoleon's probable reasoning about July 5, 1807, at Tilsit. He required the Russian alliance in order to carry out his general European policies, especially wherever these concerned England—in matters of war, the Continental Blockade, India, the Near and Middle East. He accepted alliance with Russia as a substitute for an attempted military destruction of the Russian Empire.

Hence Napoleon even more than Turkey's enemy, Tsar Alexander, found it convenient to picture in the worst light the palace revolution. The two rulers simply could not hold the conference in session long enough to await the ultimate developments. Who knows when a revolution will end? Months might elapse before Mustapha's intentions became apparent, or before the ability of his regime to survive was known. For his purpose Napoleon could deduce enough from the new council's summary dismissal of the 500 French officers and troops, together with its order that one of the Suzzo princes, a leading member of the pro-French faction, be decapitated. Napoleon nonetheless did not thereby assume an attitude of complete indifference to the Ottoman Empire, as Savary reminds us. He always considered that empire apart from its government of a given day. He found it impossible to require a liberality by his new ally that would transcend the consideration which he himself usually accorded conquered peoples. If France retained its conquests, could Napoleon abruptly require Russia to return the Principalities, which Turkey had been unable to reconquer, or Georgia, which Persia could not regain?

Did not the accounts of Suzzo's reported execution hint, moreover, that the Turks would negotiate for peace with England? The palace revolution, together with such provincial rebellions as the Serbian, seemed to establish the concept that no one could hope any longer for a really good government in alternately lethargic and revolutionary Turkey. Could such a demoralized state offer an effective strategic counterpoise to Russia in the Black Sea? What of the "new nationalism" of the Greeks, Serbians, and Egyptians, who sought "new freedom"—to borrow still another expression from the American presidential campaign of 1912? There was much to be commended in the Greek zeal, as well as in their active trade, even if that trade did tend toward coöperation with England for wartime profits.

The disturbed conditions at Constantinople had rendered it impossible for Sebastiani to send in any encouraging reports for a fortnight after May 29. Napoleon was thus confronted at Tilsit only by the reports of the reversed fortunes of the sultan in whom he had placed full confidence, and by the accounts of the anti-French manifestations which Sebastiani described. Further, there had long prevailed in western Europe an idea that the Turks must some day be pushed back into Asia. In advance of news of the palace revolt Napoleon had frankly accepted this idea in his opening conversations with the tsar. Thus his best policy seemed to be to make an arrangement with Russia, independently of the Turks. Russia by its geographical position menaced the Ottoman Empire, and always would menace it. No policy short of the destruction of Russia or of Turkey could change that condition, then or now. If Russia remained a major power, a condition clearly intended in the policies laid down at Tilsit, French policy might nevertheless prevent the immediate accomplishment of what might some day be a strategic eventuality—Russian domination of Constantinople and the Dardanelles. Savary, on the other hand, concludes that only from the standpoint of the historical tradition of French support of the Ottoman Empire can it be argued that Napoleon committed a great blunder in abandoning the Turks at Tilsit.[20]

Napoleon's treaties with Russia and Prussia, signed on July 7 and 9 respectively at Tilsit, sanctioned this abandonment. Russia and Prussia resigned from the allied coalition. England still remained at war with France, and Turkey with Russia. The secret terms of the Franco-Russian treaty included the secret agreement to meet again to discuss a partitioning of the Ottoman Empire. Modifying a stipulation of the non-ratified Clarke-Oubril treaty of 1806, the tsar surrendered to France all his debatable claims in and to the Ionian Islands, together with occupied Cattaro on the mainland.

For the two wars then in progress, the Anglo-French and the Russo-Turkish, there was now adopted a double mediation, Russia's for England and France's for Turkey. Russia must withdraw from the Principalities, upon the acceptance by Turkey of the recommended but virtually dictated Russo-Turkish armistice. Turkey could return to the Principalities, if ever, only after a treaty of peace should be mediated, signed, and ratified. The alliance stipulated reciprocal military assistance in two contingencies, namely the failure of either or both of the projected mediations. Before December 1 Russia must make common cause with France if England refused a prompt peace on the basis of freedom of the seas and the restitution of British conquests since 1805. France must make common cause with Russia if Turkey did not come to terms within three months. Their joint object thereupon would be to detach from the Turkish Empire everything in Balkan Turkey except the Straits and the European hinterland of the Straits. This stipulation bears exact reproduction:

If as a result of the [revolutionary] changes at Constantinople, Turkey refuses to accept the mediation of France, or if, having accepted it, no satisfactory result has come within three months from the opening of negotiations for peace, France will make common cause with Russia against the Ottoman Empire, and the two powers will come to an arrangement with each other to detach from the yoke and vexations of the Turks all the provinces of the Ottoman Empire in Europe, the city of Constantinople and the province of Rumelia excepted.[21]

Officer-grade couriers were without delay to spread the news of the treaty. All hostilities between Russia and Turkey were to cease immediately, on sea and land. The tsar had accepted Napoleon's offer to arrange a settlement "honorable and advantageous to the two empires." An armistice convention was to stipulate the mode of execution of the withdrawals by Russia and Turkey from Moldavia and Wallachia. Special stipulations governed Russia's forces quitting Cattaro and the Ionians in favor of France.

Napoleon personally directed to Talleyrand the procedure for making his new Turkish policy effective. One step would push Turkey into a dictated armistice. As negotiator Napoleon selected Adjutant Commander Guilleminot, who was to be known for years thereafter as a French expert in Turkish affairs, and who as ambassador to Constantinople in 1833 was to mediate a Turko-Egyptian peace. He must journey to General Michelson's headquarters, and also to the grand vizir's center of operations. Napoleon and Alexander hoped to keep secret the essential terms of alliance. Guilleminot would be given only the secret stipulations to which Turkey must conform, and he must urge the necessity for an immediate armistice with Michelson. Despite Russia's evacuation of the Principalities, the Ottomans must not occupy the territory until after the signing of a definitive treaty. Afterward Guilleminot must proceed to Constantinople, bearing a ciphered letter for Sebastiani which would say, "Napoleon's policy for the Ottoman Empire now wavers, being on the point of changing, although he has not yet decided." The ambassador could quote Napoleon as saying, "The best understanding existed between Russia and himself, following twenty days at Tilsit, and he hoped the friendship would be constant." Further, in spite of the pain caused Napoleon by Sultan Selim's fate, and the scant regard held for his ambassador and the French troops late in May, Sebastiani must win from the new sultan a promise of the execution of the anticipated armistice. Turkish police forces must remain on the Danube and Russia's must withdraw, with neither nation keeping an army in the Principalities. Talleyrand must notify Sebastiani privately that the Ionian Islands as well as Cattaro "had been given to Napoleon in full proprietorship." Sebastiani if possible must arrange for the return sailing through the Bosporus of four vessels of the line belonging to Russia's Black Sea fleet. This action was to be performed if it would not disturb the populace, and if the ships were guaranteed against capture by the new sultan personally by letter to Michelson, who in turn would forward it to Corfu.

There would be need in Paris for an Ottoman ambassador, one clearly authorized to accept Napoleon's mediation. Sebastiani should tell the sultan that the French emperor had been offended by the dismissal of his cannoneers, a dismissal carried out without even a notification of his ambassador. Sebastiani should testify, if possible, to Napoleon's interest in Selim, but in this connection was to say nothing that might hasten the regal prisoner's death. Sebastiani might chide Sultan Mustapha, emphasizing his foolhardiness in failing to write Napoleon, the sole protector of the Ottoman Empire. Manifestly the Turks could not have resisted Russia without Napoleon's protection. "I still remain the friend of Turkey," Sebastiani could quote the emperor, "but I have become a friend of Russia again." One must always seek means of conciliation, he continued, avoiding any issues that might irritate and exasperate the nations concerned.

Talleyrand must notify Vahid Effendi in Warsaw of the peace and of the fact that Turkey had been included. The foreign minister must touch but lightly on Napoleon's dissatisfaction with the scant attention accorded Sebastiani by the new Ottoman administration, and with "the disgraceful release of his cannoneers." Sebastiani must positively send all the cannoneers and other French troops back to Dalmatia. As it transpired, only Juchereau de Saint-Denys remained. The subservient Talleyrand by July 12 could report his issuance of all these orders.[22]

Such is Napoleon's own restricted statement of his policies and in some measure deceptive procedures immediately after Tilsit. Neither the conversations nor the written agreements with Alexander had specified the title under which the French would hold the Ionian Islands. Chief of Staff General Berthier wished to exercise all the rights of French sovereignty, but Napoleon contented himself with the appointment of an imperial commissioner. This divergence of opinion in part explains the lack of full information for Sebastiani. No matter what the restrictions, the fact was that Napoleon's forces occupied the Ionian Islands, ending the unpopular, really unilateral but nominally Russo-Turkish military control there. We may note here that France succeeded with difficulty in holding Corfu as late as 1814, whereas the remainder of the islands gradually fell to the British fleet. Napoleon's immediate task would be to provision Corfu. According to the treaty, Cattaro simply had been "turned over to French troops." As a sample of the usual method for notifying Turkey, we have Napoleon's letter of July 9 to Ali Pasha of Albania, who had reacted favorably to flattery by Napoleon's consul general in Albania, Poqueville, and other official Frenchmen. He had written a friendly letter to Napoleon, and the emperor acknowledged from Tilsit the proffered friendship with the statement that he would welcome any further communication. His generals had been ordered to cooperate with Ali Pasha. Peace existed between France and Russia and Turkey had been included in the treaty.[23]

The Emperor of France ruminated soon after the conference. Had he been too hasty in agreeing to evacuate Silesia? He believed he had been, this conclusion actually opening the subsequent debate with Russia that connected Silesia with Russia's policy for the Principalities. A mention of Silesia nearly always suggests the general problems of the Germanies. The treatment of the Germans after their defeat was a problem Napoleon faced over and over again. King Frederick William III had not been consulted when Napoleon and Alexander negotiated the basic provisions of the Franco-Prussian treaty as well as their own. Of Napoleon's threefold solution for the Germans, the policy of "divide and rule" was most important. By this policy the regional, detached organization of the Germans was effected. Austria and Prussia were diminished in size, and kept separated; most of the Rhineland states were organized under Napoleon's own supervision. His second plan depended upon a reconstituted Polish state, friendly to France in consequence of its isolated location to the east of the Germans. The fact that Poland, like Turkey, was through its geographical position also an enemy of Russia, suited his plans admirably. In order to keep the Duchy of Warsaw friendly and Prussia weak, the emperor decided that French forces must remain in Silesia. An historical similarity was the relatively slight diminution of Germany in 1918 and France's alliances with Poland and Czechoslovakia following the First World War. The fate of Napoleon's third solution, to limit the German armies numerically, could have taught the world long ago that this policy would never work. He tried that method by the treaty of 1807, only to discover that Prussian armies were a great factor in his ultimate defeat. Ignoring the futility of that solution, the victors of 1918 attempted it again.

Marshal Berthier and Prince Rostov issued a joint memorandum, as follows, ordering the Russian vessels of war in Ionian waters to return to the Black Sea:

[Russia's] Black Sea vessels are to remain at Corfu unless the commandants prefer, for private reasons, to sail either to Venice or to a Neapolitan port. There they are to await a letter from the French ambassador at Constantinople, who will inform them whether he has been able to obtain permission for them to pass [the Straits] to the Black Sea. Whatever the coastal point at which this squadron may elect to touch, it must always remain within reach of coast batteries and secure from surprise by sea, whether by the Turks or by the English.[24]

In spite of the decisions at Tilsit, Russian forces in August did not wish to evacuate Cattaro and Corfu. Nonetheless, the Corfu garrison of some 4,840 officers and men, together with four frigates and several transports, left and went north to Venice in September. The Russian commander apparently disliked the French orders. He sailed away to Trieste, disregarding the wishes of the local commandant; but he was ordered back by Prince Eugene, the viceroy of Italy, in a letter written September 24. These allied forces were given everything they needed in Venice and Padua, Napoleon reported to General Savary on October 6. Admiral Seniavin invented pretexts to delay for several weeks his sailing from Corfu.[25]

Russians could presume that Napoleon's recall of his officers and men from Constantinople represented the results of a deal made at Tilsit, with France winning everything Russia claimed in the Ionian Islands and Cattaro. Actually, the recall was primarily face-saving and confirmatory, after the revolutionists had themselves canceled the request for French troops. That Russia would surrender the Ionians partly satisfied Napoleon's pique at Turkey's anti-French demonstrations. Talleyrand wrote for Sebastiani's private information that the emperor's disposition toward Turkey had been altered only by events. Turkey must if possible be restrained from veering toward the British side. If the proposed mediation did not succeed, however, the Russians intended to renew the war. An armistice alone represented the safe exit for the now somewhat confused French policy for Turkey. Negotiations for a definitive peace could be delayed by the mediator, while an armistice for a time would serve as a smoke screen. Russia already had accepted Napoleon's mediation. By implication, Sebastiani might argue, this acceptance could work to Turkey's advantage. About all the nonplused Ottoman negotiator in Warsaw could do, so Talleyrand frankly told Vahid, was to await new instructions. This stalemate ended all genuine attempts by Caulaincourt or others to arrange a Franco-Turkish alliance.[26]

The record has revealed in this chapter that France left revolutionary Turkey at war with Russia at the moment when it made peace and alliance with the tsar at Tilsit. Meanwhile, Turkey had declined to enter an alliance with Napoleon against Great Britain. Hence, after Tilsit, no argument for a joint Franco-Turkish war against England could be calculated to be successful. By mediating the stipulated Ottoman armistice with Russia, France retained at least one means of holding Turkey's friendship for a while longer and perhaps of retarding an Ottoman understanding with England.

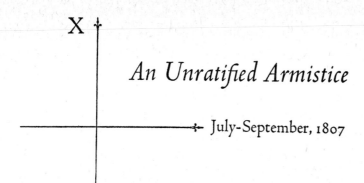

An Unratified Armistice

⊱ July-September, 1807

FROM THE MOMENT of his alliance with Russia at Tilsit, Napoleon's former policies for Turkey and Persia embarrassed him. Having sought alliances in the Near and Middle East against Russia, he had now allied himself with Alexander, the enemy of Turkey and Persia. He sought to appease the tsar while encouraging his Turkish and Persian friends to support his campaign against Great Britain. France's secret policy of alliance with Russia was not immediately revealed in the Levant. There, Napoleon's agents attempted (until the end of General Horace Sebastiani's ambassadorship in 1808) to continue the antecedent policy of alliance with Turkey. Thus, paradoxically, Napoleon for several months escaped most of the effects of his new policy of leaving these friends in the lurch.

The news of late August, 1807, revealed each region as not knowing what was happening in the other. In this chapter we shall see the Russo-Turkish armistice signed at Slobosia castle, on the Danube. Britain's Arthur Paget waited for a Turkish hearing near the Dardanelles, where Russia's blockade continued in effect. Paris reconsidered its new policy for Turkey, in the light of Sebastiani's clarification that Ottoman foreign policy still was pro-French despite the palace revolution and the new sultan; Napoleon considered it possible to retain Turkey's good will. Antoine Gardane assembled his mission to Teheran, although his original instructions now seemed to lack clarity in consequence of Napoleon's alliance with Russia, the terms of which were not fully revealed to him. Meanwhile, Teheran enthusiastically counted on French help against Russia. Official Turks fell back on Napoleon, whose military prowess transcended mere policy. The Turks believed Sebastiani's mid-June promises in their behalf and expected to be extricated from their ill-advised war against Russia. London used the Franco-Russian peace to solicit Turkey's friendship anew, seeking a good opportunity to evacuate Alexandria. It took no unnecessary chances, however, either with France or Russia. It sought to learn the secret stipulations of Tilsit. Britain sent Hartford Jones to Teheran to negotiate, and launched a preventive naval attack against pro-Napoleonic Denmark. The Russo-Turkish conferees at Slobosia congratulated themselves on handling a difficult assignment expeditiously. Turkish amenability gave Ambassador Sebastiani better spirits.

On July 9 at Tilsit, Napoleon and Alexander ratified their alliance. French and Russian officers were dispatched promptly on a hot weather journey to the Danube. Napoleon commissioned Adjutant Commander Guilleminot to accompany Serge Lazarev, a Russian officer, to the headquarters of the grand vizir and General Michelson. They must urge the Turks to an immediate armistice with Russia and thus fulfill the expectation—virtually a demand—of Napoleon and Alexander. Guilleminot seems to have been given the principal duties—obvious since France would be the mediator. He would deliver letters explaining his mission and notifying the commanders of the decision of the two emperors—that Russo-Turkish hostilities would cease whenever Turkey adhered to the Franco-Russian arrangement and accepted Napoleon's mediation for the definitive peace. It was not supposed that Turkey, so recently weakened by revolt, could refuse the proffered armistice.[1]

Guilleminot regarded his mission as more military than diplomatic. He took lightly the direction to proceed to Constantinople afterward, and there deliver the carefully penned instructions to Sebastiani. Napoleon counted upon the ambassador and Guilleminot to argue through to a parallel conclusion in Constantinople the decision adopted at military headquarters. Guilleminot as the friend of both belligerents could preside over the negotiations for an armistice or a treaty of peace. Afterward he must return to General Michelson's headquarters to follow through the local arrangements necessary for carrying out the stipulations.

A final three-hour visit between Napoleon and Alexander preceded their departure from Tilsit. Among other things they without doubt agreed to head their foreign ministries with men in full sympathy with the new alliance. Restoring diplomatic and consular relations between France and Russia constituted routine business. Talleyrand advised Foreign Minister Budberg that Consul General Barthélemy de Lesseps would return to serve also as chargé d'affaires for a time. On July 11, before leaving Tilsit, Napoleon called into conference General A. J. M. R. Savary. To the latter's surprise he was appointed interim envoy to Russia, with the title of *chargé de mission*. The emperor outlined Savary's instructions verbally, but withheld a copy of the secret alliance of Tilsit. Napoleon said that he desired peace with every nation and that the point must be stressed. He anticipated that Silesia would represent the only immediate issue with Russia. Savary might throw out the suggestion that the French ruler never gave anything back; specifically, that he intended to keep his forces in Prussia, for one reason to enforce the payment of the indemnity authorized by the new Franco-Prussian treaty. Savary must express the need for a good Russian ambassador in Paris. Talleyrand was directed to issue instructions respecting the details of other current business. If we accept Savary's later account, that constitutes the entire story. Napoleon said nothing of Turkey—indeed nothing of any details at all except the continuance of his troops in Silesia. France began immediately to evacuate the Niemen, but not the Prussian provinces.[2]

Napoleon departed for Paris. Within a few days he knew he had acted too hastily in interpreting pessimistically the Ottoman palace revolt of May 29, even though it had offered a good pretext for reversing his policy of alliance with Turkey. Sebastiani's dispatch of June 9 detailed the aftermath to the overthrow of Sultan Selim III. (Napoleon's staff deciphered this dispatch at Königsberg on July 12, on their way home.) Sebastiani revealed that the revolt against Selim had been put over by the ulema, together with the janissaries. The native-born Mohammedans had entrenched themselves in power, the individual behind the throne being the mufti of Constantinople. That superior ecclesiastical official had been long recognized as the chief interpreter, sometimes virtually the dictator, of Mohammedan law. The new foreign minister, Halet Effendi, could be presumed to be a friend of France because he had been ambassador to Paris. He, like all the rest, took orders from the mufti. For a time the government was entirely under control of the ulema. For some fourteen months thereafter that group was successful in the age-old conflict for control of the state, against the recruited Mohammedan "slave family." Many other factors were involved in 1807, among them ambitions of military leaders and the activities of several military cliques such as the janissaries in conflict with the ordinary troops in the quest for power or influence.

When on June 8 Sebastiani conferred with Halet and also with a chief of the ulema, it became clear that Turkey's foreign policy would not change. Sebastiani reported this in that dispatch; but Napoleon knew it five days too late to affect the stipulations signed with Russia on July 7. We remind ourselves that, owing to slow communications, these events at Constantinople could take no account of the significant military and political developments in the north of Europe since Napoleon's victory at Friedland on June 14. That Constantinople as yet knew nothing of the conference at Tilsit added significance to Halet's announcement of the continued pro-French policy.

Other good news for Sebastiani to report included reactions to Mehemet Ali's victory over the British in breaking their siege of Rosetta. On May 22 for the first time the Turks revealed themselves as unafraid to challenge Admiral Seniavin's blockading squadron. Turkey won a naval skirmish against Russia off the Dardanelles; both squadrons withdrew after several hours of ineffective firing. Sebastiani cited numerous physical manifestations that no change as yet had marked Ottoman foreign policy. The Ottoman fleet still guarded the Dardanelles against the watchful Russians. An official communique recounted an advance by the grand vizir's army from Bucharest toward the Russians. The proof of French favoritism included a decree by the new sultan prohibiting English commerce anywhere within the Ottoman states.[3]

Russians near Constantinople used the revolution almost immediately as a means of attempting to make peace with Turkey. Pozzo di Borgo—at this time a colonel of the army—addressed such an appeal to Halet on June 9, from his station on board Seniavin's flagship anchored at Tenedos. The Ottomans refused, their general policy being to allow themselves to be lured into further coöperation with France by the prospect of recovering the Crimea. Sultan Mustapha did not in the least suspect Napoleon's reversal of policy and virtual abandonment of Turkey. Turks of all parties counted on Napoleon's interest and consideration in a general pacification. This suggested a means whereby to respond to Pozzo. The note, prepared by Halet and altered by the mufti, was withheld until June 28. In carefully studied language it notified Russia that Turkey could negotiate only at a general peace conference. Vahid Effendi had been given such authority to negotiate. The note further stated that the Turks were remembering Russia's recent invasion of the Principalities, its move into the Ionian Islands, and its conquest of Georgia.[4]

All along the journey—through Dresden and back to Paris on July 31—Napoleon could reflect. Would Russia actually become his fighting ally against England? Would the undecided details respecting the Ottoman Empire bar the way, especially his denial of the Straits to the tsar? Must he in the end fight Russia to save the Dardanelles? Why had he not discounted the palace revolution? How could he overcome Turkey's obvious reluctance to surrender the Principalities to Russia? What of Persia? Would it not be better to send no new instructions to Gardane at all, thereby through uncertainty to cloud every issue to his own advantage? Would Turkey enter a shooting war against England? Would it even retain its "cold war" policy? How soon must he commit himself to Russia respecting a transfer of the Principalities? The longer he held off, the more chance there was of Russia's joining him against England.

Could suitable substitutes be found for Russia's ownership of the Straits? Perhaps he could offer Finland, the Principalities, Georgia, and the potential profits from a joint expedition to India. What of Austria's policy in general and of its bearing on Turkey's provinces in the Balkans? As for Prussia, should he not have withheld any agreement to evacuate Silesia? Nevertheless, he could thereby test the Russian alliance, and even profit from it. Perhaps he had the means to keep his troops in Silesia, despite his promise to evacuate Prussia. There were the unpaid indemnity and the clever treaty wording that set no date for his withdrawal. Somehow, he must escape the manifold implications—mostly adverse to him—of a specific application of an obviously contradictory policy for Turkey. His former policy had now been modified in all its essentials; going back to it assuredly would alienate Russia. If he agreed on the one hand to abandon the Principalities to Russia and at the same time sought to save them for a possibly well-behaved Turkey, no one would know what to believe. He must procrastinate, which he could readily do as the mediator. His assurance that he still considered the Ottoman Empire a friend undoubtedly would be taken with reservations at Constantinople.

Tsar Alexander must have realized after Tilsit how much had been left unsaid. Respecting the Ottoman Empire as a whole he had won only an agreement to agree later. Concerning Constantinople and the Straits, he and Napoleon had merely declared anew their strategic importance— and left them to Turkey. In order to possess the Principalities he must discover a "suitable" equivalent for France. Presumably this could be uncovered in the Balkans—although Napoleon had vouchsafed no encouragement to his first suggestion of Albania and the Morea. Indeed, Napoleon had kept the initiative for interpreting the approaching dissolution of Turkey. Napoleon's forces must at least evacuate Silesia.

The student of history may reflect on the importance of interpreting in advance the presumed collapse of Turkey. No power then or since ever permitted Russia to have its way. The plan of 1807 to concert later in some sort of enforced partition of Turkey, moreover, foretold the similar agreement between Russia's Tsar Nicholas I and three British statesmen in 1844, namely Aberdeen, Peel, and Wellington. Both agreements left the date for the fall of Turkey unstated; like the Napoleonic understanding, that of 1844 failed when really tested. Two factors account for failure: (1) no agreement concerning the date to apply the accepted principle of partition, and (2) no agreement respecting the distribution of specific territories. The first agreement failed in 1808, the other in 1853. The ultimate failure to agree on the time and details eventually led to war, in 1812 and again in 1854, between the collaborators. The secret debates between Russia and Great Britain from 1844 to 1854 paralleled to a remarkable degree those between Russia and France from 1807 to 1812. In both cases, Russia was refused the Straits. The problem continues today, the United States being the newcomer to the group of nations restricting Russia's action.

The revolution at Constantinople, and also, but more especially, the Franco-Russian alliance caused the collapse of Napoleon's scheme for a considerable French army to march across Balkan Turkey to the Dniester. Those factors likewise terminated the unworkable plan to sail a French squadron into the Black Sea. There could be no Franco-Turkish alliance against Russia. Nor, in all probability, could there be one against England. Napoleon no longer needed Turkish and Persian diversions against Russia; hence they could no longer count on support from him to regain respectively the Crimea and Georgia—if indeed he ever really intended to aid them. The subsequent events suggest his private arrangement with the tsar to abandon most of his highly successful diplomacy in both Turkey and Persia in exchange for Russia's surrender of the Ionian Islands and Cattaro.

Napoleon's deceit toward Turkey eventually caused the eclipse of influence of the successful Sebastiani, at whose behest the Turks had declared war against Russia late in December, 1806 (chap. vi). For months after Tilsit neither he nor the Turks could believe what had happened there. When they gradually learned the details, his and their disappointment became all the more appalling. In order to assure Turkey's unswerving loyalty to Napoleon's anti-Russian and anti-English causes he had recommitted France to a pro-Turkish policy in mid-June. He renewed his strong pledges of support as late as July 18. He had pledged the fair treatment of Turkey in the peace as the natural corollary of his pledges made during war. No one at the French embassy then suspected a sudden Franco-Russian treaty of peace; Sebastiani had had no chance to learn of it when he so committed France.

News of the startling Franco-Russian armistice (signed on June 22) was revealed at Constantinople on July 18. Anger at the Turkish military front on the Danube could be given expression concretely: the grand vizir arrested the French courier expediting the news, an aide-de-camp of General Savary. Any French armistice not mentioning the Turks caused them "great disquietude." Although Sebastiani as yet possessed no official information of this, it was specifically demanded of him whether Napoleon would intervene in Turkey's behalf in the forthcoming Franco-Russian treaty. Would Napoleon do so without the concurrence of Vahid Effendi—whose powers admittedly were not very extensive? Must Turkey negotiate separately? Sebastiani could not, and did not, answer these questions satisfactorily. He assured the Turks, however, that Napoleon would not sign a treaty that neglected to guarantee the independence and integrity of their empire. He thus used the formula which Napoleon accepted in the Clarke-Oubril treaty of 1806. Such a personal assurance did not fully suffice. Halet wrote an appeal to Talleyrand for Napoleon's good will in negotiating with Vahid Effendi. The latter's instructions alternatively concerned either an alliance or a general treaty of peace. The new sultan appealed to Napoleon, whom he took care to salute as "Emperor and Padishah of France." He wished Sebastiani's promise fulfilled to uphold the integrity of Ottoman territory.[5] Pozzo di Borgo and Paget, each with authority in hand to negotiate, rendered Sebastiani's position increasingly difficult. Stationed at the Dardanelles, both clamored for a hearing; they said they waited with "great offers"—disquieting Turkey even more. Sebastiani admitted to Talleyrand that never since coming to Constantinople had he faced a problem as difficult as this. He even lacked information (delayed in consequence of the arrest of the French courier).[6]

Nor could Teheran understand the change in Napoleon's policy, revealed when Gardane finally arrived there in December. No one in Teheran, far away in distance and in information, in July supposed the anticipated Franco-Persian alliance—signed only on May 4—would be stillborn. French headquarters had announced nothing respecting Persia immediately after Tilsit. Talleyrand hesitated to notify that monarchy of the new policy, for Persia probably would be needed against England. Obviously, however, the laboriously achieved beginnings of a comprehensive French policy of alliance with Persia must end, and give way to the newer policy of alliance with Russia—for the tsar and the shah were at war.

Gardane had not yet left Vidin—en route to Teheran back in July —before the first essential object of his mission had disappeared, namely to hold Persia effectively at war with Russia. Gardane knew immediately of the peace of Tilsit but not of its details. Talleyrand wrote him (on July 20, 1807) that he would advise later fully how the Franco-Russian peace might more directly concern the minister's duties in Persia. Even in the absence of better information, this dispatch meant that Gardane must proceed to Persia—whatever his duty might be after arrival. Also on July 20, Shah Feth Ali remitted to the French a long letter addressed to Emperor Napoleon, his new ally. Joannin translated it and La Blanche carried it. The shah stated that heaven willed the impossibility of any alteration or rupture of the Franco-Persian alliance and that the beautiful Franco-Persian friendship would be as "a garden, where reigned eternal spring."[7]

Before the news of Tilsit, Ottoman military officers had begun to take the Franco-Turkish alliance for granted, together with its implied joint effort with Persia against Russia. There is Yousef Pasha, generalissimo of the army of Asia, who wrote the French ambassador at Constantinople as late as September 2—apparently not yet crediting a Russo-Turkish armistice. He promised to concert with the Persians in a big offensive against Russia.[8]

The Franco-Russian armistice at a time they were negotiating for an alliance with Napoleon aroused Turkish anger. Later in July the grand vizir revealed his ire: he considered Turkey left to the mercy of Russia and frankly said so. According to him, this proved that Turkish confidence in Napoleon had been greatly misplaced.

The expected anti-French reactions eventually materialized in the Principalities and the Barbary Regencies, and in the Ottoman Empire generally. The ill feeling for France mounted each day at Constantinople. Sebastiani privately despaired of accomplishing anything further. On August 9 he expressed gloomily to Talleyrand the opinion that "the Turkish Empire seemed nearer to ruin than ever." He cited the virtually independent pashas, the insufficient governmental revenues, and the demobilizing army of the grand vizir. Turkey's ministers openly expressed themselves as no longer bound to France, for Napoleon had broken his engagements to them.[9]

The Turks all but overplayed their feigning of abused innocence. Sebastiani on August 21 reassured them with respect to the integrity of Ottoman territory. He stated again that Napoleon would make no peace with Russia which did not guarantee their independence and integrity. The Turkish ministers rejoined that they still expected an alliance with France in advance of a general settlement. They objected, however, to several provisions of Talleyrand's draft of the Franco-Turkish alliance. They remarked on the probability that the projected commercial stipulations would lead to further disputes between Turkey and England.[10] The situation eased somewhat only after Sebastiani eventually received the instructions from Tilsit to assure the Turks of Napoleon's personal friendship for them and to convey his offer to mediate the final peace.

General Savary appeared in St. Petersburg promptly on July 23. His first conversations and reports upon arrival were not very enlightening; they revealed inadequate information about the secret conversations at Tilsit. Two days before he came, they repealed the decree against the some 700 Frenchmen resident in Russia which Kochubei had countersigned on December 10, 1806. This represented a concrete application of the Treaty of Tilsit. Savary perceived his acceptance as a military man but not as a diplomat; he would be considered only as a general and aide-de-camp of the French emperor. He sensed immediately, however, that the alliance by no means solved all the French problems, owing to English influence within Russia's governing aristocracy. He averred that a well-chosen French ambassador would be the best way to counter or to silence this. Certainly it would be a mistake for him to remain there long in his admittedly temporary capacity. A simple *chargé de mission* could not reflect Napoleonic power before the Russian people. He reported Austria's ambassador, Maximilian Merveldt, to be the most pro-British individual he had encountered.

Savary in the first interview conveyed Napoleon's suggestion that pro-French Count Rumiantsov be named the tsar's ambassador to Paris. The tsar hinted that his minister of commerce would be given important additional cares soon.

The tsar lost no time in stating to Savary his preoccupation with the unfinished business of Tilsit. He issued an overture to his ally respecting the Ottomans. He recalled that Napoleon had talked discouragingly of the continued existence of the Turkish Empire; that had given him reason to hope. "I avow," Alexander stated, "that if Turkey does crumble one day, Russia's position makes us hope to inherit a share of the spoils. Napoleon gave me understanding upon this head and I leave it entirely to him when he shall consider the moment arrived."[11] He gained the distinct impression of some personal arrangement at Tilsit whereby France had abandoned Turkey in exchange for a free hand elsewhere, perhaps in Spain. Years afterwards, when writing his memoirs, he still held that opinion.

Savary remained in St. Petersburg during the second half of 1807, the honeymoon of the Franco-Russian alliance. All his communications to Russia proved pleasant. Russia also made things agreeable for him personally by showering upon him such attentions as frequent invitations to dine with Tsar Alexander.

He liked De Lesseps. If the length of his first two dispatches from St. Petersburg is any indication, the consul general took his restored position seriously. In these (of August 19 and 22) he commented on the varied attitudes of members of the tsar's cabinet, these generally contrasting with the quite favorable disposition toward Napoleon held by Alexander himself. Foreign Minister Budberg assured De Lesseps that there had been nothing personal in the circumstances that forced the latter's departure the previous year. Budberg frankly expected opposition to the alliance with France from Russians "who had not yet caught up with the rapidity of events." However, he stated, the tsar sincerely desired the new alliance. He wished Frenchmen to have free access to Russia—all whose interests or commerce commanded it.

Tsar Alexander personally expressed to De Lesseps the same general sentiments, adding that he "had spent some precious moments" with Napoleon at Tilsit; he would never forget the French emperor's wise counsel. He intended to mediate a settlement of the Anglo-French war, and he would not permit himself to be intimidated by the British squadron reported in the Baltic with an unannounced object. De Lesseps liked Rumiantsov. He found the aged minister of commerce always seeming to favor France. Budberg, on the contrary, formerly had been a partisan of the Anglo-Russian concert.[12]

News from the north rapidly deflated Turkey's plans. The fact of a Franco-Russian armistice of itself bespoke caution, and a change in Ottoman demands could be noted as the days passed. As late as June 14—with Napoleon known to be marching toward victory—official thought had turned to regaining the Crimea. Upon news of the armistice, the Ottomans seemed willing to settle with the tsar if allowed to retain only Moldavia and Wallachia. This change was illustrated by the foreign minister's letter to Talleyrand on July 25—based on news dated up to June 22—in which he said they still counted on Napoleon to help them uphold their independence and their existing territory.[13] Sebastiani that day had a new report from Vice-consul Mechain at the Dardanelles. This stated that a British squadron of seven vessels had joined the Russians, its object being to help obtain a hearing for Arthur Paget. A few days later Mechain reported positively that the Russians and British were negotiating with the Turks to arrange conferences for peace.[14]

Only on August 21 did Sebastiani receive Talleyrand's instructions addressed to him from Tilsit on July 9. Colonel Guilleminot had at length forwarded these by another officer, he himself remaining on the Danube. Sebastiani then assumed a more cheerful attitude. Upon being assured of Napoleon's mediation at Paris, the Turks indicated they would adhere to whatever stipulations of the Franco-Russian treaty concerned them. At this point, August 25, Paris reacted cautiously to the dispatches received at Königsberg on July 12, indicating that Turkey would be friendly to France. Talleyrand suggested that Sebastiani seek to hold intact all the good will he had built up in Turkey.[15]

Turkish affairs inevitably were connected with those of the Baltic, the other end of a giant arc around southern and western Europe. During the summer Britain too late dispatched a land force of 10,000 men there as a diversion against Napoleon's flank or rear. The force entered just as peace came at Tilsit, however, and hence it affected Swedish rather than Russian policy. The British remained, while the French threatened their communications. Napoleon demanded that Denmark close the Sound and the Belts against the British fleet. Britain, determined to send a squadron to support Sweden, demanded Denmark's opening of the Sound (July 16). On July 28, it instructed the fleet's commander to sail to Kiel, to demand an explicit statement of policy from the Danish prince royal. The policy must be one of alliance with Britain, attested by the surrender of Denmark's fleet for the duration.

The initial British reaction to the Treaty of Tilsit tended toward acceptance of a general pacification in duplication of the policy followed in 1801. In advance of precise information of the details secretly arranged at Tilsit, Foreign Secretary George Canning reacted favorably to the idea of general peace. On August 4, however, he directed Lord Gower to demand that he be informed of any secret stipulations.[16] Whatever its terms (which Gower soon discovered to be quite secret), the fact of peace must of itself obviously change Britain's cold-war policy for Turkey. A withdrawal from Alexandria might serve to restore Turkey's collaboration. Upon news of the Franco-Russian settlement, therefore—so Canning wrote Paget—there no longer seemed any reason for the Anglo-Turkish war; Britain favored friendship. Paget must convince the sultan's ministers of the danger inherent in a Franco-Russian alignment. Britain as a friendly gesture would withdraw from Egypt.[17]

France and Russia felt that they must notify all the world of their alliance—although not by revealing its much sought, strictly secret, terms. The new orientation of general policies could be heralded by new personalities at their foreign offices—policies always having a way of being linked with the directing personnel. Napoleon took the first move by appointing Count J. B. M. Champagny on August 9 as foreign minister. Upstairs went the pro-Turkish, pro-Austrian, faithful Talleyrand, elevated to the dignity of vice-grand elector of the empire. That honorable and lucrative sinecure permitted him the life of a grand dignitary, third in rank in the list of the great dignitaries. Napoleon could always call him back into service for anything intended to outwit Russia—as we shall see him doing preparatory to the conference at Erfurt in September, 1808 (chap. xv).

Champagny proved a mere figurehead as foreign minister. His first dispatch to General Savary (August 26) sharply criticized the latter's initial report from St. Petersburg. He said Napoleon desired complete details, whereas Savary had written only generalities. Savary debated this, whereas General Caulaincourt, his successor (appointed in November), interpreted the order as Napoleon's desire to have supplied almost stenographic reports of everything the tsar said.[18] Savary perceived gradual changes favorable for France in the attitudes of official Russians. By the end of August, Baron Budberg came over completely to the French side. Count Kochubei of the Ministry of the Interior—once ambassador to Turkey—for a time still manifested anti-French dispositions. Of the foreign diplomats, Ambassador Gower obviously promoted English interests and Austria's Ambassador Merveldt repeatedly revealed himself as pro-English.[19]

Budberg remained in office only until the tsar could select his successor, for Alexander, as well as Napoleon, marked his new policy by changing foreign ministers, choosing the genial, respected, sixty-eight-year-old Count Nicholas Rumiantsov. Savary joined De Lesseps in reporting the count quite friendly to France. Perhaps too frank in his comments for a foreign minister, Rumiantsov would continue as minister of commerce while heading the foreign office. Publicly Budberg attributed poor health as the reason for his retirement, announced on September 9, 1807. It was not mentioned that he had been a leading exponent of the international coalition which Napoleon had wrecked. Alexander also announced the appointment of Count Pierre Tolstoi, a lieutenant general and brother of the grand marshal of Russia, as his ambassador to Napoleon's court. The latter's military status matched that of Caulaincourt, whom Napoleon appointed ambassador to Russia in October. Tolstoi would be important in military affairs in Russia and Poland for many years after Napoleon's fall. Some weeks in 1807 elapsed before he could appear in Paris.[20]

Contrary to advance predictions, a reaction favorable for peace marked the reception of the Treaty of Tilsit at Turkish military headquarters on the Danube, in contrast with the violent opposition to the Franco-Russian armistice. The grand vizir considered the terms of the treaty revealed by Guilleminot to represent Napoleon's action as that of an ally of Turkey. On July 26 he commissioned Galib Effendi to negotiate an armistice with Serge Lazarev. After some delay to await Galib Effendi's letters of credence, Guilleminot and Lazarev met formally with the Ottoman plenipotentiaries in Slobosia castle, on August 12. The latter raised the serious issues of autonomy for Serbia and the type of provisional government to be set up for the Principalities. They manifested no disposition to negotiate with Serbian rebels and opposed a mention in the treaty of Russia's guarantee or sponsorship of the Serbians.[21]

On August 24 they duly signed the Russo-Turkish armistice of Slobosia. It stipulated the cessation of hostilities and the opening of negotiations for a definitive settlement. Even if no final agreement should be reached by April, 1808, the armistice meanwhile could not be broken. It was interpreted as quite favorable for Turkey, under the circumstances. The settlement elated all its negotiators simply because it was concluded. They agreed that a number of unsettled issues would be taken up by Napoleon as the mediator of a definitive peace—including the important territorial issue. The armistice stipulated Russia's and Turkey's evacuation of the Principalities, this to begin within thirty-five days from the signing. All the Russians would depart and the Turks would retain only token forces for police duty. Russia must evacuate

Tenedos and all other points held in the Aegean area. Russian vessels must move away from the Dardanelles, ending their blockade—"so that the passage should be in fact open and free." If Russian vessels encountered inclement weather upon sailing to their home ports, the Turks must not interfere but on the contrary aid them in every way. The ships of war and of commerce captured by both powers would be reciprocally returned.[22]

If Sebastiani could arrange for the passage of four large Russian war vessels through the Straits into the Black Sea—to return home from Tenedos and the Aegean Islands—Napoleon would interpret the concession as a friendly gesture by Turkey.[23] For the moment, the armistice seemed acceptable to the commanders in the field and both sides took steps to enforce it. General Michelson, ill during the negotiations, died two or three days after the signing. Lazarev sent a courier to his successor, General Meyendorff, who ratified the armistice in the tsar's name. This circumstance gave Alexander a pretext to disavow the pact, for General Meyendorff had been issued no such authority to act and, in fact, would be replaced by countermanding orders from St. Petersburg. On his own responsibility Meyendorff acted in good faith and began the evacuation for which only thirty-five days had been allowed. Meanwhile, Guilleminot and Lazarev believed their assigned task finished. The former considered it unnecessary to proceed to Constantinople as instructed. Guilleminot's report of August 29 detailed the proceedings. The first copy of the report went to Napoleon by French courier and the duplicate by means of an Ottoman courier who also wished to convey the news to Vahid Effendi in Paris. Guilleminot waited at Slobosia castle, to be on hand if he should be needed during the evacuation.[24]

About this time Gardane, uninformed of recent events, appeared in Constantinople bound for Persia. There, on August 26 he arranged to travel to Teheran in company with Mirza Riza, the returning Persian ambassador who had allied his shah with Napoleon in May (chap. viii). Already Gardane, like Sebastiani, sensed the misgivings evident on both sides respecting the new Franco-Persian alliance. In Paris, Foreign Minister Champagny on August 26 issued to Gardane the supplemental instructions promised by Talleyrand. Napoleon sought peace between Russia and Persia, as well as between Russia and Turkey. That the shah's alliance with France had not as yet been ratified in Teheran or Paris was offered by Champagny as the none too clever excuse for peace. Gardane might work for "an honorable peace" with Russia and for hostility toward England. Persia should eliminate all commerce and communication with England or the English East India Company. This meant, in brief, for Gardane to seek to fulfill the Franco-Persian alliance so far as it concerned England, but to ignore it with respect to Russia. Presumably Georgia could be saved for the allied tsar. On this day at Teheran, Mirza Cheffi, first vizir of the Persian Empire, addressed Talleyrand. As yet obviously unaware of the new French policy, he spoke of "some secrets of unanimity and good intelligence," revealing that the Persians had turned down several overtures for peace emanating from Russia owing to their alliance with France, which, he believed, precluded a separate treaty.[25]

England too had been thinking of Persia. Not long after Gardane left Finkenstein, George Canning commissioned Sir Hartford Jones, the agent ultimately to be Gardane's successful rival. Jones must sail in hot pursuit to the Persian Gulf, and head a British mission intended for Teheran. By Jones' instructions of August, 1807—drafted after consultation with the East India Company—he must obtain the reconfirmation of the company's commercial treaties, and win Persia's neutrality during the Anglo-Turkish war. Britain, in exchange, would guarantee the shah's territory.[26]

Most of Gardane's rather imposing mission, including civil and military personnel and a doctor, assembled in Constantinople in September. Among its secretaries was Ange Gardane, a brother of the minister. To assist were Joseph Rousseau, already in Teheran, and Felix Lajard, a diplomat and scholar. The six interpreters included Joannin and Nerciat, the two already in Teheran. Jean Raymond, a military figure with experience in India and at Bagdad, became an attaché. These men will figure in our ensuing account of relations in Teheran. One of them, Nerciat, we shall see much later as an ineffectual and self-conscious Napoleonic spy in Syria (chap. xviii). Gardane's military personnel numbered five captains and four lieutenants: namely, Tuilhier, Lamy, Bontemps, Verdier, Bianchi, Trezel, Bernard, Fabvier, and Reboul. Three of these were to become generals of division under the Bourbon Restoration, namely Lamy, Fabvier, and Trezel, and the latter also a minister of war. None of Gardane's assistants was over forty.[27]

A new blow to Franco-Russian peace-planning came at the north, in Britain's attack on Copenhagen on August 16. When Napoleon learned of it—within ten days—he immediately wrote his ally to propose that Alexander march an army against Sweden in order to compel it to make common cause with Denmark. Obviously Napoleon favored any means of bringing Russia and England to war. At the moment St. Petersburg knew only of the preliminaries of the attack, "astonishing" news which Budberg relayed on the same August 26 to De Lesseps and Savary. A reported squadron of two hundred or more British men-of-war, he said, including an imposing thirty-five ships of the line, had entered the Baltic. Denmark's request for an explanation elicited nothing more than quite unsatisfactory general comment from the resident British minister. A British officer signified the intention to force the Danes to turn over their fleet until the close of the war. The effort seemed quite similar to the naval move against Turkey in February. Gossip held that this proposal must be accepted on the spot or the British fleet would attack Danish coasts and ports.[28]

Hostilities between Britain and Denmark were soon under way, the Danish prince royal refusing to surrender the fleet. Even as Minister Budberg requested Gower to explain the English motives, news came of the British bombardment of Copenhagen. The naval action provoked indignation against England in France, Russia, and the Baltic countries. By thus striking a weak neutral, Britons themselves frankly admit, England suffered a loss of moral reputation that partly outweighed the immediate strategic advantage.[29] Britain bombarded Copenhagen so severely (September 2 to 5) that the Danish government surrendered the fleet. A by-product was Britain's occupation of Heligoland—which in 1890 would be transferred to Emperor William II of Germany.

During the first ten days of September, everyone at St. Petersburg discussed the happenings at Copenhagen: the British negotiations, the bombings, the capture of the Danish fleet, and Britain's cutting off all outside communication. Russia's indignation at the attack speeded its decision to improve Kronstadt's fortifications. Savary reported the events and visited that port on September 28. Denmark solicited Russia's support and good offices against England. De Lesseps—who wrote in more detail than Savary—held that England would be disposed to accept Russia's mediation, if the latter consented to inform London of all the secret stipulations of the Treaty of Tilsit and if it promised the most perfect impartiality.[30]

On September 5 Champagny drafted an answer to letters from Halet Effendi, the new Ottoman foreign minister. Halet had written in June and July about the proposed Franco-Turkish alliance—which no one mentioned seriously any longer. Napoleon's new foreign minister, replying via Sebastiani at Constantinople, evaded the issue completely by retelling the "happy news" of peace between France and Russia and of Napoleon's wish to see Turkey and Russia at peace. Issuing a veiled threat, precisely as Napoleon had directed Talleyrand at Tilsit—he stated that the French emperor thereafter would judge the new Ottoman government by its willingness to accept an armistice with Russia.

By the same special messenger Champagny acknowledged Sebastiani's reports to the end of July and sent clarifying instructions. If Guilleminot had proceeded to Constantinople as intended at Tilsit, the ambassador would have had in hand the positive instructions that would reverse his attitude. Napoleon could not reply to Sultan Mustapha's reported letter for the simple reason that he had not received such a letter. Recognizing Sebastiani's pessimism (expressed in early August), Napoleon directed him to encourage Turkey to shake off its passivity. If, upon receipt of the delayed instructions, Sebastiani should not succeed, he might turn affairs over to M. Latour-Maubourg and return home.[31] Although Consul Pierre David of Bosnia submitted a steady stream of reports, he received few replies either from Talleyrand or Champagny.[32] This dearth of replies illustrates Napoleon's general neglect of the Balkans.

In diplomacy as well as in war Napoleon defended by attacking. Blunt words emanated from Paris on September 7, 1807, in a dispatch personally dictated by Napoleon for Sebastiani. The emperor ridiculed the Ottoman call for the retrocession of the Crimea as a claim by a power which had been held at bay in the Principalities by a mere 20,000 Russians. Whereas the Turks had not been able to defend the Principalities even for a single day, he himself could do so by a stroke of the pen. Yet he had no obligation to do so. Vahid Effendi had spent fifteen days at his headquarters, in May, without signing an alliance. During that time Sultan Selim had been deposed, and the 500 French cannoneers had been summarily dismissed by Sultan Mustapha. The latter had not notified him of the change nor sent him an ambassador nor written him a letter. Was it not evident that Turkey had changed its policy? Napoleon hoped the armistice would have been concluded and the stipulated mediation assigned to him. If Turkey still followed a pro-French policy, he would guarantee its hold of the Principalities. If it made peace with the English, it might as well consider itself lost; its partition would be decreed before the end of the year. The emperor had no wish to hasten the ruin of Turkey; he would support it as long as its government remained a true friend.[33]

The Turkish governor at the Dardanelles, Hassiz Ismail, addressed to Sebastiani a friendly letter on September 7, regretting the dismissal of the French officers and engineers. He praised their good work in directing the refortification of the Dardanelles, an important project not yet completed. He remarked that Arthur Paget, supported by a British squadron of some twenty vessels, now urged Turkey to peace. Sebastiani privately supposed that with Napoleon's officers now gone the defenses of the Dardanelles would remain unfinished.

Gardane—at the time still in Constantinople—learned Sebastiani's trick of answering a question for which he really had no answer, a technique he himself employed later in Teheran. The ambassador to Turkey would contend that an apparently pressing problem in reality represented no problem at all, by reason of the probable fact that someone was working out its solution elsewhere—the farther away the better, in those days of difficult and slow communications. Sebastiani here contended that Turkey could not possibly make peace with England at the Dardanelles, at a time when the Russo-Turkish peace to be mediated at Paris certainly would include several anti-English stipulations.

Sultan Mustapha authorized a present of ten fine Arabian horses for Napoleon, in further testimony of his desire to cultivate friendly relations and, if possible, to have the French emperor forget his attachment for the imprisoned ex-Sultan Selim. With his own hand he penned a letter to Napoleon. Several months later—when Napoleon was busy with the conquest of Spain—Champagny acknowledged with thanks (on May 11, 1808) the ten horses that finally had been delivered to Paris.[34]

At Teheran, meanwhile, no news seemed to be good news. Confidence in Napoleon grew every day. Couriers set out from Teheran on September 5, bearing to their new ally friendly letters from Shah Feth Ali and Prince Abbas Mirza. At Paris, Champagny was surprised when a rumor respecting Persia was fulfilled. Someone had reported "an officer" to have been touring Europe for three months and to have left Persia some five months earlier. In mid-September Yousef Bey, presumably a second Persian envoy, arrived impressively with a suite of four persons. This individual, as we know, had come to Constantinople while Mirza Riza was still in Warsaw and had waited to learn where to go next. He delivered several letters which had been transmitted by General Sebastiani.

Without asking questions, Napoleon thought that Yousef might be the expected resident ambassador from Persia. He and Champagny decided to play safe. In the state courtesies accorded Yousef they followed the precedents of 1715, when a Persian envoy had visited Paris, and of April, 1807, in entertaining Mirza Riza (chap. viii). Yousef submitted no credentials—which should have aroused suspicions but did not. Indeed, the archives reveal the letters of credence for the important Asker Khan, naming him resident ambassador to France, to have been issued in Teheran only in that month of September, 1807. These letters were not translated in Paris—by Jaubert for the foreign minister—until August of the next year. Meanwhile, Yousef for several weeks did very well. That Napoleon blundered in entertaining a simple courier as an ambassador we shall see from Gardane's belated and blistering reaction from Teheran.[35]

Lazarev replied on September 5 to the Ottoman complaint that the Russians had not fulfilled the provisions of the armistice of Slobosia with Turkey. Anticipating the official Russian policy of disapproval of the armistice, he reasoned that the nonevacuation of the Principalities resulted from the illness and death of General Michelson and the consequent delay while another commander assumed his tasks. Moreover, Turkey had not provided adequate police protection in Bucharest and elsewhere, the areas evacuated first. Lazarev charged that Ottoman troops came to pillage rather than to protect, in some sectors their numbers being too few for effective policing. Accordingly, he had halted further evacuation until directed by Tsar Alexander himself to resume it. With respect to the fleet outside the Dardanelles, its surrendering of Tenedos and sailing for home ports also must await orders from high authority. The Russians within a few days reëntered Bucharest. Everyone knew that the Russo-Turkish argument to ensue would be bitter and that all its issues would be confused. After what he termed his own full investigation, Galib Effendi gave the lie to Lazarev's twice-repeated charges against the conduct of Ottoman troops. He reported this to Guilleminot, who undertook independent inquiries.[36]

St. Petersburg by no means shared the elation over peace expressed at Slobosia. As early as September 11 even uninformed observers there correctly surmised that Alexander would not ratify the armistice. The tsar openly opposed the stipulation that prohibited the renewal of hostilities before April; he formally repudiated the armistice as too favorable to Turkey. He did not wish to tie his hands, he said, if the Turks should manifest before April no real disposition to peace. He did not wish to abandon his blockade of the Dardanelles before actually signing the peace. His naval position at Tenedos had for months constituted one of his two toe holds on Turkey, the better one being his military position in the Principalities. General Milloradovich maintained his headquarters at Bucharest, while the octogenarian Prince-Marshal Prosorovski—active despite his age—held the over-all command from Jassy. General Kutusov directed a large army near the Dniester.[37] Milloradovich "liked war, and waged it with distinction," so General Sebastiani once characterized him.

Britain's negative reply to Russia's offer of mediation in the Anglo-French war was soon received. That action and the taking of Copenhagen gave convenient pretexts for Alexander to speed the severance of relations he had promised Napoleon. London's declination of peace presumably brought into force the stipulation of Tilsit for outright Russian military aid to France. Rumiantsov handed Ambassador Gower a second protest on behalf of Denmark. He said the news of Copenhagen had been placed before the tsar, who had read it with "infinite pain." Rumiantsov declared that, together with "this silence, this reserve" respecting the requested explanations, the situation was viewed by the tsar as contrary to Russia's interests. Russia's ruler considered himself the guarantor of the security and the tranquillity of the Baltic Sea.[38] Gower replied promptly (September 13). Although he had referred the issue to London, he could tender his own observations: the operation against Denmark obviously had been of such a nature as to preclude advance notification to anyone. The "silence" should rather be attributed to Russia for not revealing the secret stipulations of Tilsit. Turning Russia's language about, he stated, "This silence, this reserve, is an admission by Russia that these stipulations are directly contrary to the interests of Great Britain." Moreover, England had never recognized Russia's exclusive right to guarantee the tranquillity of the Baltic. On September 24 Rumiantsov sent notes to Sweden and Denmark which attempted to revive the Great Northern League of Armed Neutrality, formed against England during the American Revolution. News of the actual capitulation of Copenhagen came to St. Petersburg on September 18. As soon as the initial excitement died down, De Lesseps estimated the general effect of the British bombing to be favorable to the French cause. Some consternation was noted among English sympathizers in court circles at Rumiantsov's pro-French management of foreign affairs.[39]

In reply to Savary's first reports, Champagny in mid-September prescribed arguments to be used in support of Napoleon's Continental Blockade. Napoleon desired to seal up the entire shore line of Europe against Britain. Russia could assist in the north and Austria in the Adriatic; the restriction could be made so strong that "no Englishman could live in security as a commercialist in Europe" and England would be forced to peace.[40] Napoleon also prepared for renewed trade in the Levant, if opportunity should arise, by decreeing on September 21, 1807, Marseille's restoration of the eighteenth-century plan for inspection of all fabrics exported from there, so that their uniform qualities might be assured. Perhaps it would give hope to unhappy, impoverished Marseille, although without sea power there could be no Mediterranean trade.[41] The foreign minister simultaneously directed various arguments to be used at Constantinople to justify Napoleon's annexation of Ragusa to his Kingdom of Italy—a "kingdom" that was richly endowing a number of his favorite generals. Among the justifications was the statement that this "reunion" changed nothing in the status of Ragusa so far as concerned Turkey.

Napoleon notified Savary in mid-September that Turkey had accepted his mediation in the Russo-Turkish war. He needed Turkey, at least for the blockade against England; but he could promise it nothing that would oppose directly the interests of allied Russia. Champagny again held out the hope that the Principalities would be retained by Turkey, provided Turkey did not make peace with England (September 22).[42] If actually followed as a policy, this would mean another Napoleonic contradiction. Russia for the time must be turned toward Finland in order to postpone its acquisition of the Principalities. Thus one can understand why during the ensuing months Napoleon unsuccessfully claimed the fulfillment of Russia's pledge of active war against England.

General Sebastiani opened his official relations with Napoleon's new foreign minister by repeating his earlier request to be recalled to France; he wrote Champagny that he would leave affairs to Latour-Maubourg. He transmitted Turkey's belated official notification of the accession of Sultan Mustapha and a personal letter from Mustapha to Napoleon officially requesting the proffered mediation. Mouhib Effendi was given full authority to conclude a treaty of alliance with France. Sebastiani summed matters up on September 22. He believed Turkey would not make a separate peace with England. Arthur Paget was offering the evacuation of Alexandria and the return of any Turkish area held by the English in exchange for the pure and simple restoration of peacetime relations. Although Turkey had declined, some question of its policy remained. Gossip concerning the secret Treaty of Tilsit held that Russia had thereby ceded to France Prevesa, Parga, and Butrinto along the

Albanian coast north of the Gulf of Arta. Sebastiani also stated his belief that Turkey, in exchange for a guarantee of the remainder of its territories, would cede them, even if part of a more comprehensive proposal that included Montenegro. Guilleminot would already have reported, Sebastiani continued, that upon the arrival of a courier from St. Petersburg General Milloradovich suspended the evacuation of the Principalities—thus increasing the manifest "disquietude and alarm of the Turkish government."[43]

Vahid Effendi had come to Paris from Warsaw with returning French officials. When notified of Ambassador Mouhib's coming, he asked for his passports (October 9). The resident ambassador presented his letters of credence on October 29. As spokesman for the Turks, he blatantly issued a "pure and simple" demand that the Russians fulfill all the conditions of the armistice—a demand which everyone ignored.[44]

Official France would learn, late in December—by means of extralegal police searches of Mouhib's papers—that the Ottoman grand vizir and foreign minister were resolutely opposed to a treaty concession of the passage through Turkey of French troops bound for Persia and India. Jaubert translated for Champagny on Christmas day, 1807, the illegally inspected instructions to Mouhib, dated October 24. From these it is clear that Turkey had determined, in the treaty of peace to be arranged with Russia, to exclude Russian and all other foreign warships from the Straits in addition to stipulating the restoration of Moldavia and Wallachia. A drafted requirement read, "In a word, the passage of the Straits must be definitively closed to the vessels of war of all powers." Russia "must not be permitted any further execution of that facility accorded by the treaty of alliance in 1805."[45] We recall that Russia had been conceded the passage in order to be able to sail to Corfu but that this original reason disappeared at Tilsit.

In fact, neither France nor Russia displayed a serious disposition to comply with the stipulated withdrawals from the respective Prussian and Turkish territories. This suggests a probable secret and personal understanding at Tilsit to that effect. In any event, France's forces remained in Silesia, Russia's in the Principalities. The tsar not only refused to ratify the Russo-Turkish armistice of August 24 but also disgraced General Meyendorff, who had approved it. One explanation of Alexander's reasoning is that, preoccupied with Turkish weakness, he thought more of the idea of partition—discussed in earnest (if preliminary) fashion at Tilsit—than of the peace settlement with the sultan which the Treaty of Tilsit predicated. Another suggestion is that he hoped thereby to force the issue of a partition of Balkan Turkey, also contingently in prospect in accordance with the arrangements at Tilsit. Russia covered its failure to evacuate with the pretext of banditry among the authorized Ottoman police.

When the stipulated Russian evacuation of the Principalities was not made good, the Ottoman foreign minister urged Sebastiani to ask for its execution.[46] Late in September, Turkey—finally, and too late— yielded in principle to France's pre-Tilsit demand for an offensive as well as defensive military alliance. Sebastiani still believed Napoleon could expect Turkey to continue its war against England. Indeed, Sebastiani paradoxically felt encouraged over the paradoxical situation. "Napoleon's influence at Constantinople is greater than it has ever been," so he encouraged Paris. When Turkey could not win Seniavin's release of the Ottoman vessels captured during the war—a requirement of the nonratified armistice—it offered them as an outright gift to Napoleon. Sebastiani privately speculated that the fall of Turkey was inevitable, and that in any partition of that moribund nation—so often hinted since Tilsit—Napoleon, its only friend, could have almost all of the country. On the other hand, he did not consider it desirable to push to ruin any government already so far gone.[47]

Britain's evacuation of Alexandria in September perceptibly improved its relations with Turkey. Everyone then agreed that an Anglo-Turkish treaty of peace was primarily a question of time. Admiral Collingwood held realistically to his viewpoint, that England's war with Turkey had served to embarrass British affairs, "without the possibility of its having one good consequence." To him, the blockade of the Dardanelles seemed to be represented to the home cabinet as possessing too much importance. "The constant northeast winds during the summer months are a complete bar to regular trade," he stated. He knew of no vessel's entering that strait from April to September, 1807—and yet no one had noticed the least lack of supplies in the Ottoman capital.[48]

This chapter has demonstrated the immediate effects in the Near East of the great-power politics of mid-1807. Tsar Alexander did not ratify the armistice with Turkey, whether due to the secret Franco-Russian alliance at Tilsit or to anticipation of making a deal with France on the basis of Napoleon's new friendship. This meant that he would not be required to end his occupation of the Principalities. The upshot was to test the working value of the Franco-Russian alliance.

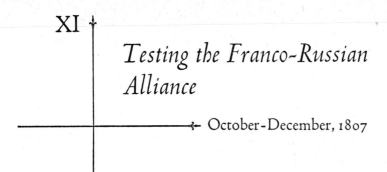

XI

Testing the Franco-Russian Alliance

THE PRELIMINARY Franco-Russian debate respecting the Straits had been held at Tilsit. In contrast to the delaying action there agreed upon, Napoleon in conference with Ambassador Tolstoi verbally conceded Constantinople to Russia—according to Tolstoi's report, which Napoleon never denied although given an opportunity to do so after the tsar quoted it to Ambassador Caulaincourt. But the question of ownership of the Straits must not be opened yet, Caulaincourt's instructions of November implied—not until Napoléon could handle personally that delicate problem. The germ had been planted by the vague allusion; Napoleon would watch its possible growth. Let Russia scheme to win the Dardanelles, as well as Constantinople and the Bosporus.

Napoleon took for granted and confidently awaited Russia's military support against Great Britain. Of greater immediate interest than that possibility, promised by the alliance of Tilsit, his policy in October, 1807, would offer to exchange other nations' territories, specifically Prussian Silesia to France for Ottoman Moldavia and Wallachia to Russia. The dazzling though vague second step of his policy would be to dangle before Tsar Alexander the prospect of a Franco-Russian general partition of the Ottoman Empire. The latter was considered a better means of attaching defeated Russia more firmly to the alliance. In this chapter we will show that the step did not necessarily involve an actual partition, but merely was the French plan to evince enough willingness in that direction to encourage Russia to enter the war against Britain. Possibly there could be joint action against British India. Thus Napoleon would handle powerful Russia precisely as he had the lesser allies of the east—Turks, Persians, Lithuanians, and Poles. The method would tantalize the tsar with the prospect of prompt fulfillment of an historic ambition in order to win support to expand Napoleon's empire. The discussions did not in 1807 approach a debate over the Dardanelles but did concern the possible Russian ownership of the Principalities, important segments of the European hinterland of the Straits.

Napoleon did not yet know, at the beginning of November, 1807, when Count Tolstoi came to Paris, of Russia's breaking diplomatic and commercial relations with Great Britain. Among the ambassador's aides was young Count Nesselrode, later to play a long and distinguished role in Russia's foreign policy. Napoleon reciprocated immediately for Tolstoi's presence by sending Ambassador Caulaincourt to relieve General Savary. With these ambassadors began the testing of Franco-Russian alliance relations under Tilsit. A general redirection of French policy —with all of its confused and contradictory aspects—was forecast in Count Champagny's instructions to General Savary at the end of September and early October, when Napoleon did not as yet know that the Russo-Turkish armistice of August 24 would be repudiated by the tsar. Napoleon's new foreign minister notified Savary that Ambassador Sebastiani had won Turkish authorization for the passage of the Dardanelles toward the Black Sea of the Russian vessels quitting Corfu, help that should be appreciated at St. Petersburg. In those days the French emperor was quoted as saying, "It is only with Russia that we wish to have an eternal alliance, against all enemies." France wished nevertheless to be on the best terms with Austria. Also, he could easily and completely forget Prussia's past conduct, if that power's future behavior did not require the Grand Army to return again.[1]

As if appointed for the purpose, the tsar's new foreign minister, Count Rumiantsov, pushed forward the issue of a possible partition of Turkey. In the initial overture to Savary, he stated that Russia did not wish to delay long "in the great affair of Turkey." An earlier hint by Budberg, thrown out in July and suggesting a further discussion of the fate of the Ottoman Empire, apparently had been ignored by Napoleon. Rumiantsov referred specifically to the preliminary general discussions between Alexander and Napoleon at Tilsit of an eventual partition of the Ottoman Empire in the Balkans. This had been included as a potentiality of the Franco-Russian alliance. Rumiantsov remarked that "it would be of great interest" to consider the details of the problem soon. Although Tsar Alexander did not desire any conquest, the Ottoman Empire appeared in such a sad state that even without conquests its succession must still be arranged. Everyone knew of the palace revolt, the Serbian rebellion, and the general insubordination of the pashas in the frontier provinces.

Rumiantsov justified Russia's declining to execute the stipulated evacuation of the Principalities, on the ground of unforeseen difficulties. If Russia evacuated, bands of Turks would roam about and massacre the inhabitants. There existed in fact other weighty considerations for postponing the evacuation. Alexander appears to have put out further hints for an overture from Napoleon on the subject. Doubtless he already had discussed with his advisers whether a territorial solution respecting Constantinople and its district—denied expressly at Tilsit—might not yet be combined with the contingent formula fixed there for a partition of the Balkan portions of Turkey. More urgent, Napoleon sought a means whereby to retain Silesia. According to the Treaty of Tilsit, that Prussian province no less than the Danubian Principalities must be restored by the signers. Napoleon probably considered the best way would be to connect the two, although the tsar later disputed any understanding at Tilsit implying a connection. Meanwhile, Napoleon employed the treaty's stipulation of Russian evacuation to prove his partiality to Turkey—although the treaty required that Russia evacuate only temporarily.

When news came in mid-October of the failure to ratify the Russo-Turkish armistice, Paris again played showman to the Turk by calling upon the tsar to fulfill his duty under the Treaty of Tilsit. The confident Turks, who did not know the secret details of Tilsit, awaited sponsorship by France.[2]

Savary meanwhile gradually awakened to his basic assignment, to attend to the full execution of Tilsit, an official copy of which Champagny forwarded to him on October 13. The interim envoy was directed to read and understand it and, if desirable, to read and clarify it to the Russians. Champagny prescribed ingenious arguments for encouraging Russia to evacuate Moldavia and Wallachia. Whereas Tilsit stipulated Russia's unconditional and absolute evacuation, rigorously stating the time for it, it required France's evacuation of Silesia only after Prussia had made its prescribed financial "contributions." Hence Russia could not really take Prussia's part in the matter of having the French evacuate without first entering to collect the indemnity on behalf of Napoleon. Of the two mediations agreed upon—Russia's between France and England and France's between Russia and Turkey—only the latter had been successful. Champagny directed Savary to confirm Russia's agreement to evacuate. That Russia had not evacuated already, he could say, was probably due to a misunderstanding. The envoy must make clear that France did not mistrust Russia's motives. The tsar's dislike of certain provisions of the Russo-Turkish armistice, however, should not hold up his temporary evacuation as promised to France. If Russia sought to justify its continuing in the Principalities by France's remaining in Silesia and Brandenburg, Savary must stress the difference between the two, the unconditional and absolute evacuation of the Principalities in contrast with that for Silesia, which would come into effect only after full payment by Prussia. Thus, he might say, Russia was failing in an existing engagement while France was not, for the latter possessed an incontestable right under treaties with Prussia and with Russia to retain its forces in Silesia.[3]

Because Ambassador Mouhib possessed authority to treat for peace in Paris, France invited Tsar Alexander to issue similar authority to Ambassador Tolstoi. The full execution of that phase of Tilsit required only two things, Champagny wrote, namely Russia's evacuation and the naming of plenipotentiaries to negotiate peace under Napoleon's mediation. The Ottoman envoy reportedly possessed extensive discretionary powers; Savary might suggest the same for Tolstoi to avoid the inconvenience of seeking new instructions at every stage of the negotiation.

Respecting Russia's mediation in behalf of France, England had let pass the stipulated month following the notice. France considered this a refusal. "Not only has England not accepted," wrote Champagny, "but by its expedition to Copenhagen (chap. x) has underscored the refusal in a most positive and most clear manner." Napoleon expected Russia to notify England of the contemplated terms of peace. If an agreement had not been made by December 1, he expected Russia to close its ports against the English, recall its ambassador to London, and begin war.[4]

Galib Effendi and the others of Sultan Mustapha's advisers relied heavily on the favorable terms of peace which Napoleon would impose against Russia in their behalf. They accorded France unusual favors but kept secret their desired terms. In mid-October Ambassador Sebastiani impressively announced the French annexation of Ragusa, to which the sultan's ministers raised not the slightest objection. The Italian flag now flew over Ragusa's merchant fleet, which claimed, and was granted, access to the Black Sea. Sebastiani observed that the Turks were still much disquieted over Russia, owing to the nonevacuation of the Principalities and to the reported renewal of former practices in Serbia and elsewhere in Balkan Europe. The Ottomans gave Sebastiani one occasion to guard Napoleon's recognized title of padishah. When the court of Austria requested the same title for its ruler, the French ambassador stated that the title accorded Napoleon must not be granted lightly to others. Thereupon the Turkish foreign minister declined Austria's request. Among other marks of favor to France, the sultan issued the orders corrective of abuses which France had solicited in behalf of Roman Catholics. Turkey no longer feared the possible coming of another British squadron into the Dardanelles and up to Constantinople. Admiral Collingwood did not enter the Straits to support any new negotiations, as had Duckworth in February. Collingwood fared no better, however, the Ottoman council remaining convinced that its best policy lay in alliance with France and in a "cold war" against England. They evinced some alarm over Russian reinforcements that were coming into the Principalities.[5]

The manuscript draft of a letter of late October, 1807, not dispatched, reveals more of Napoleon's thinking with respect to measures to avoid the consequences of the contradictions of his Near Eastern policies. He would defend his own course by attacking Turkey's. He considered saying bluntly that the actions of the new Turkish government made him wonder whether Turkey's attitude had not changed. In any event the doubt had been sufficient for him to recall the 500 French gunners. Meanwhile the arrival in Paris that month of Mouhib Effendi accompanied by Guilleminot gave ample evidence of a pro-French policy by Turkey's new government.[6]

French policy for Persia perforce favored peace between Persia and Russia, and so Champagny advised Gardane, on October 29, "The continuance of the war between Russia and Persia today would be without utility," because the Franco-Persian alliance could consider only Great Britain as the common enemy. Napoleon's eastern policies became more confused than ever, caused, in part, as always, by the handicap of slow communications. On that same October 29, in Teheran, Consul Joseph Rousseau personally delivered to the shah the friendly communication —now seven months old—which Napoleon wrote at Osterode on April 3, a month before signing the Franco-Persian alliance. Teheran expected Gardane, perhaps toward the end of November.[7] Meanwhile, Count Gudovich, Russia's commander opposing Persia, took the initiative on October 8 for an armistice. His letter to Crown Prince Abbas Mirza stressed the Franco-Russian alliance, the precise terms of which he did not know. Without mentioning the Russo-Turkish armistice—of which he could hardly know—his proposal paralleled it.

Napoleon believed it was only a question of time before the stipulations of Tilsit would call for Russia to break with England and enforce the Continental Blockade. As a result of the bombing of Copenhagen, Tsar Alexander advanced the date for his rupture of diplomatic relations with England to November 6. Observers in St. Petersburg could discern the new tendency in Anglo-Russian relations. Of its many evidences, Anglophile Budberg's being replaced by pro-French Rumiantsov was the most significant.[8] On November 4 Savary triumphantly reported the issuance of passports to Ambassador Gower and his staff. He hoped Napoleon would be pleased with that success. On the personal side, he did not accept kindly the reproaches of Champagny—sometimes for what he did, sometimes for what he did not do in the way of reporting fully. The first speculation concerning a regular French ambassador indicated that Count de Laforest, one of Napoleon's favorites, would be named, and for several weeks he was expected at the Russian capital. Official Russians did not like him, doubtless because he had been of too much aid to Napoleon in Prussia. Then came the more welcome news that General Caulaincourt soon would be on the way.

Russia's note breaking off all communications with England listed two reasons: Britain's refusal of mediation in the Anglo-French war, and the attack on Denmark. The new policy would continue, the tsar declared, until England satisfied Denmark and agreed to negotiate peace with France. Russia published a "declaration" to this effect—but not of war—on November 7, 1807.[9]

Russia and Turkey, both Napoleon's friends, were at war with each other. His best maneuvering had produced only their nonratified armistice. The tsar's nonevacuation of the Principalities did not seem so important, provided France could obtain a suitable equivalent. No longer could Napoleon ignore Russia's official interest in discussing possible successors to the Ottoman Empire. He combined boldness with caution in thus instructing Savary, on November 1: "Respecting the affairs of Turkey, I feel the need of settling that matter and I am ready to come to an understanding with Russia in regard to it. This affair is of course very interesting to me. I shall confide in you by writing after seeing Tolstoi. I might even need a personal meeting for this with the tsar—after war has been declared by Russia against England."[10]

The tsar's advisers held in common the idea that the Straits must never pass to any great power save Russia. It was wondered whether an effect of Russia's nonratification would be the alternative of the partition of Balkan Turkey—as foretold by the alliance of Tilsit. The background for Tsar Alexander's consideration of a possible partition of Turkey was a long-continued debate within Russian official circles. Proponents of partition liked Count Rostopchin's argument of 1801: as a "national" policy for Russia, a partition even with its admitted difficulties would be more readily applicable than the alternate plan to keep Turkey alive by means of stimulants. The opponents contended that Russia would do well to permit Turkey to live as a weak neighbor— Count Kochubei's plan of 1802.[11]

Napoleon and Champagny handled Ambassador Mouhib's principal business in unhurried, routine fashion. Sultan Mustapha's letter to Napoleon proved friendly. On November 6 the Turkish foreign minister let Sebastiani know that the sultan wished to coöperate with Napoleon respecting the Ionian Islands, Dalmatia, Ragusa, and Cattaro. In his first audience granted the new ambassador, Napoleon complained of Mustapha's neglecting to notify him promptly of his accession, and of the slight to Sebastiani. Worst of all, the sultan did not control the pashas in the Ottoman provinces adjacent to French Dalmatia; he needed only to solicit aid and France would send up to 100,000 troops into the disaffected areas. Napoleon said he regretted that the long absence of official news had impelled him to recall his 500 cannoneers.[12] This cleverly avoided the information received at Tilsit that Mustapha had summarily dismissed them.

Champagny notified Savary that the Turkish ambassador possessed full authority to treat for peace with Russia, whereas newly arrived Tolstoi did not. Turkey, meanwhile, insisted upon the full execution of the Russo-Turkish armistice. Embarrassed, Sebastiani had no instructions for the case that had arisen, Russia's failure to evacuate Moldavia and Wallachia. Admiral Seniavin did not release the captured Turkish vessels to France nor abandon the blockade of the Dardanelles, upon learning of the tsar's nonratification of the armistice.[13] Sebastiani called attention to the Turks' surprise and dissatisfaction at the categorical rejection of the armistice.

At St. Petersburg, Rumiantsov at first replied in general terms to Savary's request for the reasons why Russia had not evacuated Moldavia and Wallachia. He said certain stipulations of the armistice proved unsatisfactory and that the Turks had violated it by moving troops into segments of the disputed region.[14] The tsar then shifted the subject. He said, in mid-November, "My news from Constantinople is to the effect that the English are assuming a great preponderance over the Ottoman

council, so I must be more than ever on guard." Rumiantsov promised
Savary he would send Tolstoi authority to negotiate—although he made
no comment at all respecting possible terms.[15] Champagny's question
had been answered evasively: full powers would be given Tolstoi, but
not instructions as to how to use them.

A friendly if revolutionary Turkey now being evident, Napoleon again
decided to court both governments. Champagny advised Sebastiani in
mid-November that Napoleon had told Tolstoi of his astonishment that
the armistice had not been executed. However, so Champagny restricted
him, the ambassador must not convey to Turkey anything more positive
than that. Napoleon's immediate reply (November 7) to the tsar's
personal letter which Tolstoi delivered repeated an earlier expression of
pleasure at the personal conferences at Tilsit. More important, the
French emperor expedited to General Savary his initial reactions to
Tolstoi's comments, pending Caulaincourt's departure for St. Petersburg. On the same day that he spoke bluntly to Mouhib—at Fontaine-
bleau castle—Napoleon in an interesting discussion with Count Tolstoi
succeeded in covering up Silesia by dangling Constantinople before the
tsar. He issued an indirect invitation for Russia to discuss a partition
of Turkey.

France gave the new ambassador special attention socially. From Napoleon's account of his first conference with Tolstoi, the latter submitted
his letters of credence on November 6. After the formal amenities, they
talked together for an hour, Napoleon stressing Turkish affairs and Tolstoi the Prussian. According to Tolstoi's report, the French emperor
stated that General Savary had relayed Russian hints respecting their
possible acquisition of Moldavia and Wallachia. He said he would as a
matter of policy prefer to guarantee the integrity of the Ottoman Empire, although he had taken no engagements to do so. On the other hand,
he cautioned, by no means could an equivalent for France be found in
Albania and the Morea.

Quite significantly, Tolstoi reported to Rumiantsov that the emperor
said further that France wished to possess Silesia. Napoleon admitted he
would even consent to a big partition of the Ottoman Empire, if that
suited Russia's plans. He authorized Tolstoi to offer Constantinople to
Alexander—so the tsar's ambassador further recorded—because France
had no contracts with Turkey, and had no designs on that capital. (Napoleon carefully refrained from mentioning the Dardanelles or the Bosporus.) If, as a second alternative, Russia should renounce its desire for

Moldavia and Wallachia, France would evacuate Silesia. If Russia remained there, France must be compensated in Prussia. "In the third supposition," Tolstoi reported, "which would involve a complete dismemberment of European Turkey, he would consent to Russia's extension through Bulgaria to Constantinople, that capital included, in exchange for French acquisitions he did not specify."[16]

As is usual in diplomatic affairs, Napoleon did not permit the tsar to depend solely on Tolstoi's account of such a significant interview. He himself summarized it for Savary's information and guidance. In doing so he avoided all reference to Constantinople but suggested that Alexander send to Paris "any more extensive ideas" he had in mind respecting the Ottoman Empire besides the Principalities. Tolstoi spoke a great deal of Napoleon's nonevacuation of Prussia. These are the emperor's words: "I have spoken frankly to Tolstoi of affairs at Constantinople relative to Russia, in clarifying several matters. Everything that can conduce to our closer relations pleases me. The world is large enough for both France and Russia. M. de Tolstoi needs to concert always and maintain warm friendliness. I think that Russia should mobilize troops to march against Sweden, if its king refuses to make common cause with the continent. As for me, my troops are on the frontiers of Portugal and will enter there. Tolstoi spoke much of the evacuation of Prussia. . . . He doubtless took that way of entering into Russia's policy of retaining the Principalities. If such is Russia's project I shall retain as compensation some Prussian provinces. If Russia has any more extensive ideas respecting the Turkish Empire, M. Rumiantsov should send the new ambassador more precise instructions. As for me, I desire everything that can strengthen our ties."[17]

A month later, after Tolstoi's report had been received, the tsar remarked that the least concession on Napoleon's part regarding Turkey would be welcomed. From these two accounts it would not appear by any means that Tolstoi got off to a bad start in Paris. Champagny so interpreted Tolstoi's efforts, at any rate, for we find him writing Savary two days later that the new ambassador spoke too much of Silesia, both to himself and to Napoleon.

Savary long remembered the foreign ministry's rebuke for his brevity in reports. Now, for once, he sent a word-for-word report of his conversations with the tsar and Rumiantsov—those held on November 8. Russia therein transmitted officially to its ally, upon request, its specific reasons for not evacuating the Principalities. There had been an official report that Russia's forces on the Danube had caught several Turkish ships attempting to supply the garrison at Ismail with powder.[18] The sultan's inability to enforce in the Barbary Regencies the Russo-Turkish commercial convention of 1783 was another reason for hesitancy to negotiate for peace. No redress had been granted for the capture of a Russian ship in 1786, despite the successive requests of Tsarina Catherine, Tsar Paul, and Tsar Alexander. During the weeks after Tilsit Russia had devised a moderate partition scheme. If France should not be ready to take Albania and the Morea as equivalents, Russia could agree to take only Bessarabia at the time and hold open the question of Moldavia and Wallachia until the end of the Anglo-French war.[19]

Napoleon utilized General Caulaincourt, his new ambassador to Russia, as a third person, in addition to Tolstoi and Savary, to relay his suggestion that Tsar Alexander forward comments, if he wished to discuss a partition of Turkey. Instructions were ready for Caulaincourt on November 12. They reveal Napoleon's thinking six days after his signifiicant discussions with Tolstoi and Mouhib. Apparently the French emperor had purposely awaited Tolstoi's opening statements before approving Champagny's draft of the instructions.

Russia's reluctance to permit France to retain Silesia presents a convenient point of departure for summarizing Caulaincourt's instructions. The French ambassador's first duty would be to solicit the tsar to instruct Tolstoi concerning the manner of executing the Treaty of Tilsit. Tolstoi possessed no authority to discuss the prospective peace with Turkey, prescribed for French mediation. From there Caulaincourt must proceed to territorial matters—the gains from which might have proved more profitable to the "Axis powers" of that day. Rumiantsov's overtures, together with Russia's continued occupation of the Principalities, led Napoleon to suppose the tsar "had some views" respecting Moldavia and Wallachia. He would not too strongly oppose their occupation; indeed, under certain conditions this would serve his interests—if an equivalent for France could be found.

"In line with this hypothesis," Champagny continued, "France might find an equivalent in the possession of some Prussian provinces which, while weakening the Hohenzollern power, would further consolidate Emperor Napoleon's federative system. To this consideration is added that, in the existing state of decadence of Turkey, the Principalities are virtually lost to it already. Turkey can at best only extract their resources and at worst see the country ravaged and its inhabitants plundered and vexed by the competing groups there. The cries and complaints will reach Napoleon's ears. He will be called upon to intervene in their ceaselessly recurring quarrels, and the friendship of France and Russia will be endangered."

Champagny next proceeded to Alexander and Napoleon's pretexts. The tsar's personal interests sought to aggrandize his empire, as was true also of his Romanov predecessors. If Russia retained Moldavia and Wallachia in apparent violation of the Treaty of Tilsit, compensation for Napoleon could be found only in the Prussian provinces stipulated for restitution. These would provide an equivalent in population, wealth, and resources to the two Ottoman provinces; each ally thus would obtain an equal share. To be sure, Prussia would be left with only two million inhabitants; but why should Prussia not become only a minor power, having lost its great-power rank already?

Russia's leaders probably would suggest that Napoleon take compensation from certain Balkan provinces nearest his Kingdom of Italy, perhaps in Bosnia and Albania. Caulaincourt must oppose such an arrangement, because it simply would not suit. Such provinces would have to be conquered; they could by no means be counted as in Napoleon's hands already, as were the Principalities in Russia's. Napoleon thereafter would have to struggle to hold them, moreover, for the inhabitants would interpose many obstacles to peaceful possession. The western Ottoman provinces, being poor and without commerce and industry, and by location difficult to attach to the center of his empire, would not represent a valuable acquisition for Napoleon. "Instead of compensation, that legacy would become a source of vexations to be terminated by arms, without profit and without glory." Moreover, it would be unwise to detach so much of the Ottoman Empire, if that empire were to survive at all. Separating Moldavia and Wallachia could be condoned because they were as good as lost already, having been so long under Russian influence.

Champagny directed Caulaincourt to argue not so much against a partition of the Ottoman Empire as for postponement of it. Several serious consequences were foreseen from its destruction—which certainly would take place if it should be menaced simultaneously by the Russians from one side and by the French from the other. "This collapse of the Ottoman Empire may be desired by the Russian cabinet. One recognizes it as inevitable. It should be no part of the policy of the two imperial courts, however, to accelerate the collapse. They should await the moment when a partition of Turkey's vast debris could be put through more advantageously for France and Russia—after they no longer need fear that England, their enemy, in a scramble for the spoils might appropriate Egypt and several of the richest islands. This is the emperor's strongest objection to the partition of the Ottoman Empire," Champagny affirmed.[20]

Napoleon here personally dictated a supplementary statement, definitely requiring Caulaincourt to concede the Principalities for an exchange. Said Napoleon of himself, "The true desire of the emperor at the moment is also that the Ottoman Empire retain its existing integrity, living in peace with Russia and France and having for its limits the center of the Danube and the places that Turkey possesses on that river —up to Ismail—always provided that Russia agrees that France acquires an equal augmentation from Prussia."

More important, Napoleon's supplementary statement authorized a straddling position, which we shall see Caulaincourt assume in his secret debates with Rumiantsov and the tsar in March, 1808 (chap. xiii), respecting the allocation of further territories from Turkey. It was possible that a policy looking to the partition of the Ottoman Empire beyond the severance of the Principalities would be decided upon by St. Petersburg, he said. He intended, "in that case, in no sense to choke that court on that object." He preferred to make such a partition "only in concert with it, in a manner to give France the greatest possible influence in said partition, rather than through it to grant Russia the facility to intervene in Austria." Therefore, Caulaincourt "must not in any sense refuse to discuss the partition but declare that it would require a verbal meeting of the rulers." The last instruction eventually led to the conference which was held at Erfurt almost a year later (chap. xiv).

Napoleon's supplementary statement ended at that point and Champagny's instructions resumed—somewhat repetitive for so significant an issue. Caulaincourt must recall to Tsar Alexander the conversations with Napoleon at Tilsit on the subject of Turkey. The two rulers agreed to undertake nothing in respect to its partition until after an understanding arranged personally between them. If Russia contemplated any partition, however, even of severing the Principalities, Caulaincourt must stress at least one consequence. In order to be prepared strategically for any contingency, Napoleon on no account would evacuate the left bank of the Vistula. If the Russians spoke of Albania and Bosnia as compensation, Caulaincourt must demonstrate their inequality with the Principalities. He must always hold to Napoleon's possession of additional Prussian provinces as a "perfectly equal arrangement, suitable to all their interests, of prompt and easy execution, and having none of the consequences of policy which wise foresight should exclude."

The Emperor of France could not disarm (that is to say, evacuate Silesia), while such great interests stood in question. Champagny's argument for exchanging the Principalities for Silesia became more definite, more unyielding. Russia was still occupying and reinforcing Bessarabia, Wallachia, and Moldavia. Napoleon had every confidence in Alexander and wished to coördinate his own progress with the tsar's. Yet the two empires must march as equals. "Such is the principle of Napoleon's conduct. Reason, justice, and prudence do not permit him to adopt any other policy and no obstacle could swerve him from his course." Napoleon would evacuate the Prussian provinces only after Russia's negotiations for peace with Turkey began, and after the tsar should have stated his intention to restore Moldavia and Wallachia to Turkey. Alternatively, the tsar might partially evacuate the Principalities—about the joint arrangement of which Napoleon had spoken, relative to a new order of things.

Napoleon held himself ready for either policy; either one suited him. It would be more advantageous to Russia to accept the Principalities, for which reason alone he preferred it. This would require a preliminary understanding. With respect to the form of the arrangement, a secret convention could be signed so interpreting the Treaty of Tilsit. They could also guarantee to Turkey its remaining provinces. Each ally would announce publicly, under specious pretexts, its refusal to evacuate such and such province. The conclusion secretly reached would then be confirmed in the Russo-Turkish treaty to be negotiated under French mediation. A parallel convention between France and Prussia—under Russia's mediation—would sanction France's acquisition of Silesia.

Champagny concluded this section of Caulaincourt's instructions by repeating Napoleon's real object (as if revealing it anew): "Such are, on this important point of policy, the views of the Emperor of the French. He would have preferred that the Turks remain in peaceful possession of the Principalities. The desire to treat the cabinet of St. Petersburg kindly, however, and to attach himself more and more to Tsar Alexander, does not permit him to exclude the abandonment to the tsar of the two provinces, for himself moderately taking equal compensation in the Prussian provinces. Finally—although quite far removed

from the proposition of a partition of the Turkish Empire and considering this step deadly—he does not wish you, in your discussions with the
tsar and his minister, to condemn it in an absolute manner. He directs
you to represent with vigor the motives that might advise postponing
the date for it. This old project of Russian ambition is one bond that
can attach Russia to France and in consequence it is necessary to guard
against entirely discouraging its hopes." The last phrase revealed the
French emperor's essential object.

Champagny stated that winning Silesia for France and dangling the
prospect of an eventual, more general partition of Turkey must be the
most important, although not the first, service of Caulaincourt at the
Russian capital. Russia must declare war against England before his
taking up the subject of Turkey. The British conduct against Denmark
in the Baltic, a sea protected by Russia, of itself justified war and offered
the most plausible pretext for it. Russia would weaken itself by not
declaring war. Caulaincourt must minimize such a war, however; he
could state that it would obviously be followed immediately by peace.
Paris had not learned of Russia's measures short of war with England
a week before, a severance of relations without a declaration of war. The
instructions admitted the possibility of war, in which event the tsar
should demand that Sweden make common cause and should force the
issue in case of refusal.

Caulaincourt must state that Austria had adhered verbally to the views
of France, and also would go to war against England. Champagny
stated: "What a great and powerful effect of the alliance of the two
first powers of the globe! The continent of Europe against England, to
annihilate its commerce, paralyze its industry, render sterile its greatest
asset, power on the sea." They could dream even of a joint expedition
to India. It at first appeared chimerical and tentative, Champagny admitted; but could Russia and France not do it? Forty thousand French
troops, to whom passage through Constantinople would have been accorded by Turkey, joined by 40,000 Russians traveling by way of the
Caucasus, would suffice to terrify Asia and permit the conquest. From
such reasoning, he said, Napoleon had sent General Gardane to Persia.

Britain had advanced subsidies to the tsar in the war which Napoleon
won in June, a war that left his new ally in debt. To assist in Russia's
recovery, France proposed to purchase lumber and naval stores and pay
cash for delivery into warehouses in Russia. He also proposed to construct in Russian shipyards three vessels of the line, each of 74 guns.

Champagny considered that Count Rumiantsov, as the minister of commerce, should appreciate Napoleon's liberality in commercial matters. France wished no exceptional privileges. Without any quibbling over details, it would be agreeable for France to adopt the rules theretofore applicable to English traders in Russia. The essential idea was for Russia to favor French commerce and totally exclude that of England. Thus ended Champagny's instructions of November 12, 1807.[21] Caulaincourt's attractive personality could be counted a further aid. He had been chosen partly because he was a military man of smart appearance and because he enjoyed Napoleon's full confidence.

Immediately after approving these instructions, Napoleon left to attend to affairs in Italy (November 16). Champagny accompanied him to the south. On December 1 he dispatched supplemental instructions —based on Savary's and De Lesseps' latest reports—for Caulaincourt to treat with hatred or indifference the anti-French Maximilian Merveldt, the Austrian ambassador.[22] During the three weeks while Caulaincourt was en route to St. Petersburg, Savary could report the sensation created on November 18 by the departure of Britain's Ambassador Gower and his staff. Savary by now had received the instructions of October urging Russia's evacuation of the Principalities. This probably was intended for showing to Turkey so as to increase France's bargaining power in its forthcoming negotiations over Silesia. Apparently Napoleon planned to permit Savary's embarrassing questions to disquiet the Russians before Caulaincourt made his seeming concessions respecting a territorial exchange.[23]

The records reveal a gloomy Sebastiani near the end of November. The Turks would not accept Napoleon's logic that their coöperation with France was indispensable to the continued existence of the Ottoman Empire. He believed that the Turks feigned agreeableness merely to obtain more advantageous conditions of peace with Russia. He suspected Halet Effendi of being pro-English, even in English pay, judging from the fact that the Ottoman foreign minister openly protected the French-hating Prince Moruzzi. He conveyed his conjecture that the anti-French faction of the Ottoman ministry possibly had succeeded in shaping a policy of not negotiating for the military alliance with France until after the formal treaty of peace with Russia. All indications pointed to an understanding soon between Turkey and England. Despite the official friendliness, the French could no longer enjoy fully their traditional privileges in Turkey. M. de Fox, a respectable French merchant, complained violently against the treatment given him. Sebastiani recalled the torturing by Ottoman police of two subjects of France, cases later explained away by the sultan's ministers. Champagny would be able to judge whether Mouhib's instructions were not unsatisfactory, especially in reference to an alliance with France.[24]

The last point hinted that Paris now knew what it did not know in November. Champagny did not yet possess information as to the instructions. It would be a month before Napoleon's secret police, possessing their own resources, used them. As soon as Sebastiani's dispatch came to Paris, Jaubert could be found working on the Christmas holiday to translate Mouhib's secret instructions, which had been acquired extralegally. Champagny thereby confirmed at least part of Sebastiani's suspicions. Meanwhile early in November the emperor's blunt statements to the Ottoman ambassador produced a salutary effect at Constantinople. Sebastiani reported, early in January, 1808, that Napoleon's words "gave a very good direction" to the Turkish government. Napoleon ordered Sebastiani decorated again, with the *Couronne de feu*, on January 12.

Tolstoi had been confirmed as expressing the tsar's policy with regard to Silesia. Rumiantsov had written that ambassador quite frankly, on November 26, that Tsar Alexander "would see with extreme satisfaction the prosperity and aggrandizement of the French empire." He considered it unfortunate, however, that Napoleon wished aggrandizement "against Prussia, or against any weak state bordering on the Russian empire." He recalled the French emperor's caution at Tilsit against any common commercial or geographical frontier for the two allied empires.[25]

Savary noted during the first week of December that the Russians seemed to foster no foreign projects except to uphold the alliance with France. On the other hand, Napoleon's proposal to exchange Moldavia and Wallachia for Silesia displeased Alexander. The latter said Napoleon himself had offered him the Principalities, at Tilsit, and at no time had connected Turkey with Prussia. Thus such a "trade" did not conform with Tilsit.[26] In reporting Tolstoi's insistence that Prussia be evacuated, Savary said that he observed no surprise on the autocrat's part—an attitude Savary felt to be an ill omen. It seemed as if "this matter were the principal object of Tolstoi's instructions." Savary admitted, however, that the tsar and Count Rumiantsov were the "only true friends of France in Russia."

De Lesseps penned as good or better observations on political affairs as did Savary. Early in December the consul general recounted that all eyes were fixed on Sweden, where prompt Russian action was anticipated no later than the spring of 1808. The closure of the Baltic against the English would be difficult, if not impossible, without the coöperation of Sweden. Little diplomatic activity for the moment marked the relations of allied Russia and France. Napoleon wrote of the Russian troop and fleet units that had departed from Malta; Alexander thanked the French emperor for a gift of books.[27]

After some delay, on December 7, Russia dispatched the general authority we have mentioned for Tolstoi to negotiate with Turkey under Napoleon's mediation. Because it authorized no terms for discussion, one presumed the reason was to await Caulaincourt and possible suggestions from Napoleon. Paris at the time expected official news from Vienna of London's reply to the proffered mediation for peace.[28] When Russia had failed to bring England to a conference, Austria had tendered its services. George Canning replied, on November 23, by stating that the British cabinet had answered already: to both Austria and Russia it had indicated a willingness to enter negotiations for peace. He vouchsafed not a word, however, of utilizing Austrian or Russian mediation.[29] Thus whereas Russia sent no terms for peace, Britain accepted no mediator.

An exchange of letters between Sebastiani and Marshal Prosorovski clarified Russia's position in the Near East. The Russian commander at Jassy no longer desired an armistice—not even one that met the tsar's objections to certain stipulations of the nonratified arrangement of August 24. The Russians frankly did not wish to evacuate until after a definitive treaty. "Prosorovski's reply troubles and disquiets the court of Constantinople," Sebastiani reported. Ottoman ministers evinced recriminatory attitudes toward France, reminding him that Turkey had declared war against Russia only at the solicitation of France. In a discouraging mood on December 10, Halet urged Sebastiani to get action. He asked, "What has been the price of Ottoman devotion to France?" He said his government had turned back Pozzo di Borgo, together with Russia's offer to restore the Principalities and to pledge noninterference in their internal administration afterwards. It likewise had turned away Paget and "resisted a thousand British intimidations." The Turks had agreed to transfer the forthcoming negotiations with Russia from Bucharest, as originally intended, to Paris. What had been the Turks' reward?

Halet invited Emperor Napoleon to witness their position: Russia would not evacuate the Principalities, a clear violation of the Treaty of Tilsit; on the contrary that nation had stationed additional troops there. The effect would be to stimulate the Serbs to further revolt. The mortified sultan had not even had replies to the two letters he had written Napoleon. Sebastiani could assure Halet only of the general good will of the French emperor. The ambassador himself fell too ill for a time to conduct official business. He so advised Paris, repeating the request for his recall; his health was so bad he thought he would have to turn affairs over to Ruffin or Latour-Maubourg.[30]

From Milan, Champagny replied to Sebastiani's discouraging reports of late November—those complaining against pro-English Halet. The ambassador was told he must speak directly to Sultan Mustapha in certain cases, if the objectionable ministry remained long in office. Napoleon had not written the new sultan, while waiting to learn whether the Russians authorized Tolstoi to negotiate for peace. Napoleon's foreign minister held cautiously to general promises, another indication of the emperor's feeling his way with Russia. "This silence by Napoleon should not cause uneasiness to the Ottoman government," said Champagny. "The emperor always distinguishes between his friends and enemies; and he will always treat as friends those who demonstrate their affection for him." The first new proof of Turkey's friendship for France should be to press vigorously the common effort against England. "This is no time for anyone to be neutral—in this quarrel of England against the continent."[31] Napoleon is best remembered in Milan at this time (December 17) for decreeing new measures to supplement the Berlin decrees of 1806, prohibiting English and regulating neutral shipping with the continent.[32]

On December 11, Savary confirmed the offer of the Principalities in exchange for Silesia, the offer Napoleon had proposed verbally to Tolstoi on November 6. He also conveyed the emperor's admission of comments to Tolstoi: that the world was large enough for both Russia and France, and that if Russia had any more extensive ideas than the proposed exchange respecting Turkey, precise instructions must be sent to Tolstoi; as for himself, Napoleon favored everything that would unite Russia with France more closely.[33] Thus Russia had now been given both versions of the conference of November 6, Tolstoi's and Napoleon's. The significant concluding portion of this statement Caulaincourt also confirmed, when he came to St. Petersburg a few days later.

Meanwhile, impatient Napoleon solicited from General Marmont, in Dalmatia, information respecting the actual strategic value of the Turkish provinces in Europe. His thoughts seemed to be nearing concrete proposals for his ally. He once directed Champagny to caution a French agent against any comment respecting the future status of Constantinople. Everything really awaited Caulaincourt's reports.

The French ambassador's arrival in St. Petersburg on December 17 seemed to foretell some significant new orientation of Napoleon's policy. General Caulaincourt characterized the dwelling provided him as "the most beautiful in St. Petersburg, magnificently furnished." The tsar stated, at the ceremonial audience, "France and Russia will give peace to the world and Napoleon can never have an ally more faithful than myself." Rumiantsov let France know indirectly that Napoleon would not be handling affairs alone. He objected to Champagny's saluting Russia as a "confederate," in Caulaincourt's letter of credence. He said the word "ally," which Champagny also used, meant something in interpreting Franco-Russian relations, whereas the word "confederate" did not. Caulaincourt explained that Napoleon merely intended to be more friendly and cordial than ever. When, a few days later, Rumiantsov again asked the ambassador to omit the disputed word, the latter indirectly foretold the adamant position he would regularly assume: he would not drop the word until Paris so ordered.

Caulaincourt's series of dispatches began on December 21. He detailed his first debate over the proposal to exchange the Principalities for Silesia. The Russians got him badly off the directed order of discussion of the various topics, because they had broken off relations with England. Caulaincourt stated to Tsar Alexander that whereas Napoleon expected the evacuation of the Principalities as required by Tilsit, the attitude of France toward Turkey's territories must be the same as Russia's toward the Prussian provinces. Napoleon's iterated attachment for the tsar nevertheless did not permit an advantage by the tsar that would upset the balance of power created at Tilsit.[34]

On December 21, following the first of the ambassador's many dinners in the imperial palace, Alexander and Caulaincourt in the privacy of the tsar's study discussed all current business, including the issue of Silesia. Alexander commended Napoleon's appointment, saying that Caulaincourt would suit much better in St. Petersburg than would De Laforest. The tsar stated, as evidence of good relations, that Russia had advanced to November 6 its breaking of relations with England. He hinted that he leaned toward war: "Doubtless General Savary reported Rumiantsov and myself as always prejudiced for war with England." He might perhaps have declared it, he continued, had Napoleon given the signal. Respecting Sweden, he agreed he must employ force if its king would not take the steps that conduced to peace. As for Prussia, Alexander repeated that it distressed him to have that state mentioned as compensation for anything from Turkey. "It was Napoleon at Tilsit who spoke first of Moldavia and Wallachia," said Alexander, "as well as concerning other parts of Turkey. Napoleon blocked out his own share. He considered himself as entirely freed of any bonds to Turkey, in consequence of the revolutionary deposition of Sultan Selim. Certainly he said nothing about making poor Prussia an equivalent for the Principalities. As a matter of fact, in the Principalities anarchy and provincial revolutions create more issues than does Russia's interest."

Caulaincourt conveyed the assurance that Napoleon sought only the strict fulfillment of Tilsit. If an equivalent could be found, it would be the first time the emperor ever had separated his court from that of his allies—meaning Turkey. Caulaincourt thus recorded Napoleon's claim of never before having left an ally in the lurch. He continued by stating that his emperor supported Turkey in the same manner as the tsar supported Prussia and that Napoleon had full confidence in Alexander.

The tsar said that he understood, and that with the general attitude they shared, France and Russia could always agree on details; but Napoleon's mention of such an exchange distressed him.

Caulaincourt thus had permitted himself to be caught off guard by discussing Turkey first, instead of a Russian war against Great Britain. Nonetheless he proceeded unreservedly with his prescribed arguments against restricting the French territorial equivalent to the Balkans. The tsar admitted that Caulaincourt presented the case clearly, but he in no sense admitted its validity. He did not doubt Napoleon's intentions. It would be necessary, however, to accomplish something significant to prove to Russia and the Russian army that his alliance with France would not accrue solely to French advantage. He recalled Napoleon's expressions at Tilsit, in which the French emperor did not hold an opinion of the Turks of the sort to lead him to support them. He had offered to second Russia's interest in Turkey as his own. "He set our share, the Principalities, and his own, together with something to Austria to satisfy its *amour-propre* rather more than its ambition. Such were his intentions." The Turks, not the Russians, broke the armistice. If he did not have full faith in Napoleon, he would under some pretext now renew the fighting against Turkey.

Caulaincourt observed, in his analysis of this conversation sent to Paris, what the reader has observed, that the discussion had begun to move around in circles. He therefore fell back on his instructions by stating that the problem of Turkey should be arranged between the two emperors themselves in a personal meeting. If the Turks had mistrusted the Wallachians, the latter nonetheless were still Turkish subjects. So it was with Prussia, where the police power had not always taken account of the best interests of the state.

The tsar almost duplicated Napoleon's planned device of attempting to render his ally amenable by seeming to concede the area most sought. He suggested arranging a general understanding before the spring of 1808, because his army would be prepared by that time to act—either against Sweden or England. Meanwhile, he desired frequent discussions with Caulaincourt. They must work together respecting the measures to be taken if the English should attack Russia's coasts. He iterated that his reorganized army stood ready for service against either the English or the Swedes. Caulaincourt stated, as authorized, that Denmark would second the tsar's operations in Sweden.[35]

Rather than discuss a war in the north, Rumiantsov preoccupied himself with Tsarina Catherine's system of conquest in the south against the Ottoman Empire. Caulaincourt's initial discussion with that minister likewise came on December 21, in advance of the talk with the tsar. Rumiantsov raised the issue of Prussia, based on Tolstoi's report of his conference of November 6 with Napoleon. Caulaincourt argued that Tolstoi had not accurately reported Napoleon's meaning; the emperor really desired to execute the Treaty of Tilsit.

Caulaincourt separately recorded his own reactions for Champagny, after rephrasing his two virtually stenographic reports of the first conversations. By explaining the interrelationship of Prussian and Turkish situations, he had simply followed his instructions. He discovered that Russia itself had apparently decided to encourage war between Russia and England in advance of his coming by breaking off diplomatic and commercial relations. With Russia's army ready for conquest in Finland, the question of Sweden likewise seemed near a decision. The ambassador disclaimed responsibility for the initiative that had forced the premature discussion of Turkey; Tolstoi's raising the Prussian question with Napoleon and Champagny on November 6 had done that. As it was, *amour-propre* seemed to replace policy when Russia opposed France's taking an equivalent in Prussia. The tsar earlier had stated to Savary that although he did indeed desire to hold the Principalities, he would evacuate them rather than agree to Prussia's loss of a single additional village. Caulaincourt's decided impression, gained in these early talks, interpreted Russia as fearing a French province on its frontier. Count Rumiantsov said he well remembered Napoleon's caution at Tilsit, that friendly great powers should never possess a common frontier.[36]

Almost sidetracked entirely was the issue of a Russian war against Great Britain. During the next few days Caulaincourt found an occasion to refute Russia's statement that Napoleon had first suggested a partition of Turkey. Apparently an afterthought, he may have remembered to do this at the time he was writing his initial reports. He mentioned again the need for a personal meeting between the two sovereigns and re-emphasized the idea that wise policy should dictate compensation to France in Prussia. He considered—so he wrote Champagny—that his repetition of points served to stress the reasoning presented in his opening discussion with the tsar.[37]

Now returned from Italy, Napoleon read these reports on January 18, 1808. Obviously he must offer something better. In consequence, we shall see him quickly initiate—to put it bluntly—the ill-advised and insincere proposal of February 2 for a joint Franco-Russian expedition to India (chap. xii). Even if only a smokescreen for his continued occupation of Silesia, such a scheme possessed plausibility. Would the tsar accept it? Meanwhile, Champagny directed Caulaincourt to follow without deviation the same line he had been taking respecting Turkey. He explained that he had intended as a compliment the word "confederate" used in accrediting Caulaincourt, and the word was always so taken in Paris. He sent new letters which conformed literally to Rumiantsov's suggestion.[38]

The status of Caulaincourt's negotiations remained unchanged for several days. St. Petersburg lacked news of any new developments in Turkey and, so it seemed, no one said anything concerning Britain. Caulaincourt tried unsuccessfully to commit Russia to a fighting war against England. Finally, when almost at the end of his resources, he suggested to Rumiantsov, on December 28, the desirability of the joint expedition to India.

No alert Russian could possibly miss that hint of a French military expedition based at the Turkish Straits. "The Russian foreign minister did not appear to believe in the possibility of this expedition," Caulaincourt meekly observed, in his report.[39] This reaction also doubtless influenced Napoleon to appeal personally for the expedition to India—which we shall see him do in his letter to the tsar on February 2. Caulaincourt met success with the proposal that France purchase naval stores and construct three ships of the line in Russian shipyards: the tsar's government appeared disposed to permit the construction and to guarantee the safety of the goods and vessels, even during war. Caulaincourt busied himself drafting the agreement for this, although not certain he possessed the authority to do so. This permission especially demonstrated Russia's friendship, Russians pointed out, for Britain had been refused a similar request during the time of greatest Anglo-Russian intimacy.[40]

From his observations in Paris Count Tolstoi suspected Napoleon's intentions more than ever, as time elapsed. Napoleon for his part clearly suspected that Tolstoi was sending adverse reports to St. Petersburg. Never once after the meeting of November 6 did Napoleon discuss affairs with him frankly. Tolstoi's report of December 28 relayed certain gossip that seemed to him to have some foundation in fact, for Napoleon did not disavow it: France wished to create a Kingdom of Dalmatia, territorially extended; the French provinces on the eastern coast of the Adriatic would furnish the nucleus and it would be destined to embrace southern Greece and other sections of the Ottoman Empire.[41]

On December 30, Caulaincourt acknowledged Champagny's order of November 25 from Milan, to treat Herr Merveldt frigidly. He replied that he would conform—although it must have been difficult, for he added that Austria's envoy had scheduled for that evening his first diplomatic dinner honoring Caulaincourt himself.[42] General Savary finally departed for France. As 1808 opened, court circles in St. Petersburg discussed the crisis in Russo-Swedish affairs. Reports from Constantinople told on January 10 of the severity of Ottoman measures. These, illustrated by Prince Suzzo's execution, were designed to hold the loyalty of the government's personnel. Arthur Paget remained on board one of the British frigates at the entrance of the Dardanelles, to be ready to negotiate if a good opportunity offered. A delay of almost a year proved to be needed.

In Persia, Gardane's impressive mission had finally arrived. It had left Constantinople late in September and traveled by way of Ankara, Tokat, Erzurum, Khoi—a journey Gardane described as "infinitely arduous and dangerous." Crown Prince Abbas Mirza gave the party a splendid reception at Tabriz. Napoleon's minister entered Teheran on December 4, an associate reporting the reception as "pompous." Joannin and the few others had prepared in advance for the distinguished welcome.

Feth Ali appeared none too happy about his alliance with France's brilliant ruler-dictator. Minister Gardane scored an initial success, and the shah broke relations with the English East India Company soon after his coming. On December 24 the shah ordered all the English expelled from Persia, and he withdrew his envoy from Bombay. Of the belated news he brought, the details of the French peace with Russia was the most discouraging for Persia, for it canceled out the expected French aid in the Russo-Persian conflict. Nevertheless, Gardane demonstrated for several months his ability at clever persuasion. The anti-English attitude of official Persia accounted for the early success in that phase of his diplomacy.

A possible French expedition against India occupied the thoughts of everyone connected with Gardane's mission. They studied routes and facilities; Gardane believed the Levantine headquarters for it should be Syria. When the shah asked outright for Napoleon's assistance to exclude Russia from Georgia, the minister answered cleverly. He argued that that stipulation—Number 8 of the Franco-Persian treaty of alliance—simply because it occurred later in the sequence than Article 4, which called for Persia's assistance for France to go to India, could be executed only after stipulation number four had been fulfilled. The Persians agreed with this interpretation, although unconvinced of its logic. Even so, Gardane frankly advised Paris that an Indian venture by France and Persia would depend on the restoration of peace between Persia and Russia. So receptive were Persians to Napoleonic advice that Gardane had within a month accomplished much. He exchanged ratifications for the treaty of alliance and concluded a new treaty of commerce. Persia conceded to France for naval and shipping facilities the islands of Karek and Bender-Abassi in the Persian Gulf. It accorded in all Persian villages freedom of religious worship for French consuls. In accordance with his secret instructions, Gardane signed a convention calling for Persia's purchase of 20,000 muskets in France at the stated price of 30 francs each—to be payable when Napoleon delivered them to the Persian Gulf.

Meanwhile, Yousef Bey, Persia's messenger in Paris, transacted no official business. That he found himself fêted as if a full-fledged ambassador, as we have seen, was due to a mistake on Napoleon's part. In December he at last stated that he felt called upon to request with vigor that replies be handed him to the letters he had delivered from the shah and the vizir. Owing to his health he wished to return to Teheran, but he could not leave France without the replies. Napoleon accordingly, upon his return to Paris in mid-January, wrote briefly to the shah. His letter stated that it would be delivered by Yousef, an individual who had been "treated as the envoy of a Prince who is dear to me and with whose actions I have been pleased." His only mention of politics referred to England as their enemy. Champagny used the same Persian courier to carry his letter advising Gardane he had nothing to add to the latter's general instructions. Thus when the Persians should secretly unseal and read that communication, they would learn from it exactly nothing. Eventually Yousef departed, leaving his secretary-interpreter in Paris without funds. The latter appealed to Napoleon as the ally of his sovereign not to permit him to live in poverty and in debt. He tendered a bill covering accumulated debts and future needs in the amount of some 12,000 francs.[43]

The slow-moving Persian affairs were but taking their natural course.

In this chapter we have seen Napoleon connect Russia's wish to acquire the Ottoman provinces of Moldavia and Wallachia—hinterland of the Straits which Russia coveted—with his own demand to hold Prussian Silesia. Tsar Alexander, on the other hand, wished that France acquire as an equivalent to the Principalities some territory in the Balkans, perhaps in Albania and southern Greece. This problem led to overtures from Russia to discuss the details of a possibly more extensive partition of Turkey. As Napoleon's new ambassador to Russia began his work, the inferences from Napoleon's instructions were clear. Paris wished to take an Anglo-Russian war for granted. With that war under way, secret negotiations would consider a number of territorial transfers in Europe. Napoleon seemed more than ready to offer to exchange almost all of Ottoman Moldavia and Wallachia for Silesia, together with Albania and Bosnia. Sensing Russia's reluctance to concede Silesia, he lured Alexander with the Principalities and with hints of something more to follow—after peace with England. It is significant that he declined as yet to encourage (although he would not discourage) all Russia's tentative efforts toward a more general partition of the Ottoman Empire. We note an important omission in the instructions to Caulaincourt: there is no hint of a territorial adjustment at the Straits. This is all the more conspicuous by reason of Tolstoi's report to St. Petersburg in which he attributed to Napoleon the direct comment that Russia might acquire Constantinople.

XII

Shall Turkey Be Partitioned?

THERE IS no other way to check the progressive aggrandizement of the empire of a Napoleon or a Hitler than to defeat it. The
farther it extends, the farther it wishes to extend. It is never satiated,
never appeased. At Napoleon's zenith, in February 1808, he was contemplating for a moment crossing the Dardanelles and the Bosporus and
going all the way to India, in coöperation with Russia and Austria. He
never seriously considered attacking India alone, either in 1798 or at the
height of his power.

Faulty interpretations of Turkey's weakness had attracted colony-
seeking French imperialists to Ottoman Egypt in 1798. Owing to the
Franco-Russian alliance the Ottoman Empire could be virtually ignored,
from a strategic point of view, in 1808. An expedition to India might
be balanced against Russia's wish to partition the Ottoman Empire, particularly if Napoleon planned to make Constantinople the jumping-off
place—as Ambassador Caulaincourt had suggested and as the emperor
himself would propose. Napoleon's scheme for a joint thrust by land
against India, genuine in appearance, may have been merely a cover-up
for his push into Spain.

The international aspects of the manifold and shifting Levantine
problems are illustrated in this chapter by the continued Franco-Russian
debate over Silesia and by Napoleon's willingness to consider a partition of Turkey. The weakness of the Turkish government and policy
invited intervention. In the north, Denmark had drawn some British
naval strength to the North Sea; Tsar Alexander's challenge to Sweden
would draw more. With England thus occupied, allied France and Russia might by means of partition win for themselves new territories in the
Near and Middle East.

Early in the nineteenth century—precisely as before and since—an
internally divided India lured the potential invader. Official France had
long confidently held to the formula that a small number of European

troops could conquer and rule the country, owing to the competing nationalities, castes, and religions within it. Perhaps such troops could arrive there by land. Thus the problem of India itself could be reduced in Napoleon's calculations to that of excluding a few Englishmen. France and Russia might attack India from the land side, whereas Britain had to defend the sea routes to that country. The French emperor believed that with Russia's help he could circumvent the British policy—which would not be a hesitant one—for the routes to India. Certainly in February, 1808, and this is the pivotal month for our discussion here, Napoleon looked upon India as a land problem which France and Russia could solve by acting together.

Had the principal problem of the British defense of India already become, in 1808, essentially that of the defense of the land instead of the sea approaches to India? A parallel, we remember, is that of Adolf Hitler's scheming for Germany and Japan to win India. If it had been a land problem in 1941, its solution might have been attempted by Soviet Russia or Japan, or perhaps by Germany. Whether in 1808 or 1941, however, only with Russia eliminated or coöperating would India be vulnerable by land whether by Napoleon's France, Tojo's Japan, or Hitler's Germany. Later, we might have expected the inevitable: a Franco-Russian, Russo-German, or German-Japanese conflict over India.

Ambassador Tolstoi rendered himself increasingly distasteful to Napoleon by his continued insistence that France evacuate Silesia. Tolstoi inquired, on January 10, 1808, whether there were any changes in France's official opinion. Champagny replied that matters stood where they were in mid-November; Prussia would be evacuated as soon as it paid the indemnity. Tolstoi rejoined that the cost of Napoleon's troops of occupation diminished Prussia's ability to pay. When the emperor returned from Italy a few days later, Tolstoi read to him several dispatches from Rumiantsov and argued for the separation of Turkey's affairs from Prussia's. Napoleon replied tauntingly that, judged by what the tsar's ambassador contended, the destruction of the Ottoman Empire had already been decided upon at St. Petersburg. Tolstoi tacitly agreed by remarking that the French emperor seemed to be the only one who still believed that that empire, crippled by anarchy, possessed any value.

Napoleon said he could not entirely forget the services of the sultan to him in turning considerable forces against Russia during the last war. Tolstoi balanced against this all of Russia's assistance to Napoleon, notably the cession of Corfu at Tilsit and the demonstrations against

Sweden. He averred that Moldavia and Wallachia could by no means compensate for the many sacrifices to ensue from Russia's rupture with Britain. Tolstoi wrote his government that Napoleon had not closed the door to the possibility of arranging Turkish affairs independently of Prussia's.[1]

Coveted by Napoleon, Albania offered the emperor a timely pretext to proceed with Russia toward a partition. Whatever tendency its pasha had held toward coöperation with France had faded. As the starting-point Napoleon charged that Ali Pasha was dealing openly with the British. Making the charge at Constantinople, he would be able in that way also to assure himself of the nature of the real sentiments of the new sultan toward England. He properly ignored the reality of the existence of an Anglo-Turkish "war" but wished to know what attitude Sultan Mustapha IV would take if the British attacked Corfu. Could Turkey somehow be brought into effective action against Britain?

Napoleon wished Turkey to be advised that negotiations for peace between it and Russia had begun. This false advice was designed to meet the sultan's looking to him as the mediator authorized at Tilsit. He issued instructions that several questions be posed at Constantinople. If Russia wished to retain the Principalities, would Turkey enter a military alliance with France? What means did the sultan possess for waging war? If the British landed on Corfu, would that ruler order Ali Pasha to provision the fortress and defend the French troops and messengers sent along the land routes? Might France not send a contingent of 4,000 or 5,000 men through Ottoman territory to reinforce Corfu—a force sufficient for that task but not large enough to alarm Ali Pasha? He impatiently directed General Marmont to request Ali Pasha for permission to march the troops from Cattaro to Butrinto (February 2). He also boldly notified General Lauriston, commander on Corfu, that Butrinto and the other mainland points formerly held by the Republic of Venice had been turned over by Turkey to French sovereignty.[2]

Thus territories must be handed to Russia and military facilities accorded France. How could Napoleon on the one hand take Russia's part in calling for the cession of the Principalities and on the other induce Turkey to enter a fighting war against England? Turkey must pay either way, and obtain in return only the promise of security for whatever part of its empire might remain intact. In fact, to promise Turkey anything would endanger the Franco-Russian alliance. Such a program would be impossible of acceptance by any but the weakest of weak governments at Constantinople. Alexander and Napoleon had discussed the weakness at Tilsit and both were watching the gyrations of Mustapha's policy.

Napoleon blandly proceeded to a contingent program of partition. If Turkey refused what he requested, he would be given the excuse to arrange the partition with Russia. He took the diplomatic offensive, much as he would in military matters. He laid the groundwork for something to trade to Russia in exchange for Silesia or India or both. Thus on January 12 Foreign Minister Champagny bluntly instructed Sebastiani at Constantinople: "The ambassador is charged to communicate to Turkey that the emperor has sought in vain to induce Russia to evacuate the Principalities and that Turkey probably will be forced to purchase peace at the price of these two provinces." Champagny phrased the directions respecting Albania less forcefully, although he withheld none of Napoleon's intent. Napoleon wished not only to defend the Ionian Islands but to prepare Corfu for a prolonged English siege. Sebastiani must request immediate orders to Ali Pasha to assure the latter's support in Napoleon's provisioning of beleaguered Corfu. He intended some 6,000 troops (increasing the original figure) to march quickly from the Cattaro to Butrinto, whence to sail to Corfu and Sainte Maure.

In not evacuating Moldavia and Wallachia, Russia had violated a stipulation of Tilsit, although many now believed that the matter had been privately arranged between the two emperors. Champagny began to hedge when the Ottoman ambassador waited eagerly to negotiate peace in Paris. The Principalities would require a prolonged discussion, he stated. Although Napoleon had intended to make further representations in Turkey's behalf, he now believed that he should not take sides; he must be a mediator of peace in the truest sense of the term. He would remember the good dispositions of Turkey in respect to providing facilities for Corfu. Sebastiani could approach the problem of the Principalities by discovering Turkey's attitude, should Russia wish to retain Moldavia and Wallachia enough to threaten a new campaign.[3]

To make Albania a more effective excuse, Napoleon wrote (on January 22) personally to the sultan. The ambassador must deliver the letter in special audience. Napoleon wished precise orders to assure his provisioning of Corfu and, if possible, also of Sainte Maure. Whether he believed it or not, he stated his doubt that the English would besiege Corfu. Napoleon reciprocated the sultan's expression of a friendly attitude toward France. He desired the sincere reconciliation of Russia and Turkey. England remained the real enemy of France and Turkey—the

England that menaced several points of the Ottoman Empire, including the pashalics near Corfu. For the sultan's cause no less than for his own, French forces must oppose them there. He awaited with confidence the sultan's granting of facilities.[4]

In privately clarifying his letter he told Sebastiani he thus addressed the sultan in order that, if the English actually besieged Corfu, any necessary portion (again increasing the figure) of the French army of 20,000 in Dalmatia might be able to depart from Cattaro, cross Ali Pasha's Albanian territory, and appear on the coast opposite Corfu. From Butrinto the troops might readily sail to Corfu, join the garrison, and drive the besiegers into the sea. In any eventuality he expected that fortress to hold out for six months. He had requested Ali Pasha of Albania to protect the communications between Cattaro and Butrinto and wished the sultan so to order him.

A month later the effect of these two communications was apparent. The Turks gave little attention to anything said respecting Corfu but much to Napoleon's willingness to permit Russia to hold the Principalities. Although Russia had rejected the negotiated Russo-Turkish armistice, Alexander and Mustapha nevertheless were observing a working armistice—Russia meanwhile retaining its military control in Moldavia and Wallachia. New fighting might break out at any time.

If Russia had really desired a settlement with Turkey, Tolstoi like Mouhib would have been prepared by January for a discussion, under French mediation, of actual terms for peace. No directions respecting terms had accompanied his authorization to negotiate. It is apparent from the French documents, however, that the time had not yet arrived for detailed negotiations, nor indeed for any Russo-Turkish discussions. France and Russia procrastinated. Paris inquired of Turkey what it desired, as if it had not informed itself already from a secret examination of Mouhib's secret instructions. No one held a deep conviction that peace would come between Russia and Turkey. Mediator Napoleon at the moment thought rather more of Turkey as the means whereby to encourage Russia to aid in the defeat of England.

Napoleon insisted most emphatically that the Turkish and Prussian territorial questions be combined. France would give away some of Turkey's possessions provided Russia gave away some of Prussia's. Champagny phrased two alternate secret plans and handed them to Ambassador Tolstoi in writing, on January 14. In both, Bessarabia and the mouths of the Danube might go to Russia. In one plan, Russia and France actually would evacuate Silesia and the Principalities as stipulated at Tilsit; in the other they would respectively assume sovereignty over them.[5] Tolstoi at the moment troubled himself over what he imagined he had discovered, a French plot for the total dismemberment of Prussia. Champagny felt called upon to deny this to St. Petersburg.

At last in mid-January Tolstoi could advise Champagny that he had received full authority to treat for peace with the Ottoman ambassador. Accordingly, the negotiation began. Champagny suggested by letters that Tolstoi and Mouhib transmit their credentials to him. The Ottoman ambassador—one of the few Turks of the period who knew where he was going—put the French on the defensive by calling for Napoleon's support to preserve the independence and integrity of the Ottoman Empire, "as solemnly promised by General Sebastiani."[6] (Mouhib had been in Constantinople in June and July, 1807, when Sebastiani formally made a similar commitment; later, Mouhib revealed himself as a personal enemy of Napoleonic policy.) Tolstoi's dispatches reflect continued irritation with France. That of January 14 suggested that from the beginning Napoleon had never intended to evacuate Silesia.[7]

What did the Turks wish in a settlement with Russia? Mouhib's secret instructions seem never to have been communicated to France officially. Sebastiani surmised that they contained anti-French clauses. How these came into French hands unofficially is not revealed. We know only, as has been mentioned, that on Christmas Day of 1807 Jaubert translated the pertinent letters, one by the grand vizir dated September 25 and the other by the foreign minister dated October, 1807. According to these, confident Turks believed that Napoleon would have the Russians remove themselves from the Principalities. The letters directed the exclusion by negotiation of Russia's vessels from the Straits: "The passage of the Straits of Constantinople must be absolutely prohibited to Russian war vessels and this prohibition is an extremely essential object of your mission." Mouhib was required by his government, however, to make the exclusion from the Straits general, thus restricting all the foreign powers, including France.

The treaty with Russia represented only one of Turkey's intended negotiations in Paris, where official Turks were still expected to talk of an alliance with Napoleon. In the instructions, France must not be authorized to march its military forces across Turkey. The grand vizir thus directed Mouhib: "In the project of a treaty of alliance handed Vahid Effendi at Finkenstein, it is stated that the Ottoman government would not place any impediment to the passage through Turkey of any French individuals en route to Persia. Such clauses inserted in treaties in an absolute manner are evidently detrimental to the interests of the Ottoman Empire, and you must oppose these with all your might."[8] This would result in difficulties also for the passage of French troops through Albania, standing along the Balkan rim of the Ottoman and French Empires. Indeed, Napoleon eventually withdrew his request to cross Albania having found he faced so much opposition to it. From extralegal information he knew already of the Ottoman plan to forestall his sending troops through the heart of their empire. He formulated a strategic reply to be applied practically: if he could agree with Russia to send troops through Constantinople toward Persia and India, he might simply ignore the intended Ottoman intention to refuse him passage. A hint relayed by Sebastiani presented a convenient way out. The Ottomans wished to discuss the proposed alliance with Napoleon only after a treaty of peace had been signed with Russia. If there should be no such treaty, no occasion would arise for Turkey to announce its intended general refusal of transit facilities by land and sea.

These were the basic factors behind the scenes for Napoleon's proposing a joint thrust at India. The ending of any further attempt by Austria to mediate an Anglo-French peace represented the ostensible reason for the ensuing secret discussions.

Tolstoi correctly observed that Talleyrand, who had been dismissed, still possessed considerable influence on Napoleon's foreign policies. Talleyrand long had been, generally speaking, pro-Austrian and pro-Turkish. His influence would be important early in 1810, in arranging Napoleon's marriage with Maria Louisa, for Talleyrand preferred a Habsburg princess to a Romanov grand duchess. Tolstoi reported that the emperor twice consulted the ex-foreign minister in mid-January, 1808. Both seemed convinced that peace would be impossible, so long as George Canning and the adamant British ministry of that day held office. King George soon confirmed this, with a bellicose speech in Parliament.[9]

Napoleon's consultation with Talleyrand is revealed in Prince Metternich's *Memoirs*. Then ambassador in Paris, Metternich found himself engaged in discussions in January, 1807, intended as the secret preliminary of a possible partition of Turkey. Talleyrand and Metternich agreed to withhold their discussion from Tolstoi, as well as from Foreign Minister Champagny. Metternich reported to Count Stadion of Austria's government that Talleyrand desired to force the Habsburgs to adopt an anti-English policy. He wished to align them for coöperation with France and Russia in an expedition against British India. Metternich states that Talleyrand said this to him, on January 18: "Napoleon has two plans in mind. One rests on real foundations, the other is a romance. The first is the partition of Turkey, the second an expedition to India. You ought to be in on both of them. French and Russian soldiers should appear along with Austrian soldiers. And the French, the Austrians, and the Russians ought to enter Constantinople on the same day." Metternich admitted that Austria should participate, if in any event changes must come. Talleyrand made it seem attractive by suggesting that the shares of Ottoman spoils would be smaller for each power, if arranged for three instead of for two. Austria by all means should avoid being left out.[10]

Metternich as an afterthought inquired what Russia thought of this significant overture. Talleyrand replied that the first deep incisions in territory had already been made; Russia had been the first to desire a share of Turkey, and France until shortly before had favored conserving the sultan's state. He believed that Russia wished to include Austria and that both Russia and France now desired a partition. Indeed, Russia was helping itself to the first nineteenth-century slices of Turkey, the conclusion being that "France would not succeed in having the Russians evacuate Moldavia and Wallachia."

Metternich advised against counting upon an easy conquest of the Ottoman Empire. He estimated that it would cost 300,000 men and require several years, allowing for the anticipated fighting, illness, and brigandage. Nor would the country become Europeanized, no matter what the foreign rule. Talleyrand affirmed that these considerations would not stop Napoleon. He suggested that only token forces would be needed from Austria. Napoleon could direct the combined efforts from Italy.

Metternich inquired what portions France would want. He observed that many Ottoman areas would tempt the Russians and that certain portions would be absolutely essential for Austria. Talleyrand stated that the Morea, the Ionian Islands, and the Aegean islands guarding the Dardanelles, together with Egypt, would suit Napoleon. He believed Austria would want the banks of the Danube river, Bosnia, and Bulgaria. The ex-foreign minister added, after speaking of the Crimea, "Constantinople must be yours, although in the present position of affairs the Russians have the most right to it." He recommended that Austria decide promptly because the plan would in any event be executed soon.[11]

The Austrian ambassador frankly advised his court to consider seriously this secret proposal to partition a vast neighboring empire. "Everything bespeaks some great movement," he wrote. Metternich also recounted to Vienna the circumstance that when Champagny had been hastily summoned for new conscriptions, he read to the French Senate comments of exceptional violence against England. Metternich reverted to the Bonapartean philosophy of 1798: "Turkey will be attacked for want of something better to do," he wrote, "and because Napoleon long has desired to strike a blow at English commerce in the Near East." The colonization and civilization of Egypt represented a fixed idea for Napoleon.

"We cannot save Turkey," Metternich advised Stadion. We must "therefore help in the partition and endeavor to get as good a share of it as possible. We cannot resist the destructive and invasive principles of the French emperor and hence we must deflect them from ourselves." He did not accept Talleyrand's appraisal of Russia's desire to partition the Ottoman Empire at that moment. He admitted that the ambition existed but believed its extensive character had been modified. Whereas Russians would gladly aggrandize themselves at the expense of Turkey, "they feared to divide the cake with persons having such good appetites."

In Metternich's opinion, to delay taking sides would be "exceedingly dangerous." Austria held the position of being offered something definite in exchange for its coöperation, and it should not fail to heed Talleyrand's advice to be watchful of its own interests. Metternich warned that France might wish to take Constantinople: "It would be very difficult to suppose that Constantinople would be assigned to the Russians. And it seems to me extremely probable that, of the three allied generals, the French general would have the most pretension to establish his headquarters there. M. de Talleyrand said to me yesterday, 'It is necessary that we should become allies.'" France and Russia both needed Austria, each to watch the other, Talleyrand concluded; Austria by playing its part would come out very well.[12]

Notwithstanding the pledge to secrecy, Metternich could not refrain from engaging Tolstoi in conversation respecting the scheme. With the latter he discussed the possible destruction of Turkey, labeling it merely a "political dream" he had had. He admitted that Napoleon had confirmed part of the dream, however, and that the emperor in doing so had mentioned the word Constantinople. Tolstoi appeared curious respecting the details. Metternich said nothing more, except to warn that Russia and Austria must take quite seriously any mention of Constantinople by Napoleon. Adroit questioning confirmed his initial persuasion that Talleyrand had not discussed the matter with Tolstoi. He asked point blank whether Russia would fight to preserve Turkey against any French attack.

Tolstoi commented candidly, "If the cake cannot be saved, it must be fairly divided." Metternich assumed from all this that Caulaincourt must be intended as the agent to make the overture. He soon covered what he at first had not mentioned, by assuring Tolstoi that Russia would be notified and asked to concert, if the French should advance any precise proposals.[13]

Metternich had detected a decidedly official character in his two discussions with Talleyrand. He did not, however, expect the fate of the Ottoman Empire to be approached as directly as Napoleon would broach it to him in the audience granted on January 22. The emperor employed as the opening wedge the question of why Constantinople had not been brought into discussion by English ministers in their recent talks of peace with Austria. These were talks that had convinced him England did not really want peace. Metternich led the French ruler on, speculatively remarking that the English probably thought that France could not threaten Turkey's independence after being the most vociferous partisans of its preservation. He said he believed that Austria's interest in Turkey actually took precedence over the French interest there.

Napoleon met that debatable point promptly by replying, "Our interest is more decided than yours." He charged that Austria supported the sultan only because of Turkey's weakness. Although traditional in Austro-Turkish relations, questions of rivalry had never entered into Franco-Turkish relations. By location as well as tradition Austria should be Turkey's enemy; France by the same tokens should be Turkey's friend. Imperative circumstances alone would force him to strike a blow at the Ottomans—whom he really ought to sustain by every means in his power. France needed no territorial aggrandizement, although he would not deny that Egypt and some colonies would be advantageous. Such colonies could not equal "the prodigious expansion of Russia," an expansion which Austria also could not see with indifference. Indeed, the partition of Turkey should unite France and Austria quite closely.

Napoleon reverted to Constantinople. "When they [the Russians] are established at Constantinople you will need France to help you against them and France will need you to counterbalance them. It is not yet a question of partition but when it becomes so I shall advise you. You must participate in it. Whatever may be your share, you will possess a very strong interest in having a hand in the affair and you must participate. You have just and geographical claims on the course of the Danube."

Metternich expressed his surprise at this broaching of the subject of the destruction of the Ottoman Empire. Although Austria desired to preserve Turkey, if France abandoned that old Mohammedan ally it would be finished. If Turkey must crumble, he hastily added, Austria could not be indifferent, either to the choice of spoils by the partitioning powers or to its own share. With no instructions for such a problem, he could suggest only a general statement. France would do well to depend upon Austria rather than upon Russia. On the other hand, Austria felt that France, by virtue of location, could do it more harm than could Russia.

If Napoleon coöperated with Russia, he said, he must direct the common policy. He led Metternich into discussing personalities. The two agreed that generals did not really suit the diplomatic function. The emperor inveighed against General Merveldt, about whose pro-English attitude Savary, De Lesseps, and Caulaincourt in succession had complained, and reproached General Count Tolstoi with talking too much for the envoy of a defeated power. Metternich complained against Napoleon's ambassador in Vienna, General Antoine Andreossy (who became Napoleon's envoy at Constantinople in the critical year 1812).

Metternich records that he and Napoleon walked up and down the emperor's large study fifty times, Napoleon meanwhile keeping his luncheon and attendants waiting for two hours. At the end, Napoleon thus summarized what Metternich must report: "There is at present no question of a partition of Turkey but whenever there is, you not only will be allowed but called as by right to defend and discuss with us your interests and your views."[14]

Great Britain represented the principal dark cloud in Napoleon's scheming in the early weeks of 1808, for King George's speech on January 21 publicly challenged France to a fight to the finish. His speech sought new national support in "this so terrible and so imposing" struggle. Doubtless General Savary's comment, upon his returning to Paris, had convinced Napoleon that something new or sensational would be needed to bring Russia into active war.

Some sort of Russo-Turkish negotiations for peace were mentioned many times. Tolstoi and Mouhib Effendi on January 23 met with Champagny in what proved their only conference with such an object. The latter as the mediator accepted their credentials and read them aloud. Mouhib's credentials took care to use Napoleon's titles, "Emperor and Padishah of the French, King of Italy." Tolstoi objected to Turkey's statement in Mouhib's papers that an armistice existed, because the tsar, as everyone knew, had not ratified the armistice with Turkey. Mouhib manifested the wish to proceed immediately to negotiate a treaty, while Tolstoi asked for a delay, stating he must be given time to obtain necessary instructions from St. Petersburg.[15] On February 2, the day of a significant Napoleonic proposal to Russia, Champagny started on its way to Constantinople a tiny communication, the minutes of the brief conference. He thereafter recognized the stalemate but did nothing to end it. On February 19 he wrote Caulaincourt he was having "to struggle daily against the requests of the Ottoman ambassador to learn when conferences for peace would be resumed, nothing having been done since the transmission of the credentials."

The dissatisfaction of nervous Turks at Constantinople now turned to alarm at the protracted delay in the peace conferences. Fighting weather would return to the Balkans before long, and the armistice would expire at the end of March. Sebastiani relayed the Turkish official view, reporting their mention of an armistice in the present tense. Because the Russians did not admit the existence of a legal armistice, no validity attached to the terminal date. Sebastiani conducted little business; everyone awaited action in Paris. "It is to satisfy the Turks," he apologized to Champagny, "that I often send couriers to your excellency."

A long conversation between the tsar and Caulaincourt on January 29 concerned Constantinople in relation to the routes to India. Napoleon's ambassador reasoned that the two powers should not neglect any means of achieving the common goal of defeating Britain. This led to the matter of the approaches to India. Russia well understood from its many military and other experiences the difficulties of arriving there. The tsar frankly hinted of the uncertainty of success, owing to the distances, deserts, and poor means of subsistence. Caulaincourt conveyed Napoleon's suggestion that several army officers reconnoiter that country and report what would be needed to ensure success. Gardane was already mapping the routes within Persia.

It was significant that Alexander inquired by what routes the armies of Russia and France would move to Persia, in the event they adopted the plan. This suggested for the first time an idea for Caulaincourt's answer which eventually would bring the two allies into sharp disagreement. He responded with the earlier words of Champagny (although he attributed them to himself): "Geography wills that the French army should pass through Constantinople." Russia's army might travel through the Caucasus, if the tsar did not possess sufficient ships to cross the Caspian. The tsar at the time hazarded no rejoinder.[16]

Persians meanwhile could not have realized that Napoleon considered them merely as pawns useful against England and would never really help them to recover Georgia. Gardane must have known or guessed this policy, hence he went to considerable lengths to disguise it. It is less important, if we take into account the slow and difficult means of communication, that privately he minimized Persia's fighting ability. The Persians could not guess the adverse Napoleonic policy in store for them. On the basis of the facts at hand, it would appear that Napoleon's military coöperation with them had begun to be realized. Witness Gardane's convention of late 1807, which promised them 20,000 muskets and a supply of ammunition, and the French officers already training segments of Persia's army in the famous Napoleonic methods.

From his military experience Gardane believed that a French attack on India should be based in Syria, with Persia coöperating. He thought Persia certainly would demand Georgia as the price of that aid. France unquestionably enjoyed the favored diplomatic position in Persia, but Gardane did not fail to observe how British commercial interests and influence were still strong there and were still relatively permanent. He and his officers kept preparing the ground for invasion. They mapped routes to India, discussed itineraries, visited and studied the ports of the Caspian Sea and the Persian Gulf. He started frequent reports on these subjects on their slow journey to Paris.[17]

After some eight weeks in Teheran, Gardane reported that the shah and his ministers appeared sincerely devoted to the French. Abbas Mirza, the heir to the throne, seemed especially devoted. Persian policy sought above everything to regain Georgia. Gardane estimated that 40,000 to 50,000 European troops could win India, provided they included at least 3,000 or 4,000 cavalry. He asked to be recalled to France, pleading

poor health and a dislike for the air at Teheran. The shah replied to
Napoleon's letter of mid-1807 delivered by Gardane. He expressed approval of the minister and of the French officers and stated that he
would live up to all the stipulations of his alliance. He had heard that
a Russian negotiator would come to Teheran. At the end of January a
Persian negotiator went to Tiflis, armed with authority to conclude an
armistice with Russia but not to discuss the definitive peace to which
General Gudovich, the tsar's commander in Georgia, so often had alluded. He was accompanied by Captain Larry, one of Gardane's engineers.[18] Napoleon did not receive these dispatches for several months.
Illustrative of the slowness of western communications with Persia is
the fact that Gardane had at last learned of Champagny's appointment
as foreign minister. On February 12, 1808, he acknowledged Talleyrand's dispatches of August 26, 1807.[19]

Any projected land attack against British India doubtless would require passage through Asia Minor and Syria, key Ottoman areas, in
order to escape the British naval concentrations in the Mediterranean.
There would be only the protected Straits to hurdle. Napoleon's scheme
would also depend on many other favorable circumstances, all of which
could not reasonably be expected to materialize simultaneously. Unlike
the earlier expedition to Egypt, this campaign would require the collaboration of Russia, Austria, Turkey, and Persia. If tendering voluntary
coöperation, Persia would in all likelihood demand Russia's withdrawal
from Georgia. Like Turkey, however, it could be pushed aside, if need
be.

Russia more than ever preoccupied itself at the end of January with
Sweden, with the coming military attack, and with the possibilities of
war. Napoleon, like Hitler, could take whatever comfort he liked from
the prospect of Russia's conquest of Finland. The tsar's agents talked
of everything except what interested Napoleon most, a Russian campaign against England. Caulaincourt convinced himself that the Russians
were acting in accordance with the French alliance. As an illustration,
the tsar declined any isolated action to help the rebellious Serbians. St.
Petersburg meanwhile heard that the Turks and the English would possibly negotiate. It was reported that Arthur Paget was authorized to
disembark at the Dardanelles. The Turks nevertheless procrastinated, to
await the presumed negotiations between Tolstoi and Mouhib in Paris.[20]

King George's announcement of Britain's determination to continue
the war became another turning point in Napoleonic policy for the

Levant. The speech to Parliament angered Napoleon. If the British wished a fight to the finish, he would give it to them. Earlier, Napoleon had dreamed of dominating the Mediterranean—reverting to his concept of 1798—with Sicily becoming France's key to that area.

New conditions just at that moment encouraged Napoleon. England had been obliged to withdraw some naval forces from the Mediterranean to bolster Sweden. The time was thus opportune for a push in the Levant, but only if arranged in concert with Napoleon's Russian ally. French naval vessels had flaunted Britain and supplied Corfu. Napoleon would not now confine himself to the western rim of the Levant. He would go all the way to Constantinople with an army, with the announced purpose of advancing to India.

Beside the uncertainty of Turkish policy, owing to the palace revolt of late May, 1807, and its aftermath, Napoleon could advance many other pretexts for forcing the Ottoman Empire into line with his anti-English policy. As an alternative, he could unite with Russia in partitioning Turkey. The reports detailed many anti-French moves, together with general Turkish sentiment which opposed everything Christian. Once General Marmont, when building the coastal road in Dalmatia, stepped over into Ottoman territory. This drew a protest from the local inhabitants to the sultan. In Algeria, French influence continued to decline. Morocco evinced coldness. Napoleon could always complain of pro-British Ali Pasha of Albania.[21]

Napoleon knew it would be impossible to arrange a comprehensive partition of Turkey without considering Great Britain. Any transfer of such territories had to provide strategic advantages for Great Britain or, alternatively, Britain had to be ignored. If a division were arranged during peacetime, Britain might simply share the spoils. If England should be ignored during the war, however, it might with its Mediterranean naval strength annex proportionately more than its share. Inevitably associated with England, Egypt represented a special problem. Napoleon could never forget Britain's thwarting him in 1798 through its control of the Mediterranean. Early in 1808 Britons were charged by certain leading Egyptians with negotiating—unsuccessfully—to move into Alexandria once more. Mehemet Ali indignantly declined to permit the occupation of the city, declaring that his troops would defend it if necessary (February 10). French consuls believed that the visit of an English war brig to Aboukir was intended to support the warning of the possibility of a French expedition to Egypt like that of 1798. The brig tendered British assistance, stated the report, but the pasha still declined any foreign aid.[22]

The desire to enlist the tsar in a fighting war against Britain influenced Napoleon not to halt the negotiations of Caulaincourt which were concerned with a partition of the Ottoman Empire. The new instructions issued on January 29 contained many conditions, but the door at last stood open wider than it had at Tilsit. Champagny, the pro-Russian figurehead of the foreign ministry, approved Caulaincourt's initial comments in December to the Russians as expressively conveying Napoleon's views. Unenthusiastically he stated that England would feel the full effect of Russia's interruption of commercial relations within a few months. He repeated that Silesia represented the only equivalent for France's yielding in the matter of Moldavia and Wallachia.

Napoleon understood that Turkey's situation offered a means of conserving and advancing his alliance with Russia. He wished to use quite guarded language in repeating the overture to discuss a partition of Turkey. Because Caulaincourt had found the Russians opposed to a further partition of Prussia, he might tell the tsar and Rumiantsov that he could listen to proposals for a possible partition of Turkey, something he nonetheless considered bad for French policy in the long run. The Ottoman Empire must be considered in connection with more general problems. He repeated that Moldavia and Wallachia might be exchanged for Silesia, if the two allies decided upon only a small partition. More extensive territorial gains should follow a breakup of Turkey in Europe. Whereas Caulaincourt must not absolutely reject the idea of a general partition, he must not formally adhere to it. Thus Napoleon was ready either to abandon the Principalities to Russia or partition more of the Ottoman Empire. Champagny argued that the alliance would be dearly bought by the second alternative. A new era of revolutions would open in Europe, "which doubtless the genius of Napoleon would turn to his advantage but which also would delay peace with England. It would redouble for France and for Europe the calamities of long-continued war, and become more costly and more disquieting by ever-extended expeditions." He contended that Alexander's government really needed the stabilizing effect of the external French support.

"In your meetings with Tsar Alexander and Count Rumiantsov," however, Champagny cautioned again, "do not reject absolutely the idea of this partition." None-too-subtle procedure might be used to sound out the Russians. "Inform yourself how it is to be done, what are its means of execution, what nations would participate. And do not conceal that it is so little favorable to the interests of France. We cannot win an advantageous share, even if greatly extended. Show the advantage of deferring the partition until after the peace with England or at least until that power is pushed out of the Mediterranean. For the moment, it is in a position to be able to claim the most valuable spoils of the Ottoman Empire."

As an antidote for the inevitable reminder of Napoleon's angry comment at Tilsit against the revolutionary deposition of Sultan Selim, Caulaincourt must tell Russia that Sultan Mustapha now seemed even more attached to Napoleon than was the ex-ruler, his friend Selim. The new sultan had offered to place several ships at Napoleon's disposal. Ambassador Tolstoi, "still the defender of Prussia," had stated he must wait for instructions before opening discussions for peace with Turkey.[23] The wait would be from nineteen to twenty-two days, because during the winter months it took the fastest couriers that long to travel between Paris and St. Petersburg.

Champagny dispatched a long, gossipy, and uninformative instruction to Caulaincourt on February 2. He acknowledged the latter's dispatches down to January 13. Napoleon had been well satisfied with the good reception Russia was giving his ambassador. Contrary to reports received in Russia, Champagny did not believe Turkey would negotiate with Paget because Sebastiani had restored his own influence there.

Savary had returned to Paris. On that February 2 Napoleon dictated one of his most famous letters from his desk in St. Cloud palace. He proposed to Tsar Alexander a joint expedition against India and confirmed his personal authorization for Caulaincourt to discuss a partition of the Ottoman Empire. On that winter day in St. Petersburg, Russians were telling Caulaincourt of their declaration of war against Sweden, which offered proof that the tsar wished to carry out everything he promised at Tilsit. In the letter Napoleon took Britain's announcement of continued war as his starting point for his new plan to attack India by land and sea in concert with Russia and Austria. He admitted that his scheme was more intended to scare "the London merchants" into peace than actually to occupy India. In proposing the plan he ignored Turkey's official attitude of refusal to concede him the passage of troops to India, although that attitude was unofficially known to him. Russia and France would simply tell Turkey that the passage must be accorded.

Napoleon stated to Alexander that he had talked with Savary several times. Britain being determined to fight, only by means of "great and vast measures" could France and Russia bring it to terms and proceed to consolidate their system. Russia had strengthened its army; Napoleon would lend Alexander all the assistance in his power. He was not jealous of his ally; rather he desired Russia's glory, prosperity, and territorial extension. Alexander might extend Russia's frontier to the west as far as he liked. Napoleon would aid with all his resources if Russia undertook to conquer Finland.

The French emperor proposed a joint expedition to India, to be arranged and executed promptly. An army of 50,000 Russian and French troops, together with token forces from Austria, could be directed overland into Asia by way of Constantinople. These forces would hardly reach the Euphrates, he predicted, before "England would be trembling and on its knees before the continent." Because France stood in Dalmatia, and Russia stood on the Danube, the joint army could be on the Bosporus within a month after the understanding was reached. The blow would be heard all the way to the Indies and England would be beaten. Napoleon would refuse no preliminary stipulations requisite for such a great object. "However," he went on to say, "the reciprocal interests of our two states must be combined and balanced." This could be accomplished in personal conferences between themselves or in sincere discussions between Rumiantsov and Caulaincourt. Another Russian ambassador in Paris would suit him better than the "prejudiced and suspicious" Tolstoi; he would prefer someone really devoted to the Franco-Russian alliance.

Napoleon urged speed. He stated, "Everything can be signed and decided before March 15. By May 1 our troops can be in Asia and at the same time Your Majesty's troops at Stockholm." The English, thus menaced in Asia and chased from the Levant, would be crushed by events. Russia and France would have preferred peace but "the enemies of the world" did not want it that way. Napoleon concluded, "It is the part both of wisdom and of policy to do that which destiny orders, and to go where the irresistible march of events leads us. . . . The work of Tilsit will regulate the destinies of the world."[24]

Of Napoleon's more explicit accompanying instructions to Caulaincourt, the original has been lost. Only a copy of an extract from them is extant, a segment the ambassador permitted Rumiantsov to read and copy, on February 29. This segment, preserved in Russia's archives, has

been published. It is doubtful whether, even if the complete instructions
were in our hands, they would reveal what Napoleon really planned. He
hoped to intrigue the tsar and to encourage a second personal meeting
where he might perhaps again outtalk the tsar. According to the preserved segment, Caulaincourt was to say that Napoleon wanted whatever
Alexander wanted, the world being large enough for both. So he had
expressed himself to Tolstoi. He would not urge the evacuation of
Moldavia and Wallachia, if the tsar did not insist that he leave Silesia.
His partial evacuation of Prussia already had occasioned great pleasure
in England. He wished Alexander to know that he was thinking of combining an expedition to India with the partition of the Ottoman Empire. The joint army for both easy ventures would require in Asia only
20,000 to 25,000 Russians, 10,000 Austrians, and 35,000 to 40,000
French. The combined force would advance into India. Caulaincourt
must stress that Napoleon believed England would be terrified as soon
as those armies came to the Euphrates. Although the French emperor
understood that this meant the partition of the Turkish Empire, the
final arrangement of the details would require his personal meeting with
the tsar. Caulaincourt might first consider the details of partition with
Rumiantsov. They could study the map and submit their common ideas.
In their meeting the emperors would afterward decide the issue. If
no personal meeting could be arranged, Tsar Alexander could at least
send a more acceptable negotiator to Paris, since it was impossible to
discuss such important matters with Tolstoi.

He encouraged Russia to utilize this good opportunity to defeat Sweden, its geographical enemy. The general object of the allies must be
to give peace to the world by extending the regional preponderance of
both states. Russia needed movement and action. Napoleon would deny
it nothing, although it would be necessary to agree over all the details.
France was undertaking new conscriptions and maintaining an army of
40,000 in Dalmatia. Napoleon gently reminded the tsar's diplomats
that he had not, in 1807, required vanquished Russia to reduce its army,
as he had made Prussia do. He would not become jealous, Caulaincourt
must say, of further military increases by Russia. He would second the
tsar and merely request reciprocity. It would please him if the tsar visited
Paris. If Alexander could come only part way, he needed only to put his
finger on the map midway between Paris and St. Petersburg, and Napoleon would meet him there. In order to speed the meeting, he would
come without even awaiting an exchange of confirmations. If no meeting

could be arranged, Caulaincourt and Rumiantsov must work out their ideas as far as they were able. Alexander's negotiator could come to Paris, "and everything would be prepared for the great purpose."[25]

Napoleon's decision to refuse any offer of an equivalent for the Dardanelles and the Bosporus—neither of which is mentioned in the letter or in the surviving instructions—seems to have been made in advance. We know this from the ensuing secret debate in March (chap. xiii).

This significant instruction, including the portions not preserved, proved far less important in inaugurating the extensive discussions at St. Petersburg for a partition of Turkey than Napoleon's letter. The letter really impressed Alexander, even if it did not specifically mention any such partition. It promised in general, and in exchange for an equivalent, the French acquiescence to any prerequisite Russian stipulations. Although Napoleon stated that he desired to strike quickly at India, there seems no evidence that he had changed his opinion, expressed at Tilsit, of excluding Russia from a permanent foothold at the Straits. No mention of the subject, however, might lead the Russians to think he had changed. Meanwhile, if Russia went to the Straits temporarily, as a means to an end, Napoleon would be there, too. Substitute territories might be handed over to Russia: the Principalities from Turkey, Finland from Sweden, some provinces from Turkey in Asia. We know from Caulaincourt's reports that, as a last resort in order to launch the three-power expedition to India, he would concede Alexander the Bosporus, but not the Dardanelles.

Napoleon also intended to advise Alexander that although he would be prepared to study a partition of Turkey if such were necessary to defeat England, nevertheless he meant Austria to participate in that division. He may have accepted, at least partially, Talleyrand's proposal of 1805, to have Austria serve as the barrier against Russia in the Balkans. We have seen that he had Talleyrand secretly open a parallel discussion with Austria. From the viewpoint of strategy it would be better for the combined expedition to proceed against India at the same time as Russia diverted British efforts to Sweden and the North Sea, and while France diverted England to Spain and Portugal. On the other hand, it was possible that India might divert Britain from Sweden and Spain.

Napoleon gave no hint to Tolstoi of the instructions to Caulaincourt about discussing Turkey and India. On the contrary, he took the occasion of Savary's return to criticize Tolstoi anew for certain opinions (February 6). He combined abused innocence with his firm intention to remain in Silesia. He asked how Tolstoi could doubt that he would evacuate Silesia, once Russia left the Principalities.[26] Of equal significance was the fact that no hint went to Sebastiani and Gardane of the potentialities of a partition.

It is little wonder that early in March Caulaincourt's courier from Paris, and not Tolstoi's, engaged Tsar Alexander's greatest attention. By now Ambassador Mouhib began to grumble audibly, although he did not yet let his complaints reach Napoleon. He sensed something amiss, although he seems never to have known that his secret instructions were already in Napoleon's hands. Ambassador Sebastiani's dispatches during this period still reveal the original lack of comprehension of the completeness of Napoleon's change of policy at Tilsit. For one reason, that policy had not really been clarified to him before the instructions sent on January 12, 1808. The directions sent from Tilsit had related to an armistice, not to Napoleon's general policy for Turkey. Meanwhile, Sebastiani had committed himself and Napoleon, in the absence of new instructions, to a pro-Turkish French policy even if, as it did happen, Russia and France ended their war. The partial truth revealed from Tilsit led Sebastiani for months thereafter to cover up and procrastinate, and even to wait alongside the Turks to see what each succeeding courier might bring from Paris in their interest.

It was presumed at Constantinople that Napoleon was mediating between Turkey and Russia. The Turks constantly expected official confirmation. During the interval while the instructions of January 12 were on their way, the Ottoman capital speculated upon the presumed negotiations in Paris for a Russo-Turkish peace. Early in February Turkey's courier to Paris carried a letter for Champagny and supplementary secret directions intended for Mouhib's supposed negotiations. One reason for the Ottoman official fear of Russia's uncertain policy, Sebastiani believed, could be the internal ferment in the wake of revolution. Foreign Minister Halet's letter presented a pitiable plea to continue the "indissoluble bonds of friendship" between the Ottoman and French empires. He expressed renewed confidence that as the mediator Napoleon would accord the Turks just treatment.[27]

Champagny could always invent excuses for procrastinating by renewing this or that complaint against Turkey. One complaint related to offenses charged against the semi-independent dey of Algiers, who confiscated French goods to sell to the English and refused to liberate his Genoese, Ionian, and Italian slaves, all now subjects of Napoleon.

The dey's corsairs attacked French and Italian ships. Only because of friendship for Turkey had Napoleon not declared war against Algeria. However, Sebastiani must say, the emperor would declare war if the slaves should not be freed; Turkey must do what it could to prevent the rupture.[28]

Sebastiani eventually got around to the inevitable breaking of the news to the Turks of Napoleon's changed attitude toward them. Napoleon's orders of January 12, phrased by Champagny, gave him no chance to delay further the presentation of the jarring official intelligence of the fundamental change. Sebastiani admitted, on February 12, the tenor of the change, doing so in the easiest manner he knew. Napoleon's letter of January 22 for the sultan had not yet come, nor had it been announced. There was no extenuating circumstance to ease the situation. Sebastiani performed his painful duty by reading to the Turks, word for word, Champagny's instructions and questions. These asked—the trivia aside —to know Turkey's policy if Russia should wish to retain Moldavia and Wallachia. Respecting the results of this communication, Sebastiani may speak to us for himself, in the words he wrote Paris on February 15:

The communication I made contrasts much with the honorable conduct I held the last year, at the time the English appeared before Constantinople. I then supported with all the faculties of my being the dignity of my sovereign in defending, with my own arm, a nation that had rendered itself worthy of such interest by the devotion it had shown Napoleon. Today's *démarche* contrasts strangely with the assurances I renewed to the Turkish government only as late as two months ago, in the name of the emperor, namely that it should retain Moldavia and Wallachia and that it would find in the emperor's friendship a constant support against its enemies.

As his only condition, he had recommended Turkish opposition to England.[29] Sebastiani now admitted privately to Champagny that his career in Turkey had ended.

He called on Halet and Sultan Mustapha again three days later to receive their replies to Champagny's several questions. Might French forces be sent through Albania to succor Corfu? Could, and would, Turkey engage in a common effort against England, even if Russia retained the Principalities? He learned that a big Ottoman state council had been held as the result of his communication. Several counselors had spoken against France "with great vigor." Halet Effendi later made the following verbal statement to him:

The sultan has noted with extreme chagrin the change in the dispositions of France. Until now, the French emperor has given him proofs of his friendship and interest, which consoled him in the uncertainties and dangers of his position. Today, Napoleon participates in a project that might lead to extreme disorders in Turkey and accompanies his alarming communication with no offers of support, no promise of assistance. Turkey will never consent to cede Moldavia and Wallachia. It prefers war a thousand times to such humiliation. Sultan Mustapha has decided to write Napoleon personally, to reveal the critical situation in which his empire has been placed.

The Ottoman council decided that the Turks not only would not cede the Principalities, but also instead that the sultan must take steps to recruit 50,000 additional cavalry and 30,000 infantry troops. In the decision, the revolutionary and court factionalism disappeared; members of the ulema, janissaries, and government officials all spoke out in the same vein. Thus Sebastiani had not toned down "the great effect" of his transmission to the Turks of what he termed "the simple communication from M. Champagny, dated January 12." The Turks being convinced that defeat in this matter would mean the fall of their empire, he stated, Ottoman defense of the Principalities would be given immense popular support.

Sebastiani created an extenuating circumstance. Although he had not been authorized to reassure the Turks he proceeded to do so off the record. He advised them, drawing from what he characterized as "indirect" reasoning. He does not reveal in the record what he actually said, although he stated that his words somehow calmed the Turks, even if their fears were not allayed. One could hear criticisms of France in cafés, in mosques, in public places generally. He himself did not escape abuse: some Turks charged that "the infidel French ambassador had caused the war between Turkey and Russia, and between Turkey and England."[30]

Napoleon's personal letter arrived within a few days. It, and Sebastiani's strong tactics, won partial support for Napoleon's proposal to provision Corfu. The ambassador won his hard victory, however, only over the opposition of Foreign Minister Halet. At first he had communicated Champagny's dispatch of January 12 only verbally; he now gave it to Halet in writing. He argued personally before a small council of ten persons that the Turks might indirectly win the peace they desired through authorizing, as requested, the passage of French troops through Albania. The Turks then abandoned their first decision, which was for the sultan to reply personally to Napoleon's requests, to state the difficulties of such permission, and to request explanations. They decided instead to name plenipotentiaries "to seek to arrange this difficult affair" with France. Sebastiani continued his debate with them the next day, and the day after—in three conferences in all. The chief of the janissaries and the mufti opposed the French request. They and others said this affair represented a powder box which threatened "revolution more terrible than that which overthrew Selim." Sebastiani patiently met their arguments. He held that the passage of 4,000 troops (reducing the number to the lowest mentioned anywhere in the documents) would be a cheap price to pay for holding Corfu against the English.

Three officials, the foreign minister, the master of the horse, and the mufti, consistently opposed the passage of troops. Sebastiani threatened to depart from Constantinople unless they should agree. He left this proposition with them to mull over, so that they could judge the effect upon the Turkish public of a sudden withdrawal of the ambassador of the mighty Napoleon. The ambassador turned down promptly the janissaries' demand for a French guarantee of Moldavia and Wallachia in exchange for the passage of their troops. The threat to leave placed Mustapha in fear for his throne. The council accepted the French "offer" on February 27.[31]

Because of the conditions of travel in Napoleonic times, Napoleon's significant proposals of February 2 to Russia were in their special courier's charge until February 25. Meanwhile Caulaincourt's regular diplomatic business called for the starting of successive couriers in both directions. During the three weeks, the steady stream of social courtesies to Caulaincourt included frequent meetings with the tsar. After every French or Russian courier from Paris, official Russians seemed keen for news. That Tolstoi's dispatches could convey little, only heightened Russia's interest in the information sent to the French ambassador. The Russians inquired about Napoleon's reactions to everything: what he thought of their break with England and of their approaching war with Sweden and whether they had stimulated proposals regarding Turkey.

Remote Teheran likewise wished late news from Paris, although with less likelihood of receiving it. On February 19 Minister Gardane acknowledged Champagny's dispatches of September 17 and October 29, 1807—all received together—and four days later welcomed another belated courier with dispatches of early November. Napoleon sent no direct message to Feth Ali. Early in March the shah politely indicated his disappointment and displeasure by stating, in a personal letter to Napoleon: "The sincere friendship which so happily prevails between our two empires and the close alliance contracted by our two glorious courts, impose upon us respectively the obligation to give effect to our relations by writing frequently, to consolidate more and more our primary bonds. . . . We hope Napoleon for his part will deign to continue this practice."[32]

Caulaincourt continued in his reports to stress Russia's impatience for news. The tsar inquired on February 7 whether a courier just arrived had brought replies to several questions sent to Paris, some dating back to Savary's time. Tolstoi had conveyed Napoleon's statement to him that Caulaincourt would have information and that all issues might be discussed fully with the ambassador.

At Rumiantsov's house, on February 8, that minister asked point blank: "You can give us something positive, as M. Tolstoi has hoped?"

The ambassador replied that Napoleon had spoken quite positively respecting Silesia as the equivalent for Moldavia and Wallachia, and he argued pleasantly for giving Silesia to France.

Rumiantsov rejoined as expected that Russia could not permit France to possess Silesia. He repeated that Napoleon's request for it had pained the tsar. The Russians valued their alliance with France and wished it to endure. They wished every arrangement to be based on long-range calculations. Napoleon's request did not conform with his promises at Tilsit respecting Prussia.

Caulaincourt avowed that the cession of Silesia would cement the alliance.

Alexander's foreign minister said it would be to French benefit exclusively. He called attention to Russia's war against Sweden, the tsar thus proving himself neither just half-friend nor half-ally. Caulaincourt replied as he had been directed by Napoleon: France could not find an equivalent in Bosnia and the Morea, which by virtue of their location were subject to English influence. He suggested that Silesia was of no military importance owing to its remoteness from France. Russian interests would be enhanced by any sort of partition of Turkey, whereas French interests favored no partition. France must retain Silesia, the only available equivalent for the Principalities. The latter would extend Russia's frontier very greatly, even to the Danube river.[33]

That evening after dinner the tsar invited Caulaincourt to a serious discussion. At the outset he confirmed his desire to see the alliance endure and attract only permanent policies. He suggested that Napoleon could find a rich equivalent in northwest Italy and Portugal, rather than in Prussia.

Caulaincourt objected that such an offer would be really remote, almost as if the substitute were located in America. Despite Napoleon's titles, neither the "King of Spain" nor the "King of Italy" had promised anything at Tilsit but only the Emperor of France; surely it must be to France that the tsar made his offer. It was the French ambassador who was now speaking.

The tsar drew upon history to combat Caulaincourt's claim that Silesia had scant military importance; he recalled notably the line of the Oder river in the Russo-Prussian war at the time of Frederick the Great. He repeated several times the attachment that he held for Napoleon and the French alliance, and he insisted that Napoleon ought to fulfill his promise to evacuate Silesia. He finished by asking the ambassador to report to Paris everything he had said and, in addition, he requested him to suggest that Napoleon needed to reflect on all of it. Thereby he held the door open for further discussion.

The text of Russia's declaration of war against Sweden having been communicated to Paris in advance, it was known there the day of its issuance on February 17.[34] Count Rumiantsov confirmed the tsar's readiness to arrange with France for the protection and provisioning of the several French vessels of war to be constructed in Russia.[35]

Repeated reports reaching St. Petersburg held that Napoleon intended to combine Silesia with the Duchy of Warsaw. Hence Caulaincourt reported, on February 19: "The opposition that has been evidenced to consenting to permit France to take an equivalent in Prussia has not in any sense changed." When the tsar inquired whether a French courier arriving that day had delivered anything new respecting the affairs of Turkey, Caulaincourt evaded the issue, much as before. He said that France's war with England seemed to bar an immediate partition of Turkey, although France sought an equivalent in Prussia for the Principalities. The tsar spoke once more of his deep interest in Prussia and of seeing the Treaty of Tilsit fulfilled.

Caulaincourt repeated the French proposal for Russia to fulfill that treaty strictly, except for the exchange of territories already several times mentioned. The tsar now proposed as equivalents, in addition to those mentioned in Portugal and northwest Italy, the Ionian Islands, Cattaro, and—virtually —Hanover.

France had these already. Caulaincourt stated they would be covered by treaties, and that in the case of Cattaro it really appertained to Austria. He reminded the tsar that whereas the Treaty of Tilsit assigned the Ionians to France, it did not similarly cede the Principalities to

Russia. The tsar appeared indifferent to Austria's position. To him, the Turks would lose little by ceding the already devastated Principalities. The French ambassador utilized the remark that Sultan Mustapha seemed greatly attached to Napoleon, more so even than his predecessor had been, and that he had proved it by tendering his fleet for Napoleon's service. He pointed out that Russia would win a territorial advantage from Persia.

The tsar adroitly requested the ambassador to write General Gardane to second Russia's offers of peace with the shah—that is to say, to support Russia's retention of Georgia. Napoleon had apparently dodged that specific issue at Tilsit; Caulaincourt replied vaguely that although he possessed no authority to write Gardane, he would feel no hesitancy in agreeing to convey Napoleon's dispositions in that regard.[36]

Caulaincourt tells us he was reporting all his discussions in full detail and with "scrupulous exactitude." The debate concerning Silesia thus had become stalemated. Rumiantsov and the tsar always supported Prussia. They stressed the difficulties and disadvantages of their temporary withdrawal from the Principalities.

Paris corrected the erroneous report (chap. xi) that Arthur Paget had been authorized by Turkey to disembark at the Dardanelles. On February 20 Napoleon as a gesture announced the approaching withdrawal of unstated numbers of French forces from Prussia and from the Duchy of Warsaw. Yet he said nothing of recalling troops specifically from Silesia.[37]

What came of Napoleon's overture to Austria? Austria would support Turkey as long as possible, so Minister Stadion instructed Metternich. It "would join in the partition only when impossible to arrest it and upon the express condition of the most perfect agreement between the three powers." This precise reply permitted further discussions between Talleyrand and Metternich on the one hand and between Tolstoi and Metternich on the other, during the last week in February. Talleyrand commented that, although he personally wished to preserve Turkey, he believed "nothing could hold Napoleon back." He admitted that Napoleon's statements in January had suggested a less imminent partition of Turkey than had his own. "Less imminent" was actually Talleyrand's verbal substitute for Metternich's tentative conclusion that the project might have been "adjourned."

"Does Russia share Napoleon's views?" Metternich asked, repeating his question of January. "Heartily," replied Talleyrand. "The conquest of Turkey is one of the favorite ideas of Tsar Alexander. . . . He has so expressed himself in several conversations with me."

Metternich appeared somewhat eager to mention the secret discussions to Champagny. Talleyrand assured Austria's ambassador, however, that only Napoleon, Metternich, and himself were participating in them; one need not bother about the foreign minister. Metternich wished to guard against Napoleon's using Austria's announced consent to the general principle of a partition as the lever to force Russia into the scheme. He recommended that Vienna counteract such a maneuver. Without admitting to Tolstoi that he had talked with Talleyrand, he communicated to Tolstoi some instructions from Vienna in response to the "political dream" of which he had spoken. Austria would prevent the partition as long as it could and act only when it must. Both agreed, however, that the matter no longer could be considered a dream because the word "Constantinople" had been pronounced by Napoleon. Tolstoi was assured that Austria regarded the matter as of common interest.

To his own court, Metternich interpreted the French overture as quite definite with respect to the principle of partition and quite vague with respect to its details. He confessed his inability to answer Vienna's inquiry with respect to how far the discussion between Russia and France had gone. That answer must come, he said, if at all, from St. Petersburg.[38] Tolstoi faithfully reported to his court what Metternich told him: Austria would prefer to uphold the Ottoman Empire. If, however, the partition of Turkey should be irrevocably decided, Austria would accede to all the arrangements "but concerting with Russia and France," and even tendering some military support for its execution.[39]

Official Russians sensed the coming of important news from Paris, especially late in February, by which time the reactions to Savary's personal report to Napoleon must be available. When a courier from Tolstoi brought little information on February 23, they questioned Caulaincourt again. They left the impression that they felt Tolstoi might be a weak ambassador who missed the important developments. The Russians believed that Napoleon should at least demonstrate appreciation for Russia's declaration of war against Sweden. Nevertheless the feeling persisted on both sides that the "religion of Tilsit" had been carried too far.

Russia's minister of foreign affairs argued long and well, although without success, for the simple French authorization for Alexander to possess the Principalities. It became more and more difficult for Caulaincourt to parry the increasingly forceful questioning by the tsar and his minister. Here are two of Rumiantsov's questions which Caulaincourt records. What did France wish to do with Silesia—unite it with Warsaw and use it for French troops? Would Prussia be compensated elsewhere? If Caulaincourt could answer these questions, the minister would hazard referring the question of Silesia to the tsar once more. To the Russians, the affairs of Turkey were not and had never been connected with the affairs of Prussia. It was equally significant that they felt that nothing Napoleon had said to Tolstoi since his return from Italy in January had been really "in the manner" of the comprehensive alliance of Tilsit.[40]

Caulaincourt reminded them that a Russian war with England, rather than war with Sweden, should relate to a partition of Turkey. How might one indemnify Prussia, he asked, without also indemnifying Turkey? He further criticized Tolstoi. Napoleon's ambassador sensed that his weak replies had not convinced Rumiantsov; the tsar's object must be to remain in the Principalities and have France evacuate Silesia.

Thus unless Napoleon made a new proposal, the debate over the Principalities had become deadlocked. The delivery of his letter presented an electrifying new element (chap. xiii). Emperor Napoleon's project of a joint expedition to India may have been only a trial balloon, intended to test the alliance of Tilsit with respect to Russia's commitment to engage in a shooting war against England. The conditions for that participation, as foreseen at Tilsit, had now arisen.

In this chapter we have seen that Napoleon considered a policy of partition of the Ottoman Empire. The new sultan and the anti-French conduct of Ali Pasha of Albania proved as good starting points as any. Of more significance was Napoleon's new strategic plan to cross the Straits on the way to India. In this, the greatest difficulty was to win the indispensable coöperation of allied Tsar Alexander, who promptly interpreted the scheme as of benefit exclusively to France and accordingly demanded compensation elsewhere. That the tsar would insist upon possessing both the Dardanelles and the Bosporus, if he participated, will be demonstrated in the next chapter.

XIII

The Dardanelles—
"La Langue de Chat"

⤙ March, 1808

ALTHOUGH many other factors were involved, the region of the Dardanelles and Bosporus represented the special bone of contention between France and Russia from 1807 to 1812. Tsar Alexander insisted that Russia alone must possess these keys to his empire. Emperor Napoleon could not—or would not—concede this strategic center of the Near East and hence of three continents. He would have given Constantinople and the Bosporus, provided France acquired or shared the Dardanelles.

This was the primary subject matter for one of the most significant debates between great-power allies in modern history. Lessons for the present may be found in the secret discussions in St. Petersburg between Ambassador Caulaincourt and Tsar Alexander and Foreign Minister Rumiantsov in March, 1808. The as yet incompletely revealed story of Chancellor Hitler's negotiations with Marshal Stalin suggests a parallel between 1808 and 1940: that the Straits once again loomed so large as to become the pitfall issue of a cumbersome alliance.

Caulaincourt held in 1808 that Russia's being at the Dardanelles placed it at the doors of Corfu and Toulon. His contention hints another parallel, a parallel with the policy of the United States and Great Britain at the Conference of Potsdam in 1945 and after. These two powers agreed that the Soviet Union might send its warships through the Straits, upon the requisite revision of the Straits Convention of 1936. Under no circumstances, however, might the Soviet Union assume with Turkey the joint defense of the Straits.[1]

One of the many interesting and important lessons of continuing significance from the Napoleonic period was France's inability to arrange amicably with allied Russia the terms for a succession to the Ottoman Empire. Napoleon attempted what Hitler once tried, to agree with Russia to partition Europe into spheres of great-power influence. The French emperor proceeded in 1808 under cover of the Franco-Russian alliance of Tilsit, the Nazi dictator under his agreement of 1939 with the Soviet Union to partition Poland. In 1808, Russia and France would under the plan hold the lions' shares of Europe, Austria being given a morsel to satisfy its *amour-propre*. In 1940, the Soviet Union and Nazi Germany were to control Europe and Asia, with Fascist Italy thrown a morsel.

There would be set up under each project the supremacy of the major powers within the region agreed upon. The lesson is the impossibility of any dictators' partitioning of the European world into permanent spheres of influence and power, owing to their inability to agree about the inevitable strategic zones of friction to be left standing between them. Both unsuccessful negotiations came to the same end: war between the would-be dividers of the spoils. Napoleon and Hitler discovered the impossibility of an agreement respecting the details that would keep both allies happy. They could not even keep an existing alliance intact by means of feigning satisfaction. The lesson twice learned at enormous expense in lives and treasure should be well remembered.

The Straits had been demonstrated in February, 1807, to possess considerable value in modern naval strategy, a conclusion to be drawn from Admiral Duckworth's blunder and failure. He forced his way through the Dardanelles only to discover the danger of having his fleet bottled up. In spite of this, the huge backdrop for the drama of 1808 was the British Navy, which had been primarily responsible for ending the French challenge to empire in Egypt from 1798 to 1801. The specific issue in 1808 was the ownership of the Dardanelles, whether it was to be left to weak Turkey, turned over to Russia, or jointly shared by France and Russia.

This debate came to be termed *la langue de chat,* from a chance observation by Rumiantsov one day. While he and Caulaincourt studied the maps, the Russian happened to say that the Gallipoli peninsula seemed to resemble a cat. Thereafter the debate over the Dardanelles was even officially referred to by that summary and witty term.

The detailed story will unfold from the official records, primarily from Caulaincourt's stenographic-type reports to Napoleon.

The courier bearing the French emperor's justly famous letter of February 2, 1808, to Tsar Alexander braved the winter weather; he arrived at St. Petersburg late on February 25. The letter tersely proposed a joint expedition against India. As bait it authorized preliminary secret discussions looking to a partition of the Ottoman Empire.

This changed profoundly the nature of the previously halting secret discussions between Ambassador Caulaincourt and Foreign Minister Rumiantsov and the tsar on the subject. They no longer would say a great deal respecting an exchange of Silesia and the Principalities. Instead, they locked themselves in a diplomatic stalemate over the more important question of the Dardanelles.

They debated earnestly the future ownership of Constantinople, the Bosporus, and the Dardanelles, together with the European and Asiatic hinterlands of the Dardanelles. The debates during March, 1808, appear in a new light when traced in full detail and in their logical setting. The account of these is mostly behind us. A longer perspective and a new reference to the original manuscript sources reveal why the debate became deadlocked: it was the French unwillingness to concede both the European and the Asiatic banks of the Dardanelles to Russia. In this chapter we shall make an analytical translation of the reports of the pertinent phases of the negotiations. Most of these reports were first published in 1890, although without their setting. Whereas the conclusions from the debates are well known—or rather the lack of them, owing to the respectively adamant positions—the details are hardly remembered at all.

Caulaincourt's special instructions, most of which have been lost, came to St. Petersburg by the same courier who carried the letter, on February 25. Caulaincourt personally delivered Napoleon's communication the following day, and he details the immediate reactions of tsar and minister. Alexander read the letter on the spot, then reread it, stating it gave him great pleasure. He remarked at one point, "This is the language of Tilsit," and, at another, "These are great matters."

Tsar Alexander immediately assured the French ambassador that he would, if possible, travel to Paris to see Napoleon. The qualification doubtless impelled Caulaincourt to offer, as directed, "to put the compass on the map" for a joint meeting midway between the two capitals. Appropriate pleasant remarks ensued. Caulaincourt noted the secrecy implied respecting the new matters proposed for discussion. Napoleon had not even admitted the tsar's ambassador in Paris to his confidence.

Ambassador Tolstoi's expedited dispatches came to St. Petersburg on February 26. His account of that moment, his latest conversation with Napoleon, revealed only that the latter stated the tsar still urged him to evacuate Silesia. This time the French emperor had asked, in a friendly manner, "Who is pressing you to evacuate the Turkish provinces? Who is it that is telling you I do not wish to evacuate Prussia, that I will not evacuate it one day?" Embarrassing questions, these, for an ambassador whom Napoleon disliked.[2]

During an interlude at a ball that evening, the tsar beamed with pleasure. Meanwhile he had perused Napoleon's letter several times. Rumiantsov also confirmed the tsar's reaction, generally summarized by the expression that the letter represented the language of Tilsit. The French ambassador soon afterward reported orders in preparation for the Russian squadron in the Mediterranean to coöperate in the "common cause" of Russia and France.[3]

Thus began the new phase of the secret negotiations over Turkey at St. Petersburg. Although these were stalemated by mid-March, they eventually extended to late June.

The initial reaction to Napoleon's expected overture had been more than satisfactory. A series of conferences between the French ambassador and Rumiantsov considered details respecting Napoleon's double scheme of marching to India and partitioning the Ottoman Empire. These conferences began on February 29, when Caulaincourt transmitted an extract from Napoleon's secret instructions, the extract we utilized fully in the foregoing chapter when discussing Napoleon's letter of February 2. To summarize it: any evacuation of Prussia by France would please only England. Napoleon would not insist that Alexander depart the Principalities provided he himself did not evacuate Silesia. More important, he though of combining a joint expedition against India with a partition of the Ottoman Empire. Russia, France, and Austria could march together across western Asia. Caulaincourt and Rumiantsov should study the possibilities of a partition of the Ottoman Empire. The partition of Turkey, the final terms for which the two emperors must approve personally, and the joint expedition to India would offer the action Russia seemed to need. The entire program would extend the regional preponderance already enjoyed by the two allied states. It would please Napoleon if Alexander came to Paris or met him midway between their two capitals or sent him a better negotiator than the suspicious Tolstoi.[4]

Russia evinced willingness to support the French project for Asia, a joint conquest of large territories in India. When Rumiantsov inquired whether Napoleon did not wish also to exclude the Turks from Asia, as well as the British, the ambassador replied that the question concerned a partition of Turkey in Europe, western Asia being involved only in connection with the proposed military expedition.

Rumiantsov then inquired what Napoleon meant by a partition. He recalled a previous mention of France's acquiring the Morea, the Ionian Islands, and Crete. Moreover, Napoleon now proposed to admit Austria to the partition. He remarked that the French emperor kept silent respecting Silesia.

Caulaincourt thrust Silesia aside. To him that was a small matter that could be handled by Count Tolstoi in Paris, a matter foreign to "the great object." He suggested that Rumiantsov indicate on the map his views of three hypotheses, namely a partial partition of Turkey in Europe, a more general partition of the Balkans, and a dismemberment of Turkey in Asia. This opportunity Rumiantsov declined to utilize, until after discussion with the tsar. They could both confirm at once that a personal meeting between the two emperors would finally become indispensable.[5]

On March 1, Tsar Alexander personally stated his reactions to Caulaincourt. He inquired whether Napoleon had not forwarded some details of his own views respecting this "great affair."

Caulaincourt replied evasively, but read to him the same extract from Napoleon's instruction he had transmitted to Rumiantsov the day before.

Alexander made it clear that if Napoleon desired an expedition for India to assemble at Constantinople, all of Turkey should be partitioned. If, on the other hand, Napoleon wished to discuss only a partial partition, along the lines suggested at Tilsit, everything was prepared already. Only a general partition would require a new arrangement. Alexander recalled that at Tilsit Napoleon had not in any sense wished to destroy Turkey. As for himself, his own ambitions had not reached beyond Moldavia and Wallachia. He guardedly alluded to Silesia, by saying that the question of a partition of the Ottoman Empire would cancel everything said since Tilsit regarding Prussia.

Caulaincourt recalled that Napoleon had never really urged the tsar to evacuate the Principalities, so long as the continuing French war with England seemed to render it inadvisable for France to evacuate Prussia. He spoke of "confidence and reciprocal facilities," and stated that Napoleon expected of him only a preliminary exchange of ideas with Rumiantsov. Following that, a meeting of the two sovereigns could be arranged or at least a special Russian envoy could be sent to Napoleon. Alexander suggested that Minister of the Navy Chichakov would be a good negotiator.

Caulaincourt emphasized Napoleon's haste, his insistence upon speed. Thereupon the tsar suggested that the ambassador study the maps with his foreign minister, and that together they prepare a plan of partition. The tsar frankly admitted Constantinople might be considered too important to include, too far geographically from France and probably regarded by France as too important for Russia to acquire. But he had an idea for it: the Turkish capital might become a free city.

All the other details might be worked out with Rumiantsov. The negotiations could be speeded, at the same time allowing for couriers to and from Paris. Neither said a great deal respecting the projected expedition to India, yet Alexander offered to lend Napoleon as many troops as he should need. The joint expedition could only depart from Constantinople, he stated, although he would dispatch a small force from Astrabad also. Thus he would demonstrate himself "neither just half-friend nor half-ally."[6]

Diplomatic jockeying for position marked the second conference between Caulaincourt and Rumiantsov the following day (March 2). Russia's first proposal considered possible developments if it were permitted to acquire Moldavia and Wallachia in exchange for the French control of Silesia. The second discussed a general partition of the Ottoman Empire. In this, if France acquired Egypt and perhaps other places, Russia must be given more than the Principalities. Austria might share the spoils, provided it accorded equitable service in the undertaking. France had always desired Egypt, Rumiantsov remarked, whereas in the early 1780's it had been suggested to Tsarina Catherine II that Russia acquire Constantinople if Austria became master of Egypt. He announced that Alexander favored Napoleon's projected expedition to India, as desired by France and solely for French benefit. But he sympathized with Prussia, and discouraged any extension of the Duchy of Warsaw.

Caulaincourt considered that Turkey in Europe probably should be discussed first, Turkey in Asia and Africa constituting another question. In any event he did not wish to begin with Egypt, nor would he concede that "little German questions" be permitted to stand in the way of larger objectives.

Rumiantsov announced Alexander's willingness to place his Mediterranean squadron at Napoleon's disposal, to act against Britain in India and to support a new French expedition to Egypt. At Tilsit matters had been arranged, although perhaps not very well, at least well enough to assure tranquillity. Now everything had changed.

Caulaincourt suggested that Russia annex Finland, and asked what Alexander wished to have.

Rumiantsov replied the tsar had never said definitely, but it appeared to him Russia should acquire Moldavia, Wallachia, and Bulgaria, and France take the Morea and perhaps Albania and Crete.

Caulaincourt inquired further, respecting the disposition of the remainder, including what would be Austria's share.

Rumiantsov suggested allotting diminutive Croatia to Austria, together with something in Bosnia.

Caulaincourt rejoined that Bosnia represented the real route to Albania, and hence a natural share for France. He reminded that Serbia had been forgotten.

Rumiantsov suggested that Serbia might be given its independence, under Russian and French influence.

Caulaincourt considered that two big influences over one country would resemble two mistresses in one house.

Rumiantsov conceded the point, thereupon suggesting that Serbia be assigned to an Austrian archduke. Russia's only engagements toward the Serbs, he stated, concerned their protection against Turkish massacres.

Caulaincourt observed that Russia would thus win the advantage, from the standpoint of Christian populations.

At this opening, Rumiantsov raised the issue of Constantinople and the Straits, postponed at Tilsit. He contended, in a long sentence: "If the Turks are excluded from Europe, which to me appears inevitable, if an expedition to Asia is desired—for I doubt it will be possible to obtain the sultan's consent to the necessary military passage after having in advance amputated his empire's legs and arms—and even without that, if they are, I say, excluded from Constantinople—which I regard as contrary to our interests—at least if not given to a government as ill as the Turkish, this city, by its position, by ours, and by all the interests of our commerce—of which the key is at the Dardanelles and the Bosporus—comes to us, together with a considerable territory that includes these points."

Caulaincourt did not miss this opportunity to apply what we may assume were his instructions. He replied, "The key of the Black Sea and that of the Sea of Marmara, that is much for a port, Count. It would be considerable even to possess one of the Straits. It seems to me this will be proposable only if each of us has one."

"One without the other is nothing," Rumiantsov countered. "It is geography and our Black Sea, in addition to our political interests, that make us desire to possess Constantinople. You are far away, and you would acquire enough beautiful possessions to keep you from envying us. Your share is beautiful indeed and, as I have told you, we will accept with pleasure whatever acquisitions you make that do not touch us."

The ambassador reverted to the expedition to India, his primary consideration.

Rumiantsov stated this to be entirely in the French interest, although the tsar stood ready for it if compensation for Russia could be found.

Caulaincourt reminded him of Napoleon's desire for speed, an expedition to be under preparation within a month.

That factor would be clarified in a few days, the Russian minister assured him. Going back to the question of partition, he stated that Moldavia and Wallachia had been tacitly allotted to Russia at Tilsit, in exchange for an equivalent for France.

The two spoke of methods, the preparedness of the Russian army on the Danube, and other factors.

They agreed to reduce to writing their conversations up to that point, for reports to be submitted to the two emperors, this despite the admitted loss thereby of a few days' time.[7]

Let us digress to contemporize the events in Constantinople and in Teheran.

Sultan Mustapha IV appealed to Napoleon on March 4, recalling all the evidences of friendship his government had given the French emperor. The letter stressed Turkey's good faith in the execution of engagements. It recalled the promises made by Sebastiani ever since the Treaty of Tilsit. It solicited Napoleon's protection and prayed him to guarantee the integrity of its territory.[8]

In Teheran, Minister Gardane learned on March 2 that the English friend of the Persians, the military commander Sir John Malcolm, together with the negotiator Sir Hartford Jones, had come to Bandar Abu Shehr, on the coast. He immediately requested Vizir Mirza Cheffi not to receive them. To do so, he stated, would be contrary to Persia's alliance with France signed in May, 1807. In all seriousness he announced he would depart from Persia, should they be received.

In addition, the British reportedly blockaded the Persian Gulf to forestall any French attempts to occupy the islands ceded by Persia in a commercial convention negotiated by Gardane but which had not been (and would not be) ratified. Two days later, during a friendly conference, Gardane and the shah agreed to the accuracy of the reports of the British activity. Neither could propose any measures against the action itself.

The shah iterated his confidence in Emperor Napoleon. He asserted again that so loyal to the alliance was his own first minister the latter should in fact be regarded as the minister of Napoleon the Great. He requested thirty French officers, to serve as instructors to Europeanize his army. He wished also to receive the 20,000 rifles for which Gardane had contracted in January and of which nothing more had been heard.

He promised that the British would not be received, and stated he awaited with impatience the results of France's mediation between Persia and Russia. As a means of acquiring better terms he, like the sultan, shifted the responsibility to Napoleon. He counted fully upon Napoleon's aid to recover Russian-occupied Georgia. Gardane reported that the shah's ministers and favorites seemed pro-English, except for Mirza Cheffi.

At the third secret conference of the series at St. Petersburg, on March 4, Rumiantsov laid his cards on the table. He announced that Tsar Alexander had agreed Napoleon might take the Morea, the Ionian Islands, and Albania—all useful for the French Navy—together with Egypt and even Syria, if he liked.

Caulaincourt reverted to his previous consideration, the desire first to discuss the partition of Turkey in Europe, not of Turkey in Asia.

Rumiantsov proposed for Russia, in such a limited partition, Moldavia, Wallachia, Bulgaria, and perhaps also Serbia. For France there would be the Morea, Albania, the Ionians, and a part of Bosnia. Austria might take Croatia and the remainder of Bosnia. All these terms applied if Rumelia and Constantinople should be left to the sultan.

Caulaincourt immediately remarked that Russia had increased its claimed share since the conference two days earlier. If that process continued, he contended, Russia would take everything. Moreover, Austria would be dissatisfied if Serbia, geographically so near, went to the tsar.

Rumiantsov thereupon suggested that Serbia be assigned to a German or other European prince, who would marry a Russian grand duchess. The children of the union would be required to accept the Greek Orthodox religion.

Caulaincourt considered Napoleon would be willing to make some concession to Russia's imperial family, although he himself lacked any authority to refuse or agree to such a request.

Rumiantsov believed France should desire nothing more than Serbian independence, in view of the oppression and the rebellious state of affairs existing in that province.

Caulaincourt remarked that he proceeded on the hypothesis that the expedition to India, and the Franco-Russian coöperation in it, would take place as consequences of the arrangements respecting Turkey, the latter being the basis for all the matters he discussed.

Rumiantsov agreed that Alexander intended this, except that Russia desired an advantage in proportion to the support furnished. In his opinion, Austria most certainly would coöperate also, although so far as concerned Moldavia and Wallachia, Russia could handle them alone.

Caulaincourt expressed disinclination respecting Bulgaria, only to be reminded again that Russia would be going to India for France, not for Russia. Caulaincourt chided Rumiantsov by remarking that Russia presumably had entered the war against England.

Rumiantsov returned the subject to the question of Silesia.

Caulaincourt repeated his own dodge that, in comparison with "the great object that concerns us," Silesia could possess little importance for Russia, with its already vast spaces.

But Rumiantsov wished rather to speak again of Constantinople. "If," he said, "as the projected expedition seems to presuppose, all of Turkey is partitioned and this city is not left to so insignificant a government as that of Turkey, Russia wants it, together with the Bosporus and the Dardanelles." If they extended the partition to include the Straits, he stated Serbia could be given to Austria, together with a portion of Macedonia and Rumelia, down to the sea, this to separate France from Russia. "Thus Austria will separate us, and so conform with the principle expressed by Emperor Napoleon at Tilsit, the principle that, if we are to remain friends, we must not be neighbors." Moreover, Austria thus would be attached firmly to the Franco-Russian system. In such an arrangement, France would acquire the remainder of Macedonia, and the western segment of Rumelia, and, "in general, what you want: all of Bosnia, if you wish; Austria taking part of Rumelia, and Macedonia, to separate Russia and France; Egypt and Syria besides, if that suits you."

Caulaincourt stated that the proposed portions were not equal. Said he, "Constantinople alone is better than all, than everything you offer France in Europe. You are not generous today, Count."

Rumiantsov parried, "It is rather you who would have everything. What is to be done with Constantinople and its district, after it is no longer held by the Turks? How do you see the thing?"

Caulaincourt replied noncommittally, ignoring the inclusion of both

the Straits. "Constantinople frightens me, I admit. A beautiful awaken-
ing, that, to open one's eyes as the emperor of Constantinople. Between
your present frontier and Constantinople is the width of an entire empire. What a position, one may say, in two parts of the world. These are
ideas with which one must familiarize himself before speaking."

Rumiantsov pursued his argument, again including both the Straits.
Geography required Constantinople for Russia, he said. Except for its
commerce, Russia could have wished another solution. He held it would
not be so advantageous as Caulaincourt believed, being far from Russia.
It would be a city and a country without numerous inhabitants. But
Russia's position, because of the Black Sea, required that it possess the
area up to Constantinople and the Dardanelles.

Here Caulaincourt let fall the decisive reply, again presumably speaking precisely as directed by Napoleon: "I do not quite include the possibility of Russia's acquisition of Constantinople. But if it is admitted,
I declare to you that I will not consent that the Dardanelles also go to
the same power."

When Rumiantsov asked to whom Caulaincourt would give the Dardanelles, he replied frankly that he would take them for France.

"Why that?" asked Rumiantsov. "What advantage will you derive
by approaching so near us?"

Caulaincourt contended, "If one accords Constantinople to you it
would necessarily require some great, even astonishing, advantages for
France; where could they be found? In Europe, I do not see enough. In
Asia and beyond, would it be Egypt and Syria? What can compare to
it? In any event, if you offer these acquisitions to us, there will be necessary a means of communicating with them, and I can find it with safety
only in the Dardanelles. Further, I will ask whether you would support
us in the conquest of these two provinces. After all, in speaking to me
of Egypt and Syria you have meant to oblige us, Count. Of what value
is this offer, without the Dardanelles?"

Rumiantsov replied, "The tsar has not clarified his views on this
special coöperation, but you know how accommodating he is on all these
things, and how easily he adopts everything that proves the price of this
alliance and the arrangements with Emperor Napoleon. Our commerce,
Ambassador, during the lifetime of Napoleon will not be troubled, I
wish to believe; but what guarantee would it have afterwards, if you
possess this key?"

"Your commerce," rejoined Caulaincourt, "consists only of the products of your soil. All Europe needs it, France the same as other powers. Because it is their ships which transport it, and not yours, what damage will be done by our position at the Dardanelles? None, I assure you. Yours can impede everyone, ours nobody."

"You see everything that you would acquire by this method," Rumiantsov argued, "what influence; and for us, what would we have? A city with a great name and nothing more. I would a hundred times more prefer the second."

"The comparison does not injure Constantinople," Caulaincourt countered, to highlight dramatically Napoleon's strategic appraisal of the Dardanelles. "Take your army to Finland; you will arrive; we are on the march."

"The islands alone are an incalculable wealth for you," Rumiantsov insisted; "they will give you excellent sailors. You will dispose of Egypt and Syria as you wish, and what would we have in return for that? If you acquire the Dardanelles, could you not give us Serbia?"

Caulaincourt promptly met this adroit maneuver. "In that manner, you put us in your pocket," he commented, "by saying that you do not want us in yours. What will be left for Austria? Look at the map, Count. Geography decidedly opposes your acquisition of Serbia. Let us speak also of Asia; you can take more there. Trebizond is in your hands; that is a good acquisition for yourself as the minister of commerce. In all, Count, make this reflection: everything that you will acquire will affect and consolidate your power; all that you propose for us is, by our relative position, almost at the end of the world. In any event, you would be strengthened and we ourselves weakened."

Rumiantsov turned the discussion to details. "But how far do you come," he asked, "and by what route, if you have the Dardanelles?"

"At least to Rodosto [on the Sea of Marmara]," Caulaincourt replied without hesitation. "One might take as a frontier the chain of [Balkan] mountains from Pristina to near Adrianople."

All this Rumiantsov perceived at once, a proposal for France to hold sway not alone over the Dardanelles but also over a south Balkan zone from sea to sea, from the Adriatic to the Marmara.

He nipped it in the bud by announcing his own definite reply to Caulaincourt's basic proposal. "My opinion is that we can cede neither Constantinople nor the Dardanelles," he said. "As for the remainder, I will seek the tsar's orders; perhaps a decision will be easier. We wish, you may be certain, to aid and support you in every way, and we have found the same confidence in Emperor Napoleon, whose letter gave Tsar Alexander great pleasure."

Caulaincourt agreed that the matter be submitted to higher authority. "We are only exchanging preliminary ideas," he reminded. "Napoleon surely will have several ideas that will harmonize everything." That Rumiantsov also believed.[9]

Napoleon's instructions on this point are not preserved, although he obviously had directed Caulaincourt to uphold his intention to cross Balkan Europe, from southern Dalmatia across to Pristina and through Eastern Rumelia to about midway along the coast of the Sea of Marmara. Caulaincourt withheld at this conference any reference to the land frontier Napoleon expected on the Asiatic side of the Dardanelles. Rumiantsov did not raise the issue.

About all the Russians could fall back on to meet this unexpected Napoleonic demand would be the theory of permanent friendship, so much emphasized by Napoleon at Tilsit: to remain friends, the Russian and French frontiers must never touch. Napoleon anticipated as much; and he had given Caulaincourt an alternative, to permit Austria to stand between them, even at the Dardanelles. We know this from the ambassador's later statement in a report that he had not had to utilize the authorized proposal that Austria be given the debated strait. But Russia would specify Austria's extension only to the Aegean Sea, certainly not to the Sea of Marmara. The extensive French claim to all the southern part of the Balkan peninsula, introduced at this point, seems intended to pave the way for a substitute proposal which, whatever its other arrangements, would withhold the Dardanelles and its European and Asiatic hinterlands from Russia.

Caulaincourt at his first opportunity spoke with Tsar Alexander respecting Constantinople, after he had received a new letter from Napoleon. Tsar Alexander inquired whether it contained any further clarifications of the proposed partition. As Caulaincourt reported the conversation on March 7, he replied evasively, stating that Napoleon still awaited Caulaincourt's own first reports.

"That will not be long," observed the tsar, "it appears you are doing very well in the preliminary discussions with Rumiantsov."

"We differ in opinions respecting Constantinople and the Dardanelles," Caulaincourt replied, "opinions in which I have neither conceded nor refused anything. Your first idea held that this city be made independent."

"Things have changed," stated the tsar. "Napoleon now requests an expedition, which was not a question earlier. There are some things that I am obliged to possess, even in order to concert sincerely and continue your system. Napoleon desires to grant certain advantages to this country; I wish to support him as a true ally. It is necessary, however, that the conceded advantages be substantial, that they justify the sacrifices that we make. You see Rumiantsov day after tomorrow, and you will agree that I am moderate in my demands, giving due regard to my geographical position and to what I am doing for you. I assure you I shall be happy to see Napoleon."

The conversation turned to England and Sweden, Caulaincourt assuring Tsar Alexander that the French emperor wished Russia to possess Finland.[10]

Thus Rumiantsov's opinions really had been the tsar's—now confirmed in person—or else the tsar had adopted Rumiantsov's.

Another glance elsewhere reveals Count Champagny at the moment preoccupied with additional arguments to be sent Caulaincourt for France's retention of Silesia. Before he could receive any reports of the first new negotiations concerning Turkey, he issued new instructions respecting that much-debated Prussian province (March 9). He met Tsar Alexander's interpretation of the Treaty of Tilsit (as reported in December) by noting differences in the applicability of the two Franco-Russian treaties of July 7, 1807. The treaty of peace engaged France to evacuate the Prussian provinces, Russia to evacuate Moldavia and Wallachia. By the alliance, on the other hand, if England refused Russia's mediation the latter agreed to make war against the former. Similarly, France as Russia's ally would fight Turkey, if the sultan refused French mediation.

England had rejected peace, and had burned Copenhagen. Turkey in contrast had accepted the proffered mediation. It entered upon an armistice with Russia, repelled English advances. The armistice still continued, although Russia refused to ratify the formal stipulation of it. Indeed, Turkey had done everything to bring into operation the stipulation of Tilsit that guaranteed its independence. Russia possessed no basis, Champagny continued, for assuming Moldavia and Wallachia to be any different from Silesia. What had France gotten from the alliance? Nothing. Russia desired to possess Moldavia and Wallachia, and now perhaps Finland also.

Caulaincourt must reason with Rumiantsov. "This is not to say that you reject all the opinions of Russia respecting the Ottoman Empire,"

Champagny wrote, "or that you refuse to coöperate in that sphere. It is to say that you examine the consequences of their execution, this being of extreme importance. For this execution France cannot stand ready, if they involve a treaty violation, unless Russia grants it proportional advantages. The matter should be maturely considered, not decided suddenly." Napoleon would give his best attention to any overtures from Russia.[11]

Tsar Alexander at length in 1808 formally declined any undertaking to assist France, even if an ally, to go to India, to conquer Syria, or to reconquer Egypt unless he himself should be given satisfaction at the Straits. The fourth secret conference on the problem came March 9; it was a long debate that produced only an impasse. "The same questions, the same replies," almost summarized it, as Caulaincourt observed in his virtually stenographic report.

Witness his significant evaluation: "Rumiantsov concluded by stating that Alexander could not consent to see France possess the Dardanelles, that this was to displease his friends for *une langue de chat,* an allusion to the form of the Gallipoli peninsula. Neither could he see Constantinople in other hands than his own. Austria must stand between France and Russia and possess, besides Serbia, Macedonia down to the Aegean. Although the Tsar would agree with pleasure that France, for its part, take anything else that suited us, it would not work for the future and for the great object of the existing alliance between the two countries unless they agreed between themselves respecting the point which would become a continual source of difficulties, forcing each to station an army there, and which in any case opposed the principles of wise policy."

Caulaincourt argued that Russia's offer of the ports of the Levant and of Syria practically negated this seeming difficulty. Russia by its proposal would acquire immense possessions for which France would have no just equivalent. While wishing to do what would please the tsar, France, it appeared, could not permit Austria to take everything proposed, including Salonika, which would place it too near the suggested new French acquisitions in Albania and Greece.

Had Alexander stated whether or not he would coöperate in the proposed conquest of Syria and Egypt? Rumiantsov replied in the negative, but admitted this as probably beyond the realm of possibility, for then Russian forces would be engaged simultaneously in Sweden, on the coasts, on the frontiers of Persia, in war with England, and would be needed, finally, for the conquest of Turkey and for the Franco-Russian expedition to India.

Caulaincourt remarked that, in such a state of affairs, it would be better to revert to Alexander's first idea, and establish an independent government at Constantinople.

At this Rumiantsov protested strongly. He stated, "That idea does not mean anything. . . . It represented only a general reflection." Without compensation one could not justify Russia's government, in the eyes of the nation, in placing at French disposal an army for the conquest of India. "If we do not win Constantinople in the partition," he continued, "there will be more dissatisfaction with the new order than there is at present. Let us work for the future. You are making difficulties respecting the possession of Constantinople. Napoleon would not do so, I am sure. He himself offered Tolstoi this acquisition, when speaking of other matters." He insisted Russia must have a conspicuous acquisition in the great partition. "It would be a mistake for us to do without that, I repeat to you, because we are giving you an army. Do not dispute over some parcels of land, over some advantages which our position can offer us. Bulgaria is without numerous inhabitants, while the portion of Rumelia we would acquire is without advantages . . . give us Serbia."

Caulaincourt repeated his comment of the preceding conference. Serbia was not near Russia, and such a disposal of it would be unsatisfactory for Austria. "I added," he reported to Napoleon, "that I could not see why Russia, if it considered impossible its consent to our acquisition of the Dardanelles if it possessed Constantinople, could not consent to an independent government at Constantinople, together with some territory in Europe, especially since Tsar Alexander had been the first to sense the probable necessity of perhaps adopting that idea." Caulaincourt stated he could not understand why Alexander had changed his original opinion.

Without replying positively, Rumiantsov again protested the proposal, but with added vigor. "Every consideration gives Constantinople to us, if you wish to do something that will endure, and which treats us as we deserve to be treated. I repeat, Napoleon offered it to us."

As before, however, he asked for details. To whom would Caulaincourt propose to assign the sovereignty of the free city of Constantinople?

The ambassador suggested the scheme for the Duchy of Warsaw but again made an impossible proposal, doubtless laying the groundwork for his anticipated mention of Austria as the substitute for both France and Russia. He suggested a French prince as sovereign, reasoning that that solution would balance the geographical and religious influence of Russia. "Because this is a position you value in relation to commerce," he added, "it needs a mixed influence."

Rumiantsov did not hesitate to record that as inadmissible. He choked off any substitute proposal, repeating that Russia must have Constantinople and the Dardanelles. To prove to France, however, that Russia had no other desires than to establish affairs there on a footing of stability and to avoid all disputes in the future, he proposed that if Russia should be given Constantinople and the Straits, it not only would agree that France acquire the ports of the Levant, but would guarantee them against both Turks and English.

Caulaincourt asked whether such a guarantee would extend to Egypt and Syria, and whether France at all times would possess the right to send troops into Asia, to Smyrna and elsewhere, and whether Russia would coöperate in the conquest of Smyrna and the ports of the Levant against a Turkey perhaps supported by England.

Russia could not coöperate by land in such conquests, Rumiantsov replied, but would place a fleet at French disposal. Moreover, Russia would formally guarantee these ports of the Levant by land and by sea. Such a guarantee would not extend to more distant Egypt and Syria.

Caulaincourt asked whether Russia, in the guarantee, would agree by treaty to intervene against England.

Rumiantsov replied in the affirmative, provided war came in a struggle for the ports. He offered a joint Russo-Turkish control as a substitute, an offer parallel with Marshal Stalin's proposal of 1945 and 1946. Rumiantsov referred again to the necessity of giving Russia additional compensation for the proposed coöperation against India, and repeated several times that such coöperation in fact would be contrary to its interests if Russia did not obtain Constantinople and the Dardanelles. However, he stated Russia did not wish the exclusive influence over the Straits: it would agree with pleasure that the castles in Asia, or at the Bosporus, or at the Dardanelles, remain in Turkish hands. Moreover, it did not claim anything on the Adriatic banks.

Caulaincourt responded that Rumiantsov well knew that Russia would be the mistress wherever faced only by Turks. Another guarantee beside Turkey would be needed to satisfy the commercial world. If

Russia believed itself too wronged by abandoning to a foreign prince the Dardanelles or Constantinople, together with their hinterland in Europe, it might seek compensations in Asia. It might acquire Trebizond.

Rumiantsov held firmly for Constantinople and the Dardanelles. He assured Caulaincourt, jokingly, that Napoleon would be more just than his ambassador. In all this Russia desired nothing that would warrant any suspicion by France. His further statements revealed that Russia desired only an agreeable arrangement and, in consequence, Alexander counted upon proofs of full reciprocity.

Caulaincourt said France would second Russia against Sweden, had agreed to discuss this proposed partition, "etc., etc."

This conference of four hours' duration had produced nothing concrete, so Caulaincourt prepared to write a statement for Napoleon. He asked Rumiantsov to dictate it. The resulting memorandum eventually went to Paris, along with Caulaincourt's reports for Napoleon. It is entitled, "The views of Count Rumiantsov respecting the partition of Turkey at the end of the conference of March 9."

Rumiantsov's memorandum listed two sets of terms of partition for the Ottoman Empire. (1) If they arranged only a partial partition, in pursuance of the alliance of Tilsit, Russia would acquire Moldavia, Wallachia, Bessarabia, and Bulgaria. France would acquire Albania, part of Bosnia, the Morea, and Crete. Austria would be given Croatia and a portion of Bosnia. Serbia would be independent, and assigned to the administration of a prince of the Habsburgs, or to another foreign prince who must marry a Russian grand duchess. (2) If they arranged a big partition, the following terms were proposed: Russia would acquire Moldavia, Wallachia, Bessarabia, Bulgaria, and that part of Rumelia along the mountain chain from the existing Serbian frontier and thence along the Maritsa to the Aegean Sea, the hinterland of the Dardanelles and the Bosporus. France would acquire Bosnia, Albania, the Morea, Crete, Cyprus, Rhodes, all the Ionian Islands, Smyrna and the other ports of the Levant, Syria, and Egypt. Austria would acquire Serbia, and Macedonia to the sea, except such segments as France might desire in order to fortify her Albanian frontier, provided that Salonika be given to Austria. Croatia would go either to Austria or to France, whichever Napoleon desired. The three powers would coöperate in the projected expedition to India, Russia asking nothing there for its contribution.

Caulaincourt possessed no authority to put anything into writing.

He nonetheless recorded the five principal counterproposals he had interposed to Rumiantsov's observations during the conferences. (1) He opposed Russia's possession of Constantinople. (2) It would be necessary to assign the Dardanelles to France if Russia should take Constantinople, Austria being compensated in Croatia or Bosnia for the losses in Macedonia. (3) Otherwise, an independent government at Constantinople must be established. (4) Russia might be requested to reply formally to the question whether it would coöperate in the projected conquest of Syria and Egypt, provinces which Alexander had offered to France. (5) If France took the Dardanelles, or if a free city were established, Russia would be compensated in Asia, in the area of Trebizond.[12]

Thus Caulaincourt's addition to Rumiantsov's memorandum represented a written version of what Napoleon had intended should be verbal only. He had not expressly forbidden this method to his ambassador, however, and the damage was done. Napoleon himself would not fall into this error of policy. He would reply in writing neither to Caulaincourt's nor Rumiantsov's statements of details.

He had intended the preliminary results to be vague, nothing specifically granted or denied in advance of the time he and Alexander would make the decision in personal conference. Preoccupied as he was in Spain, we shall see that Napoleon near the end of May forbade Caulaincourt to put any further current verbal discussion into writing for official transmission to the Russians. He made the prohibition so strong at that time, that Caulaincourt's announcement to Russia that he could not sign a written statement must itself be made only verbally.

The immediate result, before Rumiantsov's memorandum could be approved for submission to Napoleon, was Russia's proposal of a military corridor across the Dardanelles—recalling the proposal of a corridor across the corridor in the unsuccessful Nazi-Polish negotiations of 1939. Russia's proposal resulted logically from Caulaincourt's question as to a military passage to Smyrna and beyond.

Rumiantsov carried his and Caulaincourt's written statements to Alexander. The following day, he advised the French ambassador that the tsar held out formally for Constantinople. Any big partition of Turkey that did not assign this to Russia would oppose the interests of the Russian nation and would be even worse than the existing situation, bad as it was.

With respect to the Dardanelles, Russia considered it impossible to furnish troops for the expedition to India without acquiring the advantages at the Straits which geography, more than ambition, assigned to it.

Alexander's desire to concert with Napoleon, however, had suggested to him a probable means of meeting any interests France might have in the Dardanelles—which prudent foresight required him to reserve for himself. He proposed a military corridor; that is, to establish by treaty a military route over which France at all times might traverse the Dardanelles from Europe to Asia and from Asia to Europe.

Caulaincourt observed that this met only part of his objections, and not at all satisfactorily even there. He reverted to the need for an independent government at Constantinople, but stated that his instructions limited him to outlining the French position, that he could not formally stipulate anything. He said that, properly speaking, France should possess the "Dardanelles of Asia" (underscored in the original of the report) as belonging with the Levantine ports that Russia had tendered.

When Rumiantsov demurred, the ambassador said that this should not disturb Russia, for a French colony there would be only a feeble means of assuring the actual possession of the ports and the passage of the French troops, whereas Russia could sail her fleet within the Black Sea and into the Sea of Marmara. France, he stated, must take suitable precautions against the Turks, and not be at their mercy.

Rumiantsov stated that he had anticipated this idea and already discussed it with the tsar, who had entirely refused it.

Caulaincourt regretted not finding Russia more conciliatory in "little things." Respecting the other items, Alexander approved of what Rumiantsov had said. Russia would guarantee the French ports, but accord no military and naval support to conquer and hold Egypt and Syria.

When Caulaincourt inquired how Russia's promised naval forces would be employed, Rumiantsov did not recall having said they would be available. Upon being reminded, he stated that Tsar Alexander had not given any general consent to employ his fleet. When Caulaincourt affirmed that Rumiantsov had told him so, quite positively, the latter replied he did not doubt Alexander would place the fleet at Napoleon's disposal.

Caulaincourt wrote Napoleon that he had been advised that the fleet's own chief, however, would be the person with whom he must discuss naval methods. Rumiantsov invited Caulaincourt to discuss such matters directly with Admiral Chichakov, while the foreign minister would help as much as possible.

Caulaincourt said this attitude appeared to change matters materially. It would embarrass him at Paris, owing to his earlier report that the Russian fleet would be available. He hoped everything concerning that factor would be decided as promised within a few days. He asked to see the tsar the following day, before forwarding the report, to confer respecting the fleet, as well as to debate further the "Dardanelles of Asia."

Rumiantsov clearly appeared concerned as to whether Caulaincourt's views were his own or those of the Emperor of France. He still professed to hold the conviction that Napoleon would consent to everything Russia requested in Rumiantsov's memorandum.[13]

The French ambassador talked with Chichakov in advance of his requested conversation with Tsar Alexander, which took place during the afternoon of March 12.

To the tsar he boldly stated he had accepted "without conditions" the fleet which Russia had offered France.

"All that will be arranged, you may be sure," Alexander replied, "but let us speak of the great affair. Rumiantsov has read me his memorandum. I have made a few changes, and all to your advantage. My word, you have a beautiful and good share."

Caulaincourt rejoined that Russia instead would possess the advantages, both in geographical position and in population.

To this Alexander remarked, "And you, what a number of provinces, not counting Albania and the Morea!"

Caulaincourt called all these mere morsels and far away from France.

The tsar disputed this, referring to Napoleon's Kingdom of Italy. He insisted he considered himself very moderate in his requests.

Caulaincourt once more reverted to the subject of an independent government at Constantinople, the solution first proposed by the tsar.

Alexander explained, "I had not then foreseen the importance of what Emperor Napoleon has requested." If Russia furnished an army for India, it must have commensurate advantages. He felt sure Napoleon would be of that same opinion. No doubt must be left respecting his possession of Constantinople.

"But the Dardanelles, sir?" Caulaincourt protested. "If Your Majesty possessed them, together with Constantinople, the passage would be less free than the Sound, which has a different power for each bank."

Alexander repeated, in pleasant tones, his adamant position: "Let us not be immediate neighbors. I recall the good advice of Emperor Napoleon. . . . I cannot give way on this point. If you were there, no one could come to Russia, or depart, without your permission. I have no doubt regarding the good intentions of Emperor Napoleon, but I can do nothing that will disturb public opinion, or create uncertainty between us. . . . I shall write to Napoleon. The ports of the Levant—you know that these are the richest and most populous! Smyrna, what wealth! In general, your position is superb, everything considered. . . . Warsaw, and your troops there, give you a menacing position against us, if we were to quarrel some day."

Caulaincourt argued the French position was only what English rivalry rendered necessary, nothing more. Warsaw had been turned over to the King of Saxony, not to Napoleon. "After all," he asked, "can we ever be the natural enemy of Russia? We are located far from you, and if our frontiers never touch we can only march together. Russia's enemy is Austria. If the partition takes place, this will become more so than ever. Geography can not make Austria your ally. But, thanks to our own wars with it, Russia will have nothing to fear there for half a century."

Caulaincourt observed that Russia offered France some territories in Asia, territories not requested.

"Without Asia," replied the tsar, "you still have the best share, because of your navy."

"Your Majesty offers us a military route to the ports of the Levant," came the answer, "but where is the point of departure for the ports? The Dardanelles of Asia, probably. Without that, where is the safety for this route?" Only if Tsar Alexander helped to conquer those regions, independently of the campaign to India, would the new places acquire value for France.

"Take all you wish in Asia," said Alexander, "except what touches the Dardanelles. That would remove all value to what you will be giving us. Respecting our coöperation in the French conquest of the ports, heretofore I have always refused to aid. But I do not wish to refuse everything you request this afternoon. If the solutions I have proposed are adopted, so that the big partition takes place and, in consequence, I am at the Dardanelles and Constantinople, I will coöperate with you in this conquest, but not including Syria and Egypt."

Caulaincourt ended his part of the discussion by disclaiming any authority to announce a decision. He lacked any further instructions, he stated, than those conveyed in Napoleon's letter of February 2.

The tsar then said he would be glad to talk with Napoleon again. He expressed some impatience to arrange a meeting, probably at Erfurt.[14]

Thus the memorandum would be sent to Napoleon as Russia wished it, the unyielding position respecting the Dardanelles to be submitted for decision. That same March 12, Rumiantsov questioned Caulaincourt respecting the nature of the tsar's reply to Napoleon's personal letter. The ambassador suggested that there be included the latest discussion concerning a partition of Turkey in Asia, upon which there had been no agreement. Rumiantsov again spoke encouragingly of the prospect of an agreement with Napoleon personally.

He redrafted his memorandum outlining the discussions to that point. The note is now phrased to indicate the lack of any tentative agreement respecting Constantinople and the Dardanelles. It outlined the two plans we have seen, one fulfilling the tacit objects of Tilsit by assigning the Principalities to Russia, the other meeting Napoleon's enlarged proposal of early February. The only changes were Russia's disclaimer of any desire to conquer Asia Minor, previously admitted in the discussions as a possibility, and its denial of any claims to territory to be jointly won in India. France might take as much of India as it liked, disposing of it as it pleased. He stated the object of the memorandum to be to establish, with "a sort of precision," the matters which would be discussed and agreed upon by the two emperors when they conferred personally.[15]

Alexander confirmed his approval of the demands and outlines of Rumiantsov's memorandum in a letter of March 14, in reply to Napoleon's letter. "It was left to a genius to conceive so vast a plan," he patronizingly wrote. He said he had expressed himself with frankness and without reserve to General Caulaincourt concerning the interests of his empire. If Napoleon concurred, he offered a Russian army for the expedition to India, and another to aid France to conquer the ports of Asia Minor. Moreover, Russia's fleet in the Black Sea would be placed entirely under Napoleon's orders. If Napoleon approved his ideas, he stood ready for the joint meeting that Napoleon suggested. Erfurt seemed the best place for it. Meanwhile, his conquest of Finland proceeded satisfactorily.[16]

Caulaincourt's private letter to Napoleon, submitting his personal reactions to all this, completed the parcels for the couriers to be expedited to Paris. He believed that Russia's official opinion had vacillated from day to day, but that Rumiantsov dominated it. He admitted he had never gotten round to Napoleon's alternative proposition, tentatively assigning the Dardanelles to Austria. (This had presumably been authorized in those parts of the secret instructions that have not been preserved.) It intrigued Caulaincourt to reflect that he had thus avoided, inadvertently, drafting an article for a possible subsequent treaty of alliance between Austria and Russia. Moreover, he wondered whether Russia, if under the necessity of deciding, would have preferred Austria or France at the Dardanelles, since it was not always a political or military idea that dominated Russia's cabinet. The Russian court held out for Constantinople out of vanity, and for the Dardanelles out of interest, to assure its Black Sea commerce and indeed, the commerce of all its empire.

Russia's ministry of commerce, he continued, of course must follow Rumiantsov's ideas. Indeed, he was finding it difficult to negotiate with a foreign minister who, also being minister of commerce, could defend commerce so vigorously. In Rumiantsov it really seemed to be two men against one.

The suggestion of an independent government at Constantinople had been opposed by all of Alexander's advisers. They preferred instead to leave it to weak Turkey, the principle recommended for Russia's policy by Foreign Minister Kochubei in 1802.

Tsar Alexander seemed genuinely to desire the new personal conference with Napoleon, whereas Rumiantsov favored it only if assured in advance of the bases on which he would negotiate.

Finally, in Caulaincourt's opinion Napoleon might change the map of the world by giving Russia Constantinople and the Dardanelles. In exchange for that, Napoleon certainly could do what he pleased elsewhere, annex Italy and perhaps even Spain, change dynasties, found kingdoms, arrange anything concerning Austria, all without arousing Russia's suspicions. And he could have the Black Sea fleet and the land army to conquer Egypt.[17]

In summary, Napoleon's proposal of February 2 that the projected joint expedition assemble at Constantinople became the point of departure for debate on various hypothetical partitions of the Ottoman Empire. Of significance was the ultimate disposal of the Turkish Straits. When Napoleon opened the subject of India, it evoked the tsar's counterproposal for compensation at the Dardanelles and Bosporus. Only if the Straits were conceded would Russia coöperate in invading India.

Caulaincourt drew the Russians out, having them indicate the details for a partition. He did not commit himself or Napoleon for or against most of their suggestions. The debate was stalemated over two alternate projects of partition, one excluding and one including Constantinople and the Straits. The negotiators discussed the latter project in much the greater detail.

The secret Franco-Russian negotiations had many times involved the recognition of the primary strategic position of the Turkish Straits. It may be suggested that Napoleon's inability or unwillingness to concede both of them to Russia caused the ultimate failure of his empire. Because Napoleon refused Russia compensation at both Straits (chap. xiv), the India bubble burst. As the eventual consequence, moreover, Russia did not coöperate effectively in Napoleon's European policies thereafter, either against Austria in 1809 or against the continentally blockaded British.

XIV

"The Bases Cannot Be Accepted"

THE DIPLOMATIC stalemate over the Dardanelles was perhaps chiefly responsible for eventually killing the Franco-Russian alliance. Caulaincourt had held inadmissible every formula that excluded a division of the Straits between Russia and France, should any partition of Turkey include the zone of the Straits. Alexander had refused every proposal that permitted France to share that zone; Constantinople and the Straits must be Russian or Turkish. In this chapter we attempt to trace Napoleon's reactions to these propositions.

The reasons for Napoleon's insistence upon sharing or owning the Dardanelles are none too clear. His failure to recover security at sea suggests one factor. For another, such ownership would figure in the reëstablishment and extension of French commerce throughout the Levant. The French consuls in Egypt repeatedly recommended as desirable the establishment of protected land routes from Egypt around to Constantinople and to western Europe. The only water barrier would be the narrow Straits. The Dardanelles and the Bosporus might be expected, moreover, to become a base for the subsequent conquest of Syria and Egypt—and the same logic would apply to a route of conquest and supply for British India.

Caulaincourt's withholding of the Dardanelles from Russia's ownership in March, 1808, merely reflected Napoleon Bonaparte's fixed idea dating back to Syria in 1799, whereby the land bridge to western Asia must be made accessible to France. His bitter experience there taught him, once and for all, the strategic value of the Dardanelles. As a Turkish ally, Russia had stood astride the Straits, and Great Britain, another Turkish ally, barred the sea. He could not return to Europe by the Syria-to-Asia Minor land bridge. His unsuccessful campaign at Acre had demonstrated how difficult would be French conquests in western Asia, when communications depended solely upon the sea lanes. Obviously, to use the land bridge from Europe one must control southeastern Europe, not merely a position in Africa. Conceivably, the bridge could be broken by the Straits, its water link. The value of the Dardanelles and Bosporus would be incomparably greater, everyone recognizes, if held by the greatest and nearest land power. As a modern parallel, Turkey's alliance with Great Britain from 1940 to 1945 had the effect of withholding from Mussolini and Hitler the use of the Dardanelles. Turkey's policy of neutrality effectively closed the land bridge against the Italo-German forces marooned in northern Africa—forces which of necessity returned westward to Tunis, always hoping in vain for the relief that did not come from across the short distance by sea from Sicily.

Rumiantsov and Alexander had steadily increased their offers to win French acquiescence. They provisionally granted Silesia and various Turkish islands and provinces, together with joint Franco-Russian military expeditions to India and elsewhere. From Russia's first mention of compensation at both Straits, Caulaincourt had insisted that France be dominant at the Dardanelles if Russia acquired Constantinople and the Bosporus. Russia considered such a solution worse than the existing weak Ottoman control of the gateway to its fertile southern provinces. In this big argument neither side would yield. We have seen Caulaincourt once report to Napoleon, "The same debates, the same conclusions." He conceded Moldavia, Wallachia, and Finland to Russia. The several suggested partitions, debated without result, eventually included most of the Ottoman Empire except its heart, the Straits, and included Tsar Alexander's offer to employ his Black Sea fleet to support France in conquering Smyrna and the ports of Asia Minor. This would involve his first Russian sailing of the Straits under the arrangement he proposed.

The impatient tsar believed that he would be able to agree with Napoleon within a half hour, were the latter with him in person. The negotiators had submitted the entire matter to Napoleon, by means of a carefully worded Russian memorandum to which Caulaincourt appended written reservations. Afterward, at a personal conference between the two emperors, the final decision would be taken.

French difficulties mounted at Constantinople itself. Sebastiani reported (March 14) that Mouhib had stressed from Paris that Turkey could not count on French support. According to the Ottoman ambassador, Emperor Napoleon had irrevocably engaged to follow Russian policy and, if the new ally insisted, he would not hesitate to sacrifice

Turkey in the same manner in which he was sacrificing Sweden. "France is considered an unfaithful ally who has betrayed Turkey," so Sebastiani relayed Mouhib's testimony. "This conviction is general. It is impossible to destroy it, and today Turkey hates France more than Russia."[1]

Mouhib's anti-French feeling was attested fully by unofficial information volunteered by Theologue, his embassy's first interpreter in Paris. In an unannounced visit to the Ottoman embassy on the afternoon of May 22, Verninac, former French ambassador to Turkey, learned that Mouhib was asleep. Theologue invited him for a private discussion in the garden. The latter discounted Napoleon's possible arrangement to extend the period for the *de facto* Russo-Turkish armistice—which in any event amounted to nothing if ultimate peace remained in doubt. He considered it obvious that the powerful Napoleon need not permit Russia to violate the Treaty of Tilsit by remaining in the Principalities. Hence Turkey must conclude that Napoleon had permitted it. If Russia did not make peace, he confided, Turkey would be beaten and its ruin would inevitably ensue. Theologue revealed that he had had the courage to say as much to Mouhib and to argue that the difficulty could be met only by abandoning some territory. Mouhib had replied that "the French were Turkey's enemies, the same as the Russians and all infidels." The ambassador boasted that the Mohammedans would be able to handle the situation by force of arms and cede nothing. Theologue called attention to the military defeats, only to have Mouhib accuse him of being a Christian himself and in sympathy with Christians. Theologue revealed the incredible weakness of the Ottoman Empire, its empty treasury, and its inability to raise more than 30,000 troops, mostly in Asia. Frontier provincials went their own way, as did the Greeks.[2]

Gardane sent gossip from Teheran. Among Shah Feth Ali's many troubles in March was the likelihood that his government would break relations with Turkey. It was assumed that the new sultan was in accord with the English. Although Russia and Persia were observing a *de facto* armistice, no Persian envoys had been named to negotiate peace, and the expected Russian negotiators had not appeared. If they came to Teheran, the preponderant French influence there would be threatened. More important was Gardane's preoccupation with the English ships off Persia's coasts. The reported conferences of Hartford Jones with Persian officials at Bandar Abu Shehr, on the coast, forced the French minister to urge that the English be expelled. Feth Ali dodged a direct reply, although speaking in generally favorable terms from the French standpoint. Gardane's interpreter seemed convinced by the interview that the Persians really wished to chase the British away. The Persians held off under the assumption the English would soon leave anyway.[3] In Paris, for once only three months behind with news from Persia, Foreign Minister Champagny on March 18 acknowledged Gardane's reports of December 24, giving the details of his reception and initial results. He directed Gardane to encourage a *rapprochement* between Russia and Persia and to hold Persia to its anti-English course.

Having broken with England, Russia wished to let Napoleon worry about its ships in the Adriatic. Caulaincourt revealed this in his routine business of late March, 1808. He stated: "News arriving from Constantinople in recent days affirms that the Turks have signed a secret treaty with the English and that the Turkish commandant of the Dardanelles, who was believed to have been replaced, has been ordered to Malta to conclude the new arrangements." The tsar ordered precautionary measures against Turkey, to assure a favorable result in the Principalities. In a friendly manner, he tendered Napoleon the more or less marooned Russian ships in the Adriatic. Tsar Alexander personally favored placing at Napoleon's disposal not the main squadron but his several vessels of war at Lisbon, Portoferraio, and Trieste. In July his government directed Admiral Seniavin to deliver a frigate from his squadron to any French officers designated to receive it.[4]

Turkey yielded to the French claims against Algeria by directing the dey—against whom Napoleon had ordered reprisals—to restore all confiscated French property. By March 20 Constantinople had a copy of General Berthier's abrupt letter to the pasha of Albania. This communication was intended to facilitate the passage of Napoleon's troops through the province. The letter had "troubled the spirits." The Ottomans appeared to be at last realizing that in Dalmatia France held a strategic position with regard to Balkan Turkey similar to that of Russia and Austria. The sultan feared that Albania might revolt and all of Rumelia be inflamed if Berthier carried out his threat to attack Ali Pasha in the event that the passage of troops were denied. This letter, written before the Turkish concession of passage, embarrassed Sebastiani.

Champagny marked time with Mouhib, leaving the latter uninformed of Napoleon's intentions. He did make one slight concession, on April 1. He called attention to the conditional character of his words in mid-January, when he said, ". . . if the Russians should wish to keep Moldavia and Wallachia." The Turks had seemed to interpret this as positive and inevitable. He dampened whatever remained of the Turkish hope for peace, however, by stating that the negotiations with Russia did not require frequent conference. He said that Napoleon desired a durable peace between Russia and Turkey, not merely peace.[5] A further illustration of the procrastination is Champagny's reply in mid-March to the Turks' letter written January 30, before they learned of the single preliminary conference on January 23. He referred to that conference and stated that the reason for the delay concerning explanations and instructions was only the great distances to be spanned. Napoleon's good offices were available for a *rapprochement;* England should be recognized as Turkey's real enemy. Napoleon busied himself in 1808 in Spain and Portugal, not in the Near East and beyond. His early February plan to solicit Alexander's coöperation against Britain in India—at the territorial expense of Turkey in the Balkans—came significantly at a time when it could cover his policy and action against Bourbon Spain. The emperor's initiative, early in 1808, taken to unseat the Spanish monarch raised the issue long contested by French and British armies there. His invasion of the Iberian Peninsula moved swiftly, the first successes being achieved only against insurrections and a British land force. The contest remained indecisive, and twice forced upon him a two-front situation, when he attacked Austria in 1809 and Russia in 1812.

Napoleon apparently did not like Russia to consider the winning of the Principalities a foregone conclusion. Champagny directed Caulaincourt (on April 2) to inform Russia of Turkey's absolute refusal to cede Moldavia and Wallachia. Napoleon soon authorized the communication to Russia of two reports from Sebastiani, unfavorable to Russia.

Early in April Alexander closed Russia's frontiers against English merchandise, thus conforming with Napoleon's Continental Blockade. No doubt remained of the quite limited meaning of the tsar's "declaration" issued in November against England.[6] The tsar thanked Caulaincourt for freeing the remaining Russian prisoners of war. Champagny opposed the measure as soon as he learned of it, thereby revealing that Napoleon was displeased with Russia's adamant policy of withholding aid for a campaign against India unless compensated at the Straits.

Napoleon's reactions to the secret discussion of partition had to be gleaned mostly by inference. Upon Alexander's inquiry, Caulaincourt stated that Napoleon had simply acknowledged his first dispatch which had told of the delivery of Napoleon's letter of February 2. In mid-

April, the curious tsar again asked for official information. The conversations of the tsar and Caulaincourt now related to operations against Spain and England and merely speculated concerning the time when Napoleon would get around to an answer respecting Turkey. Reports from Generals Prosorovski and Kurakrin hinted that Sebastiani twice had been on the point of leaving Constantinople, although they understood that Napoleon's ambassador finally won authorization for the passage across Albania. Sooner or later Sebastiani would be forced to leave, owing to his growing conviction that Turkey and England would reach an understanding. The Turks began to talk of renewing the fighting war, in order to regain Moldavia and Wallachia. Tolstoi wrote to temporarily absent Champagny that his news from Constantinople pictured the Turks as arming heavily, in consequence of which Alexander might alter his dispositions regarding them.[7] Alexander's foreign minister related all this to Caulaincourt on April 11, whereupon the latter remarked that the Turks had fulfilled Tilsit's condition by the very fact of offering to make peace. It could not be Turkey's fault if Count Tolstoi always waited for, and never received, instructions to negotiate peace with Turkey.

The sultan had agreed to the passage of the French troops although, owing to insubordination by Ali Pasha, he did not feel able to advance assurances of Albania's compliance with the order. He admitted the fear of unfavorable reaction by the janissaries, who still resisted any type of foreign intervention. Accordingly, Sebastiani assured several of their chiefs that Napoleon did not intend to use Ionian military relief as a ruse to get his troops down into Greece. This negotiation during April —left in part unfinished—proved to be Sebastiani's last important discussion with Turkey. Paris recalled him by a letter of March 17.[8]

Before Sebastiani departed from Constantinople on April 26, so Latour-Maubourg affirmed, he had restored the confidence of the Ottoman ministry in Napoleon's good will. He transmitted certain directed explanations, notably Champagny's interpretation of the conditional character of Russia's claim to Moldavia and Wallachia. The Turks felt they were lost if Napoleon withdrew his support. At that time their troops threatened to renew the shooting war with Russia on the Danube, with or without orders from the Ottoman central authority and notwithstanding that negotiations under French mediation conceivably could be under way in Paris. For the time being Russia was still observing the working armistice. Sebastiani announced to the Turks that he had been permitted to return to France for his health. He promised to concern himself with Turkish interests during his sojourn in Paris.[9]

By the time Caulaincourt's fully detailed secret reports came to Paris, Napoleon had departed to superintend personally Joseph Bonaparte's seizure of the Spanish crown. This left in the air the decision respecting Rumiantsov's memorandum (chap. xiii). Alexander remarked to Caulaincourt on April 27, "I hope incessantly that you will have news from the emperor. It is reported to me from Paris that he will be absent for at least two months. This is a long time, in view of the position in which it leaves us. He is irrepressibly active. After having regulated the affairs of Turkey and of India, which will force England to peace, the emperor will need rest, and especially sleep." Reflecting Napoleon's adverse reactions, Champagny sent only routine instructions to Caulaincourt—on April 18 and 26 and May 31—after receiving the latter's detailed accounts of the secret discussions. More than ever, Napoleon's Spanish problems took the spotlight. Only in mid-August did the emperor return to his favorite palace, St. Cloud. Late in April, at Bayonne, he received Caulaincourt's secret reports of March, together with Rumiantsov's summary of the sharp debate over the Dardanelles. It is evident that Napoleon and Champagny studied these documents with interest but without conviction.

Napoleon never abandoned his original decision to exclude Russia from the acquisition of Constantinople and both Straits. His absence from Paris ostensibly explained his neglect to transmit a direct reply. Offering another convenient means of evading a reply was the admitted magnitude of the issues, requiring that the two sovereigns meet personally. On April 26, Rumiantsov believed that the pending negotiation could not be concluded so long as Napoleon was preoccupied with Spain. He advised Caulaincourt that Tsar Alexander would wait until he heard from Napoleon, before taking any further action against Turkey. The minister wondered aloud whether Napoleon had not forgotten Russia. Neither side said anything further of Napoleon's original proposal to speed a joint campaign against India.[10]

A slight clue to Napoleon's afterthoughts concerning his secret proposal to attack India was a communication from Bayonne whereby he directed Consul David of Bosnia (on June 1) to counter the "false, absurd report" that the French planned to launch an expedition to Persia by way of Turkey. The consul must state the pertinent fact, he said, that France at the time had not a single soldier in Turkey.[11] If this was based on his actual policy, it reveals an abandonment of serious consideration of India, once he learned it would cost Constantinople, the Dardanelles, and the Bosporus. The proposed personal conference already threatened to be merely a post-mortem examination of the project (chap. xv).

That the emperor seemed to lack a real interest in Turkey is suggested by the circumstance that the sultan's letter to Napoleon dated in April was not translated (by Jaubert) until mid-August, 1808. The Ottoman ruler therein expressed confidence that Napoleon's imperial word had guaranteed officially the independence of the Ottoman government and that the treaty to be arranged between himself and Russia would conform with Ottoman interests. He expected a "prompt and favorable result" from the negotiations.[12]

News of the assassination of four French officers at Antivari caused Napoleon's policy for Turkey to turn to coldness. Anticipating formal approval for his troops to pass through Albania, Marmont early in March had dispatched in advance four officers and a French interpreter to notify the several pashas. The reports from these four ceased when they reached Antivari, on March 13. Champagny at first assumed that they had been arrested by the pasha of Scutari or of Berat. He wrote from Bayonne to Ambassador Mouhib for information and at the same time threw in complaints against various abuses permitted by Ali Pasha. He demanded satisfaction for the latest outrage. Constantinople learned at that time that the four French officers had been temporarily imprisoned, then assassinated, at Antivari. Early in May, David officially confirmed the assassinations. The latter himself took refuge in Dalmatia, the move being caused more by pique at not winning satisfaction for Antivari than by any personal danger.[13] In Sinop, the Turks insulted and later murdered Consul General Fourçade.[14] The courier carrying to General Marmont the Ottoman approval of the passage of troops finally arrived on April 13 in Travnik, Bosnia, the seat of David's consul generalship. Enforcing the order represented the next problem and it was accomplished only with caution.

Three factors ended Sebastiani's brilliant diplomatic career in Turkey: his poor health and spirits, the change of general policy in consequence of Napoleon's alliance with Russia, and the potentialities for Turkey in the secret discussions at St. Petersburg. He turned the embassy's affairs over to Latour-Maubourg as chargé d'affaires. An immediate and conspicuous further decline ensued for French influence. No one could obtain satisfaction for grievances.

While Sebastiani's recall represented an important change in French policy, Ruffin's presence and personality seemed to give it a changeless character. The latter, jealous of Latour-Maubourg, sought to return to Paris. As at other times, the foreign ministry refused to sanction his return because he was still too valuable in the heart of the Near East. Constantinople might again become a key center for action instead of observation. Latour-Maubourg would serve until mid-1812, although never with the title of ambassador. Far more important, he never possessed adequate instructions from Paris.

Ange Gardane, the brother of the minister to Persia, had traveled slowly and came to the Turkish capital en route to France. He and La Blanche, one of the most used and most trusted secretary-couriers of the time, left Constantinople simultaneously with Sebastiani. Asker Khan, Persia's resident minister assigned to Paris, was still visiting in Constantinople, seemingly disinclined to proceed promptly to his new post. Later, according to a dispatch of July 12 from Teheran, when Shah Feth Ali and his ministers learned that their ambassador stopped at Constantinople for a casual visit of several months, they were "astonished."

The significant new development in Persia was British interference with French policy. Upon learning of the treaty cession of two islands to France, the English sent a squadron to the entrance of the Persian Gulf. Minister Gardane prepared to break off relations with the Persians. When Hartford Jones extended them the olive branch, Gardane—no less than Sebastiani in the case of the Turks—was embarrassed to have nothing of consequence to say to them. Although Gardane had frequently requested instructions, he could complain in mid-April that he had had no news from the French foreign minister since the unimportant dispatch of November 13, 1807—which he received in mid-February.

Perforce, Gardane proceeded on his own judgment. He threatened to leave Teheran, writing this to Mirza Cheffi, the shah's grand vizir. He assured them he would still be interested in Persia's affairs. He found Mirza Cheffi, as always, ready to be useful to France. Gardane held what he termed a "final" conference with Crown Prince Abbas Mirza. Through him the latter requested France to send three or four regiments for war against the Russians or the English, two or three additional officers, and a surgeon, together with a nonaccredited journalist, to inform the French public of affairs in Persia. Indirectly revealing a phase of Persian official thinking, Abbas Mirza stated that in the event of war with Turkey he would expect only the officers, not the regiments. Gardane did not answer a question as to whether he was leaving upon orders from Napoleon or upon his own initiative.

Gardane forbade Teheran to receive Jones. Nevertheless, French sources reported the latter as en route to Teheran on April 24. Unsubstantiated and sometimes contradictory gossip of pertinence in the Persian capital included stories that French forces from Dalmatia had moved near to Constantinople, that other French troops had arrived in the Crimea on the way to Persia, and that Napoleon personally was commanding a powerful army in the Balkans as a result of Turkey's refusal to allow French troops to cross its territory. Gardane privately supposed that the Persian court had decided to make the most of the situation by playing off the French, Russians, and English against one another. In his conversations with the shah he could fall back on something. Having sent his brother to Paris in Persia's interest, he could speculate with them that probably Ange Gardane would return with secret information which would please the Persians. The shah let it be known that he kept putting off Russia's field commander regarding peace because he knew his interests were being cared for by Napoleon in Paris.[15]

Mirza Cheffi confidentially revealed to Gardane certain reports received from Asker Khan at Constantinople. According to these, the Ottoman government had sought by various arguments to turn the latter away from his journey to France. They told him that he would be embarrassed in Paris and his mission would lack utility. He would be representing an alliance with Napoleon which, sooner or later, could be nothing less than deadly. They argued that it would be better to cooperate with Turkey and to consolidate Persia's influence in Asia. Asker Khan stated that he had thrust aside all these insinuations, boldly upholding the durable character of Persia's alliance with France and advising that the sultan show equal esteem for Napoleon.[16]

Rumiantsov utilized France's capital city to reveal, through Russia's diplomatic channels early in May, the tsar's expectation of possessing the Principalities and Georgia. He announced that Russia desired to live in peace with the Ottoman Empire and Persia. The tsar had confided to Napoleon as the mediator the only conditions he considered suitable for a stable and solid settlement. Russia's ruler would be charmed if the sultan and the shah should recognize "the existing situation." That meant that they should cede the occupied Principalities and Georgia.[17]

From Bayonne, Champagny said nothing of Turkey when on April 27 he acknowledged all of Caulaincourt's key summaries of his debates through March 24. Champagny did reveal Napoleon's unfriendly calculations, however, by reprimanding Caulaincourt for ordering General Claude Victor to release the Russian prisoners held in Prussia. The foreign minister recognized but evaded the "other matters" discussed in Caulaincourt's ciphered dispatches by stating that Spain required Napoleon's entire attention.[18] The latter also used Spain as an excuse, when he wrote to the tsar on April 29. Furthermore, Napoleon amply confirmed his agent's apparent evasiveness in a direct written reply to Alexander's overtures. He recounted in friendly tone the problems in Spain and promised he "would soon be free to plan the great affair" with the tsar. He neither conceded the Dardanelles to Russia nor even mentioned that subject directly. He merely stated that he had found Rumiantsov's memorandum "far from conciliating the different interests." Work would be needed to reach a conclusion—work that must be done. Alexander might count on him with respect to Austria. Turkey "and its hundred pashas, each going his own way," annoyed him. His squadron had scored no little success, in supplying Corfu with munitions and food for two years. He would be very glad to see the tsar personally again.[19]

Believing that "no news is good news," Russia had evidently continued to hope for a partition of Turkey. Indirect news now shattered the hope. Notwithstanding everything Caulaincourt and Rumiantsov had said, agreement with Napoleon respecting the Straits was doubtful. This became even more apparent when Napoleon threatened, in devious fashion, to take Turkey's side against Russia. Doubtless such a threat was intended to draw attention from Alexander's demand for the Dardanelles.

Caulaincourt acted upon new instructions when, on April 29, he officially communicated to Russia the two ciphered anti-Russian reports by Sebastiani. In these Napoleon's ambassador spoke of Turkey as the ancient ally of France. They reported the affairs of Turkey as of February and stressed the Turkish disquietude. Russia's failure to state whether the armistice would be prolonged had disturbed them. Sebastiani seemed to fear Russia as the master of Turkey, even before it crossed Turkey's frontiers. Rumiantsov took these reports to the tsar, meanwhile remarking on Turkey's considerable preparation for war.[20] The tsar promptly invited Caulaincourt to dinner, and the latter after-

ward reported Alexander as apparently uneasy over Napoleon's purpose
in communicating the dispatches. Russia's autocrat said, "Speak to me
plainly. What is the object of these letters? Has the emperor changed?
Does he wish to prepare me for a change?" He stated that Napoleon
had announced "some great projects" to him and that he had simply
desired to second his ally; certainly his conduct since Tilsit spoke
loudly in that respect.

Being a good diplomat, Caulaincourt expressed "astonishment" that
such doubts had entered the tsar's mind. To him, it seemed only natural
for Sebastiani to defend the Turks.

Alexander retorted, "The Turks are of a savage species. And Napoleon
at Tilsit was more animated against them than myself." Had Caulaincourt spoken with Rumiantsov respecting the armistice between Russia
and Turkey—the continuance of which Sebastiani and the Turks so
much desired? Caulaincourt interpreted this as a threat to terminate the
de facto armistice. He found Rumiantsov noncommittal when, three days
later, he asked the tsar's foreign minister whether the armistice was to
be broken without using the mediator.

Both sides could play the same game. Rumiantsov stated that he considered, in strict right, that the armistice might be interpreted as broken
already, owing to Turkey's new military preparations and to Alexander's
sending reinforcements into the Principalities.

Caulaincourt spoke to the tsar again, to complain of not being able
to report an assurance that the armistice would be extended.

Alexander replied that new hints from Constantinople foretold an
Anglo-Turkish understanding—hints supported by General Sebastiani's
departure. However anxious he was to please Napoleon, he would have
to do "what the Turks forced him to do."[21]

With Caulaincourt's reports of the debates in hand, did the French
emperor now prepare to move against Albania—always frankly included
as within his share, in the event of a partition of Turkey? Champagny
in mid-May directed new complaints against Ali Pasha, this time for his
enslaving France's Balkan and Ionian subjects. Napoleon's headquarters
clarified to Russia that it was Admiral Ganteaume's squadron which had
reinforced and provisioned Corfu. (Frenchmen always remember Ganteaume for his having facilitated Bonaparte's escape in 1799 through the
Anglo-Turkish blockade of Egypt.) Champagny notified Turkey that
the relief of the island rendered a crossing of Albania less necessary. On
the other hand, he made it clear that Napoleon was still watching Tur-

key's policy concerning the request: the Ottoman Empire must understand it could be supported only by Napoleon, that it would fall without his support. He interpreted Turkey's Balkan record for the moment, including the assassinations at Antivari and the pro-English conduct of Ali Pasha, as unsatisfactory. The French claimed that they had sent the alternate sea expedition to Corfu as a means of demonstrating moderation toward Turkey.[22]

Napoleon's instructions to Caulaincourt during this period have not been preserved—if indeed he ever sent anything more than restrictive generalities and stressed the importance of a personal meeting. We can read the instructions, however, in the mirror of Caulaincourt's responses. After the arrival of each French courier in St. Petersburg, he consistently held to vague replies to Russian questions. Once he answered that "he had replied in the affairs of Turkey as Napoleon had directed." Alexander appeared anxious for the personal meeting, "in order to put the compass on the map." Caulaincourt frankly estimated Alexander's personal confidence in Napoleon as being the one certain Russian factor favorable to France. The tsar's advisers, in contrast, tended toward suspicion and vacillation. Alexander repeatedly expressed his confidence while they discussed the preliminary arrangements for the meeting at Erfurt. The tsar unsuccessfully defended Rumiantsov's opinion that most of the details for a partition could be worked out in advance, leaving only the final decisions for the sovereigns personally.

Caulaincourt opposed this opinion more definitely than ever. He dodged an answer, when asked point-blank on May 21, "Are there some difficulties concerning *la langue de chat?*" Evidently Napoleon's secret instructions restricted his saying anything at all concerning either a tentative or a final disposition of the Dardanelles; a matter of such importance must be left to Napoleon himself. Caulaincourt evasively remarked in reply that thirty couriers could not accomplish as much as three days of meetings between the two rulers. He said that this great affair included "delicate matters" which they alone could handle. He suggested that the tsar agree to meet at Erfurt without any advance stipulations. He maintained that the tsar, not Napoleon, desired the partition; the latter was only consenting to it to be agreeable. "He cannot sacrifice in this circumstance all the interests of France to those of his ancient ally." Here Napoleon himself repeated Sebastiani's offense of terming Turkey a French ally. Caulaincourt remarked, however, that in matters of this importance, diplomatic effort stopped almost as soon as begun. The tsar agreed to a personal meeting without advance stipulations. He ruled out June, in order to await the more complete military results in Sweden. He considered July would be better, when more would be known also of the attitudes in England.[23] Actually, the meeting came late in September (chap. xv).

Napoleon thus abandoned the proposed expedition to India, at least if it must cost the Dardanelles. England might sue for peace. He directed Champagny, on May 22, to have Caulaincourt withhold any commitments and especially to avoid putting into writing for the Russians anything discussing current affairs. Quite obviously he did not like Caulaincourt's putting in writing such interpretations as the ambassador had appended to Rumiantsov's memorandum—a memorandum which the French emperor never answered in writing. Caulaincourt's communication, he stated specifically, must not be considered as an official communication. Even this slight notice, he directed, must be given to Russia only verbally and not in writing. The ambassador in subsequent discussions might remark that France had nothing to gain by Russia's arriving at Stockholm.[24] One finds no direct mention by Napoleon of the secret conversations at St. Petersburg or mention of Turkey. Champagny mentioned them, however, when acting in part under this directive. To Caulaincourt he stated exactly nothing: that the emperor—still away from Paris—had not found time to consider Caulaincourt's reports of his conferences with Rumiantsov on the subject of Turkey. The important Spanish business that called him to Bayonne left him as yet even less time than before to examine Rumiantsov's memorandum.

Ambiguous comment on Russia's sojourn in the Principalities continued Napoleon's game with the tsar. Champagny's words could be taken either as mild criticism or as praise:

During this time, the Russians have continued to occupy Moldavia and Wallachia and to consume its products. Not remaining within their protected military position, they have accustomed the Wallachians and Moldavians to their domination, have effaced or destroyed all that could attach the latter to the Turkish government. They have rendered themselves more and more able to attack with advantage the miserable Turks who, despite extensive publicity and claims, have only been able to form an army corps of 6,000 men under the orders of the grand vizir. None of the interests of Russia have been compromised.

He thus minimized Turkey's striking power by not counting the many thousands of troops commanded by the pashas, and purposely contradicted Sebastiani in the two dispatches transmitted to Russia.[25]

What had Napoleon intended by communicating Sebastiani's pro-Turkish dispatches? On June 4 Champagny tried to write something in reply to that question as asked by the tsar on April 30. If the matter had been forgotten, Caulaincourt need not haggle over it. One answer was that those important letters had been communicated because France considered that they would interest Russia as a friendly court. In particular, they revealed Turkey's disposition not to cede Moldavia or Wallachia. Thereby the French government had simply conveyed general information, without considering how Russia might interpret this or that sentence. The transmission of Sebastiani's dispatches by no means implied France's abandonment of anything in its relations with Russia. One glaring error needed correction, Champagny stated, namely Sebastiani's statement that the Turks were raising a very large army for service at the Danube. Actually, their army there numbered only 4,000. Nor was it true the Turks wanted an understanding with the English. Reinforcements of some 8,000 Russians were sent into the Principalities.[26]

In Persia, Gardane was still without new instructions and with very little news from Constantinople or elsewhere in Europe. Late in May 1808, his treaty of commerce with Persia had come into Champagny's hands. The latter renewed the instructions for the minister to speed up a Russo-Turkish agreement and to hold Persia to its anti-English course. He said nothing of French mediation or of Georgia.[27] Gardane took occasion to ridicule official France for the entertainment given messenger Yousef Bey during the preceding autumn. The minister said he could not imagine how French officials "had not observed the latter to be only a simple servant." He stated that Yousef was a very ordinary doorkeeper at the court, who had been sent to carry the shah's letter to Napoleon. "He was a simple courier. He left Teheran in September, 1806, traveling by way of Aleppo. This man did not merit any of the honors with which he has been overwhelmed." Gardane commended Asker Khan, the actual Persian ambassador en route to Paris, as a "person of distinction, honored in his tribe, rich, powerful, esteemed, and employed by the shah. He had, it was said, given several proofs of his bravery."[28]

Britain's Captain Malcolm, who came in support of Hartford Jones, had not sailed away from Persia after his rebuff early in March. Grand Vizir Mirza Cheffi informed Gardane, on June 1, of Malcolm's being in the Persian Gulf with four vessels of the line to complement the six vessels and four transports already there. The shah reportedly would send 4,000 troops to the coast to oppose an English landing.[29]

Certain official Persians began to evince willingness to be persuaded by the English, being tired of waiting for action by Napoleon. In conference with Gardane, the pro-French vizir and pro-English minister of war asked if Napoleon's minister would consent to Malcolm's sending a simple courier from the British squadron to visit Teheran. Gardane refused absolutely, citing the alliance with Napoleon which required the cessation of all communications with England. When the two Persians inquired what would be the effect, Gardane replied with a question. What had become of the 4,000 troops Persia supposedly sent to the coast? He was informed that the number had been reduced by a thousand and that in any event any such small force could not successfully hold back the English. The war minister preferred to receive the courier, but Gardane suggested Persia's reinforcement of the coast.

Feth Ali made the decision and it was favorable to France. The vizir apprised Gardane immediately that the coasts would be defended. The commander there, Ismail Bey, with his 3,000 men had been ordered to open hostilities if the British should land.[30] This flurry of activity led Gardane to speculate on the general conditions (June 2). Observing the situation from distant Teheran, he considered that the general situation in Europe alone had prevented the fall of Turkey as a consequence of Russia's advances. The Russo-Persian war concerned him more. Shah Feth Ali directed Asker Khan to speed up his negotiations at Paris for Russia's evacuation of Georgia. Such an evacuation, he said, accorded with the Franco-Persian treaty of alliance—which he considered "of eternal duration." General Gudovich, Russia's commander in Georgia, sought peace on the field rather than by means of French mediation. He sent Lieutenant Colonel Baron Wrede to Teheran and a friendly letter to Gardane. Paris would not learn of these acts until September 5.

Napoleon did nothing less than turn his back on a Persia which more than ever needed the mediation of a third power. Unaware of this, or unwilling to give credence to it, Gardane stated to the shah that he believed that Tolstoi and Asker Khan might work out the problem with Napoleon. Feth Ali decided to dispatch authority to his ambassador to sign peace with Russia on whatever terms Napoleon approved. Thus Napoleon acquired another unsolicited role, that of mediator, one which he did not fulfill. Meanwhile, the shah asked Wrede to return to Tiflis to conclude a temporary armistice to endure throughout the negotiations. Champagny argued, in a delayed letter from Paris, that the treaty of alliance with Persia did not impose on Napoleon the positive obligation to recover Georgia. The treaty merely stated that Napoleon recognized Georgia as appertaining legally to the shah of Persia. Napoleon had engaged, he said, "to use all his efforts to have Russia evacuate it. . . . However, since the peace of Tilsit this obligation is only that of employing his good offices; it does not guarantee the evacuation."[31] News of another fragile eastern policy now came: General Decaen, who commanded a handful of French troops on Mauritius Island, had, after a year, signed a commercial treaty with the Imam of Muscat. The foreign ministry, however, decided not to put the arrangement into effect for the time being, nor to give any publicity to it.[32]

Champagny had an unimportant question to ask Ange Gardane and La Blanche upon their return from Persia. He remembered Mirza Riza's hotel bill, left unpaid in Warsaw in May, 1807. With resident Ambassador Asker Khan and his staff at last actually approaching Paris, the problem would be likely to come up again. Who should defray their living expenses? Champagny inquired into Persia's reciprocity, writing Ange Gardane at Marseille for positive information. Did the shah pay all the French expenses, and from the time the legation touched Persian frontiers? Were all members of the French staff given free lodging, food, and supplies? It would seem from the reply that the Persians had been good hosts. Ange said that they had assigned without cost a hundred horses, lodging, food, and necessary supplies. After the establishment of the group in Teheran, they made special provision for Gardane and Joseph Rousseau and authorized daily pay and traveling expense for the military officers. Other hospitable contributions and a guard of honor were provided.[33] For Asker Khan the foreign ministry at Paris proceeded to rent a house in suburban Corbeil.

Whereas French agents in the Near and Middle East still interpreted France as wishing to support Turkey and Persia, Napoleon and his colleagues in Paris seemed little interested. En route to Paris, Sebastiani visited Ambassador Andreossy in Vienna, where Russian Prince Kurakrin asked him embarrassing questions concerning Turkey. The ambassador to Turkey returned on June 12, physically weak from recurrent illness. To Mouhib Effendi he spoke as he had to official Turks along the way, in a manner to inspire full confidence in Napoleon's intentions toward them. He spoke thus at their army headquarters on the Danube, and he also took care to visit Russia's General Prosorovski in Jassy. La Blanche, to his surprise, found little Parisian interest in fresh information of Persia and almost no concern about the developments in Teheran.

Champagny wrote him to visit his family, because the campaign in Spain fully occupied Napoleon. Meantime, in Persia, the shah's summer camp near Teheran provided the setting for new exchanges of courtesies with Gardane and for dispatching to Paris several new letters from the French minister and the Persian leaders (June 30).[34]

A further indication of policy was Napoleon's insistence on supporting not all of the Ottoman Empire but rather the segments of especial concern to him. An example was Albania, interrelated with French Dalmatia and the Ionian Islands.[35] Temporary headquarters at Bayonne issued more—and increasingly bitter—complaints against Albania in mid-June. They charged that Ali Pasha conspired with the English and that he intended to participate in an expedition against the Ionians. He had refused to help the French provision Corfu. Napoleon insisted that Ali Pasha obey the sultan's order to facilitate the sending of provisions to the adjacent ports for embarkation. If Sultan Mustapha could not force Ali Pasha to obey the ordinary law, Napoleon advised, he should declare Ali Pasha a rebel and proceed against him accordingly. Consul David reported himself as insulted rather than given satisfaction for the outrage against four of Napoleon's officers at Antivari. In August, he angrily left his official residence.[36]

Two months after Sebastiani's departure, Latour-Maubourg compared the words of the Turkish government with its deeds. By words, its relations with France seemed satisfactory. The assassins of the four French officers would be punished severely. In answer to a news report that a representative of the East India Company prepared to travel to Bagdad, it was said that any Englishmen discovered there would be chased away. As to deeds, Latour-Maubourg admitted that the expulsion of anti-French Halet Effendi from the ministry had discouraged, though not destroyed, the several Turkish parties opposing France. But Prince Moruzzi bribed freely and spread tales that Napoleon only retarded the coming of peace. He said the French gave Turkey only promises, rather than a settlement with Russia, and that Austria's diplomatic envoy supported the "insinuations." Moruzzi asked what Napoleon would reply to a possible Albanian refusal to permit passage of the requested 4,000 or so French troops? It was whispered that Sebastiani had made the request only in order to terrify the Turks.

By late June, Latour-Maubourg noted special coldness in communications to him after a courier came from Ambassador Mouhib. Thereafter, it was difficult to discuss either Bagdad or Albania with the Turks, and they neglected the envoy's other current business. They inquired into the French occupation of Ragusa, theretofore ignored. Latour-Maubourg demanded punishment for the assassins of Fourçade and reparation for several insults to Frenchmen in other sea ports. In all these matters, whereas they promised prompt relief, they postponed action.[37]

Caulaincourt did not see the tsar for several days during May, a period of mourning for a grand duchess. On May 29 Alexander inquired whether Napoleon had made any overtures to the Austrians respecting the Turkish question. The inquiry had not been raised earlier, and now Caulaincourt was not free to answer, even if he had known. We may surmise from accounts we have seen by Tolstoi of Talleyrand's "political dream," that the Russians may have suspected the affirmative. The French ambassador reported no secret conversations respecting Turkey during the first three weeks of June. The tsar evinced a lively interest in all the news from Spain.

The allies had shown fear of each other at the Dardanelles. French policy for the Dardanelles could be stated quite definitely: Russia must not be installed there. Caulaincourt gave the Russians only one clear reply to their proposals of March. The verbiage aside, he simply stated that the bases of their proposals could not be accepted. He revealed no disposition to discuss details. Such may have been Napoleon's terse direction to him from Bayonne, together with the noncommittal point that such weighty matters must be decided by the emperors themselves.

A simple denial of the bases of Russia's proposals without other comment left much to be desired, adequate as it is for us today because it meant denying Russian ownership of the Dardanelles. The discussion, which was a sequel to the foregoing, came between Caulaincourt and the tsar on June 24; it was almost the final chapter of the long debate. The French ambassador assured Alexander that Napoleon continued to desire a personal conference. He wished that it be held without advance stipulations, "because M. Rumiantsov's project presented some difficulties which could be resolved only by the sovereigns themselves." Alexander confirmed his agreement for a personal meeting with Napoleon and postponed the date for it until late August.

It is more important that the tsar asked, "But what are the difficulties?" Caulaincourt replied that Alexander himself had foreseen one; Rumiantsov and he, the others. "Constantinople is a point so important that its possession, together with the entrance of the Dardanelles, would make you doubly masters of all the commerce with the Levant, even with India. Without discussing any details, the bases of M. Rumiantsov's project cannot be accepted."

"Constantinople, upon replacement of the Turks," the tsar contended, "will be only a provincial city at the extremity of the Russian Empire. Geography wills that I have it, because if it goes to another I would be no longer master of my house. And yet it would be without inconvenience to others that I hold the key to the door of my house."

Caulaincourt rejoined, "It is also the key to Toulon, to Corfu, to world commerce."

Alexander stated, "Such an arrangement could be devised as to make impossible any closing of that route to commerce."

Caulaincourt repeated the difficult and evasive consideration he had put to Rumiantsov early in March:

If your Majesty ruled always, this guarantee would possess great value. Yet prudent foresight decrees, in an affair that determines the destinies of the world, that Emperor Napoleon take all the safeguards possible for his empire. Will the successor to your Majesty be the friend and ally of France? Can you guarantee that? Rumiantsov outlines Russia's share as something which would be certain and permanent. Although Napoleon wishes to aid you, he nonetheless can not sacrifice to you, in an arrangement of this importance, the interests and safety of France. To conciliate each other is not always to be found by means of appropriation.

Alexander thus justified himself:

I do not ask more than I think proper. But when you have the greatest share, and when all the results of this great event will be to your advantage, it is indispensable that I possess what geography assigns me. . . . Emperor Napoleon can not want the Dardanelles. Does he wish to give them to someone less inconvenient than if I had them?

Caulaincourt ignored this implied reference to Austria, which, as we know, was actually covered in his secret instructions. Three months earlier, he had reported this phase as never having been used. He now merely declared, by way of rebuttal, "If you possess them, you will be at the doors of Corfu, of Toulon."

"Much less than you are at the doors of Portsmouth, and than England is at the doors of Brest and Cherbourg," Alexander countered.

Caulaincourt concluded:

Thus we are rivals, even in peace. Perhaps we will not always be friends, certainly not allies. Permit me to reply that your comparison provides a reason opposing the project: your wish that we remain friends. For that, the advantages must be reciprocal. If we follow Rumiantsov's views the real power in the Levant will be Russia, whose acquisitions will be bound up with its vast empire. No longer would a balance of power exist that could preserve peace. France, in contrast, if it acquired territories far removed, at the Dardanelles, even at Constantinople, would not be redoubtable to anyone, because this would be distant property, the hope of a colony. In the hands of Russia it becomes a formidable establishment. All these reasons demonstrate to you that only a meeting can harmonize such interests. These are weighty transactions, in which the sovereigns alone can reach an accord.

Alexander terminated his comment on that occasion by summarizing Russia's position, for then and for later. "I agree with you," he said, "but I do not want to place my country in worse position than it is found as a neighbor of the Turks. With France at the Dardanelles, we would lose more than we gain."[38]

The next day, Caulaincourt learned from Rumiantsov that Russia had acquiesced in Napoleon's plan to keep the matter open. The foreign minister "seemed to adjourn all idea of an arrangement and even of discussion of Turkish affairs until the personal meeting." Caulaincourt tells us further that he himself "did not let pass any opportunity to convey to Russia's minister that the bases he proposed in the memorandum of March could not conciliate the two parties, that anything satisfying only Russia's interests could not be accepted."[39] The agreement to meet at Erfurt without advance conditions meant exactly that.

The significant debates at St. Petersburg over the Straits were definitely adjourned and thrown back to Napoleon and to the joint conference. Thus Tsar Alexander, after the weeks of patient waiting for the reactions, had to content himself with the prospect of discussing the Turkish question later. He knew definitely that Napoleon would not concede the Dardanelles to Russia. In turn, he could deny France his armies for India and Egypt and the vessels of war intended also for mentioned and unmentioned potential adventures.

The intervening wait could serve as a period for cooling off. By the time the conference actually assembled at Erfurt late in September— France meanwhile saying nothing more—the Russians would be likely to conclude (as they did) that Napoleon's negative reply transmitted by Caulaincourt meant what it said.

By way of summary we shall note that Napoleon withheld from Russia a positive answer to all the suggested schemes for Ottoman partition except to state that Russia's acquisition of both Straits could not be accepted. If Russia took the Bosporus, France must have the Dardanelles or at least its Asiatic half. Yet the acquisition of both sides of this vital aquatic gateway was the basic Russian requirement.

XV

Post-mortem at Erfurt

THE PROSPECT of the easy territorial extension of Russia into adjacent areas was as tempting to Tsar Alexander I as later to Marshal Stalin. Adolf Hitler's bribery of the Soviet Union in August, 1939, by support for the latter's acquistion of territories, was thus by no means unique in principle. It may be compared with the Franco-Russian arrangement at Erfurt in 1808, when Napoleon conceded Russia's expansion into Finland, Bessarabia, Moldavia, and Wallachia, in exchange for Alexander's coöperation. Lands so situated as to be zones of friction between Russia and its European neighbors could be used for the purpose. Hitler conceded to Stalin a portion of Finland and three other Baltic states, much of Poland, and the selfsame Bessarabia.

Spirited but indecisive debating between Napoleonic France and tsarist Russia over various plans for a contingent partition of the Ottoman Empire reflected the important map-changing potentials of the Franco-Russian alliance. In the debates from March to June, 1808, Tsar Alexander at first apparently accepted with enthusiasm Napoleon's plan for a joint move against India. He required, however, that Russia be given Constantinople, the Bosporus, and the Dardanelles. The tsar also wished to possess Moldavia, Wallachia, and Bulgaria. Ambassador Caulaincourt secretly revealed to the Russians Napoleon's wish to sever Silesia from Prussia and the Dardanelles from Turkey, together with Albania, Bosnia, and Greece. He did not deny a French interest in Egypt, Syria, and Smyrna, all proffered by Russia if France conceded Constantinople and the Dardanelles. Both allies agreed that Austria might be given some territory between their two regionally dominant empires—perhaps considerable portions of Serbia and Rumelia down to Salonika—in order to stand between them all the way to the Aegean Sea and thus to meet Napoleon's formula for holding France and Russia to their policy of friendship.

An agreement probably could have been reached respecting Egypt and the zones to be partitioned in the Balkans and western Asia. No agreement respecting the Straits seemed likely, however, so long as France and Russia both wanted the Dardanelles. They talked of a personal meeting intended to harmonize their views, although the tsar apparently would accept nothing less than his own control of both of the Straits. He refused to partition the Straits as between Russia and France, or even to partition between themselves the respective European and Asiatic banks of the Dardanelles alone. The tsar's alternative was to call off a general partition and thus leave both Straits to weak Turkey. In that case he would withdraw his promise of a joint expedition to India, Asia Minor, or Egypt. Neither side openly admitted the magnitude of the gulf between the conflicting points of view. If Caulaincourt could not agree with Rumiantsov and Tsar Alexander, perhaps Napoleon himself could do so. They said that, neither side taking it seriously. The two rulers had agreed to meet in personal conference at Erfurt in Thuringia and there to reach a decision. Caulaincourt won Alexander's consent to come to the meeting without any advance understandings, however, and the limited result will be seen in this chapter.

Napoleon's policy could not be pro-Turkish; for then the alliance with Russia would have to go. He counted Russia's friendship as far more valuable than Turkey's. He adopted no program in 1808 that could be construed in St. Petersburg as conspiring to give assistance to Turkey as against Russia. To convince himself of Napoleon's loyalty, the tsar had only to glance at the nature of Napoleon's hesitant policy at Constantinople and his weak diplomatic representation there. Latour-Maubourg, the competent French chargé d'affaires, won no great personal influence with the Turkish ministers. It is more important that Champagny never once in three years sent him any significant instructions. Nor was Pierre Ruffin given any important assignments, although he had become France's traditional watchdog of policy at the Straits. There was little French policy for application within Turkey. One glimpses the weakness of policy, or the lack of it, in all the dispatches to and from Constantinople. There could be no close Napoleonic relations with Turkey so long as the Franco-Russian alliance of Tilsit existed. The Turks, for a long time not appreciating this, hoped that that alliance might bring Russia and Turkey to peace and the retrocession to them of Russian-occupied Moldavia and Wallachia.

Having no official policy of complete coöperation with Turkey, Napoleon by mid-1808 really had no such policy left with allied Russia in respect to Turkey. His policy could not be fully pro-Russian, for then the Dardanelles must be yielded. When discussing arrangements for the conference at Erfurt, Alexander asked Caulaincourt on July 10, "Did the emperor write to you of his views on the partition of Turkey?"

The ambassador replied in the negative, but iterated the unacceptability of the project of giving Russia both Straits (chap. xiv).

"It is that *langue de chat*, without doubt," Alexander said resignedly, using again the nickname by which they referred to the Dardanelles.

"And Constantinople, eh, sir?" asked Caulaincourt, for *la langue de chat* referred exclusively to the Dardanelles.

"Have you informed Emperor Napoleon that Rumiantsov called this *la langue de chat?*" asked the tsar.

"Yes, sir," came the reply. "I have not withheld anything from the emperor. It is the best way to serve you both."

Alexander concurred. He stated that he would likewise speak frankly with Napoleon at Erfurt. He did not doubt the influence of that scheduled conference "on the affairs and tranquillity of the world."

Caulaincourt changed the subject, hinting at possible English evasions of the Continental Blockade in Russia—a factor to become more of a reality in the following years.[1]

One divines, rather than reads in the documents, Napoleon's hesitant groping behind the scenes for a Turkish policy. He liked to distinguish a Turkish government from Turkey as a state. Of the former he might occasionally disapprove. But, apart from sometimes ignoring a given Ottoman cabinet, Napoleon wished to preserve most of the Ottoman Empire, at least until England should agree to another general peace. In their feuding among themselves the Turks endangered their chances of holding his approbation.

In preparation for the conference of Erfurt, Napoleon requested the opinions of General Sebastiani. The latter's analysis of July 12, 1808, characterized Sultan Mustapha IV—enthroned by revolution—as having none of the wisdom and all of the faults of his predecessor, Selim III. If a popular movement should reverse Mustapha and enthrone his brother, Prince Mahmud, the country would still be governed by a weak prince.

Sebastiani wrote prophetically, for within less than three weeks such a reversal came as the result of a second revolution in as many years at Constantinople. Turkey boasted many troops in the aggregate, although Balkan troops generally disliked to fight outside their own provinces.

During the campaign on the Danube, of some 40,000 Ottoman troops available, 15,000 remained in Constantinople and 10,000 in Adrianople. The sultan had ordered a special corps of 7,000 troops to defend the castles of the Dardanelles and the Bosporus. The centrally controlled army which opposed Russia at the Danube numbered only 15,000, mostly of troops recruited in Asia. The existing local armies added considerably to the fighting power, notably the 25,000 troops commanded by the strong Mustapha Bairakdar of Ruschuk, and some 8,000 under the ineffective pasha of Vidin, the successor to deceased Passvan Oglu. Sebastiani considered the provincial troops as infinitely better than those in the central army under the grand vizir. On the sea, the sultan commanded twenty-two seaworthy ships of the line and other vessels of proportionate power, all well fitted out from the large resources of the arsenal at Constantinople. Good crews were lacking, for the Turks were not seafarers by nature.

The reason for revolution in 1807 had been the age-old conflict between the native-born Mohammedans and the recruited Mohammedans over wielding the temporal power. The new sultan at least twice had attempted to eliminate the influential mufti of Constantinople, who had sanctioned his enthronement, only to find his imperial position endangered. There were the janissaries, whose actions no one could predict. The sultan and the mufti controlled only the center of the empire, according to Sebastiani; outside, the provincial governors ruled. An ancient dynasty, the ancient customs, and the common religion bound the empire together; a serious religious schism would rend it. A great many Turks still believed that the maintenance of their empire depended on Napoleon's good will, this being their sole reason for the cold war against England. Of the princely Greek families, those of Suzzo and Callimachi were sincerely devoted to France, but their weight was over-balanced by the rich and powerful anti-French Moruzzi family and their associates.

Due to geographical location and to theocratic system, said Sebastiani, Turkey feared and hated Russia. Nevertheless, only with French support had it had the courage to declare war in rejoinder to Russia's occupation of the Principalities. The Turks were also afraid of Austrian expansion in the Balkans. They could readily believe, on the other hand, that all of Europe was dominated by the powerful Napoleon. The ex-ambassador estimated that the Russian army encamped on the Danube could come to Constantinople within eighteen days. The batteries on the Bosporus would be powerless to resist an attack by land—a situation parallel to that of Singapore in 1941. Once in Constantinople, the Russians would have the support of the Greek Orthodox Christians, their religious cousins.

A French naval exploit in the Dardanelles was considered advisable by General Sebastiani. Of two routes of attack open to the French army in Dalmatia—should a push to Constantinople be ordered—he said that the one through Bosnia required seventy-five days of marching and the one by way of Albania was virtually unknown. The more convenient approach, except for English interference, would be to attack Turkey from the sea, forcing the Dardanelles and debarking an army to occupy Constantinople. He warned, however, of real danger in an attempt to force the Dardanelles. The Aegean islands, except for Crete, could be occupied with little difficulty. An invasion of southern Greece by land would be a simple operation, the French bases in the Ionian Islands facilitating it. Official Ottoman thinking might be estimated as running like this: if France decided to defend Turkey against the Russians it would be difficult to win approval for the admission of a French army. Only in desperation would the Ottoman pashas invite it.[2]

Persian politics assumed a slight new interest for Paris in mid-July, 1808. Champagny learned of the approach to Paris of Asker Khan, Persia's resident ambassador, and received Gardane's hint that the shah expected Napoleon to obtain the evacuation of Georgia. Feth Ali wished to avoid direct negotiation with Russia and leave the terms of peace to Napoleon. He assumed his good ally would certainly save Georgia for him, whereas if he himself arranged with the tsar's field commander, the outcome might be as unsatisfactory for him as the military struggle had been up to that time. General Gudovich's forces revealed no intention of departing from Georgia. The French foreign ministry's analysis of the Persian situation, based on reports dating back to April, concluded that the Persians had turned the negotiation over to Napoleon as their best way to escape the loss of Georgia. Accordingly, Napoleon might properly ignore any private instructions respecting Georgia which Asker Khan might bring, his primary concern being his alliance with Russia.

Champagny expressed regret to Gardane that the Persian negotiation with Russia must be moved to Paris. Asker Khan arrived inopportunely, shortly before the meeting at Erfurt. He came to Paris on July 22— the date placed in the official records by his official guide-host, P.

Amédée Jaubert. Now an "auditor to the Council of State," Jaubert met the ambassador at Napoleon's frontier. He details the trip from Strasbourg to Paris: Asker Khan arrived at Lunéville on July 16, on a Saturday, came to Château-Thierry on Tuesday, and entered Paris on Wednesday. En route the host displayed Napoleonic power to best advantage, calling attention to the order that prevailed everywhere in France and to the regularity of the postal service and the other physical evidences of an efficient government. The Persian envoy remarked several times: "It is easy to see I finally have arrived in a country submitting to the laws of your emperor."[3]

Asker Khan requested an interview with Napoleon, but had to await the emperor's return from the south. Meanwhile Napoleon's aides accorded him special attention, well remembering the emperor's penchant for overdoing courtesies to official Persians. The foreign ministry, with the definite knowledge of the hospitable, cost-free treatment accorded Ambassador Gardane, determined to entertain the Persian with like munificence. The ambassador and his staff installed themselves in the dwelling in Corbeil. The renting of the house led to amusing difficulties. It had been rented by a relative of the absent owner. When the owner returned, he complained to the magistrates of Corbeil against letting his house for an indefinite term and against the requirement that his furniture be moved out. They had given him no guarantee, moreover, that the house would be left in good order, with its windows and doors intact. He did not wish to move his furniture, the renter's tenure being indefinite, but wished to store it in two unused rooms of the house. Persian habits of life annoyed him, and he was sufficiently annoyed to have his complaints filed with the foreign ministry (where they were forgotten).[4]

Meanwhile, Feth Ali in Teheran was telling Frenchmen that Napoleon was free to accomplish the impossible, the occupation of the two ceded islands in the Persian Gulf which had been blockaded by a British squadron. Ismail Bey—commander of the Persian coastal forces ordered to intercept the British—issued to Gardane from the Persian Gulf a friendly if sharp reminder of the lack of concrete results from Napoleon's mediation. He had heard nothing to reassure him; he hoped Gardane's efforts would match his words. Ismail's letter suggests that Gardane was justified in suspecting that the English had begun to have influence; it recounted Sir John Malcolm's arguments against a Persian liaison with France. He had said that a Persian war with Great Britain

would last ten years. England distrusted Russia, Persia's enemy, he continued, and was therefore Persia's friend. England, if an ally, could offer
Persia 30,000 men equipped for war. Ismail stated that he had refused,
his government not being on friendly terms with England and its agents.
He had replied that what England offered possessed no utility for Persia
and that Persia could not permit a British landing anywhere on its coasts.
"This response desolated the English," wrote Ismail.

Thus, while Persia did not as yet officially permit an English courier
to Teheran, a simple Persian officer was making himself accessible for
discussions. Here we can detect the beginning of the end of Gardane's
transitory one-man victory over a British naval squadron in the Persian
Gulf. Thereafter he rapidly lost his direction of Persian foreign policy
—the fault being too little action by Paris in Persia's behalf.[5] Most of
the discussions in Persia had concerned Napoleon's general policy rather
than any specific orders. Russia relieved the emperor from the embarrassment of once having admitted that Persia should possess Georgia
again. Rumiantsov directed General Gudovich on August 4, 1808, to
say that, much as Russia trusted Napoleon and no matter what the great
advantages Russia might acquire from his mediation, it nevertheless
would not request his mediation of its dispute with Persia. France was
too far removed geographically to understand fully Russo-Persian problems. If Persia desired peace, let it negotiate directly with the field
commander. Rumiantsov believed the shah sought only an armistice of
a year, in order to allow time for further military preparations. Gardane's
later explanation that this decision was taken to save General Gudovich's
amour-propre seems weak.[6]

Feth Ali faced a crisis by the end of August, 1808, when Gudovich
threatened to nullify the existing armistice and the British became more
insistent. Hence he wrote his French ally, emphasizing what a loyal
collaborator he had been. He announced that France might occupy
Karek and Bandar Abass and that the British had been excluded. Britain's
would-be ambassador had been turned away: Captain Malcolm had left
in a huff because the Persians would not listen to his propositions. The
shah's letter, together with Ismail's warning, suggested the possible
reversal of Persia's policy. Indeed, a few days earlier a minister of the
shah confidentially revealed to Gardane the minutes of a verbal communication in which Feth Ali hinted at changing his conduct toward
France, if his hopes should not be realized. Gardane suspected that the
English fleet had not actually sailed from the Persian Gulf. Gudovich

wrote Gardane and others that he had been given extensive discretion
to negotiate a treaty, the essential being the cession of Georgia. This
jarring conclusion could not be accepted, in the absence of information
as to Napoleon's possible action in Persia's behalf. Accordingly, they
reached not a Russo-Persian peace but an armistice, in mid-September
1808. Gardane himself was willing to mediate a definitive treaty, his
difficulty being Gudovich's insistence upon retaining Georgia. Gudovich
used the tsar's alliance with Napoleon as a threat: Russia's main army
now being free, it could be employed against Persia if necessary.[7]

Western Europe would not learn of all this for many months. Napoleon's new instructions eventually arrived in Teheran; these directed
Gardane to work for an understanding between Persia and Russia, but
they offered nothing resembling a pro-Persian policy. It did not surprise
the minister to learn, in mid-October, that Tsar Alexander had declined
Napoleon's mediation. That Gudovich should threaten to renew the war
if the Persians did not negotiate peace did surprise him. Accordingly he
sent Felix Lajard, the dependable secretary of his legation, to Gudovich.
En route, Lajard sought to placate the official Persians by using Gardane's formula, which was designed to soothe both sides. France might
thereby win credit for maintaining the armistice. He cleverly stated that
Napoleon, the shah's ally, "had guaranteed the existing territories of
Persia."[8] The statement would seem to the Persians to demonstrate a
strong stand to prevent a renewal of fighting. To the Russians, on the
other hand, it would indicate no real support for Persia's recovery of
Georgia because it was actually occupied by Russia. Hence Russia might
retain Georgia simply by not reopening hostilities. Gardane penned dispatches to Paris regularly, although he could rarely send them promptly.
He let them accumulate while he waited for a courier and for changing
general conditions. He always complained of being absolutely deprived
of political news. Letters to him received late in October from the
foreign ministry were dated the preceding May 24.

Paris meanwhile focused its attention on Napoleon's military campaigns and governmental changes in Spain. The activity there still
covered up the emperor's failure to discuss with Russia any details for
a partition of Turkey. The tsar maintained his friendly attitude with
Caulaincourt. On July 24, he said he had prepared his declaration of war
against England and would continue to be as true to the alliance of Tilsit
as he had demonstrated already he was, by breaking off relations with
Britain. He directed attention to Turkey anew by the remark that Aus-

tria's envoy at Constantinople seemed to be working against France and Russia. The Austrians reportedly intrigued in Serbia and opposed the Turks in Bosnia and Albania. Accounts also indicated that an agreement between Turkey and England was quite remote because Turkey feared to displease Napoleon.

Caulaincourt reminded Alexander that the tsar himself had been the first to foresee the difficulties presented by the possession of Constantinople and *la langue de chat* (the Dardanelles). He added, "Napoleon wishes only to cement the Franco-Russian alliance in such a manner that nothing will break it."[9]

Napoleon and Champagny were still at Bayonne when the second palace revolution began in Turkey. The preliminary revolt came at Constantinople on July 28, 1808. On that day the rebels strangled the reforming ex-Sultan Selim who had been in prison, they deposed Sultan Mustapha, and they enthroned his brother, Mahmud II (1808–1839), another of Selim's cousins. The principal leader against Sultan Mustapha IV was another Mustapha, nicknamed Bairakdar, which means "the bearer of the holy flag." He was the powerful and respected pasha of Ruschuk and an admirer of deposed Selim III. He wished to restore legality to the rule and to the succession. His followers found the hidden young Prince Mahmud, the only remaining legitimate claimant, and they deposed and imprisoned Sultan Mustapha. The latter was forced to occupy the prison apartments until so recently used by the far more renowned and able Selim. They quickly completed the ceremonies of deposition and installation, all moves being upheld by a friendly new mufti. Amid confusion much like that of 1807, they proclaimed Mahmud to be sultan. It is understandable that Sultan Mahmud II should reward such devotion to legality; Bairakdar became his first grand vizir. Although the latter had arrived too late to save Selim, as Mahmud's grand vizir he considered that he might save the former Sultan's policies.

The second revolutionary reign began like the first, with utter disorganization in government, finance, and in the armed forces. Latour-Maubourg could only watch the developments. Mahmud's retention of Galib Effendi as foreign minister was considered a pro-French gesture. After several days, the French chargé d'affaires found an opportunity for a few words with Galib, who assured him the change did not mean a change of foreign policy. Turkey would not negotiate with the Russians and English without French approval. Some months later, the inevitable consequent revolt brought the murder of the imprisoned

Mustapha. Only shortly before that event in mid-November did Mahmud write Napoleon of his accession.[10]

That a dearth of business marked the French palace at Constantinople for several weeks after the change of sultans was not due to a lack of problems but to the general situation.[11] The Russo-Turkish armistice continued to be effective, primarily owing to Russia's disposition not to disturb Turkish affairs in advance of the conference between the two emperors. Apathy and the turmoil of the revolution prevented the Turks from renewing the fighting and many still hoped that Napoleon would take care of their interests. For a moment at the end of July the French emperor concerned himself with the conduct of Ali Pasha of Albania. Champagny phrased the complaints as questions for Constantinople. What did the pasha really want? Did he seek the Ionian Islands for himself? Did he expect the English to give him enough troops and ships? Did he wish to make Albania independent?[12]

As Talleyrand remarked in August, 1808, a whole year of Franco-Russian negotiations had left the allies about where they were at Tilsit. The scheduled conference at Erfurt might offer an opportunity to negotiate in detail. As a preliminary, doubtless for added bargaining power, the tsar stiffened his policy respecting Silesia by returning to his original point of view. According to this view the evacuation of Silesia by France had never been contingent upon his own evacuation of the Principalities. However, he admitted to Caulaincourt: "We must come to terms and act in concert to obtain mutual advantages." He said he considered his pledged word fully as sacred as treaties. This probably accounts for his accepting at Erfurt Napoleon's innocuous draft of a treaty.[13]

The second Turkish revolution suggested to Alexander that Napoleon might interpret it as he had the first one, as presenting an opportunity to consummate the partition of Turkey. Late in August, Alexander forwarded to France the news of the revolution that had ended the life of ex-Sultan Selim, jailed Sultan Mustapha, and begun the rule by Sultan Mahmud, whom he termed "a phantom of a sovereign." To the tsar, all this portrayed Turkey "as weak in body and in spirit, the circumstances adding new facilities for the execution of the great plan." He believed that the revolution had severed Napoleon's last bonds with Turkey.[14] Alexander justified his position respecting Georgia and stated that the Treaty of Tilsit had superseded the Franco-Persian alliance.

Reports persisted that Turkey seemed to wish an understanding with England. Latour-Maubourg's dispatches of late August—deciphered on

September 30—were the latest official news on hand at Erfurt of the events in Turkey. He sent word that the new government planned to reunite the Ottoman empire by reducing all its rebels to submission—some by menace, others by reward. Ali Pasha especially would be forced to obey. The new ministers had solemnly informed Latour-Maubourg that they intended to force that governor to break off all his dealings with the English and to be friendly with the French. Napoleon's envoy indirectly learned later that such directions were issued. In consequence, he had refrained from following Champagny's instruction of June 14 to ask Turkey to declare Ali Pasha a rebel. Latour-Maubourg well understood that the Turks would not hasten to heed such a request owing to the greater Russian danger. Moreover, they recalled how Bonaparte in 1798 had solicited them to declare the beys of Egypt rebels, only to learn that he really intended thereby to render easier his own invasion of Egypt. They could recall that Napoleon Bonaparte had said he entered that Ottoman province to accord assistance—which had not been requested—to force the local rulers of Egypt to submit to the sultan's authority.

A petition to Tsar Alexander by a number of Wallachians and Moldavians asked deliverance from the Turkish yoke. Political expediency dictated a strong stand by the sultan for the Principalities, moreover, to win support for the new Ottoman government. Pro-English Turks played up the latest news from Spain and Malta, to the disadvantage of confidence in France. Latour-Maubourg most disliked the story that foretold the formation of a new coalition to defeat the French empire. The Austrian internuncio, who practically never called on the Ottoman foreign minister, owing to cool official relations, now reportedly asked Turkey to join such a league. Grand Vizir Mustapha Bairakdar wished to assemble 200,000 troops to regain the Principalities, so reports had it. Some also hinted at a secretly planned expedition against the Crimea. A year earlier, such potential activities would have pleased a Napoleonic agent; now, Latour-Maubourg relayed the gossip without interest. He could do little toward enforcing Napoleon's Continental Blockade. Once a number of Ionian and Ragusan commercial ships subject to Napoleon sailed into the Black Sea. He declined to authorize their departure until Champagny so directed, owing to the danger of their capture by the British off the Dardanelles. He likewise feared that they might join the British and become carriers of commerce. Champagny drafted a request to the navy that such ships be accorded naval protection, but he thought

better of sending it.[15] Among the continuous court intrigues, one reported scheme was to reverse Ottoman foreign policy by having the
Russians connive with the grand vizir to set up still another sultan. The
new sultan in turn would surrender the Principalities and sign a defensive and offensive military alliance with Russia.

France feared an old project, the opening of a port to the English
opposite Otranto, at the entrance to the Adriatic. Latour-Maubourg announced bluntly that France would consider any hostility by Albania as
hostility by Turkey. Ruffin discussed with the new government the current French demands. By these, Turkey should discover and punish the
assassins of Fourçade, guarantee against all vexations the religious persons
of the Holy Land, and give satisfaction for the four assassinations at
Antivari. He expressed Napoleon's surprise at Turkey's negligence. The
foreign minister immediately transmitted in writing his concurrence in
all this. Consul David, who upon his own responsibility had quit his
official residence at Travnik, was reprimanded for this by Champagny
on September 13.[16]

At the eve of the conference at Erfurt, Russia's conquest of Finland
was still going on. Tsar Alexander closely followed the events there,
while Emperor Napoleon, in spirit at least, was in the midst of his
campaign in Spain. The meetings at Erfurt hardly caused a lull in the
latter's stream of steady orders dealing with Spain and the other myriad
affairs of state. There was still speculation upon whether Emperor Napoleon intended to attack Austria, once he settled matters in Spain.[17]
Official circles in St. Petersburg were discussing the reported disorders
in Turkey, Austrian armaments, the Anglo-French war and its block-
ades, and the probable duration of the Franco-Russian alliance. Caulaincourt conveyed to the tsar "the happy news of the arrival of the King
of Spain in Madrid." We do not discover in the documents any hint
of his conveying the later news of Joseph Bonaparte's hasty departure
from the Spanish capital.[18]

In advance of the conference, it had become quite clear to Napoleon
that timid Champagny could not really handle the delicate negotiations
over Turkey. Everyone seems to have taken his incompetence for granted.
Nor could even Napoleon himself attend to Turkish matters, without
considerable planning in the midst of rapidly changing conditions. The
French finally planned to do almost nothing at Erfurt—to leave matters
much as they were. On the other hand, something had to be devised to
deal with the unfinished negotiations begun by Caulaincourt. Who could

best assist Napoleon in the plans? Undersecretary Hauterive won permission to try his hand. In recommending the most advantageous French policy for Turkey, he borrowed and enlarged upon the old idea of setting up a dependable Christian ally in the Balkans. Hauterive suggested dividing European Turkey into six areas, three Mohammedan and three Christian, all under the imperial overlordship of Constantinople and all enjoying the guarantee of France. The Moslem states would be Albania, Rumelia, and Bosnia, and the Christian would be comprised of Greece, Serbia, and the Ionian Islands.[19]

Napoleon called in Talleyrand as the principal assistant. To the latter he turned over all of Caulaincourt's secret dispatches. The ex-foreign minister "found them everything that could be desired," and Napoleon privately revealed himself as believing he had outmaneuvered Alexander in the debate of March (chap. xiii). He set Talleyrand to drafting a convention to be proposed. "I do not desire," he directed, "to be engaged in too precise a manner with Russia concerning affairs in the east."

Talleyrand's draft of a treaty was taken to Erfurt. In it the Principalities were given to Russia but the Straits were withheld. According to the original draft, France and Russia must preserve the Ottoman Empire, except for Moldavia and Wallachia. Talleyrand assigned these provinces to Russia outright, whereupon Napoleon added a corrective, pledging Russia for the time being only to occupy but not to own them. The ruler added a stipulation, moreover, whereby France would agree to support Russia against Austria, if that state should ever align itself with Turkey. It may be noted that Austria had evinced no likelihood of joining Turkey.

Not Champagny, but the redoubtable Talleyrand went to Erfurt with Napoleon. The emperor directed the ex-minister in his discussions to emphasize the youth of both rulers, there being no need to rush through the final arrangements for Europe. "You will insist upon that," Napoleon cautioned, "for Rumiantsov is sanguine about the Near Eastern question." It could also be argued that any settlement would have to be approved by public opinion in France. Freeing the Greeks would be a popular philanthropic gesture and suggest a change of emphasis from partition to liberation. Talleyrand also must suggest to Foreign Minister Rumiantsov that the emperor would soon be seeking a divorce from Empress Josephine, that his destiny demanded a dynasty, and that a sister of the tsar was of an age that suited him. "Tell him also," he said, "that once my affairs in Spain are settled, I will enter into all his views

for the partition of Turkey." Talleyrand demurred, believing such matters should be mentioned to the tsar only by Napoleon himself.[20] Such
devious planning doomed in advance all Russian hopes that the stalemate
respecting the basic issue of the Dardanelles could be broken. Nonetheless Chargé d'Affaires Rayneval, who wrote routine reports from St.
Petersburg during Ambassador Caulaincourt's absence at Erfurt, on
October 21 expressed the general belief in the Russian capital that one
of the primary results of the meeting would be a definitive arrangement
of the affairs of Turkey.[21]

When Napoleon and Alexander met at Erfurt on September 27, uncertainty still marked the political situation at Constantinople. Was
Mustapha Bairakdar's government stable? The two emperors, together
with their advisers, came for what proved to be glittering conferences
that extended to mid-October. Napoleon's bringing Talleyrand should
have warned Foreign Minister Rumiantsov. Always the showman, the
French emperor also brought along the generals who had helped him
defeat Prussia in 1806. He so maneuvered the entertainment-filled days
as to delay serious business long enough to make Alexander sense the reflection of his great personal power and prestige.

At last, Napoleon personally slipped the drafted convention into the
tsar's hand; this had to be a secret shared only between themselves.
Afterwards they signed it, with little change and almost without comment.[22] Owing to their inability to agree in advance respecting the
Straits, the conversations at Erfurt proved far less cordial, paradoxically,
than those held when victor and vanquished had met immediately after
the fighting some fourteen months earlier. Although Napoleon expected
to save the benefits of his alliance with Russia, it seems clear from Talleyrand's memoirs that he was far from willing to agree to a general partition of the Ottoman Empire in order to do so. On the contrary, he held
to his original plan to uphold most of Turkey, through yielding only the
Principalities. These would be accorded—although not immediately—
and thus the tsar would not go home empty-handed.

The conference thus officially adjourned the never-concluded debate
respecting the Dardanelles. There was almost no rebuttal; there were no
spoken recriminations. No jury existed to decide the issue. That continuous and common world problem of the Straits would be debated
many times thereafter. It would be the principal issue of the Crimean
War, from 1853 to 1856. Hitler and Stalin would debate it in 1941,
along lines similar to those of 1808, and a similar stalemate would result.

In the Convention of Erfurt (signed October 12) France and Russia renewed the alliance of Tilsit but modified it to cover the actualities of the day. Alexander agreed to support the French policies in the Germanies, while Napoleon sanctioned Russia's appropriation of Finland from Sweden and, eventually, of Moldavia and Wallachia from Turkey. The agreement promised to require England to recognize Russia's possession of these and to recognize Joseph Bonaparte's rule in Spain. The Principalities must be sought first through friendly negotiation, Russia's pretext to be "the revolutions and changes that agitated the Ottoman Empire," which allowed no security for persons and property. Furthermore—the opposite of Tilsit's stipulation—if Turkey did not consent, the *casus belli* would arise for France only if Austrian or other unlikely support accrued to Turkey. Russia accepted two precautions to preserve France's prestige at Constantinople and to prevent Turkey from gravitating toward England: the understanding respecting the Principalities was kept secret and all the other possessions of the Ottoman Empire were guaranteed.[23]

Napoleon put aside all further scheming for a land expedition against India. His unwillingness to concede the Dardanelles as the required compensation seems to account for this, even more than his immediate problems in Spain and Austria. He had once thought that Russia might be his eastern policeman while he cleared Spain and Portugal of British troops. Yet he could not permit his ally to become established at the Dardanelles. The fate of Turkey was aided also by Alexander's unexpected difficulties in Finland. Thus definitely and formally ended all the discussion of a general partition of the Ottoman Empire. The two emperors said nothing more of a joint expedition to India, Asia Minor, Egypt, or Syria. Erfurt thus sharply reversed the policy of contingent partition adopted at Tilsit. Except for the Principalities, its results seemed to indicate Napoleon's return to sponsorship of the weakened Ottoman Empire.

A report of early October in St. Petersburg stated that the Turks had broken the armistice, making a surprise attack against Russian forces in the Danube Valley.[24] Doubtless the negotiators at Erfurt knew of this report, and it was probably another reason for their decision to sever the Principalities. A more important report concerned the new revolutionary disturbances at Constantinople. Napoleon and Alexander apparently could not bother with small affairs, however, except when, as here, they offered a pretext to do what they planned to do anyway.

Although Turkey's foreign policy was not clear, Latour-Maubourg recorded one estimate of it. When sending the complete details of ex-Sultan Selim's death and the accession of Sultan Mahmud (received at Erfurt on September 30), he conveyed the assurance given France of an unchanged Ottoman foreign policy. The new sultan promised he would follow Selim's footsteps, not Sultan Mustapha's. At Paris, Ambassador Mouhib took the opportunity to display again the same impatience that had characterized him for months; he did not like the alleged "negotiations" for peace with Russia. Only routine business marked the instructions to Latour-Maubourg which Napoleon dispatched from Erfurt (and Champagny sent from Paris) during the period. The task to be done at Constantinople was "to maintain the Ottoman government's policy of friendship toward France."[25]

Whatever Turkish confidence still remained in France as mediator of a Russo-Turkish peace faded during the further weeks of inaction. Latour-Maubourg called Napoleon's attention to the several reasons for Turkey's veering toward England. The Turks listed first Napoleon's failure to accomplish anything as mediator despite the *de facto* armistice. They contrasted their sultan's official support of France in the Continental Blockade. Their nervousness arose from the constant danger—even if at variance with French advice—of renewal of the fighting war with Russia. Latour-Maubourg could observe redoubled efforts by the Moruzzi family, "the declared enemies of France." They dispensed additional bribes to a court reeking with intrigue. They treated Frenchmen generally as people who had delivered portions of their territory over to Russia. English partisans questioned the basic vitality of Napoleon's empire. There was more than a whispering campaign; Anglophiles capitalized on the adverse developments in Spain, and they played up the uncertainty of the French policy for Turkey.

The effect of the conflicts of French and Ottoman policies on the Balkan rim may be discounted, for these were mere pinpricks, associated as they were primarily with individual governors and notably with the pro-British attitude of Ali Pasha of Albania. But the general situation was a grave matter, so Latour-Maubourg told Paris in his dispatch of October 10. He stated frankly, "The Turks are losing all confidence in French mediation. . . . They are beginning to believe they have been abandoned by Napoleon. . . . The Turkish people detest the Russians as their natural enemies." On the other hand, there remained the chance that Turkey would still wait a short time for possibly favorable reports from Paris of Mouhib's final efforts to see that the mediator acted. If Mouhib's efforts should prove unsuccessful, wrote Latour-Maubourg (who did not know of the newest change of French policy), the Turks undoubtedly would turn to England. That they had not done so was due solely to France's promise of mediation. Latour-Maubourg warned that an arrangement for the technical restoration of Anglo-Turkish peace would not terminate the efforts of the English and their partisans. They would proceed from there to an Anglo-Turkish alliance.

The original authority to mediate still represented an immediate French advantage, for no one at Constantinople yet knew how thoroughly that role had been bartered away in the Convention of Erfurt. In the longer view, moreover, the tradition of Franco-Turkish coöperation represented a basic French asset. Enemies could whisper against France, but Frenchmen on the scene could recall a long tradition of friendship, now supported by the brilliant showmanship of a Napoleon with a powerful empire and a strong eastern ally.[26]

French Vice-consul Mechain at the Dardanelles transmitted a revealing report on October 14. Governor Hakki of the castles of that strait at first sent no one of official character to visit the English vessels. The English made no move to land, although they got through a message to Constantinople despite the absence of official representation in Turkey. Ambassador Arbuthnot's interpreter, Pisani, had remained within easy call since early in 1807. Pisani, who had been out of sight and action since Duckworth's exploit, was now found by Mechain at the Dardanelles as a member of Raguil Pasha's suite. Mechain related that the correspondence of Governor Hakki became quite active with the English frigate from October 11 to 13, at which time an English negotiator was waiting. Several times Hakki sent officials to the ship. When, on October 12, he granted a ceremonious audience to the negotiator, Mechain protested strongly. Mechain frankly doubted the sincerity of the Ottoman government.[27]

Latour-Maubourg did not know what course to follow. He did know that the situation called for positive action. In view of the English diplomatic activity he ended his temporary voicelessness by taking the diplomatic offensive. Without instructions he demanded explanations of the reported negotiations at the Dardanelles. That a Napoleonic agent acting in the very center that had just been withheld from Russia lacked pertinent instructions was curious. Latour-Maubourg wrote: "Since the departure of General Sebastiani I have not had any sort of instruction respecting matters of this importance." He reported several anti-French utterances by Austria's internuncio. To make bad matters worse, he observed that many Turks definitely favored renewing the fighting against Russia. He characterized Grand Vizir Bairakdar as being "the real sovereign and of a tyrannical and brutal character." The latter headed those impatient Turks who were eager to cross the Danube, but who held back to learn of Mouhib's possible success in Paris.[28]

Ruffin was quite ill and could not be of any help during that month. However, Lieutenant Colonel Boutin, a traveling "strategic services" agent for Napoleon, who reported with the same courier, substantiated the opinions of Latour-Maubourg. This spy revealed the contrast between Turkey's official decree, which ordered its agents to enforce the Continental Blockade, and that nation's actual practice, which was to engage in considerable trade and shipping with the English. "The English are masters of the merchant navigation of the archipelago," he wrote.[29]

At the moment Paris was paying scant attention to Turkey. We find Champagny in a casual dispute with Mouhib arising from the French sequestration of an Algerian vessel at Marseille and of a Greek vessel sailing the Ottoman flag at Leghorn. The reports of Latour-Maubourg and Boutin did not disturb Napoleon's foreign minister. As soon as he received them (November 5), he interpreted them to Napoleon as containing nothing new. "Mustapha Bairakdar still governs the Turkish Empire with vigilance and severity," he stated, "by braving both the ulema and the janissaries." The Turkish people did not wish peace with Russia, and they were losing confidence in France, as they became increasingly aware of their virtual abandonment. Before renewing the fighting in the Principalities, they only awaited the courier from Paris, who set out the day Napoleon departed for Erfurt. Boutin estimated that some 40,000 Turkish troops were on the Danube and that plans called for doubling the number; the Russians had 30,000 there and considerable reserves beyond the Dniester. He believed the Turks would not succumb suddenly but would fight on in desperation.[30]

Tsar Alexander returned to St. Petersburg on October 29. As one result of Erfurt, he recalled Count Tolstoi from Paris. Private reports at St. Petersburg late in November—based on news received from Constantinople by way of Vienna down to October 25—correctly hinted that Ambassador Robert Adair had been received, although not as yet in Constantinople. Caulaincourt did not transmit any Russian reactions because subsequent reports explained that Adair had been rebuffed, the Turks meanwhile saying they could not receive him because of their friendly relations with France. They planned to send a confidential messenger to the Dardanelles, however, to learn what proposals he wished to offer.[31]

Latour-Maubourg's request to be informed of the status of Ottoman negotiations with England provided Foreign Minister Galib Effendi with an opportunity for a forthright written statement of Ottoman policy; this statement was intended as a warning to France that negotiations with England were about to begin. He said that everyone knew that England broke off relations early in 1807 solely to be able to assist Russia. Because for some time this had not been a factor, he saw that the only reason to continue the breach was Napoleon's demand for it. While the intimate official associations with France were admitted, equity demanded that he remind France of Napoleon's failure to bring Turkey to peace with Russia. Napoleon had entered a separate peace with Russia, Galib complained, and even maintained an active alliance with the sultan's enemy. The sole remaining consideration for not listening to Adair lay in the faint hope that the French court might even yet redeem its promises. In plain truth, however, he said the negotiations authorized for a treaty with Russia had remained "immobile" for a year. Russia had not evacuated the Principalities, nor had France given a single reassuring reply to Ottoman suggestions respecting what the eventual treaty should include.

Just what were the French intentions toward Turkey? These could be revealed, Galib taunted, even before the latest reports of inaction at Paris. When Ambassador Mouhib had visited Champagny before the emperor's departure for Erfurt, to announce the accession of the new sultan, what reception was he given? He had simply been told that he must present new letters of credence to Napoleon, owing to the advent of the new sultan, and obtain new authority to negotiate the treaty with Russia.

It was an amazing verbal communication to Napoleon's empire at its height, not alone for its frank comment but for its delivery by a power torn by internal dissension. Latour-Maubourg sent it to Paris promptly, together with his analysis of other recent happenings. His analysis revealed a complete contrast to the ascendant French position of 1806. Here was another remarkable appraisal of French policy and of the status of Frenchmen who were subjects of the mighty Napoleon.

Latour-Maubourg admitted—from his personal knowledge of what had happened during the preceding six months—the correctness of the claim that Champagny had given Mouhib no word of assurance or of consolation. Nor had Mouhib been given any kind of assurance at all of positive nature. Latour-Maubourg, himself without instructions, had had to confine his comments to vague generalities. "Thus the Turks by degrees have lost the confidence they had in us," he concluded, the greatest reason for this being the Franco-Russian alliance. In any event, Turkish sentiment for peace with England had become very strong since late October. From a practical point of view, the Turks felt that to uphold the integrity of their territory they should prepare for renewed fighting against Russia. Latour-Maubourg reminded Paris of the arrest of Frenchmen resident in Turkey in 1798. If affairs developed as far as a breach of relations with Turkey, all Frenchmen there again would be exposed to "a certain danger." He interpreted Turkish exasperation as quite strong, with Frenchmen suffering insults every day.[32]

The parting of the ways for Turkey and France had taken place gradually. The outright admission of the existing coolness was made at Constantinople on October 28. By an understandable coincidence the conference between Latour-Maubourg and the Ottoman foreign minister was held at the moment Champagny was drafting France's new statement of policy for Turkey. The foreign minister's first draft became too long and involved, and he replaced it with a series of three instructions for Latour-Maubourg which applied the decisions of Erfurt. France awaited the response to a new tentative proposal for peace which had been presented to England, Champagny stated. The tsar believed anarchy would come if he withdrew from Moldavia and Wallachia. Probably the ultimate ownership of the Principalities could be decided in a general settlement. France held itself ready to guarantee the remainder of the Ottoman Empire, provided that empire continued to oppose England. Champagny authorized arguments intended to convince the Ottoman Empire that it no longer needed the Principalities. The Danube could be its convenient frontier and its strategic line of defense. Religion and customs separated the people living north of the river from the Ottoman government; they always had been secret enemies of the Turks. Turkey derived little revenue from the Principalities, could levy no troops there, and exercised no direct authority over them. It could appoint no Turkish official there, all local government being under the Greek hospodars. In a practical sense, the new sultan had been bequeathed an empire already shorn of Moldavia and Wallachia. Latour-Maubourg must say that Russia, not France, desired the cession of that Ottoman territory. Russia definitely would accept peace on that basis.[33]

Count Rumiantsov came to Paris after Erfurt, in order to be near, if an opportunity to negotiate with Great Britain should arise. Napoleon went to Spain. The Russian foreign minister took occasion to discuss general policies with Prince Metternich, Austria's ambassador. Of interest to us is Rumiantsov's holding secret conferences with Mouhib. These were unknown to Champagny until they were revealed by Theologue, the Ottoman ambassador's secretary-interpreter, who sometimes served Napoleon. Champagny disliked to think of Theologue as his intermediary with the allied foreign minister, but transmitted to Napoleon the information acquired from that source (December 1). Rumiantsov confided that Marshal Prosorovski would attempt, through an agent sent to Constantinople, to arrange for conferences directly with Turkey without French mediation. Champagny's preliminary conference with the Ottoman envoy had prepared him for the "quite astonishing" proposal to cede the Principalities.[34]

Slower and more erratic communications with Teheran contributed to the slowness with which Persia accepted the shift of policy by Emperor Napoleon. One notes from the documents a considerable reticence on the part of officials in Paris to discuss a policy for Persia. Whereas the Persians assumed that there had been considerable negotiation for peace between Persia and Russia at Paris, the fact was that there had been exactly none on that subject and little on any other Persian subject since Tilsit. Yet shortly after Erfurt the French foreign ministry got around to making up a large parcel for a courier to Persia. The scanty instructions must have annoyed Minister Gardane and his assistants; he read of desultory official studies in the French capital respecting possible fulfillment of the agreement to sell arms, which he had negotiated several months earlier. More important new instructions were started on November 2. These would not actually be received and deciphered until August, 1809, almost a year later.

The foreign minister reported to Gardane that Asker Khan had held a conference with Tolstoi respecting peace. Champagny had served as the intermediary, only to discover that Russia's ambassador possessed no instructions to negotiate. Paris then directed Gardane to find ways to relieve France of the necessity of having to decide the terms between Russia and Persia. He might warn that such a delegation of authority could only weaken relations of France with Persia. Champagny ignored Gardane's treaty of commerce, signed in January, and directed that before signing such a treaty the minister must forward the draft to Paris for approval. Champagny correctly reminded Gardane that the latter had not been given instructions with respect to the clauses to be included.[35]

Meanwhile, Felix Lajard found Persia's army camp in considerable confusion and on half-rations (November 17, 1808). The shah's army on active duty totaled only 9,830 men, a surprisingly low figure. Gardane repeatedly told the shah that he had received no official news from France, and Feth Ali reproached his grand vizir many times for the silence from that country. He summoned Gardane into conference on November 23, only to be informed once more that the minister expected a courier. He promised that when the courier came the Shah would certainly see authentic proofs of Napoleon's high affection for him. "They are long in coming here," interrupted Feth Ali. Gardane renewed his warning that he would leave if the English were permitted to enter Persia. The shah for the first time took a reproachful attitude toward Napoleon's alliance with Russia, and gave Gardane sixty days of grace (until January 20, 1809) to learn what measures Napoleon had taken in behalf of Persia.[36]

On the basis of Gardane's dispatches, the foreign ministry in Paris advised Napoleon that French agents in Persia believed that the British would attack Karek, one of the islands assigned to France. The shah had confirmed his permission for a French army to pass to India but insisted that it include only Frenchmen and Italians. No Russians were to be among the troops. Asker Khan transmitted several letters to Champagny, among them one by Prince Abbas Mirza complaining of the lack of results from the negotiations for peace. Grand Vizir Mirza Cheffi insisted that the Persian ambassador's only object at Paris was to obtain Russia's evacuation of Georgia, that Persia awaited Napoleon's keeping his promise. He reminded Champagny that Persia had adopted Gardane's advice to seek an armistice with Russia and friendship with Turkey.

Champagny answered Mirza Cheffi in a friendly but general manner. He wished "to cultivate precious relations of friendship" and to affirm that Asker Khan was aiding this amity materially. In a similarly noncommittal way he addressed Abbas Mirza. He advised Gardane to stress Persian friendship with Turkey, moderate Persian conduct toward Russia, and aversion to the English. The foreign minister considered what must be done regarding Gardane's convention, which called for the delivery to the Persian Gulf of 20,000 French muskets and a large supply of ammunition. He privately inquired of his official associates in Paris whether Napoleon could not send Persia a limited quantity of the promised supplies. The convention had also requested but not required a number of French technical workers intended for the military establishments and for peacetime manufacturing. He advised Napoleon that it would be well for the war department to approve these stipulations before ratifying the agreement.[37]

Gardane faced new difficulties. His long dispatches of November 25 discussed factors preparatory to an expedition to India, including routes, numbers of troops, and equipment. But the rumor that the British would soon be permitted to enter Persia disturbed him. He conferred with the shah and afterwards stated in writing to Mirza Cheffi: "I declare, in accordance with the audience I had with the shah, that I deem it my duty, and due the honor of my august master and of our great nation, to leave your court with all the legation the instant the English are admitted to your territory." The grand vizir addressed Champagny the next day—in another letter that would be long en route—to express his hope that no event would transpire to sever the Franco-Persian alliance. If Napoleon did not live up to his engagements toward Persia, it would be to the "eternal dishonor of France." The shah wrote the emperor in similar vein.[38]

Lajard learned that Russia's army in Georgia totaled 16,000; it was larger and more efficient than Persia's. He discussed affairs with Gudovich at the latter's camp before Erivan. The latter thereupon wrote Gardane that he was acting under superior orders and from the point of view that the Treaty of Tilsit had replaced any or all French support of Persia's claims to Georgia (on November 25). Gudovich interpreted Gardane's letter, which Lajard had delivered, in light of conditions more than of words. Lajard favored Persia by proposing an armistice based on the status before the war, while Gudovich insisted that Russia's new frontier include conquered Georgia. Nothing came of the new overture. The sporadic fighting was resumed.[39]

Gardane contributed a new idea, that Napoleon send a French army into Persia for defense against the English and permit it to remain there. His proposal resulted from the vizir's assertion that without French aid Persia could not defend itself against Russia and England. Gardane suggested at least 10,000 men—slightly more than Lajard's report of the effectives in Persia's army. Mirza Cheffi was still wondering, as he had, many times, what had become of the French muskets ordered almost a year before. The question might have embarrassed a minister less resourceful than General Gardane. "Sending 20,000 muskets is such a little thing for France," he said, lightly passing it off, "and His Majesty himself is so great that he will condescend personally to inspect closely those trifles." The next day Gardane appealed to the Persians to spare four Russian prisoners of war scheduled for execution at Teheran.[40] This appeal revealed an attitude the Persians did not fail to notice.

What of Persia in Napoleon's calculations? Did he promise at Erfurt to remain aloof from Turkish and Persian affairs, so far as concerned Russia, or did he merely lose interest in the shah's cause? As one indication, the archives reveal that Champagny forwarded Gardane's instructions of November by way of Ambassador Caulaincourt at St. Petersburg. He hoped the latter could arrange for a Russian courier to get them through to Russia's enemy country. The foreign ministry read with care the official estimates of prices for the guns and ammunition for which Gardane contracted, the actual cost being much higher than the figures that had been set. Of greater consequence was that the order would require three years to fill unless Napoleon's primary arsenal was utilized. Napoleon's advisers thought that it would be of advantage to station the requested technical workers in Persia, even if only to produce goods for sale to India. Such an arrangement would work only if the English themselves could be kept out. On December 17 Champagny advised Gardane of the "happy news" that French forces had entered Madrid. This bit of news came to Gardane only on the following August 22, along with the other packets sent through Russia. Ignoring Gardane's commercial treaty, Champagny drafted a convention which omitted all reference to the sale of arms to Persia. He proposed commercial relations similar to those under the Ottoman capitulations; with complete extra-territorial jurisdiction for France, the low 3 per cent import and export rate, and the other customary terms of such unequal "treaties."

To summarize, we may observe that after Erfurt scant activity marked the alliance between France and Russia. There seemed little prospect of sensational developments from it. As had been hinted in Paris, Russia sought to negotiate directly with Turkey for the cession of Moldavia and Wallachia. A Russian officer appeared at Constantinople on November 12, representing Prince Prosorovski, the military commander in Wallachia. He stated that "the Europeans" had agreed to guarantee the

Ottoman Empire after severing the Principalities for Russia. He left in company with Turkish negotiators because he asked for peace parleys on the field without French mediating aid. The Turks accepted his offer to negotiate but with the reservation of preserving the integrity of all Ottoman territory. The Turks and the Persians, always reluctant to disbelieve Napoleon, began vaguely to perceive the disadvantages to them produced by his secret shift of policy. In the autumn of 1808, Napoleon still counted many partisans in Turkey. Yet the British could count more. The key Ottomans of October, 1808, did not turn over to the French the secret communications which Britain sent them, as they had done in December, 1806. It is more important that the British sought to restore peacetime relations with Turkey and normal relations with Persia.

XVI

Near Eastern Policy at Loose Ends

✦ 1808-1809

THE EMPEROR of the French never escaped from his changing and ever dangerous contradictions in Near Eastern policies. How could he be a genuine ally of Turkey's enemy while at the same time retaining the sultan's friendship? At first he had feebly explained his course by the revolutionary change of rulers and by his own mediating role under the Treaty of Tilsit, whereby the new sultan was led to hope that the mediation would benefit the Ottoman Empire.

It must have been expected that Turkey's normal reaction would be to veer eventually toward Napoleon's perennial enemy, England. By late 1808, Turks of all factions were aware of the disappointing news of Napoleonic policy in their behalf. Austrian partisans appeared to wish the English to enter Constantinople, while the Moruzzi family and most of the Greek politicians aligned themselves on the Russian side. Napoleon's indomitable spirit no longer influenced a large segment of the Ottoman people. In Turkish foreign relations the essentials of the ensuing weeks, as we shall see in this chapter, were the coming of peace and alliance with England early in 1809 and the rupture of the *de facto* armistice with Russia.

Ever since (and perhaps even before) uniting with Russia to defend Turkey against Bonaparte in Egypt, Britain had claimed an interest in the Dardanelles. Its policy of coöperation with Russia being completely upset by the Franco-Russian alliance, it had had little opportunity to restore official relations with the sultan, broken off through its fleet's unsuccessful cruise in the sea of Marmara (chap. vii). The summer of 1808 had seemed to offer a chance to negotiate. The anti-French developments in Constantinople did not pass unnoticed by London, where on June 26 the cabinet had commissioned Sir Robert Adair to oppose any Napoleonic plan to march an army through the Ottoman Empire to attack India. "War" presumably existed between England and Turkey, yet the British cabinet authorized only another threat of force against

Turkey—the threat to become reality if Adair deemed it necessary. By the latter's instructions, if Turkey capitulated to the Franco-Russian system, he must support friendly Ali Pasha of Albania and elevate Albania to be the new center of British influence in the Balkans. Russia having gone to the other side and the existing "war" with Turkey boasting neither battles nor interest, Foreign Secretary George Canning saw no reason why the sultan could not sign peace with Great Britain. The treaty might simply declare, "The two countries are restored to a state of peace, and unrestrained commercial intercourse is revived."

It was foreseen that Russia might also sign a treaty of peace with Turkey. In that case Canning gave Adair the alternative of simply adhering to the Russo-Turkish treaty, provided it excluded a formal guarantee of the Ottoman Empire. Britain's expired alliance with Turkey might be revived, Adair here being authorized to stipulate the promise of British naval protection for Constantinople. In such a case, however, Turkey would be requested to turn over an island guarding the Dardanelles—either Crete, Chios, or Melos. Adair would invite Turkey to undertake active operations, if they were practical, against Russia in the Black Sea. It was important that Turkey "require the liberty of passage for a British squadron through the Dardanelles and the Bosporus with the occupation of such points as might be necessary for effectually securing the safe return of that squadron."[1]

The attitude of Turks and Persians in late 1808 presented Great Britain with its new opportunity. Peace with the sultan was by now considered a mere matter of formality. Britain also wanted to weaken or nullify the Ottoman decrees favorable to Napoleon's Continental Blockade, to legalize its existing wartime trade with Egypt, and to restore the former British privileges of trade with all other Ottoman provinces. Britain wished to ally itself with Turkey and if possible stipulate its naval navigation of the Straits. It would like a new treaty with Persia in order to reopen full relations with that buffer for India. Officials commented upon Persia's few direct trade relations with Europe, all former British trade having been conducted through the East India Company.

The English had learned all the secret provisions of the Treaty of Tilsit. They could use their information with telling effect in dealing with Turkey. Napoleon and Alexander did not know, while at Erfurt, that two English naval vessels had appeared off the Dardanelles near the end of September. On board the frigate *Seahorse* waited the negotiator, Sir Robert Adair, with authority in hand to arrange a settlement with Turkey. He demonstrated Britain's good will by suspending all interference with Greek and Turkish shipping. He soon learned of the reluctance of the Turks at the capital to hasten into the negotiations proposed by him.

According to an unsigned dispatch which they phrased on October 12, the British argued that the Turks were entitled to suspect something in Napoleon's conniving. The dispatch reasoned from the ascendant position of France in Russia and the nature of the Franco-Russian agreements. The Ottoman government could not ignore that the partition of the Ottoman Empire in Europe had been decided. Russia's failure to carry out the ostensible clause of Tilsit by evacuating Moldavia and Wallachia underscored the interpretation. The British advised the Turks to break with "Bonaparte."[2]

On November 2 Vice-consul Mechain sent Latour-Maubourg news from the Dardanelles to the effect that the exchanges between the British and Turks were continuing. Hakki Pasha had been deposed and removed to Crete, his successor under Sultan Mahmud II being the restored Raguil Pasha, a former partisan of Selim and an exile during Mustapha's administration. Later, when Bairakdar was eliminated at Constantinople, Raguil would in turn be exiled again and the Dardanelles would be entrusted to Hakki.[3] Vahid Effendi, who had been special envoy to Napoleon in 1807, came personally to the Dardanelles to deliver several letters and to meet Robert Adair. Raguil and Vahid treated Consul Mechain politely, although they revealed to him absolutely nothing of their secret discussions. On November 12 Adair requested permission to sail through the Dardanelles, in the frigate anchored near the castles guarding the entrance to the strait. His request came to Constantinople at a time of confusion, an aftermath of the palace revolt that had enthroned Sultan Mahmud in July.

Until mid-November Mahmud could be only a puppet of the mutinous soldiery responsible for his elevation. The Ottoman public bitterly resented the harsh rule of Grand Vizir Mustapha Bairakdar. He maintained a splendid palace and adjacent buildings resembling the sultan's seraglio in everything save size. Eventually the janissaries, shocked by his brutality, withdrew their support and turned against him. The time seemed ripe for another revolution. This did not necessarily mean a replacement of sultans, there being no other Ottoman princes in the line of direct descent except the imprisoned ex-ruler, Sultan Mustapha IV, who was unpopular. The janissaries thus decided to revolt only against the grand vizir. Bairakdar's troops numbered some 5,000 loyal Albanians, scattered in various sections of Constantinople. He commanded perhaps an equal number of auxiliaries. Altogether they were too few to cope with the janissaries, the traditional and unruly center of the Ottoman infantry.

At this time Latour-Maubourg was writing his observations for Paris about the new Ottoman government. He related that although Bairakdar exercised absolute authority, he did so with justice. The janissaries had been steadily weakened, with a corresponding increase in the power and influence of the so-called "irregular" or ordinary troops, their insistent and far more numerous rivals headed by Bairakdar. Sultan Mahmud returned to one of Sultan Selim's unpopular reforms by ordering the latter trained somewhat on the European pattern.

The janissaries overthrew the grand vizir on the night of November 11; the Albanians appeared unwilling to fight it out with them. As a warning, the janissaries burned a building near the palace of the grand vizir, hoping also thereby to provoke such a violent clash as to annihilate the party that had enthroned Sultan Mustapha in 1807 by deposing Selim. Not long afterward, a clash occurred within the grand vizir's palace. During the night of November 14 the janissaries forced their way into that palace and disposed of Bairakdar's guard. When they were frustrated in their search for Bairakdar, they started a huge fire. They thought he must have escaped, and so they hunted him not only in his own palace but also in the sultan's palace and on board Ottoman naval vessels. Bairakdar did escape for the moment by hiding first in the harem, then in a subterranean secret tunnel, linking his palace and the seraglio, which included a sort of arsenal room. A frightful night ensued. All parts of the grand vizir's palace blazed simultaneously from fires set to cremate the grand vizir and any of his friends hiding in the building. They caught the kiaya bey, an intimate adviser to the sultan, and the treasurer; both were cut to pieces. The grand vizir never reached the sultan's palace; trapped in the tunnel, he was killed by an explosion. They found his body two days later and displayed it publicly. They claimed the grand vizir had committed suicide to prevent capture.

Several days of utmost confusion followed: there were additional fires, pillage by various troops, and attacks against the sultan's palace. A body of janissaries soon made themselves masters of that palace, where they discovered another corpse, that of ex-Sultan Mustapha. Indeed, some of their leaders had helped Mahmud to dispose of that figure on November

17. By now, Bairakdar's Albanians and auxiliaries had been killed or dispersed and the revolution had spread to the controlling authorities of the fleet and to the military arsenals of the capital. Many leaders perished and virtual anarchy for a time shattered all order. The janissaries compromised with Mahmud because he alone remained as the legal claimant to the throne.[4]

None of Mahmud's new ministers figured personally in Napoleonic policy. We need only refer to Galib Effendi, who continued as before to be Mahmud's foreign minister. During this time Adair at the Dardanelles—without any knowledge as yet of the anarchy in Constantinople —held his first conference with Raguil and Vahid (November 16). Vice-consul Mechain at first seemed to be making some progress in countering Adair's hope of restoring normal relations between England and Turkey. This the French consul believed, when the new governor at the Dardanelles evinced friendliness toward Napoleon. Turkey's foreign minister did not change, however, and Mechain reported Adair as conferring further with the Turks, on November 21 and 26.[5]

Meanwhile, Spain became once again the central concern in Napoleon's affairs. The emperor, after having returned from Erfurt to St. Cloud, soon left again (on November 3) for Bayonne, from whence he could direct the army of Spain. On December 5 we find him in Madrid, the city governed by General Belliard, another trusted colleague of the well-remembered long days of the French expedition to Egypt in 1798 and 1799. So great was the confusion of Spanish affairs that for a time the French embassy at Constantinople had to guarantee credit for the expenses of the Spanish legation.

Two revolutions had occurred at Constantinople since Latour-Maubourg had been sent any real instructions. The chargé d'affaires could not meet with authority so important a development as that of the Russians' taking the initiative to demand Turkey's cession of the Principalities. He thus entreated Champagny again, on November 25: "I pray Your Excellency to take account of my position. Since the departure of General Sebastiani I have not received any instructions."[6] The new Turkish council seemed weaker than ever, according to his speculation, and further serious menace by the English would endanger it.

Latour-Maubourg's mild diplomatic offensive requested from the Turks full information of their negotiations with the English at the Dardanelles. He complained against these and threatened, not to break relations, as did Gardane, but to expedite a courier to Paris to ask for instructions. As another example of the foreign ministry's routine neglect, early in December Champagny merely acknowledged the dispatches from Constantinople down through October 30 and relayed military news. The foreign minister said that Latour-Maubourg must seek to maintain the usual friendship between France and Turkey. Russia's wish to negotiate directly with Turkey would provide another opportunity for him to remind the sultan's ministers that the tsar, and not France, wished to detach the two Ottoman provinces.[7] In mid-December, to counter in kind the anti-French propaganda which cried up Napoleon's difficulties in Spain, Champagny directed attention to Turkey's own adverse problems—in Asia the Wahabis, and in Europe the menace of Ali Pasha. Why, one might ask, did Turkey tolerate any English agents at all? Latour-Maubourg must tell the Turks that Napoleon's victory in Spain duplicated his blitzkriegs in all of his other wars. Champagny added that Paris had deduced from Adair's negotiations at the Dardanelles that Britain and Turkey were likely to come to terms.[8]

On December 19 Latour-Maubourg could report further on the actual and attempted negotiations by Adair. To keep himself in the clear, the chargé d'affaires called attention to his repeated references since October 2 to these negotiations and to his lack of instructions. He could not evaluate the decision at Erfurt. He reminded Paris that he had reported the coming of the Russian officer to Constantinople as an injury to French prestige. When the interpreter for the Ottoman foreign office died on November 16, gossip for several weeks held that he would be replaced by an anti-French Moruzzi. Latour-Maubourg blocked the appointment. For some twenty-six days, Turkey had no such liaison officer at all, a circumstance without parallel.

Such was the general picture when the new orders by Champagny came to Latour-Maubourg. These required him to support Russia's acquisition of the Principalities. As directed, the chargé d'affaires stated that Russia and not France had taken the decision to sever the Principalities. He gloomily admitted to Champagny that all matters affecting French policy in Turkey were indeed bad, despite the solemn assurance to him by several of the sultan's ministers that they would never enter a separate peace with England. Moruzzi reportedly would aid in the peace conference with Prosorovski. "Any favor to the Moruzzis, the declared enemies of the French name," Latour-Maubourg wrote Paris, "is an insult to France." The Turks had "irrevocably decided" not to cede the Principalities. From his summary dated December 19, 1808, the chargé d'affaires apparently did not guess—notwithstanding Mechain's hints—that an Ottoman treaty with England was near.[9] While Galib Effendi was at military headquarters on the Danube, Atif Effendi temporarily directed Ottoman foreign affairs.

The Anglo-Turkish negotiations languished for a time in consequence of the revolutionary disturbances of mid-November. Adair forced the Turks to a decision by threatening a strict blockade of the Dardanelles and of Smyrna. They feared, so Mechain reported on December 20, that this might deprive Constantinople of supplies and in turn stimulate the diverse factions to renewed revolt; the disaffected elements could employ the pretext of famine, because it would not take long to feel the effects of such a blockade.[10]

A combination of circumstances thus enabled Adair to conduct serious discussions at the Dardanelles in December. The indirect revelation by Russia of the essential of the Franco-Russian agreement at Erfurt had its effect, together with the seeming approach of renewed Russo-Turkish war. Austria's friendly offices aided England. In mid-November Vahid Effendi appeared at the Dardanelles with full authority to negotiate. He and Adair admitted their mutual object of restoring peace. The negotiations eventually revolved around two factors, the economic —adjusted with difficulty—and the political, from the discussions of which nothing emerged conceding a permanent or even temporary British naval use of the Straits. Not only did Turkey refuse, but Britain went so far as to agree in the future to respect the Turkish closure of the Straits to all foreign vessels of war so long as Turkey remained at peace.

Vahid requested virtual free trade with Great Britain as a reciprocal concession, but he won only the assurance that Britain would manifest "general favor and protection to the Ottoman flag." He personally promised that negotiations would be undertaken for a commercial treaty. Britain, like France, had several pending pecuniary claims, which Vahid refused to satisfy. Adair requested the restoration to trading status of several Turkish merchants whose British warrants of protection had been canceled several years earlier. Vahid declined because Turkey wished to terminate the abusive foreign use of such warrants. Turkey was willing, however, to concede everything of practical commercial importance which Britain might properly request. Vahid accepted Adair's request for a treaty basis for the capitulations, this alone constituting a new landmark. The restored prerogatives included the low tariff of 3 per cent on all exports to Turkey, together with the commercial navigation of the Straits and the Black Sea.

Vahid refused Britain a blanket concession of the military navigation of the Straits, whereupon Adair attempted to arrange that during the Anglo-French war the naval vessels of Great Britain should have permission to sail the Dardanelles for Constantinople, provided they carried diplomatic dispatches. This Vahid also declined. Not until 1840 did Britain force acceptance of the latter principle. Even then, it was restricted to light vessels (which meant, under the capitulatory regime, vessels of not more than 450 tons). Vahid stated that Turkey wished to take the opportunity of its war with Russia "to put an end absolutely to the passage of ships of war of that power through the Dardanelles."[11] It might be expedient in 1809 for England's navy to possess treaty access to the Black Sea, he said, in view of the Franco-Russian alliance. This could have little practical effect, however, if Turkey remained a neutral in the Anglo-French War. Thus Adair had no good reason not to agree to the Turkish restriction, which always had been applied at the sultan's discretion alone. Adair pledged Britain's support to a unilateral stipulation: it thereafter would conform with "the Turkish rule" of closure of the Straits during times of Ottoman peace.

The archive records indicate that up to 1809 foreign warships did not navigate the Straits—except those of Russia as an active Turkish ally from 1798 to 1805. Aside from Duckworth's discomfiture inside the Dardanelles in 1807, the British had never suffered any serious inconvenience by their exclusion. Thus their agreement to respect Turkey's closure did not surrender any privilege. In order to renew the sultan's friendship, Adair simply promised that Britain would not again force the Straits as long as Turkey remained at peace. Britain would hold all its warships outside the Dardanelles.

The Anglo-Turkish Treaty of the Dardanelles was duly signed on January 5, 1809. The agreement restored the capitulations, the tariff of 1805, and the privilege of British retail trading within the Ottoman Empire. British officials thereafter must not issue warrants protecting any subjects of the sultan.[12] The political sections are ordinarily termed a peace and an "alliance," although the latter contained no obligation on Turkey's part to fight Napoleon. A stipulation common to the agreements of 1799 and 1809 was Britain's exclusion from the Dardanelles. Hence the political stipulations are of interest mainly because Britain's war flag did not follow its restored commercial flag into the Black Sea.

England became in fact the first of the major powers to recognize officially these Turkish interpretations: that the Straits must be closed to foreign warships during times of Ottoman peace, and that the Mediterranean could sometimes be considered a sea in which Turkey had the status of a neutral power. This represented an important, although limited, treaty development toward the general internationalization of the Turkish rule of closure. The treaty thus recorded Britain's pledge: "As ships of war at all times have been prohibited from entering the canal of Constantinople, viz., in the Straits of the Dardanelles and of the Black Sea, and as this ancient regulation of the Ottoman Empire is in the future to be observed by every power in time of peace, the court of Great Britain promises on its part to conform to this principle." Secret annexes established a defensive Anglo-Turkish alliance against France, with Great Britain assuming the duty of protecting Turkey with an adequate fleet. Turkey accepted no reciprocal duty.[13]

Thus in the interest of peaceful relations with Turkey, Britain recognized the sultan's right to close the Straits whenever that ruler should be at peace. England simply accepted what Turkey had asserted to be its rule. The treaty did not preclude Turkey's changing that rule. It did not authorize any joint strategic operations in the Black Sea, to give effect to the one-sided alliance against a nonexistent French fleet there. On the other hand, the sultan's ministers could and did employ Britain's pledge of abstention to declare boldly to France in 1809 that if an English fleet appeared at the Dardanelles, it would be refused admission.[14]

The Treaty of the Dardanelles did not authorize British warships to serve as the carriers of diplomatic dispatches to Constantinople. With no exceptions whatsoever, it simply pledged Great Britain to respect the sultan's closure during times of Ottoman peace. Moreover, whereas the treaty stated that "every power" would observe the Turkish rule, obviously Britain and Turkey could not obligate other powers; the treaty in fact bound only Great Britain and Turkey and only British ships of war. A rule if observed in practice only when convenient or politic to the powers was not transformed by this first important treaty recognition of the Straits as closed into an international obligation binding all the powers. That development would come only in 1840 and 1841, when the major powers themselves accepted the restriction.

It can be argued that in 1809 Great Britain pledged Turkey, through the latter's own sovereign action while it remained at peace, to exclude Russian, French, and other foreign vessels of war from the Straits. Without a joint control of the Straits—such as the Soviet Union unsuccessfully sought in 1946—perhaps it was well to leave the matter to Turkey. There then existed no international body upon which the responsibility could be laid, should Turkey authorize exceptions to the rule it had proclaimed. Britain possessed no territories at the Straits or on the Black Sea. Its nineteenth-century wars, moreover, except when it was an ally of Turkey against Russia during the Crimean War, really gave it no political responsibilities allowing it to claim the naval navigation of the Straits.

Frenchmen at the Turkish capital considered the defection of Turkey from their policy as fully consummated by the Treaty of the Dardanelles. The treaty having been agreed upon, the English squadron sailed away from the entrance of the Dardanelles, ending its anchorage of three months and four days. French Vice-consul Mechain, who had reported the fact of many English-Turkish conferences, could not relay their subject matter. He appreciated that the Turks generally assumed that the council had decided to come to an understanding with England.[15] Normal relations with Britain being stipulated, Sir Robert Adair impressively sailed into Constantinople on board a British war frigate. His coming on January 12 pleased many Turks, observed Latour-Maubourg —who now could, like Jaubert, sign as auditor of the Council of State. They saw in the treaty a probable partial relief from the scarcity of foreign goods. Other Turkish subjects seemed less happy. Among these were several Greek politicians, and all those who did not desire a strong Turkish government to function with English backing.[16]

The first confirmed report of Adair's successful negotiations infuriated Tsar Alexander. He hurried off a courier early in February, 1809, with a message designed to prod the authorities at Constantinople into action —even if too late to affect the result. He would break off the armistice if Turkey gave in. Russia would consider the admission of an English agent to Constantinople as a renewal of the fighting war. If, within twenty-four hours of the delivery of the notice, Adair and his party should not be expelled from Constantinople and Ottoman territory, Russian armies in Moldavia and Wallachia would cross the Danube to exact a "glorious vengeance." At the same time, the Turkish negotiations with Britain really seemed to Alexander to offer a convenient pretext for renewing the war when the spring fighting weather should return in April. At Erfurt Napoleon had guaranteed him eventual possession of the Principalities. He stated to Caulaincourt, on February 11, "To exclude Great Britain from the continent of Europe is merely a part of the common Franco-Russian plan. The basic fact, however, was Turkey's refusal to cede the Principalities, as Prince Prosorovski had demanded in December. The bluntness of the language directed at Constantinople suggested that the tsar might overstep the limits set by the secret Convention of Erfurt. He added, to correct this impression, "I do not expect any aggrandizement beyond the Danube. The Turks remain where they are. They are necessary there for the tranquillity of everyone. What we said last year I only agreed to in deference to Napoleon and did not intend to circumscribe the system we adopted against England."[17]

Rebellious Serbia might have been of interest to France. Karageorge addressed Napoleon from Belgrade on August 16, 1809, soliciting the emperor to become the "august defender and legislator of the Serbian people." The Serbs offered Napoleon special forts in exchange for his support. In the spring of 1809 various Frenchmen contended that it was absolutely necessary for France to occupy Crete and Lemnos, important guardian islands of the Dardanelles. They also anticipated Hitler's wish to control southern Greece.[18] If Russia remained faithful to the French alliance, which was now often doubted, any Levantine location would be beneficial for expanding French trade in Asia and for proceeding against the English. If the partition of Turkey in Europe came—and the gradual internal dissolution of the Ottoman government made it seem inevitable—these Frenchmen felt that Bosnia and Albania should come to France in order to give uninterrupted access by land to Greece and to complete the French control of all ports around Europe from the Morea to Holland.[19]

On the basis of such clever considerations, Napoleon hoped to acquire something for nothing, perhaps the most perilous of international procedures. France would give Russia nothing. Champagny recorded his own reactions to recommending the partition of Turkey. Writing from Vienna, he agreed with its principle but denied its applicability (August 5). Although he accepted the arguments, the conditions favoring a partition might be so long delayed that the general situation could well have changed. He said that Napoleon possessed an interest in preserving the Ottoman Empire and that the circumstances of the moment did not permit an examination of the question.

In Persia, likewise, French policy suffered an eclipse. General Gardane acknowledged in mid-January, 1809, Champagny's inconsequential let-

ters—those started from Bayonne and Paris the preceding July and
August. His unattainable object was the exclusion of English negotiators. He entreated the shah to send Hartford Jones away, in the wake
of Sir John Malcolm, who had been denied a hearing in 1808. Napoleon's envoy again cited the obligation of Feth Ali's alliance. On January
24 the shah and Grand Vizir Mirza Cheffi rejoined that France also had
duties under that alliance; despite the displeasure to France, Persia might
be forced by circumstances to admit the English ambassador. Gardane
took the next step, declaring his intention to retire from Persia the moment Jones entered.

Thus began the slow termination of Napoleon's representation in
Teheran. Mirza Cheffi remarked that the minister's departure was un-
thinkable. Must Asker Khan also depart from Paris? French honor, he
taunted, required Gardane to remain in residence near the Persian court.
The grand vizir charged that Gardane had absolutely refused to permit
two French officers to accompany Abbas Mirza in a campaign against
General Gudovich near Erivan. Napoleon's minister cleverly argued that
this was a prudent refusal: by withholding such aid, France retained the
possibility of filling the role of mediator for Persia's benefit. He stressed
that his own attitude was too well known for him to remain in Persia,
should Jones be received. Without the slightest basis for the speculation
and merely to gain time, he said that he felt assured that Napoleon must
have negotiated Persian affairs while at Erfurt. Finding the Persians
adamant, Gardane resorted once more to the vague generality that no
news was good news. With impressive earnestness he contended, on
January 24, 1809, that a definite reply to the English should be put off
at least until the latest news came from Paris. Feigning abused innocence,
he introduced a challenge: if it should then be found that France really
had neglected Persia, there would be time enough for any arrangements
under discussion with France's enemies; that would be the time to make
peace with Russia and to rescind all the promises given Emperor Napoleon.

At this point in the conference, so Gardane frankly admitted, the shah
haughtily and impressively said the discussion was being prolonged in
a disagreeable manner and begged leave to retire. The next day the ruler
relented slightly, sending word that he would seek precise information
respecting whether General Malcolm still remained in the Persian Gulf
with his reported force of 30,000 men.

On February 4, Persia authorized Jones to come to Teheran. Persian officials did not actually invite him; rather the Briton repeatedly invited himself. To make good his threat, Gardane withdrew to the frontier town of Tabriz. He intended to wait there, near Prince Abbas Mirza, for news or instructions from Napoleon. The shah expressed unhappiness at having been abandoned by France. He stated that at least it seemed he was deserted, since he received no replies to his several letters to Napoleon. The minister obviously could say little. He did suggest once more, however, that perhaps Asker Khan was negotiating in Paris, and he renewed the hope that the conference at Erfurt would have taken some decision in Persia's behalf.

Neither development could possibly have had any further influence on Persia's policy. In Paris, officialdom just barely thought of Persia. Napoleon's foreign minister inquired of the navy what could be done to deliver to the Persian Gulf the stipulated 20,000 muskets and munitions ordered by the shah a year earlier. One may correctly surmise that the French navy, in those days of British supremacy at sea, would recommend no steps at all. As for the high prices, Napoleon instructed that the cost set in Gardane's convention be adhered to, even if lower than the actual cost of the guns and ammunition. The emperor suddenly ordered the beginning of the execution of the order, the sending of 3,000 of the muskets.[20] Such a demand, everyone knew, was meant only to have something to show Ambassador Asker Khan and to send Gardane, for France possessed no practical means by which to make the delivery. Napoleon did not intend the actual delivery; he used the order as a method of clarifying Persia's policy toward him or postponing the apparently inevitable success of British negotiations at Teheran.

What was Asker Khan doing at the time? Whether from instructions or from his own initiative, Asker Khan took official leave of the French government on January 30, in order to force a showdown. Champagny sensed that the interoffice discussions in Paris respecting the shipment of arms would not be enough to hold him there, hence he recommended that Napoleon ratify the convention which stipulated the sale of the muskets and ammunition. He proposed that the ratification clarify that only the sale involved an obligation, and that Persia's request for special French workers must be merely a request. For show, Napoleon issued another order that could be transmitted to Teheran; Asker Khan could take it. Through Secretary of State Maret he directed that no exceptions be made, that the entire convention be "inviolably observed" (February 20).[21] To be certain that Gardane's dispatches matched Asker Khan's information in content, Champagny notified the minister belatedly, on March 1, 1809, of Napoleon's approval of the sale of the muskets and munitions. This news he expedited—indeed exceptional—so as to arrive in Tabriz on July 24. Many weeks before that, however, all thought of France's fulfilling the contract had been abandoned by Gardane and Feth Ali.

The appearance of Hartford Jones in Teheran on February 14 signified the end of an epoch in French policy. Gardane reported that the Englishman requested the termination of the Franco-Persian alliance and the cession of islands and coastal points for British naval stations in the Persian Gulf.[22] Gardane and his staff left Persia a few at a time. Joannin and Nerciat, two of the interpreters on the staff, remained in charge of the legation. Joannin advised Gardane, by letter to Tabriz on March 12, of gossip that revealed his own nervousness: he had heard that Jones had paid to have him and Nerciat assassinated. For several days Gardane continued writing to the Persians—to the shah, the crown prince, the grand vizir—still seeking to have them mend their conduct by sending Jones away. All three avoided the issue. Felix Lajard had remained at Tiflis, following his failure to bring General Gudovich and the Persians to the peace table. There seemed no place for him to go. At the end of March he complained of being without official news for five months. He believed the Persians were intercepting his communications from Gardane. The latter authorized him to return to Paris, ostensibly because of his poor health.[23]

Gardane retreated very slowly, in the unrealistic expectation that some development would remove Jones from the scene and permit his return to Teheran. In a conference with Abbas Mirza in mid-April, he issued a final warning. He would depart from Persian soil within four days. Again assuming his now characteristic attitude of abused innocence, he would not permit himself to be talked into waiting a few days longer. Probably to Gardane's surprise, Abbas Mirza did not press the issue.

Persians in Teheran, far from conceding Gardane anything more, talked of how France had failed them in every major project. They correctly charged that Napoleon had not mediated the war with Russia to restore Georgia to them. He had not ratified the Franco-Persian treaty of commerce. He had not sent the 20,000 muskets. Joannin kept Gardane posted on this comment. When the minister actually fulfilled his threat to leave Persia, he commissioned to remain in Tabriz another Napoleonic agent, Jean Raymond, an artillery officer once named provisional vice-consul at Bender-Abouchir. Because Abbas Mirza requested it, Gardane authorized Raymond to give artillery instruction to selected Persians, provided that he did not accompany Persia's army into any fighting against the Russians.

Asker Khan, always unhurried in movement, began to make good his own bluff also. Thus he could almost duplicate Gardane's calculated but readily transparent planning to win breathing spells. Whatever aid a delay in the breach of relations might have afforded to general policy, he requested his passports only on April 19. The arrangements were duly completed for his departure and Jaubert again accepted the commission as his guide. The Persian thus would have the company of a recognized Napoleonic favorite as far as Strasbourg. There was a striking nearness in the dates for the departure of Gardane and Asker Khan, each unaware of the other's intentions. Asker Khan, like Gardane, changed his mind. On July 10 he was still in Paris, his preparations proceeding slowly. Subtly, he announced that his departure was due exclusively to the fact that his mission originally had been intended to be only temporary. No motive of discontent or any coldness between the two courts led him to decide to go.

Gardane decided to return to France by way of Russia. He was shown similar courtesies, several of Abbas Mirza's officers accompanying him to Persia's frontier. Gardane came to Tiflis on May 20, to be for a time, like Lajard, a guest of Persia's enemy and Napoleon's ally. Joannin remained in Teheran for several weeks, writing many speculative letters to Gardane but accomplishing little otherwise. During the summer he too retired to Tabriz, leaving self-conscious Nerciat to carry on the letter-writing.[24]

Commercial shipping in the Bosporus became an issue with France. For Turkey, so far as concerned Russia and France, the terms of Russo-Turkish settlement had been decided at Erfurt. Whether Britain's warships would sail the Black Sea had been answered in the negative. Britain could pass the Dardanelles and Bosporus with its merchant vessels only. Would Russia sail the Straits? Ambassador Adair won Turkey's closure of the Straits against commerce with Russia. The sultan's notice of the prohibition of all intercourse with the tsarist realm, "by sea or land," assigned as the reason fear of a sudden attack by sea (April 10, 1809). Adair approved the stoppage, although it involved a momentary cessation of British commerce to the Black Sea. "It will prove prejudicial in some degree to English commerce," he admitted to London, "but the advantages upon a larger scale which our cause will derive from it are so manifest that I consider myself fully justified in having advised and enforced it." In his opinion, Great Britain would have done the same, had it possessed the Dardanelles. The measure proved detrimental to the new commercial position of Odessa, whose exports in 1808 had exceeded imports. Adair admitted that Turkey needed the wheat available from the coasts of the Black Sea. He contended, however, that "with the least degree of application—which the Turks' necessities will teach them— they might obtain enough grain from Syria, Egypt, and other parts of their extensive dominions."[25] Austria's envoy did not support Adair in this matter. Russia met the issue as best it could, by ordering trade kept open for all neutral flags at Odessa.

Latour-Maubourg protested the Turkish action. He did so without specific authority from Paris, not so much for allied Russia as in the interest of France. Throughout the *de facto* Russo-Turkish armistice the Straits had been open to commercial shipping; upon renewal of the fighting Turkey simply had proceeded as before, by closing the Bosporus to all commercial vessels. Latour-Maubourg's protest cited the Franco-Turkish treaty of 1802, which reserved to Turkey no restrictions whatever against neutral French shipping in the Straits. He admitted the difficulties of commerce during any war, however, and asserted that France would follow in the Russo-Turkish war the principles customary for neutrals. If France took on board prohibited produce at Odessa, he promised it would be unloaded at Constantinople, in conformity with Ottoman regulations.[26] Latour-Maubourg pretended to consider the Ottoman closure of the Straits and the Black Sea as directed against French and Italian shipping. He always liked to think of the Black Sea as one region safely away from British warships, protected by a friendly Ottoman Empire and an allied Russia. French trade had flourished there in 1808, utilizing Russian-protected carriers.

In Turkey's reply it was insisted that Frenchmen properly enjoyed the privilege of such navigation only at those times when other powers also enjoyed it. The exclusion ordered in 1809 being made general, it did not contravene the treaty with France. The Ottoman government treated frigidly and even with hatred Latour-Maubourg's consequent stronger protest, filed on April 30. He asked, in writing, that Turkey permit French ships to navigate the Black Sea "in virtue of existing treaties." The Ottomans held those treaties to apply only during times of Turkish peace; in war no nation could permit enemies to use its facilities.

Napoleon's chargé d'affaires then asked, merely to establish the principle, that permission be granted for a few French officers to enter the Black Sea on a small boat.

Turkey replied that it positively would not permit any foreign boat to navigate there.

At that point, Latour-Maubourg began to use menacing language. This led only to the response that Turkey stood ready for war, if France employed violence.

Latour-Maubourg duly reported these exchanges. With no instructions he could scarcely declare a one-man war or leave as a warning. Yet the implied danger of war alarmed all Frenchmen residing in the Ottoman capital. Many of them hastened to take the precaution of soliciting foreign protection, for their confidence in Napoleon's power had ebbed. Many ships of the Ionian Republic sought the English flag.[27]

In Egypt, Latour-Maubourg's protest appeared to be a threat of war. Consul General Drovetti asked Mehemet Ali to clarify his position, should war come. The pasha did not neglect this opportunity to court Napoleon's favor. Yet he offered to aid France only behind the scenes —another low point for Napoleonic prestige in the Near East. The pasha said he would seize no French ships upon a Franco-Turkish rupture, if they should be disguised by sailing the Barbary flag and by anchoring at Rosetta instead of Alexandria.[28]

On May 7 the embassy at Constantinople relayed to Paris the first news of Gardane's withdrawal from Persia, his departure being due to the fact that English policy had prevailed. Additional news and speculation that day included the rumor that the British fleet would soon unite with the Turkish, the combined squadron to undertake an expedition against Russia's establishments on the Black Sea. Turkish vessels of war were observed being provisioned.

The Near East represented a sounding board for general policies. Most important of the general events in Europe in 1809 was the new war whereby three Austrian armies undertook an ill-advised offensive against Napoleon in March. The Habsburg venture may be attributed in part at least to a misconception of French power by the people of the Near East. If neutrals could judge Napoleon with the indifference or contempt we have seen in the records, his power must be fading. Austria could observe the demoralization of French policy in Turkey. Britain and others could testify that it extended elsewhere, including Persia, so much so as to encourage the belief that the time had come for revenge.

For the first time a real two-front war against Napoleon was possible, Spain representing the first front and Austria the second. Austria's attack in the east would furnish the element lacking in resistance to Napoleon's lightning campaigns before. Russia failed to make common cause with Napoleon, which would have placed Austria itself in a pincer.

Napoleon's lightning movements eastward went into full swing once more in this his fourth campaign against the Habsburgs. So unrealistically did he appraise Spain and Portugal that he no longer considered them a major matter. He deemed laborers and naval gunners sufficient to guard Brest; he thought that his prestige would keep the English away. In those days, 50 francs a month maintained a bread wagon, including the wages of the driver, its upkeep, and the harnessing and feeding of its four draft horses.

The war at first did not lighten Latour-Maubourg's tasks, for no one suspected a sudden French victory over Austria. The military champion must ever demonstrate his right to the title; the Near East considered it likely that Napoleon's armies had grown soft. The fighting between Russia and Turkey got under way again. Everyone believed that Russia's alliance with France sharpened Turkey's reactions against everything French. Britain's Ambassador Adair seemed to have all the answers, although few Turks remembered to ask him for them. In the Austro-French war a preliminary climax was recorded in April and May. It suggests a parallel to the Nazi march to the English channel in 1940. Napoleon forced the Austrians to the defensive from the outset. He did not really need Russia, any more than Hitler needed Italy in 1940; he counted on Russia's military support only if Austria attacked on the side of Bohemia or Warsaw. By May 13 the war was largely over, with Napoleon issuing orders from Schönbrunn palace in Vienna, the palace built for the renowned Maria Theresa of eighteenth-century Austria. Napoleon maintained his headquarters there for several months, until October 4. The lightning engagements continued, French forces accounting for the principal Austrian armies in a manner which anticipated the mopping-up operations of the Nazis in western France in June, 1940. Early in July, 1809, Napoleon's victory at Wagram over Archduke Charles, the Austrian commander, sealed Austria's confusion and defeat.

Proudly from Vienna, early in June, Napoleon's foreign minister suddenly burst into dispatch-writing to Latour-Maubourg. Because nothing must disturb the concert with Russia, however, his comments were numerous but unimportant. He announced no new policies, only the hesitant revival of interest in old ones. There were vague generalities respecting trade possibilities in the Levant.[29]

Adair visited England during the summer of 1809. Upon returning to his post in September, he hinted he might be able to win authorization for Britain to sail a naval squadron up to Constantinople, in order to coöperate with the Ottoman fleet in the Black Sea. Such a potential arrangement illustrates the historical and legal inapplicability of the Ottoman closure of the Dardanelles and Bosporus to foreign warships at times when the Ottoman Empire was at war. The Turkish foreign minister responded favorably, requesting a British fleet. London soon considered the project inadvisable, however, in view of the larger perspectives of the day.

Napoleon did what he could to counteract and repudiate Gardane's withdrawing from Persia and thus turning over an allied state to exclusive English influence. Joannin, who was given the title of chargé d'affaires, admitted late in July that Hartford Jones "seemed to have attained the object of his intrigues." When news of Gardane's departure came to Napoleon's headquarters in Vienna, Champagny wrote Mirza Cheffi soliciting the continuance of friendly relations (June 3). "The interests of the two empires have not changed," he said. "It is to be desired that their relations do not change." Napoleon penned a friendly reply to the shah's old but recently received letters. "We count on the word you have given our minister, that you will be cordially attached to us," he stated. He authorized special decorations for Raymond and Joannin. Meanwhile Abbas Mirza cordially welcomed Joannin, when the latter took the hint and moved from Teheran to Tabriz.

Champagny's basic idea was to hold Persia to friendship if possible, and not permit the English to dictate its policy. In a letter dispatched in the same June—to be received by Joannin instead of Gardane, on October 13—Champagny bluntly told Gardane that he should not have left Teheran; that move virtually had turned Persia over to the English. All the good will so carefully built up would be endangered. Although the minister must judge on the spot whether he could return to his post, the communication clearly implied that Napoleon desired him to do so.

Meantime, however, Gardane had returned to eastern Europe. He addressed Champagny on July 17, attempting to explain his departure, and how Persia actually called his second bluff, as they had not his first. He had kept out England's Captain Malcolm in 1808 by threatening to leave. He explained that he tried the same device to have Hartford

Jones denied. When Persia nevertheless admitted the latter, there remained nothing for him to do except to carry out his threat. Gardane wrote Joannin from Warsaw (on July 25) of Champagny's reprimand and directed the latter not to depart from Teheran unless forced to do so. Champagny also instructed him, on August 21, to hold firmly to his post, although Joannin had left already. The foreign minister revealed that Gardane had fallen into disgrace before the emperor because he had left. This instruction Joannin also received on October 13, at Trebizond rather than Teheran. Gardane did not consider his reprimand justified. Champagny almost ignored the minister's first explanation and asked him to put his motives into writing. This Gardane did, in August, in a curt letter that said even less than before and which revealed nothing new. The foreign minister thereupon replied with venom that none of the reasons listed could justify the departure. Gardane returned to Paris.[30]

Champagny countermanded Gardane's authorization for Lajard to come to Paris. Lajard must return to Persia—an onerous task for almost any Frenchman—and reside at the Persian court until the coming of a new chargé d'affaires. The three French officers still training the Persian army were complimented and promoted. Napoleon likewise bluntly informed the presumably remaining French staff that he did not consider the French mission terminated simply because of the appearance of an English negotiator in Persia. The foreign minister attempted some clarifications for the shah. Conditions admittedly had changed, owing to the French alliance with Russia at Tilsit. France now could hold only a mediating position, being friends of both the Persia and Russia who were at war. He sent word once more that Napoleon had ratified the all-but-forgotten convention promising to sell muskets to Persia, and he asserted that this certainly represented an act of friendship.

Meanwhile, Joannin had had a difficult time. He steadily lost in the diplomatic skirmishes with the British. His dispatch of September 12 from Tabriz indicated that it would be impossible for any French legation officer to remain in Persia, so successful had been Hartford Jones' campaign against Napoleon. On the other hand, Feth Ali wrote Napoleon a long, friendly letter that month. He expressed the real or feigned hope that France would still aid him to recover Georgia. The shah recalled the friendly relations of the preceding several years and stated that he had done what Gardane advised until at last it seemed that the French would not fulfill their pledges. Now, he had been encouraged anew by a communication from Asker Khan indicating that the French government would see that Georgia was restored to Persia. The latter had advised him that this would require time and patience, however, with Napoleon so busy in Spain and elsewhere.

Abbas Mirza feebly attempted to restore the connection. Joannin went to Trebizond, intending to proceed to Europe (this intention being known in Paris by mid-December). However, in mid-October he received the packet of dispatches revealing Napoleon's intention to maintain diplomatic relations with Persia. In caustic rejoinder to the dispatch of June 8 from Vienna, he said it seemed quite late to try to stop the progress of English influence in Persia.[31] There was no need to lock the door after the horse had been stolen.

All of Champagny's orders notwithstanding, the remnant of the once-imposing French staff had finally left Persia in September. These orders were in any event not received in time. Nerciat came to Trebizond also and proceeded to Constantinople. He had done little to justify his feeling of self-importance from the moment Gardane departed. Later, he served ineffectively as a spy in Syria. Raymond likewise went to Constantinople, to be ready to guide to Paris Asker Khan's successor, when and if the latter should appear there. The shah appointed Hussein Khan as the new envoy, although quite understandably the latter was recalled before he arrived in Paris. Unbelievably, Asker Khan was still in Paris, where he remained until June, 1810.

Lajard had not yet acted on his authority to return to France, although he could have returned to Persia as directed. Symbolic of the floundering indifference of French diplomacy in the Near East, was the slowness of the communications. Lajard went the other way, northward into Russia.[32] Of the dispersed staff, the always-obedient Joannin alone for a time heeded the direction received on October 13. His return to Tabriz early in December served little purpose. He engaged in several conferences there with Abbas Mirza and with Hassan Mirza, the crown prince's minister. The latter ordered him to move to Erivan. Again he left Tabriz, on December 18, the Persians getting him away by a ruse. They handed him the friendly letters of mid-September from the shah and the crown prince, together with directions to deliver them to Napoleon immediately. He actually departed from Persia on January 31, 1810. His dispatches place him in Constantinople on March 31 and in Paris on June 3.[33]

Napoleon's lightning campaigns having settled Austria's fate, Metternich, who was gradually achieving the ascendant position in foreign affairs over Count Stadion, negotiated the preliminaries for the Peace of Schönbrunn, together with Nugent and Champagny. In that peace of mid-October, Napoleon won much. Among the results was his organization of Carniola, Carinthia, and Croatia as the Illyrian Provinces and their addition to the command of Governor Marmont of Dalmatia.[34] He also directed his minister of the interior to intimate in a speech to the French legislative body that the severance of Galicia from Austria was not really political. Caulaincourt must show Russia the emperor's disinterestedness in that province by citing the protocols of the secret conferences preceding the peace. He cited his policy of concert with Russia in the Near East and in the Baltic. "Tsar Alexander has perceived how I have settled the question of Moldavia and Wallachia," he wrote. "I have helped along the peace with Sweden. A sentence in my speech will procure him peace with Turkey. What more can I do?" If the presence of a French consul at Bucharest should be an inconvenience to Russia, he would be recalled. Napoleon directed: "Caulaincourt must not fail to tell M. Rumiantsov that, all Frenchmen being born with the idea that France must protect Turkey, there are certain things which depend on protocol, and on circumstances. I cannot publicly proclaim the fact that I am abandoning Turkey but my speech leaves no doubt respecting the cession of Moldavia and Wallachia."[35]

Russia and Turkey continued at war, with little enthusiasm on either side. The tsar moved larger forces to the Danube, in order to take the initiative upon the end of the Austro-French war. Most of Constantinople's reports of Ottoman successes in the field against Russia in 1809 proved untrue. Certain Turkish commanders simply covered up their losses by fictitious reports which aroused false hopes. The correct information of Russia's occupation of the fortress of Ibraila early in 1810 came as quite a shock to the sultan's ministers. Thereupon, orders were issued to commanders of the Dardanelles castles to defend the entrance against a possible British attack. By friendly advice they prevented the British from sending a large ship of war through the Dardanelles; this hindrance was one act which angered Ambassador Adair.[36]

To recapitulate, we observe that Napoleon's Turkish and Persian policies fell to their nadir in the interlude following Erfurt. Upon his own initiative Gardane broke off diplomatic relations with Teheran. In 1809 the sole French political policy within the Ottoman Empire appeared to be to mark time. The French policy for the Ottoman Empire was to coöperate with Russia in the maintenance of most of that realm.

France could not act alone, owing to its alliance with Russia. The routine French Near Eastern official papers of the day were devoid of real interest. The reports of Latour-Maubourg from the key center of Constantinople assumed almost the same speculative character as the dozens from Consul David in inconsequential Bosnia.

London lost no time in attempting to capitalize on the great opportunity that might arise from the revolutionary change of governments at Constantinople and from Napoleon's coöperation with Russia. The new sultan seemed to represent an exceptional chance for the pro-English factions, helped along as they were by the absence of a French ambassador. British sympathizers within official Ottoman circles did not delay in concluding the Treaty of the Dardanelles with Great Britain. This treaty was not only the first significant international recognition of the sultan's rule of closure of the Straits to foreign warships while Turkey remained at peace, but also it loomed brightly in the eclipse of the remnant of Napoleonic policy in the Levant.

XVII

Rim of the Blockade

⊰ 1809-1814

NAPOLEON'S Continental Blockade proved ineffective in the Levant from its inception. He sought to close Europe to England, while the British counterblockade intended to cut off from Europe all neutral trade with Napoleon and his satellites. The dual blockade increased prices and profits, especially for the Egyptian producer and the Greek carrier. The deciding factor from the standpoint of the Near East was not policy but sea power. Only Britain possessed the naval strength requisite to enforce its orders. It is anyone's guess how the remnant of Napoleon's navy could have enforced on the high seas his order for neutrals to stay away from England. He decided he could enforce it at least on the land side. He ordered confiscated every neutral ship that allowed itself to be searched by the British, a rule which could be applied whenever such ships touched at ports controlled by himself and his dependable allies.

French agents in the field ordinarily were the last to admit—even if they recognized it—the collapse of the magic of the Napoleonic legend. If at a given time Napoleon nurtured no policy for their guidance, they counted on the fear of his blitzkriegs to hold his natural allies to a course of coöperation. More important than any given Napoleonic policy for Turkey was the policy which the Turks accepted for themselves. They earned their reputation for vacillation. They admitted divided loyalties. They habitually adhered to a given foreign policy only in such a hesitant manner that the shift of attitudes of a few men within the governing inner circle could change it. During the first half of 1809, the pro-English group was clearly in the ascendant at Constantinople. In this chapter we shall see how Latour-Maubourg labored, for the most part without success, to rebuild some pro-French sentiment and to have Turkey enforce the Continental Blockade.

According to an analysis by the chargé d'affaires at the end of September, 1809, Napoleon's occupation of Vienna encouraged Ottoman attitudes favorable to France. At the moment, "the alarming progress of the Russians" hinted at another shift of Ottoman policy. Napoleon's friends could make a better showing, convincing themselves once more of his indulgence and friendship at this time of new dangers. Latour-Maubourg could not as yet assume that this friendship was definite. There were the constant palace intrigues and the continued occupancy of the most important ministerial posts by the enemies of France. Foreign Minister Galib Effendi, "ordinarily a man of wise spirit, had gone over to the Moruzzis." Vahid Effendi, the leading negotiator at Paris and Finkenstein, who "pretended to be France's friend," negotiated the Treaty of the Dardanelles and thus proved to be pro-English. Vahid, like Galib, kept Latour-Maubourg uncertain of Turkish attitudes most of the time. While Galib was at military headquarters on the Danube, the important officers in foreign policy were the two Moruzzi brothers. A vociferous minor officer, Iset Bey, stood at the forefront of France's enemies within the governing circle. France's friends disclosed to the embassy many secret developments, the faithful Eugene and Antoine Franchini creating the contacts. These interpreters still had influence. They procured copies of two important secret documents, one a letter from Adair written at the Dardanelles in December and the other a missive revealing the anti-French views of the Moruzzis. They believed the letter had been written by the Moruzzis, then sent to Adair to be signed as his own.[1]

Napoleon improperly relegated the war in Spain almost to a side issue. He contented himself, throughout most of the period of 1809 to 1812, with personal rule from St. Cloud or from some other palace of suburban Paris. That the French policy for the Near and Middle East came to loose ends may by no means be attributed wholly to the Franco-Russian alliance and to the new peace settlement with Austria. Britain's sea power and its economic warfare figured significantly. Without adequate sea power, Napoleon's blockade of Europe against England could not be really effective. On its Levantine fringe, conditions weakened it.

What Near Eastern factors occupied Napoleon's interest at the time the British settled their quarrel with Turkey by the Treaty of the Dardanelles? For one thing, he did not like General Marmont's recommendation to arm 15,000 Croats without first making certain of their loyalty. He retained his unwarranted confidence that the Continental Blockade actually would restrict British trade in the Near East and in the Mediterranean generally.

way into the Levant by means of their own merchants, together with
the coöperation of the sultan's profit-taking Greek and other non-Mo-
hammedan subjects. The British government facilitated this trade by
granting Malta virtually a free-port status.[5] Western trade with Ottoman provinces could be reciprocal, for the Turkish agriculturalist ordinarily looked with disdain upon commerce and manufacture. He liked
to sell agricultural staples to Britain, taking its manufactures in exchange. England regarded such trade as highly desirable, especially for
its forces in Spain, although its eighteenth-century Tory type of governing aristocracy always talked of protecting indigenous agriculture.

As Britain steadily won the upper hand in the economic warfare involving Egypt, French agents dreamed of French-controlled land routes
to and across Constantinople and the Straits. The only alternative during war appeared to lie in the dormant plan for routes, primarily overland, around the eastern Mediterranean, with Salonika and Constantinople as the important intermediary depots. The French consuls never
tired of urging Paris to attempt to open up from the European side a
safe land route through Constantinople, at least for commerce. Bonaparte had failed to achieve such a route in 1799 by starting around from
Egypt. It was also suggested that neutral Turkish boats might carry
Egyptian produce through the Dardanelles to the Turkish capital, from
whence it would find markets in Europe by way of Balkan roads.[6]

Until 1811, Napoleon avoided anything in the Near East likely to
disrupt his coöperation with Russia. There seems little doubt, however,
that he planned an eventual utilization of the Balkans, possibly along
the line of the minimum territorial accretions he meant to win from
bartering with his Russian ally. Caulaincourt's refusal to block out all
of Serbia for Austria in his secret discussions of March, 1808 (chap.
xiii) suggests that Napoleon may have welcomed negotiations with certain Serb leaders. The rebel leader, Karageorge, sent his representative,
R. Vucinich, to contact Napoleon in Vienna in October, 1809, and
tender to France several Serb fortresses. M. Meriaze took it upon himself to aid this Serbian agent, who in 1810 went to Paris, where he was
encouraged to remain at French expense for nearly three years. Yet he
was never given a favorable decision.

French agents could inveigh against Ali Pasha of Albania, for they
despaired of bringing him around to their cause. Latour-Maubourg complained ever more earnestly against the pasha's jealousy of the French in
the Illyrian Provinces. The documents reveal that the French chargé

d'affaires was watching everything and interposing objections when he could. When Turkey slightly delayed Adair's audience of leave, Latour-Maubourg wished to know the reason. He also complained of the barbarity of a Turkish naval commander, who allowed the ears of a slave, a French subject, to be cut off. In consequence of changes in theTurkish cabinet in July, 1810, we find Ali Pasha ordered once again to hold good relations with the governor of Corfu and to furnish him with supplies.[7]

The general trend toward insubordination in the Ottoman provinces stimulated Near Eastern nationalism. The intermittent rebellions among the janissaries at Constantinople indicated the trend, while the insubordination became constant in Albania, Serbia, and Egypt. Mehemet Ali of Egypt led the governors who consistently earned heavy profits from the wartime grain trade with Malta. The French not only lost this contest, but also the internal politics there subjected their agents to what they considered more or less dangerous exposure. Drovetti, Napoleon's consul general at Cairo, once lamented Egypt's being a country from which Europeans could hope for little while fearing all. Mehemet Ali tolerated British commerce in defiance of Napoleon's blockade and even encouraged Egypt's lucrative trade with Malta. In that British-held island he established an Egyptian depot from which he could expedite the grain intended for British forces in Portugal and Spain. British manufactures often came to Alexandria on board neutral Austria's vessels, these in turn carrying away local produce destined for Malta. French agents persevered, largely without success, in their attempts to halt the trade with Malta.

In defiance of the capitulations, of the Continental Blockade, and of all the iterated decrees by Sultan Mahmud, Mehemet Ali established a monopolistic system for Egypt's foreign trade. He steadily augmented the export rates in order to meet his growing military requirements, among them the campaigns to conquer Arabia. He proceeded to liquidate his weakest neighbors in the characteristic manner of dictators. In 1811 he destroyed the Mamelukes who had been responsible earlier for his elevation to power.

Greek and Turkish ship captains, often friendly to Napoleon, felt themselves in constant danger from the enemies of the French throughout the Levant. Consul Saint Marcel at Alexandria often complained of his inability to obtain enforcement of the Continental Blockade. Upon the receipt of instructions, the French agents held themselves aloof from the internal politics of Egypt. British intimations, rather than concrete developments, kept alive the threat of a new French invasion of Egypt. The appearance of an armed French merchantman at Alexandria in March, 1808, had alarmed the pasha, according to consular accounts. The Treaty of the Dardanelles had ended the uncertainty of legal trade so far as concerned England; three English vessels arrived at Suez from India in May, 1809.[8] The restoration of trade authorized by that treaty encouraged the increases recorded in the exchanges between Alexandria and Malta. French agents early in 1809 arrived at a belief, without documentary evidence for it, in a secret British understanding with Mehemet Ali for this trade, which was thought to have been entered into at the time the British evacuated Alexandria in September, 1807.

Over French protest Mehemet Ali facilitated the trade with England in every particular except price. British purchasing agents usually had gold in hand to discharge their trade balances. The governor's monopolistic prices caused them to disburse more gold sooner. His scheme would work so long as he had no competition from Russia and little from Turkey's Danubian provinces. He interposed handicaps to anchoring British vessels of war in Egyptian ports, as always evincing the attitude that it would be well to play safe with Napoleon. He craftily excused himself to Drovetti for permitting and encouraging the growing trade with England, when confronted by the sultan's nonrescinded order for him to enforce the Continental Blockade. He wished to finish with the Mamelukes, he explained, whom Bonaparte knew well from his battles with them in 1798. He could thereby render it impossible for them to align themselves with their British partisans. He needed the stronger army, and its strength had to come from the profits from the trade with Malta.

Because the British encouraged both pasha and Mamelukes, Mehemet Ali on occasion encouraged the French and at other times kept a watchful eye on them. He always listened alertly to British news of the sailings of French warships to and from Toulon. No one could forget that the French emperor was the selfsame Napoleon Bonaparte who had conquered Egypt through a surprise attack in 1798.[9] Egypt's trade increased, as did Mehemet Ali's profits. At the opening of 1811, one could expect thirty or forty cargo ships from Malta. Egyptian attitudes toward the British had changed materially by then. The lush profits brought the pasha completely around from his hesitant acceptance of them. The sultan, for his part, more and more often accorded Napoleon only lip service. He repeated his prohibition against the Egyptian and the Greek trade with England. Mehemet Ali ignored the decree, as was expected, explaining to Drovetti that he feared an English invasion of Egypt if he halted the trade.[10]

Mehemet Ali intended to strengthen his own position in Egypt and to prepare that province, if not for full independence, at least for the rank of a detached Barbary Regency. A portion of his profits therefore went into the beginnings of an Egyptian navy. In November, 1810, he suggested to Drovetti that France might profit by aiding him. Because Drovetti had been instructed to refrain from taking sides in Ottoman internal politics, however, he tendered no encouragement. For a time thereafter the pasha looked coldly on all Frenchmen. The importance lay in Mehemet Ali's moves not at that time, but afterwards. Drovetti later favored France's indirect mastery of Egypt through the use of Mehemet Ali as its lieutenant to conquer Algeria. The France of the Bourbon restoration eventually adopted Drovetti's scheme, in 1829. When the scheme failed, France alone went into Algeria in 1830.[11]

With Britain gradually taking most of Smyrna's trade, Vice-consul Fourçade of Sinop had recommended earlier a plausible, if desperate, remedy: he would open French commerce with Asia by way of the Germanies and the Black Sea. He envisaged a substitute there for Smyrna and at the same time a means to avoid the long caravan journeys at the south. He considered Sinop an excellent center for commerce coming from across the Danube. From Sinop, he believed commerce could radiate to Samsun, Amasia, Tokat, Caesarea, and Adana. It was readily appreciated that no route to those areas could be direct. He had also suggested an alternative route, south from Odessa to Constantinople and thence to Smyrna and Adana.[12] Several French commercial houses in Smyrna and Corfu solicited authorization to arm merchant ships. Champagny recommended these suggestions to the navy in November, 1809. The navy sent six letters of marque to Latour-Maubourg and Governor Donzelot, to be distributed to French producers of armaments. These permitted the arming of merchant ships at Constantinople, Smyrna, and the Ionian Islands.[13]

Much speculation and some news concerned the progress of Russia's army in 1810. When April brought campaign weather once more, the Turks hoped to renew the fighting. The grand vizir became seriously ill at camp, however, and Russia's campaigning also was less vigorous than expected, partly from illness in the Russian army and partly from the relatively small numbers engaged on both sides. The renewed conflict became a struggle in the field for Wallachia, Moldavia already being in Russian hands. General Kemenski, the conqueror of Finland, entered the picture. He scored the greatest successes of 1810, successively occupying Silistria, Sistova, and Ruschuk, the large fortresses guarding the passages of the Danube.

Occasional fragments in the relatively uninteresting archive records for 1810 suggest that Napoleon was already beginning to play the difficult and dangerous game (not manifest before) of secretly circumventing his alliance with Russia. As an example, there was Theologue, the first interpreter of the Ottoman embassy in Paris, who engaged in occasional off-the-record discussions in the private service of Napoleon and Champagny. If his service were good, he might be well paid for it. We find him revealing a conversation with the Ottoman ambassador, who expressed disquietude at the continued marks of consideration accorded Russia's personnel in Paris. Theologue argued to the ambassador, pretending to reveal a high state secret, that all such demonstrations represented only surface manifestations necessitated by policy. When Napoleon read Theologue's report, he considered it to possess such "an air of truth" that he authorized 6,000 francs for him.[14]

When Ambassador Asker Khan finally departed from Paris in June, 1810, he carried away presents and other objects of English manufacture. Champagny issued his passports, announcing that Jaubert would travel with him to Strasbourg and that Georges Outrey, appointed vice-consul at Bagdad, would be his guide-companion all the way to Persia. Napoleon acceded to the ambassador's parting suggestion by authorizing the service in Persia of several French officers, a surgeon, and three mechanics. Asker, however, did not avail himself of the service after requesting it.

Asker Khan's journey seemed to present to Napoleon a new opportunity to reopen his legation in Teheran, and hence the French emperor made an—overcautious—attempt in that direction. From the time of the ambassador's arrival in Paris on July 22, 1808, Outrey had served as interpreter for Asker. To him Napoleon assigned the task of rediscovering or reopening relations with Persia. According to the secret instructions given him, he must serve as Napoleon's chargé d'affaires in Persia if the circumstances permitted. He could reside in Teheran under that title and thus reëstablish the French mission.

Outrey's instructions were issued May 28, 1810. They recalled that Minister Gardane left because of the arrival of the successful British

competitor, Sir Hartford Jones, and that Chargé d'Affaires Joannin also
departed because of the successful British intrigues. Napoleon, however,
did not consider that this constituted an interruption of his official relations with Persia. Outrey must work cautiously, at first revealing only
his title of vice-consul to Bagdad; that of chargé d'affaires could be
used whenever the time was ripe. Outrey would travel to Teheran ostensibly as an interpreter. If, upon arrival, he found suitable conditions,
he then would present the letter accrediting him to Persia and settle
down to combating English influence. He carried letters to Abbas
Mirza and others, these also to be transmitted only if he remained in
Persia under the desired title.

Champagny directed Outrey to follow a pro-Russian policy. He stated
in the instructions that Persia had lost Georgia in a military sense,
several years earlier. Its army had not succeeded in recovering that province. Napoleon by no means had guaranteed Persia's recovery of Georgia.
He had promised his best efforts to have Russia evacuate it. He had
done all he could, the interests of one ally being in direct conflict with
the interests of another ally. Since Gardane had committed France beyond that policy, Napoleon disavowed him. The minister should not
have made any statements to give Persia exaggerated hopes of assistance.
If Persia should be found friendly (of which Outrey would advise) Napoleon would begin to send the 20,000 muskets and the ammunition
which Gardane had promised. Earlier the emperor had ratified the agreement and had issued orders to fulfill it but had suspended the execution
of the order when news came of Persia's pro-British conduct.

Alternative instructions outlined Outrey's duties as vice-consul in
Bagdad, a position envisaged as more political than consular. France
maintained no political agent there at the time, although it was an important point for the observation of English activities. No suggestion
was revealed that Napoleon intended to play off the pasha of Bagdad
against the shah, taking advantage of their well-known rivalry. Outrey
thus possessed instructions to reopen relations in Persia, if he could, or
alternatively to proceed to Bagdad.[15]

The Persian ambassador's considerable party included his staff assistants and personal servants; it required fifty horses to pull the several
stagecoaches they needed. Outrey duly accompanied the group to Constantinople. Joannin, who arrived in Paris in July, 1810, fared better
than had Gardane, for Napoleon approved his return. Lajard was ordered
home from Russia, Napoleon at last being convinced that Gardane had

judged correctly the pro-English conduct of Persia. Lajard finally arrived in Paris on November 7, to be paid a full salary as resident chargé d'affaires in Persia, although he had not actually served in that capacity.[16] One reason for Napoleon's approving the departure of these agents, in contrast with his hostile reception of Gardane, had to do with an official confession. With the departure of Asker Khan from Paris, Napoleon at last recognized that his Persian policy had collapsed. That is to say, not until mid-1810 did both France and Persia publicly acknowledge the reality of what had happened upon Napoleon's alliance with Alexander at Tilsit in July, 1807.

Asker Khan and his party remained in Constantinople for several weeks, Outrey thus having a good opportunity to report developments promptly. The failure of Napoleon's policy was soon reflected by Asker Khan's treatment of him. Also, the guide reported (September 26) the treason of one of the ambassador's staff, who deserted, presumably to the British, upon their arrival on August 21. Throughout the journey from Paris to Constantinople, Asker Khan had daily protested his devotion to Napoleon and to France, so Outrey's report reveals. The ambassador had assured the latter of his perfect welcome in Teheran. However, after a month in Constantinople Outrey reported that Asker turned his eyes toward the English and perhaps talked with them. The ambassador certainly changed his attitude toward Outrey. This became clear when he discouraged the latter from making the trip to Teheran. Like all French officials arriving in the Turkish capital throughout the Napoleonic period, Outrey consulted Ruffin. Thereupon he informed the Persian ambassador that he must travel all the way to Teheran as Napoleon had directed, after which he would proceed to his assigned post in Bagdad. Then Asker Khan requested Outrey not to leave with him but to journey two days behind him for some distance out of Constantinople, when they would meet and enter Persia together. The latter consulted Latour-Maubourg, who advised reliance on the Persian ambassador's promise to wait for Outrey to catch up. In consequence, the ex-ambassador departed from Constantinople on October 14 and Outrey two days later. But Napoleon's envoy never caught up with the Persian.[17]

Among the military personalities on the rim of the blockade, General Marmont seems to have seen the handwriting on the wall more clearly than others. He had long smarted at the lack of activity of his command in Dalmatia. That it represented the key control area for the Balkan rim of policy did not measure up to his personal ambition. Spain and Portugal held the spotlight so consistently that Napoleon transferred Marmont there, appointing General Dondolo to succeed him in 1810. Marmont could at last command a large army and assist Marshal Soult to fight the indomitable Arthur Wellesley.

Piracy by the Barbary corsairs also restricted what little Mediterranean trade remained to France. The British doubtless would have suffered from their raids also, if they had not been so able to protect their commerce. The virtually independent ruler of Algeria, markedly hostile to France since 1807, refused to deal with French consuls in 1809. He exacted financial levies from French subjects and neglected to pay reparation for damages. To strike back, Napoleon ordered sequestered all Ottoman vessels entering the ports of the Illyrian Provinces. Their papers must be sent to the director-general of customs in Paris, who reported to Napoleon himself in "commerce council." From the papers they would decide which ships to confiscate and which to release (October 2, 1810). Latour-Maubourg's complaints produced two lip-service correctives by Sultan Mahmud in February, 1811. These, directed respectively to Tripoli and Tunis, were without practical result. Britain, moreover, saw to it that France could not aid Turkey to enforce such orders, even had the latter really wished to do so.

Napoleon virtually finished with his activity in the Near East by having surveys made of the segments where he had started, Egypt and Syria. He commanded two travelers to go there in 1810. What a contrast to the 40,000 he had led to Egypt in 1798! Interesting among the unexciting developments in a French approach to a more active policy for the Near East in 1810 was Napoleon's order of June 20, out of a clear sky, for secret information respecting these two Ottoman provinces. He desired Boutin to extend his Near Eastern "commercial" mission to Egypt, in order to study anew the fortifications of the delta of the Nile and to consider methods for troop movements. This agent of his strategic services fell into English hands, however.

Without awaiting Boutin's results, Paris dispatched a second envoy with the same objectives. In this case Champagny used the ambitious but hesitant Nerciat, recently returned from Persia. The foreign minister spent several hours drafting Nerciat's special instructions in June, 1810, only to have them canceled by Napoleon and a letter dated October 17 substituted for them. Napoleon wished Nerciat to content himself with visits to Egypt and Syria. It was intended that the agent should remain away for a year, and that he should acquire the latest information about the places Napoleon personally knew so well, namely Acre, Jaffa, Rosetta, Alexandria, and the citadel of Cairo. He must study the political situation, including factionalism within these Ottoman provinces. He would travel, like Boutin, as a naturalist, "under pretext of science and medicine."[18]

Let us follow the Nerciat mission. His assignment proved long and difficult, owing in part to his excessive caution. He advanced slowly, always fearing arrest by Napoleon's enemies and always overestimating his own importance. He visited in Vienna long enough to confuse his imaginary enemies. He arrived in Constantinople only on May 6, 1811. There he believed his secret mission was viewed with suspicion; in his opinion, some official Frenchmen had been indiscreet. His reports show him to have been in Smyrna on July 22 and at Rhodes, where he learned of Boutin's capture, on August 16. Nerciat entered Syria in September, by way of Alexandretta. He was at Acre and its environs during the summer of 1812. He wandered about, unable even to send in reports, during 1813 and 1814. He finally took passage on a boat for France from Cyprus on March 28, 1815, only to turn back to await the outcome of events involved in Napoleon's "hundred days" of restored rule. He finally landed at Marseille, on December 17, 1816. His peregrinations had done neither himself nor the fallen emperor any service.[19]

Halet Effendi, the foreign minister of Mustapha IV's regime in 1808, whom the French hated, returned from exile in March, 1810. He attempted to use Latour-Maubourg as a steppingstone for his return to power. If he could have his old position again, he promised, he would follow a pro-French policy. The chargé d'affaires could not listen to so well-known an opponent of Napoleon. Foreign Minister Galib died in 1811, after three years of generally pro-English and anti-French policy under Sultan Mahmud II. The documents of the time reveal no cordiality, no intimacy, in fact little business of any kind, for Latour-Maubourg.[20]

British frigates retained their mastery of the Mediterranean. The official dispatches throughout 1811 and 1812 uniformly verified the fact that Napoleon's blockade did not function anywhere in the Levant. Egypt's wartime trade reached its peak in 1811, the British being the only important European traders there. Mehemet Ali's extraordinary profits from the grain exports made him the richest and most powerful of Ottoman pashas. As he successively (he would say necessarily) extended and protected his monopolies, he became the exclusive export merchant for Egypt. Drovetti and Saint Marcel despaired of enforcing the blockade. They agreed that Egyptian trade could not really come again to France until after peace, or until after a miraculous restoration of France's sea communications in the Mediterranean.[21]

Latour-Maubourg reluctantly admitted, in September, 1811, the failure of the Continental Blockade. He stated in a significant report that, owing to the Treaty of Tilsit, violent language had had to be employed to obtain any concessions at all from Turkey. The sultan's ministers gave France neither their confidence nor their good will. He attributed the attitude to Napoleon's silence respecting a policy for the Ottoman Empire. Sometimes any statements by the chargé d'affaires to Turkey had a worse effect than his saying nothing. He urgently renewed his plea—of three years' standing—to be given some new basis for restoring French influence. He observed that no inactive foreign envoy could live in Constantinople in dignity and honor. French shipping suffered thousands of affronts in the neighboring islands, he said, and the sultan seemed powerless to prevent them. Gloomily, he stated, "If we insist energetically on obtaining satisfaction, we expose our dignity to entire loss. English war frigates in the Aegean Sea always have more effect than our threats. If, on the other hand, we submit to abuse without protest, we set a pernicious example." He recommended that all French trading vessels remain far away from Turkey. The Continental Blockade troubled British commerce only a little, but it harmed French influence at Constantinople greatly. Latour-Maubourg believed the one chance to accomplish something might be to station a few French frigates at Smyrna, "if under a very prudent commander." Despite Turkey's orders, he stressed, in not a single port of the Levant did the British find their trade actually excluded.[22]

Napoleon resumed for a moment in February, 1811, during a war scare over Poland, his long-defunct negotiations for an alliance with Sultan Mahmud. He proceeded under the strange assumption that he could pick up at will where he had left off when going over to Russia's side in 1807. At a time when everyone sensed exceptional coolness in French relations with Russia, Napoleon directed Latour-Maubourg to reopen the discussions automatically disrupted by the Franco-Russian alliance at Tilsit. Instructions of April authorized an overture for a permanent alliance with the sultan: France offered to support Turkey's regaining the Principalities and the Crimea, the same lure used in 1806. Turkey remembered well being left in the lurch, and hence Latour-

Maubourg could accomplish nothing. It would have been impossible for the Turks not to perceive Napoleon's real object: again to employ their power and position for a diversion at the south against Russia's military forces while he invaded Russia.

The recall of Ambassador Caulaincourt testified to Napoleon's displeasure with Tsar Alexander. In May, he notified the world of a change of foreign policy by replacing Champagny (the Duke of Cadore), the personification of his policy of alliance with Russia. He named as foreign minister the nonentity who had long served as his secretary of state, Maret (the Duke of Bassano). Marshal Jacques Lauriston went to St. Petersburg, and Caulaincourt was received coldly in a five-hour conference at Saint Cloud on June 5, 1811. The ex-ambassador still held the opinion with respect to the Dardanelles that had marked his secret negotiations of 1808, namely that Russia must not have them (chap. xiii).

Constantinople did not for a long time know of a new war scare, the fear renewed in late 1811 of a Franco-Russian conflict. The city finally heard whispers of it. The practical conditions for a *de facto* Franco-Turkish alliance, without a formal treaty, would emerge if France attacked Russia. This would, in effect, restore conditions to what they had been before the Franco-Russian battle of Friedland in June, 1807, provided Russia and Turkey did not make peace beforehand. Yet autumn reports heralded a pending Franco-Russian *rapprochement* which stimulated new talk of Turkish peace with Russia, near the end of December. Would no big war come at the north, after all? Latour-Maubourg felt himself called upon to deny the rumor, as a means of holding Turkey at war.[23]

The approaching French invasion of Russia obviously altered the course of the Russo-Turkish war.

On the one hand, there was the French overture to Turkey. Maret repeated Napoleon's proposal for an alliance with Turkey, on January 21, 1812. Too impatient to await the arrival of Nedjib Effendi, the new Turkish ambassador in Paris, the emperor sent to Latour-Maubourg draft agreements of an ostensible treaty, a secret alliance, and a military convention as a basis for his negotiations in Constantinople. The secret treaty promised the restoration of Moldavia and Wallachia to Turkey, together with the Crimea; it required Turkey to enforce the Continental Blockade against Great Britain. If France attacked Russia through Poland, the military convention called for Turkey to attack simultaneously along the Danube.[24]

On the other hand, there was the British navy. The English sea power could threaten a pincer against Turkey in concert with Russia's action on land. Reports suggest that England threatened to force the Straits and burn Constantinople, if the sultan acceded to Napoleon's demand.

The Russian influence remained the most direct of the several influences bearing on Turkey. Foreseeing the need for relief on his Balkan front, Tsar Alexander moderated his terms early in 1812 to ask for Moldavia only, together with an indemnity. He demanded virtual independence for Wallachia and Serbia, however, which Sultan Mahmud could not concede. Everyone expected a compromise. Alexander gave way once more, to facilitate the negotiations. He offered to return both Moldavia and Wallachia to Turkey. Thus ended, on May 28, 1812, the Russo-Turkish war fought primarily for the benefit of Emperor Napoleon.

The treaty settlement is known as the Peace of Bucharest. By it the tsar restored Moldavia and Wallachia to Turkey, although he renewed their considerable local autonomy, originally stipulated in 1774. Russia acquired most of Bessarabia. The treaty stipulated autonomy for Serbia but permitted Turkish forces to garrison the fortresses there. Russia would hold the large islands comprising the Danube delta, these thenceforth to be unfortified. The merchant vessels of Turkey and Russia must possess complete freedom of commercial navigation on the Danube River, with Russian vessels of war forbidden to sail beyond that river's confluence with the Prut. The treaty confirmed Russia's general commercial prerogatives contained in the capitulations, those respecting Tunisia, Algeria, and Tripoli being especially mentioned.

All the previous Russo-Turkish treaties were confirmed, except those which "the effect of time" rendered obsolete. Such phrasing, among other results, had the effect of terminating legally the long-defunct Russo-Turkish alliance of 1805, together with its exceptional permission for Russian warships to navigate the Straits. It ended Russia's claims to transit connections with the Ionian Islands; these dated back to 1800, but they had actually been handed over to France in 1807. The Peace of Bucharest mentioned neither the Turkish rule of closure of the Straits nor a Russian acceptance of the exclusion of foreign warships so long as Turkey remained at peace—the restriction which Great Britain had accepted in 1809.

The treaty gave Turkey another day of grace as to territorial integrity, a respite which was useful also for internal reconstruction. With the peace it emerged almost unchanged in a territorial and military sense, perhaps even stronger than before. Only a dispute over the Russo-Turkish frontier in Asia marred Turkey's relations with Russia. This unfinished business would be taken up by Tsar Alexander with vigor after Napoleon should be eliminated from the European scene.[25] Napoleon's invasion of Russia, in June, 1812, broke off for the time any further negotiations with Turkey respecting the contested lands. Except for the disputed frontier, the Peace of Bucharest removed the Near East from the general diplomatic scene of Napoleon's activities for the last three years.

Meanwhile, the French emperor had returned to his policy, best personified by Sebastiani, of strong diplomatic representation at Constantinople. Napoleon never personally visited the Dardanelles, nor did he even enter southeastern Europe. Although he had campaigned in 1798 and 1799 across the eastern Mediterranean, in Egypt and Syria, and had led armies into northeastern Europe in 1807 and 1812, he never did learn firsthand of conditions in Constantinople. He now appointed as ambassador another military figure, this time General Andreossy, who had served as ambassador in Vienna. Andreossy was instructed to urge Turkey to reconquer all the provinces taken by Russia. The new ambassador appeared in Constantinople six months too late, however, for the Turks were unwilling to be left in the lurch a second time. Unaware of the approach of Russo-Turkish peace, Napoleon moreover agreed with the Habsburgs to uphold Turkey's integrity, in an alliance made on March 14. They reciprocally guaranteed their territories. They promised mutual support if either power should be attacked or menaced. Of potential significance for our problem, they guaranteed the integrity of the Ottoman territories in Europe. They invited the sultan to accede to their alliance.[26] Thus Austria almost accidentally inaugurated the Turcophile policy which would become one of the most notable factors in the Near East situation during the ensuing decades.

Napoleon was successful so long as he did not fight on two military fronts. His armies usually triumphed, down to the venture initiated by himself in Russia in 1812, when his best army was left to continue its indecisive struggle in Spain. Shrewd observers could foresee the Napoleonic invasion of Russia. It proved a blitzkrieg, launched characteristically without warning. There seems no need to retrace here its details or the details of the other wars of 1812. The Russo-Persian war remained inactive. France's war against England in Spain and Portugal would reach a new climax when Wellington entered Madrid in August, 1812, although that particular occupation proved temporary. The United States declared war on Great Britain in the month in which Napoleon invaded Russia.

The well-known Franco-Russian war of 1812 proceeded much according to Napoleon's schedule for several weeks.[27] Meanwhile, there was little diplomacy. The impatient Napoleon, now in Moscow, thus summarized, at the end of September, what he did not know of affairs elsewhere: he had had no news from Warsaw, little from Vienna, none from Constantinople, and none from America. Travel conditions normally required six days for communications between Vilna and Moscow. Even without news from the Near East, Napoleon did not miss a great deal, for little of consequence occurred there. French issues dragged along with aloof Algeria. He could have read about these in the official correspondence of the day from Constantinople. France still did not wish to break with the Algerian Regency, out of fear that the only result would be to increase Britain's commercial superiority there.

Napoleon exercised his troops and waited in Russia while a series of military disasters sealed the doom of his army in Spain. He finally procured a copy of the Russo-Turkish treaty, discovering it in a newspaper in Moscow. Sending the discovery to Foreign Minister Maret at Warsaw, he stated, "It appears that you have not received it from Constantinople, for you have not sent it to me."[28]

While in ignominious retreat across Lithuania,[29] early in December, Napoleon quitted the remnant of the French army to hasten back to Paris with Caulaincourt, Duroc, and Lefebvre. He decided to transfer his command to Murat before returning to Vilna, making the announcement to his principal marshals on December 4. He wished to cross the Germanies in advance of news of the collapse of his Grand Army. Should it become known at a time of his absence, it would perhaps precipitate a general insurrection against him. He must be in Paris as soon as possible to take measures in person to meet the serious situation. In less than fifteen days the small party traversed Poland and Germany.

Their rapid travel placed them back in Paris on December 18, 1812, where Napoleon promptly set to work to restore the shattered confidence. A dispatch to Ambassador Andreossy on December 22, four days after the return, furnishes an illustration of his fictitious official statements. He spread the pious fraud that the Grand Army would be forced to winter between the Niemen and the Vistula, owing to losses of war material and horses and the winter's coming too early that year. The losses would be repaired; everything would be changed by March, 1813. He had had his old ally Turkey in mind, he said, when fighting Russia. Another dispatch on December 29 advised against any credence being given to the published Russian reports of French losses. Maret advised Andreossy on January 13 that 350,000 men had been recruited by the Ministry of War.[30]

The outstanding illustration of Napoleon's initial attempt to conceal the catastrophe is his letter of January to Emperor Francis in Vienna, his father-in-law. This he laboriously redrafted several times, the letter finally overdoing the falsehoods of his communication to Turkey. In words and phrases added with his own pen, he assured the emperor that Maria Louisa would not be sent home. The annotated original of this letter is now a prized piece among the emperor's specially bound original papers reposing in the "secret room" of the Ministry of Foreign Affairs in Paris.

Turkey could not yet know positively the magnitude of Napoleon's blunder and defeat in his Russian adventure. Official reports in February sharply conflicted. Word from Paris seemed to give credence to the French emperor's claim that he would take care of Russia that spring. Turkey had no special need to seek Napoleon as an ally, however, having signed peace with Russia. The Ottoman Empire simply stood between the rival camps of the great powers, as they proceeded to form themselves into what some at the moment called a new balance of power, but which we know to have been Napoleon versus the sixth coalition against him, the one which held the preponderance of power.

As long as Napoleon's empire remained intact, Turkey benefited by a balance of European strength; if neutral between the great-power contenders, it might be protected by either side. Turkey's blatant announcement of policy in January and February, 1813, reflected the situation. The coalition considered an expedition into Italy, and Foreign Secretary Castlereagh sought favors from Turkey, including permission for Russia's vessels of war to pass the Straits. The Ottoman ministry refused positively, still being hostile to Russia and not wishing to risk an offense to Napoleonic France whose remaining potentialities could not be underrated. The legend of Napoleon had reappeared. British Ambassador Robert Liston counterproposed that Russian soldiers make their way through the Straits as unnoticed passengers, since Russia's merchant vessels under the new treaty were free from search. This was not attempted, because of the difficulty of keeping secret the transport of horses and heavy war equipment.

Castlereagh thought it might be a good plan for Russia and Turkey to form an alliance in order to help terminate Napoleon's imperial career. The truth of his complete defeat in Russia was now no longer concealed; there was talk of a knockout blow. Liston attempted in March, 1813, to teach Turkey's ministers the theory of permanent hostility between nations—the theory that Napoleon had used with telling effect in discussions with Tsar Alexander at Tilsit. Liston told the Ottomans:

When two great nations [Russia and Turkey] are placed near each other and become rivals and what is termed natural enemies, they have it in their power to follow three different lines of conduct. They may live in a state of constant enmity and painful suspicion, in a succession of quarrels and hostilities which, without having a decisive effect upon the fate of either country, consume their strength and mar their prosperity. They may go to war with their utmost energy and obstinately continue the contest until one of the parties is reduced to such a state of inferiority as to give the other no further alarm. Or they may determine amicably to adjust their differences, to settle their reciprocal interests and claims in such a manner as to leave no room for future dispute, and thenceforward live on a footing of amity and concord which may promote the happiness of each and inspire other powers with sentiments of respect.[31]

When the sixth coalition formed, in direct consequence of Napoleon's debacle in Russia, Turkey still guarded its neutrality. Thus the Near East remained virtually outside the Napoleonic theater from 1812 to 1815. These were interesting years for Turkey, years when the Ottomans attempted to interfere with Russia's grain trade through the Dardanelles and when Castlereagh haltingly developed a British policy for Turkey.

The Ottoman Empire took advantage of the changing conditions to try, without success, to win back the economic prerogatives given or bartered away long before or lost by defeat at arms. Turkey soon realized it must handle its new commercial treaties, now in effect with several powers, not merely in the casual manner it treated the former unilateral capitulations. Great Britain and Russia stood at the forefront in seeing to it that Turkey did not unduly restrict their trade. Tsar Alexander's minister to Constantinople, A. Italinski, had returned to his post immediately after the Peace of Bucharest.

French influence now could win only lip service from Constantinople.

It had not seemed so weak in January, 1813, before Turkey became aware of Napoleon's disaster. Sultan Mahmud then issued special orders for Napoleon's benefit. He directed the dey of Algeria to redress the French grievances and restore the capitulations. Everyone understood, however, that the dey would do as he pleased, as he always did. Napoleon's Ambassador Andreossy admitted that that governor was quite powerful enough to act independently of the sultan. Reports after nine months confirmed that nothing resulted from the new directive.[32]

Italinski consistently endeavored to hold the Straits open for the bumper harvests of Russian grain now available to the allies. With better and cheaper cereals than those from Egypt, the Russian competition cut into Mehemet Ali's profits from his wartime monopoly. The Peninsular War at last was ended, and less grain was required in Spain. Moreover, the pasha's general trade with Malta diminished sharply upon the reopening of the Black Sea. The latter region presented to European merchants, so they believed for the moment, their chance to break Mehemet Ali's monopoly. But they fruitlessly invoked the Ottoman capitulations to restrain the pasha from interference with their trade in Egypt.[33]

More pertinent for Ottoman policy was Turkey's claim that a grain scarcity existed in January, 1813. That nation's efforts to solve the problem were concentrated in the Dardanelles and Bosporus. Whether the scarcity was real or fancied, any preëmption of foreign grain discovered in transit through the Straits conceivably would aid Egypt as Russia's competitor. At the time, Turkey took for granted that Napoleon would extricate himself from the reported difficulties in wintertime Russia. Whatever the extenuating circumstances, the sultan, in defiance of the promises to Russia, boldly prohibited shipments of grain through the Straits. Of the Russian concessions renewed by the Peace of Bucharest, one had restored the immunity from any Ottoman search of Russian vessels. Italinski regularly insisted that this immunity be respected.

The Russian minister and the Turks held firmly to their opposing views. Several grain freighters appeared in the Bosporus and their masters properly refused to permit Ottoman searches. These vessels threatened to force their way through the Straits, whereupon Turkey ordered sunk any vessels that attempted to pass in defiance of the prescribed search. A renewal of the Russo-Turkish war threatened. It was avoided by a combination of the resourcefulness of the ships' masters with the willingness of Ottoman officials to accept comparatively high bribes. The receipt of more accurate news of the fate of Napoleon's armies in Russia also blunted the edge of Turkey's insistence. The ships in question duly sailed into the Mediterranean.

To provide for all cases, however, Italinski accepted a compromise whereby one-half the Russian grain found in the Straits should be turned over to Turkey. The prescribed Ottoman prices would be accepted, on condition that the other half be accorded unhindered passage. Turkey thereby obtained an adequate supply of grain and Russia's merchants expected augmented profits from the remaining half. In practice, however, Turkey and the Ottoman agents lost in the arrangement. Not one-fourth of the grain was actually landed at Constantinople, and thus the Russians saved the bribes.[34]

In any event, the Dardanelles would be a factor against Napoleon whenever Russia's grain helped to supply British forces in Malta, Spain, or elsewhere. Britons argued that if Russia could enjoy unrestricted commercial navigation of the Straits, so could they. Castlereagh and Liston contended that British rights must equal the Russian respecting all commerce with and through Turkey, in virtue of the Treaty of the Dardanelles in 1809.

Britons also entered into a working compromise arrangement for their trade and navigation. They could hardly debate the general issue at a time when further Napoleonic potentialities clouded Europe's skies. They also argued against the existence of any extreme urgency, for fear that pressure might again force Turkey into a pro-Napoleonic policy. The plain truth is that Britain and Russia desired to leave Turkey undisturbed in its neutrality. A recent parallel may be found in the policy of the Anglo-Russian-American coalition in 1943, when it employed gentle persuasion toward Turkey, not coercion, for there was a Hitler to humble. When by 1944 the Allies wished Turkey to participate in the war, they came out about as well with the Republic of Turkey as did the allied coalition of Castlereagh's time with Sultan Mahmud's Turkey: Castlereagh had no success.

The compromise economic arrangement of 1813 also forestalled a possible Russian advantage over England. Liston thus sanctioned the practice of the embassy's issuing or approving fictitious manifests to cover the prohibited produce. If labeled something else by an embassy official, wheat and tallow could be sent through the Straits without fear of preëmption by Turkey. The documents reveal that Turkey illogically considered that it had won this diplomatic skirmish.

The British merchants for fifteen years thereafter found little occasion to complain of their method, even if it differed from Russia's. In consequence of the precedent of 1813, Turkey later argued that Great Britain had accepted a modification of the long-sought principle of absolute commercial equality with Russia. The British documents do not seem conclusive respecting this; they do show that Liston coöperated with Italinski in a "course of forbearance and partial concession toward the Ottoman Porte."[35]

Several merchants recommended that Liston insist upon complete trading immunities. By mid-1813, in consequence of Liston's urgent and repeated representations, Turkey restored a partial British free outlet from the Black Sea. According to the rule as it apparently was accepted by the ambassador, British ships must not take out of the Black Sea the prohibited grain, tallow, or other produce desired by Turkey without first offering it for sale to the Turkish government at the prescribed low prices. Turkey could accept whatever part it needed, not necessarily half, and permit the remainder to pass the Straits.[36]

The Anglo-Turkish tariff negotiation in May, 1813, further evinced British compromise with Turkey. The last tariff had been signed in 1805, when goods were cheaper than in 1813. Turkey discovered it could not collect through specific duties set years before the full 3 per cent ad valorem duty prescribed. Turkey requested a new tariff, for a tariff traditionally must be negotiated at fourteen-year intervals. When Liston refused, Turkey announced it would collect the tariff in kind. It thus intended to make reciprocal the scheme of the capitulations whereby foreign merchants who believed themselves overcharged possessed the option of paying the tariff in goods. Andreossy could do little but watch, although France, unlike Britain, had nothing to lose because it had no trade there. As a gesture, he accepted a new and higher tariff, whereupon Liston gave in. The latter believed that "the inconvenience would be but temporary and ultimately would be set aside in consequence of private arrangements with the collectors of the customs."[37]

In May, Liston attempted by fictitious manifests to send through the Dardanelles and Bosporus three ships loaded with guns and powder for Russia. Someone betrayed the secret, after the ships had sailed through the Dardanelles and up to Constantinople. Turkey's threat to confiscate both ships and cargoes forced them back into the Aegean.[38] This, together with Duckworth's withdrawal in 1807, led Turkey to the unrealistic conviction that it could make Britons and Russians back down every time.

In 1813 everyone at Constantinople admitted preoccupation with Napoleon, and properly so. The French emperor launched another characteristic offensive in the Germanies that year. Once more he attacked before his enemies could unite their forces against him. At first his venture recorded successes. But miserable failure came at Leipzig, where he lost the so-called Battle of the Nations on October 13-16. With difficulty Napoleon extricated most of his army, retreating across the Rhine. The end of his military operations in Spain was attested by his treaty with the restored King Ferdinand in December. Soon Italy and Holland accepted other jurisdictions.

The year 1814 found Napoleon at last on the defensive in France's national territory. Could he save his empire from complete ruin? Russia, Austria, England, liberated Spain, Prussia, and several other German states gave the answer: their military contest with him resulted in their occupation of France early that year. In the end, France alone of Napoleon's states remained loyal—and even that much loyalty discredited Prince Metternich's calculations.

When the allies signally defeated Napoleon east of Paris on February 1, his fate could no longer be in doubt. The armies of the coalition entered Paris on March 31, and the frustrated emperor on April 11 accepted sovereignty over the island of Elba in the Mediterranean.

We have traced the growth and effects of Napoleon's policies in the Near East from the peace of Europe in 1802 to the debacles in Spain and Russia in 1812. His early programs, we have observed, were distinguished by unity and coherence. This carefully woven web was ruptured by the tension in French relations with other great powers, notably with Russia and England. From 1802 to 1807 Napoleon favored Turkey, then a shift in relations with Russia brought the emperor to debate with his ally, Tsar Alexander, the partition of the Ottoman realm. At the same time, the idol of France signed with Persia an alliance which he never really applied. The heart of the problem for the entire Near and Middle East was the Dardanelles. From the Gallic viewpoint, if France could not possess the Dardanelles, neither should Russia. In Muscovite eyes only Russia, of all the major powers, could possess the Straits. There was no yielding by either nation on this fundamental issue. The impasse forced the emperor to policies in the Near East which became one of the chief causes of the dissolution of his empire. The hub of Napoleon's turning wheel of fortune was his adamant demand to have at least a share in the ownership of the Dardanelles.

XVIII

Epilogue: The Last Phase

1814-1815

THE RESTORED Bourbon dynasty won allied blessing. The new ruler of France, His Very Christian Majesty King Louis XVIII, appointed the influential and vacillating Talleyrand to be his minister of foreign affairs. Thus ended the latter's easygoing life as an idle Napoleonic grand dignitary. Nearly always pro-Turkish, Talleyrand urged the Bourbon king to write Sultan Mahmud II immediately (May 20, 1814). The new ruler recalled the old-time reciprocal advantages of the friendship between Bourbon France and Turkey and stated that he wished to draw close again the bonds of friendship with the Ottoman Empire. He wished to facilitate Franco-Turkish communications and commerce. Forgotten were the Bonapartean expedition to Egypt in 1798, the consequent Franco-Turkish war, and the anti-Turkish alliance with Russia. From his "Imperial Palace of the Tuileries," Louis XVIII termed Sultan Mahmud his "dear and perfect friend." The Bourbon king eventually named the Marquis de Rivière to replace Andreossy at Constantinople (September 24). The venerable Ruffin once again would be chargé d'affaires temporarily, according to his orders, during the changeover which proved to be of several months' duration.[1]

The sultan's formal and friendly reply to King Louis XVIII came to Paris in due course. It came to the wrong recipient, however, for it was received by the returned Emperor Napoleon. The archives show that it was translated on March 15, 1815, early in the "Hundred Days," by our friend Amédée Jaubert, Napoleon's secretary-interpreter for Oriental languages. The sultan had written of "the friendship that had not ceased to exist between the Bourbons and the noble race of Ottomans." He agreed with Louis that reciprocal advantages had accrued from the friendship during several centuries. He assured France of his renewal of the antecedent treaties with the Bourbons.[2]

The sultan watched with interest the growing jealousies among the allies. Several factors combined to give his empire considerable advan-

tages in the discussions at the Congress of Vienna. That congress debated, as a matter of course but without urgency, every phase of the
over-all problem of Turkey, although it was a side issue. No one considered seriously annoying Turkey; the congress did not even extend to
the Danube its general principle calling for the unhindered commercial
navigation of certain international rivers. Britain assumed the protectoral
function for the Ionian Islands, having learned well its lessons of sea
power in the Mediterranean. Moreover, the entire Napoleonic period
had accustomed England to vigilance at and near the Dardanelles. Austria
even more than Great Britain championed Turkey's cause. Metternich
wished to guarantee Turkey's territory, a proposal Russia and Britain
rejected. They requested Turkey's stricter enforcement of treaties. Russia desired the unhindered navigation of the Straits for its commerce
and the adjustment of the disputed Asiatic frontier. Because Great
Britain opposed Russia on the question of the frontier, the congress left
the matter unsettled.

Andreossy of France had urged Turkey, at the time the negotiations
opened, to require Russia to evacuate the territories occupied on the
eastern shores of the Black Sea, or to declare a new war. Sultan Mahmud
wished a long breathing spell instead. The Ottoman Empire indeed
needed time to reconsolidate its position in southeastern Europe, in
western Asia, and in northern Africa. The sultan wished also to modern-
ize his army.

Such had been the state of the discussions of Turkey at the time
Napoleon escaped from Elba. He had landed at Cannes on March 8,
1815, to be accepted promptly by the French public as its emperor
again. Russia still debated its most expedient policy, in view of the support accorded Turkey by Austria and Great Britain.

The return of the emperor places under the spotlight for curtain calls
Caulaincourt, Ruffin, and Amédée Jaubert. The loyal Caulaincourt became the restored emperor's foreign minister in Paris during the Hundred Days extending to mid-June of 1815. Ruffin had assumed his duties
as chargé d'affaires on November 14, 1814, the day Ambassador Andreossy actually left Constantinople. Thus the hero of the entire Napoleonic
program in the Levant served at Constantinople to inform and guide
the French colony there through the rapidly changing loyalties of the first
half of 1815. Assigned his new post by the Bourbon king, Ruffin's status
became as confused as anyone's in consequence of the return from Elba.

Louis XVIII still ruled, although not at Paris. From Vienna, Talleyrand issued orders as the king's foreign minister; from Paris, Caulaincourt carried out Napoleon's directions. Both demanded loyalty.

"*Vive le roi! Vive l'empereur! Vive le roi!*"

Who at Constantinople could know which foreign minister to obey? The French colony survived the crisis of the Hundred Days better than did western Europe for a simple reason: at that distance it could never be sure what constituted the really up-to-date news.

The emperor never forgot the Near East, even in the anxious days of his transitory comeback. As an immediate step to regain his control of the embassy at Constantinople, he dispatched the trusted Jaubert to be his chargé d'affaires.

Jaubert experienced some delay in reaching the Dardanelles, not a novelty to him after the dangers and delays of his long journey to Teheran in 1806. At length he appeared, on June 5, 1815. He found Jerome Mechain still vice-consul at the Dardanelles, as he was to remain until 1817. Mechain was probably as much in doubt as everyone else respecting who might be his overlord on a given day. The consul could not obtain a boat to take Jaubert to Constantinople, hence Napoleon's envoy proceeded by land, arriving on June 9. Ruffin immediately bowed to the *fait accompli*. He welcomed his old friend and notified the Ottoman government of the French people's acceptance of Napoleon again. He announced that Jaubert, not himself, should be recognized as the chargé d'affaires. As for himself, he would again be only the counselor of embassy. Friends thought the latter's sacrifices probably would include his moving out of the French palace back to his old private residence, to the house near the embassy which he had occupied so long. Ruffin would not have cared, for Jaubert represented the miracle-working Napoleon and a brilliant decade of French history.

Ruffin's official announcement met Turkish ridicule and the strong opposition of Britain's Ambassador Liston. Jaubert knew that this time he would fail, in contrast with his successes at Constantinople a decade earlier. As events proved, Ruffin did not move out of the embassy. With Jaubert also in residence there after June 9, the embassy staff members could adjust their loyalties quite readily. Ruffin had temporized as much as he could, during the month after receiving Caulaincourt's instruction to support only Napoleon. Now Jaubert and Ruffin must decide, among other things, the weighty question of whether to fly the Bourbon or Napoleonic flags at the French ambassador's palace. Should the fleur de lis flying over the chief doorway be replaced by the imperial eagles?

There was more hesitation. Jaubert impatiently gave the answer respecting the flags by personally exchanging them during the night of June 12. During the evening of June 14, Ruffin clarified his own position before the assembled staff. He led the way in pledging loyalty to Napoleon and was followed by all except two members. On June 18 came Napoleon's defeat in the Battle of Waterloo.

Of the two men who would no longer shift with the tide, Mathieu Deval, the first secretary of the embassy since 1810, proved to be an ardent Bourbon royalist. He revealed Jaubert's arrival by a letter to Talleyrand at Vienna, telling of the Napoleonic envoy's excellent welcome by Ruffin and the official personnel. The French merchants at the capital divided their loyalties. In addition to Liston, the watchful included Russia's Italinski and Austria's Baron von Stürmer. Deval moved out of the French embassy and into the Russian minister's palace.

Several times Ottoman officers summoned the French to remove the Napoleonic ensign, but Ruffin and Jaubert refused. Ruffin argued that he lacked the authority, having reverted once more to the position of counselor. He insisted that the unrecognized Jaubert alone held the position of chargé d'affaires. However, Jaubert admitted failure when Turkey firmly refused to accept him in that capacity. On June 26 he retired from Constantinople.

Pierre Ruffin resided in the French palace four months longer, until October 23. The schism ended at Constantinople only when confirmed official news at last told of the Battle of Waterloo and of the second Bourbon restoration in Paris. When, in August, 1815, orders eventually came from the Marquis de Rivière, Ruffin changed sides again. His royalist protestations availed him little, however. Talleyrand dismissed him, recalled him to Paris, and disgraced him, an action revealing Talleyrand's true character. Tale-telling Deval moved back into the ambassador's palace in October, being authorized to handle French affairs until De Rivière came (early in June, 1816). Not until 1818 did the Bourbon ministers restore the venerable Ruffin to their good graces. They then returned him to Constantinople in an inferior capacity for a year, and restored his title of counselor of embassy in 1819.[3]

Napoleon ranted as he reviewed the past, walking about the island of St. Helena. All of Tsar Alexander's flattery and cajolery of him, he said, had been intended to win his consent to Turkey's cession of the Dardanelles to Russia.

Although he had lost an empire, he remained content with his persistent refusal to grant that incomparable strategic jewel in exchange for delusive enticements. What did his extravagant declamation matter? He would succumb in 1821 to cancer of the stomach, which for him might be termed the cancer of destiny. His interpretation of his policies at the Dardanelles would survive, and the policies would be imitated by succeeding generations of Frenchmen and others. Foremost among these policies was that Russia should be excluded from the Dardanelles.

NOTES

Abbreviations Used in Notes

AE: Archives du Ministère des Affaires Etrangères (Paris)

AEMD: Archives du Ministère des Affaires Etrangères, Mémoires et Documents

AN: Archives Nationales (Paris)

CCM: Archives Modernes de la Chambre de Commerce de Marseille

CNI: *Correspondance de Napoléon I*^{er}

FO: Archives of the British Foreign Office (London)

MG: Archives du Ministère de la Guerre (Paris)

MM: Archives du Ministère de la Marine (Paris)

Noradounghian: G. Noradounghian (ed.), *Recueil d'actes internationaux de l'Empire ottoman*

Picard: E. Picard and L. Tuetey (eds.), *Unpublished Correspondence of Napoleon I*

Sbornik: *Russkoe Istoricheskoe Obshchestvo Sbornik* [Publications of the Russian Historical Society]

Sup.: Supplément

Testa: I. de Testa (ed.), *Recueil des traités de la Porte ottomane*

Notes

I. Observer on the Bosporus (1802-1803)

1. AE Turquie Sup. 23; AEMD Turquie 63; Noradounghian, II, 50–54; Testa, II, 146.
2. AE Turquie 204.
3. AE Turquie 204.
4. AE Turquie 204; FO 78 Turkey 37.
5. CCM, B.214 Lettres, and AE Turquie 214.
6. AE Turquie 204.
7. AE Turquie 204; AEMD Turquie 14, 64.
8. AE Turquie 205.
9. AE Turquie 205.
10. AE Turquie 204.
11. H. Dehérain, *La vie de Pierre Ruffin*, II, 254.
12. AE Constantinople 74.
13. AE Constantinople 74.
14. AE Turquie 206.
15. AE Turquie 205.
16. AE Constantinople 75.
17. AE Turquie 205.
18. Testa, II, 264–269.
19. FO 78 Turkey 119.
20. FO 78 Turkey 37, 136.
21. AE Turquie 204.
22. AE Turquie 206.
23. AE Turquie 205.
24. AE Turquie 206.
25. *The Problem of the Turkish Straits* (1947), Department of State Publication No. 2752, 47–68.
26. AE Turquie 204.
27. AN, AF IV, 1687; AE Turquie 205.
28. AE Turquie 207.
29. AE Turquie 207; AE Russie 143.
30. S. M. Goriainov, *Le Bosphore et les Dardanelles*, p. 5; AE Turquie 208.
31. AE Turquie 205.
32. G. Douin and E. C. Fawtier-Jones, *L'Angleterre et l'Egypte: La politique mameluke, 1801–1803*, p. 398, quoting War Office p. 346.
33. AE Turquie 206; AE Constantinople 75.
34. AE Turquie Sup. 23.
35. AE Turquie 207.
36. AE Turquie 207.
37. AEMD France 1774; AE Turquie 206.
38. FO 78 Turkey 40, in G. Douin, *La politique mameluke, 1803–1807*, pp. 37, 42.
39. Douin, *ibid.*, pp. 91–94.
40. AE Turquie 208.
41. V. J. Puryear, *France and the Levant* (1941), pp. 113–134.
42. AE Russie 143.
43. AE Turquie 207.

II. "Emperor and Padishah" (1804)

1. AE Turquie 207; CCM, dossier: Commerce du Levant, 1802–1855.
2. AE Turquie 207.
3. AE Turquie 207.
4. AE Turquie 207.
5. CNI, IX, 368; Testa, II, 255.
6. AE Russie 143.
7. AE Turquie 208.

8. AE Turquie 208.
9. AE Turquie 208.
10. Testa, II, 261–263.
11. Testa, II, 256–263.
12. AE Turquie 208.
13. AE Turquie 208.
14. Testa, II, 341–343.
15. *Ibid.*, pp. 270–271.
16. AE Turquie 208.
17. AE Turquie 208.
18. AE Russie 143.
19. AE Turquie 208.
20. Testa, II, 344; AE Russie 144.
21. Testa, II, 344–346.
22. *Ibid.*, pp. 346–347.
23. *Ibid.*, p. 348.
24. Testa, II, 348.
25. AE Turquie 209.
26. AE Turquie 209.

27. AE Turquie 209.
28. Testa, II, 349.
29. *Ibid.*, p. 350.
30. AE Turquie 209.
31. Testa, II, 273.
32. *Memoirs of Prince Adam J. Czartoryski* (2 vols., 1888), II, 52–55; AE Turquie 63.
33. Czartoryski, *Memoirs*, II, 49–50.
34. Puryear, *England, Russia, and the Straits Question, 1844–1856*, pp. 1–75, 189–256.
35. Goriainov, *Le Bosphore et les Dardanelles*, pp. 4–8.
36. G. Douin, *Mohamed Ali, pacha du Caire*, pp. 62–63, quoting AE Alexandrie.
37. AE Russie 144.
38. AE Turquie 209.

III. Scheming for Persian Coöperation (1805)

1. AE Turquie 209.
2. Testa, II, 271–272.
3. AE Turquie 209.
4. CNI, X, 276.
5. AE Turquie 207.
6. AE Turquie 207.
7. AE Turquie 208.
8. CNI, X, 362.
9. FO 78 Turkey 771; FO Stratford Canning Papers 32.
10. AE Turquie 209.
11. CNI, X, 295.
12. AE Perse 8; AE Turquie 209.
13. AE Perse 8.
14. AE Turquie 209; AE Turquie Sup. 23.
15. AE Turquie 209.
16. AE Perse 8.
17. AE Perse 8; AE Turquie 210.
18. AE Turquie 210.
19. AE Turquie 210.

20. Sbornik, vol. 82, pp. 8–12.
21. P. Bertrand (ed.), *Lettres inédites de Talleyrand à Napoléon*, p. 122.
22. AE Turquie Sup. 23.
23. AE Constantinople 76; AEMD Turquie 63.
24. Drovetti to Talleyrand, September 21, 1805; AE Alexandrie 18.
25. AE Turquie 210; AE Perse 8.
26. P. A. Jaubert, *Voyage en Arménie et en Perse*, pp. 4–6.
27. AE Turquie Sup. 23.
28. AE Perse 8.
29. AE Perse 8.
30. AE Turquie 210.
31. AE Russie 144.
32. AE Turquie 210.
33. AE Turquie 210.
34. AE Turquie 210.
35. Dehérain, *Ruffin*, II, 188.

IV. Ottoman Policy Veers Toward France (October, 1805–February, 1806)

1. AE Russie 144.
2. Parandier reported himself on October 9, 1805, as being well received in Transylvania; AE Turquie 210.

3. AE Turquie 210.
4. P. Bertrand, in *Revue Historique*, XXXIX (1889), 64–75, and *Lettres inédites*, pp. 156–174, from AEMD 658 and 659.

5. Goriainov, *Le Bosphore et les Darda-nelles*, pp. 4–8; Noradounghian, II, 70–77; F. F. Martens, *Recueil des traités conclus par la Russie*, XI, 87; cf. T. Schiemann, *Geschichte Russlands unter Kaiser Nikolaus I*, I, 266.
6. Sbornik, vol. 82, p. 159.
7. S. Tatischev, in *La Nouvelle Revue*, LXIV (June, 1890), 496; *Cambridge Modern History*, IX, 259.
8. AE Turquie 210.
9. AE Turquie 211.
10. CNI, XII, 242.
11. AE Turquie 211.
12. AEMD Turquie 64.
13. Sbornik, vol. 82, pp. 240–241.
14. Sbornik, vol. 82, pp. 244–251.
15. Sbornik, vol. 82, p. 260.
16. Sbornik vol. 82, pp. 251–264.
17. AE Turquie 211.
18. AE Turquie 211.
19. AE Turquie Sup. 24.
20. AE Turquie 215.
21. AE Turquie Sup. 24.

V. New French Courses are Charted (March-July, 1806)

1. Sbornik, vol. 82, p. 361; P. Pisani, *La Dalmatie de 1806 à 1809*, pp. 157–173.
2. Sbornik, vol. 82, pp. 315–322.
3. Sbornik, vol. 82, pp. 325–328.
4. Goriainov, *Le Bosphore et les Darda-nelles*, pp. 8–10.
5. AE Russie 145.
6. AE Russie 145.
7. Sbornik, vol. 82, pp. 362–363.
8. AE Russie 145.
9. AE Turquie 211.
10. AE Turquie 211.
11. AE Turquie 211.
12. CNI, XII, 472.
13. Testa, II, 274–275.
14. AE Turquie 212.
15. AE Turquie 212.
16. AE Perse 9.
17. AE Perse 9.
18. AE Turquie 211.
19. AE Turquie Sup. 24.
20. AE Perse 9.
21. AE Perse 9.
22. AE Perse 9.
23. AE Perse 9.
24. CNI, XII, 555.
25. AE Turquie 212.
26. AE Turquie 212; CNI, XII, 580–581.
27. AE Turquie 212.
28. AE Turquie 212.
29. CNI, XIII, 7.
30. CNI, XIII, 5.
31. Testa, II, 276.
32. AE Turquie 212.
33. AE Turquie 212.
34. CCM, dossier: Commerce du Levant (1802–1855).
35. AEMD Turquie 64.
36. AE Turquie 211.
37. Sbornik, vol. 82, p. 392.
38. Sbornik vol. 82 pp. 367, 380.
39. AE Turquie 212.
40. Sbornik, vol. 82, p. 397.
41. Sbornik, vol. 82, pp. 410, 415.
42. CNI, XII, 657.
43. Sbornik, vol. 82, p. 442.
44. AE Russie 146.
45. AE Russie 146.
46. AE Russie 144.
47. AE Turquie 212.

VI. Breaking the Russo-Turkish Alliance (August-December, 1806)

1. FO 78 Turkey 136. Parliament abolished the Levant Company in 1825. Puryear, *France and the Levant*, pp. 37–40.
2. AE Turquie 212.
3. AE Turquie 212.
4. AE Turquie 212.
5. AE Turquie 212.
6. AE Turquie 212.
7. FO 78 Turkey 51.

8. AE Turquie 212.
9. Testa, II, 279–291.
10. AE Turquie 212.
11. AE Turquie 212.
12. AE Turquie 212.
13. J. Barrow, *Life and Correspondence of Sidney Smith*, II, 211–215.
14. AE Turquie 212.
15. AE Turquie 212.
16. AE Turquie 212.
17. AE Turquie 212.
18. AE Turquie 212.
19. AE Turquie 212.
20. CNI, XIII, 602.
21. Great Britain, War Office, 6.56, quoted in Douin and Fawtier-Jones, *L'Angleterre et l'Egypte*, III, 1.
22. AE Turquie 212.
23. CNI, XIII, 682.
24. AE Turquie 212.
25. AE Turquie 215.
26. AE Turquie 212.

27. AE Turquie 212; CNI, XV, 5; Testa, II, 284–285.
28. AE Turquie 212
29. Testa, II, 282.
30. AE Turquie 212.
31. Testa, II, 285.
32. AE Turquie 212.
33. Testa, II, 287.
34. AE Russie 144.
35. AE Perse 9.
36. AE Perse 9; cf. Dehérain, *Ruffin*, II, 41.
37. AE Turquie 212.
38. AE Turquie 212.
39. Sbornik, vol. 82, pp. 488–494.
40. AE Turquie 212.
41. AE Turquie 212; AE Russie 144; Sbornik, vol. 82, pp. 473–479.
42. AE Turquie 212.
43. AE Constantinople 76.
44. AE Turquie 213.
45. AE Turquie 213.
46. AE Turquie 217.

VII. *"That Infernal Strait"* *(January-February, 1807)*

1. Barrow, *Life of Sidney Smith*, II, 217–222.
2. Testa, II, 288.
3. Loyd, Mary (ed.), *New Letters of Napoleon I* (1898), p. 36.
4. AE Turquie 213; CNI, XIV, 160.
5. AE Turquie 213.
6. Czartoryski, *Memoirs*, II, 168–173, 178–182; Schiemann, *Geschichte Russlands unter Kaiser Nikolaus I*, I, 266.
7. Testa, II, 290.
8. Testa, II, 290.
9. AE Turquie 213.
10. Testa, II, 291–293.
11. Testa, II, 293.
12. AE Turquie 213.
13. AE Turquie 213.
14. AE Turquie 213.
15. AE Turquie 213.
16. AE Turquie Sup. 24.

17. AE Turquie 213.
18. AE Turquie 213.
19. AE Perse 9.
20. Testa, II, 295–296.
21. AE Turquie 213.
22. Testa, II, 297.
23. AE Turquie 213.
24. AE Turquie 213.
25. AE Turquie 211; Testa, II, 298.
26. AE Turquie 213.
27. AE Turquie 213.
28. AE Turquie 213.
29. AE Turquie Sup. 24.
30. AE Turquie 213.
31. AE Turquie 213; Testa, II, 299.
32. Douin and Fawtier-Jones, *L'Angleterre et l'Egypte: la campagne de 1807*, pp. 66, 105–107, quoting British War Office 6.56.

VIII. *Persia Enters the French Orbit* *(March-May, 1807)*

1. AE Perse 9.
2. AE Perse 9.

3. Bertrand, *Lettres inédites*, pp. 313–315.
4. Testa, II, 298.

5. Bertrand, *Lettres inédites*, p. 326; AE Turquie 213.
6. AE Turquie 213.
7. AE Perse 9.
8. Bertrand, *Lettres inédites*, pp. 326–328, 332–333, 356–357.
9. AN, AF IV 1686, first dossier No. 7.
10. AE Turquie 213.
11. AE Turquie 213.
12. Testa, II, 300–301.
13. AE Perse 9.
14. Cf. Bertrand, *Lettres inédites*, p. 357.
15. AE Turquie 213.
16. AE Turquie 213.
17. Dehérain, *Ruffin*, II, 77.
18. AE Turquie 213.
19. CNI, XV, 17, and AE Turquie 213.

20. AE Perse 9; CNI, XV, 19.
21. Bertrand, *Lettres inédites*, p. 412.
22. AE Turquie 213.
23. AE Turquie 213.
24. Bertrand, *Lettres inédites*, pp. 453–454.
25. *Mémoires du duc de Rovigo*, II, 46–48.
26. AE Perse 9. See A. de Gardane (ed.), *Mission du général Gardane en Perse sous le premier Empire*, pp. 81–94.
27. *Mémoires du duc de Rovigo*, II, 49–50.
28. Bertrand, *Lettres inédites*, pp. 445, 449.
29. AE Perse 9; De Clercq, *Recueil des traités de la France*, II, 201–203.
30. AE Perse 9.
31. AE Perse 9; CNI, XV, 261–265.
32. AE Turquie 214.
33. AE Turquie 214.

IX. *Napoleon Abandons the Ottoman Empire (June–July, 1807)*

1. AE Turquie 214, 215.
2. AE Turquie 212.
3. AE Turquie 214.
4. AE Turquie 214.
5. AE Turquie Sup. 24.
6. AE Turquie 214.
7. Sbornik, vol. 83, p. 180.
8. *Memoirs of the Duke of Rovigo*, II, 79.
9. AE Turquie 214.
10. AE Perse 9.
11. AE Turquie 214.
12. Arthur Paget, *The Paget Papers*, II, 286–298.
13. Douin and Fawtier-Jones, *L'Ang eterre et l'Egypte*, p. 66 (Castlereagh to Fox, April 25, 1807; British War Office, 6.56); 105–107 (May 17, 1807); 134, 143 (Admiralty to Collingwood, June 16, 1807, British Admiralty records, 2–1364).

14. Sbornik, vol. 89, pp. 33–39.
15. CNI, XV, 457–458; AE Turquie 214.
16. CCM, B.146.
17. AE Russie 144.
18. AEMD Turquie 63; Sbornik, vol. 83, pp. 6–7.
19. L. A. Thiers, *Histoire du consulat et de l'Empire*, VII, 654.
20. *Mémoires du duc de Rovigo*, II, 80–85.
21. Martens, *Recueil des traités russe*, XII, Nos. 494, 495; Sbornik, vol. 89, pp. 51–59, 60–62, 66–70.
22. CNI, XV, 404; AE Turquie 214.
23. Testa, II, 302.
24. Picard, I, 602; cf. Sbornik, vol. 89, p. 69.
25. Sbornik, vol. 83, pp. 45, 73; vol. 89, p. 99.
26. AE Turquie 214.

X. *An Unratified Armistice (July–September, 1807)*

1. Picard, I, 602; Sbornik, vol. 89, p. 69; AE Turquie 214.
2. *Mémoires du duc de Rovigo*, II, 96–97.
3. AE Turquie 214.
4. AE Turquie 214.
5. AE Turquie 214.
6. AE Turquie 214.

7. AE Perse 9.
8. AE Turquie 215.
9. AE Turquie 214.
10. AE Turquie 214.
11. Sbornik, vol. 83, pp. 6–7.
12. AE Russie 144.
13. AE Turquie 214.

14. AE Turquie 214.
15. AE Turquie 214.
16. AE Russie 144.
17. *The Paget Papers*, II, 321.
18. AE Russie 144.
19 Sbornik, vol. 83, p. 30.
20. AE Russie 144.
21. AE Turquie 215.
22. Sbornik, vol. 83, pp. 93–97.
23. AE Turquie 214.
24. AE Turquie 215.
25. AE Perse 9.
26. FO 60 Persia 1.
27. Dehérain, *Ruffin*, II, 47.
28. AE Russie 144.
29. AE Russie 144.
30. AE Russie 144.
31. AE Turquie 215.
32. AE Turquie 215.
33. Testa, II, 303.
34. AE Turquie 215, 216.
35. AE Perse 9.
36. AE Turquie 215.
37. AE Turquie 215.

38. AE Russie 144.
39. AE Russie 144.
40. AE Russie 144.
41. AE Turquie 215.
42. AE Turquie 215; AEMD Turquie 63.
43. AE Turquie Sup. 24.
44. AE Turquie 215.
45. AE Turquie 215.
46. In common with many key ambassadors then and since, Horace Sebastiani did not profit financially from his embassy. He lost money and went into debt. At this point in 1807 he discovered his private fortune in France threatened by costly litigation, in consequence of his wife's demise in April. He appealed to Napoleon for 40,000 francs on October 5, in order to try to save his fortune, a request fulfilled immediately. AE Turquie 215.
47. AE Turquie 215.
48. *A Selection from the Public and Private Papers of Cuthbert Collingwood*, p. 314.

XI. Testing the Franco-Russian Alliance (October–December, 1807)

1. AE Russie 144.
2. AE Russie 144.
3. AE Russie 144; Sbornik, vol. 83, p. 136.
4. AE Russie 144; Sbornik, vol. 83, pp. 137, 139.
5. AE Turquie 215.
6. AE Turquie 215.
7. AE Perse 9.
8. AE Russie 144.
9. AE Russie 144; Sbornik, vol. 89, pp. 200–207.
10. CNI, XVI, 157.
11. Goriainov, *Le Bosphore et les Dardanelles*, p. 49.
12. AE Turquie 215.
13. AE Turquie 215.
14. Sbornik, vol. 89, pp. 218–222, 263–266.
15. Sbornik, vol. 83, pp. 215, 233.
16. Sbornik, vol. 89, pp. 177–180.
17. Sbornik, vol. 83, p. 207; CNI, XVI, 173.

18. AE Russie 144; Sbornik, vol. 89, pp. 266–267, 315.
19. Sbornik, vol. 89, pp. 273, 279.
20. AE Russie 144.
21. AE Russie 144.
22. AE Russie 144.
23. AE Russie 144.
24. AE Turquie 215.
25. Sbornik, vol. 89, pp. 259–262.
26. Sbornik, vol. 83, pp. 165, 238; vol. 88, p. 360.
27. Sbornik, vol. 88, pp. 342–346.
28. AE Russie 144.
29. AE Russie 144.
30. AE Turquie 215.
31. AE Turquie 215.
32. AE Russie 144.
33. CNI, XVI, 171, 230.
34. AE Russie 144.
35. AE Russie 144; Sbornik, vol. 88, p. 361.
36. Sbornik, vol. 88, pp. 362–369; AE Russie 144.

37. AE Russie 144.
38. AE Russie 146.
39. AE Russie 144.
40. AE Russie 146; Sbornik, vol.89, p. 329.

41. Sbornik, vol. 89, p. 317.
42. AE Russie 144.
43. AE Perse 9.

XII. Shall Turkey Be Partitioned? (January-February, 1808)

1. Sbornik, vol. 89, pp. 325–326.
2. CNI, XVI, 288; Picard, II, 43.
3. AE Turquie 216.
4. AE Turquie 216.
5. Sbornik, vol. 89, pp. 356–359.
6. AE Turquie 216; AE Russie 146.
7. Sbornik, vol. 89, pp. 352–354.
8. AE Turquie 215.
9. Sbornik, vol. 89, p. 342.
10. *Memoirs of Prince Metternich*, II, 175–177.
11. *Ibid.*, II, 178–180.
12. *Ibid.*, II, 180–183,
13. *Ibid.*, II, 194–199.
14. *Ibid.*, II, 183–193.
15. AE Turquie 216; Sbornik, vol. 89, pp. 383–384.
16. AE Russie 146.
17. AE Perse 9.
18. AE Perse 9.
19. AE Perse 9.
20. Sbornik, vol. 88, p. 453; AE Russie 146.
21. AEMD Turquie 64.
22. AE Alexandrie 18.
23. AE Russie 146; cf. A. Vandal, "Documents relatifs au partage de l'orient," *Revue d'histoire diplomatique*, IV (1890), 425–427.
24. CNI, XVI, 586–587; Sbornik, vol. 88, pp. 456–458.
25. S. Tatischev, *La Nouvelle Revue*, LXIV (June, 1890), 713.
26. Sbornik, vol. 89, pp. 396–402.
27. AE Turquie 216.
28. AE Turquie 216.
29. AE Turquie 216.
30. AE Turquie 216.
31. AE Turquie 216.
32. AE Perse 9.
33. AE Russie 146.
34. AE Russie 146; Sbornik, vol. 88, p. 480.
35. AE Russie 146.
36. AE Russie 146.
37. Sbornik, vol. 89, p. 418.
38. *Memoirs of Metternich*, II, 198–201.
39. Sbornik, vol. 89, pp. 417–418.
40. AE Russie 146.

XIII. The Dardanelles—"La Langue de Chat" (March, 1808)

1. *The Problem of the Turkish Straits*, Publications of the Department of State, No. 2752 (1947), 47–68.
2. AE Russie 146.
3. Vandal, "Documents relatifs au partage de l'orient," *Revue d'histoire diplomatique*, IV (1890), 431–434.
4. Tatischev, *La Nouvelle Revue*, LXIV (June, 1890), 713.
5. Vandal, *op. cit.*, pp. 434–437.
6. *Ibid.*, pp. 437–440.
7. *Ibid.*, pp. 440–446.
8. Testa, II, 308.
9. Vandal, *op. cit.*, pp. 446–451.
10. *Ibid.*, pp. 451–452.
11. AE Russie 146; Sbornik, vol. 88, pp. 525–530.
12. Vandal, *op. cit.*, pp. 452–457.
13. *Ibid.*, pp. 457–460.
14. *Ibid.*, pp. 460–463.
15. *Ibid.*, pp. 463–465.
16. AE Russie Sup. 17; Sbornik, vol. 86, pp. 535–537.
17. Vandal, *op. cit.*, pp. 465–467.

XIV. "The Bases Cannot Be Accepted" (March-June, 1808)

1. Testa, II, 308.
2. Testa, II, 308.
3. AE Perse 9.
4. AE Russie 146, 147.
5. AE Turquie 216.
6. AE Russie 146.
7. AE Russie 146.
8. AE Turquie 216.
9. AE Turquie Sup. 24.
10. AE Russie 146.
11. AE Turquie 216.
12. AE Turquie 216.
13. AE Turquie 216.
14. AEMD Turquie 63.
15. AE Perse 10.
16. AE Perse 10.
17. AE Russie 146.
18. AE Russie 146.
19. CNI, XVII, 55; Sbornik, vol. 88, p. 670.
20. AE Russie 146.
21. AN, AF IV, 1697; AE Russie 146; Sbornik, vol. 88, pp. 674–692.
22. AE Turquie 216.
23. Vandal, "Documents relatifs au partage de l'orient," *Revue d'histoire diplomatique*, IV (1890), 467–468.
24. CNI, XVII, 210.
25. AE Russie 146.
26. AE Russie 147.
27. AE Perse 10.
28. AE Perse 10.
29. AE Perse 10.
30. AE Perse 10.
31. AE Perse 10.
32. AE Perse 10.
33. AE Perse 10.
34. AE Perse 10.
35. AE Turquie 216.
36. AE Turquie 217.
37. AE Turquie Sup. 24.
38. AE Russie 147.
39. Vandal, *op. cit.*, pp. 468–470 (and, briefly, in AE Russie 147).

XV. Post-mortem at Erfurt (July-November, 1808)

1. AN, AF IV, 1697.
2. Testa, II, 310–327.
3. AE Perse 10.
4. AE Perse 10.
5. AE Perse 10.
6. AE Perse 10.
7. AE Perse 10.
8. AE Perse 10.
9. AN, AF IV, 1697.
10. AE Turquie 217.
11. AE Turquie 217.
12. AE Turquie 217.
13. Talleyrand, *Memoirs*, I, 299.
14. Tatischev, *Revue Nouvelle*, LXIV (June, 1890) 719.
15. AE Turquie 217.
16. AE Turquie 217.
17. AE Russie 147.
18. AE Russie 147.
19. Cf. F. Charles-Roux, *France et les chrétiens d'orient*, p. 121.
20. Talleyrand, *Memoirs*, I, 300, 305–309.
21. AE Russie 147.
22. Talleyrand, *Memoirs*, I, 310–342.
23. De Clercq, *Recueil*, II, 284–286.
24. AE Russie 147.
25. AE Turquie 217.
26. AE Turquie 217.
27. AE Turquie 217.
28. AE Turquie 217.
29. AE Turquie Sup. 24.
30. Testa, II, 329.
31. AE Russie 147.
32. AE Turquie 217.
33. AE Turquie 217.
34. Testa, II, 330.
35. AE Perse 10.
36. AE Perse 10.
37. AE Perse 10.
38. AE Perse 10.
39. AE Perse 10.
40. AE Perse 10; AE Russie 147.

XVI. Near Eastern Policy at Loose Ends (1808-1809)

1. George Canning to Robert Adair, June 26, 1808; FO 78 Turkey 60.
2. AE Turquie Sup. 24.
3. AE Turquie 217.
4. AE Turquie Sup. 24.
5. AE Turquie 217.
6. AE Turquie 217.
7. AE Turquie 217.
8. AE Russie 147.
9. AE Turquie 217.
10. AE Turquie 217.
11. R. Adair, *Negotiations for the Peace of the Dardanelles*, I, 105–109; FO 78 Turkey 60; Puryear, *England, Russia, and the Straits Question, 1844–1853*, pp. 257–339.
12. Noradounghian, *Recueil*, II, No. 27. The far more comprehensive Anglo-Turkish commercial convention signed in 1838 is discussed in Puryear, *International Economics and Diplomacy in the Near East*, pp. 84–91, 107–124.
13. Noradounghian, *op. cit.*, pp. 81–85. For an evasion of the pledge in November, 1829, see Puryear, *France and the Levant*, pp. 62, 96–98.
14. AEMD Turquie 64. For the 1830's, pertinent records are in FO 195 Turkey 116, 122.
15. AE Turquie 218.
16. AE Turquie 218.
17. AN, AF IV, carton 1698.
18. Testa, II, 331.
19. AE Turquie Sup. 24
20. AE Perse 11.
21. AE Perse 11.
22. AE Perse 11.
23. AE Perse 11.
24. AE Perse 11, 12.
25. Adair, *Negotiations for the Peace of the Dardanelles*, I, 171.
26. Testa, II, 333–336.
27. AE Turquie Sup. 24.
28. AE Le Caire 26.
29. AE Turquie 219.
30. AE Perse 12.
31. AE Perse 12.
32. AE Perse 12, 13.
33. AE Perse 13.
34. See Vandal, *Napoléon et Alexandre Ier*, II, 546–548, 549–559, citing AE Russie 150, 151, and Vol. III, *passim*.
35. Loyd, *New Letters of Napoleon I*, 166.
36. AE Turquie Sup. 24.

XVII. Rim of the Blockade (1809-1814)

1. AE Turquie Sup. 24.
2. AE Russie 147.
3. Picard, III, 787.
4. Picard, III, 604.
5. AE Le Caire 26.
6. AE Alexandrie 18, 19; AE Constantinople 77.
7. AE Turquie Sup. 25.
8. AE Alexandrie 18.
9. AE Le Caire 26; AE Alexandrie 18.
10. AE Le Caire 26; AE Alexandrie 19.
11. AE Le Caire 26. Respecting the Drovetti plan in 1829 and 1830 see Puryear, *France and the Levant*, pp. 112–146.
12. AEMD Turquie 14.
13. AE Turquie 217.
14. AE Turquie Sup. 24, 25.
15. Consul General Corancez, Napoleon's political agent who observed Persia and India from Bagdad, had replaced the deceased elder Rousseau at that station in 1808. AEMD Turquie 64.
16. AE Perse 13.
17. AE Perse 13.
18. AE Turquie Sup. 25.
19. AE Turquie Sup. 25.
20. AE Turquie Sup. 25.
21. AE Alexandrie 19.
22. AE Turquie 222.
23. AE Turquie 222.
24. AEMD Turquie 64; AE Turquie 222.

25. Puryear, *France and the Levant*, pp. 14–15.

26. De Clercq, *Recueil des traités de la France*, II, 369–372.

27. Illustrative references are: *Memoirs of the Duke of Rovigo*, III, 157, 161; De Pradt, *Narrative of an Embassy*, pp. 10, 29, 46, 74; E. Tarle, *Napoleon's Invasion of Russia*, pp. 59–135; Karl von Clausewitz, *La campagne de 1812 en Russie, passim*.

28. AE Turquie Sup. 25.

29. Tarle, *Napoleon's Invasion of Russia*, pp. 326–412.

30. AE Turquie Sup. 25.

31. FO 78 Turkey 81.

32. AE Constantinople 77.

33. AE Alexandrie 19.

34. FO 78 Turkey 81.

35. FO 78 Turkey 136.

36. FO 78 Turkey 81.

37. FO 78 Turkey 81.

38. FO 78 Turkey 81.

XVIII. Epilogue: The Last Phase (1814–1815)

1. AE Turquie Sup. 25.

2. AE Turquie Sup. 25.

3. AE Turquie 229 and Dehérain, *Ruffin*, II, 119.

Bibliographical Note

THE important background of the eighteenth century constitutes a separate story. Because the Ministry of Marine directed French affairs in the Levant for most of the century, a large collection of reports by French agents in the Levant and in Barbary is to be found in MM (housed in AN). MM, B7, carton 449 includes a political report dealing with Egypt by M. Saint-Priest at the end of his ambassadorship in 1785. The historian may consult an uninterrupted series, if scattered and often contradictory, of official statistics for trade from 1700 on. MM, B7 includes some 44 cartons on the general problem; carton 452 has comparative figures for trade in the period 1781–1787. The series AEMD Turquie is useful: Vol. 8 has a report by Ambassador Bonnac covering 1725–1740 (duplicated as Vol. 12); Vol. 9 includes a compilation of value for French commerce in the Levant in 1789; Vol. 17 has an historical sketch by Saint-Priest which stresses the negotiations of 1740 and 1783 and covers the scheme for a Suez canal; Vol. 29 has translations of various treaties down to 1740; Vols. 7, 14, and 30 are miscellaneous consular reports; Vol. 63 (duplicated as Vol. 69) and Vol. 64 include lengthy and valuable historical sketches (not always reliable, but clear and well organized) by M. Pellissier, consul at Bagdad, dated 1855, covering the period 1789–1815 from the French archives; AE Constantinople 74 gives consular material, 1795–1802. Paul Masson, *Histoire du commerce français dans le Levant au XVIIIe siècle* (Paris, 1911), summarizes a great many of the rich archive resources up to 1789. F. Charles-Roux, *Le project français de commerce avec l'Inde par Suez* (Paris, 1925) analyzes a venture of 1785–1789.

C. de La Jonquière, *L'Expédition d'Egypte* (5 vols., Paris, 1899–1907), is a documentary work useful for all aspects of the Bonapartean expedition to Egypt, from the time of the substitution of the invasion of that Ottoman province for the proposed descent on England to the return of Napoleon Bonaparte to France. Five or six volumes of CNI (32 vols.,

Paris, 1855) represent a rich storehouse of information, although by no means complete; Vols. 29 and 30 reproduce the emperor's retrospective *Guerre d'Orient,* appraising his campaigns in Egypt and Syria. Among the countless secondary works discussing the expedition, I mention two by F. Charles-Roux: *Les origines de l'expédition d'Egypte* (Paris, 1910), and *Bonaparte, gouverneur d'Egypte* (Paris, 1936).

Respecting the French army in Egypt following the departure of Bonaparte, from a long list of references I cite: M. F. Rousseau, *Kléber et Menou en Egypte* (1900), letters and orders of the day; G. Rignault, *Le général Abdallah Menou* (1911), a doctoral thesis of merit; F. Charles-Roux, *L'Angleterre et l'expédition française en Egypte* (2 vols., 1925), based on selected documents and contemporary writings. The manuscript documents dealing with Kléber's negotiations with the Turks leading to the nonratified convention of El Arish (March, 1800) are in AE Turquie 201. Menou's surrender of Alexandria to the British on September 2, 1801, finished the expedition. See G. F. Martens, *Recueil des principaux traités,* VII, 1–37; R. T. Wilson, *History of the British Expedition to Egypt* (2 vols., 1803).

Upon the return of the French army to France, various of its members recounted its history and described Egypt and its resources. At the outset appeared as authors Reynier, Vivant Denon, and Desgennettes. Almost a third of the personnel of the Institut de France of the future were represented among the returned scientists. They produced a stream of publications, as did the principal military officers.

Documents illustrating French economic interest in the Black Sea, 1767–1820, are in AEMD Turquie 14. The contemporary book dealing with the potentialities of commerce in the Black Sea, written by its principal proponent, did not appear until 1805: Anthoine de Saint Joseph, *Essai historique sur le commerce et la navigation de la mer Noire* (2 vols.). It is based on studies preliminary to the Franco-Turkish treaty of 1802, which opened the Black Sea to French commercial shipping. Talleyrand approved this publication, and mentioned its author to Emperor Napoleon I, who appointed him an officer of the Legion of Honor. The work became a standard textbook for the subject in France and remained so for some twenty years; it was reissued in 1820. The essay is a popularized account of the author's own and other enterprises to establish commercial and maritime relations between the ports of the Black Sea and those of the Mediterranean in the 1780's. Marseille was the center of all the French trade in the Black Sea, as throughout the

Levant. Jules Julliany, *Essai sur le commerce de Marseille* (Paris, 1842); Volume I sketches the beginnings of that city down to 1840.

The various standard collections of treaties and other documents are convenient aids throughout the Napoleonic period, as is especially true of CNI. The object of much writing is the perennial minister of foreign affairs under the Directory, the First Consul, the Empire, and the Bourbon Restoration. A general picture of the personality is G. Lacour-Gayet's *Talleyrand* (4 vols., Paris, 1930–1934), a work inadequate for any questions of diplomacy.

Confusing manuscript records greet the researcher for Levantine policy during Bonaparte's Consulate. An example is the Franco-Turkish treaty of 1802. The best of the scattered and incomplete papers respecting its background, negotiation, and immediate results, are: AE Turquie 203–205; AEMD Turquie 14; CCM: dossier, Commerce du Levant et de Barbarie, généralités, 1802–1855; B.213–214, and B.143–144 (Lettres 1801–1804); B.256, Mémoires; FO 78 Turkey 37, 119. Pierre Ruffin, the chargé d'affaires before Ambassador Brune's appointment late in 1802, always wrote full, and fully detailed, reports. His frequent dispatches account for the bulky character of the archive materials for this period. H. Dehérain, *La vie de Pierre Ruffin* (2 vols., Paris, 1919) is much better for the personality than for his problems. The student might consult M. P. Coquelle, "L'Ambassade du maréchal Brune à Constantinople, 1803–1805," *Revue d'histoire diplomatique*, XVIII (1904), 53–73. G. M. V. de Conchard, *Le maréchal Brune* (Paris, 1936), does not include Brune's activity at Constantinople.

Horace Sebastiani's important political report to the First Consul concerning Egypt at the end of 1802, a preliminary of the breach of the Peace of Amiens, is in AN, AF IV, carton 1687. Other useful papers for the period are: AE Constantinople 75 (1802–1804); AEMD France 1774, letters and orders of Bonaparte, 1802–1803; G. Douin and E. C. Fawtier-Jones *L'Angleterre et l'Egypte: la politique mameluke* (1801–1803) (2 vols., Cairo, 1929–1930).

Russo-Turkish relations are summarized in S. M. Goriainov's authoritative monograph, based on Russia's archives: *Le Bosphore et les Dardanelles* (Paris, 1910). P. H. Mishev, *La mer Noire et les détroits de Constantinople* (Paris, 1899) is suggestive of broad general developments. Russian Foreign Minister Czartoryski's interesting suggestions in 1804 for a partition of Turkey may be glimpsed in A. Gielgud (ed.), *Memoirs of Prince Adam J. Czartoryski* (2 vols., London, 1888). Talleyrand's project of 1805 on the same subject is sketched in P. Bertrand, "M. de Talley-rand, l'Autriche, et la question d'Orient en 1805," *Revue historique*, XXXIX (1889), 63–75.

Copies of Ambassador Arbuthnot's secret negotiations with Turkey at the end of 1806, turned over to General Sebastiani, the most-favored ambassador, are in AE Turquie 212. Ottoman methods sometimes required a stenographic report of conferences with foreign diplomats, in order that the precise wording could be studied by the Ottoman council afterward. This led to many detailed reports, copies of which otherwise would not be available in the French archives. Friendly Turks turned them over to Sebastiani, or to Pierre Ruffin. All of Ruffin's conferences respecting the pecuniary claims against Turkey (1802–1804) are so recorded and transmitted. This Ottoman custom also made possible handing to Sebastiani accurate information concerning Ottoman secret ministerial conferences. This would be true only for an ambassador on the inside track as adviser, and during times of crisis—such as for Sebastiani and his time.

AE Turquie 212–216 contain Sebastiani's reports down to 1808. CCM, B.146 relates to trade problems. Admiral Duckworth's forced passage of the Straits is recorded in AE Turquie 213. Reference might also be made to M. P. Coquelle, "Sébastiani, ambassadeur à Constantinople, 1806–1808," *Revue d'histoire diplomatique*, XVIII (1904), 574–611. E. Driault, *La politique orientale de Napoléon* (Paris, 1904) deals with the activities of Sebastiani and Gardane. Ever the partisan of the emperor, this author maintains without creditable logic in *Tilsit à Erfurt* (Paris, 1893), p. 193, that Napoleon by the alliance with Russia at Tilsit saved rather than abandoned Turkey.

The typical Napoleonic imperial decree naming General Clarke to negotiate with Baron Pierre d'Oubril in 1806 is in AE Russie 146. Russian documents covering D'Oubril's mission to Paris, the Clarke-Oubril treaty of July 20, 1806, and its equally unsuccessful aftermath negotiations, are in Sbornik, Vol. 82, 383–472. The best French sources are AE Russie 144–146, much utilized in Sbornik. Sbornik, Vols. 83, 88, and 89 are of great value for Franco-Russian relations for 1806–1808 except for the omitted secret negotiations respecting the Straits. For the Clarke-Oubril treaty, see also P. F. Shupp, *The European Powers and the Near Eastern Question, 1806–1807* (New York, 1931), 81–130. Text of the treaty: De Clercq, *Recueil des traités de la France*, II, 180–182.

General Savary, the *chargé de mission* at St. Petersburg in 1807, before

Caulaincourt took over as Napoleon's ambassador to the allied state, is a poor dispatch writer (AE Russie 144). He contributes in retrospect brief sidelights of his six months in Russia: *Mémoires du duc de Rovigo* (1828), (also in English trans., 1828), II.

Documents for Egypt, 1805–1807 are: AE Constantinople 76 (1804–1807); AE Le Caire 26 (1803–1812); AE Alexandrie 18, consular reports of Drovetti; G. Douin, *Mohamed Aly, pacha du Caire, 1805–1807* (Cairo, 1926), the reports by Drovetti to Talleyrand. G. Douin and E. C. Fawtier-Jones, *L'Angleterre et l'Egypte; la campagne de 1807* (Cairo, 1928) stresses the activities of British officials rather than the policy at London. *A Selection from the Public and Private Correspondence of Cuthbert Collingwood* (2 vols., London, 1837) discusses naval affairs. A. Paget, *The Paget Papers* (2 vols., London, 1896), includes diplomatic and consular correspondence, Vol. II giving important documents respecting changes in British policy in reaction to the Treaty of Tilsit. E. Driault, *Mohamed Aly et Napoléon, 1807–1814* (Cairo, 1925) is another of the valuable series, mostly of documents, published under the auspices of the Société Royale de Géographie d'Egypte. Douin compiled several volumes, Driault a few. The discrepancies in Driault's numbering of repository cartons for the beginning of *Mohamed Aly et Napoléon,* in comparison with AE, may be explained by the subsequent binding of the documents into volumes at the French foreign ministry. F. Mengin, *Histoire de l'Egypte sous le gouvernement de Mohamed-Ali* [to 1823] (2 vols., Paris, 1823) is a general account by a contemporary.

For the period when Napoleon transacted his business at Finkenstein, and Talleyrand maintained his office in Warsaw, there are concise summaries in print of French policy as it evolved. For example, there is Napoleon's coolness to the Austrian offer to mediate a general peace in March, 1807. Perhaps more informative than CNI for this particular period is P. Bertrand's edition of *Lettres inédites de Talleyrand à Napoléon 1800–1809* (Paris, 1889), mostly of the spring of 1807. The extracts are from AEMD France 658, 659.

All general histories of the Ottoman Empire discuss the palace revolutions. Two special works are: A. Juchereau de Saint-Denys, *Révolutions de Constantinople en 1807 et 1808* (2 vols., Paris, 1819), the observations of a French army officer; O. Schlecta-Wssehrd, *Die Revolutionen in Konstantinopel in den Jahren 1807 und 1808* (Vienna, 1882).

A remarkable short, published selection of French documents for Napoleonic relations with Turkey in 1806 and 1807 is in Testa, II,

270–337. One important correction for Testa may be noted: Document No. 93 (II, 303–306) is credited to Champagny instead of to its author, Talleyrand, and is incorrectly dated November 28, 1807, instead of January 28, 1807.

The archives of the French Ministry of Foreign Affairs—as a result of a clerical error when the manuscripts of the period were arranged for binding—date as of October 8, 1807, the memorandum of Napoleon's first conference with Ambassador Tolstoi in Paris. That was the important discussion of a possible partition of Balkan Turkey in which Russia might acquire Constantinople, after his refusal at Tilsit. Other references in the manuscript volume AE Russie 144 make clear the heading should be "8/9bre" instead of "8/8bre." The conference actually occurred on November 6, the date correctly used in Sbornik, Vol. 83, pp. 207 and Vol. 89, pp. 177–180.

Caulaincourt's memoranda of his unsuccessful alliance negotiations with Vahid Effendi early in June, 1807, are bound incorrectly, in AE Turquie 212 (June, 1806) instead of in 214 (June, 1807).

The significant instructions of November 12, 1807, to Caulaincourt were utilized at the source, AE Russie 144. They are published, with an introductory note, by A. Vandal, in the *Revue d'histoire diplomatique*, IV (1890), 54–78, and in Sbornik, Vol. 88, pp. 292–302 and Vol. 89, pp. 736–739.

From 1806 Napoleon's embassy at Constantinople handled the diplomatic and consular business for Italy as well as for France. More important—the Ottoman Empire remaining intact throughout Napoleon's period—the political series for "Turquie" includes the relations with Greece, the Balkans in general, western Asia, and the other provincial areas. Tracing the policy in this series reveals the policy of the Napoleonic empire for the entire Near East.

Regional studies are inadequate. F. R. Chateaubriand, *Itinéraire de Paris à Jerusalem, précédé de notes sur la Grèce*, was a popular travelogue in western Europe for many years, heightening contemporary French public interest in the Levant. E. Driault, *Napoléon et la résurrection de la Grèce* (Paris, 1924) includes a brief general summary of Napoleon's Mediterranean policy. W. H. Hardman, *A History of Malta, 1798–1815* (London, 1909) gives a collection of English and foreign documents referring to events in its history, 1792–1815. E. Rodocanachi, *Bonaparte et les îles Ioniennes, 1797–1816* [sic] (Paris, 1899) has a documentary appendix for 1814–1819. Consul Pierre David, stationed in Bosnia from 1806 to

1814, is needlessly resuscitated. The bulky character of his reports encourages undue emphasis of him, illustrated by extracts from his journal at Travnik in 1807–1808 published in *Revue d'histoire diplomatique,* XXXIX (1924), 129–169, 301–328. A. Boppe, *l'Albanie et Napoléon, 1797–1814* (Paris, 1914) is useful; his *Documents inédites sur les relations de la Serbie avec Napoléon I*er *de 1809 à 1814* (Belgrade, 1888), give extracts from AE hinting a negative policy. G. Yakshich, *L'Europe et la résurrection de la Serbie, 1804–1834* (Paris, 1907), stresses Serbia in international relations; it may be complemented by B. von Kallay, *Die Geschichte des serbischen Aufstandes, 1807–1810* (Vienna, 1910). Quite general are J. D. Ghika, "La France et les principautés danubiennes, 1789–1815," *Annales de l'École libre des sciences politiques,* XI (1896), 208–229, 321–352, and N. Iorga, *Histoire des relations entre la France et les Roumains* (Paris, 1917). AE Turquie 216 includes an important summary of the career of Passvan Oglu of Vidin.

For Persia I have utilized AE Perse 8–11. Also available is P. Amédée Jaubert, *Voyage en Arménie et en Perse, 1805 et 1806* (Paris, 1821), an interesting nonpolitical travelogue which reveals nothing of the great purposes of Napoleon's planning in 1805. The manuscript documents of AE Perse 8–11 should be used with FO Persia 1, the mission of Hartford Jones. Alfred de Gardane (ed.) *Mission du général Gardane en Perse sous le premier Empire* (Paris, 1865) presents documents that conform with the originals in AE Perse 8–9.

Two of many articles may be mentioned. E. Driault, "Napoléon à Finkenstein," *Revue d'histoire diplomatique,* July, 1899, treats problems in general and has some material on Persia and Turkey. H. Dehérain, "Le voyage du consul Joseph Rousseau d'Alep à Bagdad en 1807," *Syria* (1925), 174–187, recounts the hardships of French travel in the Middle East. Clément Huart, *Histoire de Bagdad dans les temps modernes* (Paris, 1901) is quite general. The several volumes of E. Driault's *Napoléon et l'Europe* cover the period generally. G. Roloff, *Die Orientpolitik Napoleons I* (Weimar, 1916) is a brief survey for 1798–1814.

Ambassador Caulaincourt's negotiations of 1808 with Foreign Minister Rumiantsov and Tsar Alexander I establish the general role of the Straits in the ultimate failure of the Franco-Russian alliance of Tilsit. The conversations are covered by Albert Vandal's publications of most of Caulaincourt's reports to Napoleon from January to June, 1808, *Revue d'histoire diplomatique,* IV (1890), 420–470, and his analysis, *Napoléon et Alexandre I*er (Paris, 1891), I. I have carefully compared the published reports with the originals (AN, AF IV, carton 1697), and the few omitted have been utilized in the foregoing study.

Napoleon's letter of February 2, 1808, which opened the way for the secret debate of March is in CNI, XVI, 586–587. AE Russie Supplément 17, gives the tsar's reply to the letter. Napoleon's supplemental instructions to Caulaincourt during this period have not been preserved, although the general statement of policy on November 12, together with Napoleon's letter of February 2 are adequate for most points. What is lacking, really, are the complete instructions that accompanied the letter of February 2. It has been well suggested these can be deduced from Caulaincourt's reports after March, 1808, available in the Archives Nationales, most of which have been published. A. Thiers, *Le Consulat et l'Empire* (Vol. VIII), presents a textual reproduction of the draft proposals sent to Paris by Rumiantsov.

Caulaincourt's official reports to Foreign Minister Champagny reveal too little. Nor do the latter's instructions to Caulaincourt near the end of January, 1808, tell enough, either of Napoleon's new ideas or of his methods: AE Russie 146. There is duplication of many points of the secret discussion; whenever Caulaincourt sent summaries to Champagny at the same time he sent the full details to Napoleon. Selections from Napoleon's letters to Champagny for 1808 are in AEMD France 1780. The original reports to Napoleon are among the Imperial archives, in AN.

For the negotiations on Poland, see E. Driault, *Tilsit; France et Russie sous le premier Empire, 1806–1809* (Paris, 1925), especially follows the negotiations respecting Poland. Marcel Handelsman, *Napoléon et la Pologne, 1806–1807* (Paris, 1909), has general information. *Alexandre Ier et prince Adam J. Czartoryski* (Paris, 1865) presents selections from their personal correspondence, 1801–1823.

Jean Hanoteau (ed.), *Mémoires du général Caulaincourt, duc de Vicence* (3 vols., Paris, 1910), makes fairly interesting reading, but is strangely silent on his secret conversations of 1808 with Tsar Alexander and Count Rumiantsov. S. Tatishchev, *Alexandre Ier et Napoléon, 1801–1812* (Paris, 1891), gives lengthy quotations from the documents without source references. A convenient source for the conference of Erfurt is J. V. A. de Broglie (ed.), *Mémoires du prince de Talleyrand* (Paris, 1892). I. P. Bertrand upheld the exactness of these memoirs (*Revue historique*, 1892). A. Vandal, *Napoléon et Alexander Ier* (3 vols., Paris, 1891–1894) is a comprehensive history of Franco-Russian diplomatic relations under the alliance of Tilsit.

The Anglo-Turkish Treaty of the Dardanelles (1809): FO 78 Turkey 60, and 136, the Levant Company; Robert Adair, *Negotiations for the Peace of the Dardanelles* (2 vols., London, 1845), the leading British account, with some quotation from the documents.

The essential records of Franco-Russian relations in 1809 are in AN, AF IV, carton 1698, Caulaincourt's reports. Bound as AE Turquie 217 are the inconsequential reports of M. Latour-Maubourg at Constantinople for that year, when Foreign Minister Champagny sent him no consequential instructions. E. Driault, *Le grand empire, 1809–1812* (Paris, 1924) is useful for its bibliography, and for the chapter that traces the Franco-Russian conflict of ideas in 1810.

The failure of the Continental Blockade in the Levant is well illustrated by AEMD Turquie 14, AE Turquie 222, AE Constantinople 77, AE Odessa 1 (1802–1811). No detailed study is available for the grain trade in the Mediterranean during the Napoleonic period. Such a study would include Egypt as a source of grain for the armies in Portugal and Spain, Malta as a center of distribution, and the Austrians as carriers. A general study, W. F. Galpin, *The Grain Supply of England During the Napoleonic Period* (New York, 1925), suggests that grain from other sources minimized the commercial importance of the Mediterranean for England at that time.

The Peace of Bucharest (1812) is reported in AE Turquie 222, and FO 78 Turkey 81.

Three fresh accounts for 1812 may be indicated. The well-known tragic retreat of the Grand Army from Moscow has been reëxamined, with its details made more precise and graphically pictured: Eugene Tarle, *Napoleon's Invasion of Russia* (Oxford University Press, 1942), pp. 326–404. Napoleon's laments during his disheartening trip back from the frozen wastes of Russia in December, 1812, as recorded by his companion, Caulaincourt, may be found in *With Napoleon in Russia* (1935), based on memoirs not unearthed until the twentieth century. B. Dundalis, *Napoléon et la Lituanie en 1812* (1940) is excellent.

Anglo-Turkish commercial problems in 1813 are important: see FO 78 Turkey 81, the reports of Ambassador Robert Liston. Consul General Cartwright's report to the Levant Company on May 25, 1822, reproduces in FO 78 Turkey 136 a letter by Liston dated July 28, 1813, partially agreeing to Turkish preëmption: that part of the British and Russian produce found in transit through the Straits might be purchased by Turkey.

For Persian relations with Russia and England, 1813–1814, see FO 97 Persia 294; Hertslet, *Commercial Treaties,* I; C. V. Aitchison, *A Collection of Treaties . . . Relating to India,* VI. P. M. Sykes, *A History of Persia* (2 vols., London, 1915), II, is a convenient textbook reference. J. F. Baddeley, *The Russian Conquest of the Caucasus* (London, 1908) discusses the contemporary military campaigns there.

For the Congress of Vienna, AE Turquie 229 has the reports of Lauriston and the restored Bourbon's Ambassador De Rivière. Among the numerous references are: G. Pallain (ed.), *Correspondance inédite du prince de Talleyrand et du roi Louis XVIII pendant le congrès de Vienne* (Paris, 1881); Hertslet, *Commercial Treaties,* I; T. Schiemann, *Geschichte Russlands unter Kaiser Nikolaus I* (4 vols., Berlin, 1904–1919), I.

V. J. Puryear, *France and the Levant* [1814–1833] (1941), continues the general account, as does his bibliography (pp. 223–235).

Index

Abbas Mirza, pro-French Persian crown prince, 45, 150, 350, 367, 375

Adair, Sir Robert, British ambassador at Constantinople: negotiates peace with Turkey, 355, 360-364; returns to England, 373

Albania: coveted by Napoleon, 253; passage of the French troops through, 312

Alexander I, Tsar of Russia: joins Third Coalition, 61; communicates with Napoleon, 66, 185; conferences of, with Napoleon at Tilsit, 187-200; discusses Ottoman Empire, 210; rupture of relations of, with England, 230; 243; conversations of, with Caulaincourt respecting Dardanelles, 262, 285, 293-294, 299-302, 318, 325-327, 331, 337; effect of Napoleon's letter on, 270, 282-284; infuriated by Turkey, 364; issues terms for peace with Turkey, 394

Alexandria: British occupy, 146; British troops withdrawn from, 184

Algeria: abuses of, to Frenchmen, 124; French claims against, 310

Ali Pasha, master of Albania, 9, 29, 91, 197, 253, 265

Ancona, 382

Andreossy, General Antoine: French minister to Vienna, 112; 261; ambassador to Turkey, 395; 399; 404

Anglo-French war, renewed in 1803, 16-18

Anglo-Turkish tariff negotiations (1813), 401

Anglo-Turkish Treaty of the Dardanelles, 362, 364

Anglo-Turkish war, 144

Antivari, assassination of French officers at, 314

Arbuthnot, Charles, British ambassador at Constantinople: 52; 59; warns Turkey, 104; mediates Italinski's dispute with Turkey, 108; supports Russia's actions, 121; bolstered by British war vessels, 122; 134; fails in negotiations with Turkey, 137-147

Asker Khan, Persian ambassador: at Constantinople, 316; arrives in Paris, 331; lives in Corbeil, 334; conference of, with Tolstoi, 349; 366; threatens to leave France, 367; departs from Paris, 387; 389

Atif, foreign minister of Turkey, 36

Austerlitz, battle of, 67

Austria: natural enemy of France, 63; Talleyrand's plans for, 64; included in possible partition of Turkey, 257-261, 277-278; and proposed expedition to India, 269; war of, with France, 371; Turcophile policy of, 395

Bagdad, Outrey appointed vice-consul in, 388

Bairakdar, Mustapha, Ottoman grand vizir, 346

Barbary corsairs, piracy by, 390

Barker, John, English consul general at Bagdad, 86

Bayazid, scene of imprisonment of Jaubert, 55

Berthier, General, Napoleon's chief of staff, 197

Bessarabia, 70, 234

Bibliographical note, 421-430

Black Sea: French ships win admission to, 2; new positions opened for, 7; French trade in, 9; 19; scheme to send French warships into, 165; French ships excluded from, 371

Bonaparte, First Consul: writes Selim, 3, 24; vague guarantee of, for Turkish territory, 3; Levantine policy of, 19; assumes title of Emperor, 27. *See also* Napoleon

Bosporus. *See* Straits

Bourbon dynasty, restored in France, 403

Boutin, 346, 390

Britain. *See* Great Britain

British policy in Egypt, 20

British fleet: summoned to Dardanelles, 106; enters Dardanelles, 107

Brune, General, French ambassador in Constantinople: 2; observer on the Bosporus, 1-21; appointed ambassador, 5; secret instructions to, 6; negotiations with Turkey, 8-23; encourages Black Sea trade, 8; likes Napoleon's title, 27; fails to win Turkish recognition of Napoleon's titles, 28-40; decorated, 31; breaks with Turkey, 32-40; 43

Bucharest, peace of, 394

Budberg, Baron, Russian foreign minister:

431

93; disapproves of Clarke-Oubril treaty, 96-97; appraises Turkey, 121; orders and letters of, 115, 127, 157

Callimachi, Prince, replaces Prince Moruzzi as hospodar, 102
Canning, George, 147, 241
Canning, Stratford, British ambassador, contributes to coming of Crimean War, 12
Capitulations: treaty basis for, 4; of 1740, 81-82; 154; defiance of, 384
Cattaro: issue between France and Russia, 76; Russian evacuation of, 198
Caulaincourt, General: 100; negotiates with Vahid, 173; ambassador to Russia, 234; instructions to, 234-239; discussions of, with Tsar Alexander, 243, *passim;* discussions of, with Rumiantsov, 244, *passim;* conversations of, with Tsar Alexander respecting Dardanelles, 262, 275-277, 285, 293-294, 299-302, 318, 325-327, 331, 337; views of, on Russian policy, 264; debates ownership of Dardanelles with Russia, 281-305; reports secret debates with Russia, 318; recall of, 393; 404
Chamber of Commerce of Marseille, 8
Champagny, Count J.B.M.: succeeds Talleyrand as foreign minister, 125; instructions of, to Savary, 226; prescribes ingenious arguments, 227; accepts conference credentials of Mouhib and Tolstoi, 262; instructions of, to Caulaincourt, 266-267; aloofness of, with Turkey, 311; writes Mirza Cheffi, 350; debate of, with Gardane, 374; letters and orders of, 212, 231, 252, 294
Choderlos, French consul at Smyrna, 20
Clarke, General H. J. G., negotiates with D'Oubril, 95
Clarke-Oubril treaty, 96
Collingwood, Admiral, does not enter Straits, 229
Constantinople: anti-Russian developments at, 97; French troops proposed for, 133; disposal of, debated at Tilsit, 190-191; disturbed conditions at, 194; effect of revolution at, 195; issues of, discussed by Napoleon, 232; disposition of, considered by Napoleon, 260; ownership of, debated in St. Petersburg, 281-305; importance of, for Russia, 287, 291; French difficulties at, 308; news from, 310; second revolution at, 337
Continental Blockade: 113-114; 162; ineffective in the Levant, 379
Corancez, French consul at Aleppo, 20, 44, 45, 86, 87
Corfu: Russian forces pass Straits for, 11; 197; 253; supplied by French vessels, 265; 381
Council of Commerce of Marseille, advocates trade in the Black Sea, 4
Crete, favorable location of, 63

Crimea, the: expedition to, suggested, 133; retrocession of, proposed, 159, 204, 217
Crimean War, background for, 206
Czartoryski, Prince Adam, foreign minister for Tsar Alexander: 21; considers plans to partition Turkey, 37; drafts treaty with Turkey, 64; 69; 77; negotiates with De Lesseps, 77-79; replaced, 93

Dalmatia: held by France, 68; under General Marmont, 91; French army in, 105, 255; French officers arrive from, 143; arms from, 161; 381
Dardanelles, the: English at, 115; forts of, 123; resistance at, 135; British fleet forces way through, 141-147; fortified by Turks, 143; ownership of, debated by Russia and France, 281-305; diplomatic stalemate over, 307; guardian islands of, 365. *See* Straits
Dardanelles, treaty of: background for, 356; negotiated, 360-362; terms of, 362-364
David, captain of ship halted at Constantinople, 8
David, Pierre, French consul in Bosnia: 84; 169; 217; reprimanded by Champagny, 340
Decaen, General Charles: expedition of, to Mauritius Island, 17; news of, 24
De Lesseps, Barthélemy, French consul general at St. Petersburg: 30; 38; 61; 69; negotiates for Franco-Russian rapprochement, 77-79; 78; assists Savary, 210
De Lesseps, Mathieu: French consul general at Cairo, 20; transferred to Leghorn, 84
De Meneval, hears important debate over Straits, 191
De Sacy, Silvestre, 60
Deval, Mathieu, Bourbon royalist, 406
Di Borgo, Pozzo, Russian negotiator at Dardanelles, 184, 204, 241
Djezzar Pasha: Bonaparte's implacable foe in Syria, 9; visited by Sebastiani, 15
Donzelot, General, governor of the Ionian Islands, 381, 386
D'Oubril, Baron Pierre: 20; Russian chargé d'affaires at Paris, 30; ordered home, 31; negotiates at Paris, 79; 93-96
Drovetti, French consul at Alexandria, 20, 54, 385
Duckworth, Admiral John T.: ordered to Dardanelles, 112, 128; forced passage of, through the Dardanelles, 134-147
Dupré, French vice-consul at Trebizond, 20, 87

Egypt: French invasion of, 1; deceptive policy for, 38; French influence in, 54; wartime trade of, 391
Elgin, British ambassador, orders British brig into the Dardanelles, 16
England. *See* Great Britain

English vessels, in the Dardanelles, 118
Erfurt, conference at: preparations for, 331,
340; 342; convention of, 343, 365
Esseid Ismail, 53

Feth Ali, shah of Persia: 40; receives Romieu
in audience, 57; writes Napoleon, 57; discussions of, with Jaubert, 156; irritated by
Franco-Russian alliance, 248; supports
France, 322; 334. *See* Persia
Foreign warrants of protection: sold to non-
Turks, 100; issue of, 101
Fourçade, V. T.: 5; French consul general
at Sinop, 7; 314
France: neighbor of Ottoman Empire, 71;
opposes navigation of Straits by Russian
vessels of war, transport, or military supply, 105; announces treaty with Persia,
153; alliance of, with Russia, 186-200;
held out of Straits by Turkey, 256; commerce of, with Asia, 386
Franchini, Antoine: travels to France, 51;
in Paris, 85
Franchini, Eugene: 7; French embassy's interpreter, 26; 46; 49; clever negotiations
of, 51-52; 59
Franco-Persian alliance: 163-166; terms of,
167; virtually nullified by Tilsit, 207
Franco-Russian: treaty of 1787, 2; alliance
of 1807 (Tilsit), 181, 187-200; debates
over Straits, 281-305, 307-308, 329; negotiations at Erfurt, 342; war of 1812, 396
Franco-Turkish treaty of 1802: 2; ratified,
4; 21
French expedition to Egypt (1798): 2; causes
Turkish arrest of French civilians, 13, 93;
imperial and colonial objectives of, 53;
General Menou last commander of, 53;
109; reasons for, 147; 339; 385
French senate, convoked, 140
Friedland, battle of, 161

Galib Effendi, foreign minister of Turkey: 2;
107; proves anti-French, 123, 380; negotiates armistice of Slobosia, 213; 228; complains of Napoleon's policies, 347; Mahmud's foreign minister, 359
Gandin, E., 4
Gardane, Ange: returns from Persia, 315;
in Marseille, 323
Gardane, Brigadier General Antoine: appointed minister to Persia, 164; instructions to,
168; trip of, to Persia, 182; 208; travels
with Mirza Riza, 214; imposing mission
of, 215; in Constantinople, 218; maps
routes to India, 263-264; writes routine
reports, 274, 309; scanty instructions to,
349; coolness of, with Persia, 315, 349-
352; clever arguments of, 366; leaves Persia, 368; news of, 371; returns to Europe,
373
General Council of Commerce of France, 19

Georgia: Russia's conquest of, 77; 167; not
retroceded at Tilsit, 189
Ghika, John, 124
Gouvion, General Jean Baptiste: governs
Warsaw, 130; entertains Mirza Riza, 164
Great Britain: becomes Turkey's ally, 10, 37;
wins navigation of Black Sea, 10; opposes
Soviet plan, 65; defeats French in Egypt in
1798, 67; continues wars with France, 99,
261; Turkey refuses new alliance with, 103;
policy of, at Straits, 127; naval exploits of,
at Straits, 135-147; sends squadron to support Sweden, 211; attack of, on Copenhagen, 215; declines Russia's mediation,
220; Napoleon awaits support against, 225;
and a possible partition of Turkey, 265;
claims interest in Dardanelles, 355; naval
power of, 382
Greeks, evade Napoleon's blockade, 382
Guilleminot, adjutant commander, mediates
Russo-Turkish armistice, 196

Halet, Turkish ambassador at Paris: 24; 35;
73; Turkish foreign minister, pro-French
policy of, 180-181; complains of Napoleon's attitude, 242; opposes French passage of troops through Albania, 273; 391
Hauterive, of French foreign ministry, 39
Hedouville, French minister in St. Petersburg, 16
Heligoland, Britain's occupation of, 216
Hitler, Adolf, 61, 127, 252, 372, 400
Hundred Days, the, 403-406

Ibrahim Effendi, friend of France: 13; 65;
71; favors Franco-Turkish entente, 72-73
Illyrian Provinces, 381, 383, 390
India: joint action against, proposed, 225,
248; lures potential invader, 251; problem
of, for Napoleon, 252; expedition to, proposed by Napoleon, 268; expedition to,
abandoned, 320; vessels arrive at Suez from,
385
Ionian Islands: Russian communications with,
11; Russia's plans for, 38; 39; Russian
military forces in, 85; 106; 381
Ismail, Hassiz, Turkish governor at Dardanelles, 218
Italinski, Russian minister at Constantinople:
8; debates with Brune, 12; questioned by
Brune, 23; opposes Jaubert, 25; opposes
Brune, 34; negotiates for renewal of alliance with Turkey, 34; 45; 76; issues ultimatum to Selim, 102; outwitted by Sebastiani, 105; leaves Constantinople, 122; 399

Jafez, Ottoman grand vizir, 54, 59
Janissaries, the, precipitate revolution, 176
Jaubert, Amédée, French linguist: travels
with Sebastiani in 1802, 14; delivers Bona-
parte's letter to sultan, 24-26; 36; sent to
Constantinople, 41; commissioned to Per-

sia, 44-60; 45; delivers Napoleon's letter
to sultan, 46-48; arrested by Ottoman
frontiersmen, 52; publishes travelogue, 55;
reports to Constantinople, 87; in Teheran,
88; letters of, to Ruffin, 89; 138; questioned by Talleyrand, 151; certifies secret
report on Persia, 155; 222; guide for Asker
Khan, 334; 403; 404

Jena, battle of, 112

Joannin, 374, 375

Jones, Hartford: commissioned to Persia,
215; 366; in Teheran, 368

Karek, conceded to France, 248, 350

Kherson, French agent at, 7

Kieffer, teaches Oriental languages in Paris,
7, 60

Kochubei, Count, adviser to Tsar Alexander,
21, 69, 212, 231

Laforest, Count de, 230

Lajard, Felix, 336, 350, 351, 374, 375, 388

Latour-Maubourg: second secretary at Constantinople, 92; French chargé d'affaires at
Constantinople, 314; reports anti-French
Turkish actions, 324-325; writes routine
reports, 339; no instructions sent to, 345;
fears arrest by Turkey, 348; protests Turk-
isk closure of Straits, 370; supports Continental Blockade, 379; 384; 386; admits
failure of Continental Blockade, 392

Lauriston, General Jacques, minister to
St. Petersburg, 393

Lazarev, Serge, negotiates armistice with
Turkey, 213

Levant Company, the, 100

Levant, the. *See* Near East

Liston, Robert, British ambassador to
Turkey, 397, 398, 401, 405

Mahmud, sultan of Turkey, installed, 337

Malcolm, Sir John, 366

Maret, becomes Napoleon's foreign minister,
393

Marmara, Sea of, British fleet enters, 135-147

Marmont, General: in Dalmatia, 91; orders
to, 132; sends 500 cannoneers to Turkey,
175; information from, 243; 265; 380;
389

Marseille, city of, 186

Mechain, Jerome, French vice-consul at the
Dardanelles: 137; 345; reports on British
negotiations at Dardanelles, 357; 364; 405

Mehemet Ali, governor of Egypt: 54; 62;
breaks British siege of Rosetta, 204; 384;
385; strengthens position in Egypt, 386

Meriaze, French agent at Vidin, 134, 382, 383

Merveldt, Maximilian, anti-French Austrian
ambassador, 239, 247

Metternich, Prince, discusses partition of
Turkey, 257-261, 277-278

Meyendorff, General, 214, 222

Michelson, General, Russian commander on
Danube: 76; enters the Principalities, 118;
occupies Jassy, 121; orders of, to treat for
peace, 158

Mirza Cheffi, Persian premier, 316, 366

Mirza Mohammed Riza (Mirza Riza), Persian ambassador to France: 58; at Constantinople, 111; 138; first meeting of, with
Napoleon, 149; conversations of, with Talleyrand, 153-154; leaves Warsaw, 167

Moldavia. *See* Principalities

Moniteur, the: publishes Sebastiani's report on
Egypt, 17; Napoleon's fictitious reports in,
9, 46, 52, 95, 129

Moruzzi, prince of Moldavia, attempts to
placate France, 124, 239

Mouhib Effendi, Ottoman ambassador to
Paris: 73; received by Napoleon, 85; 228;
229; secret instructions of, obtained by
French palace, 240, 256; uninformed of
Napoleon's intentions, 310

Mustapha Bairakdar, of Ruschuk: 125; grand
vizir, harsh rule of, 357; overthrown, 358

Mustapha IV, sultan: succeeds Selim III,
179; 218; deposed, 337; murdered, 358

Napoleon I, Emperor of the French: policies
of, for Near East, 1; continental blockade
by, 1; anti-Russian policy of, for Constantinople, 23, 29, 40, *passim*; wants Turkey
to close Straits against Russia, 30; recalls
envoy to Russia, 31; wishes aid of Turkey
and Persia, 41; interest of, in western Asia
in 1799, 44; sends special messengers to
Persia, 44-60; opposes Russian passage of
Straits, 58-59; general policies of, respecting Near East, 21, 40, 60, 73, 75-97, 125,
147, 169, 199, 223, 249, 279, 305, 327,
353, 377, 402; military position of, in
Europe, 61; favors Greece, 62; declines
Talleyrand's plan for partition of Turkey,
66; effect of victories of, 66; appeased by
Ottomans in 1806, 67; titles of, recognized
by Turkey, 72; victory of, over Austria influences Turkish policy, 73; sends Sebastiani to Constantinople, 79; safeguards Turkey, 83; expands political policy for Turkey,
85, 89; confers with Mouhib, 85; opposes
partition of Turkey, 92; blitzkrieg of 1806
by, 99-100; supports Turkey, 112; writes
Selim, 41-42, 113, 119, 130, 161; encourages a Turkish war against Russia, 116;
dictates fictitious war news, 129, 158; in
eastern Europe, 131; proposes French ships
in Black Sea, 131; writes to Shah Feth Ali,
43, 149, 158; first meeting of, with Mirza
Riza, 149; at Finkenstein, 150; audiences
of, for Mirza Riza, 165; abandons the
Ottoman Empire, 171-199; enters Vilna,
185; communicates with Tsar, 185; conferences of, at Tilsit, 187-200; Ottomans
dismiss cannoneers of, 196; thoughts of,

after Tilsit, 197-199, 204-205; misinterprets Ottoman palace revolt, 203; complains against Sultan Mustapha, 231; once concedes Constantinople to Russia, 232; supplements Caulaincourt's instructions, 236; in Italy, 239; at his zenith, 251; contingent program of, to partition Turkey, 254; connects Turkish and Prussian territorial questions, 255; proposes thrust at India, 257; marriage of, with Maria Louisa, 257; considers disposition of Constantinople, 260; writes Tsar Alexander (February, 1808), 267-268; at Bayonne, 313; excludes Russia from Dardanelles, 313; at Erfurt, 341; policy of, for Turkey in 1808, 330; contradictions in Near Eastern policies of, 355; war moves of, in 1809, 372; repudiates Gardane's break with Persia, 373; surveys Egypt and Syria, 390; resumes negotiations for alliance with Turkey, 392; invades Russia, 395; hastens back to Paris, 396; falsifies his disaster in Russia, 397; defeated at Leipzig, 402; abdicates, 402; return of, from Elba, 404; at St. Helena, 406. *See also* Bonaparte

Near East, French policy for, 23

Near Eastern routes, 82

Nedjib Effendi, Turkish ambassador to Paris, 393

Nelson, British admiral, victory at Trafalgar, 61

Nerciat, Andrea de: in Persia, 89; mission of, to Syria, 391

Nesselrode, Count, 226

Notes, 413-422

Noviltsov, 21

Odessa, French consular representation at, 7

Ottoman Empire, the: neutral in 1803, 18; alliance of, with Great Britain ineffective, 21; refuses to recognize Napoleon as emperor and padishah, 28-40; position of, in international affairs, 36; possible partition of, 37, 58, 62-64, 71, 188-200, 257-261, 277-278; allied with Great Britain, 37; French relations with, 41; refuses to recognize French emperor, 42; renews alliance with Russia (1805), 52; Russian secret plans for, 68-71; change of feeling of, toward France, 73; alliance of, with Persia and France desired by Napoleon, 75-97; held suspect by Russia, 76; westernizing of, 83; partition of, opposed by Napoleon, 92; expects alliance with France, 92; Frenchmen in, arrested in 1798, 93; policy of, gauged by policy for Straits, 99; importance of location of, 100; guarantee of, by Napoleon, 101; seeks alliance with France, 114; declares war on Russia, 120, 124; dangers to, 140; proposed treaty of, with France, 171-172; deadlock over, in treaty plans, 175; excludes foreign ships from

Straits, 256; defects from French policy, 364; closes Straits to commerce, 370; neutral in Mediterranean, 382; commercial treaties with, 398

Ottoman revolutions of 1807-1808, reasons for, 177-178

Outrey, Amédée, 56

Outrey, Georges: guides Romieu to Persia, 56-57; 86; 88; 89; accompanies Mirza Riza, 120; 138; questioned by Talleyrand, 151; interpreter for Asker, 387; instructions to, in 1810, 387-388; at Constantinople, 389

Padishah, title of, coveted for Napoleon, 27-40

Paget, Arthur, English negotiator at Dardanelles, 183

Parandier: French first secretary at Constantinople, 7; chargé d'affaires after departure of Brune, 34; weak negotiator, 39; 42; 43; 47; 49; Ruffin keeps secrets from, 50; 52; 59

Partition of Turkey, plans for, debated by France and Russia, 281-305

Passvan Oglu, pasha of Vidin, 116, 138

Persia: French relations with, 41; Napoleonic policy for, 43; Napoleon wishes information of, 46; 49; news of, 57, 138; alliance of, with Turkey and France desired by Napoleon, 75-97; French policy in, 86; paucity of news from, 111; 133; French announce treaty with, 153; secret report on, 155; couriers needed for, 158; and possible extrusion of Britain from, 164; French policy for, 165, 229; Gardane's mission arrives at, 247; war of, with Russia, 334-336; Napoleon's calculations of, 352; French policy in, suffers eclipse, 365

Pisani, English embassy's interpreter, 135, 345

Poqueville, Hugues, 84, 91

Pressburg, peace of, 68

Principalities, the (Moldavia and Wallachia): 7; new hospodars in, 11; 64; 70; 75; 102; 89; 90; 92; 103; 108; issue of dismissed hospodars of, 108-110; 118; Russians enter, 119; 121; 122; 140; 157; Ottoman recovery of, 159; Russia's possible acquisition of, 191, 226; stipulated Russian withdrawal from, 196; no Russian evacuation of, 223, 225, 227, 230; proposed exchange of, for Silesia, 236; 254; not to be ceded to Russia, 273; 294; Russians occupy, 320; bartered away at Erfurt, 345; 348; 387; 393

Prosorovski, Marshal, clarifies Russia's position in the Near East, 241, 349

Prussia: French overture to, 43; 63; 77; beaten by France, 111; supported by Russia, 266

Ragusa, French annexation of, 82, 90, 228

Rayneval, French envoy at St. Petersburg, recalled by Napoleon, 31

Republic of Turkey, during Second World War, 67

Romieu, Alexandre: consul general at Corfu, 9; Russia objects to, 21; 29; commissioned to Persia, 44-60; 45; 50; journeys to Teheran, 51, 56-57; death of, 82; 86

Rostopchin, Count, adviser to tsar, 231

Rousseau, Jean François, French consul at Bagdad, 20, 42, 43, 44, 56

Rousseau, Joseph, 56, 57, 163

Roux, Talleyrand's secretary, negotiates at Constantinople, 71-73

Ruffin, Pierre: French chargé d'affaires at Constantinople, 2; imprisoned in 1798, 6; new title for, 7; negotiates with Ibrahim Effendi, 13, 25; observes Russian forces in Straits, 32; dislikes Verninac, 38; 42; 43; negotiates with Ibrahim Effendi, 48-49; a hard worker, 49; outlines Romieu's trip to Persia, 50; 58-60; 62; 65; 67; counselor of embassy, 84; 389; 404; 405; 406

Rumelia: pashas of, form garrison at, 75; rebellion in, 104

Rumiantsov, Count Nicholas: 69; Russia's minister of commerce, 78; succeeds Budberg as foreign minister, 212; breaks relations with England, 220; overture of, to Savary, 226; opposes French expedition to India based at Straits, 246; debates ownership of Dardanelles, 281-305; visits Paris, 349

Russia: access of, to the Black Sea aids commerce, 11; military sailing of, in the Straits, 11, 16 (*see also* Straits); critical relations of, with France, 33; seeks to annex Georgia, 41; ally of England, 53; alternate policies of, for Near East, 68-71; continues war with France, 97; army of, on Dniester, 103; opposes Turkish policy, 107; and debate over hospodars, 108-110 (*see also* Principalities); losing policy of, in Turkey, 117; alliance of, with France, 186-200; alternate plans of, for Turkey, 231; position of, in Near East, clarified, 241; proposed exclusion of, from Dardanelles, 256; writes of partition of Turkey, 275; closed against English merchandise, 311

Russo-Turkish alliance: 11; of 1798, 53; of 1805, 65; nullified, 105

Russo-Turkish armistice at Slobosia (August, 1807): 201; negotiations for, 213; terms of, 213-214; nonratification of, by Russia, 219, 222

Russo-Turkish Peace of Bucharest (1812), terms of, 394

Russo-Turkish treaty of 1774, 161

Russo-Turkish war, 161

Saint-Denys, Juchereau de, 197

Saint-Joseph, Antoine de, 92

Saint Marcel, French consul at Alexandria, 384

Savary, A. J. M. R., General, Napoleon's aide-de-camp: 66; 165; appointed envoy to Russia, 202; in St. Petersburg, 209; 233

Schönbrunn, peace of (1809), 376

Sebastiani, General Horace: visits Alexandria, 14; secret instructions to, 14; reports on Egypt, 15; ambassador at Constantinople, 79; instructions of, 80-84; delayed arrival of, at Constantinople, 91-92; develops French political influence, 102; negotiates at Constantinople, 104, *passim*; confidence of Turks in, 109; reports on Turkey, 112; shares Turkey's confidences, 117; requests French military aid for Turkey, 120; promises of, 139; aids Turks to defend Straits, 143; negotiates secretly with the sultan, 145; decorated, 162; reports Turkish revolution, 176-179; gives Turkey false pledges, 181; influence of, eclipsed, 206; assured of Napoleon's mediation, 211; 221; 228; admits career in Turkey ended, 272; departs from Constantinople, 312; dispatches of, communicated to Russia, 317; advises France to go to Constantinople by sea, 333

Sebastiani, Madame, death of, 160

Selim III, sultan of Turkey: gift of, to Bonaparte, 18; policy of, in 1805, 41; personally accepts letter from Napoleon, 47; writes to Napoleon, 48, 108, 139, 145; favors France, 72; to be aided by Napoleon, 86; asks for alliance with Napoleon, 118; agrees to fight Russia, 120; defends Dardanelles, 135-147; writes to King George III, 151; reign of, ended by revolution, 176-179

Seniavin, Russian admiral, 139, 146

Serbia: question of Russian aid to, 59; revolt in, 84

Silesia, French evacuation of, an issue, 228-250

Slobosia, armistice of, 213-214, 219, 222

Smith, Sidney, 106, 128

Smyrna, visited by Sebastiani, 15

Soviet Union, the: passage of Straits approved for (1946), 12-13; 39; 65; seeks passage of the Straits, 364

Spain, problems of, 313, 359

Straits, the: Turkey mistress of, 29; and policy of Soviet Union, 40; French policy at, 21, 40, 60, 73, 75, 83, 97, 125, 147, 169, 199, 223, 249, 279, 305, 327, 353, 377, 402; 47; 53; issue of Russian ships of war, passage through, 24, 27, 31, 42, 45, 58, 62, 64, 65, 72, 77, 83, 92, 103, 110, 114, 226; Russian land routes to, 64; opened to Russia by treaty with Turkey, 65; Russia's plans for, 68-71; Russia restricts its use of, 76; unrestricted commercial navigation of, sought by France, 78; closed against Russia, 104; British threat at, 112; defenses of, 132; British passage resisted at, 160; debated at Tilsit, 188-191; issue of, left un-

settled at Tilsit, 205; Russia refused, 206;
Collingwood does not enter, 229; tsar's
advisers' idea for, 230; French expedition
based at, hinted, 246; France held from, by
Turkey, 256; partition of, between France
and Russia proposed, 281-305; strategic
position of, 305; summary of Franco-Russian debates over, 307-308, 329; French
policy for, 325; debate over, is adjourned,
342; Britain accepts exclusion from, 363,
376; commercial shipping in, 369; Italian
shipping in, 370; routes across, 383; Turkish preemption of foreign grain in, 399-
400. *See also* Dardanelles
Stuart, General, British commandant at
Alexandria, 14
Suzzo, Alexander: replaces Prince Ypsilanti,
102; pro-French Prince, 122; 136; 162; 169
Syria: French consuls in, 7; bridge to Asia, 307

Talleyrand, Napoleon's foreign minister: 2;
disputes Russia's quarantine at Constantinople, 12; issues instructions to Brune, 18;
letters and orders of, 31, 33, 38, 41, 44, 46,
53, 58, 59, 62, 66, 68, 72, 86, 90, 116,
131, 150; instructions of, apply Napoleonic policy, 35; overture of, to Prussia, 43;
instructs Sebastiani, 80-84; negotiates with
D'Oubril, 94-95; communicates with senate, 140; drafts proposed treaty with Turkey, 171-172; Napoleon consults with,
257; assists Napoleon at Erfurt, 341
Teheran. *See* Persia
Tenedos, British squadron at, 113
Theologue, Ottoman embassy's interpreter
in Paris, 309, 387

Tilsit: Franco-Russian treaty of, 181; conferences at, 187-200; alliance of, 194-195;
British reaction to, 211
Tolstoi, Count Pierre: 21; ambassador to
Napoleon's court, 213; at Paris, 226; reports Napoleon's concession of Constantinople, 232; discusses Turkey with Napoleon, 252; criticized by Napoleon, 270;
recalled to Russia, 346
Turkey. *See* Ottoman Empire
Turks, the, impatient for French mediation,
271

United States: rumors of French alliance with
(1804), 25; opposes Soviet plan, 65; refuses control of Straits to Soviet Russia, 206

Vahid Effendi: negotiates with Napoleon,
123; in Warsaw, 150; conversations of,
with Talleyrand, 154-155; negotiates with
Talleyrand, 171; negotiates with Caulaincourt, 173-175; nonplussed, 199; 222;
negotiates with British at Dardanelles, 357,
361-362
Vassilovitz, Osep, Persian messenger,
43, 50, 55, 85
Verninac, Directory's ambassador to Turkey
in 1795, 38
Victor, General Claude, 317

Walewska, Countess Maria, 130
Wallachia. *See* Principalities
Warsaw, Duchy of, 130

Yousef Bey, Persian messenger, 166,
218-219, 248